# making sense of sports

"Ellis Cashmore's text is a clear and eloquent outline of many of the important areas in the broad field of sports sociology . . . an original, interesting and timely interpretation of a fast-moving field of academic study."

*Times Higher Education Supplement*

"One of the strengths of Cashmore's book is that he does not limit himself to one particular perspective . . . the multi-disciplinary approach to sports studies which is employed here is certainly an attractive and integrative alternative to the more traditional sub-disciplinary approach."

*Culture, Sport, Society*

Ellis Cashmore's unique, multidisciplinary introduction to sport studies is completely revised, updated, enlarged, and enhanced with new chapters that reflect the changing character of contemporary sport.

Already established as a standard text, Cashmore's challenging approach to the study of sport has been improved and augmented with new chapters on:

- The mind of the athlete – a probe into the psychological qualities and processes that separate winners from also-rans;
- The rise and rise of celebrities – about the rise of celebrity culture and how this has affected the status of athletes.

Among the questions that are addressed in the new edition are:

- Cyborgization – will the human body be redesigned in a way that meets athletic needs – in much the same way as cosmetic surgery has enabled the redesign of bodies to suit aesthetic preferences?
- Nature or nurture – have advances in genetic science helped us solve whether great athletes are either born or made and, if so, how will this affect our understanding of competition?
- Masculinities – does masculine power still dominate in sports and, if not, what does this tell us about the state of men?

**Ellis Cashmore** is Professor of Culture, Media and Sport at Staffordshire University. His latest books include *Beckham* (Polity, 2002), *Tyson* (Polity, 2004), and *Sports Culture – An A–Z Guide* (Routledge, 2000).

# making sense of sports

## of sports

### Fourth edition

**Ellis Cashmore**

**R** Routledge
Taylor & Francis Group

LONDON AND NEW YORK

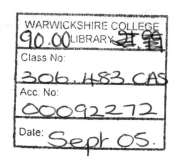
First published 1990 by Routledge
2 Park Square, Milton Park, Abingdon, Oxon OX14 4RN

Simultaneously published in the USA and Canada
by Routledge
270 Madison Ave, New York, NY 10016

Second edition 1996
Reprinted 1998 (twice)

Third edition 2000
Reprinted 2001, 2003, 2004

Fourth edition 2005

*Routledge is an imprint of the Taylor & Francis Group*

© 1990, 1996, 2000, 2005 Ellis Cashmore

Typeset in Times and Futura by Keystroke, Jacaranda Lodge, Wolverhampton
Printed and bound in Great Britain by TJ International Ltd, Padstow, Cornwall

*British Library Cataloguing in Publication Data*
A catalogue record for this book is available from the British Library

*Library of Congress Cataloging in Publication Data*
Cashmore, Ernest.
    Making sense of sports / Ellis Cashmore.— 4th ed.
        p. cm.
    Includes bibliographical references and index.
    ISBN 0–415–34854–4 (hardcover) — ISBN 0–415–34853–6 (pbk.)
    1. Sports—Social aspects.  I. Title.
GV706.5.C38 2005
306.4′83—dc22

                                                              2004022358

ISBN 0–415–34853–6 (hbk)
ISBN 0–415–34854–4 (pbk)

# contents

CONTENTS

# abbreviations

| | |
|---|---|
| AA | American Association (baseball) |
| ABA | American Basketball Association |
| ABC | American Broadcasting Company |
| ABL | American Basketball League |
| ACB | Australian Cricket Board |
| ADP | Adenosine diphosphate |
| AFC | American Football Conference |
| AFL | American Football League |
| AL | American League (baseball) |
| ANC | African National Congress |
| ANS | Autonomic nervous system |
| ATP | Adenosine Triphosphate |
| ATP | Association of Tennis Professionals |
| BAF | British Athletics Federation |
| Balco | Bay Area Laboratory Co-operative |
| BBC | British Broadcasting Corporation |
| BDO | British Darts Organization |
| BSkyB | British Sky Broadcasting |
| CBS | Columbia Broadcasting System |
| CNS | Central nervous system |
| DNA | Deoxyribonucleic acid |
| ECB | England and Wales Cricket Board |
| EPO | Erythropoietin |
| ESPN | Entertainment Sports Programming Network |

| | |
|---|---|
| FA | Football Association |
| FAME | Falk Associates Management Enterprises |
| FCC | Federal Communications Commission |
| FDA | Food and Drugs Administration |
| Fifa | *Fédération Internationale de Football Association* |
| FINA | *Fédération Internationale de Natation* (swimming) |
| HBO | Home Box Office |
| HRM | Heart rate monitor |
| hGH | Human growth hormone |
| IAA | Intercollegiate Athletic Association |
| IAAF | International Association of Athletics Federations |
| IBF | International Boxing Federation |
| ICC | International Cricket Conference |
| IGH | Insulin growth hormone |
| IOC | International Olympic Committee |
| ITF | International Tennis Federation |
| ITV | Independent Television |
| LH | Luteinizing hormone |
| MCC | Marylebone Cricket Club |
| MHR | Maximum heart rate |
| MLB | Major League Baseball |
| MLS | Major League Soccer |
| NABP | National Association of Base Ball Players |
| NASCAR | National Association for Stock Car Auto Racing |
| NBA | National Basketball Association |
| NBC | National Broadcasting Company |
| NCAA | National Collegiate Athletic Association |
| NFC | National Football Conference |
| NFL | National Football League |
| NHL | National Hockey League |
| NL | National League (baseball) |
| NOW | National Organization for Women |
| NSE | Nike Sports Entertainment |
| NYSAC | New York State Athletic Commission |
| PAC | Pan-African Congress |
| PFC | Perfluorocarbon |
| PGA | Professional Golfers' Association |
| PNS | Peripheral nervous system |
| ppv | Pay per view |
| RAS | Reticular activating system |
| RFU | Rugby Football Union |
| RSPCA | Royal Society for the Prevention of Cruelty to Animals |

| | |
|---|---|
| SANROC | South African Non-Racial Olympic Committee |
| SARU | South African Rugby Union |
| TBS | Turner Broadcasting System |
| T–E ratio | Testosterone to epitestosterone ratio |
| THG | Tetrahydrogestrinone |
| TNT | Turner Television Network |
| UCI | *Union Cycliste Internationale* |
| Uefa | *Union des Associations Européennes de Football* |
| USATF | USA Track and Field |
| USADA | United States Anti-Doping Agency |
| USOC | United States Olympic Committee |
| USTA | United States Tennis Association |
| WADA | World Anti-Doping Agency |
| WBA | World Boxing Association |
| WBC | World Boxing Council |
| WNBA | Women's National Basketball Association |
| WPBSA | World Professional Billiards and Snooker Association |
| ZCU | Zimbabwe Cricket Union |

# introduction

## why competition excites us

**WHY?**

*Question*: How many people would stand at the roadside for anything up to six hours, come rain or shine, just to catch sight of the brief blur of 198 cyclists hurtling past en route for Paris?

*Answer*: 15 million. That's the number of spectators who regularly crowd along the 2,130-mile route of the Tour de France, along a track that takes in Champagne country, the Alps, the Pyrenees, and the Atlantic coast and takes 21 days to cover.

It's an exceptional event, of course: most major competitions are over in a fraction of the time and take place in confined spaces that can accommodate thousands rather than millions. But, thanks to television, anyone who's interested can watch from anywhere in the world. Soccer's World Cup is even longer than the Tour and draws an overall audience of 30 billion over 25 days, the final game alone drawing 1.7 billion people to their tv sets. That's about a quarter of the world's population. A figure like this makes the NFL's Super Bowl seem like a private gathering of 200 million.

You could interpret this as a case of certifiable lunacy. After all, the sight of grown men cycling at breakneck speeds for three weeks, or 11 supremely fit and trained men trying to move a ball in one direction while another 11 supremely fit and trained men try to move it in the opposite direction serves no obvious function. Nor will the fruits of their labors bring any lasting benefit to civilization. It's not as if they'll take us anywhere nearer curing cancer, or bringing peace on earth, or saving the planet. And, unless we've staked a substantial wager on the outcome, we don't stand to gain anything in material terms. In fact, we will, for the most part, be out of pocket. Enthusiasm for sports is truly universal and seemingly unquenchable: no matter how much we get, we thirst for more. And there's no apparent let-up to our spending.

We pay out inordinate amounts of money either to watch or to bet on events; we travel often great distances; in some cases, we even fight – to the death – over sports. We should properly feel at least slightly uncomfortable about this. Challenge is important to the human condition: it's one of the oldest preoccupations. Where obstacles – natural or artificial – exist, we always attempt to surmount them. And, where they don't exist, we invent them. Countless episodes of triumph or folly and, sometimes, disaster have followed our attempts to conquer obstacles. Witness the yearly catalog of deaths resulting from mountaineering expeditions.

The human tendency to rise to challenges rather than just accept them is no doubt part of our evolutionary adaptation. If we didn't rise, we wouldn't have survived as a species. Sports kick in when we've taken on all the challenges germane to our survival and then lust for more; when the challenges no longer exist, we invent them. Sporting competition has everything: the challenge, the confrontation, and the climactic finality of a result. Someone, or something, always wins, loses, or ties. And this goes some way toward understanding our fundamental fascination with sports. But we still need to dig deeper for the sources.

No human institution is immune from critical investigation. Not even ones that provide us with so much pleasure. This is why there are theories of and investigations into art, humor, and, of course, sex. Ask anybody why he or she likes any of these and odds are you will get a stock response along the lines of "because they give us pleasure," or "they're good fun." Fair comment. But the analyst of sports uses this only as the starting point of his or her examination.

Often, there's resistance to approaching sports on any other terms other than those of the fan, the reporter, or the athlete. Sports practitioners and journalists have warned off those who bring too much intellect to what is, after all, a joyous human activity. Theoretical contemplation is all very well; but sports are for doers, not thinkers. If you intellectualize over an activity too much you lose sight of the basic reason why people like it. That was the jaundiced view once encountered by sports analysts. Now it's changing. Sport as an institution is just too economically big, too politically important, too influential in shaping people's lives not to be taken seriously as a subject for academic inquiry. ("Sport" refers to the entire institution and is preferred in Britain to the plural "Sports" which describes the various activities and organizations and is more popularly used in the USA.)

Those whose emotions are left undisturbed by sports are often bewildered and sometimes disgusted by the irrational waste of sports. Readers of this book will probably not be among this group. But they'll be looking for explanations: they'll want to make sense of what is, on the surface at least, a senseless activity. This book, as its title suggests, tries to do exactly that. In the chapters that follow, we'll go beyond surface appearances to reveal new perspectives on sports.

None of what follows denies the validity of the views of the fans, the athletes, the sports journalists, nor indeed the cynics. I'll integrate as many different perspectives as necessary in the attempt to make sport comprehensible as an enduring, universal phenomenon. The reader will find contributions from a range of behavioral and physical sciences, such as anthropology, biology, history, psychology, and sociology. None of these disciplines has been able to supply a single unifying answer to the question of why people are so drawn to sports. But, by piecing together various insights, we can assemble a broad understanding.

In the balance of this chapter, I'll offer three general observations on the reasons for the existence and longevity of sports. They all begin from the premise that life has deficiencies. Sports are a way of compensating for those deficiencies.

## Because life's too predictable

"The why of a fan" is the title of a classic article published in the *North American Review* way back in 1929 in which A. A. Brill argued that "life organized too well becomes monotonous; too much peace and security breed boredom; and old instincts, bred into the very cells of the body . . . still move the masses of normal men" (1929: 431). (Year of publication followed by a colon and page numbers quoted appear in brackets throughout the book.)

Brill wrote in terms of the "restrictions of modern life" depriving people of their "activity and scope, the triumphs and *réclame*" which were achievable through physical prowess under "more primitive conditions" (*réclame* means renown or notoriety – what we'd now regard as celebrity, as we'll see in Chapter 16). In explaining the fans' attraction to sports, Brill exposed what he took to be a dark truth about human nature; he described the human being as "an animal formed for battle and conquest, for blows and strokes and swiftness, for triumph and applause" (1929: 434).

As the civilizing process and rise of governing states removed the necessity for physical struggle and modernity brought with it order, stability, and security, so the nasty and brutish qualities were made redundant – but not irrelevant. They were of great use in sports. The sports that began to take shape in the middle of the nineteenth century required physical prowess. Of course, not everyone could excel in physical activities; but the ones who couldn't, were able to identify with those who could.

In Brill's view, this enabled them to recover something resembling their natural state: they could "achieve exaltation, vicarious but real" and be "a better individual, better citizen." Sports, or at least its precursors, actually contributed to building a better citizenry for the modern nation state.

Improbable as Brill's argument might have been as a total theory of sports, it offered a timeless insight about the drabness and uniformity ushered in by modernity, which is often thought to have begun in the Enlightenment of the eighteenth century and had effects across all facets of society – as we will see. One of the effects of the modern effort to bring shape and coherence to human affairs was that life became more directed, more patterned, and more predictable.

The German social theorist Max Weber used the term *calculability* to capture the ethos of modern bureaucracy; he meant that the workings of the complex organizations that proliferated all around him (he was writing around 1904–20) strained towards regulation. Their rules and procedures were designed to minimize the intrusion of the personal emotions or whims of those who administered its policies. As a result, the performance of a bureaucracy was highly predictable. (We'll return to Weber's theories in Chapter 5.)

Once the applicable regulations and procedures are known, it is possible to calculate exactly how a bureaucracy is going to deal with a matter and predict the likelihood of a certain kind of outcome. So bureaucracies stabilize a society, order its policies, regulate its citizens, and make it reliably predictable. All this makes for a rational and smooth-running society. It also affects the mentality of the people who live in such a society.

Calculability is an organizing principle in all contemporary societies, apart from those in the throes of upheaval. Spontaneity and randomness may be pleasant diversions but, in large doses, they can prove disruptive and threaten the citizenry's sense of security. Still, there's a residual attraction in the unplanned, surprise happening; everyone knows the pleasant sensation of an unexpected gift or a turn of events that are completely unexpected. On an occasional basis, surprises are fine; were they to invade our working, or public lives, they would lead to disruption and, possibly, disorientation.

In the main, we try to confine the fascination for the unpredictable to our private lives. Office workers can approach their daily tasks with a strangulating regard to rationality and precision. Once out of the office, they might retreat to the tumult of home where chaos, clutter, and utter confusion reigns. One set of the rules for work, but another for home.

The separation of life into public and private spheres is itself a product of the modern age. It has the advantage of allowing the individual to compensate in one sphere for the tensions and frustrations that build up in the other. How many of us have quietly boiled in rage during a lecture or at work? We might keep a lid on it, but explode once we're in a different context. Most of us experience bureaucracies, if only indirectly, and, equally, most of us have been irritated or angered by them; but we typically don't scream or assault people. Instead, we find outlets for these emotions elsewhere – like in sports.

Kicking or throwing balls, riding horses in a circle or inflicting damage on others might look like irrational pursuits. But, that's precisely the point: whether watched or performed, they guide the participant clear of the formal limits of bureaucracies and into areas where the outcomes of situations are wholly unpredictable; the opposite of bureaucracies.

For all of the layer-on-layer of organization that sports have acquired, especially in recent years, the actual sporting activity has retained one special nucleus: *indeterminacy*. You can never predict the result with unerring success. That is, unless the result is fixed; but then it ceases to be a genuine sport and becomes a fake or just plain theater. The indeterminate qualities of sports make them constant challenges to the bureaucratic spirit of predictability. The result of a competition can never be determined in advance, even when the odds overwhelmingly favor one party over another. Athletic competition is an area where fairytale endings occasionally do come true. Every underdog has a shot at winning.

In a world in which certainty has become the norm, uncertainty is a prized commodity. And, of course, sports are commodities in the sense that they are packaged, visually moving and colorful displays that excite our senses. Not that they would excite us if their outcomes were known ahead of schedule: contrast the rush of watching an event as it happens to watching a tape delay transmission once the result is known. It's not knowing what will happen that makes sports attractive. They can't be determined, their outcomes are uncertain and, calculate as we may, the formbook will never tell us what is going to happen once the competition begins.

Bureaucracy predominates in most countries where there are organized sports and the shift from goods-producing to service economies promises no significant reduction in organization and standardization. As economies develop, so do sports and, for that matter, religion, education, science, and many of the other important institutions that have been subject to bureaucratic imperatives.

The irony here is that, while sports are exciting because of their separation from other parts of life, the organizations that govern and administer sports have increasingly reflected those other parts. For example, sports have accumulated their own bureaucracies and some of their policies have resulted in administrative decisions that seem to go against the grain of sports. Boxing champions have had their titles stripped from them without even fighting in the ring; European soccer teams have been made to play games behind locked doors with no fans allowed in. Track athletes are suspended for taking products bought over the counter of a pharmacy to ease nasal congestion.

We might rail against the rulings, but most sports have become so vast that they need complex, bureaucratic organizations to function effectively and policies to maintain continuity. Imagine the amount of intricate organization and planning that goes into an event like soccer's four-week World Cup championship, or the summer Olympic Games, both of which occur every four years.

Even the day-to-day activities of sports performers have come to resemble those of other workers. Divisions of labor; deadlines; monotonous regimes; computer-enhanced analyses: these are all elements of work that have infiltrated sports. Much of sports today is routine and predictable. But not everything: the uncertainty that hangs over the actual competitive matchup can never be eliminated. Nor can the inspiration, innovation, vision, and moments of bravura skill that emerge in the competitive encounter. These are like lightning bolts that interrupt an otherwise continuous skyline. The unpredictability of sports provides an agreeable, perhaps even necessary, divergence from the certainty that prevails in much of our everyday lives.

## . . . and too civil

The British writer Howard Jacobson has offered a short but provocative account of our fascination with sports. Like Brill, he relies on a primitive model of the human being as engaged in a sort of struggle against the civilizing influences of contemporary life. Sport is an outlet for our lust for killing, "the aestheticization of the will to murder," as Jacobson calls it in his article "We need bad behaviour in sport, it's the way to win" (in *The Independent*, June 6, 1998).

Jacobson appeals to Darwin's theory of natural selection: he believes that life is itself a form of competition, though human society cannot function on a win-at-all-cost principle. So, we've devised manners, customs, protocols, the patterns of restraint by which we live in civil society. "Which is why we have invented sport," writes Jacobson.

Our primary instincts incline us toward competition in order to survive yet civil society forces us to curb those instincts or at least channel them into "the means whereby we can obey our primary instinct to prevail while adhering to the artificial forms of civilized behaviour." Jacobson goes on: "We watch sport in the hope that we may see someone die, or failing that, humiliated. We give up our weekends to witness rage, violence, unreason . . . to be part of the unrelenting hysteria of species survival, but at a safe distance."

In other words, it is bloodletting by proxy: we let others – the athletes – play out our instinctual impulses. This is why we feel indifferent about some sports performers who are technically good, but "nice," yet we give our hearts to headcases who seem to epitomize the rage we sometimes feel inside us.

On this admittedly extreme view, a pool table or a tennis court, a football field or a baseball diamond is a symbolic killing field; a refined Roman Colosseum, where real deaths actually did occur. All fulfill the same function: providing a stage on which to mount a ritualized Darwinian survival of the fittest. We the spectators are effectively electing others to do the dirty work for us. This makes for an attractive spectacle; murder rendered aesthetically pleasing for the masses.

Jacobson's perspective is open to many objections, not least because it crudely reduces a complex series of activities to a basic survival impulse. Yet, it provides an intriguing starting-point for discussion: sports as symbolic expressions of an impelling force that has its sources in our survivalist instincts. If we didn't have sports, we might be still splitting other people's heads open.

Sigmund Freud explained that civilization is a sort of mutilation that the civilized being never completely accepts; the civilized individual unconsciously tries to recover a natural wholeness. It is the pursuit of this wholeness that endangers him or herself as well as others. It is a form of primitive death wish.

We stand as privileged citizens of a world that has taken over a millennium to reduce the despotism, poverty, ignorance, and barbarity that were features of primitive cultures. But, on this view, we've renounced some part of our natural selves. We'll see in later chapters how the conversion from barbarity to civilized culture has formed the basis of more elaborate and sophisticated theories of sport.

---

## Modernity

From the Latin *modernus*, meaning just now, modernity refers to the state of the present and recent times, a period beginning, according to some, in the 1500s. The scientific revolution of the seventeenth century, the Enlightenment of the eighteenth and the industrial revolution of the late eighteenth and early nineteenth centuries instigated changes that brought an age in which modern values predominated. Modernity was characterized by a confidence in scientific knowledge and the explanatory power of theories (such as those of Darwin, Freud, and Einstein), a decline in the social importance of religion and the emergence of a more secular culture (i.e. more worldly rather than sacred) and a striving toward universal standards, absolute principles, and uniformity. The bureaucracy exemplified modern life: a large organization run by a central administration, it ran on rational rules and hierarchies and became a slogan for sameness, lack of imagination, and an absence of spontaneity.

## . . . and too safe

Both perspectives covered so far consider that life has become too organized and too laden with rules for our own good. There is something primeval inside us being stifled by the containing influences of modernity. Complementing this is the view that the massive changes wrought over the past two centuries have made life not only predictable and rule-bound, but also safe.

Of course, there are road deaths, unconquerable diseases, homicides, fatal accidents, and other unseen malefactors lurking in society, especially since 2001. Whether life is safer or less safe as a result, not so much of the September 11 attack as the response to it, remains an unanswered question. One thing is certain: the intricate security arrangements that have developed since that fateful day have been designed to safeguard life rather than expose it to more risk.

Even allowing for 9/11 and its aftermath, our lives are a lot more secure than they were even 40 years ago, let alone in the days of barbarism. Of course, we also create new perils, like environmental pollution and nuclear energy plant catastrophes. It seems the more we find ways of minimizing danger in some areas, we reintroduce them into others.

The sociologist Frank Furedi argues that, by the end of the twentieth century, societies all over the world had become preoccupied, if not obsessed, by safety. Risk avoidance became an organizing principle for much behavior. Safety was not something that people could just have: they needed to work toward getting it. So, human control was extended into virtually every aspect of cultural life: nothing that was potentially controllable was left to chance.

The title of Furedi's book *Culture of Fear* describes an environment in which risks are not so much there – they are created. We started to fear things that would have been taken for granted in previous times: drinking water, the nuclear family, technology; all came to be viewed as secreting previously unknown perils. Furedi despairs at this "worship of safety," as he calls it. The most significant discoveries and innovations have arisen out of a spirit of adventure and a disregard for perils.

While we avoid risks that lie outside our control, we're quite prepared to take voluntary risks. The so-called "lifestyle risks" such as smoking, drinking, and driving are examples of this. But sports present us with something quite different: manufactured risks that are actually designed in such a way as to preserve natural dangers or build in new ones. Horse racing always contains some risk for both jockey and horse, particularly in steeplechases. Lowering fences would reduce the hazard; but the governing associations have resisted doing so.

On the other hand, boxing, especially amateur boxing, has done its utmost to reduce the dangers that are inherent in combat sports. Yet both sports are fraught with risk and both continue to prosper. According to Furedi's thesis, it is probable that they would continue to prosper with or without safety measures. He cites the example of rock climbing which had some of its risks reduced by the introduction of improved ropes, boots, helmets, and other equipment. Furedi writes: "The fact that young people who choose to climb mountains might not want to be denied the *frisson* of risk does not enter into the calculations of the safety-conscious professional, concerned to protect us from ourselves."

Furedi is one of a number of writers who have speculated on the rise of what Ulrich Beck calls the *Risk Society* (1992). Beck believes that advances in science and technology have expanded our knowledge not only of how the world works, but of the perils it holds. Many of the perils have actually been fostered by our desire to know more. In other words, many of the anxieties we have, have been produced by knowledge not ignorance.

Author of the book *Risk*, John Adams believes we have inside us a "risk thermometer" which we can set to our own tastes, according to our particular culture, or subculture: "Some like it hot – a Hell's Angel or a Grand Prix racing driver, for example; others like it cool . . . But no one wants absolute zero" (1995: 15). We all want to restore some danger to our lives. How we do it is quite interesting: for instance, the same people who go white-water rafting or bungee-jumping will probably steer clear of a restaurant declared unsafe by state sanitary inspectors.

A game of chess or pool might offer no hint of danger, but skiing, surfing, Xtreme sports, and all motor and air sports certainly do. Even sitting in a crowd watching these sports carries a sense of danger. And, if the crowd happens to be at a game of soccer, the danger may be not just vicarious. The risk in some sports may be tiny; but its presence is what counts; and where it doesn't exist, we invent it.

Seekers for the source of our attraction to sports have found it in the ways culture has changed. Complex industrial societies and the maze of bureaucratic rules and procedures they brought stifled our natural spontaneity and made life too boring, according to Brill. Our primitive urges to do battle were suppressed by the development of civility and good manners in Jacobson's view. And, for others, contemporary life has become organized in such a way as to minimize risks. Sports re-inject these missing elements back into our lives. None of us is willing to sacrifice the benefits of an orderly life in which we are relatively safe and can go about our business without having to wonder what tomorrow will bring. At the same time, we need activities that give vent to what some writers believe to be natural impulses.

It seems that humans are bored: they yearn for the uncertainty, risk, danger, life lived because of instinct and passion. Sport provides an occasion for exhibiting the excesses that are prohibited in other aspects of life. It has parallels with the North American Indian Potlatch ceremonies and in the carnivals of the

Middle Ages (in which competitions featured, as we'll see in later chapters). Both presented occasions for breaking rules. In particular, the "carnivalesque," written of by Mikhail Bakhtin (1981), presented an occasion for violating rules. The penalties for such offenses would be severe in any other context. The carnival was an escape from ordinary life.

Sports have obviously morphed over the years, but we can still find in them the kinds of escape attempts that inspired early industrial workers in the nineteenth century to enrich their laborious lives by organizing games. Their efforts were gropings toward what we now regard as legitimate sports. Their pursuits were as lacking in purpose as today's sports: they were simple activities enjoyed purely for their own sake. Professionalism has ensured that sports are no longer as simple as that; today's athletes compete for money, gamblers bet for the same reason, and there are an assortment of others, including agents, coaches, and owners, whose motives may include a pecuniary element. But, for the overwhelming majority of fans and amateur players, sports still have an *autotelic* quality – the act of competing is the main pleasure. Their function lies in avoiding what we do during the rest of the working week.

Sports, at least those of today, have nothing to do with anything at all, certainly not work. They do not resemble anything, represent anything, and do not actually do anything apart from providing a momentary release from other, less pleasurable facts of life. We savor sports as ends-in-themselves.

Even sports which appear plain stupid have stood the test of time and measure up to the strict criteria of sport. There has even been a campaign to have melon-seed spitting in the Olympic program: every August in Le Frechou, France, about 50 well-trained competitors line up for this traditional country contest. Before we dismiss it as a huge prank, we should take note that spitters regularly make distances over 30 feet, suggesting that there is technique involved. While on the subject of distances, the world record for cow-dung throwing is 266 feet. Every year in Beaver, Colorado, championships are held and rules applied (like the "chips," as they are known, being 100 percent organic and non-spherical in shape!). There is even a World Dwarf Throwing Authority that has defied political correctness and still holds its 100-year-old championships in Australia. Wacky they may seem, but they are only as irrational and purposeless as the competitions we take seriously and, in many cases, fight over.

There is symmetry between our enthusiasm for sports and our embrace of other gestures, displays, and even fantasies that have no underlying reference points. We visit theme parks, like DisneyWorld in Florida and Alton Towers in England, and surround ourselves with artificial articles that have no reality outside themselves. We decamp to fantastic communities where image is everything. Our voyages into cyberspace can also be seen as flights away from the gray mundanity and toward a lusciously unrestricted universe where former identities are swapped for new ones.

At various points in history, sports have held practical value, military, industrial, and commercial; now sports beckon as a way of restoring excitement. This makes them no less powerful or compelling than they once were. Far from it: sports are more arresting now. As John Hannigan writes in his *Fantasy City: Pleasure and profit in the postmodern metropolis*: "Sports has become a defining part of our life and culture, infusing a wide range of events, activities and institutions . . . professional sports have taken the role of a common cultural currency" (1998: 142). This cultural currency is exchanged by more people than at any time in history. Sports are watched by more people, turn over more money, and probably bear more responsibility for hope and heartache than ever before. The precise reasons for this remain obscure, but we'll reveal them in the chapters to come.

**OF RELATED INTEREST**

"The why of a fan" by A. A. Brill is still worthy of serious attention, despite its age. Published in the *North American Review*, in 1929, it retains its relevance to our attempts to explain contemporary sports.

*Culture of Fear* by Frank Furedi (Cassell, 1997) is a strong argument that explains our continuing fascination with danger and may profitably be read in conjunction with Michael Bane's *Over the Edge: A regular guy's odyssey in extreme sports* (Gollancz, 1997) and an interesting study published in the journal *Physician and Sportsmedicine* "Why do some athletes choose high-risk sports?" by D. Groves (vol. 15, no. 2, 1987)

*Risk* by John Adams (UCL Press, 1995), while not about sports, is full of insights about how our obsession with security has created as many problems as it solves.

"Introduction: immersed in media sport" by David Rowe opens the second edition of his *Sport, Culture and the Media* (Open University Press, 2004a) and discusses "the extent to which sport has insinuated itself into the warp and weft of everyday life."

## ASSIGNMENT

Reviewing a previous edition of *Making Sense of Sports*, Timothy Chandler, of Kent State University, wrote: "I was surprised to find that Cashmore had not attempted to make sense of sports as a ritual sacrifice of human energy" (*Culture, Sport, Society*, vol. 1, no. 1, 1998). Make the attempt.

# naturals

## how evolution, culture, and our genes shape us

### BORN OR MADE?

Bill Reef, the race director of the "Bolder Boulder" event in Colorado found himself at the center of a controversy when he restricted Kenyan entrants to three. Reef's defense was that Kenyans were not as media-friendly as their American counterparts and the race sponsors were concerned about the way in which Kenyans were dominating. In 1996, Kenyans took eight of the first ten places; in 1997, they took seven of the first eight. Reef was insuring against a repetition in 1998.

A single nation has rarely dominated a sport as completely as Kenya did men's middle- and long-distance running in the 1980s and 1990s. The extraordinary capabilities of Kenyans both on the track and cross-country was expressed time and again through two decades, but never more so than in 1997, when an unprecedented seven world records fell in a one-month period, all but one to Kenyan athletes. While Reef did not actually say this, one could almost hear him thinking that Kenyan runners were physically advantaged when it came to running. They seemed as close as anything to "naturals."

There are some athletes who seem to have qualities that suit them ideally for a successful career; qualities that might even be seen as wondrous or peculiar, that no amount of training can duplicate in lesser beings. Bernard Malamud's allegorical novel *The Natural* was the story of one such athlete, Roy Hobbes, an invincible baseball player, who brandished his bat like King Arthur's Excalibur. Barry Levinson's 1984 movie of the book emphasizes the mythological aspects of the "natural."

The world of fact is not too far away from the world of fiction. For example, has there ever been such a complete golfer as Tiger Woods, or a female tennis player to match Martina Navratilova? Wayne Gretzky was as peerless in hockey as Michael Jordan was in basketball. Juan Manuel Fangio, who was unbeatable in the 1950s, was acknowledged as the best ever racing driver before the advent of Michael Schumacher, who, many believe, has surpassed him. Winning the Tour de France six times established Lance Armstrong among the crème de la crème of cyclists, which included five-time winners Jacques Anquetil and Eddy Merckx. These performers all seemed to have gifts that made them as naturally suited to their events as Kenyan runners, it seems, are to middle distances.

Yet, we're all "naturals" in one way: endowed with some capacity for a sporting activity. Yet, in another way, none of us is natural. Some more than others may possess great mechanical efficiency and skill in performing certain tasks and will even refine these to the point where their expertise appears effortless; so effortless in fact that it appears to be the product of a gift. Watch Roger Federer wield his racket, Sachin Tendulkar swing his bat, or Michael Phelps course through water; there appears to be no great exertion. On closer inspection, their command, like that of any other athlete, is more likely to be more the result of painstaking training than special inborn ability.

Rejecting the old adage "great sportsmen are born, not made" (and the sexism it implies), takes us so far in explaining why certain consummate performers have risen to the top. They have worked harder, have more determination to succeed, are resilient enough to withstand defeat, and can get focused at precisely the right time in a competition (Joe Montana's remarkable facility for this distinguished him from quarterbacks with better arms). But athletes are simply not born equal: a 5 foot 4 inch South Korean, no matter how hard he practices throwing hoops, is not going to prove much of a match for Kobe Bryant. A native of Nairobi, who works out over a mile above sea level, will not threaten Hermann Maier on the ski slopes. In the first case, training will simply not provide what genetics has not. In the second, environment prohibits the development of skills that are integral to some sports.

All human beings have some natural ability: sports express this in exaggerated and often extravagant forms. They provide opportunities to wring from our natural mental and physical equipment behavior that deviates dramatically from normal responses. The deviation has, it seems, no limits. Runners, rowers, and swimmers cover distances faster and faster; gymnasts perform with staggering technical proficiency; tennis players hit with ever-greater velocity.

Those who can't squeeze such efforts from their bodies are often drawn to watch, admire, and be awed by the efforts of others, efforts that sometimes last for only a few seconds. An Alex Despatie dive, spectacular as it may be, takes less than 1.5 seconds. Shaquille O'Neal slam-dunks in 2 seconds tops.

Allyson Felix runs 100 meters in the time it takes to start a car. Alex Rodriguez can steal a base while spectators are taking a swig of beer. No matter what the sport, fans will go to great lengths and pay money to witness a human performance that may well be fleeting.

We learn to appreciate sports performances, just as competitors learn basic techniques and styles on which they later innovate. The sports fan is like the art critic who acquires a knowledge of what to look for, how to evaluate, the meaning of certain properties, and so on. The athlete needs not just knowledge, but a physical mastery; in other words, a skill. This involves a lengthy and, sometimes, complex process in which he or she is made to call into service devices, ingenuity, and powers that might have gone undiscovered had the athlete not been urged or even forced to develop them. During this time, a sports competitor changes, physically and mentally: he or she learns how to control bodily movements, in many cases calibrating those movements with inanimate objects, like bats and balls.

Looked at this way, sports are learnt. But they're also completely natural: without the basic anatomical and behavioral apparatus, we couldn't perform even the simplest of operations, let alone the more complicated maneuvers needed for decent sporting action. There are what we might call limiting "givens" in the physical makeup of humans, just as there are in those of other animals. Humans have succeeded in overcoming all manner of limitations set by nature, basically by creating and employing technologies. Not that we are totally alone in this: some other species use rudimentary technologies, though not on anything like the scale of humans.

Technology has assisted sports performance and been integrated into most spheres of sports. As artifacts, technologies are manufactured items that we create and use to assist us. Poles help us vault higher, surfboards help us travel across the ocean surface. We monitor the results and modify the technologies, then transmit them to successive generations. This is not only true of sports technologies, of course: we're constantly passing on information about technologies in the effort to improve life.

Our ability to use technology derives from natural abilities: specifically, a brain large and complex enough to imagine a product, movable limbs and prehensile hands and feet to create and utilize it, and an acute sense of sight to envisage the product and gage distance. These are not properties unique to humans, but the way in which they're combined in the human species is very particular and is resembled only in other higher primates, namely monkeys and apes. The question is: what is it about the special combination in humans that enables them to develop the potential of their animal nature to levels far removed from those of other species?

Sports, as I'll argue in detail later, have only been possible because of such advanced developments; other animals engage in activities that look like sports, but aren't. Pursuing this logic, not only sports but religion, industry, warfare, education, and so on – all conventionally regarded as social institutions – are grounded in our animal origins. The entire discipline of physical (sometimes called biological) anthropology is dedicated to the task of assessing the relative contributions to social life made by heredity and environment.

Different subjects examine the same things, but in different ways. Humanities and social sciences generally find natural science approaches too reductionist in their attempt to break down (or reduce) phenomena into their constituent parts to understand how they work. For example, the sociologist sees the human effort to challenge, manipulate, or transcend the physical and biological facts of life giving rise to distinct patterns of thought and behavior. These are cultural patterns and can't be explained by reference to biological factors alone. The interaction between human beings and their natural environments results in events and processes that defy explanation in purely biological terms.

Between the two extremes, there's a whole range of diverse attempts to describe and analyze human behavior, each with its own version of why we do the things we do. In the course of this book, I'll consider several of them and assess what contributions they may make to our comprehension of just one element – sports.

---

### Reductionism

This is a method for analyzing phenomena based on the philosophy that matter is best understood once divided into its component parts. So, human societies can be approached in terms of individual beings, who, in turn, may be reduced to genes, which in turn may be reduced even further, and so on. In other words, complex wholes can only be fully understood by isolating their parts. Critics argue that the "sum of the parts" is frequently not the same as the "whole" and that *emergent* qualities are produced when all the elements come together; these are distinct and need to be analyzed in terms of the whole. "How can one understand something like fashion by reducing it to its constituent parts?" they might ask, adding that it becomes meaningful as fashion only when people act together in a collectivity, however loosely assembled. This approach is known as holism.

---

# SEVEN KEYS

Stripped to their bare elements, human beings are mobile, multi-celled organisms that derive their motive force from eating other organisms. In taxonomic terms, humans are Animalia, as distinct from members of the plant kingdom, these being bacteria, single-celled organisms, and fungi. So, we have a great many characteristics in common with other animals, especially those with whom we share common ancestors, our closest evolutionary relatives being other primates, a taxon that includes monkeys, apes, lemurs, tarsiers, and others (a taxon is the unit of classification used in biology).

There are seven key characteristics of primates that set them apart from the rest of the living world and afford them special advantages for survival. Humans have extra-special advantages, but, for the moment, we'll focus on similarities. The seven features are: an ability to grip and control, complemented by a relatively great strength of limb; stereoscopic eyes positioned at the front of the head; small numbers of offspring; a high degree of interdependence; a corresponding tendency toward living in groups; a use of reliable, efficient communication systems; and a large brain relative to body size. Now, let's deal with each of these key characteristics in more detail.

*Grip* All primates have prehensile hands and feet: they can catch, grip, and hold, thanks to relatively long, flexible digits. The ability to grip and control is enhanced by opposable thumbs or big toes which make it possible to lock around objects rigidly and so control an object's movement, as a golfer carefully guides the arc of a club's swing. From an evolutionary point of view, the origins of prehensility are not difficult to trace: distinguishing primates from other mammals was their tree-dwelling capacity. Prehensile hands and feet were useful for climbing up and down and to and from trees in forests, and additionally for plucking fruits and berries and overturning stones to pick up insects to eat.

The ability to grip is complemented by a strong versatile set of forelimbs. Suspending full body weight and swinging needs extremely powerful, long arms and legs. The very specialized functions of arms and legs for primates are reflected not only in the size and heavy muscle of the limbs, but in their range of movement: they can flex (bend), extend, and rotate. Combined with the dexterity of the hands and feet this assists fast, multidirectional travel sometimes over great distances. Gymnasts offer examples of how this ability has not been completely lost despite the human's transition from the trees to the ground.

*Stereoscope* Related to this mobility is the position of the eyes, which are typically to the front rather than the sides of the head. Two eyes enable stereoscopic vision that permits reasonably accurate estimates of distances. The sense of vision is highly developed in primates, as opposed to, say, dogs which see the world in monochrome, but have sensitive snouts and use their acute sense of smell as their chief source of information about their environments. It's no accident that no sport is based on smelling or sniffing ability, whereas a great many are organized around the ability to gauge distance and coordinate hand movements accordingly, archery and shooting being obvious examples. (It seems feasible to imagine that if humans were sensitive to smell we might have devised a sport in which an acute sense of smell was employed in conjunction with other capacities; a modified form of orienteering perhaps.) We'll return to the human capacity for making and using tools and technology in the concluding chapter.

*Small families* With other primates, humans share a tendency to give birth to one or two infants at a time; larger births are known, of course, but they are deviations from the norm. Mammals that have large litters lose some offspring at, or shortly after, birth. Primates have a smaller number of births, usually after a relatively long pregnancy, and accentuate the role of the mother in caring for and protecting the infant in an environment uncomplicated by the kind of competition that comes from large litters.

*Interdependence* One very important consequence of having small families with intense mother–infant contact is that primates learn interdependence. They rely on each other far more than many other species, members of which are abandoned at a young age and learn to adapt and survive individually, or else perish. Primates, by contrast, never learn the skills associated with lone survival. Having a protective mother, the infant has no need of such skills. What an infant does acquire is an ability to cooperate and communicate with others. And this helps explain why primates spend their lives in groups, caring for and cooperating with others.

*Groups* Individual survival for humans as well as other primates is a matter of communicating effectively in groups. So, all primates are gregarious: they grow and mature socially and not in isolation. Sports reflect this; most are organized in terms of a club structure with high degrees of interdependence and mutual cooperation needed. Even the famously lonely long-distance runners need coaches to plan their training and other competitors to make their racing meaningful.

*Communication* A lifetime spent in the company of others on whom one has to depend for survival necessitates a high degree of communication. The process of inculcating communication skills begins with the passing of auditory, visual, and tactile (touch) signals from mother to infant. It continues through life; in fact, group life is contingent on the successful storage and transmission of large volumes of information. At its simplest level, the warning conveys perhaps the single most important communication for survival. The human cry of

"Fire!" imparts much the same effect as a screech of a panicking baboon. In both cases, the first communicator supposes the recipients have some facility for recalling the image of impending danger.

*Big brains*  It seems that the necessity of communicating and the ability to do so quickly and efficiently has a connection with the large size of the brain of the primate compared to other mammals. Human beings have the largest brains and are clearly the most adept at communicating. They are, as a direct result, most developed socially. A growth in the size of the human brain can be traced back to two periods. The first, between 1.6 and 2 million years ago, witnessed a rapid expansion in cranial capacity, a change which accompanied the origin of what we now call *Homo erectus* (probably in Africa) and the use of new types of primitive tools. Bipedalism emerged as a result of a transference from the trees to the ground; the change in habitat necessitated a behavioral adaptation in posture and, eventually, an anatomical change of great significance, particularly in relation to arms and hands which were no longer employed to suspend the body and could be used for many other purposes, like making tools, building, and generally shaping the material environment to suit one's own purposes.

Anthropological evidence suggests that the size of the typical skull then remained stable for about 1.3 million years, before a second, sudden increase in brain size. The appearance of *Homo sapiens* about 0.2 or 0.3 million years ago was followed by a burst of cultural change in the spheres of manufacture, settlement, and subsistence. This is important, as there is much contention about the precise relationship between the growth of what is now the human brain and changes in habitat and activity. What is absolutely certain is that there is some form of close relationship, though the direction and way in which it worked is still in dispute.

The idea of a spontaneous expansion is not supportable. More plausible is a scenario in which the actual size of the brain after the advent of *Homo erectus* stayed the same, but the number of brain cells and neural pathways between them continued to increase. This made it possible for *Homo erectus* to become a more effective bipedal hunter and gatherer, operating at the time of day when other predatory creatures (and, therefore, competitors) were sheltering from the intensely hot midday sun. Growing extra brain cells, in this interpretation, was a defense mechanism against the harmful effects of the sun's rays on the brain; that is, the humans grew bigger brains, leaving many of the cells redundant, as mere "fail safe" devices in the tropical heat. (There are other explanations, which we'll consider in Chapter 4.) This might well have established a neural potential for more sophisticated communication and imaginative thought, which, in turn, stimulated a phase of modifying physical environments rather than adapting to them. The phase marks the beginning of sports, as we'll see later in Chapter 3. One often hears of triathletes, who swim, cycle, and run for seven hours or more, sometimes in hot atmospheres, described as "mad." Ironically, they may be demonstrating the extraordinary adaptive brilliance of the human brain in acquiring an ability to function effectively all day in extreme climates. The adaptation dates back to *Homo erectus*'s pursuit of game animals.

## THE HUMAN EDGE: LANGUAGE

The human brain is the organ responsible for the difference between *Homo sapiens* and the rest of Animalia. The enlarged neural capacity introduced the possibility of ever-more elaborate forms of communication. The physiology of the human ear and vocal tract meant that audible messages could be sent with a high probability that they would be received with reasonable efficiency. These elements, combined with the enhanced capacity for imaginative thinking, laid the foundations for human language and, by implication, new systems of word-associated thought.

Language assists the accumulation of information to be stored in the brain and confirms the awareness that other humans have similar stores of information. At the blandest level, we might ask how a game of hockey would be possible unless the players were cognizant of the rules and aware that all other players had the same knowledge. Any sport has the same prerequisite. Without language or, at least, some derivative communication system, abstract rules wouldn't be possible; so there would be no sports.

Humans aren't alone in being able to pass on knowledge from one generation to another and so perpetuate cultures, but they have the special ability to add to, or recreate, cultures whereas other primates merely inherit and receive. A verbal language as opposed to sign-based systems of communication makes this possible. Culture, we should note, refers to anything acquired and transmitted by learning and not by physical inheritance. While other animals most certainly maintain recognizable cultures, even higher apes are quite limited in their capacity to communicate and, as a result, do not pass on a vast amount of experience to new generations. The transmission has to be direct and immediate (for example, modeling and imitation); apes lack the linguistic capability to standardize, encode, classify, and concentrate meanings and experience.

By contrast, humans can transmit sometimes quite abstract meanings through several generations without any significant loss of informational accuracy. Ancient Greeks, as we will see in the next chapter, left a largess of information about themselves in the form of inscriptions, mostly on walls or clay tablets. A comprehension of these inscriptions tells us that the Greeks pursued athletics in a recognizable, rule-governed form more than any other ancient culture. Language which articulates this information is such that we can actually use it to project into the future. A future tense permits the communication of imaginative schemes and the transmission of such activities as sport. The unique elements of human language that provide for this type of knowledge of ancient cultures almost certainly arise from our genetic adaptations related to social cooperation and interdependence and changing patterns of subsistence. We have the neural equipment for picking up language; that much is clear. Less clear is the reason for the bewildering diversity of human cultures. Our biological equipment scarcely changes at all over time and space; languages, customs, religions, laws, etc. vary greatly from society to society and from one time period to another.

---

### Culture

From the Latin *cultivara* (*terra*), meaning land suitable for growth, this is often used in contrast to *nature* and refers to the learned traditions that are acquired socially and appear among mammals – especially primates. Human culture means the lifestyle of a group of people, including their repetitive, patterned ways of thinking, behaving, and even feeling. These ways are picked up through learning processes rather than through natural inheritance. The anthropologist Edward B. Tylor, in his classic text *Primitive Culture* (first published in 1871), proposed a definition of human culture that included "knowledge, belief, art, morals and habits acquired by man as a member of society." This is a very inclusive definition and others prefer to restrict the use of "cultural" to refer to rules for thought and behavior, the ways those rules are put into practice, and the manner in which they are represented or portrayed.

---

The suggestion is that, once acquired, the developed language, and the new styles of thought it ushers in, launches its users into all manner of trajectories. Humans plan and create complex organizations and institutions of a quite different quality and order than those found among other animals. Obviously these elaborate phenomena are ultimately dependent on biological factors; but their accomplishment can't be exclusively traced to biological equipment and inheritance. The often extraordinary transformations in human performance engendered by an inspirational coach, for example, remind us that we should approach biology as a license not a limit.

My prehensility and neural circuitry make it possible for me to write this book, but there are countless other non-physical influences on my ability and disposition to write – and on your willingness to read. The very concept of a book to be produced and used reflects an extremely sophisticated and unique level of communication. Books are needed for records, and records have been vital to the evolution of sport. Any balanced comprehension of sports clearly needs a range of scientific approaches: one "–ology" isn't enough. We must refer to hereditary nature; equally, though, we must examine environmental life experience, how organisms react to physical conditions surrounding them. Between the gene and the environment there are all sorts of intervening factors and processes that must be studied if we are to reach an understanding.

The biological characteristics, which distinguish humans from other animals – bipedalism, prehensility, large and more complicated brains, and language – are necessary conditions for culture building. Necessary, but by no means sufficient. Yet in recognizing this, we must at least begin our analysis of sports with a scenario: creative human beings striving to satisfy at least the minimal requirements for subsistence while subjected to the physical constraints imposed by their own biology and the material world around them. Their primary needs are to produce food, shelter, tools, and to reproduce human populations. Unless they can complete these tasks, they will have no opportunity to believe in religions and ethics, create political and economic systems, engage in war, or perform any of the other activities associated with culture. These activities, almost by definition, depend to some extent on genetically predetermined capacities. But, what does "to some extent" actually mean?

## Inspirational coaches

Sports history is full of individuals who seem to be able to inspire athletes to accomplishments beyond what seem to be their natural limitations. They have been able to take ordinary players with seemingly limited natural ability and turn them into great athletes. Among the most inspirational coaches are:

*Vince Lombardi*, who led the Green Bay Packers from an ailing outfit to two Super Bowl victories in the 1960s and was known to be a strict disciplinarian. His martinetish style was described by one of his players: "Lombardi is very fair – he treats us all like dogs." Contrary to popular myth, Lombardi did not utter the oft-quoted maxim about winning not being everything, but the only thing. His message actually had a very different import: winning, he insisted, "is not everything, but trying to win is."

*Brian Clough*, who won a total of 12 major titles for English soccer clubs between 1969 and 1993, when he retired, his most notable success being with Nottingham Forest which was twice European champion. Clough achieved his success with limited resources and at unfashionable clubs. He allowed no stars at his clubs, all players being equal parts of one unit; only his status was bigger than that of the team. "His sheer presence transformed players," one of his ex-players wrote of him. An observer reflected on his coaching: "He would be god one day, the devil the next."

*Franz Stampfl*, an Austrian track coach who, in the 1950s, moved to England where he transformed training methods: his innovative interval training, in which repeated punishing attacks on a specific distance replaced the old notion of trying to improve one's time for the whole distance. He demonstrated that ferocious pace and not mere stamina was the key to middle-distance success. In the process, his charges became accustomed to physical pain. Stampfl's principal success was Roger Bannister's historic 3:59.8 mile, the first under 4 minutes, but he also guided Chris Chataway, Chris Brasher, and a squad that dominated middle-distance running in the mid-1950s.

*Emanuel Steward*, who presided over the Kronk boxing gym in Detroit, where training was designed to weed out the weak through a grueling ordeal of near-inhuman floor and bag exercises and give-no-quarter sparring. Multiple world champion Thomas Hearns was one of his products, but his supervision of Evander Holyfield, before his tactical win over much-heavier Riddick Bowe, indicated Steward's mastery of strategy as well as conditioning techniques. He also guided Lennox Lewis through his period as world heavyweight champion. Commenting on a beaten boxer who had shown little resilience, Steward said: "He wouldn't be allowed to shadow box at our gym."

## GENOME: NATURE VIA NURTURE

We know that we share many characteristics with chimpanzees and other apes, but it's still a bit of an indignity to be reminded that we are about 98 percent the same. Well, in one sense, anyway: we share that amount of genetic material. Of course, the genetic bits we don't share are important, though perhaps not important enough to account for the colossal differences between apes and humans.

In nearly every cell of every living organism there is a complete set of instructions for creating that organism and regulating its cellular structures and activities over a lifetime. The set of instructions is called a *genome*. Imagine the genome as a vast library inside which there were once thought to be thousands and thousands of units called genes. Genes themselves are sequences of deoxyribonucleic acid, which is usually abbreviated to DNA, and this is like two rubbery ladders twisted together to form a spiral. It's called the "double helix" and there are about 3.5 billion of them in the human genome. To get some idea of the size of DNA, think of the genome library as 100 miles wide and the DNA as the size of a filament of a spider's cobweb in the corner of a shelf. If human DNA was uncoiled and stretched out, it would measure six feet.

Genes themselves are units in the thread-like structure known as the chromosome and they are the instructions for producing proteins. Proteins perform a variety of physiological functions, such as facilitating digestion, breathing, immune responses, and the movement of fluids. Most members of a species have the same collection of genes, differences resulting from very slight variations in the sequences of nucleotides. Your own DNA will probably be only 0.1 percent different from the person closest to you. So: chromosomes carry the genes which are arranged into sequences of DNA, all housed in the genome, which is the total complement of DNA genes.

Mention of genes rattles the eternal question of nature or nurture. Genetic reductionists favor the nature argument, believing that our genes fix the instructions for our development. Genes have been discovered that are allegedly responsible for all manner of human conditions, ranging from intelligence to alcoholism. Some even claim that there is a "gay gene." Following this line of thought, we'd be drawn to the conclusion that we could theoretically isolate genes that determine attributes that lead to sporting excellence, such as muscular strength or speed. We'll return to this idea shortly.

The DNA double helix was discovered in 1953 by Francis Crick and James Watson and, following the discovery, it was widely assumed that the DNA was a kind of absolute monarch of inherited development: its rule was total. The assumption reduced inheritance, a property that only living things possess, to molecular dimensions. What we look like, what we do and, indeed, who we are were seen as the product of inherited traits and DNA genes had unique, complete control over that inheritance. If the suspected 100,000 or so genes stitched into 23 pairs of chromosomes that were thought to make up the genome act as a script for the body to make proteins, then nature rather than nurture, or upbringing, seemed to make the decisive contribution to directing, or shaping us.

The surprise was that, 25 years later, further research revealed that the human genome was not as chock-full as imagined: we have only around 30,000 or 40,000 genes – about twice as many as a worm or a fly and only about six times as many as baker's yeast. In terms of genetic profile, we humans were found to be astonishingly similar: every human being on the planet was 99.9 percent the same – and 98 percent the same as chimps, of course. Yet, the evidence of our senses tells us that there is an overwhelming diversity among the human population, a diversity that manifests culturally as well as psychologically and physically; and, of course, we're very different from chimps. The Human Genome Project began as an attempt to decode the more than three billion letters of the complete human genome. What it showed was that there are far too few human genes to account for the complexity of our inherited traits or for the huge inherited differences between people and other life forms, even plants. In this sense, the project delivered a body blow to the nature thesis, offering fresh hope to the proponents of nurture. As Barry Commoner puts it in his article "Unraveling the DNA myth": "There are far too few human genes to account for the complexity of our inherited traits or for the vast inherited differences between plants, say, and people" (2002: 39).

Genetic engineers were less concerned about the philosophical implications of the breakthrough and more concerned with what could be done with genes. They sought to modify an assortment of life forms, including a rhesus monkey that carried the gene of luminescent jellyfish (which made it glow), pigs with bovine growth hormone, a mouse with a human ear, and, perhaps most famously, Dolly, the fatherless sheep who was cloned from her mother's cells. Why not introduce a gene for muscular development into an aspiring sprinter, or even clone another Muhammad Ali from the DNA of the Greatest? These are questions some geneticists pondered, though, obviously, the more immediate questions revolved around how to screen for and control disease-causing variant genes.

Of the more fantastical and maybe nightmarish applications was the attempt to synthesize DNA, as in Roger Donaldson's 2002 movie *Species*, in which scientist Ben Kingsley does exactly this, downloading information on the sequencing from extraterrestrial sources and creating a fast-maturing athletic female. Escaping the confinement of the lab, she goes in search of a mate and develops the upsetting habit of killing every man who fails to live up to her exacting standards. Used more beneficially, genes, whether real or, as in the movie, manufactured, could be introduced into the body like a rescue squad to help the body fight a faulty gene that causes, for example, cancer, Huntington's disease, or premature Alzheimer's. Duchenne muscular dystrophy, a fatal wasting disease, was among the targets for the technique. The more people learn about genes, the greater their chances of isolating them and controlling them. There is another sci-fi movie that explores the consequences of this: Andrew Nichol's 1997 *Gattaca*, in which perfect health is the norm and those with physical imperfections are consigned to an underclass.

Genetic enhancement, which has the aim of improving physical health, appearance, mental, or athletic abilities, is one consequence of the genetic discoveries of recent decades. Another is the recognition of the inadequacy of trying to explain overall human development by reference only to genes. If we humans are so genetically close to other life forms, say, dogs, which share about 95 percent of our genome, why do we turn out to be so different? The differences are obvious and pronounced, leading to the strong suspicion that they aren't caused solely by genetic dissimilarities. Then what?

### Genetic engineering

Social control over human genetics has been made possible by scientific advances, though the ethical issues rising out of the science have not been settled. While it's fanciful to think about shopping for children in a genetic supermarket or designing people the way we design cars, it's likely that we will develop the ability to make changes in the human genome that may significantly affect the physical and mental health, opportunities, and life prospects of future generations. Identifying the gene(s) responsible for inherited diseases and removing them is one application that typically meets with approval. Introducing genes responsible for the development of a desired trait is more controversial. Something similar has been tried before. Eugenics describes the production of human (or other animal) offspring by the improvement of inherited qualities and was popularized in the nineteenth century by Francis Galton (1822–1911). *Eu* is Greek for well or good. While eugenics was practiced in Europe and the USA through sterilization programs (to remove the genes of those thought to be mentally deficient, criminally-inclined, dangerously ill, etc., from future populations), it was used by Nazi Germany to justify the killing of whole categories of persons.

Matt Ridley has remarked: "The more we lift the lid on the genome, the more vulnerable to experience genes appear to be" (2003b: 59). He suggests dumping the age-old nature versus nurture dispute and replacing it with *Nature via Nurture*. Genes don't determine our development any more than PowerPoint or Explorer determine what our computers can do. They actually enable us to develop, like the computer applications enable us to open more files, search websites, check email, and so on. So, the metaphor of genes as supplying a set of instructions is misleading, according to Ridley; they make things happen, but don't decide how they happen. Nature works by way of the cultural circumstances in which we find ourselves – which is why Ridley prefers *via* (meaning through) instead of *versus* (which is Latin for against, or toward).

When it comes to talent, athletic or any kind, Ridley argues that the original genetic differences between us may be very slight. "Practice has done the rest." This might seem as if he is heading full-tilt for nurture, but here's the twist: the appetite for nurturing talent may itself be an instinct, that is, something natural, in the genes. A young schoolgirl might discover she is usually more accurate when throwing a ball at a target than her peers and this intensifies her desire for throwing the ball. She enjoys demonstrating her preeminence and practices; her throwing improves, which intensifies her appetite even further. So, although her initial edge over others was small, it becomes considerable after practice. But, that practice itself may depend on an instinct that dictates that, as Ridley puts it: "Enjoy doing what you are good at; dislike doing what you are bad at."

Ingenious as this argument is, it's not provable. Still, it suggests a way of recognizing the crucial part played by cultural factors without dismissing the role of genes in making us. Athletes are often described as talented or multi-talented, meaning they are highly proficient in a particular skill or set of skills. While the term talented might once have been used uncritically to suggest a genetic basis for skill, we now have the knowledge to recognize that genes provide only the potential for achievement, often called *aptitude*. Converting that potential into actual capacity, or capability (both meaning undeveloped faculty) and eventually skill depends on the routine performance of the skill – practice makes perfect. That inclination to practice may itself be genetically based, as Ridley argues. Maybe nature/nurture is not such a puzzle after all.

Extending the *Species* scenario, we might imagine a top soccer coach who receives mysterious information through his email that describes the genome of an unknown organism. With the help of friendly genetic engineers, he helps synthesize the DNA described in the messages and the resulting creature turns out to be a ringer for Pelé, the Brazilian player widely credited as being the best of all time. Test results show that the newly created organism is genetically the same as the great soccer player. The thrilled coach takes him out on the practice field, tosses him a ball, only to see him fall clumsily to the ground in his awkward attempt to trap it. The creation may have Pelé's genes, but he doesn't have his upbringing in the streets of Brazil, his motivation to succeed, his determination to overcome serious injuries, or any of the other social and psychological experiences that affected his eventual ability to play soccer.

Nature operates through nurture. Every gene has potential, but it's only that – potential. Whether it will realize that potential depends on what it's allowed to do, by other genes, the rest of the cell, the body, and, crucially, the entire physical and social environment at large.

The Human Genome Project confirmed what we already know: that we are all natural. But, it also disclosed something else: we're not *just* natural; there are a great many other factors involved in making us human. While its remit wasn't to explain sporting prowess, the project actually reminded us of the limits of biology and the necessity of history, culture, and the whole gamut of other forces that affect human development.

*Culture, People, Nature: An introduction to general anthropology*, seventh edition, by Marvin Harris (Addison-Wesley, 1997) is an introduction to general anthropology and a model of clarity. Harris favors a materialist approach, which complements the one taken in this book. His view is that the shaping of thought and behavior is the outcome of adaptations to ecological conditions. Taking a Darwinian starting point, Harris argues: "As a result of natural selection, organisms may be said to become adapted to the needs and opportunities present in their environments." And further: "All individuals are the products of the interaction of their genes and their environment." More extreme versions of materialism would insist that thought and behavior can be understood by studying the constraints to which human existence is subjected; these constraints arise from the need to produce food, shelter, tools, and machines and to reproduce human populations within the limits set by biology and the environment. Harris replies to critics of his approach in *Theories of Culture in Postmodern Times* (AltaMira, 1998).

*Human Evolution, Language and Mind: A psychological and archaeological inquiry* by William Noble and Iain Davidson (Cambridge University Press, 1996) emphasizes the critical role played by the distinctly human trait of symbol-making in communication; other primates use utterances that are like symbols, but probably not with intentions.

*So Human an Animal: How we are shaped by surroundings and events* by Rene Dubos (Transaction, 1998) is, as its subtitle suggests, an argument about how human "nature" is something of a misnomer. It contrasts nicely with E. O. Wilson's *Sociobiology: The New Synthesis* (Harvard University Press, 1975), a hugely ambitious attempt to explain differences and similarities in living forms by reference to the tendency to optimize reproductive success; the theory has been criticized by many who oppose Wilson's emphasis on biological factors rather than social or cultural ones.

*Nature via Nurture: Genes, experience and what makes us human* by Matt Ridley (HarperCollins, 2003a) is one of a number of contributions by one of the most illuminating writers on genetics. Among his others are: "Sex, errors, and the genome" (pp. 45–51 in *Natural History*, vol. 110, no. 5, 2001), "The genome is decoded; be happy" (p. A22 in the *Wall Street Journal*, February 14, 2001), and "Listen to the genome" (pp. 59–65 in *The American Spectator*, vol. 36, no. 3, 2003). The website for the Human Genome Project is at: <www.ornl.gov/sci/techresources/Human_Genome/project/timeline.shtml>

"Designer people" by Sally Deneen in *E: The Environmental Magazine* (vol. 12, no. 1, 2001) explores the possibilities and dangers of genetically engineering humans. Athletic ability and intelligence, she writes, rely "to a significant degree on nurture instead of nature."

*The Structure of Evolutionary Theory* by Stephen Jay Gould (Harvard University Press, 2002) explains the development of systematic thought on evolution; it's complemented by *What Evolution Is* by Ernst Mayr and Jared Diamond (Free Press, 1998). *How Homo Became Sapiens: On the evolution of thinking* by Peter Gardenfors (Oxford University Press, 2003) is also instructive, examining the evolution of human thinking.

## ASSIGNMENT

"Between the gene and the environment there are all sorts of intervening factors and processes that must be studied" (see p. 22). List as exhaustively as possible the factors and processes that contribute to the creation of what we might regard as "natural" sports performers; in other words, the kinds of factors and processes that show that performers learn and develop as much as they inherit.

# built for action

what the human body is made
of and how it works

## ALL SYSTEMS "GO" – FOR 1 MINUTE 44.71 SECONDS

August 16, 2004: the body of Ian Thorpe breaks the water of the Olympic pool in Athens. Under two minutes later, Thorpe surfaces, having traveled 400 meters through water 0.64 seconds inside Pieter van den Hoogenband's Olympic record. In 1 minute 44.71 seconds exactly, Thorpe has set in motion processes and mechanisms of immense complexity: every one of his 600 muscles has contracted, stretched, and twisted; his lungs have filled and emptied repeatedly; his heart has pumped at least 50 gallons (227 liters) of blood into all areas of the body. All this has been made possible by the intricate organizing and synchronizing capacity of his brain, which has submitted his entire body to one purpose for the duration of the race, the performance.

Question anyone who has witnessed a sports event first hand, or even on television, and they'll be unlikely to disagree with the view that the essence of sports lies in the actual sporting performance – the body in motion. The moment when competitive humans bring to an end their preparations and make visible their self-willed mastery of a particular set of skills is an engaging experience that easily surpasses reading reports, watching interviews, studying form, or any of the other ancillary activities associated with sports. The performance itself occupies center stage in sports. And while the stage itself – its structure, scenery and props, and the audience – will occupy our attention in the pages to follow, we must provide some analysis of the performance before progressing. The body will command a great deal of attention in this book: how our perceptions of it have changed, how it relates to gender and race, how it responds to drugs, how it has been visualized by artists, how it will become "cyborgized" and augmented with prosthetics, and so on. We can't address the questions without at least a basic understanding of how it works.

When we watch sports, we watch bodies move. That's what excites us. The thrill of anticipation, the arousal of the build-up, and the tension of the preliminaries are all pleasurably stimulating; but nothing beats action. Even in a chess game, the peak moments are when the players extend their arms to propel pieces across the board.

Obviously, we all control our bodies; the sports performer just controls his or hers in a particular kind of way. The more control they have, the better their chances of imposing their wills to bring a ball under control, make a vehicle travel faster, or lift their legs off the ground – and the more likely the chances of success. So, what enables us to control our bodies? It seems a ludicrously obvious question, but one that needs an answer if we're to understand better the complexities of sport.

Imagine Thorpe as a series of systems, interacting so as to produce motion. When the starter's gun fires, his central nervous system receives the signal and very rapidly relays messages to his muscular system which is stimulated to move by electrical impulses. Muscular contractions move his limbs mechanically, this being made possible by the fact that the muscles are attached to the bones of Thorpe's skeleton, which is yielding, yet tough enough to withstand the stress of movement without fracturing. Fuel is needed for the athlete to be able to repeat the motion and this comes via breathing, circulation, and digestion; once burned up, the waste matter of fuel has to be disposed of.

Viewed as a lump of matter, Thorpe's body is a bundle of about 60 billion living units called cells, each of which has the same basic structure, comprising membrane (which holds the unit together), ribosomes (which manufacture proteins), lysosomes (which destroy harmful substances and diseased parts of the cell), golgi complex (which stores endoplasmic substance), reticulum (which transports substances throughout a cell), cytoplasm (which is the liquid in which the other elements float), mitochondria (which are powerhouses, where oxygen and food react to produce vital energy to keep the cell alive), and a nucleus (which contains the chromosomes carrying coded instructions for the workings of the cell).

Cells often cluster together to form other substances, such as tissue and muscle (which comprises 50 percent of cells, being a type of tissue) and these tissues can also work in groups to become organs (heart and lungs, for instance). When organs operate together to perform a particular function, like transporting blood around the body, we usually talk in terms of systems.

For an elite swimmer like Thorpe to perform at his maximum, all his systems need to be working maximally and synchronously. We'll probe the body as if it was a series of interlocking systems. A logical first step is to ask how a swimmer, or indeed any living animal, is able to move at all and here we're drawn to an examination of the skeletal and muscular systems.

> ### Mitochondria
>
> These are the power stations of a cell where glucose and oxygen react together to create energy which converts the chemical adenosine diphosphate (ADP), which is like a flat battery, to charged-up adenosine triphosphate (ATP). This then supplies the rest of the cell with power. As its energy is used up, the ATP reverts back to ADP and returns to the mitochondria for recharging. ATP is most likely the supplier of energy for every activity in animals and plants. Energy, of course, is needed for muscular movements, but also for nerve conduction and other functions.

## MOVING THE SKELETON

The skeleton isn't just a framework, an elaborate coat hanger on which we drape skin and muscle. It's a rather elaborate, living structure that serves four important functions: protection, support, storage, and movement. Structurally, it has two aspects: the axial comprises the skull, backbone, ribs, and sternum; the appendicular refers to appendages (legs and arms), the pelvic girdle (to which the legs are attached), and the pectoral girdle (to which the arms are connected). In total, there are over 200 bones.

The human brain is disproportionately large compared to those of other mammals and, together with the spinal cord, controls in large part the movements of the whole body. As a complex, yet delicate, piece of equipment, it needs maximum protection: this is why we have a skull (or cranium), a resilient helmet composed of plates of bone fused together to form a hard casing around the brain. The interstices between the bones are called sutures and allow growth in the size of the brain until around the age of 20, after which they weld together. The skull affords sufficient protection for the brain in most activities, although motor sports, hang-gliding, and other sports in which the risk of direct collision is high (e.g. football, cricket, and cycling) use headgear for additional protection.

The other main part of the central nervous system, the spine, also needs the protection of bone; in this case a long, flexible column of vertebrae separated by discs of cartilage. In functional terms, the spine represents a remarkable adaptation, affording protection to a sensitive cable of nerves that runs from the brain to all areas of the body. The spine is articulate so as to permit the movement and flexibility so necessary to survival.

This flexibility is bought at a cost, for in certain parts of the back the spine has little or no support. Hence weightlifters strap broad belts around their waists so as to maintain rigidity in and give support to the vulnerable areas of their lower back when it is likely to be exposed to stress. Some other sensitive organs, like the lungs and heart, are also given skeletal protection, but, unlike some vertebrates (armadillos and tortoises), humans have discarded external physical protection and rely more on the wit and ingenuity that derive from the large brain, and the fleetness of foot made possible by bipedalism to protect themselves.

The conventional notion of the skeleton as a means of support is true for the majority of bones. But this needs qualification. The bony material itself is not solid, but is a composite of collagen protein fibers and inorganic mineral crystals ordered in a meshwork of cylindrical layers. This honeycombed arrangement prevents brittleness and gives bone some degree of elasticity: should stress be applied, bone distributes it to prevent a concentration. Excessive stress will cause cracks or breaks, of course, but bone's yielding capacity, or "give," reduces the danger of breakage. These qualities make it ideal as a supporting apparatus because it combines tensile strength with the yield needed for a wide range of motions.

As a rule, the heavier the load a bone must bear, the greater its diameter must be. Human thighbones, or femur, are large, as are tibia and fibula connecting the knee to the foot; they are responsible for supporting the upper body weight. But, while the femur has some protection from the quadriceps, the tibia and fibula are exposed and may need artificial cushioning from direct knocks in sports like soccer and hockey.

The skeleton can support effectively only if it grows in correspondence with the rest of the body. And bone does grow; it receives food and oxygen from blood vessels. New layers of tissue encircle existing material and form new bone, thus increasing the diameter (growth in length ceases before the age of 20). Bone grows in response to force, as does muscle. Bend, twist, compress, load, or combine these and, over time, the bone will grow to meet its task and fulfill its function, within limits of course. It will react to certain pressures or movements by fracturing, breaking, or shearing. (When this happens, cells in the outer layer of the bone – the periosteum – multiply and grow over the break, joining the two parts together.) At the other extreme, bone will lose mass if deprived of function. Stored inside bone are the minerals calcium and potassium which are delivered to the cells by blood (and which give bone its hardness) and marrow, a soft jelly-like tissue that produces red and white blood cells.

The fourth major function of the skeleton – and the most important for our purposes – is that of providing mechanical levers for movement. Bones are connected to each other at joints, which serve as axes for rotation. For instance, the forearm, the upper-arm bone or the humerus, acts as a fulcrum, and the radius and ulna as a lever. The elbow joint, which is a hinge, makes possible a simple range of movement: flexion (bending) and extension (stretching). Other joints, like the biaxial (between forearm and wrist and at the knee), the pivot (at the wrist), and the ball-and-socket (at the shoulder and hip), are more complicated arrangements and permit multiple movements in different planes and directions.

Were the joint a manufactured piece of equipment, the articular surfaces would grind together and need WD-40 or some other lubricant sprayed onto them. The human body takes care of this by interposing a film of lubricating fluid between opposing bone surfaces (in which case, they are called synovial joints), or by sandwiching a tough pad of gristle between articulating bones (cartilaginous joints). An engineer would love this natural bearing, which reduces friction.

Cartilage belongs to a class of connective tissues which, as the name suggests, joins or ties together the various parts of the body and makes movement smooth. Its capacity isn't limitless, however, and cartilage can wear out. Ligaments, which are flexible collagen bands that connect and support joints, are also liable to wear-and-tear, especially amongst sports performers, such as throwers or shot putters, who maximize the intensity or repetition of stresses on shoulder and elbow joints and are therefore prone to sprains (torn ligaments) and dislocations of joints.

Perhaps the most troublesome connective tissue for sports competitors is tendon, which is basically a collagen cable that joins muscle to bone and so transmits the pull, which makes the bone move. Tendons make it possible to use a muscle to move a bone at a distance. In the case of fingers, which are clearly vital in dexterous activities (e.g. table tennis, darts, and spin bowling in cricket), we need muscular control of the fine movements without the invasive presence of muscles at the immediate site. Were the necessary muscles attached directly to the finger bones, the size of the digits would be so large that catching, holding, or even forming a fist would be a problem. Without the action permitted at distance by slender tendons, primate prehensility would be severely restricted. Special nerves in the tendon are designed to inhibit over-contraction, but tears do occur often when fatigue or poor skill impairs coordination. Tendon tears may be partial or complete and, although any muscle tendon is at risk, those subjected to violent or repetitive stresses, such as the Achilles tendon and shoulder tendons, are most frequently involved.

The way the skeleton is framed and its levers fitted together give the body the potential for a great variety of movements through all planes. But we still need to analyze the source of its motion. Plainly stated, muscle moves our bones; it does so with two actions, contraction and relaxation. Usually, the arrangement features tendons connecting bones to one or more muscles which are stimulated by nerves to contract, causing the tendons to tighten and the bone to move.

(Some muscles appear to be attached directly to bone, obviating the need for tendons, but motion is accomplished by basically the same process.)

Muscle use is present in every sporting activity, right from sprinting where muscles are maximally in use, to playing chess where muscles function perhaps only to position eyeballs in their sockets or to move a finger by inches. The various types of muscle present in humans differ in structure and properties, but the striated muscle, which acts as the motor of the skeleton, is our chief concern. Striated muscle is under our control in the sense that we voluntarily induce its contraction and hence movement. Other types of muscles contract in the absence of nerve stimulation: cardiac (heart) muscle, for example, contracts independently of our will and has the property of "inherent rhythmicity" (we'll return to this).

Skeletal muscle consists of fibers, which are long tubes that run parallel to each other and are encased in sheaths of the ubiquitous collagen. Each fiber is made up of strands called myofibrils, which are themselves composed of two types of interlocking filaments. Thick filaments are made of a protein called myosin and thin ones of actin, and they are grouped in a regular, repeated pattern, so that, under the microscope, they give a striated, or streaky, appearance. The lengths of myosin and actin filaments are divided into units called sarcomeres, the size of which is recognized as the distance between two "Z-lines" (the structures to which the actin filaments are attached).

Although the filaments can't change length, they can slide past each other to produce the all-important contraction. We'll see later how messages from the central nervous system are taken to muscles by nerve impulses. When such an impulse reaches a muscle fiber with the instruction "Move!" energy is released in mitochondria and the filaments move closer together, shortening the muscle. As they pass, a chemical reaction occurs in which: (1) calcium is released from storage in the tubular bundles; (2) in the calcium's presence, myosin molecules from the thicker filaments form bonds with the actin filaments; (3) the myosin molecule is then thought to undergo a change in shape, yanking the actin filaments closer together; (4) the contraction of the muscle fiber ends when the calcium ions are pumped back into storage so as to prevent the formation of new chemical bonds.

The effect of the contraction is a pull on the bones to which the muscles are attached and, as the four phases take no more than a few thousandths of a second, we are capable of mechanical movements at very high speed. The flexion and extension of boxer Erik Morales's left hook took a few hundredths of a second. Such a punch, which had a concussing effect, required a great force of movement, so many fibers would have been required to contract together at speed. Ernie Els's putt, by contrast, would involve fewer fibers.

In both instances, opposing, or antagonistic pairs of muscles would be working to allow free movement. For the hook or the putt, biceps muscle would contract to bend the elbow, which its opposing member, the triceps, would relax. To straighten the arm in the action of a shot putter the triceps need to contract, while biceps relax. Muscles are equipped with special receptors that let the brain know the extent of contraction and the position in three-dimensional space without having to look constantly to check. We can close our eyes, but know the movement and position of our limbs.

The 206 bones of the adult skeletal system form a protective casing for the brain and the spinal cord, a sturdy internal framework to support the rest of the body, and a set of mechanical levers that can be moved by the action of muscles. All of these make the human body a serviceable locomotive machine for walking, running, and, to a lesser degree, swimming, climbing, and jumping. But, like other machines, the body depends on fuel supply for its power, a method for burning the fuel, and a system for transporting the waste products away. Again, the human body has evolved systems for answering all these needs.

## NOT BY FOOD ALONE: ENERGY

As a living organism, the human being depends on energy. Plants get by with light and water; animals need food. In particular, humans need protein (built up of chemical units called amino acids), carbohydrates (comprising sugars which provide most of our energy), lipids (or fats for storage and insulation), vitamins (about 15 types to assist various chemical processes), minerals (like iron and zinc), and water (to replace liquids). These provide raw energy sources that drive the machinery of the body; that is, making the compounds that combine with oxygen to release energy, and ensure the growth and repair of tissues. (The combination with oxygen will be dealt with later on.)

Obtaining food is of such vital importance to survival that the entire plan of the human body is adapted to its particular mode of procuring food. Sports, as I'll argue later, reflects our primitive food-procurement even to this day. For the moment, we need to understand not so much the way in which food is obtained, but how it's used. In their original forms, most of the above substances are unusable to human beings. So we've evolved mechanisms for rendering them usable as energy sources. Processing food is the function of the digestive system, which consists of a long, coiled tube, called the digestive tract, and three types of accessory glands.

Typically, food is introduced to the body through the mouth where it's chewed, pulped, and mixed with saliva in a process of ingestion. After being formed into lumps, it's swallowed and drops into the pharynx (throat) and, then, to the epiglottis, which is a small valve that closes off the windpipe. Water falls under the force of gravity, but food is ushered along by a wave of muscular contractions called peristalsis. Fibers in the wall of the esophagus tube (gullet) push the food downward to the stomach (which explains why cosmonauts can still eat in the absence of gravity).

From here, the food passes into the stomach, a sausage-shaped organ that can expand to about a two-pint capacity. At this stage, a churning process starts in which the food is mixed with mucus, hydrochloric acid, and enzymes (chemical substances that speed up processes – in this instance, the breaking up of protein). The effect of this is to liquefy the food, so that after between three and four hours the churned-up mass (called chyme), which now resembles a cream soup, gets transferred, via peristaltic waves, to the stomach's exit point and then to the duodenum which is the first chamber of the small intestine. Contrary to popular belief, it's here rather than the stomach where most of the chemical digestion gets done: bile from the liver and enzymes from the pancreas are released. (An exception is alcohol, which is readily absorbed in the stomach and doesn't pass through.)

A note here about the role of the brain in regulating the discharge of naturally secreted juices that aid digestion: seeing, smelling, tasting, or even thinking about food can stimulate the brain to send messages to the glands in the mouth and stomach to release a hormone called gastrin that is quickly absorbed into the blood and then to glands where it triggers the release of gastric juice. So athletes who chew gum to enhance their concentration are usually doing a disservice to their stomachs by producing gastric juices when there is no food. Gastric juices have enough acidity and protein-splitting capacity to burn human flesh. The stomach has natural protection against this, although resistance can be lowered by alcohol or aspirin and by overproducing the juices when no food is available. A possible result is an open sore in the wall of the stomach, or a duodenal ulcer.

Basically, the idea is to reduce the parts of the food that can be profitably used by the body (the nutrients) to molecular form and allow them to seep through the cells lining the long digestive tube, through the minuscule blood or lymph vessels in the stomach wall and into the blood or lymph. All the cells of the body are bathed in a fluid called lymph. Exchanges between blood and cells take place in lymph. Lymph is derived from blood, though it has a kind of circulatory system of its own, filtering through the walls of capillaries, then moving along channels of its own (lymphatics), which join one another and steer eventually to the veins, in the process surrendering their contents to the general circulatory system. Food is absorbed through the wall of the intestine, which is covered in villi, tiny absorbent "fingers" that give the tube a vast surface area. Not all food passes directly into blood vessels: the lymphatics are responsible for collecting digested fats and transporting them to the thoracic duct which empties into one of the large veins near the heart.

Once absorbed the nutrients are carried in the blood and lymph to each individual cell in the body where they are used up; that is, metabolized. The residue of indigestible or unabsorbed food is eliminated from the body by way of the large intestine. En route, bacteria in the large intestine feed on vestiges and, in return, produce certain vitamins, which are absorbed and used. Some of the unwanted water is converted to urea and passed out via the bladder. The body has precise control over what it needs for nutrition, growth, and repair. One of the many functions of the liver is to store surplus nutrients and release them together to meet immediate requirements. This large abdominal organ receives digested food from the blood and reassembles its molecules in such a way as to make them usable to humans. Different cells need different nutrients, so the liver works as a kind of chef preparing a buffet for the blood to carry around the rest of the body.

---

## Lymph

From the Latin *lympha*, for water, this is a body fluid derived from the blood and tissue and returned to the circulatory system in lymphatic vessels. At intervals along the vessels there are lymph glands which manufacture antibodies and lymphocytes that destroy bacteria. The lymph system has no pump like the blood system and the movement of lymph is brought about largely by pressure from contracting skeletal muscles, backflow being prevented by valves. The lymph system doubles as the body's immune system in that it produces proteins called antibodies, lying at the surface of certain white blood cells (lymphocytes). When needed, antibodies and cells rush into the blood stream and "round up" the harmful bacteria and viruses. While the lymph system can make thousands of antibodies, its vital adversaries are constantly mutating so as to find ways of defeating it, as the Aids pandemic indicates.

---

A supply of glucose is needed by all body and especially brain cells, particularly as they have no means of storage. If, after a sugar-rich meal, the body has too much glucose in the blood, the liver cells remove it and store it, later pushing it back into the blood when the glucose level drops. After a carbohydrate-rich meal, the level may increase briefly, but the liver will take out the surplus for later use. Muscle cells are also able to store large amounts of glucose molecules, packaged as glycogen, which is why endurance-event competitors, like marathon runners, try to pack muscle and liver cells with stored glycogen prior to competition in the expectation that it will be released into the blood when levels fall. After the glucose is used up, liver cells start converting amino acids and portions of fat into glucose and the body shifts to fat as a source of fuel.

Metabolism refers to all the body's processes that make food usable as a source of energy. The success of these depends on how effectively the body can get the nutrients and oxygen it requires to the relevant parts of the body and, at the same time, clear out the unwanted leftovers like carbon dioxide. The substance employed for this purpose is blood, but it's actually more than just a convenient liquid for sweeping materials from place to place. Cells, cell fragments (platelets), proteins, and small molecules float in liquid plasma, which is mainly water (and makes up about 60 percent of the blood's composition). The plasma contains red and white blood cells; the latter are capable of engulfing bacteria and combating infections with antibodies. Red cells are more numerous and contain hemoglobin, a chemical compound with a strong affinity for oxygen.

## Muscle-packing or muscle-loading

Carbohydrates (carbs) provide most of our energy and can be ingested in many forms, after which they are reduced to simple sugars before being absorbed into the bloodstream. Carbs are an economical source of fuel. Liver and muscles store carbohydrates in the form of glycogen, which converts rapidly to glucose when extra energy is needed. Mindful of this, endurance performers sometimes seek to "pack" or "load up" their muscles with glycogen by consuming large amounts of carbohydrate foods such as bread, cereals, grains, and starchy products for about 72 hours preceding an event. The idea is to store as much glycogen as possible, making more glucose available when energy supplies become depleted.

Hemoglobin allows blood to increase its oxygen-carrying capacity exponentially. Long- and middle-distance runners have exploited the advantage of having more hemoglobin in their blood by training at high altitudes, where there is less oxygen naturally available in the air. Their bodies respond to the scarcity by producing a chemical that triggers the release of larger numbers of red cells in the blood. After descending to sea level (or thereabouts), the body will take time to readjust and will retain a high hemoglobin count for some weeks, during which an athlete may compete and make profitable use of a generous supply of oxygen to the muscles (blood doping, as we will see later, involves extracting hemoglobin-packed blood during altitude training, saving it, and administering a transfusion to the athlete immediately prior to a race). At the other extreme, excessive bleeding or an iron-deficient diet can lead to anemia, a condition resulting from too little hemoglobin.

So, how do we manage to circulate this urgently required mixture through-out the body? The internal apparatus comprises the heart, blood vessels, lymph, lymph vessels, and some associated organs, like the liver. These form a closed system, meaning that the blood that carries the vital substances all over the body is confined to definite channels and moves in only one direction, rather than being left to swim about. It travels in three types of tubes. The thickest are arteries in which blood moves at high pressure from the heart to the body's tissues. These arteries split over and over again to form microscopic vessels called capillaries that spread to every part of the body.

A single capillary is only about half a millimeter long and a single cubic meter of skeletal muscle is interlaced with 1,400 to 4,000 of them. Laid end-to-end the length of all the body's capillaries would be about 60,000 miles or 96,500 kilometers – twice the earth's circumference. While coursing around, oxygen- and nutrient-rich liquid, plasma, seeps through the ultra-thin walls of the capillary. At the same time, capillaries, like vacuum cleaners, suck up waste products from cells. Gradually, capillaries merge together to form larger vessels that turn out to be veins; these keep blood at a lower pressure as they deliver it back to the heart.

A fist-sized muscle weighing less than a pound, the heart is a four-chambered pump that pushes blood into the arteries, gets it back from all parts of the body (except the lungs), pumps it out to the lungs, takes it back from the lungs, then returns it to the body. The chambers of the right side of the heart consist of one atrium and one ventricle. Connected to the right atrium are two large veins, one of which brings blood from the upper body and one from the lower. Blood flows from the right atrium into the right ventricle via a one-way valve; it leaves this chamber through a pulmonary artery that branches and services the lungs. Another valve stops any backflow. Blood returns from the lungs via pulmonary veins which drain into a left atrium and, then, to a left ventricle.

From here, the blood is squeezed into the aorta, the single largest artery of the body, which runs into several other arteries connected to the head, arms, and the upper chest, and, later, to abdominal organs and body wall. In the pelvis, the aorta branches and sends arteries into the legs. Blood returns to the right atrium of the heart through veins. The direction of the blood is ensured by a series of valves (blood, controlled by the valves, moves in one direction only). We call the movement away from ventricles systole and its opposite diastole. At any one time, there are about 1.5 gallons of blood in the mature human body. It takes less than a minute for the resting heart to pump out this amount and considerably less for the exerting sports performer, who can push out as much as 6.6 gallons per minute when active.

As mentioned before, the heart muscle has inherent rhythmicity and the pump acts independently of our volition. It will (given a suitable atmosphere) pump even outside the body, and with no stimulation; this makes heart transplants possible. Not that the heart is indifferent to outside influences; a sudden shock, for example, can cause sufficient stimulation to slow down, or skip, the heartbeat.

During exercise or competition the action may accelerate to over 200 beats per minute. The heart muscle itself would stretch and automatically increase its strength of contraction and flow of blood. Athletes work at increasing blood flow without the corresponding heartbeat. The extra blood flow results in a heightening of the pressure of blood in the arteries of the chest and neck, which are detected by special sensory cells embedded in their walls. Nerve impulses are sent to the brain, resulting in impulses being relayed back to the heart, slowing its beat rate and lowering potentially harmful blood pressure levels. So, the brain has to monitor and feed back what is going on during intense physical activity.

The rate of heart action is also affected by hormones, the most familiar in sports being adrenaline which causes an immediate quickening of the heart in response to stressful situations. The reaction is widespread; amongst other things, blood vessels in the brain and limbs open up, and glycogen is released from the liver. In this type of situation, the skeletal muscles might receive up to 70 percent of the cardiac output, or the total blood pumped from the heart. Under resting conditions, the liver, kidneys, and brain take 27, 27, and 14 percent respectively. Immediately after eating, the digestive organs command great percentages (to carry food away), thus reducing the supply to the muscles. So, activity after a meal tends to be self-defeating; you can't get as much blood to the muscles as you would if you waited for three hours or so.

I mentioned before that food alone does not give the body energy, but needs the addition of oxygen, which is, of course, inhaled from the surrounding air, taken to the lungs, and then transferred to all parts of the body via the blood. Once it arrives at cells, the oxygen reacts with glucose, supplied by courtesy of digested carbohydrates, and produces energy at the mitochondria sites. During this process of respiration, unwanted carbon dioxide and water are formed in the cells. Exhaling gets rid of them.

Lungs and windpipe make up the respiratory system, though the actual process of breathing is controlled by the contractions of muscles in the chest, in particular the diaphragm muscle beneath the lungs and the muscles between the ribs. The diaphragm moving down and the ribs expanding create space in the lungs. Air rushes in mainly through the nostrils where it is filtered, warmed, and moistened, and then into the lungs via the windpipe, or trachea. To reach the lungs, the air travels along tubes called bronchi which, when inside the lungs, divide into smaller and smaller tubes, ending in small bunches of air sacs called alveoli. Oxygen seeps out of the alveoli and into surrounding capillaries, which carry hemoglobin, a compound which, as we noted, readily picks up oxygen.

While oxygen leaves alveoli, carbon dioxide, produced by the body cells, enters ready to be exhaled, a motion initiated by a muscular relaxation of the diaphragm and ribs. Air rushes out when we sigh "Phew!" to denote relief and relaxation; the ribs close in and diaphragm lifts up.

The motions are more pronounced during continuous physical exertion; the body makes a steady demand for more oxygen and to meet this we breathe more deeply and more fully. The heart responds by pumping the oxygen-rich blood around the body faster. The process involves sustained use of oxygen in the breakdown of carbohydrates and, eventually, fats to release in the mitochondria of cells where the raw fuel ADP is energy charged up as ATP. This is why the name aerobic (meaning "with air") is applied to continuous activities, such as cycling, swimming, and running over distances. In contrast, weightlifting, high jumping, and other sports requiring only short bursts of energy are anaerobic. In this case, food is not broken down completely to carbon dioxide and water, but to compounds such as alcohol or lactic acid. An incomplete breakdown means that less energy is released, but what is released can be used immediately.

"Oxygen debt" affects many sports competitors, particularly ones whose event requires explosive bursts, but over a reasonably sustained period. Four hundred-meter runners often tie up in the home straight; they can't get the oxygen and glucose round their bodies fast enough, so their muscles use their own glycogen stores for releasing ATP anaerobically (without oxygen).

The product of this process is lactic acid, which needs oxygen to be converted into carbohydrate to get carried away. As runners need all the oxygen they can process for the release of energy they "borrow" it temporarily, allowing the lactic acid to accumulate in the muscles and cause fatigue. After the event, the debt has to be repaid, so rapid breathing invariably carries on. Shorter-distance sprinters also incur oxygen debts, but the build-up of lactic acid in their muscles is not usually great enough to hinder contraction. Longer-distance

---

### Hyperventilation

Carbon dioxide ($CO_2$) is a waste product and needs to be flushed out of the blood. Even a small increase in $CO_2$ content of the blood stimulates deep and, later, more rapid breathing to reduce the $CO_2$. The action is brought about involuntarily, usually during physical activity because of the fast breakdown of carbohydrates to release energy (impulses are sent to the medulla, resulting in increased breathing). Occasionally, this can lead to an over-reduction and a loss of consciousness. When this happens, hyperventilation is said to occur.

performers tend to get second winds: an increase in heartbeat rate and breathing enables the runner to take in enough oxygen to convert and dissipate the lactic acid without over-extending the oxygen debt.

## COMMUNICATIONS AND CONTROL

Let's return to Ian Thorpe for a moment. We now have an idea of how his movements are possible: how the supporting scaffold of his skeleton is urged into motion by the contraction of muscles; how those muscles are fed a supply of fuel to turn into energy; and how that fuel, in the form of food and oxygen, is pushed to its destination by blood which, at the same time, picks up waste products to dispatch. Although we've examined these processes separately, this is a device; in actual performance, all the processes are closely connected and dependent on each other.

The digestion of food, for instance, would be of no value without a blood-stream to absorb it and to distribute the products; release of energy in a contracting muscle would cease if the lungs failed to supply oxygen via the circulatory system; a contracting muscle has to be connected to articulated bone to get a movement. The working together of these is no haphazard affair. During strenuous activity, when muscles need to lose excess carbon dioxide and take in more glucose and oxygen, the rate of breathing increases automatically and the heart beats faster, so sending a greater amount of oxygen-rich blood to the muscles.

Crudely stated, the information we receive about the environment arrives by way of cells called receptors, which respond to changes in, for example, light and sound. They produce pulses of electricity which travel along nerves to the brain, which quickly interprets the meaning of the changes and issues instructions to the relevant other parts of the body (e.g. "loud noise – cover ears"). Some of the information received by the brain is stored for future use, a facility of crucial importance in the acquisition of skill, which involves the capacity to react in precisely the same way to similar stimuli time after time.

The two components of the whole nervous system are: (1) the central nervous system (CNS), comprising the control center of the brain and its message conduit, the spinal cord; and (2) the peripheral nervous system (PNS), which is the network of nerves originating in the brain and spinal cord and which is responsible for picking up messages from the skin and sense organs (sensory nerve cells) and carrying messages from the CNS to the muscles (motor nerve cells).

Nerves are spread throughout the entire body; each one consists of a bundle of minute nerve fibers and each fiber is part of a nerve cell, or neuron, of which there are about 100 billion woven into each body in such a way as to bypass the packed body cells. To do this, the network needs a shuttle service provided by connector neurons that carry signals back and forth. Further physical facts about signals are, first, that the nerve fibers that pick up sensations from receptors and deliver them to the CNS, do so with electrical impulses that are chemically charged; changes in the balance of the minerals sodium and potassium in the cells cause the impulse. Second, the speed of the impulse varies from fiber to fiber and with environmental conditions. And third, fibers covered in sheaths of myelin (a fatty substance) conduct impulses faster than naked fibers.

---

### Heart rate monitor (HRM)

A device comprising a chestband transmitter and a wrist-worn receiver that indicates how fast the heart is beating. The principle of exercising within a certain percentage of maximum heart rate has been known for years; but only with the advent of the HRM has the ability to apply those benefits been available to athletes. It is necessary to know the maximum heart rate (MHR) of the athlete and the threshold heart rate, the point at which exercise moves from aerobic effort to anaerobic. By exercising at slightly below the threshold, one can gradually force it up. Olympic 4,000-meter pursuit cycling champion, Chris Boardman, used an HRM in setting the world hour distance in Bordeaux in 1994. He had to cope with severe heat – which makes the heart beat faster – so adjusted to ride at six beats faster than he'd originally planned.

---

Perhaps the clearest way of depicting the role of the nervous system is by tracing its stages. Suppose you are a gun marksman (or woman); you must use primarily the senses of sight and touch when focusing on the target and aligning the gun and make adjustments to these environmental factors. A first step is made by bringing the target into focus: the eyes are, of course, sense organs (i.e. an assembly of receptors) and their surface, known as the retina, will react to rays of light by changing its chemical structure; this triggers off an electrical impulse that travels along nerve cells, or neurons, to the brain.

There are no direct connections between neurons, so the impulse may have to travel a circuitous route. The tiny gaps between neurons are synapses and these are bridged by a chemical neurotransmitter that takes the impulse across the synapse to the next neuron. The points of connection with the next neuron are called dendrites, which are in effect short, message-carrying fibers. One long fiber, called an axon, carries messages away from one neuron to the dendrites of the next. It takes only fractions of a second for the impulse to make its way through the synapses and neurons to the brain.

The fine web of nerves running through most of the body pale beside the densely complex mesh of neurons in the brain. Senses gleaned from our contact with the environment provide inputs that are sent to the brain; this processes the information before sending out instructions to muscles and glands. Most of our behavior in and out of sports is controlled in this way. A fast pitcher in a baseball game may choose to do many different things based on his sense impressions, mostly picked up by his vision and touch. He may notice a shuffle in the hitter's gait; he may feel moisture rising in the air that may affect the trajectory of his ball. His brain sends messages to his muscles so that he deliberately bowls a short, rising delivery.

But not all of our behavior is produced by such a process: the receiving hitter may not expect the fast ball which zips sharply toward his head, prompting him to jerk his head away almost immediately to protect it from damage – as we'd withdraw a hand inadvertently placed on a hot iron. The spinal cord section of the CNS controls this type of reflex action. The nervous impulse defines an arc that short-circuits the brain, so that the message never actually reaches it.

The behavior resulting from the reflex arc is sudden and often uncoordinated because all the muscle fibers contract together to avoid the danger. A boxer drawing away from a punch, a goalkeeper leaping to save a short-range shot, a volleyball player blocking an attempted spike; all these suggest automatic responses that need not involve conscious will for their successful completion. We hear much about reflex movements in sports and, clearly, sports in which fast reaction is crucial do exhibit such responses. But most sports action is governed by the brain and, for this reason, we need to look in more detail at the structure and functions of this most vital of organs.

While the brain itself is an integrated unit which, like any other living organ, needs a continuous supply of food and oxygen to produce energy, it can be seen in its component parts, each of which has specific functions. The medulla, for instance, controls involuntary activities that we can't control consciously, but which are essential for survival (such as breathing and heart rate). Also of interest for athletic performance is the cerebellum, which receives messages from the muscles, ears, eyes, and other parts and then helps coordinate movement and maintain balance so that motion is smooth and accurate. Injury to this component doesn't cause paralysis, but impairs delicate control of muscle and balance; for instance, the ability to surf or skate would be lost. All voluntary and learned behavior is directed by the cortex, the largest portion of the brain; this forms the outer layer of the area known as the cerebrum lying at the fore of the brain.

The cerebrum is divided into two halves, or hemispheres, each of which is responsible for movement and senses on its opposite side. Nerves on the two sides of the body cross each other as they enter the brain, so that the left hemisphere is associated with the functions of the right-hand side of the body.

In most right-handed people, the left half of the cerebrum directs speech, reading, and writing while the right half directs emotions; for left-handers, the opposite is true. So, Marat Safin's service would have been controlled by the right side of his brain, while his emotional outbursts would be associated with the left. Physical movement is controlled by the motor area: motor neurons send impulses from this area to muscles in different parts of the body. The more precise the muscle movements, the more of the motor area is involved; so a hammer thrower's actions wouldn't use up much space while a dart player's would, as he or she would be utilizing fine movements of the fingers.

The only other zone of the brain I want to note at present is the thalamus, which is where pain is felt. Pain, of course, is principally a defensive phenomenon designed to warn us of bodily danger both inside and outside the body. Impulses originating in the thalamus travel to the sensation area so that a localization of danger can be made. This is a mechanistic account of our reactions to pain: it's actually affected by all manner of intervening factors, including self-belief. In other words, if people do not believe they will feel pain, they probably won't – at least under certain conditions. There are also cultural definitions of pain: we learn to interpret pain and react to it and the thresholds may differ from culture to culture.

Such is the nature of competitive sports nowadays that few concessions to pain are allowed. Inspirational coaches encourage performers to conquer pain by developing a kind of immunity, just ignoring pain. Chemical ways of "tricking" the brain have been developed. Some drugs, for example, cause nerve cells to block or release a neurotransmitter (the chemical that carries nerve impulses across synapses to the dendrite of the adjacent neuron), the idea being to break the chemical chains linking brain to cell. We'll look at the use of drugs more closely in Chapter 10. The point to bear in mind for now is that the CNS generally, and the brain in particular, plays a central role, not only in movement, but in the delicate sensory adjustments that have to be made in the operation of all sports, even those such as power lifting, which seem to require pure brawn. The lifter's cerebellum enables him or her to control the consequences of the lift; without this, initiation might be possible but corrective feedback coordination would be absent. In short, there would be no balance and no instruction to the opposing (antagonistic) muscles to make a braking contraction on the lift's completion. The whole operation would collapse.

While we exert a large degree of control over our bodies through the CNS, many vital activities, such as heartbeat, peristalsis, and functioning of the kidneys, simply can't be controlled voluntarily. Handling these is a secondary system of nerves called the autonomic nervous system (ANS). Many of the cell bodies of the ANS lie outside the brain and spinal cord and are massed together in bunches, each bunch being a ganglion. These ganglia receive information from receptors in the various organs of the body and then send out the appropriate instructions to muscles, such as the heart, and glands, such as salivary glands. The instructions are interesting in that they are twofold and antagonistic.

Unlike skeletal muscle which is either stimulated to contract or not (it needs no nerve impulse to relay), cardiac muscle and the smooth (as opposed to striated) muscle of other organs must be stimulated either to contract more than usual or to relax more than usual. To achieve this the ANS is divided into two substrata: the sympathetic system (more centrally located) and the parasympathetic system (more dispersed). The parasympathetic system constricts the pupil of the eyes, increases the flow of saliva, expands the small intestine, and shrinks the large intestine; the sympathetic system has the opposite effect. Impulses are propagated continuously in both systems, the consequences of which are known as *tone* – a readiness to respond quickly to stimulation in either direction. (Sympathetic derives from the Greek *sym* for have and *pathos* for feeling).

Tone is rather important in certain sports: for instance, a panic-inducing visual stimulus will cause an increase in sympathetic impulses and a decrease in parasympathetic impulses to the heart, eliciting a greater response than just a sympathetic stimulation. Impulses from the two systems always have antagonistic effects on organs. The name autonomic nervous system implies that it's independent and self-regulated, whereas, in fact, the centers that control ANS activity are in the lower centers of the brain and usually below the threshold of conscious control. The appeal of bringing ANS functions under conscious control is fascinating; yogis have for centuries been able to slow heartbeat quite voluntarily, with corresponding changes to the entire body. The potential for this in sports, particularly in the areas of recovery and recuperation, is huge.

In sports, responses to change in the environment have usually got to be swift and definite. Consequently, our treatment of the nervous system has focused on its ability to direct changes and issue instructions to the relevant parts of the body in order that they react quickly. The quickest communication system is based, as we have seen, on electrical impulses. But the body's response to an internal change is likely to occur over a period of time and be brought about by chemical adjustments. The substances involved are hormone molecules and they are manufactured by a group of cells called endocrine glands, the most important of which is the pituitary attached to the hypothalamus on the underside of the brain. This produces a growth hormone by regulating the amount of nutrients taken into the cells. Hormones themselves are messengers, secreted into the blood in which they travel to all body parts, interacting with other cells and effecting a type of fine-tuning.

Because some hormones have very specific effects – many of them local rather than body-wide – they have been of service to sports performers seeking to enhance performance (as we'll discover in later chapters). The male testes secrete the hormone testosterone, which regulates the production of sperm cells and stimulates sex drive. Testosterone has been produced chemically and the synthetic hormone introduced into the body of competitors. Among the alleged effects are an increase in muscle bulk and strength and a more aggressive attitude.

Adrenaline is another example: as we have seen, it pours into the blood, stimulating the release of glycogen from the liver, expansion of blood vessels in the heart, brain, and limbs, and contraction of vessels in the abdomen. Fatigue diminishes and blood coagulates more rapidly (which is why boxers' seconds apply an adrenaline solution to facial cuts). Competitors pumped-up with adrenaline will usually have a pale complexion, on account of their blood being diverted from skin and intestine, and dilated pupils; hearts will be pounding and the breathing will be fast. The muscles will have the capacity to contract quickly and effectively either for, as the expression goes, fight or flight. This is an unusually fast hormonal change and most influences are long term, concerning such features as growth and sexual maturity. When they pass through the liver, the hormones are converted to relatively inactive compounds that are excreted as waste product, or urea, by the kidneys; this is why urinalysis is the principal method of detecting banned substances. It determines hormonal products in urine.

The chemical fine-tuning of the body is extensive and, in the healthy body, works continuously to modify us internally. Sweat glands are largely responsible for our adjustment to heat and, as many sports activate these, we should recognize their importance. The glands' secretions cover the skin with millions of molecules of water and they begin rising to the surface (epidermis) when external temperatures exceed about 25°C/77°F, depending on weight of clothing or the rigor of the activity performed. When blood reaching the hypothalamus is 0.5–1°C/35°F above normal, nerve impulses conveyed by the ANS stimulate sweat glands into activity.

Fluid from the blood is filtered into the glands and passes through their ducts so that a larger amount of moisture is produced on the skin surface. As it evaporates, the heat in the molecules escapes, leaving coolness. The internal temperature of the body is kept within acceptable limits, as long as the sweat continues to take away the heat. (When temperatures drop, a reflex action is to shiver, which is a spasmodic muscular contraction that produces internal heat.) Most, but not all, sweating results from the eccrine glands; secretions around the armpits and nipples of both sexes and the pubic area of females come from apocrine glands, which discharge not only salt and water, but odorless organic molecules that are degraded by skin bacteria and give off distinct smells. In mammals, the smell has a sexual function, though the lengths to which humans go in trying to suppress or disguise the smell suggests that the function has been discarded in our species.

A general point here is that sweat is not just water but a concentration of several materials and profuse sweating may deprive the body of too much salt. Heat prostration and sunstroke are curses to marathon runners and triathletes and their efforts to conquer them include swallowing salt tablets before the race, drinking pure water at stages during the race, and taking Gatorade or other solutions of electrolytes (salt and other compounds that separate into ions in water and can therefore help in the conduction of nerve impulses and muscle contraction). Problems for these athletes multiply in humid climates where the air contains so much vapor that the sweat can't evaporate quickly enough to produce a cooling effect; instead, it lies on the skin's surface forming a kind of seal. The result is known as heat stagnation. Even more dangerous is the situation when, after prolonged sweating due to activity in hot atmospheres, sweat production ceases and body temperatures soar to lethal levels.

Sweat glands perform a vital compensatory function in minimizing the effects of heat during physical activity and, under instruction of the brain, try to stabilize body temperature at around 37°C/98.6°F. But their thermostatic powers have clear limitations when tested by athletes, for whom 26 miles is but the first station of the advance toward the boundaries of human endurance.

The journalist who coined the now-clichéd term "well-oiled machine" to describe some highly efficient football team actually, and perhaps unwittingly, advanced a rather accurate description of the collection of trained and healthy individuals in question. Machines in the plural would have been more correct because, when examined in one perspective, that's what human beings are: a functioning series of systems made of cells and based on principles that any engineer, biologist, or chemist would find sound. But this is a partial and inadequate description and this chapter has merely set up a model; now it must be set in context and seen to work. We now have a grasp of the basic equipment and capabilities of the body; we still know little of its properties and motivations. Sports as activities derive from natural faculties, but the particular form or shape they have taken and the way they have been perpetuated and mutated over the centuries is not understandable in purely biological terms. It needs explanation all the same and this will be the task of the following chapters.

## OF RELATED INTEREST

*The Biophysical Foundations of Human Movement* by Bruce Abernathy, Vaughn Kippers, Laurel Mackinnon, Robert Neal, and Stephanie Hanrahan (Human Kinetics, 1997) takes a multidisciplinary approach to biophysics, integrating contributions from functional anatomy, exercise physiology, and other disciplines.

*Basic Biomechanics*, fourth edition, by Susan Hall (McGraw-Hill, 2004) is a clear general introduction which comes with a CD-ROM. This should be followed with the second edition of Roger Bartlett's *Introduction to Sports Biomechanics* (Routledge, 2005).

*Physiology of Sport and Exercise*, third edition, by Jack Wilmore and David Costill (Human Kinetics, 2004) is a general introduction to the study of the structure and functions of the human body and its parts and how these are affected by the exertion of muscles and limbs.

*Practical Skills in Biology*, second edition, by Allan Jones, Rob Reeves, and Jonathan Weyers (Longman, 1998) is an interesting approach to the understanding of the human body, providing practical laboratory-based exercises and field studies.

## ASSIGNMENT

In the seventeenth century, the French philosopher René Descartes tried to explain living processes like digestion, growth, and reproduction in terms of a mechanical model, i.e. the human as a machine. Repeat the exercise: break the human body down into its component parts and analyze the relations between them as if you were studying a machine, then do a specification sheet (rather as car manufacturers do), incorporating dimensions, safety ratings, replacement parts, insurance, maintenance costs, unique features, etc.

Finally, create some copy for a possible advertisement, for example: "Beneath the sleek contours of its outer shell is an engine incorporating all the latest technological advances – from electronic microchip management systems controlling fuel injection and timing through to the latest 16-valve system with turbo charger and intercooler together with 170-brake horsepower. With an acceleration of 0–60 mph in 7 seconds and a top speed of 140 mph the machine runs well with minimal adjustment on unleaded or diesel fuel. The fully independent multi-link suspension, disc brakes on all wheels, power steering, and electronically controlled 4-wheel antilock brake system combine to offer precise handling. Climate control air conditioning, leather interior, and 6-speaker radio/CD/MP3 player provides comfort, while ABS and front and side airbags afford security. 3-D mapping, voice-guidance satellite navigation is standard."

# animal origins

## how history turned hunter-gatherers into champions

### AFTER THE *PLANET OF THE APES*

Recognize anything in the following activity that merits description as a sport? Time: early 1800s. Place: Birmingham, England. Players: a tied-up bull and a ferocious dog.

> Sometimes the dog seized the bull by the nose and "pinned" him to the earth, so that the beast roared and bellowed again, and was brought down upon its knees . . . The people then shouted out "Wind, wind!" that is, to let the bull have breath, and the parties rushed forward to take off the dog . . . However, the bulls were sometimes pinned between the legs, causing [them] to roar and rave about in great agony.

The passage is from Richard Holt's book, *Sport and the Working Class in Modern Britain*, which is full of other lurid details of what passed as sports in the eighteenth and nineteenth centuries (1990: 16). As well as bull-baiting, as the above activity was known, there was cockfighting, which involved pitting two highly trained fowl together, and dog-fighting, which goes on in Britain and the USA today, albeit in an illicit way. Legislation made such contests illegal, though cruelty to animals has by no means disappeared. The persistence of fox-hunting in the face of protests confirms this and the success of new legislation in banning it is yet to be seen.

These types of activities in which animals were made to fight, maim, and often kill each other, were regarded as sports. Before you rush to deny any connection between such barbaric contests and what we now recognize as sports, consider some of the similarities.

*Competition* for no reason apart from competition itself: unlike animal fights in other contexts, there were no evolutionary functions (such as "survival of the fittest") served by the fights.

*Winning* as a sole aim: spectators were interested in a result rather than the actual process of fighting, and animal contests typically ended with one either dead or at least too badly injured to continue. Holt adds to his description of the Birmingham bull bait: "Blood would be dropping from the nose and other parts of the bull" (1990: 16).

*Spectators*: the tournaments were set up with an audience in mind – in specially dug pits around which a crowd could stand, in barns, or other public places where the action was visible to spectators.

*Gambling*: the thrill of watching the contest was enhanced by wagering on one of the animals and money frequently changed hands among the spectators.

*Animals* were trained and used: although the contests were unacceptably cruel by today's standards, we still train and employ animals in sports, such as horse- and dog-racing, pigeon-racing, polo, and (though repugnant to many) bull-fighting. Perhaps the most remarkable legacy is the Iditarod, a 1,180-mile race through Alaska featuring packs of huskies pulling a person in a sled. The original trail was forged by dog-sleds carrying freight to miners and prospectors; the latter-day contest recreates the hunger and exhaustion of driving for eight days and nights at temperatures of –51°C/–60°F. Competitive and recreational fishing remains one of the world's most popular pursuits.

All these elements are present in human cultures that extend far beyond the Industrial Revolution of the late eighteenth and early nineteenth centuries, which is the conventional starting point for studies of sports. True, the distinct shape or form of sports developed in that crucial period and the organizational structure that distinguishes sports from mere play was a product of the industrial age. But we can go back much further: it's possible to trace the origins of contemporary sports back to primitive matters of survival; which is precisely what I intend to do in this chapter.

The methods we once used for getting nutrition have been reshaped and refined, but are still vaguely discernible. Track and field events such as running and throwing are virtually direct descendants of our ancestors' chase of prey and their attempts to stun or kill them with missiles; some events still consciously model themselves on the disciplines and aptitudes associated with hunting, modern pentathlon (riding, fencing, shooting, swimming, and running) being the clearest example. Today's versions are, of course, more enjoyable than the originals in which hunters might return from a day's pursuit minus a couple of their associates.

More advanced tool use, which enhanced the ability to survive, and improved nutrition, also generated a new adaptation that we see reflected in current sports. Tools that were once used for killing or butchery have been transformed into symbolic instruments like bats, rackets, and clubs and used in a fashion which disguises the functions of their predecessors. The origins of others, such as epées, are more transparent. The purpose of this chapter is to provide an account of the beginning of sports and its subsequent development up to the last century.

The model of sports I'm building suggests the entire phenomenon has human foundations that were established several thousand years ago. It follows that any chronicle must track its way back through history to discover the reasons for the human pursuit of what are, on this account, mock hunts and battles and the purposes they serve at both individual and social levels. The latter point will be answered in the next chapter, but the immediate task is to unravel the mystery of ancestry: how did sports begin? It's a question that requires an ambitious answer, one which takes us deep into history for a starting point.

The popular image of humans emerging from their caves before progressing to ever-higher levels of civilization has given film makers some wonderful raw material. Kevin Connor's *The Land That Time Forgot* (1974), featuring marauding ape-men, and Don Chaffey's *One Million Years BC* (1966), made memorable by a young Raquel Welch clad in animal-skin bikini, are two of several films that have capitalized on appealing but erroneous premises. Our species developed in a series of relatively sudden lurches. Traveling on two legs is one of them; tripling of brain size is another.

*Homo sapiens* first appeared 100,000 to 200,000 years ago. In evolutionary terms, this is an eyeblink. Several discoveries of remains have undermined efforts to trace what used to be called the "missing link" – the creature that was more intelligent than apes but had not yet become the finished human article. In all probability, such a creature didn't exist at all. The more we know, the less simple it seems.

Every new find indicates that there is no single line of descent with a few evolutionary dead-ends branching off it. For hundreds and thousands of years, a bewildering number of different species and subspecies of ape-like and then human-like (hominoid) animals adapted, migrated, and then perished. Only one thing is clear: the species we call human beings came out of Africa, not in a single process of migration, but after a series of waves of migration.

The earth was once like the *Planet of the Apes*: they were everywhere 10 million years ago. There were about 50 different ape-like species, some of them tree-dwellers, others living on the thickly forested ground. And, though they didn't talk or dominate humans as in the movies, some may have even used sticks and stones as crude tools. Then, they began to die out, leaving only the most adaptable and so most intelligent species. Exactly why so many species perished is not absolutely clear, but the strong likelihood is that, around 8 million years ago, there was a dramatic environmental change that turned much of the earth's surface to grassland. The species that could adapt to this survived, leaving other forest-dwellers to die out.

It's probable that, out of all the survivors, several species were bipedal, walking erect across the grassy, flat terrain. Many of these would have perished, leaving those best-equipped species to remain and propagate. One of these species was a hominoid that emerged about 3.2 million years ago. Its brain was only about a third of the size of a human brain and it stood only just over three foot (one meter), but there are clear signs that it was a human ancestor. Its unusual pelvis enabled it to move on two legs and this had important evolutionary consequences. The two upper limbs used by other species for locomotion were unhindered, allowing Lucy, as her discoverers named her, to use the arms for other purposes. Prior to the discovery of Lucy's fossil in 1974, it had been thought that big-brained creatures started using tools and, to free up their hands, began to walk upright. Lucy walked on two feet and even had "modern" hands, yet showed no evidence of using tools. She was an example of *Australopithecus afarensis*, and other examples of this species have been found since then. *Australopithecus* is the generic name of small-brained fossils.

Yet, there were larger-brained creatures around by about 2 million years ago and the discovery of skull KNM-ER 1470 (it's always been known by its museum classification) with a cranial capacity of 785 cc (compared to a human's 1,400 cc), suggested a coexistence of bipedal species. There may have been several other two-legged creatures for which the grassland was, at first, suitable but which failed to make later adaptations and died out. By contrast, one of the most successful creatures in evolutionary terms, *Homo erectus*, arrived on the scene in East Africa and, later, spread to Asia and Europe between 1.5 to 2 million years ago and survived up to about 100,000 years ago. According to some theories of evolution, *Homo erectus* instituted some significant adaptations and evolved into the earliest members of our species *Homo sapiens*, who were succeeded in Africa by the anatomically modern *Homo sapiens sapiens* and in Europe by *Homo sapiens neanderthalensis*, or Neanderthals. (*Sapiens* is Latin for wise.)

*Homo erectus* was a respectful and cautious scavenger, though much evidence points to males banding together in predatory squads and becoming proficient hunters of large animals like bears, bison, and elephants and using equipment such as clubs and nets. Layers of charcoal and carbonized bone in Europe and China have also suggested that *Homo erectus* may have used fire. Physically, the male of the species might have stood as tall as 5 feet 11 inches (1.8 meters) and, while his brain was smaller than our own, the animal had enough intelligence to make primitive tools and hunting devices.

Neanderthals, who were well-established in Europe by 70,000 BCE, certainly had sufficient intellect to use fire on a regular basis and utilized a crude technology in making weapons which, as predatory creatures, they needed. As their prey were the large and mobile bison, mammoth, and reindeer, they made good use not only of physical weapons but also of tact, or stealth. They'd hunt in packs and allocate assignments to different members. Other hints of social life are found amongst Neanderthals. Evidence of burials, for example, indicates an awareness of the significance of death; ritual burials are not conducted by species other than humans.

There is also something uniquely human about the rapport with other species: the relationships humans have with other animals is an unusual one and Neanderthals may have been the first to forge this special link. It's possible that Neanderthals attempted to domesticate as well as hurt other species. The cartoon depiction of Fred Flintstone adorned in bearskins is a bit more accurate than it seems: it's quite probable that the wearing of skins was thought to invest the wearer with some of the animal's qualities (such as strength of the mammoth or speed of the deer). The close association between many sports and animals is undoubtedly connected to this type of belief.

Some see Neanderthals as distinct from and having no breeding with *Homo sapiens*, while others see them gradually replaced by *Homo sapiens* after long periods of genetic mixing. Whether or not they were replaced or just became extinct, two facts are clear: one is technological, the other cultural. Neanderthals exploited raw materials for tool manufacture and use; they also displayed collective behavior in the division of labor they used to organize and coordinate their hunts. Related to these two activities is the fact that the reciprocal obligations systems used in hunting were carried over into domestic life. Neanderthals were cave dwellers and so used a home-base arrangement; this leads to the suggestion that they most probably constructed a stable pattern of life, possibly based on role allocation.

*Homo sapiens* shared these features: they used tools, hunted in groups, and had division of labor at the home base and especially in the hunting parties. Accepting responsibility for specific duties had obvious advantages for survival: coordinating tasks as a team would have brought more success than pell-mell approaches. Signals, symbols, markers, and cues would have been important to elementary strategies. Complementing this was the sharing of food at the central home base. Maybe this awakened humans to the advantages of pair-bonding and the joint provisioning of offspring: the mutual giving and receiving, or reciprocity, remains the keystone of all human societies.

The hunter-gatherer mode of life is central to our understanding of the origin of sports. It began with foraging and scavenging as long as 3 million years ago; hunting as a regular activity followed a period of feeding off carcasses or spontaneous picking. Including more meat in the diet brought about nutritional changes, but also precipitated the invention of more efficient means of acquiring food. The response was to hunt for it – and this had widespread behavioral repercussions, not only in terms of social organization but also in physical development. Covering ground in pursuit of quarry required the kind of speed that could only be achieved by an efficient locomotion machine. The skeleton became a sturdier structure able to support the weight of bigger muscles and able quickly to transmit the force produced by the thrust of limbs against the ground. Lower limbs came to be more directly under the upper body, so that support was more efficient in motion; leg bones lengthened and the muscles elongated, enabling a greater stride and an ability to travel further with each step. The human evolved into a mobile and fast runner, and, though obviously not as fast as some other predators, the human's bipedalism left upper limbs free for carrying.

Where quarry was near enough to be approached, but also near enough to be disturbed, hunters would need short bursts of explosive speed, an ability to contract muscles and release energy anaerobically. In short, they needed the kind of power which modern sprinters possess. Hunts might take up an entire day and would demand of the hunter stamina, endurance, and the capacity to distribute output over long periods – precisely the type of aerobic work performed by middle-distance and marathon runners, not to mention triathletes.

Effective synthesis of ATP from ADP and the removal of waste lactic acid was enhanced by respiratory evolution. Ribs expanded and the muscles between them developed to allow the growth of lungs, which permitted deeper breathing to take in more and more air. Since the sustained release of energy depends on a supply of glucose and other foods, the hunter's diet was clearly important. While we can't be certain exactly what proportion of the diet was taken up by meat, we can surmise that this protein-rich food source played a role in balancing the daily expenditure of energy and providing enough fats and proteins for tissue repair.

Habitual meat-eating was not unqualified in its advantages; it introduced the very severe disadvantage of bringing humans into open competition with the large mammalian carnivores and scavengers like hogs, panthers, and tigers which roamed the savannas looking for food. Ground speed was, in this instance, a requisite quality for survival, the clawless, weak-jawed biped being ill-equipped to confront the specialist predators. In time, evolution yielded a capacity to make and use not only tools but also weapons like clubs and stones, which at least evened up the odds. The physical clash with other animals continues to fascinate elements of the human population, a fact witnessed in such activities as bear-baiting, boxing kangaroos, and the type of man *vs* horse races in which Jesse Owens performed during the undignified twilight of his career (as we will see in Chapter 6). A big advantage that tilted the balance was the increase in the human's most important asset.

Compared to body size, our brain is a truly exceptional organ; it's one of the most obvious physical features that distinguishes us from the rest of the animal world. How did we acquire our large brains? One theory holds that cooking our food enabled us to digest nutritionally rich vegetables with thick skins that could not be eaten raw. Cooking food made it more easily available, cracking open or destroying physical barriers such as thick skins or husks, bursting cells and sometimes modifying the molecular structure of proteins and starches; all of which gave us the extra calories necessary for brain growth – food for thought, so to speak.

This view opposes the more traditional view of meat as the trigger behind brain development. The larger brain, with its larger neurons and denser, more complex circuitry of dendrite branches, may well have been related to the long days spent beneath the hot sun, hunting in comparative safety while the bigger predators sought shade and rest. As carnivores, we would scavenge what the big cats lcft bchind. Thc mcat gavc us cncrgy and the effect of the sun on our heads caused the brain to swell. Yet another perspective favors bipedalism as a prime mover: freeing up arms enabled our ancestors to explore and discover, prompting further curiosity about the world and a desire to reshape it in a way we desired. The results of our handiwork stimulated further enquiry, the development of knowledge and technology, and an evolutionary cerebral adaptation.

Obscure as the relationship between brain growth and behavioral change may remain, we should at least recognize that neither is independent of the environment in which the processes take place. For instance, survival success would have depended on the ability to identify in the surrounding environment things that were needed: rocks for tools and weapons, tracks of game and competitive predators, sources of vegetable. The need to discriminate perceptually encouraged larger brains and better communication skills, which in turn occasioned bigger and better brains; these more complicated organs needed nourishment in terms both of food and social stimulation, and this would have been reflected in subsistence methods and social arrangements. The process had no "result" as such, for the brain constantly developed in response to behavioral change but at the same time led to new thoughts that were translated into action: a continuous feedback motion.

Hunting, gathering, and, to a decreasing degree, scavenging were the main human adaptations. Among their correlates were division of labor, basic social organization, increases in communication, and, of course, increase in brain size. Slowly and steadily the species evolved ways of satisfying basic biological drives and needs: food supply, shelter against the elements and predators, sex and reproduction. In the process, a prototype emerged: "man the hunter" (and I choose the phrase with care, as evidence suggests that the more robust males assumed most responsibility in catching prey). The species' greater brain capacity gave them the advantage of intellect, an ability to devise methods of tracking and capture, to utilize cunning and stealth as well as force. Concentration became important; intelligence enabled our ancestors to ignore distractions (what sport psychologists later called gating out, as we'll see in Chapter 6) and fix attention, or focus, on the sought-after game. Hunts, especially for large animals, would be more effectively performed in squads and these required a level of coordination, synchronization, and communication. Cooperation and reciprocity were qualities of great use in hunting and at the home base, where the spoils would be shared.

The accumulated experience of the hunt itself would impart qualities – like courage in the face of dangerous carnivores who would compete for food. Risks were essential to reproductive success; if they hadn't been taken, the species would still be picking fruit. Among the specific skills refined in this period would have been an ability to aim and accurately deliver missiles, a capacity to judge pace in movement, and to overwhelm and conquer prey when close combat was necessary. We should also take note of the fact that humans became impressively good swimmers and divers, evolving equipment and functions that aided deep diving and fast swimming; this aquatic adaptation may have been linked to hunting for fish.

By now, you'll have detected where I'm headed with this argument. All these features are responses to the manner in which the species procured its food: this is essential to life and so has a strong, if not determining, effect on every aspect of both lifestyle and personality. If an existing method of obtaining food doesn't yield enough nutrition, then bodies suffer and the species either perishes or makes new adaptations, perhaps formulating alternative methods. In the event, what seems to have happened in the case of *Homo sapiens* is that they hit upon a novel way of guaranteeing a food supply which eliminated the need for many of the activities that had persisted for the previous 2 million years or more, and had carved deeply the features of human character and capacities. As recently as 10,000 years ago, *Homo sapiens* devised a way of exploiting the food supply which was to remove the necessity of hunting and release humans to concentrate on building what is now popularly known as "civilization."

Instead of exploiting natural resources around them, the species began to exploit its own ability. In short, the ability to create a food supply. This was accomplished by gathering animals and crops together, containing them in circumstances that permitted their growth and reproduction, then picking crops or slaughtering animals as necessary, without ever destroying the entire stock. In this way, supply was rendered a problem only by disease or inclement weather. The practice of cultivating land for use, rather than for mere existence, gave rise to farming.

## RECREATING THE HUNT

Although now open to debate, the beginnings of agriculture are seen in orthodox teaching to coincide with the end of what's called the paleolithic age. The transition was seen by some as swift and dramatic, though this view has been challenged by others who accentuate the uneven process of development over periods of time. For example, in Europe, following the recession of the ice age, there appears to have been an interlude in which certain animals, especially dogs, were domesticated, some cereals were harvested, and forms of stock management were deployed, but without the systematic approach of later agriculturists.

Obviously, regions differed considerably ecologically, and the period characterized by the transition from hunter-gatherer to farmer was neither smooth nor uniform. But it was sudden – in evolutionary terms, that is. We started the systematic domestication of animals – a process central to agriculture – only 10,000 years ago. It may have taken the form of controlled breeding or just providing fodder to attract wild herds, but the insight was basically the same: that enclosing and nourishing livestock was a far more effective and reliable way of ensuring food than hunting for it. It was also safer, of course.

### Paleolithic age

From *palaios*, the Greek for ancient times, and *lithos*, meaning stone, this describes the period in which primitive stone implements were used. Beginning probably 2 million years ago when our ancestors put an edge on a stone, pressed its thick end against the palm of the hand and realized its power to strike and cut, this age saw the arrival of the hunter-gatherer, as opposed to the simple forager cultures. It ended as recently as 10,000 years ago, when the domestication of animals and cultivation of plants started.

Complementing this discovery was the realization that planting and nurturing plants and harvesting only enough to meet needs so that regrowth was possible was an efficient exploitation of natural resources compared to the cumbersome and less predictable gathering method. The breakthroughs led to all manner of toolmaking and other technologies that added momentum to the agricultural transformation that's loosely referred to as the neolithic age (from the Greek *neo* meaning new and *lithos* meaning stone: a period when ground and polished tools and weapons made out of stone were introduced).

Remember: hunting and gathering had been dominant for more than 2 million years before. During that period the lifestyle and mentality it demanded became components of our character. Chasing, capturing, and killing with their attendant dangers were practiced features of everyday life. The qualities of courage, skill, and the inclination to risk, perhaps even to sacrifice on occasion, were not heroic but simply human and necessary for survival. What we'd now regard as epic moments were in all probability quite ordinary. The coming of farming made most of these qualities redundant. The hunting parties that honed their skills, devised strategies, and traded on courage were no longer needed. Instead, the successful farmer needed to be diligent, patient, responsible, regular, and steadfast. A farmer was more interested in breeding animals than in hunting them. The switch was bound to introduce strains.

Hunting and gathering affected us not only culturally but perhaps even genetically, so long and sweeping was its reign. No organism is a product purely of hereditary nature or of environmental experience. Humans are no different in being products of the interaction between genes and the environment: nature via nurture, to revive the phrase used in Chapter 2. But the kind of evolutionary change we're interested in proceeded at different levels: the human way of living changed, but not in such a way as to incur an automatic switch in human beings themselves. After all, even rough arithmetic tells us that the 10,000 years in which agriculture has developed represents at most 0.5 percent of the period spent hunting and gathering. Sport, in this scenario, is the evidence that we're still catching up with the changes. It's as if cultural evolution sped ahead of biological evolution: we didn't completely change from one type of organism into another as quickly as the cultural pace required. There was – perhaps *is* – still too much of the hunter-gatherer in us to permit an easy settling down to breeding animals and sowing crops.

One response to this strain was to re-enact the hunt: imitate the chase, mimic the prey, copy the struggle, simulate the kill, and recreate the conditions under which such properties as bravery, fortitude, and resolve would be rewarded. It was a fairly minor but important adaptation in which the customary skills, techniques, and habits were retained even when their original purpose had disappeared.

OK, it made far more sense to enclose, feed, and domesticate animals than to hunt them, as it did to sow crops rather than gather wild fruits and grains. It was perfectly possible to acknowledge this, while growing bored by it. How many times have you wanted and chased something or someone and when you finally get it or them, you feel an anticlimax and yearn for the excitement of the chase? Maybe the tyro farmers craved the thrill the hunts used to bring. How could the spirit of the hunt be recaptured?

The answer was: let it continue. Hunt for its own sake rather than for food. No matter that hunting served no obvious purpose any longer, let people engage in it for the sheer pleasure or tingle it generated. In this way, people played at hunting: they didn't direct their efforts to meeting the immediate material needs of life, or acquiring necessities. Hunting became instead an *autotelic* activity, having no purpose apart from its own existence.

---

### Autotelic

From the Greek *auto*, meaning by or for itself, and *telos*, meaning end. An autotelic activity is one which has an end or purpose in itself and is engaged in for its own sake.

---

Once it became detached from the food supply, the activity took on a life of its own. When survival no longer depended on killing game, the killing became an end; what was once an evolutionary means to an end became an end in itself. The new hunt no longer had as its motive the pursuit of food but rather the pursuit of new challenges. Although in behavioral terms much the same activity as hunting, the new version was an embryonic sports or at least an expression of the drive or impulse underlying sports right to the present day. Stripped of its original purpose, the mechanical aspects of the activity came to prominence. Team coordination, stealth, intelligence, daring, physical prowess, and courage in the face of danger were valued more than the end product and, over time, these became integrated into a series of activities, each in some way mimicking the original activities.

It sounds trite to say that the roots of sports lie in our primeval past when so many of today's sports operate not in response to survival but as adjuncts to commercial interests. At the same time, we should recognize that the impulses that make sports attractive enough to be commercially exploited are part of our evolutionary make-up. Sport was the result of the attempt to reintroduce the thrill of the hunt into lives that were threatened with mundane routines in unchallenging environments. As such, it was and remains both precious and profound. It may owe nothing to the hunt nowadays; but it still owes a good deal to the attempts at replacing the hunt with something comparably as exciting.

So, there is perfect sense in Gerhard Lukas's claim that "the first sport was spear throwing," or *speer worfen* (1969). Javelins, darts, blowguns, and bows and arrows were modifications of the basic projectile and unquestionably featured in mock as well as genuine hunts. The use of the bow is interesting in that it stimulated the construction of an artifact, the target, the bullseye, which, as its name implies, represented the part of the animal to be aimed at. Archery, as a purely autotelic behavior, actually had the quality of compressing a symbolic hunt into a finite area and allowing a precise way of assessing the results. As such, it had potential as an activity that could be watched and evaluated by others, who wouldn't participate except in a vicarious way. That is, they might experience it imaginatively through the participants – which is what most sports spectators do, even today. This vicariousness was, as we now realize, absolutely crucial to the emergence and development of spectator sport.

The facility for bringing the rationality and emotion of a hunt to a home base made it possible to include dozens, or hundreds, of people in the whole experience. Just witnessing an event offered some continuity, however tenuous, within change: spectators could "feel" the drama and tension of a supposed hunt from another age, through the efforts of the participants.

The obvious acknowledgment of this came with the custom-built stadium. Stadiums, or stadia (as some prefer the plural), came with the clustering together of human populations and the creation of city-states. Irrigation was crucial to farming, of course, so most of the earliest known civilizations had their urban centers near rivers, as in China, India, and the Near and Middle East. Richard Mandell, in his *Sport: A cultural history* (1984), urges caution in gleaning evidence of what we now call spectator sports in ancient civilizations. But he does show that the Mesopotamians, for example, left traces of evidence that suggest physical competitions. These might have been tests of strength and skill; though they may also have been more military training regimes than amusements for the masses.

The seminal Egyptian civilization of some 5,000 years ago left much material in the form of documents, frescos, tombs, and bric-a-brac. In these we find depicted one of the most essential, enduring, and unchanging activities, and one which we will consider in the next section: combat.

---

**City-state**

A city that is also an independent state with its own organized administrative apparatus in which a single government is empowered to rule. Governments changed, but the bureaucracy stayed essentially intact, giving a stability and continuity to the city-state and its main institutions. Inhabitants were *citizens* and their rights, entitlements, duties, and obligations were described as *civic*. From the Latin *civitas*.

---

# IN PURSUIT OF *ÁTHLON*

At some stage in ancient history, the idea of rivalry seems to have struck chords. The straightforward drive of the hunt, in which packs pursued game, acquired a provision. The object was not merely the climax of a kill, but in administering the kill faster or more effectively than others. Competition between individuals or groups added a new and apparently appealing dimension to an already perilous activity, turning it into a game with some semblance of organization and a clear understanding of what constituted an achievement. The amusement value, it seems, was boosted by the introduction of a human challenge and by spectatorship.

It's probable, though undocumented, that physical combat activities between humans and perhaps animals coexisted with the autotelic hunts. We needn't invoke the Cain and Abel fable to support the argument that intra-species fighting, for both instrumental and playful purposes, existed throughout history. It is one of the least changeable aspects of *Homo sapiens*. Combat has many different forms, ranging from wrestling to fencing; stripped to its basics, it expresses the rawest type of competition. As such, it seems to have held a wide appeal both for participants seeking a means to express their strength and resilience and for audiences who to this day are enraptured by the sight of humans disputing each other's physical superiority.

The hunt, or at least the mimetic activity that replaced it, would have satisfied a certain need for those closely involved, but the actual behavior would have been so fluid and dispersed that it would not have been closely observed, certainly not as a complete and integrated action. Spectators would have been much more easily accommodated at a home base where fighting could be staged in much the same way and with a similar purpose to mock hunts: to break up tedious routines and raise emotions with brief but thrilling and relatively unpredictable episodes of violent action. The emphasis may well have fallen on animal fighting, unarmed human combat and, possibly, armed humans pitched against large animals such as bears or tigers. Given the purpose of this type of combat, some loose structure or framework governing the fight was likely; combatants fighting to kill or disable an opponent in order to save themselves in any way possible would be warring rather than engaging in a sport.

A fresco excavated from the tomb of an Egyptian prince and dated to about 4,000 years ago looks similar to a modern wall chart and shows wrestlers demonstrating over a hundred different positions and holds. Mandell suggests that there may have been professional wrestlers in the Egyptian civilization. Artwork shows fighters also using sticks about one-meter long; even today, stick fighting persists in parts of Egypt, though in a more ritualized form. It's quite possible that the proximity to the Nile encouraged competitive swimming and rowing. In the plains of the Upper Nile region, hunting of large game, including elephants, was commonplace, the chariot being an effective vehicle for this purpose. Pharaoh Tutankhamun (fourteenth century BCE) is shown on one fresco hunting lions from his chariot. Amphibian Nile dwellers like crocodiles and hippopotamuses were also hunted. Crete (to the south of Greece in the Aegean Sea) had trade contacts with Egypt and some kind of cultural cross-fertilization is possible.

---

### Mimetic

From the Greek *mimesis* for imitation, this describes an activity that imitates or resembles another, and which is carried out especially for amusement. A child may mimetically play cops 'n' robbers or adult members of Round Table organizations may imitate battles, albeit in a mock way.

---

Certainly, Cretans were avid hunters and their relics suggest they were combat enthusiasts also, though the form of fighting they favored seems more akin to boxing than wrestling. According to J. Sakellarakis: "One finds in Crete, the first indications of the athletic spirit which was to evolve and reach a high pitch in subsequent centuries" (1979: 14). The games that had been played in Egypt and to the East developed into more exacting performances with set rules. We also have evidence of a version of bull-fighting, and a type of cattle wrestling that resembles the modern rodeo in the United States. Bull-leaping was a dangerous game that involved grasping the horns of an onrushing bull and vaulting over its body. Bull games are still popular today, of course.

The mythical and the mundane are intertwined in our knowledge of Greek civilization, popularly and justifiably regarded as the first culture to incorporate sports or, more specifically, competition, into civic life. The compulsion to pursue public recognition of one's supremacy through open contest with others was known by the Greeks as *agōn*. Athletic excellence achieved in competition was an accomplishment of, literally, heroic proportions. Myths of Hercules sending discuses into oblivion and Odysseus heaving boulders are important signifiers of the high value Greeks placed on physical feats, but the less spectacular evidence shows that they approached, organized, and assessed the outcomes of activities in a way which is quite familiar.

"The spirit of competition and rivalry extended to every area of Greek life," writes Manolis Andronicus in his essay "Essay and education: The institution of the games in ancient Greece" (in Yaloris 1979: 43). The Greeks' approach was to win, and here we find the almost obsessive drive for success that characterizes contemporary sport: winning was quite often at any cost and scant respect was paid to such things as "fairness." Some may argue that the search for supremacy is a primordial competitive instinct. It's more likely that particular social arrangements in which inequality and distinct strata are key components encourage individuals to strive hard and better themselves by whatever means they can. Athletic prowess was one such means in the ancient civil society of Greece – the *polis*. Victors could acquire *arete* (excellence), the ultimate attainment. Greeks were also very keen on physical perfection and part of the purpose of athletic competition was to display the brawny bodies of men, but not women. One of the ideals embedded in Greek games was *kalos kagathos*, meaning the "good and beautiful man."

In terms of organization, Greeks created events which exist today without major modification. They are credited with being the first organizers of sports on a systematic basis, the Olympic Games, which began in 776 BCE, being the clearest expression of this. This event integrated sports into a wider religious festival, drawing disparate competitors and spectators together at one site every four years in an effort to convince themselves they were in some sense united. Greeks were also influential in their attempts to determine outcomes. Despite aphorisms about competing being more important than winning, victory was crucial and systems were designed to ensure accurate assessment of performance.

Exact distances were measured and staggers were introduced on racing circuits. Tallies of points were kept in multidiscipline events like the pentathlon (the Greek *āthlon* meant award, or prize, from which came the noun *athlētēs* to describe those who competed for the award). Records of performances were kept (each Olympiad took the name of the victorious sprinter at the previous festival). The games may have been less important as a spectacle than they were as a focal point around which to organize training. Physical fitness, strength, and the general toughness that derives from competition were important military attributes, and so the process was tuned to producing warriors as much as sports performers.

Sparta is the best-known city-state in this context: it was a site of phalanx training in which youths would be taken from their families and reared in an austere garrison where they would be honed for combat. There was also a religious element to competition, for the Greeks believed that athletic victory indicated that the victor would be favored by the capricious gods in whom they believed.

It's important to remember that, while today's Olympics bear the same name as their ancient forerunner, they were not games in the way we understand them – competitive activities in which winners, no matter how single-minded, find time to shake the hands of their rivals and show their respect. Winning was ruthlessly pursued and no prisoners were taken. There were no silver or bronze medals and only winners were recorded. If competitors died or were seriously injured, it went with the territory. Winners were competing not simply for glory but for the grace of the gods and this was a powerful motivation.

We can be sure that the Greeks went to great lengths in their preparations and so provided something of a prototype for what we now call training. Spartans in particular used a cyclical pattern of increasing and decreasing the intensity of preparations which is used in most modern sports. The very concept of preparation is important: recognizing that excellence does not spring spontaneously but is the product of periods of heavy labor and disciplined regimes prompted the Greeks to provide facilities. So, in the sixth century BCE, we see a new type of building called a *gymnasium* (meaning, literally, an exercise for which one strips).

By the time of the Greeks' refinements, sports had undergone changes in purpose and, indeed, nature. While the content showed clear lines of descent connecting it with more basic hunting and combat, the functions it served were quite novel: it was seen as a military training activity, as a vehicle for status-gaining, or what we might now refer to as social mobility, and as a way of securing divine favor. This doesn't deny that the impulses associated with hunting and gathering were present, but it does highlight the autonomy of sports once separated from its original conditions of creation and growth. The Greek adaptation was a response to new material and psychic requirements.

Powerful Greek city-states needed defense against outside attacks and they ensured this by encouraging and rewarding warriors. Accompanying the development of the *polis* was the growth of the state's control over human expressions of violence; sophisticated social organization and internal security were impossible without some regulation of violence. The state's response was to obtain a legitimate monopoly over violence and establish norms of behavior which discouraged the open expression of violence by citizens and encouraged saving violence for the possible repulsion of attacks from outside powers. Contests, challenges, and rivalries were ways in which the impulse could reassert itself, but in socially acceptable forms.

The value of athletic competition earned it a central place in Greek civilization and the importance of this is reinforced by writers such as Johan Huizinga and Norbert Elias, who stress that the process of becoming civilized itself implicates a culture in controlling violence while at the same time carving out "enclaves" for the "ritualized expression of physical violence." We'll return to the theory in Chapter 5, but should note the basic observation that sport serves as a legitimate means through which primitive, violence-related impulses and emotions can simultaneously be engendered and contained. Much of what the ancients would have regarded as expressions of civilization would be seen as barbarous from the standpoint of the early twenty-first century. Gouging, biting, breaking, and the use of spiked fist thongs were all permissible in Greek combat. But these were occasions for the exhibition of warrior-like qualities and mercy was not such a quality. While victory was a symbolic "kill" it was also, at times, a quite literal kill.

Much of the glory and honor that Greeks had invested in athletic competition were removed by the Romans. For Romans, who conquered Greece, part of the appeal of sports lay in the climax of killing. One of their innovations on Greek sports was in establishing preparatory schools exclusively for gladiators, who would sooner or later be publicly applauded or slaughtered. The actual events would be staged in hippodromes, cavernous stadia where spectators would joyously witness the death of one human being either by another or by beasts. Scenes such as these are vividly depicted in Ridley Scott's movie *Gladiator* (2000).

Influenced by some Greek activities, Romans held foot races, chariot races, and many types of one-to-one combat in the centuries either side of the start of the Christian era. They were also aware of the immense military advantages of having a fit, disciplined, and tempered population. It was expensive to train gladiators, especially if they were all to be killed, so convicted prisoners and slaves were virtually sacrificed.

Adding to the extravagance was the cost of importing animals: wild beasts from throughout the world were captured, transported, and nourished. For five or more centuries, hundreds of thousands of beasts were brought into the Colosseum and other stadia and, watched by massed audiences, pitched against each other or against humans. Death seems to have been an accepted part of this activity. There was nothing curious about the Romans' apparent lack of fascination when it came to hunting (no artifacts to suggest much interest). They had no need to leave their cities: the hunts were effectively transferred to the stadia where audiences could satisfy their appetites for violence, or their "blood lusts," as some might say. Gladiatorial conflicts featuring wild animals were comparable to the primitive hunts; the comparisons between human combat and today's fighting sports are clear.

Nowadays, there are few deaths to observe in sporting combat, and when tragedy does strike it leads to a period of earnest self-reflection as well as attacks from medical authorities on the "barbaric" nature of such activities. The fact remains: audiences are amused and excited by the prospect of human combat, as they are by animal conflict – about which there is far less restraint, as the slaughter in bull-fighting and hare-coursing suggests. The threshold of tolerance has dropped, but this is largely a function of the cultural forces that emanate from civilization: the human proclivity to watch, enjoy, and appreciate the infliction of damage during combat does not seem to waver. Perhaps we're not so dissimilar to our Roman ancestors who wallowed in the bloodletting and cheerfully pointed their thumbs to the floor to answer the question, life or death. As Mike Tyson told a journalist from the *Albany Times* back in January 1986: "When you see me smash somebody's skull, *you enjoy it*."

The gladiatorial schools finally closed after Christian opposition in CE 399. In the following century, the combat grew less deadly and was superseded as an entertainment by less expensive chariot racing, which was arguably the first mass spectator event, drawing crowds of up to 250,000 to the Circus Maximus. Chariot racing required teams, each team wearing different-colored uniforms, and the winners receiving prize money as well as garlands. It has been argued that Roman sports assumed a political character in this period. With no genuinely democratic means of representation, the populations may well have grown restless and demanded change were it not for the diverting effect of the combat and racing.

The entertainment that drew crowds in their hundreds of thousands diverted their attention, if only temporarily, from their grievances and so served the function of maintaining the status quo. Masses were distracted and amused, if not by bread by circuses. The theme was updated in the 1987 Arnold Schwarzenegger movie *The Running Man* (directed by Paul Michael Glaser) set in a totalitarian future in which "have-nots" are kept docile by a competition in which convicted criminals are pursued through a maze by "stalkers" – athletes trained to kill. "The public wants sports and violence," observes the competition's MC. "We give them what they want." We'll consider the scholarly attempts to portray today's sports in a similar way in Chapter 5.

## THE RUSH OF THE SPECTACLE

Beside the civilizations of Egypt, Greece, and Rome, other cultures emerging in the pre-Christian era had activities resembling sport, though in this historical context we should observe Mandell's caveat that "the boundaries that we moderns use to separate 'sport' from other areas of human endeavor have been indistinct or not worth noticing in other cultures" (1984: 93).

So, we can't be certain that the swimming, diving, and combat, armed and unarmed, practiced by inhabitants of South Asia around 2,500 years ago approached what we would recognize as sport; they may have had a more specific traditional significance, possibly bound up in the caste system. Similarly, the equestrian pursuits of the Chinese, together with their competitive archery, may have been based less on recreation or amusement and more on military training. Yet, as with Greeks and Romans, the activities themselves have been adapted to suit changing circumstances. For example, the sport we call polo almost certainly started life as a Chinese method of target practice. Many of China's martial exercises, which could be used competitively, were functional and were used to maintain a high level of fitness amongst the working population. Japanese industries have successfully adopted this ancient policy, holding exercise sessions before work in today's factories.

The Chinese were probably the first to employ a ball effectively, though there is evidence that the Egyptians experimented. In northern China there was a primitive kicking game. The Chinese invented a projectile that was the fore-runner of the shuttlecock and, presumably, propelled it by means of some sort of racket or bat.

The military importance of the horse, especially fast and maneuverable breeds, is obvious and the Japanese perhaps more than any other population recognized this in their sporting traditions. Their competitive shows of speed and intricacy have clear counterparts in today's horse-oriented events, including dressage. Japan's legacy of martial arts is large and well known; combat in the feudal age of the samurai was based on several ancient disciplines and included the mastery of horses, weapons, and unarmed conflict.

Many of the skills survive, though with modifications. The pattern that emerged in Japan as elsewhere is the use of sport as a military exercise as well as a pursuit to retain interest and capture enthusiasm while preparing its participants for the more practical discipline of defense. Wherever we find a cavalry, we almost invariably discover some form of competitive endeavor involving the horse. Typically, the competitors would be something of an elite, with resources and possibly patronage enough to compete and serve; they may well have been lionized as Greek heroes were. Certainly in medieval Europe, armed knights were the basis of the continent's supremacy and glory. The knights would be served by peasants and would enjoy status, though in material terms they may not have been much better off.

Practice fights between mounted knights gave rise to a form of combat known as jousting and, as modern fans are drawn by sparring sessions or exhibition games, spectators stood in line as the combatants galloped toward each other, lances extended. The object was to tilt the lance at the adversary in an attempt to unseat him. As the jousts gained popularity in the fifteenth century, they were surrounded by pomp, pageantry, and ritual, and formal tournaments were lavish affairs attended and heavily patronized by nobility. Jousting became an expensive pursuit quite beyond the reach of the peasantry, and indeed beyond all apart from the wealthy landowners whom the jousters served. Peasants would merely look on as the often huge and elaborate tournaments unfolded.

The combat was frequently along territorial lines, as in a 1520 tournament in northern France between King Henry VIII of England and King Francis I of France. A truly "international" event, it was spread over three weeks and attended by dozens of thousands. As well as the equestrian contests, tournaments might also have included sword fights and more theatrical displays of acrobatics and horsemanship – in the age of chivalry, women were strictly spectators.

Jousting, as with the many other forms of combat, had the military purpose of keeping knights in good fighting shape, but may have been transformed into an alternative to warring. Disputes could be settled less expensively and more enjoyably by tournaments than by costly internecine battles. From the twelfth to sixteenth centuries, tournaments became more organized and orderly, as did European society as a whole. Accommodation was made for spectators, scaffolds and stands being built as the jousts grew more popular and attracted large crowds in Italy, France, Germany, and other parts of Europe.

After the sixteenth century, the grand tournaments faded and rural events emerged, though tilts were often at targets, not humans. The tournaments gradually changed character from being hard-edged and competitive; "from sports to spectacle" is how Allen Guttmann describes the change in his book *Sports Spectators* (1986). The process is familiar to anyone who has witnessed the transmutation of wrestling after it became a popular pseudo-sport.

Hunting and archery coexisted with jousting and outlasted it, though never attracting comparable numbers of spectators. Archery survived virtually intact and is today an Olympic event; the old longbows have been considerably modified, of course. Civic festivals were organized around competitions and were grand occasions, drawing vast crowds to pageants all over Europe. The stag and fox hunts were direct predecessors of the modern fox hunts, with the rich amusing themselves by setting free their hounds and giving pursuit; the poor would amuse themselves by pursuing them all.

Hunts and other "blood sports" continued to enjoy popularity among lower classes, whose penchant for watching tethered bears prodded with sticks and then set upon by fierce dogs is similar to that of the spectators who gathered at the Roman Colosseum centuries before. Cockfights, which have almost

---

## Blood sports

Recreational pursuits that involved inflicting harm on animals were of three types, all very popular between 1780 and 1860 and modestly popular beyond. Baiting involved chaining, tethering, or cornering an animal and setting trained dogs to torment or attack it: this was favored by the British and American plebeian, or working class. Typically, a bull would be brought by a butcher or farmer who would be paid to have it secured to a post while specially trained dogs were allowed to snap at and bite it. The bull, having been ripped by the dogs, would be slaughtered and its meat sold. Badger-baiting involved releasing dogs down a badger's sett to chase it out. Fighting consisted of goading trained dogs or cocks into fighting each other until one rendered the other unable to continue. This was a more commercialized activity followed by the English aristocracy, according to Holt (1989, 1990). Hunting for amusement was also popular in the period, the quarry being ducks, cats, bullocks, among other animals. Some of these activities persist to the present day.

universal appeal, were held in England from about the twelfth century and attracted audiences from the various classes. As we saw from the description at the beginning of this chapter, the activities frequently ended in dead, dying, or seriously hurt animals.

Hugh Cunningham, in his *Leisure in the Industrial Revolution*, relates a Sunday morning meeting in London in 1816 at which several hundred people were assembled in a field adjoining a churchyard. In the field, "they fight dogs, hunt ducks, gamble, enter into subscriptions to fee drovers for a bullock." The Rector of the nearby church observed: "I have seen them drive the animal through the most populous parts of the parish, force sticks pointed with iron, up the body, put peas into the ears, and infuriate the beast" (1980: 23).

Although condemned systematically from the eighteenth century, blood sports persist to this day, most famously in the Spanish bull rings and in the streets of Pamplona. England's Bull Ring, in Birmingham, reminds us that such events were not always confined to Spain; bull-running ceased in England in 1825, a year after the founding of the Royal Society for the Prevention of Cruelty to Animals (RSPCA). The same organization brought pressure against cockfighting, which was banned in 1835, only to go underground as an illicit, predominantly working-class pursuit.

The decline of cockfighting, bull-baiting, and the like coincided with cultural changes that brought with them a range of alternative leisure pursuits. The whole spectrum of changes were part of what some writers have called the civilizing process – which we will cover in more detail in the next chapter.

But, before we are tempted into assuming that barbaric tastes and activities have completely disappeared, we should stay mindful of Richard Holt's caution: "The tendency by members of all social classes to maltreat animals for excitement or gain is by no means dead even today" (1990: 24). Dog-fighting in particular persists in the West to this day and dogs are bred for the specific purpose of fighting. In the early 1990s, amid a panic over the number of ferocious breeds proliferating, the British banned the import of American pit bulls (such animals are required to be registered in Britain under the Dangerous Dogs Act, 1991; there are about 5,000 unregistered pit bulls trained for fighting rather than as pets). For a while the law seemed to work, though dog-fighting made a comeback in the early twenty-first century, especially in England. And, as if to remind us of our retrograde thirst for blood, a police operation in 2004 resulted in the seizure of 73 trained dogs, many of which had signs of fight injuries, and the confiscation of equipment used in dog-fighting. A year before, 19 roosters and more than $17,000 (£11,000) were seized in a raid on a cockfighting den in New York City. Seventy people were arrested.

Blood sports in general and fox-hunting in particular are seen as having central importance by Norbert Elias and Eric Dunning in their book *Quest for Excitement*. The "civilizing" of society demanded greater personal self-control and a stricter constraint on violence, but the process of hunting or just observing allowed "all the pleasures and the excitement of the chase, as it were, mimetically in the form of wild play" (1986). While the passion and exhilaration associated with hunting would be aroused, the actual risks would be absent in the imagined version (except for the animals, of course) and the effects of watching would be, according to Elias and Dunning, "liberating, cathartic."

The comments could be applied without alteration to all of the activities considered so far. They are products of a human imagination ingenious enough to create artificial situations that human evolution has rendered irrelevant. But, once created, they have seemed to exert a control and power of their own, eliciting in both participants and audience a pleasurable excitement that encapsulates the thrill or "rush" of a hunt, yet carries none of the attendant risks.

History shows that activities which at least resemble sports are rarely purely autotelic and can be augmented with other purposes. From ancient to medieval ages, the tendency was to imbue supposed sporting activities with a military purpose, often encouraging qualities within participants that were of obvious utility in serious combat. We also find a theme in sports history in which many of the main roles were occupied by privileged or elite groups who performed, while most of the supporting roles were played by peasantry or plebeians who watched. The public provision of entertainment by the powerful had a latent political function in diverting attention away from practical realities and material needs and animating sentiments and emotions that were not challenging to the established order of things.

Human relationships with other animals have been peculiarly ambivalent. Dogs, for instance, have been domesticated and cared for, and used to hunt other more vulnerable creatures, and to retrieve birds which have been killed. Many other animals have simply been used as expendable prey, an observation that gives credence to the view that, while the hunt as a survival mechanism has receded, the violent impulses that it once fostered remain. Animal abuses very gradually declined in the long period under review and, though they have been under pressure this century, they certainly have not disappeared in the modern era. Animal uses, as opposed to abuses (though the distinction may not be acceptably clear-cut for everyone), are still very much with us, as dog-racing and horse-racing, remind us. The previously mentioned Iditarod in which packs of huskies pull a sled for eight days and nights in temperatures of −51°C/−60°F is an organized competition in which the driver talks to, becomes as tough as, and even sleeps with his dogs, according to Gary Paulsen, in his *Winterdance* (1994).

This close relationship with animals suggests a continuity in sports and one which, if traced back, has its origins in the transition from hunter-gatherer to farmer. While the connecting thread appears at times to be only slender, we can infer that there is surely some human property that elicits a desire for a form of autotelic enterprise based on competition. The way in which it manifests itself differs from culture to culture, and so far in this chapter I have pulled out only fragments from history to illustrate the general argument. The impression is still clear enough to draw a plausible scenario and one in which a basic impulse continues to operate in widely different contexts. In most of these contexts, some spectacle was made of violence.

Despite the ostensibly civilizing forces at work, physical cruelty and the infliction of damage on others continued to attract and entertain people. But, in the nineteenth century, very sharp and dramatic changes took place, particularly in Europe, that were to affect the sensitivity to, and public acceptance of, violence, and this was to have an impact on the entire shape and focus of sport. It was also to establish the framework of what would now legitimately pass for sports.

---

## Cockfighting

This probably has origins in ancient China and Persia. Greeks may have become aware of it after their victory over Persia at Salamis in 480 BCE and, in turn, introduced it to the Romans. For Greeks, the courage of fighting birds was regarded as exemplary: youths were encouraged to watch and emulate the birds' tenacity and valor in combat. Later, it became a mere source of entertainment, especially for gamblers. It first appeared in England in the twelfth century, though its popularity waxed and waned until the sixteenth century when Henry VIII built a royal cockpit at his palace. In the eighteenth and nineteenth centuries, cocks were bought and sold, bred and trained in a more organized way; one trainer, Joseph Gulliver, acquired quite a reputation. Cockfighting was banned in 1835 but is known to persist in the USA and Britain.

---

## TENOR OF LIFE, TEMPO OF WORK

One of the fashionable haunts of the nobility and upper classes in the early eighteenth century was James Figg's amphitheater in London. Figg, himself a swordsman and all-round fighter, opened the venue in 1719 and attracted large crowds to watch displays of animal-baiting as well as human contests, featuring swords, fists, and staffs. No sexism here: Figg held contests between and among men and women. Figg's reputation brought him appointments as a tutor to the gentry, instructing in the art of self-defense, which was regarded in those days as very much a gentleman's pursuit.

There was very little gentlemanly restraint in the actual contests, which were bare-knuckle affairs without either a specified number of rounds or a points-scoring system. A match was won when one fighter was simply unable to continue. Three- and four-hour contests were commonplace, with wrestling throws, kicks, and punches all permissible. Such types of combat were rife in England in Figg's time (he died in 1734) and drew on what was ancient tradition, as we've noted. No doubt similar forms of combat took place in other parts of the world in the eighteenth century though, in England, fighting was to undergo a special transformation.

At about the same time as Figg's venture, another combat activity was gaining popularity, at least in parts of Britain. Ball games such as "hurling" and "knappan" were loosely organized according to local customs rather than central rules and were played with inflated animal bladders. Ancient Greeks and Romans also used pig or ox bladders, though they tended to fill them with hair and feathers, more suited to throwing than the fast kicking games that became popular much later. In the intervening centuries ball games were always peripheral to activities such as combat, racing, or archery, but in the nineteenth century they seemed to take off.

I describe ball games as different to "combat activity" although it seems that at least some variants of what was to evolve into football allowed participants to complement their delicate ball-playing skills with cudgels, clubs, and other instruments that Mr. Figg and his associates would have been adept at using. Meetings would have resembled an all-out struggle much more than a practiced, rule-bound, timed game with clearly defined goals and final results.

But violence was popular and the rough and wild folk games, as Eric Dunning and Kenneth Sheard call them in *Barbarians, Gentlemen and Players* were "closer to 'real' fighting than modern sports" (1979). The authors suggest that football's antecedents reflected the "violent tenor of life in society at large" and also the low threshold of repugnance "with regard to witnessing and engaging in violent acts." Sometimes, the distinction between witnessing and engaging became blurred and spectators would join in the action.

It's rather synthetic to link these pursuits of the eighteenth century with today's boxing or wrestling and types of football; first, because of the regional variations and, second, because of combinations of rules and characteristics that made any systematic differentiation of games impossible. Yet, somehow, the essentials of both activities have dropped into the stream of history and arrived in the twenty-first century as well-ordered, highly structured, and elaborately organized sports. I use the two examples of fighting and football because they embody currents and changes that have affected the entire assortment of activities that have become contemporary sports. The decline in spontaneity and open brutality in sports mirrored trends in society generally.

## Folk ball games

Ball games were played all over England from the fifteenth century and possibly before. The custom was to play after church services on Sundays and on Holy Days. One of the most celebrated and dangerous games was played in Swaffham in the eastern county of Norfolk. Games were typically played between rival parishes and involved passing the ball by hand. Scoring involved a player carrying the ball to a specific zone. In this respect such games were precursors to rugby and American football, though scores were known as "snotches" rather than tries or touchdowns. Games would run to about three hours. Violence was a feature of most folk ball games. Serious injuries always resulted from games and deaths were not uncommon. In fact, the flagrant violence was a factor in its eventual demise in the mid-nineteenth century. Revulsion at the violence combined with the popularity of alternative ball games led to the demise of the Swaffham and other regional games.

The new rules of prizefighting, instituted in 1838, introduced some measure of regulation, including a "scratch" line which was a mark in the center of a 24-foot square ring which competitors had to reach unassisted at the start of each round, or else be judged the loser (that is, "not coming up to scratch"). It was a small but significant modification that removed the necessity of a beating into submission or a knockout to terminate a bout. In 1886, Queensberry Rules were devised to reduce the degree of bodily damage possible and to increase the importance of skill as a decisive factor in the "noble art."

Far away from Figg's boxing ring and the raucous folk ball games, another set of forces were helping shape sports; they came from Britain's public (independent) schools, which were strictly for the children of the aristocracy or very affluent. Despite the popular beliefs that public schools in the nineteenth century were upholders of the virtues of sports, they actually echoed many of the sentiments of the Puritans, who disapproved utterly of any activity that seemed frivolous, including dancing, blood sports, and wagering (betting). Such entertainment was seen by Puritans as the mindless pleasure of flâneurs and, of course, such idlers were ripe for the devil's work. From the sixteenth century, Puritans suppressed any activity resembling a contest in their attempts to create an atmosphere of strict moral discipline and the universities of Oxford and Cambridge banned ball games.

Public schoolmasters initially tried to prevent the development of soccer in particular, believing it to be disruptive of order and morally debilitating. There was also the feeling that it was demeaning for the sons of the upper classes to practice activities that were, as one headmaster of the day described them, "fit only for butcher boys . . . farm boys and laborers" (quoted in Dunning and Sheard 1979: 47). Gentlemen scholars became the new Corinthians in sharp contrast to the laboring commoners.

Intellectual trends in Germany and France were influenced by the philosopher J. J. Rousseau whose treatise *Emile* (first published in 1762) argued that physical training and competitive sport would yield positive results in the overall education of a child. Ideas drifted across to English public schools, so that, by the 1850s, two main revisions were made to the original ideas on sports. Expressed by Peter McIntosh in his *Fair Play*: "The first was that competitive sport, especially team games, had an ethical basis, and the second was that training in moral behavior on the playing field was transferable to the world beyond" (1980: 27).

Together, the ideas formed the core of "Muscular Christianity." Unselfishness, justice, health: these were the type of ideals that were manifest in sport, but also in any proper Christian society. Public schools, influenced by the doctrine, began to integrate a program of sport into their curricula. Team games were important in subordinating the individual to the collective unit and teaching the virtues of alliances. It was often thought that England's many military victories were attributable to the finely honed teamwork encouraged by public schools. Again, we glimpse the notion of sport as a preparation for military duty: the playing fields of public schools were equated with battlegrounds (Eton and Waterloo, for example). Thomas Hughes's classic, *Tom Brown's Schooldays* (first published in 1857) is full of allusions to the role of public schools in producing populations suited to rule over an empire.

The physically tough and toughening version of football, as practiced by Rugby School under the headship of Thomas Arnold and his assistant G. E. L. Cotton, gained acceptance in many public schools. Its toughness was useful in sorting out those fit enough to survive and perhaps later prosper in positions of power. The frail would either strengthen or perish. Its appeal to the prestigious

---

### Muscular Christianity

The term was first used in 1857 by a reviewer of *Tom Brown's Schooldays*. It became applied to a doctrine about the positive moral influence of physical exercise and sport, which had its intellectual roots in the philosophy of J. J. Rousseau in France and GutsMuths in Germany, and which was approvingly adopted by the public schools of England in the late nineteenth century. See Tony Money's *Manly and Muscular Diversions: Public schools and the nineteenth-century sporting revival* (1997).

public schools bent on turning out Great Men was soon apparent as the sport of rugby spread through the network and, in time, to a number of "open" clubs in the north of England (which admitted nouveaux riches and working-class members).

Exporting its sports has been a major trade for England over the decades. Versions of the football played at Rugby and other public schools were popular among college students at North America's principal universities in the 1880s. The throwing and passing, as opposed to kicking, game was played at a competitive level. As early as 1874 there is a record of a game between Harvard and McGill. Interestingly, Wilbert Leonard documents a game of soccer between Rutgers and Princeton back in 1869. Harvard refused to play soccer and Yale responded accordingly.

Muscular Christianity was also instrumental in carrying the other principal variant of football to the working class. Soccer was encouraged by churches. A quarter of today's English clubs were founded and, for a while, sustained by churches eager to proselytize in urban centers which by the 1880s were humming with the sound of heavy machinery. Industry itself wasn't slow to realize the advantages of possessing a football team comprising members of its workforce. Places like Coventry, Stoke, and Manchester can boast enduring soccer clubs that were originally works outfits. Arsenal was based at Woolwich Arsenal, a London munitions factory. Games which were only played on designated holy days and other festive occasions became more and more regular, routine, and organized.

In a similar way, many North American professional football franchises started as factory teams. The Indian Packing Company, of Green Bay, Wisconsin, had its own team in the first decade of the twentieth century; as did the Staley Starch Company, of Decatur, Illinois. Players were paid about $50 per week and given time off to train. In 1920, both companies affiliated their teams to a new organization that also had teams from New York and Washington, DC. The teams evolved into the Packers, Bears, Giants, and Redskins respectively.

We might stretch the point and describe the early works teams as para-industrial: organized much as an industrial force and intended to supplement the strictly industrial. It was a very deliberate policy pursued by factory owners. In some ways, sport was a foil for industrial order; a potent instrument for instilling discipline in the workforce. But, if sport was an instrument, it had two cutting edges for as well as carving out new patterns of order it was also responsible for outbreaks of disorder. Work and leisure were cut in two by the imperatives of industry. The more fluid way of life in which the manner in which one earned a living blended imperceptibly with the rest of one's life disappeared as the factory system issued its demands, which were a workforce ready to labor for a set amount of time at a specific site.

During that time workers operated under virtual compulsion; outside that time they were free to pursue whatever they wished, or could afford. Sport was a way of filling leisure time with brief, but exhilarating periods of uncertainty: the questions of who or which team would win a more-or-less equal competition was bound to prompt interest and speculation, as, it seems, it always has. The spell of physically competitive activity, far from being broken, was strengthened by the need for momentary release from a colorless world dominated by the monotonous thuds and grinds of machinery. Competitions, whether individual combat, ball games, or animal baits, drew crowds; but public gatherings always carried the potential for disruption.

Public gatherings and festivals, and other staged events attracted a working class which was in the process of becoming industrialized but which had not yet done so by the mid- to late nineteenth century. It was still adjusting to what John Hargreaves in *Sport, Power and Culture* calls the changes in "tempo and quality of industrial work" (1986). Hargreaves argues that the English Church's efforts in building football clubs had the effect of controlling the working class so that it would be more pliant for ruling groups. In fact, Hargreaves's entire thesis revolves around the intriguing idea that sport has helped integrate the working class into respectable "bourgeois culture" rather than struggle against it.

But the integration was never smooth and police or militia were regularly called to suppress riots and uprisings at football matches, prize fights, footraces, cockfights, and so on, as large groups spontaneously grew agitated and unruly. Boxing events to this day employ whips who are promoters' chargés d'affaires responsible for most of the minor business. But, as the etymology suggests, the original whips were employed to encircle the ring, cracking their whips or lashing at troublesome members of the audience (ancient Romans also employed whips to lash riotous crowds at their gladiatorial contests). Local laws were enacted, prohibiting meetings in all but tightly policed surroundings, sometimes banning sports completely. The rise of the governing bodies within individual sports represents an attempt to absorb working-class energies within a formal structure, thereby containing what might otherwise have become disruptive tendencies.

The same forces affecting combat helped reshape football, taking out some of its ferocity and establishing sets of rules in what was previously a maelstrom. In 1863, the Football Association was formed to regulate the kicking form of the sport (the word soccer probably derives from "assoc," an abbreviation of Association). The version that stressed handling was brought under the control of the Rugby Union, which was created in 1871. *Rugby's Great Split*, as Tony Collins calls it, into distinct amateur and professional organizations came in 1895, the latter being known as Rugby League, which remained confined to the northern counties of England where it was favored by the working class. The other major change in rugby came in North America, where in 1880, the addition of downs to replace the to-and-fro of rugby and a straight line of scrimmage instead of the less orderly scrummage gave American football a character all of its own (the forward pass rule was introduced in 1906).

Baseball's governing body has its origins in 1858 when the National Association of Base Ball Players was formed. The game was played for many years before, probably evolving out the English games, base-ball and rounders, in which players struck a ball with a bat and ran through a series of bases arranged in a circle, or a "round." Baseball was the first fully professional sport in America, charging admissions to ballparks and attracting a predominantly blue-collar fandom.

The changes in the organization of sports were responses to demands for orderliness and standardization. England and, later, North America metamorphosed into an industrial society where the valued qualities were discipline, precision, and control. Sports not only absorbed these qualities, but promoted them, gradually influencing perceptions and expectations in such a way as to deepen people's familiarity with the industrial regimen.

Industrialization drew populations to urban centers in search of work; not work quite as we know it today, but uncomfortable, energy-draining activities performed for long hours often in squalid and dangerous conditions. This type of work needed a new mentality. People were expected to arrive at work punctually and toil for measured periods of time. Their labors were planned for them and their efforts were often highly specialized according to the division of labor.

Behavior at work was subject to rules and conditions of service. Usually, all the work took place in a physically bounded space, the factory. There was also a need for absoluteness: tools and machines were made to fine tolerances. Underlying all this was a class structure, or hierarchy, in which some strata had attributes suited to ruling and others to being ruled. The latter's shortcomings were so apparent that no detailed investigation of the causes was thought necessary: their poverty, or even destitution, was their own fault.

All these had counterparts in the developing sports scene. Time periods for contests were established and measured accurately thanks to newer, sophisticated timepieces (up to the mid-eighteenth century, clocks and watches didn't keep accurate time). Divisions of labor in team games yielded role-specific positions and particular, as opposed to general, skills. Constitutions were drawn up to instill more structure into activities and regulate events according to rules. They took place on pitches, in rings, and halls – in finite spaces. Winners and losers were unambiguously clear, outright, and absolute. And hierarchies reflecting the class structure were integrated into many activities. Captains of teams, for example, were "gentlemen" from the upper echelons. The sense of order, discipline, location, and period which sport acquired helped it both complement and support working life.

As the form and pace of sport imitated that of industry, so it gained momentum amongst the emergent working class seeking some sporadic diversion from its toil, something more impulsive and daring than the routine labors that dominated industry. While sport was assuming a symmetry with work, it still afforded the working class an outlet or release from labor; it was pursued voluntarily during the time spent away from work.

As the nineteenth century drew to an end, most sports took on a much more orderly character: both participants and spectators came to recognize the legitimacy of governing organizations, the standards of conduct they laid down, and the structures of rules they observed. The whole direction and rhythm of sport reflected the growing significance of industrial society. In his *Sport: A cultural history*, Richard Mandell writes: "[L]ike concurrent movements in law and government, which led to codification, and rationalization, sport became codified, and civilized by written rules which were enforced by supervising officials (the equivalent of judges and jurors)" (1984: 151).

The reasons for concentrating on nineteenth-century England are: (1) it's here we find something like a factory's smelter shop where rationalized, organized sport appears as an extract from the molten historical trends; (2) the English experience radiated out amongst the imperial colonies and ex-colonies, including North America, with sports, as well as trade, "following the flag"; and (3) it's this period of history that has excited many writers sufficiently to produce theories of the rise of sports in modernity. In the next chapter, I'll consider five theoretical approaches that shed light on the reasons for the rapid growth of sports in the late nineteenth and early twentieth centuries and, indeed, for their persistence into the twenty-first.

## OF RELATED INTEREST

*Ancient Greek Olympics* by Stephen G. Miller (Yale University Press, 2004) is a detailed account of the original Olympiad, right down to how competitors tied their foreskins. Nigel Spivey's *The Ancient Olympics* (Oxford University Press, 2004) complements this, while *The Eternal Olympics: The art and history of sport* edited by Nicolaos Yaloris (Caratzas Brothers, 1979) is a large format book, packed with pictures of artifacts and reproductions of artwork, many from the pre-Christian era.

*Sports in America: From wicked amusement to national obsession* edited by David Wiggins (Human Kinetics, 1995) collects 19 essays organized into five parts: (1) pre-1820; (2) 1820–70; (3) 1870–1915; (4) 1915–45; (5) 1945–present. The third part, dealing with industrialization and urbanization is especially relevant; in this, various writers focus on the period 1870–1915.

*History of Sport and Physical Activity in the United States*, fourth edition, by Betty Spears and Richard A. Swanson (Brown & Benchmark, 1995) is one of the most respected and durable histories of North American sport and should be read in conjunction with *Sports Spectators* by Allen Guttmann (Columbia University Press, 1986) which is densely packed with historical detail on the emergence of sport. Guttmann's focus is far wider than that implied by the title and actually provides a basis for understanding sport. "We are what we watch," writes Guttmann toward the end of the book that captures how sports can be used as a barometer of historical change and one which should be read by any serious student of sport.

*Crossing Boundaries: An international anthology of women's experiences in sport* edited by Susan Bandy and Anne Darden (Human Kinetics, 1999) is a collection of materials on the largely undisclosed history of women in sports.

Richard Holt's books, *Sport and the Working Class in Modern Britain* (Manchester University Press, 1990) and *Sport and the British* (Oxford University Press, 1989), examine what now seem to be crude forms of sports and reveal the links between these and today's versions. Older activities gradually faded as industrialization encroached and cultural patterns changed, but Holt emphasizes the continuities and "survivals" from old to new. Complementing these is Hugh Cunningham's *Leisure in the Industrial Revolution* (Croom Helm, 1980).

*Combat Sports in the Ancient World* by Michael Poliakoff (Yale University Press, 1987) describes in fine detail the early forms of combat, such as the Greeks' *pankration* ("total fight") and Egyptian wrestling. "The will to win is a basic human instinct, but different societies give varying amounts of encouragement (or discouragement) to the individual's attempt to measure himself against others," observes Poliakoff in his chapter entitled "The nature and purpose of combat sport." Elliott J. Gorn's *The Manly Art: Bare-knuckle prize fighting in America* (Cornell University Press, 1986) updates the argument.

*Sport History Review* edited by Don Morrow (Human Kinetics) is a biannual journal that concerns itself with sports history.

## **ASSIGNMENT**

Cockfighting and boxing: these are two sports that have deep historical roots, but which have aroused controversy. Cockfighting is illegal; and both American and British Medical Associations lobby for a ban on boxing. Despite its illegality, cockfighting persists underground. Defenders of boxing argue that, if banned, boxing would also go underground, making it more dangerous. But, one might contend that drug-taking is a widespread underground activity and that does not mean we should legalize it. Compare boxing and drug-taking, taking into account that both cost lives, yet both are engaged in by young people on a voluntary basis. If one is legal, should the other be?

*burning* **QUESTION**

### *how old are sports?*

4,000 years, if you accept the theories of Nicolaos Yaloris, who detects evidence of what he calls "true athletic spirit" as long ago as the second millennium Before the Common Era (BCE). There is evidence of activities resembling sports in the Aegean civilization that centered on Crete, as there is evidence of high standard art, work in copper and bronze, and linear script all around the same time.

Others date sports much more recently. Some say the Renaissance, beginning in the fourteenth century, while others maintain that sports as we understand them today started in nineteenth-century England. It depends on how you define "sports." Most historians tell us to guard against exaggerating the similarities between ancient and medieval contests and contemporary competitions. The actual activities may resemble what we now recognize as sports, but the cultural milieux were completely different and the meanings given to the activities quite unlike today's.

The boundaries we use to separate sports from other areas of life "have been indistinct and not worth noticing in other cultures," writes Mandell. Ancient Greeks, for example, believed winners of events were chosen by gods and the competitions they held were of profound religious importance; as such, athleticism was all-pervasive. Pre-Meiji (before 1868) Japan held archery and equestrian contests, but these were linked to military purposes rather than being purely athletic competitions.

The first Olympiad took place in 776 BCE and was animated by the same spirit that guided the intellectual inquiries of Pythagoras, Hippocrates, and Socrates: to explore the boundaries of human possibilities. Evidence of this can be discerned in the dramas of Sophocles and Aeschylus and the military conquests of Alexander the Great. They form disparate parts of a wider enterprise to control and subordinate nature to human requirements, using both physical and intellectual means.

By combining the efforts of various historical scholars, it is possible to construct a timeline that allows us to trace the existence of athletic activities. The dates are, of course, approximate and indicate the time of the first appearance of the activities. The places are often vague, referring to regions rather than the countries as we define them nowadays.

## BEFORE THE COMMON ERA (BCE)

| | |
|---|---|
| 4000 | **Mycenae, Hellas (Greece)** Horse racing |
| 3000 | **Mesopotamia, Sumeria** Chariot racing. Archery contests. Stick fighting. Paramilitary athletic training. |
| 2300 | **Indus River region (Pakistan, India)** Horse and chariot races. Combat contests. |
| 2000 | **Crete, Hellas** Athletic competition with rules. Bull-leaping, combat contests linked with religious festivals.<br>Throughout Hellas (Greece) Gloved combat contests; foot races, chariot races. Athletic training. Emphasis on victory.<br>**Egypt** Ball games, staff and knife, and wrestling contests. |
| 1600 | **Minoa** Combat sports using thonged fists. |
| 1360 | **Egypt** Hunting on Nile. |
| 1200 | **Olympia, Hellas** Beginning of Hellennic Middle Ages. Jumping events, discus, spear throwing, foot and chariot racing, armed combat contests. Funeral games to honor the dead. |
| 776 | **Olympia, Hellas** Inaugural Olympic Games. Foot races only. |
| 708–680 | Pentathlon, wrestling, boxing, *pankration*, horse races added to Olympic program. |
| 600 | **Hellas** Integration of athletics and education. Physical and moral courage intertwined. Healthy body, healthy mind. Rivalries valued in all cultural spheres, including musicians, poets, sculptors, etc. Competition for excellence, fame, and honor, i.e. *agōn*. |
| 576 | **Sparta, Hellas** Specialized physical training with specialized role of trainer. Athletics part of military education. |
| 400 | **Hellas** Purpose-built athletic stadium. Professional athletes receive subsidies from cities to train full-time. |
| 146 | **Greece** subjugated by Romans. Athletics continue, but with increasing emphasis on killing sport, e.g. gladiatorial contests (featuring slaves), *pankration*, archery. |

## COMMON ERA (CE)

300    **China** Equestrian sport, including polo. Competitions with military utility, including archery, boxing, wrestling, and paramilitary gymnastics.

393    **Rome** Christian Roman ban on all pagan festivals, including Olympic Games.

410    **Rome** Fall of Rome. Beginning of Dark Ages → tenth/eleventh centuries.

500    **Middle East** Horse racing.

646    **Japan** Archery. Equestrian events, including dressage.

900    **Europe** Equestrian sports. Jousting.

1000    **Japan** Ball games, possibly adapted from Chinese versions. Sumo.

1100    **Rheinland Pfalz (Germany)** Tournament attended by 40,000 knights.

1150    **England** Archery contests.

1400    **Europe** (especially Burgundy, Brabant). Tournaments with equestrian events (including jousting), fencing and sword duels.

1450    **Scotland** Early forms of golf/hockey ("driving").

1500    **Europe** International tournaments featuring archery, swordfights, jousts and other contests.

1555    **Europe** Ball games, e.g. *calcio* in Italy, *Faustball* in Germany and elsewhere (earlier) among Aztecs, Inuit, Japanese, Maoris.

1570    **Japan** Paramilitary sports. Equestrian events. Archery. Swordfighting. Spear-throwing. Shooting. Martial arts, principally competitive jujitsu.

1600    **England** Rural hunting. Hounds, horses. Prey included boars, wolves, and red deer.

1600    **Europe** Animal-baiting. Dog pits, bear pits, cock pits, etc. Rise in gambling. Rural horse racing.

1660    **Germany** and elsewhere in Europe. Formal competitive dueling.

1787    **England** Marylebone Cricket Club (MCC) formed.

| 1800 | **England** Horse racing in enclosures, early in century. |
| 1836 | **Japan** Weightlifting. |
| 1851 | **USA** First America's Cup yacht race. |
| 1858 | **USA** National Association of Base Ball Players (NABP) formed. |
| 1863 | **England** Soccer and rugby divide into distinct sports with own federations. |
| 1870 | **Europe, North America, Japan** Rationalization of sports. Training and trainers appear, growth of organizations to codify and regulate activities and record results. American football acquires its own rules (as distinct from rugby). |
| 1880 | **USA, Europe** Cycling craze among women and men. |
| 1886 | **England** Queensberry Rules instituted in boxing. |
| 1891 | **USA** Basketball invented at YMCA training college in Springfield, Massachusetts. James Naismith credited with being originator. |
| 1896 | **Greece** Modern Olympics (amateur) created. Baron Pierre de Coubertin credited with being originator. |

*Sources*: Coombs (1978); Kühnst (1996); Mandell (1984); Miller (2004); Poliakoff (1987); Spivey (2004); Vandervell and Coles (1980); Yaloris (1979).

*More questions . . .*

- Why were Roman contests so different from Greek athletics?
- Is it fair to describe ancient competitions as "sports"?
- What would happen if we stopped children under the age of 11 playing competitive sports?

*Read on . . .*

- Peter Kühnst, *Sports: A cultural history in the mirror of art* (Verlag der Kunst, 1996).
- Richard D. Mandell, *Sport: A cultural history* (Columbia University Press, 1984).
- Michael B. Poliakoff, *Combat Sports in the Ancient World: Competition, Violence, and Culture* (Yale University Press, 1987).
- Nigel Spivey, *The Ancient Olympics* (Oxford University Press, 2004)
- Nicolaos Yaloris (ed.) *The Eternal Olympics: The art and history of sport* (Caratzas Brothers, 1979).

# the hunt for reasons

## how theories help us understand sports

## THE FIGURATIONAL APPROACH

Sportization. That's how Norbert Elias refers to the process in which sports as we recognize them today came into being. Raucous and rowdy folk games were brought into a common fold through the application of precise and explicit rules governing competitions. Strict application of the rules ensured equal chances for rivals and supervision by officials guaranteed fairness. So a mixed bag of chaotic and often disordered activities developed into distinct, rule-bound contests, refereed according to strict standards and evaluated according to clearly defined criteria.

Elias argues that all this took place in the nineteenth century and accompanied the English Industrial Revolution. Yet, he is wary of theories that explain one in terms of the other. "Both industrialization and sportization were symptomatic of a deeper-lying transformation of European societies which demanded of their individual members greater regularity and differentiation of conduct," he writes in "An essay on sport and violence" (1986a: 151). Elias is often credited with offering the most encyclopedic theory on the origins and development of sport.

Theories are collections of ideas or suppositions that try to explain something – in this case, the existence of sport. They're often based on general principles, not always with supporting evidence. The intention is that the theory can be converted into conjectures or propositions that can then be set against reality. Not that this always works in practice: some theories are hard to test and those that can be are often challenged. Rival theories criticize them for interpreting facts in a way that supports the original principles. So they become circular.

The problem is: we just can't get to grips with the reasons for something without theory. We have to have some sort of organizing framework in which we can arrange our facts in a way that makes them comprehensible. Whatever the lawyers say, the facts do not speak for themselves. So, when Elias wrote about the sources, expansion, and direction of sports, his theory was not intended as a definitive statement, but rather as a possible answer to some of the more taxing questions about sports. His is but one theoretical approach; we'll begin with it, before moving on to alternatives.

The "transformation" so central to Elias's theory had roots as far back as the fifteenth century and involved the gradual introduction of rules and norms to govern human behavior and designate what was appropriate conduct in a given situation; it also involved the rise of impersonal organizations to maintain rules. These reflected a general tendency in Europe toward interdependence: people began to orient their activities to each other, to rely less on their own subsistence efforts and more on those of others, whose tasks would be specialized and geared toward narrow objectives. In time, chains of interdependence were formed: a division of labor ensured that each individual, or group of individuals, was geared to the accomplishment of tasks that would be vital to countless others. They in turn would perform important activities, so that every member of a society depended on others, and no one was separate or completely independent.

The pattern of relationships that emerged is called a *figuration*. For this kind of system to operate with reasonable efficiency, people would have to be discouraged from pursuing their own interests and whims in an unrestrained way. There had to be a method of control over emotions and behavior, particularly violent behavior. The need for control grew more acute in eighteenth-century England, where, in the aftermath of civil strife, many people feared a recurrence, according to Elias and Dunning (1986: 171). The

---

**Figuration**

While, in a general sense, this refers to the form, shape, or outline of something, Elias has applied it to interdependent relations between people and used it to represent "chains of functions" between them. Some have found in the concept a new approach to study, while others, like Bauman (in *Sociology*, vol. 13, 1979) have found it reminiscent of more orthodox notions, like "pattern" or "situation," and question the value and originality of the concept.

state was the central authority responsible for internal orderliness and overall organization and planning. With the formation of state control came what Elias calls a "civilizing spurt."

Here we come across Elias's more general historical account, *The Civilizing Process* (1982), which describes a sweeping trend, or even evolution, in which human societies have controlled the use of violence and encouraged an observance of manners. The two aspects are part of one general tendency. So, for example, the decline of dispute settlements through violence and the rise of social prohibitions on such things as spitting and breaking wind are not unconnected in Elias's scheme. They both represent new standards of conduct in changing figurations. The level of acceptable violence drops as the emergent state takes over the settling of disputes and monopolizes the legitimate use of violence. As rules and conventions develop, they spread to all areas, so that standards are imposed, both externally and internally – as well as being controlled by the state, individuals control themselves according to accepted or "correct" codes of conduct.

Since the days of the ancient Greeks, which is Elias's starting point, civilization has progressed with the state's power and therefore control over violence within the family and between neighbors, clans, and fiefdoms, increasing at a pace roughly equivalent to our internal controls over emotions and behavior; in other words, self-restraint. (The similarity to Freud's conception of society taming our more primitive urges through the super-ego is quite pronounced here.) In their essay on "Figurational sociology and sport," Patrick Murphy *et al.* point out that Greek combat sports "involved much higher levels of violence and open emotionality than those permitted today, and were less highly regulated" (2000: 95–6).

According to Elias, inhibitions about violence were also lower, so there would have been little queasiness or sense of guilt after either witnessing or engaging in actions that would today be deplored as savage, brutal – in other words, uncivilized. If we jumped on H. G. Wells's time machine and zipped back to watch a *pankration* in the ancient Greek games, we'd find it rebarbative, that is repellent and obnoxious.

The civilizing process is a vast world trend, but not a completely linear one: there are phases in history when a figuration may "decivilize" and regress to barbarism, tolerating a higher level of violence and ungoverned behavior. Elias describes this as a "reverse gear." Equally, there is allowance for sharp accelerated movements forward, such as in the civilizing spurt Elias believes is so crucial to our understanding of modern sport.

While it would caricature the civilizing process to equate it with changes in self-control, this particular aspect of the wider development acted as an agent in generating "stress-tensions" which, in turn, agitated the need for organized sport. How does Elias see this happening? First, an abstract observation from

Elias's introduction to *Quest for Excitement* (co-edited with Eric Dunning): "In societies where fairly high civilizing standards all round are safeguarded and maintained by a highly effective state–internal control of physical violence, personal tensions of people resulting from conflicts of this kind, in a word, stress-tensions, are widespread" (1986b: 41).

Next, most human societies develop some countermeasures against stress-tensions they themselves generate and, as Elias writes in the same introduction, "these activities must conform to the comparative sensitivity to physical violence which is characteristic of people's social habits (customs and dispositions) at the later stages of a civilizing process" (1986b: 41–2).

So, the ways in which people "let off steam" mustn't violate the standards that have become accepted by society at large. Watching humans mauled by wild animals might have provided stimulating and enjoyable release for the ancient Romans, as might burning live cats or baiting bulls for the English in the nineteenth century. But, the civilizing process, according to Elias, changes our threshold of revulsion for enacting and witnessing violence, so that, nowadays, some cultures in the West find a sport like boxing – relatively mild in historical terms – intolerably violent (boxing is banned in Sweden, for instance). The methods we choose to discharge tension closely reflect general standards and sensitivities.

Fox-hunting is Elias's favorite example. Once synonymous with the word "sport," fox-hunting is now an anachronism and pressure against it would no doubt have prompted its demise were it not a pursuit practiced exclusively by the landowning elite. Developing in the late eighteenth century, this peculiarly English custom was quite unlike the simpler, less regulated, and more spontaneous forms of hunting of other countries and earlier ages where people were the main hunters and foxes were one amongst many prey, boar, red deer, and wolves being others. Fox-hunting was bound by a strict code of etiquette and peculiar rules, such as that which forbade killing other animals during the hunt. Hounds were trained to follow only the fox's scent, and only they could kill, while humans watched.

The fox itself had little utility apart from its pelt; its meat was not considered edible (not by its pursuers, anyway) and, while it was considered a pest, the fields and forests were full of others which threatened farmers' livestock and crops. The chances of anyone getting hurt in the hunt were minimized, but each course in the wall of security presented a problem of how to retain the immediacy and physical risk that were so important in early times. Elias believes that the elaboration of the rules of hunting were solutions. The rules served to postpone the outcome or finale of the hunt and so artificially prolong the process of hunting. "The excitement of the hunt itself had increasingly become the main source of enjoyment for the human participants," argue Elias and Dunning (1986: 166).

What had once been foreplay to the act of killing became the main pleasure. So the fox hunt was a virtual pure type of autotelic hunt: the thrill for participants came in the pace and exhilaration of the chasing and the pleasure of watching violence done without actually doing the killing. And, remember, this was sport: it lacked the competitive element so vital to contemporary definitions, but it was practiced to elicit the arousal of the hunters. Apart from that, it had no utility. In other words, the chasing itself was the purpose and, in this sense, it bore similarity to today's sports. After all, the thrill of sports is in trying to score as much as scoring.

The influence of the civilizing spurt is apparent in the restraint imposed and exercised by the participants in fox hunts. The overall trend was to make violence more repugnant to people, which effectively encouraged them to control or restrain themselves. Elias stresses that this should be seen not as a repression but as a product of greater sensitivity. The fox-hunters didn't secretly feel an urge to kill with their own hands; they genuinely found such an act disagreeable, but could still find pleasure in viewing it from their horses; what Elias calls killing by proxy (this bears some resemblance to Jacobson's argument covered in Chapter 1).

Despite all attempts to abolish them, hunts persist to this day, probably guided by appetites similar to those whetted by the sight of humans being masticated by raptors. Hundreds of millions of *Jurassic Park* fans can attest to the enjoyable tension provided by the latter, albeit through the medium of film. While Elias doesn't cover contemporary hunts, we should add that their longevity reveals something contradictory about the civilizing trend and the impulse to condone or even promote wanton cruelty. Recent legislation to ban hunting with dogs is being contested by hunt supporters, many of whom say they are prepared to risk prison to continue their sport.

To ensure a long and satisfying chase, and to be certain that foxes are found in the open, "earth stoppers" are employed to close up earths (fox holes) and badger setts in which foxes may take refuge. Many hunts maintain earths to ensure a sufficient supply of foxes through the season (foxes used to be imported from continental Europe). The hunt doesn't start until after 11 a.m. to allow the fox time to digest its food and ensure that it's capable of a long run. During the course of a hunt, a fox may run to ground and will either survive or be dug out by the pursuant dogs, a virtual baiting from which even the dogs emerge with damage. New hounds are prepared by killing cubs before the new season, a practice observed and presumably enjoyed by members of the hunt and their guests.

In Elias's theory, fox-hunting was a solution to the problems created by the accelerating trend toward civilization and the internal controls on violence it implied. The closing up of areas of arousal, which in former ages had been sources of pleasurable gratification (as well as immense suffering), set humans on a search for substitute activities and ones which didn't carry the risks, dangers, or outright disorder that society as a whole would find unacceptable – the quest for excitement.

The English form of fox-hunting was only one example of a possible solution, but Elias feels it is an "empirical model," containing all the original distinguishing characteristics of today's sport. Other forms of sport, such as boxing, football, cricket, and rugby, showed how the problem was solved without the use and abuse of animals; the first two of these were appropriated by the working class. All evolved in a relatively orderly manner, well matched to the needs of modern, bureaucratic society with its accent on organization and efficiency and ultimately in line with the general civilizing process.

The explanation of sport is but one facet of Elias's grand project, which is to understand the very nature and consequences of the civilizing process. It follows that critics who are not convinced by his general model are certainly not by his specific one. The actual idea of a civilizing process has the tinge of a theory of progress in which history is set to proceed through predetermined stages, which can't be altered. Elias's mention of the irregularity of the process and the reverse gear are marginal to the main thesis which suggests that, as Paul Hoggett puts it, "civilization seems to march onwards fairly straightforwardly without any collapsing back into barbarity" (1986: 36).

Many contemporary observers of sport might want to argue that collapses are quite commonplace and point fingers in the direction of soccer stadiums, once the sites of open, almost ritualistic violence between rival fans. Elias and his devotees would recommend a more detailed examination of history to appreciate that violence has for long been related to soccer; only the media's amplification of it has changed. Presumably the same could be said about fox-hunting. But this response is only partially satisfactory, as many other sports have developed violent penumbra quite recently and it is hard to establish any historical connections with, say, boxing, cricket, and rugby, all of which have experienced major crowd disorder over the past few decades.

It's interesting that the nucleus of Elias's model has not been attacked. A basic proposition is that "pleasurable excitement . . . appears to be one of the most elementary needs of human beings," as Elias puts it in his "An essay on sport and violence" (1986a: 174). Yet, Elias never documents the sources of such needs and, considering that the entire project rests on them, one might expect some expansion. This is mysteriously absent. Is it a biological drive? Part of a survival instinct? A deep psychological trait? Elias's treatment seems to suggest that the need for "pleasurable excitement" is of a similar order to the need for food, shelter, sex, and other such basic needs, rather like ones in Abraham Maslow's theory of motivation (which we'll cover in Chapter 6). Certainly, the need for excitement appears to be basic; though social and ecological conditions might change the way in which we interpret our needs as well as our wants. They might not be as static as Elias supposed.

This may seem a small quibble with what is after all a hugely ambitious attempt to illuminate the nature and purpose of modern sport by connecting its changing character to the civilizing transformation of the past several centuries. Far from being an autonomous realm separated from other institutions, sport is totally wrapped up with culture, psyche, and the state. Human "stress-tensions" are linked to large-scale social changes.

Yet, the analysis still seems caught in a time warp; as Vera Zolberg concludes, it does "not devote adequate attention to one of the most striking features of sport in modern society, that of the business of sport" (1987: 573). The way in which sport has been seized upon by commercial organizations has tended to show Elias's theory as adequate at a certain level, but unable to cope with the developments imposed on sport by the pressures of professionalism in recent years. The state may once have played a key role in precipitating organized efforts to satisfy basic needs for excitement, but global corporations have become powerful forces.

## NARCOTIC EFFECTS: CRITICAL THEORY

Sport is a remarkably ironic thing, its chief characteristic being that it provides an entertaining relief from work while at the same time preparing people for more work. This is the central insight of a group of theorists who have, in one way or another, been influenced by the work of Karl Marx. Although Marx himself didn't write about sport, others have interpreted his theories in a way that provides insights into the political and economic utility of sports.

Marx wrote in the mid-nineteenth century and his focus was modern capitalism, an economic system based on a split of the ownership of the means of production (factories, land, equipment, etc.). Owners of the means of production are bosses, or bourgeoisie, in whose interests capitalism works and who are prepared to milk the system to its limits in order to stay in control. The working class, or proletariat, is forced to work for them in order to subsist. As the system doesn't work in their interests, they have to be persuaded that it could if only they were luckier, or had better breaks, or worked harder. In other words, the system itself is fine; it's actually the workers who need to change for the good. As long as workers are convinced of the legitimacy of economic arrangements, then capitalism is not under threat. So the system has evolved methods of ensuring its own survival. And this is where sport fits in.

Because Marx's own thought was subjected to so many different interpretations, it was inevitable that no single analysis would emerge that could claim to be "what Marx would have written about sport had he been alive today." When theories of sports bearing Marx's imprimatur began to surface in the early 1970s, they were far from uniform, their only linking characteristic being that sports were geared to the interests of the bourgeoisie, or middle class, had the effect of neutralizing any political potential in the working class, and contributed in some way to the preservation of the status quo. Sports were, in other words, to be criticized, not just analyzed.

The principal scholars claiming to work with a Marxist approach were the American Paul Hoch, Jean-Marie Brohm, a French writer, and the German theorist, Bero Rigauer. Other commentators, such as Richard Gruneau, John Hargreaves, Mark Naison, Brian Stoddart, and William Morgan, later contributed toward what has now become a respectable body of Marxist literature on sports. The work of Hoch, Brohm, and Rigauer is informed by the spirit of the Frankfurt School, and which we can summarize as Critical Theory. The other group of theorists take as their starting point the theories of the Italian Marxist Antonio Gramsci, whose central concept of hegemony has provided a focus for studies of sport and which we will cover in the next subsection.

Sports serve four main functions for capitalism, according to John Hargreaves. First, organized sport helps train a "docile labor force": it encourages in the working class an acceptance of the kind of work discipline demanded in modern production; hard work is urged in both sport and work. We've noted before how the organization and tempo of industry became reflected in sport and Hargreaves sees the congruence as almost perfect. In his *Sport, Culture and Ideology*, Hargreaves compares the features of sport and industry: "A high degree of specialisation and standardisation, bureaucratised and hierarchical administration, long-term planning, increased reliance on science and technology, a drive for maximum productivity, a quantification of performance and, above all, the alienation of both producer and consumer" (1982: 41). Major events, like the Olympic Games and Super Bowl, are given as examples of the final point.

Second, sport has become so thoroughly commercialized and dominated by market forces that events and performers are treated as – or perhaps just are – commodities that are used by capitalist enterprises: "Sport is produced, packaged and sold like any other commodity on the market for mass consumption at enormous profits" (1982: 41). The trading or transfer of players typifies the commodification.

The third area in which sport fits in is in "expressing the quintessential ideology in capitalist society." What Marxist theorists have proposed here is that sport works in subtle ways at indicating qualities or imperatives in people; all these qualities have counterparts in society at large. Aggressive individualism, ruthless competitiveness, equal opportunity, elitism, chauvinism, sexism, and nationalism: all these are regarded as admirable. Their desirability is not questioned in sports and the uncritical approach to them is carried over to society. Fourth, there is the area of the state: this bureaucratic administration represents capitalist interests. It follows that every intrusion into sport by the state must be seen as some sort of attempt to link sports participation with the requirements of the capitalist system.

Four areas, then, but hardly a theory; they are really only lowest common denominators for all those favoring a Marxist conception of sport. Beyond these, there are a variety of theories all taking their lead from Marx in the sense that they see the split over the means of production as central. In other words, sport has to be analyzed in terms of class relations. In 1972, Paul Hoch published his *Rip Off the big Game: The exploitation of sports by the power elite*, in which he advanced one of the most acerbic Marxist critiques of sport, which he likened to the mainstream religions about which Marx himself wrote much. Religion was regarded as little more than a capitalist convenience, absorbing workers' energies and emotions and supplying a salve after the week's labors.

Sport has much the same significance. Both religion and sport work as an opiate that temporarily dulls pain and gives a false sense of well-being, but which is also a dangerous and debilitating narcotic that can reduce its users to a helpless state of dependence. The attraction of sport is as compelling as that of religion and its effects are comparable: it siphons off potential that might otherwise be put to political use in challenging the capitalist system.

The title of Jean-Marie Brohm's book indicates his position on contemporary sport: *Sport: A prison of measured time* (1978). By this, Brohm means that the institutional, rule-governed, highly organized structure of modern sport has been shaped by capitalist interest groups in such a way as to represent a constraint rather than a freedom. Sport is in no sense an alternative to work, less still an escape from it "since it removes all bodily freedom, all creative spontaneity, every aesthetic dimension and every playful impulse" (1978: 175).

---

### Homo faber/homo ludens

From *homo*, the zoological name of the human genus; *faber* being the Latin for work, *ludens* for play. These describe two images of the supposed natural state of humans. In *homo faber*, work is the primary activity and the human existence is based on productive activity; humans express their creativity through the objects they make. Marx's stress on the liberating potential of unfettered labor did much to popularize this. The Dutch historian Johan Huizinga opposed this view, advancing the concept of *homo ludens*, in which irrational play is a primary human capacity that is often stifled by the demands of work, especially in contemporary society. Self-realization comes through free, perhaps frivolous, play.

---

The competitor is merely a prisoner, whose performances are controlled, evaluated, and recorded, preferably in measurable terms. Capitalism as a system stifles the human imagination and compresses the human body into mindless production work; and as sport is but one part of that system, it can do little more than reproduce its effects. It just obeys the "logic" of the system. As Richard Gruneau writes in his *Class, Sports and Social Development*: "For Brohm, capitalism has shaped sport in its own image" (1983: 38).

Others, like Bero Rigauer, in his *Sport and Work* (1981), agree with the basic assumptions and emphasize how corporations have penetrated, or completely taken over, sport. It is as if sport has been appropriated by one class and used to bolster its already commanding position in the overall class structure. For Rigauer, sport has aided the economic system by improving the health of workers and so minimizing the time lost at work through illness.

Like Brohm, he sees a "technocratic" takeover of sport, with performances being subject to rationalization and planning, and training becoming more time-absorbing and important than performance itself. Initiative and creativity are stifled, rendering the human performer as the "one-dimensional man," so called by the Marxist philosopher Herbert Marcuse (from whom Brohm and Rigauer draw inspiration). For Rigauer, sport is part of "the social processes of reproduction" in the sense that it contributes to the continuation of capitalism without our ever seeing it as such (2000: 44).

In all accounts, the human beings are depicted as passive dopes, pushed around by factors beyond their control. But are humans just like hockey pucks? Do they really respond so readily and easily? Those who think not find the work of Hoch and Brohm rather too deterministic – all thoughts and behavior are determined by outside forces emanating from the capitalist system. Sport is but one tool for maintaining the domination and exploitation of the working class.

In contrast, other writers prefer to see the working class playing a more active role. Certainly, there is reciprocity between the way in which modern sport is organized and the functions it fulfills on the one hand, and the requirements of capitalism on the other. But this doesn't deny that different groups (classes) are involved in different sports and at different levels at different stages in history. Sport is not, as Hargreaves puts it, "universally evil." Its meaning and significance have to be investigated more closely. Other Marxist writers, including Gruneau and Hargreaves himself, have attempted to do this. All would go along with the more orthodox Marxist approach, but only so far.

Sport is much more multifaceted than the others acknowledge. It may give substance to wider ideologies and exfoliate working-class energies, but it can also be useful as a builder of solidarity within working-class groups, which are brought together with a common purpose. "It is precisely this type of solidarity that historically has formed the basis for a trenchant opposition to employers," observes Hargreaves (1986: 110).

Public gatherings at sports events have always generated a potential for disorder and have attracted the state's agents of control. Some writers have even inferred a form of political resistance from the exploits of soccer hooligans. So, involvement in sport can actually facilitate or even encourage challenge rather than accommodation. Far from being a means of controlling the masses, sport, on occasion, has needed controlling itself. On the issue of sport as a preparation for work, Hargreaves reminds us that not all sports resemble the rhythms and rationality of work. Fishing and bowling provide relaxation and relief in very stark contrast to work.

Hargreaves (1986) argues against a firmly negative view of sport as providing only "surrogate satisfactions for an alienated mass order . . . perpetuating its alienation" and instead argues for a more flexible, spontaneous interpretation. Sport may perform many services in the interests of the status quo, amongst them a belief in the ultimate triumph of ability ("if you're good you'll make it" – in sport or life generally). It also helps fragment the working class by splintering loyalties into localities, regions, etc. But it can also provide a basis for unity and therefore resistance to dominant interest groups: "Part mass therapy, part resistance, part mirror image of the dominant political economy," as David Robins puts it (1982: 145).

## BRITISH AND AMERICAN EMPIRES

Even those who stick valiantly to Marx's first principles are embarrassed by the literalism of the type favored by Hoch and others of his persuasion. Staying true to Marx and applying his class-based formula to virtually any phenomenon is like trying to vault with a pole made of timber: not only is it heavy, but it's rigid (actually, ancient Greeks did use wooden poles). Other writers have opted for more flexibility, taking basic Marxist ideas as they have been reinterpreted by later theorists, in particular Antonio Gramsci, whose central contribution was through the concept of hegemony. Those who followed Gramsci wanted to restore the role of the human being to that of an agent, someone who was active and could intervene in practical matters rather than just respond to the logic of capitalism.

According to hegemony theory, there is nothing intrinsic to sports that make them conservative or subversive: they have no essential qualities. Under capitalism, sports have been supportive to the existing order of things; but there's no necessary reason why, given different circumstances, they could not have a liberating effect.

For Richard Gruneau, as sports become more structured in their institutional forms, they constrain and regulate much more than liberate their participants. The kind of liberating features of sport he has in mind are

> ## Hegemony
>
> From the Greek *hegemon*, meaning leader, this refers to leadership, supremacy, or rule, usually by one state over a confederacy, or one class over another. It has been used in a specifically Marxist way by Antonio Gramsci, who sought to understand how ruling or leading groups in a capitalist society maintain their power by indirect rather than direct economic or military means. They do so by creating a culture that is shared by all but which favors one class over another, usually the most deprived. It is domination, but of intellect or thought rather than body, though ultimately there is a relation because the labor of subordinate groups is exploited. It is important to appreciate that hegemony is not some artificial contrivance: it is a genuinely felt set of beliefs, ideas, values, and principles, all of which work in a supportive way for the status quo and hence appear as common sense. According to Gramsci, an entire apparatus is responsible for diffusing ideas that complement and encourage consensus. These include the Church, education, the media, political institutions, and, if Stoddart, Naison, and others are to be accepted, sports.

spontaneity, freedom of expression, aesthetic beauty. Politically, sports can yield the kind of solidarity that contributes toward the women's movement, civil rights campaigns, and other types of protests against injustice and inequality. In sports, there are opportunities to mobilize against the status quo, not just comply with it. Historically, this has not been the case and the enthusiasm for sports, particularly among the working class, has bolstered the social order.

Flocking to sports as amusement, the working class assimilates its values and principles, most of which dovetail perfectly with those of the wider society. Fair play and the opportunity to go as far as one's ability allows are sacrosanct in sports: meritocratic ideals are important in society too. One legitimates the other. Forgotten is the fact that, in any capitalist system, there are gross, structured inequalities in the distribution of income, wealth, and prestige and that these are replicated one generation after the next through an inheritance system that favors rich over poor. For hegemony theorists, it is important that those at the poorer end of the class structure regard this as commonsensical; that they are not constantly questioning the legitimacy of a system that consigns them to also-rans. Sports encourage this by promoting the good of meritocracy and the equality of life chances that seem to be available to everyone, but, in reality, are not.

Two oft-neglected writers, Mark Naison and Brian Stoddart, have offered studies of sports that draw on Gramsci's concept of hegemony and its role in supporting empires. Naison's early article, "Sports and the American empire" (1972) and Stoddart's analysis of the "Sport, cultural imperialism, and colonial response in the British empire" (1988) advance our understanding of the economic and political utility of sports in stabilizing what might otherwise be disruptive colonial situations. Both writers acknowledge the work of C. L. R. James (1963), whose historical analysis of cricket showed how the values supposedly embodied in the sport were disseminated throughout the Caribbean and how these were of enormous benefit to a colonial regime endlessly trying to manage the local populations.

Sport for both Naison and Stoddart is a means of cultural power, not direct political power as suggested by the others. "Athletic events have increasingly reflected the dynamics of an emergent American imperialism," writes Naison (1972: 96). "As the American political economy 'internationalized' in the post-war period, many of its most distinctive cultural values and patterns, from consumerism to military preparedness, have become an integral part of organized sports." And Stoddart: "Through sport were transferred dominant British beliefs as to social behavior, standards, relations, and conformity, all of which persisted beyond the end of formal empire" (1988: 651).

---

### Imperialism

From the Latin *imperium*, meaning absolute power or dominion over others, this refers to the political and economic domination of one or several countries by one other. The union of the different countries, known as colonies, is the empire. There is an unequal relationship between the ruling sovereign country, sometimes known as the metropolitan center, and the peripheral colonies, which are reduced to the status of dependants rather than partners. Technically, the USA's colonial dependencies have been few compared to, say, Britain or those of other European powers in the nineteenth and early twentieth centuries. But its indirect political influence and its economic pre-eminence over a vast network of other countries have convinced many that there is North American imperialism.

---

By participating in sports, populations who came under American and British influences were taught teamwork, the value of obeying authority, courage in the face of adversity, loyalty to fellow team members (especially the captain), and, perhaps most importantly, respect for rules. Stoddart writes of cricket, though it could be applied to any sport: "To play cricket or play the game meant being honest and upright, and accepting conformity within the conventions as much as it meant actually taking part in a simple game" (1988: 653).

Ruling over colonies in far-flung parts of the globe could have been achieved by military force; indeed, it was initially. But coercion is not cost-effective, especially so when the geographical distance between the metropolitan centers and the peripheral colonies was as great as it was, particularly in the British case. But, if a population could be persuaded that the colonial rule was right and proper, then this made life easier for the masters. Sports provided a way of inculcating people with the kind of values and ideas that facilitated British rule and a "vehicle of adjustment to American imperialism, its popularity an index of America's success in transmitting adulation of its culture and values" (Naison 1972: 100).

None of this suggests a passive acceptance of the rule of America or Britain. As Thomas Sowell writes in his *Race and Culture: A world view*: "Conquest, whatever its benefits, has seldom been a condition relished by the conquered. The struggle for freedom has been as pervasive throughout history as conquest itself" (1994: 79).

By exporting institutions as strong as sport it was possible to create shared beliefs and attitudes between rulers and ruled, at the same time creating distance between them. Organized sports, remember, were products of the imperial powers, most of the rules being drawn up and governing bodies being established between the 1860s and 1890s, exactly the period when the imperialism was at its height. The rulers, having experience with sport, were obviously superior and this reinforced the general notion they tried to convey – that they were suited to rule, as if by divine appointment.

The rules of sports were codified at a central source, transferred to all parts of the vast imperial web, then adhered to by people of astonishingly diverse backgrounds. The colonial experience in general was not unlike this: ruling from a center and engineering a consensus among millions. Impoverished groups over whom Americans and British ruled were introduced to sports by their masters. When they grew proficient enough to beat them, that posed another problem. West Indian cricketers became adept at repeatedly bowling fast balls that were virtually unplayable. South Africa developed a style of rugby that made it almost invincible. Australia beat England regularly at cricket. The problem as it was seen on British soil was that such achievements might be "interpreted as symbolic of general parity," as Stoddart puts it (1988: 667). Baseball was "popularized by the increasing number of American corporate and military personnel" in Puerto Rico, the Dominican Republic, Venezuela, Mexico, and elsewhere, writes Naison (1972). Now, many players from those countries play in US leagues.

The concept of sport as a purveyor of imperial culture is a powerful one, especially when allied to a Marxist analysis of the role of ideas in maintaining social structures. Sport, in the eyes of critics like Naison and Stoddart, is not the blunt instrument many other Marxists take it to be. For them, its value to ruling groups is in drawing subordinate groups toward an acceptance of ideas that are fundamental to their control. This was appropriate in the empires of America and Britain, where orders and directives came from a central source; just like the rules of any sport.

For theorists influenced by Marxism, sports can never be seen as neutral. They can be enjoyed; indeed they must enjoyable to be effective. If we spotted the surreptitious purposes of sports, they could hardly gratify us at all. For them to work, sports must be seen as totally disengaged from the political and economic processes. In the colonial situation, it was crucial that sports were enjoyed and transmitted from one generation to the next. Yet, according to Marxism, this should not deflect our attentions totally away from the valuable functions sports have served – and probably still serve – in the capitalist enterprise at home and abroad. This gives a different slant to the variety of Marxism that sees sports in a one-dimensional way: as politically safe channels or outlets for energies that might otherwise be disruptive to capitalism. Yet, it clearly complements it in identifying the main beneficiary of sports as capitalism.

## RATIONALIZATION AND THE PROTESTANT ETHIC

Max Weber's theories are typically seen as either a direct challenge to Marx's or an attempt to augment them with additional ideas. Unlike Marx and his followers who emphasized the role of material, economic, or productive factors in shaping all aspects of social life, Weber believed ideas and beliefs played a significant role; not in isolation, but in combination with the kind of material factors Marx had played up. In particular, Weber argued that the rise of modern capitalism is, in large part, a result of the diffusion of Protestant tenets throughout Europe and America. Protestantism did not cause capitalism, but its principles and values and those of early capitalism were so complementary that Weber detected an "elective affinity" between them. The attachment is what Weber, in the title of one of his major books, called *The Protestant Ethic and the Spirit of Capitalism* (1958).

The Protestant ethic that emerged in the sixteenth century and, over the next 300 years spread through Europe and the United States, embraced values, attitudes, and behaviors; it encouraged rational asceticism (or austerity), goal-orientation (ambition), constancy (determination), thrift, individual achievement, a consciousness of time, and work as a "calling." In other words, the ethic encouraged the very beliefs and action that were conducive to the rise of business enterprises and, eventually, capitalist economies. While it was originally a religiously inspired protocol, the Protestant ethic transferred to everyday life, promoting human labor to a central position in the moral life of the individual and elevating the business entrepreneur to an exalted status. Laboring in one's chosen vocation was extolled in sermons and in popular literature (for example, the writings of Cotton Mather, Benjamin Franklin, and Thomas Carlyle) as both a duty and vehicle for personal fulfillment.

To understand how all this ties in with the growth of sports, we need to go back to the time before the Protestant ethic had risen. The Renaissance was a period beginning in the early fifteenth century, in which individuals seemed to find release. Starting in Italy, then spreading throughout Europe, creativity, self-expression, and imaginative construction became watchwords. Europe underwent an extraordinarily fertile period of cultural rebirth in which many great masterworks in art, architecture, and engineering were produced.

One of the effects of this was a growth in play and recreation. As artists and scientists were released to exercise their imaginations on new, previously undreamed of projects, so others were released to express themselves in playful physical activities. Ball games in particular enjoyed a surge in popularity. Elementary forms of tennis and handball emerged, known as *pallo della mona*, *rachetta*, and *paletta*. A rough and often dangerous version of football called *calcio* was also played. These and other games had none of the organization or regulation of contemporary sports and they were played in a rather different spirit: the object was to take pleasure from the activities – not necessarily to win.

As playful games gained in popularity, they fostered occasions for spectators to watch. Not that this made them any more competitive. For example, fencing contests were closer to acrobatic exhibitions than outright conflicts: opportunities to express one's physical abilities in front of audiences. In this sense, they had some resemblance to the ancient Egyptian games of the second millennium BCE. Of the latter, J. Sakellarakis writes: "The sole purpose of such displays of athletic prowess was to entertain a spectacle-loving people rather than to serve an ideal similar to that expressed by the later Greek Olympic Games" (1979: 14).

In the Renaissance, no higher values of glory or honor were embodied in games: they were to be enjoyed and watched, plain and simple. Urban festivals and tournaments became popular throughout Europe in the fifteenth and sixteenth centuries. Inter-town rivalries were friendly, if raucous. The predominant Roman Catholic Church at first tried to outlaw the carnival-like activities; they had no obvious utility, either practically or spiritually. Faced with a gathering momentum of interest in games such as *calcio*, the Church eventually conceded and actually recognized such pastimes by allowing them to be played on Holy Days, a tradition that has endured in one way or another.

Catholicism's influence waned as the belief that human beings could shape their own destinies gained currency. Among the most influential Protestant reformers was John Calvin, who lived between 1509 and 1564, and taught that humans, rather than remain subservient to papal dictates, could save their own souls and change the world around them in the process. Human conduct should be ordered according to divine ends, according to Calvin: discipline, abstinence, and the avoidance of pleasures of the flesh were among the many principles he laid down. So, the playful activities about which the Catholic Church had been reserved were quite definitely opposed. Those accepting the ethic of Protestantism were forbidden from taking part in anything so frivolous and cheerful as game-playing.

The Catholic Church's response to the challenge of the Reformation was to reinterpret tournaments, festivals, and carnivals at which games were played as representations of the Catholic faith, performed for the greater glory of God and serving the added purpose of maintaining a healthy body. But, as Protestantism grew and the science it encouraged developed, magic, mysticism, and many theological doctrines were driven out in a process Weber called the "disenchantment" of the natural world. Catholicism came under attack, as did all activities that involved expressive human movement.

In his book *The Influence of the Protestant Ethic on Sport and Recreation*, Steven J. Overman pays close attention to the consistency between the ethical principles and the impulses that led to the rise of what he calls "rationalized sport" which was "built on the prerequisite that sport was to be taken seriously" (1997: 161). Activities that were once regarded as useless and trivial were rationalized in a way that made them agreeable to Protestants. By this, Overman means that the casual, impromptu, and hit-or-miss nature of games and sport-like activities were turned into pursuits that bear much closer resemblance to today's regulated sports.

Older cultures, including Spartan and Roman, had exploited the utilitarian potential of sport, linking training and competition to military purposes. The athletic field was perfect preparation for combat. In *Max Weber: From history to modernity* (1992), Bryan S. Turner notes that, while never enthusiastic about athletic contests in themselves, nineteenth-century Protestants were prepared to interpret athletic activities as having a rational motive: they promoted healthy bodies, strengthened "character," and assisted the production of a hale and hearty population that was habituated to discipline and hard work.

In other eras, athletic competition or games might have been pleasurable escapes from the grind of everyday life. But the Protestants preferred to stress their pragmatic value. The seriousness of purpose that directed action toward goals, the stress on calculable outcomes rather than sheer chance, and the avoidance of pleasures of the flesh were features of the Protestant ethic; but they were also features of the newly rationalized athletic contests that emerged in the late eighteenth and nineteenth centuries.

The labor-intensive character of sports and recreation had been recognized years earlier. The late seventeenth-century scientist Robert Boyle observed that "tennis . . . is much more toilsome than what many others make work"; and the philosopher John Stuart Mill mused "many a day spent in killing game includes more muscular fatigue than a day's plowing." Such views chimed well with Protestants who championed hard work: they denounced monks as lazy parasites because their lifestyle did not count as work. Early settlers in North America were even suspicious about American Indian males who hunted, while females did the real physical work – laboring in the fields, rearing children, and preparing food.

The conception of athletics as paid work goes way back before 1869 when the Cincinnati Red Stockings became the first salaried club, or 1864 when the English instituted the "gentlemen *vs* players" distinction to ensure that the working-class players who were paid were not genuine "sportsmen." But, after the 1860s, professionalism began to change sports. For example, an old practice first used in fifth-century BCE Sparta was revived: employing a specialist person to supervise training. The coach, or trainer, was given the responsibility of ensuring that athletes prepared adequately for their event; this meant taking sports seriously, using rational planning, systematic routines, and, perhaps most importantly, exercising self-discipline. All had analogous features in the Protestant ethic.

If the devil makes work for idle hands, there was no room for his enterprise in sports. Work and productivity replaced pleasure and recreation in several sports, a notable exception being the Olympic Games, which were reintroduced in a modern form in 1896. The Olympic movement strove to create a tenuous and largely artificial link with the ancient games that ceased in CE 393. As such, it prohibited professional competitors and allowed only those who participated in athletics for the honor and pride of competing. Early games were not the spectacles we have become used to in recent decades: programs of events were smaller and competitors were poorly prepared – training was frowned on by amateurs.

Yet, by the 1924 Olympics, a more goal-directed approach had begun to appear. Hugh Hudson's 1981 film *Chariots of Fire* captures the emergent trend nicely. Leading up to the games, the two central athletes, Harold Abrahams and Eric Liddell, are steadfast in the training, Abrahams actually using a professional coach Sam Mussabini (who is not even allowed into the stadium because he has been paid) to oversee his regimen. Yet a third competitor, Lord Andrew Lindsay, presents an alternative portrait of the English gentleman competitor of the 1920s: he places champagne flutes on the edge of his hurdles during practice runs to deter him from clipping them and spilling his favorite tipple. After training (and, occasionally, before) he partakes in a few glasses of champagne. He is the complete gentleman-amateur, with no trace of the single-mindedness, less still the ruthlessness, that gradually takes hold of his fellow Oxford student Abrahams.

While amateurism – from the Latin *amorosus*, pertaining to love – was not sacrificed by the International Olympic Committee until much later, the elevation of winning over just competing became a more prominent feature. And winning required hard work, discipline in training, and efficiency in performance. A further point of symmetry between the Olympics and the ethic that guided society into industrial modernity was the exactitude of its record keeping. Quantification was absolutely vital for industrialism, of course. The Olympic Games, like their ancient predecessors, kept strict registers of results. With the technological benefit of accurate timepieces, the modern games were able to log times and distances, setting in motion a quest for record-breaking performances.

This is one of the characteristics Allen Guttmann believes marks out the traditional from the modern society, the others being secularism (decline of religion), equality, specialization, rationalism, and bureaucratic organization. In his book *From Ritual to Record: The nature of modern sports* (1978), Guttmann argues that, while sports, or at least their progenitors, were originally intended as alternatives to work, they became reflections of it. Overman goes even further: "The Protestant sport ethos succeeded in transforming sport into a regimen of goal-directed behaviors which the are antithesis of pure play" (2000: 338).

By the end of the 1920s, the meaning and purpose of sport had completely changed: they had become organized, regulated, and subject to rules. The rational planning that Weber had analyzed as a major feature of modernity had supplanted the spontaneity and freedom of earlier forms of play. The focus of sports narrowed: to coin a phrase, winning was the only thing. And this was consistent with a Protestant ethic that praised and honored the accomplishment that derives from exertion, perseverance, abstinence, and self-control. Rewards are not given; they are earned.

In presenting a model of the Protestant ethic and its pivotal role in the rise of capitalism, Weber did not intend to explain the mutation of sports into the rational activities we witness today. But his analysis offers a way of recognizing how the ethic that conferred on work a positive status, stressing its benefits and condemning idleness, made a considerable impact on reshaping sports.

---

### Corinthians

From the ancient Greek city of Corinth, site of the Isthmian games, which was known for its wealth, luxury, and licentiousness, Corinthians being its inhabitants. In the early nineteenth century, this took on sporting connotations when it was appropriated by wealthy gentlemen-amateurs, who could afford to ride their own horses, sail their own yachts, and pursue sports for no financial gain – in contrast to the professional players. The self-styled Corinthians believed they embodied the true spirit of sport for its own sake.

## ETHOLOGY'S MAGIC MIXTURE

While he dismisses most of the Marxist approaches to sport as "political clap-trap," Desmond Morris discerns a "small grain of truth" in the idea that events that fascinate, excite, and entertain people also distract them from "political terrorism and bloody rebellion." But, on examination, this aspect of sport "is not political after all, but rather has to do with human nature" (1981: 20). Morris, as a student of animal behavior and who affords humans pride of place in his perspective, has turned his sights to sport in his book *The Soccer Tribe*.

Morris begins from an observation of the 1978 soccer World Cup Final between Argentina and Holland, an event comprising 22 brightly clad figures "kicking a ball about in a frenzy of effort and concentration" on a small patch of grass, and watched by something like one-quarter of the entire world's population. "If this occurrence was monitored by aliens on a cruising UFO, how would they explain it?" asks Morris. His book is a kind of answer.

Morris adopts the role of the puzzled, detached observer, recording notes in the ship's log in an effort to discover "the function of this strange activity" and, while his sights are fixed on soccer, his records have relevance for all sports. His rejection of the Marxist "social drug" approach is understandable, for Morris is an ethologist (a scientist of animal behavior) and follows the approach of *On Aggression* (1966) author Konrad Lorenz, who believed that aggression is instinctive in all animals, including humans. Sport is truly a "safe" diversion from violent behavior. But were political systems to change, the aggression would still exist and would still need an outlet. Political frustrations may aggravate aggressive tendencies, but they do not cause them. This removes the need for any detailed social or psychological theory: sport in general and soccer in particular are grand occasions for venting instinctively violent urges.

Morris goes on to expose several interesting facets, the first being the ritual hunt. Morris's initial premise is much the same as the one offered in this book: that the predecessors of sport were activities that "filled the gap left by the decline of the more obvious hunting activities." The activities passed through a series of phases, the final one being symbolic in which players represent hunters, the ball is their weapon, and the goal the prey. Football players "attack" goals and "shoot" balls. Sport is a disguised hunt, a ritual enactment.

Morris calls today's athletes "pseudo-hunters" whose task of killing the inanimate prey is deliberately complicated by introducing opponents to obstruct them, making it a "reciprocal hunt." Goalkeepers of a soccer team resemble "claws" of a cornered prey "lashing out to protect its vulnerable surface." Its parallels with hunting have given soccer global appeal. Some sports, such as archery, darts, bowling, billiards, snooker, skeet, skittles, curling, croquet, and golf, all concentrate on the climax of a hunt in the sense that they all involve aiming at a target. They lack the physical risks and exertions of a headlong chase and the necessary cooperation between members of the hunting pack. Tennis and squash are more physical, but, unless played in doubles, lack team-work. Some sports, especially motor racing, capture the chase aspect of hunting and also retain dangers.

Basketball, netball, volleyball, hockey, cricket, baseball, lacrosse, and rugby football have plenty of fast-flowing movement and a climactic aiming at targets. Yet the risk of physical injury isn't too high. Morris believes that, apart from soccer, only Australian rules football and ice hockey approach what he calls the "magic mixture." The former has been isolated geographically and the latter suffers because the small puck (the "weapon") makes it difficult for spectators to follow the play (while Morris doesn't mention it, attempts have been made to resolve this by experimenting with a luminous puck that is easier for television cameras to pick up). Soccer seems to capture all the right elements in its ritual and has the potential for involving spectators to an intense degree, which makes watching all the more satisfying.

For all its ritual, soccer – and for that matter many other sports – has a tendency to degenerate into what Morris calls a stylized battle. At the end of play there is usually a winner and loser, and this is not a feature of hunts. Soccer caricatures many other sports in arousing its spectators; fans seethe and fight, they are outraged at bad play or decisions, and euphoric at good results. Other sports engender similar reactions, but at a milder level. At least one piece of research has put this to the test, focusing on hooliganism at football grounds as "ritualized aggression" in that it is not typically violent in a destructive way, but conforms to an "order" with unwritten rules and codes of behavior. As befits an ethological approach, comparisons are made with nonhuman species which use ritual displays of aggression for various purposes, but do so without transgressing boundaries. The stylized war for Peter Marsh and his co-writers, Elizabeth Prosser and Rom Harré, is bounded by *The Rules of Disorder* (1978).

In a similar vein, Morris argues that sport serves as a safety valve through which people vent their spleen in a way that would be unacceptable in many other contexts. But attending an emotional event, as well as providing an outlet for anger and frustrations built up during the week's work, may add a new frustration if the result isn't satisfactory and so make the spectators and players feel worse than before. So, the fan (who happens to be male in Morris's example) "goes home feeling furious. Back at work on Monday, he sees his boss again and all the pent-up anger he felt against the soccer opponents wells up inside him" (1981: 20). So, every game is therapeutic and inflammatory "in roughly equal proportions."

Another ambiguous function of sport is its capacity to act as a status display. Again, Morris writes about soccer, but in terms that can be adapted to fit other sports: "If the home team wins a match, the victorious local supporters can boast an important psychological improvement, namely an increased sense of local status" (1981: 20). Soccer, like most other organized sports, developed in a period of industrialization; as we have noted, many British clubs began life as factory teams. A successful side conferred status not only on the team, but on the firm and even the area. Winning teams and individuals are still held in esteem locally because a victory for them means a victory for the community or region.

The conferment of status is quite independent of objective material positions. Since the publication of Morris's book, this aspect of his argument has become more relevant, as depressed areas in which local manufacturing industries have collapsed or in which communities have been destroyed have yearned for success through sport. The troubled West Midlands city of Coventry was boosted by the local football club's first-ever English Football Association (FA) cup win in 1987. Northern Ireland gained respite from destruction and bloodshed on fight nights when boxing occupied center stage in the sports world. On a national level, staging a major sports event can have an uplifting effect economically and politically as well as culturally on a whole country, as Hugh Dauncey and Geoff Hare show in their collection of essays *France and the 1998 World Cup* (1999). The 2004 Olympic Games were a vital part of the regeneration of Athens as a major capital city and an integral part of the European Union.

Morris's fourth function of sport as a religious ceremony is arguably the most underdeveloped in his assessment, but others before him have expanded on this concept. Like a religious gathering, a sporting event draws large groups of people together in a visible crowd; it temporarily unites them with a commonly and often fervently held belief not in a deity but in an individual sports performer, or a team. Sport is a great developer of social solidarity: it makes people feel they belong to a strong homogeneous collectivity, which has a presence far greater than any single person. Morris equates the rise of sport with secularization: "As the churches . . . emptied with the weakening of religious faith, the communities of large towns and cities have lost an important social occasion" (1981: 23). The function has been taken over by sport.

This argument has been expressed by a number of writers, perhaps most famously by Michael Novak, whose book *The Joy of Sport* (1976) is a reverent acknowledgment of the ecstatic elements of sport. Certainly, the general view that sport has assumed the position of a new religion is a persuasive one and is supported by the mass idolatry that abounds in modern sport. (For the most complete study of the relationship, see Shirl Hoffman's *Sport and Religion*, 1992.) We need look no further than the opening or closing ceremonies at the Olympic Games, or half-time at the Super Bowl, to see the most stupendous, elaborate displays of ritual and liturgy. These are precisely the types of rituals that have been integral to mass religious worship in the past.

The purposes they serve would be similar. In measurable terms, one could suggest that sport is more popular than religion: far more people watch sport than go to church; sport gets far more media attention than religion. Sports performers are better known than religious leaders. In all probability, people discuss sport more than they do religion. So, it seems feasible to say that sport occupies a bigger part of people's lives than does religion.

But religion is intended to provide transcendental reference points beyond everyday experience; it gives moral guidelines; it instructs, informs, and enlightens. Some fanatics may believe sport does all these things. Realistically, it does not, though this is not the thrust of the argument. Do religious believers follow the guidelines or learn from the enlightenment? Some might respond that sports fans do. Otherwise, why ask Mika Hakkinen to tell people to wear TAG Heuer watches, or Mario Lemieux to appear in Old Spice ads, or Roberto Carlos to promote Pepsi? People follow sports with much the same zeal and commitment as active church-goers follow religion and, although it might seem insulting to religious adherents, sports fans do pursue a faith, albeit in their own way.

The comparison between sport and religion extends beyond superficial resemblances when we recognize that sport has become a functional substitute, supplying for the follower a meaningful cause, an emblematic focus, and a source of allegiance, even belonging. But there is still another way in which sport fills a vacuum left by religion and here we move on to the concept of sport as a social drug. Morris, who is dismissive of Marxist theories of sport, fails to make the connection between the two functions. The "opiate thesis" we encountered earlier, when applied to sport shows how sport can function to keep workers' minds off political revolt and so preserve the status quo – which is, according to Marx, what religion was supposed to do. Morris, in rebutting this, states the argument rather crudely, making sport seem a "bourgeois–capitalist plot," a conspiracy orchestrated by the bosses. As we saw in previous sections, this isn't quite the intention of Marxist writers.

There are two residual functions, both of which Morris concedes are exaggerations. As big business sport is commercialized and run effectively as if making money was the sole organizing principle. This is partly true, but misses the reason for the involvement of the "vast majority" which is because they "love" sport. "Money is a secondary factor," according to Morris. As theatrical performance, showbusiness influences are very evident in sport nowadays and the suggestion is that sport has become a mass entertainment. This is true for football, boxing, baseball, and other sports, but not for bowls, netball, judo, and many other minority sports. Even then, sport, by definition, can never be pure entertainment for as soon as the unpredictable element of competition is gone, it ceases. It then becomes pure theater.

Morris's treatment is not a formal theory, but a catalog of functions which soccer serves, as indeed do all sports at various levels, from the psychological to the political. There is no attempt to link the functions together, nor much evaluation of which functions are most effective. Its minor strengths lie in drawing our attention to the many ways in which sport has embedded itself in modern culture and the modern psyche. Try thinking of something that can simultaneously function as a stylized battle, a religious ceremony, and a status display. Morris offers what is really no more than a preamble to his "dissection" (as he calls it) of soccer, but even in this he dismantles the notion that sport is "only a game" and indicates that a match is "a symbolic event of some complexity."

So much for attempts to make sense of sport through grand theories, all of which have merits yet none of which is without problems. At least they provide frames of reference within which we can operate when investigating some of the more specific issues concerning sport. In the following chapters we'll do exactly that, in each case looking at popular ideas that circulate in sport and exposing some of their shortcomings.

| THEORY | Marxist | Figurational | Weberian | Ethological |
|---|---|---|---|---|
| DYNAMIC | Class conflict | Social configuration | Rationalization | Human nature |
| CENTRAL TREND | Hegemonic control | Civilizing process | Growth of capitalism | Instinct suppression |
| SOURCE | Economic power | Control of violence | Religious beliefs/ economic change | Innate aggression |
| REASON | Distraction | Quest for excitement | Reflection of social organization | Symbolic hunt |
| EFFECTS | Pacification of working class | Stress-tension release | Rationalization of sports | Outlet for violent behavior |

**theories of sports**

"Part One: Major Perspectives in the Sociology of Sport" in *Handbook of Sports Studies* edited by Jay Coakley and Eric Dunning (Sage, 2000) consists of seven chapters all devoted to theory; they include illuminating chapters on figurational and Marxist approaches. One of the book's editors, Eric Dunning, has his own *Sport Matters: Sociological studies of sport, violence and civilization* (Routledge, 1999) which provides an elegant defense of figurational theory while remaining alive to the contributions of Weber, Marx, and several other theorists.

*Leftist Theories of Sport: A critique and reconstruction* by William J. Morgan (University of Illinois Press, 1994) is a challenging evaluation of the major tendencies in critical theories of sports. After examining the varieties of Marxism, Morgan offers a "reconstructed critical theory." Morgan argues that the "mass commodification" of sports amounts to "the capitulation of the practice side of sport to its business side."

*The Influence of the Protestant Ethic on Sport and Recreation* by Steven J. Overman (Avebury, 1997) is a brilliant Weberian analysis of the development of contemporary sport in North America. As the title suggests, Overman is concerned with identifying the ways in which religious ideas impacted on the emergence of sports.

*The Soccer Tribe* by Desmond Morris (Jonathan Cape, 1981) describes the way an alien might descend to earth and try to get to grips with the strange customs and practices of soccer fans and players, which Morris likens to tribal behavior; while the author doesn't offer a theory to explain the behavior, he suggests an ingenious historical account of how soccer evolved.

## ASSIGNMENT

On page xxxii of the introduction to their *Handbook of Sports Studies* (2000), Jay Coakley and Eric Dunning write: "The viability of our field depends on our ability to develop collective agreement about rules for making 'truth' or, perhaps better, claims about the 'reality congruence' of our propositions and findings. In the absence of such an agreement, we cannot share and criticize each other's ideas and research in a manner that produces general understanding as well as a foundation of knowledge." Do you spot any possible ways in which the theoretical approaches covered in this chapter might lead to such an understanding or "foundation of knowledge"?

# in the mind

## what makes winners win and losers lose

### THE BIGGEST CHOKE IN HISTORY?

It was the 128th British Open at Carnoustie, Scotland, in 1999. Jean Van de Velde had led for three days, having played some of the most sublime golf of his career. He'd been something of a prodigy, starting playing as a 6-year-old in his native France. Having qualified for the PGA Tour in 1988 after a distinguished amateur career, he won the Roma Masters in 1993. But, as he approached the 72nd hole with a three-stroke lead, he knew that the biggest prize so far was within reach. There was nothing in his bearing or behavior to suggest he would play this hole with anything but the same adeptness and composure he had brought to the previous 71. Gathering momentum, Van de Velde looked set for a peak performance, all facets of his game gelling together at exactly the right time. Then, something extraordinary happened. There followed 15 of the most incomprehensible minutes in sports history.

Faced with a relatively innocuous hole and needing to make a double bogey (six or better) on the par-4, 487-yard hole, an element of caution was all that was required to seal victory. There was no logical reason to suppose the Frenchman would play anything but conservatively. His decision making had been flawless thus far. The voice of reason was surely whispering to him. Yet his behavior suggested that he just wasn't listening. Let's eavesdrop.

*Voice of reason*:  OK, the title is there for the taking. The main thing is: don't get anxious about the prospect of your first major trophy. Just play conservative, risk-free golf, keeping composed and relaxed, but just sufficiently aroused to perform at maximal efficiency.

*Response*: VdV elects to hit a driver off the tee, sending it 20 yards to the right and almost drives into the notorious Barry Burn. The ball flies over the water and comes to rest on dry ground, sitting up on low rough.

*Voice of reason*: Not a good start, but far from disastrous. Now, let's make the rational choice by taking a wedge and chipping safely back into the fairway. This will pave the way for an easy approach shot onto the green. Then it's two putts for the championship.

*Response*: VdV pulls a 2-iron from his bag and strikes for the green. It's a wildly ambitious attempt and completely unnecessary in the circumstances. The shot screws to the right, hits the grandstand, and ricochets back about 25 feet into knee-high heather.

*Voice of reason*: The title's still winnable. The sensible route is now to punch the ball sideward back into the fairway as a prelude to the green. No need for panic. Keep the poise. Don't even think about the shot itself. Just choose it and let your body go through the mechanics. Over to autopilot for the rest of the tournament. Let it guide us safely to the title.

*Response*: VdV goes straight for the green. It's a brave though heedless shot and the ball comes to rest in the water.

*Voice of reason*: Now, we have a little problem. Not an insurmountable one, but sound decision making is called for. What are the options? (a) Take a penalty stroke and a drop. (b) Avoid the penalty stroke and play the ball from the water. With a big title on the line, this is something of a no-brainer. Go with (a).

*Response*: VdV kicks off his shoes and socks, hitches up his pants to his knees and wades into the water. As he does so, he notices the ball sink even further under the water so that it's submerged by two inches. This is a huge moment. If he fails to scoop the ball out of the burn, he remains stuck in the water and title hopes evaporate right there. He changes his mind and takes the drop.

*Voice of reason*: We're still alive, but we're now in the rough about 60 yards from the pin. The main thing is to avoid the bunker, so make a mental picture of the ball sailing comfortably to exactly where you want it to land. Don't rush this one. Pace yourself carefully, bring your heart rate down and, whatever you do, don't snatch at it.

*Response*: VdV clears the water, but his ball lands in the front greenside bunker.

*Voice of reason*: Now we have a little tension creeping in. If we don't make this shot, our rival, who seems to draw sustenance from every error we make, is going to win without even having to fight for it. Make a mess of this one and we don't even get to a play-off. Ah, what the hell, we've probably blown it anyway. Just get it over with.

*Response*: A nice bunker shot from about 25 feet rolls 6 feet past the hole. VdV smiles, as if he hasn't a care in the world. He looks relaxed and still confident.

*Voice of reason*:  All's not lost: we're one shot away from a play-off. Remember: this cup has to be won and, if we manage it, we can dismiss the last few shots as a blip and get back to the kind of golf we were playing earlier.

*Response*:  VdV looks loose and at ease as he makes the putt.

The game goes to a play-off with Paul Lawrie and Justin Leonard, but VdV struggles to find his earlier form, while Lawrie, a Scot playing with strong home support, gathers impetus and triumphs.

It's often been said that the French would rather lose in style than win without it. But national stereotypes can't fully explain Van de Velde's almost inconceivable downfall. His skill wasn't in doubt: he'd played efficiently, even masterfully, up to the point where victory was in sight. The *Atlanta Constitution* echoed many, many others when it described Van de Velde's failure as "the biggest choke job in all the history of golf" (July 19, 1999). Van de Velde dismissed this: "I couldn't live with myself knowing that I tried to play for safety and that I blew it . . . So I made my choices . . . it's a game and I play at that game because I enjoy it," he told *The Independent* (July 19, 1999). (Van de Velde's fortunes declined further in 2002 when he suffered a serious knee injury, which needed surgery.)

His account evoked thoughts of the Kevin Costner character in Ron Shelton's 1996 film *Tin Cup* who, when faced with the choice of playing safe for a win, opts for a series of ambitious, but ultimately self-destructive shots. Neither, it seems, were flexible enough to adapt their approach to suit conditions. There are few constants in sports and champions need to be able to adjust to changing circumstances. Many have the game, as they say; only a few have the mind.

Lawrie confessed that his "mind was racing" as he watched Van de Velde fold, leaving him the opportunity to pull off the unlikeliest win of his life (quoted in the *New York Times*, July 19). He meant that, while he must have started the hole believing he would just go through the motions, he experienced a state of alertness after witnessing Van de Velde's faltering. He began to anticipate a different outcome to the one everyone (including himself) had expected. His attention narrowed as he prepared to respond to the newly evolving situation. Glimpsing the possibility of the title, Lawrie's task would have been to maintain his form without becoming over-aroused and tightening up.

In terms of skill, Van de Velde and Lawrie were evenly matched. Leonard was also arguably their equal. Analyze the physical profiles of the top hundred players of golf or any sport and there would probably be little difference in terms of visible skill, nor in their manifest capacity to endure the elements or withstand injury.

The phrase *primus inter pares* means first among equals and it's not a self-contradiction. Even when athletes of identical physical mettle meet, there's

> ## Mind
>
> Mind is a convenient term rather than a precise concept with empirical referents. It's used, often loosely, in contrast to body to suggest mental properties and processes, such as consciousness, volition, and feeling. Some schools of thought, such as psychology's behaviorism or philosophy's physicalism, find the term unhelpful and prefer to include only observable phenomena in their investigations. Others tend to employ the term cautiously, concentrating on specific features, such as memory, perception, or cognition – the action of knowing. While the investigation of the mind, or the soul, dates back to antiquity, systematic analysis began in earnest in the mid-eighteenth century. Two seminal publications appeared in 1855: Herbert Spencer's *The Principles of Psychology* and Alexander Bain's *The Senses and the Intellect*. Over the next several decades, scholars as diverse as Sigmund Freud (1856–1939) and Edward Thorndike (1874–1949) took the study away from the realms of philosophy and toward a more scientific examination.

always difference. There are still champions and runners-up. Advantages always exist. This raises questions. What are the sources of the advantages and how do some athletes acquire them, while others find them elusive? In answering these questions, we'll notice how the distinguishing features are rarely physical. The differences between athletes lie in, for instance, their motivation, commitment, discipline, confidence, emotional control, and a cluster of other features that constitute their psychological make-up.

In this chapter, we'll follow the example of Clarice Starling and colleagues in building a profile, in our case, of the model athlete. We'll focus in particular on elite athletes – those who have become champions. By definition that makes them a minority. But, they have characteristics that virtually every athlete of any level needs in order to progress. We'll also look at some of the reasons why other athletes don't progress.

## MOTIVATION: THE SPUR TO ACTION

In the late nineteenth century, two minor experiments turned out to have major importance. Max Ringelmann was an engineer at the French Institute of Agronomy (that's the science of soil management and crop production) whose research focused on the relative work efficiency of oxen, horses, and men, and involved elementary tasks such as rope pulling, measuring the amount of force exerted per subject. With each new person added to the human group, the amount of force for each individual was diminished. Contrary to Ringelmann's expectations, there was a shortfall of effort as the size of the team increased. The suspicion was that mechanical problems were not the source of what became known as the Ringelmann effect: the cause was motivational loss.

A few years later, in the USA, Norman Triplett compared the performances of cyclists riding alone with those paced by the clock and those racing against each other. There was a pronounced improvement across the three situations, leading Triplett to conclude: (1) the presence of others aroused the "competitive instinct" which, in turn, released hidden reserves of energy; (2) the sight of others' movements had the effect of making riders speed up.

Together, the experiments showed that the physical performance of humans is significantly influenced by factors that would today be described as psychological and these factors were themselves affected by different environmental conditions. Both experiments discovered that the presence of others affected the level of performance, in Ringelmann's case the reason being a change in motivation, or "social loafing" – slackening off when working toward a common goal with others. The idea that motivation, that is, an internal state or process that energizes, directs, and maintains behavior, can have such an overwhelming effect on physical performance sounds obvious. Maybe it was obvious in the nineteenth century, too, though no one seems to have been too inclined to test it, at least not until these two experiments.

The realization that internal states had a bearing on athletic performance, or indeed any kind of goal-directed physical activity, opened up the possibility that, if we could study them, we could probably change them. Pitch a motivated athlete against one who is unconcerned about the outcome of a contest and the chances are that the former will prevail. Not always, though; for reasons that we'll cover later. But, the message was clear: find the sources of motivation and that will provide the clues as to how performance can be modified.

During the first half of the twentieth century, a kind of architecture of the human mind was drawn up. Different schools offered their own designs on the structure of intellect, cognition, emotion, and other human faculties associated with mental life. Motivation featured in most analyses. It referred to the mainspring of action: the force, drive, or impetus that impels movement (the Latin source of motivation is *motus*, to move). It's what makes us tick, so to speak, and, as such, provides us with an entry point for the inspection of the mind of the athlete.

Motivation is what spurs us into action: it directs us toward certain objectives or in specific directions. The resulting behavior is always intentional, in the sense that we mean something to happen; though the outcomes don't always turn out the way we intended. Where there's no conspicuous link between behavior and an outcome, there's usually no motivation. So, for example, if you want to be a chess grand master, then you probably won't be motivated to train with weights (unless for another, unrelated purpose). The anticipated outcomes, effects, or consequences of a motivated behavior are vital. This is why motivation is such a priceless commodity: physical skills are insufficient in themselves.

The big question is: what induces us to act? In other words, where does motivation come from? Abraham Maslow's answer in the 1950s was based on his celebrated hierarchy of needs, which was a structure based on human imperatives, the primary one of which was biological (hunger, thirst, temperature maintenance, and so on). Imagine these as the bottom tier of a pyramid. Above this are other layers of ever-more cultivated needs, including the need for affiliation with others, aesthetic needs, and the need for self-actualization – to find fulfillment in realizing one's own potential. Motivation works upwards: once we satisfy basic needs, we ascend to the next tier. In Maslow's theory, motivation has origins in human needs, or drives. Sigmund Freud too believed humans are motivated by primal drives, in his approach by sex and aggression. In childhood, parents forbid the free expression of sex and aggression and these become repressed, remaining in the unconscious. For Freud, these unconscious motives manifest in later life, exercising an influence over conduct, though in disguised ways, such as in illness, accidents, mannerisms, or Freudian slips (of the tongue).

Neither account is of much use to sports analysts – not unless they're intending to deprive an athlete of a basic need and make the satisfaction of that need contingent on an appropriate performance. Alternative theories of motivation center on cognition and are based on the view that we're motivated to action in areas where we experience positive feelings of competence and esteem. In other words, if I like ice dancing, but look about as graceful as donkey when I hit the ice, I'm unlikely to be motivated in this pursuit. But, I might casually pick up a basketball and throw it clean through the hoop every time, without even trying. The display draws the acclaim of my peers and I sense a contented afterglow as I walk away. Chances are that I'll be motivated to get back on the court and improve even more. Secretly, I might still harbor thoughts about ice dancing, but I'll be motivated to improve my ball skills in preference.

Self-based approaches, as they're called, explore the ways in which we become motivated and how we maintain that motivation. If someone desires to look like a supermodel but regards themselves as podgy, their motivation might be to exercise and eat less as a way of closing up the discrepancy between what they are currently like and how they want to be. The desire functions as motivation. Whether their original equation is accurate isn't relevant. The person might already look like Kate Moss. They just want to be even thinner. Subjective evaluations are all-important; there's no presumption of rationality. A middle-distance runner might think that by doubling his or her mileage in training, they will run faster in competition and they'll be motivated to do so; at least until they find themselves out of the medals (the British runner of the 1970s,

David Bedford, thought and did exactly this. Although he started favorite to take gold in the 1972 Olympics, he failed).

If we feel we can demonstrate competence in an endeavor, we'll be attracted to it and will sense a locus of control in our attribution of success or failure: we're the ones who will determine how well we do in an event, not fate, nor the weather conditions, the referee, luck, god, or any other external factor. Believing that we control our own destinies is a powerful impulse to succeed and, correspondingly, avoid defeat. It can work the other way too: if an athlete believes he or she is responsible for a sequence of disappointing performances, they may lower their sights, experience a drop in motivation, and slide to further losses.

---

### Locus of control, or causality

If someone believes they should accept blame or praise as the architect of their own destiny, the locus of control is internal. On the other hand, if they believe they're at the mercy of forces beyond their control, the locus is external (*locus* is Latin for place). How they attribute the causality can shape an athlete's development, though not always in a straightforward way. For example, a skilled performer who has experienced success might attribute a loss to unstable, external factors, like poor officiating or bad luck. They'll interpret the setback as temporary. Combined with a willingness to attribute success (whether individual or as part of a team) to effort or other internal variable, they'll sustain self-confidence and protect their image of themselves. A less skilled athlete, who has tasted defeat more often, might attribute a loss to their own deficiencies, leading to low future expectations, a drop in motivation, and the likelihood of further defeats.

---

Most athletes are motivated to achieve, but the level at which they strive to achieve is, of course, variable. They may just want to demonstrate their ability at playing golf at the club, for instance. Or they may seek the approval of peers. Or they may simply set themselves goals, such as to beat their fellow players at the club, or perhaps go all the way to major championships. These goals can either change as a player matures, or they may stay the same. A professional golfer who has never won a major may have a burning ambition to win one. Once he or she wins one, they may feel that they've accomplished their mission.

What seems clear is that successful athletes all hold what's called an achievement motivation: they personally seek success and, in their quest, will look for challenges, show persistence, remain unafraid of losing, and blame themselves in a way that allows them to improve when attributing wins and losses. They'll also value *extrinsic* rewards. While some players are urged to perform at their best and derive feelings of satisfaction from turning in a competent display, the athletes we popularly regard as "winners" are the ones who measure their success against others. They'd prefer to perform poorly and win, rather than well and lose.

Clearly, we act because we want to achieve something, even if it's only getting out of bed in the morning. This in itself is motivated action. It strikes us as obvious that athletes have different motivations to the rest of us, but we should guard against regarding these as fixed. How many potentially good athletes do we know who seem suddenly and perhaps inexplicably to lose motivation? The world is full of people who had the skill, but not, as sports writers often say, the hunger. The metaphor is not such a bad one: it suggests an uneasy or discomforting state that the subject desires to avoid or escape. Competitors at every level want to avoid failure. Coming eighth out of eight sprinters is not a failure if the last-placed runner records a personal best time. Being beaten on a points decision is not a failure if the loser was up against a vastly more experienced boxer and turned in a career-best performance. The ultimately successful athlete can assimilate reversals of fortune such as these and manage to maintain motivation for the next competition.

Being motivated is clearly the most basic requirement of a competitor: action needs to be aimed at an end or goals, short or long term, or the individual never even gets near athletic competition. Of course, many sports careers have been brought to an abrupt halt: injury, distractions, setbacks, an aversion to training are a few of the countless reasons why people drop out almost as soon as they get into sports. The ones who stay adapt. They have to, if only to survive in such a competitive environment.

## COMMITMENT – WHY SOME KEEP IT AND SOME LOSE IT

"You only get out of this game what you put in." How many times have we heard this adage? It refers to commitment. Committing yourself to something or someone means pledging or obligating yourself and implicating yourself in a course of action from which there are limited escape routes. Clearly, progress in sports requires some level of commitment, whether it's in terms of time dedicated to training or abstinence from other satisfying endeavors. Yet, commitment isn't the same as monomania (an inflexible fixation on one thing), but an adaptable orientation that allows an athlete to pursue specific objectives, although not to the exclusion of other potentially fulfilling pursuits. At least that's what the manuals will tell you. Familiarity with some of the top athletes of recent eras suggests that their commitment was more demanding. Gabriela Szabo, the pre-eminent female middle-distance runner of the early twenty-first century, spent her entire waking day training and needed between 12 and 14 hours sleep because of the physical demands of her sport. Anastasia Myskina, the French Open champion of 2004, trained from 8.00 a.m. till 8.00 p.m. every day after the age of 11. Steve Redgrave, who won five gold medals at successive summer Olympics, dedicated himself to a grueling training program almost every day for over 24 years. Buddy Lazier postponed surgery on a broken back to allow him to train seven days a week in preparation for his successful shot at the Indianapolis 500 in 1996. Such levels of commitment are not uncommon among athletes.

The relationship between motivation and commitment is clear: an athlete who is motivated to achieve is more likely to submit him or herself and voluntarily impose restrictions on their freedom as long as they believe it will yield benefits. But, there's always change. A small-scale study of a swim school by Robert Rinehart (1998) captured the most irresistible change in sports. Young swimmers arrived committed and ready to accept the discipline necessary to become successful. The discipline was both "inscribed by others, including coaches and parents, and it is inscribed by itself," meaning that the athletes submitted their bodies to frequently rigorous demands necessary for cultivating skills.

The swimmers were initially attracted to the sport because of the "love of water" or the sheer joy of swimming, but they soon surrendered any notion of enjoyment and accepted that competitive success would only come through regular, predictable, systematic training. Drawing on the work of Michel Foucault, Rinehart shows how what he calls "the relative freedoms of swimming" were replaced by a "disciplinary system both insidious and tenacious." Movements were broken down into minute fragments, each analyzed and subject to electronic surveillance; attendance was checked, progress was monitored, goals were set. The study illustrates how the denial that's so important to discipline in competitive sports isn't simply imposed: it's internalized by the athletes themselves.

It's a minor study with a major point to make about how athletes, if they are to make progress, incorporate the rules and codes of training rather than just have them dictated to them. Again, we see the importance of motivation: without an achievement orientation, the required behavior can't be induced; it needs to be forced. Typically, as an athlete ascends in competition, the incentives that motivate become palpable. The intrinsic pleasure of competing might still exist, but the more powerful rewards are extrinsic – money, titles, records.

There are also disincentives at work: the monotony of repetitive exercise, the abstinence, and, perhaps most importantly, the absence of tangible proof of potential are among the reasons why athletes drift away from the sport they once found so attractive. Some athletes regress or just withdraw from competition. Among the more obvious reasons for this are alternative career opportunities or new responsibilities (like parenthood) that leave insufficient time to devote to sports. But, then there is the sense of failure that sometimes results from repeated exposure to defeat. We've all been in unpleasant, negative situations. If we feel we can do something about them, we'll do it, and, if we don't, we get out.

If prospective athletes experience their failure to reach goals as the result of inevitable factors that lie beyond their control, then redoubling efforts, changing tactics, or modifying training are seen as futile. They see themselves as helpless. In 1980, Carol Dweck published an influential paper in which she drew on Martin Seligman's earlier book *Helplessness: On depression, development and death* (1975). Dweck argued that children who attributed failure under competitive conditions to such things as lack of ability, luck, or other factors over which they had no control, showed a tendency to concede defeat and opt out of sports. They avoided challenges, believing that they could do nothing to influence the course of events. Failure became certain, in their eyes. Dweck coined the term *learned helplessness*.

Failure in itself matters far less than how a young athlete interprets that failure. So, helplessness is linked to how they explain outcomes or results. We learn to think of ourselves as, in some way, lacking the power to change matters. Like dogs which were systematically subjected to unpleasant treatment and refused to escape, even when presented with an opportunity to do so, humans become habituated to failure (the dog experiment provided one of the early insights into this condition).

Unforgiving coaches ("you're useless") or indifferent peers ("you didn't deserve to win") are likely to promote learned helplessness. While assurance ("a slight change in your technique will yield a big improvement") will convey a sense of empowerment. The reason why many would-be athletes drop out is not so much because of their technical inability – even limited athletes can view their sheer participation as a success if it's a source of pleasure to them – it's the sense of helplessness that many find so disagreeable, if not obnoxious.

## SWITCH TO AUTO

Contrary to what commentators occasionally say, skill is nothing to do with instinct: it's learned, developed, improved, and refined through practice. Skill comprises three types: motor skills, which are sequences of physical movement; perceptual skills, which involve receiving information about the environment; and cognitive skills, which relate to thinking, and depend on anticipation and decision making. In all three types, extended practice reduces the need for conscious involvement: the performance of the skill becomes automatic.

Different sports demand different permutations of the three types of skill, of course. Few perceptual or cognitive skills are needed for weightlifting, for instance. Whereas success in golf depends on choosing and carrying out strokes that are appropriate to particular conditions, and so involves all three types. Both need gross motor ability, including short bursts of muscular effort and body coordination. Actually, many sports that ostensibly demand different skills share several. Historically, players like Bo Jackson and, before him, Denis Compton, have excelled at two sports, in Jackson's case baseball and football, in Compton's cricket and soccer. Each pair of sports shared perceptual and cognitive skills, if not motor skills. The strategies employed to master one of the sports were presumably used to master the other.

Typically, improvements in skill acquisition are rapid at first, then slow down to a gradual pace and some athletes insist that, in maturity, decreases in one type of skill are compensated by increases in another (injury, loss of ambition, or lack of physical condition rather than the erosion of skill ends sporting careers). Improvements in accuracy and coordination aren't achieved by repetition of the same skill, but by new, unrelated challenges, which means that highly skilled athletes rarely shirk different, possibly awkward, tasks.

It barely needs stating but skill alone means very little outside the competitive environment. There are several reasons why, the most obvious being that we're confronted by people who have much the same skills as us and often deploy them to nullify ours. In the fictional scenario cited earlier in which I can throw the ball unerringly through the hoop, I might still never be much good at basketball. I might outstrip everyone when allowed to stand and compose myself when preparing to take a free shot, but, confronted by lightning-fast rivals in open play, I'm slow, lose composure, and become fazed. There's no necessary carry-over from a self-paced skill (when the player has complete control over the execution of the skill) and externally paced skills (when other players' movement affect if and how the skill can be realized). The competitive environment also dictates whether an athlete can use *closed* skills: the exact conditions under which the skill is going to be performed is established in advance and incalculable factors are minimized, such as in ice dancing, gymnastics, or synchronized swimming. By contrast, *open* skills are needed in situations in which change and inconsistency are the norm. Any sport in which confrontation and collision are ingredients needs open skills: athletes have to make quick decisions and react to movement, either of other athletes or of missiles, in order to perfect the skill.

Some individuals appear to have natural aptitude, but this is a potential to perform a task; it only means that the person can be trained to perform a skill. They may have ability, that is unlearned qualities that enable them to accomplish the task without much, or even any, instruction or practice. Training enhances that ability, so that they can perform it with greater degrees of proficiency. But, we shouldn't make the error of assuming skills are natural or species-specific properties. In his 1972 study of feral children, *Wolf Children and the Problem of Human Nature*, Lucien Malson records how children deprived of human contact and reared in the wild by animals in their formative years, are usually mute quadrupeds who begin to stand erect only after painstaking tutoring. One boy could use his hands only for picking up objects between his thumb and index finger. Some eventually use language but not competently. Yet many were adept at tree climbing and other dexterous acts not usually associated with humans – skills that they presumably acquired through imitation and repetition.

Most, if not all, aspiring athletes set goals. Time and again, this is shown to be the most effective method of improving competence. Prescribing limited, realistic objectives yields results, though the range of results differs, depending on the athlete. Overall, goal setting is a superior technique to the "go out there and do your best" approach. Here we sense the importance of commitment again: failure to reach a goal can be disheartening, perhaps even humiliating, and few athletes reach every single goal. Yet a success has several positive consequences, the most visible of which is a rise in self-efficacy. While self-efficacy is extremely changeable, some athletes have relatively stable levels. These are the kind of people who relish challenges, persevere at meeting them, show resolution, and achieve at consistently high levels. When athletes

---

### Self-efficacy

This describes a person's or team's belief in their capacity to produce sought after results under specific conditions. As conditions change, so might someone's belief in their competence to reach a certain level of performance. The word efficacy shares a common root with efficiency, the Latin *efficax* which means, essentially, bringing a desired outcome. The term was first used systematically by the psychologist Albert Bandura. Self-efficacy (s-e) isn't constant and mediates between skill, or proficiency, and outcomes, or performances. In this sense, it tends to be more fluid than self-confidence and is susceptible to change in four ways: (1) repeated success raises s-e, while lack of success depresses it; (2) watching teammates doing well can boost s-e; (3) being persuaded verbally that you're doing well (even if you're not) has an impact; (4) athletes who experience high arousal can be persuaded that this state is beneficial, in which case their s-e is raised (some studies suggest this, others show that anxiety is not so amenable to change).

are evenly matched in all other respects, self-efficacy can prove a crucial difference, especially over longer competitions (involving overtime, extra time, tiebreakers, etc.).

We've all practiced a skill over and over without quite mastering it until we arrive at a point when it suddenly clicks and we can do it. Then, every time we do it, we wonder why we struggled so much before. We assemble it in our repertoire of other skills and consign it to memory. This is the point where automaticity, which I alluded to previously, takes over. Surrendering conscious effort to motor control involves a belief in one's own capacities; in other words, self-efficacy releases us to concentrate on other aspects of our game. This is how we build the repertoire.

Repeated success enhances self-efficacy to the point where occasional defeats are insignificant and have little impact on an athlete's self-confidence. Confident athletes enter contests certain in the knowledge that they'll achieve whatever goal they've set themselves. We all know what a valuable resource confidence is: trusting one's own ability and judgment, being self-reliant, assured, and, on occasion, bold confers a sizeable advantage. Over-confidence, on the other hand, is a different matter: being pre-emptory, assuming that the desired outcome is already secure, often leads to the kind of bombastic complacency that proves ruinous. The difference between self-efficacy and self-confidence is narrow and some scholars, such as Robin Vealey (1986), have drawn criticism for failing to distinguish the two (see Manzo's (2002) critique, for example). One way of understanding the two is by visualizing increments of self-efficacy as courses of bricks in a wall, which is eventually a solid – though not indestructible – structure of confidence.

An achievement-oriented athlete, who commits herself to a course of action, inscribing self-discipline and obedience to a regimen in the pursuit of a set of skills, typically sets goals in a steady, piecemeal acquisition. Those in search of overnight success are always disappointed: skills come in small degrees until most of them can be performed automatically. As skills are mastered, so self-efficacy builds and the type of confidence one often associates with competitors manifests prior to or even during competition. But, what actually is going on in the mind of an athlete when the competition is in process and how does this separate the winners and losers?

Often, a victorious athlete is one who stays focused throughout a competition. Focused refers to a state of arousal in which concentration is unwavering. It means operating at the highest possible level of attention, so that a competitor is able to screen out all irrelevant stimuli in the environment and select only visual and audible information that's relevant to the immediate task. Some athletes can be focused in the lead-up to a competition, train steadfastly, perhaps for years (if their goal is an Olympic medal, for example), but lose focus in competition. Others can focus in both training and competition.

Even though the concept has become a little too elastic in recent years, focus remains a valuable tool that can be used to ascertain what separates the champions from the also-rans. Lapses in concentration or distractions can be disastrous in competition; so the facility for gating out extraneous stimuli for long periods is crucial. Imagine the focus required of Formula 1 drivers: while their visual focus falls on the track ahead, they are constantly receiving instructions through their helmets from their pit crew and must respond alertly and accurately, not just for a few minutes, but for several hours.

Competitors in team sports, on the other hand, must focus in a different way: both visual and hearing foci must be wider to take account of movements and sounds of others. They can't afford to focus only on their own game: they have to listen to the instructions of others and take note of players in their peripheral vision. This is called "scanning" (see Van Schoyck and Grasha 1981). A team player must stay alert to the behavior of colleagues and opponents, anticipate what will happen, and has little time to think about how he or she is going to execute a particular skill. There's a general point to be made: effective athletes tend to be those whose mastery of skills is so consummate that they can virtually perform them automatically. In other words, they think about what they're going to do, not how they're going to do it. Lance Armstrong, whom I will consider in more detail shortly, remembers how his cycling improved when he learned this lesson: "I was pushing too hard, not realizing it. I sat down, and focused on execution."

Like anything else in sports, focusing is worked at: athletes cultivate the facility for gating out, or filtering, features of the environment that are not relevant to them. They either devise or are advised on methods of perfecting this. Rugby's Jonny Wilkinson performed a personal ritual prior to attempting conversions: he visualized a target in the crowd, then imagined the ball hitting the target. As he progressed through the procedure, he was able to eliminate extraneous sounds or objects.

## Automaticity

Having mastered a basic skill, athletes can often execute it without conscious control. They have no need to concentrate on the mechanics of, for example, passing the ball or effecting the double pike, but can focus on other aspects, such as tactics or their opponent's intentions. Aspiring golfers are discouraged from thinking about their swing: once the basic technique has been mastered, they are told to emulate proficient golfers and allow the swing to be automatic. Automaticity is the property of a process that operates independently of our attention.

Other athletes self-talk: they literally say out loud scripted sequences of words. In Sam Raimi's 1999 movie *For Love of the Game*, Kevin Costner plays a pitcher who is able to obliterate crowd noise by quietly uttering "clearing the mechanism." Whereas Pat Rafter lost a Wimbledon final in 2000 to Pete Sampras, despite self-talking "Relax. Relax" throughout the match. He reached the final again the following year. "This time I'll be saying: 'Choke. Choke'," said Rafter. It was to no avail: he lost in five sets to Goran Ivanisevic.

Self-talk is one of a number of techniques athletes employ to key themselves to a peak performance. Sports history is full of one-off episodes in which athletes hit a career peak, which they're never able to scale again (Buster Douglas's win over Mike Tyson in 1990; Bob Beamon's record-shattering long jump in 1968). Other athletes maintain peak performances year after year. People like Sergei Bubka, who set 35 world outdoor and indoor pole vault records. In tennis, Martina Navratilova won 167 single titles and remained as the world's number one for a total of 331 weeks (that's almost six-and-a-half years). Michael Jordan won six NBA championships with the Chicago Bulls, retired, then came back to play with the Washington Wizards. Michael Schumacher had won seven (and counting) Formula 1 championships by 2004.

These athletes possess no essence of greatness. Extraordinary as they were and are, they have the same biomechanical features as their peers and, in objective terms, their skills were not of a qualitatively different order. The difference is that they were able to reproduce their best form consistently and in a variety of contexts. (Interestingly, they all played into their thirties and, in Navratilova's case, forties.) Lance Armstrong is another great athlete of recent history. He is, in many ways, exemplary: he clearly had an unerring capacity to reach a peak performance at precisely the right time, not just for a year or two, but consistently over a period long enough to constitute an epoch in sporting terms.

## INTENSITY PERSONIFIED: ARMSTRONG

Armstrong finished 111th, dead last, in his first professional cycling race, the Classico San Sebastian, a one-day 120-mile event through Spain's Basque country. He was 27 minutes behind the winner. In 1992 – the year he came 14th in the Olympic road race – he was 20. Five years later, he had advanced testicular cancer, which had spread through his lungs and brain. Specialists told him that there was a 60 percent chance he was going to die. Yet, he underwent surgery and chemotherapy, survived, and resumed his cycling career. In 1999, Armstrong won the first of his straight Tours de France with a winning margin of almost seven minutes. There followed a period of total hegemony. His sixth victory in

2004 placed him ahead of the sport's legends, Eddy Merckx, Jacques Anquetil, Bernard Hinault, and Miguel Indurain, all of whom won five titles. His coach, Chris Carmichael, reckons that to have set Armstrong a goal of emulating any of these would "have been almost dooming him for failure." Armstrong himself admitted to having little appreciation of cycling history, an innocence he put down to being a Texan, as opposed to a continental European.

After the inauspicious start to his professional career, Armstrong developed into a world-dominating athlete. His recovery from cancer makes him untypical, of course. Yet, in many other senses, he presents an object lesson. On his own account, he went into hospital as one man and emerged another. In physical terms, he had lost about 15 lb (6.8 kg), but the real changes came in his mind.

Armstrong remained ambitious, structuring his career around goals, though without ever envisioning a career of legendary proportions. But, even the step-by-step goals he'd set for himself must have looked beyond him when he was diagnosed with cancer. Small incremental targets rather than great ambitions became the order of the day.

There is a sense of reclamation with anyone who has successfully fought a life-threatening illness: having got their lives back, they can approach any other achievement as a kind of bonus. After his recovery, Armstrong returned to the road a more relaxed rider. The benefits of relaxation have long been recognized in sports, either as part of an athlete's preparation for a contest, a winding down technique after competition or, occasionally, a way of restoring composure during competition. Anxiety is one of the greatest impediments to effective performance, so an athlete who enters a competition calmly, emotions under control, with breathing, heart rates, and muscular tension all within desirable limits is well poised. What was there to get anxious about after you'd just beaten cancer?

Armstrong's first Tour win was seen by many as an aberrant result. A rank outsider, he took the favorites by surprise with a plucky, carefree series in which he showed more adventure than in his previous career. He wasn't burdened either by his own or others' expectations. Nor, it seems, was he constrained by his previous form. "The only way to make advances is to try out new things and to work on new regimes and protocols," he told Carol Lin on the *CNN Saturday Night Show* in 2003 (Lin 2003). He was talking about cancer treatment, but he could just as easily have been referring to cycling tactics.

Then, improbably, he repeated the win. It's often said that becoming a champion improves an athlete. Apart from the obvious upgrade in self-efficacy, there is self-esteem, that is, how worthy or valuable a person considers themselves. They're more likely to interpret failings or setbacks as attributable to others rather than their own deficiencies. This is a dangerous tendency and can lead to complacency or arrogance. But, it can also be a boon in reinforcing the all-important quality of confidence. After two successive wins, this is a quality Armstrong had in abundance. It must have been worth a five-minute start every day of the tour.

There were other changes: Armstrong produced about 6 percent more muscular power than in previous years. Allied to a newfound openness to new tactics, this turned him into a top climber – something he'd previously never envisioned. The old belligerence and tenacity in his cycling were no longer in evidence. The origins of this became clear in his own memoirs when he recounted how he regarded cancer as an opponent that had to be conquered. After this, rival cyclists must have seemed relatively compassionate. He also discovered – to his surprise – that he wasn't as efficient in one-day events any more, so his move to the classics was born of necessity.

Armstrong's astonishing comeback marks him off as a singular athlete. Yet, in many other ways, he personifies characteristics shared by a great many consistently successful performers. We've already noted the imperative property of motivation, the indispensability of commitment, and the requirement for discipline. Armstrong allied these to an anxiety-free approach, openness to new ideas, and a sheer doggedness. Success generated its own self-fulfilling dynamic. (Armstrong's detractors suspected that he used performance-enhancing dope, though he never returned a positive test. Even if he had, he would hardly have been the only one in the world of elite cycling.)

Once in the heat of competition, Armstrong, like other champions, was able to perform at a peak, in his case for 21 days at a stretch. Hitting a peak at precisely the right time and maintaining it for the appropriate period is arguably the most valuable asset of accomplished athletes. We hear talk of being in the *zone*, or in full *flow* when athletes reach a *peak* performance. Athletes sometimes groan that they've peaked too early or just couldn't get into the zone. There are no secret formulas for reaching a peak when it's required, though some researchers argue that practice enhances its likelihood. Others reckon that those periods of total congruity between objective excellence and subjective satisfaction are impromptu and occur fortuitously. For athletes who hit peaks every so often, maybe. But, for an athlete, such as, in cricket, the effortlessly fluent Brian Lara, who becomes completely absorbed at the crease and remains that way for hours on end, game after game, there is more than chance.

Some athletes practice autogenic relaxation prior to a game, others opt for Zen techniques. There are a variety of methods for trying to induce a level of awareness that facilitates peak performance. Myriad accounts of elite performers suggest no common routine, apart from a narrowing of attention and a visualizing of the immediate objective – for example winning the next hole, batting the coming ball, leading the next stage – rather than winning the whole competition. Once into the flow, the various elements of skill come together, eliciting automaticity, which helps maintain the momentum.

---

### Flow, peak, and zone

These all refer to a mental state in which athletes believe they are performing at peak levels. Flow was originally coined in 1990 by Mihaly Csikszentmihalyi to describe an athletic performance that seems to move by itself without any undue effort. He later collaborated with Susan Jackson to write *Flow in Sports: The keys to optimal experiences and performances* (1999). As the title suggests, there is a relationship between the sensation of flow and objective performance. If one is optimal, the other should correspond. A key feature of flow is the balance between an athlete's perception of the challenge and his or her skills. Confronted by a formidable yet not insurmountable obstacle, an athlete might rise to the challenge and reach the zenith of a personal performance. An easier task won't elicit that kind of response. This is why some high quality performers disappoint in everyday competitions, yet excel in the big matchups.

Athletes have a sense of control, confidence, and effortless momentum. Doubts and any other kind of negative thoughts dissolve. The goal is clearly visualized throughout the whole performance, facilitating complete concentration.

*Peak performance* also tends to stress the subjective elements, describing a feat that's experienced as maximal even though objectively it may not be at or near an athlete's best effort in quantifiable terms (Ravizza 1984). It also comes close to being what many nowadays call being *in the zone*, which Cooper (1998) suggests is spontaneous and probably random and has "spiritual dimensions."

Boris Becker alluded to this in his 2004 autobiography where he recalled entering a "trance-like stage" as he approached the climax of big games. He attributed this to an "erotic" relationship between himself and his audience: "They not only want to see you. They want to have you."

---

Any event at all can effect a shift in momentum: a fielding error, a mishit, a flash knockdown – potentially anything. An event works as a catalyst, prompting a response from the athlete. Cognitive, physiological, and behavioral changes combine to produce a driving force that affects the athlete's behavior and, in turn, elevates or depresses his or her performance (Taylor and Demick 1994). Change in perceptions (in particular, of self-efficacy) and arousal, translates into performance. Conversely, losing momentum, or experiencing negative momentum, can prove detrimental to performance, especially if a lead has been depleted and one's opponent is coming from behind. So even momentum-assisted athletes encounter interruptions during competition.

In his memoir *On and Off the Field* (2004), the cricketer Ed Smith offers an insight into how better players are able to rescue the momentum. His view is predicated on the assumption that the best players aren't necessarily better than the norm: their technique is not necessarily superior and they're not gifted. What they do better than most is listen to one of two voices, weak and strong, which start to "battle" in the midst of competition. When the player lacks momentum, the weak voice provides a rationale for failure: "a teammate will get the runs," "you're tired," "this is just an off day," "your adversary is in exceptional form." So, there is a compelling reason for escape: embarrassment – "you can make it right another day." Even the best players succumb to the weak voice sometimes, but less often than more modest players. More usually, they'll listen to a stronger voice that's willing them to persevere until they recover the momentum. The so-called "clutch players" are those who thrive in adversity, and who, on this account, pay attention only to the stronger voice no matter how much momentum has been lost.

Listening to the strong voice works when striving to get back into a game, though, in the Van de Velde calamity, it seems the stronger voice urged the golfer to play exuberantly if irrationally with victory in sight. The voice of reason must have been drowned out.

Voices in the head might well be heard by some athletes, but they are best regarded as a convenient metaphor for the conflicting demands experienced by athletes in stressful situations. The more searching questions include why athletes hear the contrary voices at all and why they respond to them in sometimes starkly different ways.

Fear is common in sports: it goes some way toward understanding the rapid disintegration of some athletes' form at crucial stages in competitions they seem poised to win. Those who are unafraid either of losing or winning hold a significant advantage: they'll continue to trust their game, rather than switching their attention to it and, in the process, trying too hard. Their effort goes into completing the task rather than the execution of specific skills.

One of the perils of becoming a champion is satiation. Once the mission is accomplished, an inevitable period of self-satisfaction follows and the weaker voice becomes dominant. For some, complacency sets in and they retreat into mediocrity or perhaps retirement, safe in the knowledge that they achieved what they set to do. Others, like Armstrong, of course, use the boost in confidence that accompanies a major triumph as fuel for the next mission. The difference is simple: some athletes are attracted to their sport. At least, this is a view offered by Laura Finch (2001), who points out that if an athlete is drawn toward a sport, he or she is likely to exhibit high intensity in pursuing it. By intensity, we mean the quality of eagerness or passion an athlete brings to both training and competition.

Finch's point seems manifestly obvious: if we like doing something, we'll approach it with more enthusiasm than if we didn't. But, this isn't always the case. Changing coaches or switching to a different club, for example, can increase (or decrease) an athlete's intensity. For instance, in the early 2000s, Bolton Wanderers of England's Premiership became known, in the words of its manager, as a "refuge for battered footballers." Players of proven capabilities, who were seemingly past their best, typically found new leases once at the club. Manager Sam Allardyce believed the secret lay in providing a player with "an environment where he can feel happy again and enjoy his football again."

Professional athletes rarely enjoy their sports in the same way as children or youths. Think about it: by the time an athlete is 32, they've been repeating more or less the same routines for 16 years, possibly more. They may be well paid for their endeavors and content themselves with the thought that, if they weren't in sports, they'd be in a less lucrative and more tedious line of work. But, there are the injuries to consider too: training helps promote a healthy body, but competition involves damage, the long-term effects of which manifest themselves years later. The temptation to quit and find a new career path is countered by the possibility of earning more money from competing. *Or*, by passion.

Some athletes just love their sports. Why else would someone like Jerry Rice, wealthy and with every accolade his sport had to offer, continue to play in one of the meanest leagues in sport even as his fortieth birthday approached? Similar questions can be asked of many, many more athletes, who show no signs of mellowing in their maturity and approach their game with a level of intensity others can match but rarely surpass. There is an intrinsic attachment holding them fast, something akin to what Michael Novak called "the joy of sport." Joy is also what fastens many athletes to their sport even when their skills have diminished.

This isn't a romantic vision of sports. Most elite athletes dislike and some even abhor the monotony of training and the ruthlessness of competition. They may still be highly proficient in what they do. But, the ones who relish both are best equipped to maintain the level of intensity required to excel for sustained periods.

For these athletes, there is invariably physical decline: loss of muscular power, speed, and flexibility can be minimized through training. Slowing reaction times can't. But, the big compensation is decision-making capacity. Making choices in the conditions of uncertainty that prevail in sports, involves often complex deliberations, like predicting probable consequences and imagining the likely impact of a course of action on opponents' future decisions. Like any other skill, decision making is learnt, though, in this case, slowly and painstakingly over years. Some young athletes are able to make decisions with a mastery that belies their youth. Most, however, acquire the skill through experience drawn through the years.

## EMOTIONS, IN AND OUT OF CONTROL

Despite the *Atlanta Constitution*'s verdict, Van de Velde's failure probably didn't deserve the dubious accolade of the biggest choke in history. That distinction is awarded, by common consent, to Jana Novotna who led Steffi Graf 4–1 in games and 40–0 in the third set of the 1993 Wimbledon women's final. Novotna, who had looked confident and in control, inexplicably crumbled and lost. It became known as The Choke. A technically able player, Novotna was left wanting again in the French Open of 1995, when leading 5–0 and 40–30 with serve against Chanda Rubin, who survived nine match points. Even in golf, Van de Velde is rivaled by Greg Norman who held a six-shot lead over his nearest rival with one round remaining of the 1996 Masters. On the ninth through twelfth holes, he relinquished his lead to Nick Faldo, then went on to lose the trophy by five strokes. For collective chokes, the Houston Oilers have a claim: having run up what seemed an unassailable 32-point third quarter lead over the Buffalo Bills in the 1992 NFL play-offs, they contrived to lose 41–38.

Sudden surges of severe anxiety at critical stages are common in sports. Typically, they are experienced by athletes who are approaching victory, but become tense and apprehensive at the prospect and abruptly lose form. They call it a choke because it bears resemblance to a temporary suffocation. The sufferer rarely has chance to recover composure before his or her rival capitalizes.

When winning becomes an active possibility, arousal levels increase to the point where physiological functions interfere with performance. Obviously, all athletes need to be aroused to some level. No one wants to go into a competition too mellow or chilled. They want their sweat glands open, blood vessels constricted, pupils dilated, and respiratory volumes and metabolic rates elevated. But, there is an optimum level of arousal. The athlete needs to align these physical changes with the required level of composure, so that the appropriate level of arousal is maintained throughout a contest. If the levels are too low, the performance might be sluggish; too high and it might be too frenetic to be effective. Think of the level of arousal defining an inverted U, with the arc at the top of the ∩ being the target area. Too little arousal (to the left of the ∩) or too much (to the right) and the performance is adversely affected.

This "inverted-U hypothesis" as it's called (by, among others, Fazey and Hardy 1988) looks good on paper, but real examples from sports expose its limitations. How can it explain Novotna's abrupt descent from peak form to the abyss? Players are often stricken with anxiety and disintegrate as if falling from a cliff top. It's as if their arousal levels equip them well for most of the competition, then, faced with the likelihood of victory, the levels shoot up, prompting a catastrophe. Presented graphically, this "catastrophe" theory would suggest a kind of ⌐. High levels of arousal in themselves don't cause the downfall:

only when combined with anxiety. So what brings about the anxiety in some competitors and not others?

Many competitors are able to coast into early leads, but become afraid when the prospect of a win looms. They become stricken by what they believe to be the heightened expectations of others. This translates into the sensation of pressure and they become temporarily disabled and choke. Large crowds tend to multiply the perceived expectations, which turns up the pressure.

Some of the famous chokes we have covered earlier involved athletes who played effectually in early stages of a competition, when little was anticipated of them. Then, as victory came into view, they seemed to become frantically aware that they were actually expected to win and, instead of continuing to play as they had, began attending to what we might call the mechanical features of their game. Other athletes may be able to do this in some circumstances, yet not in others. When they experience the type of stress brought on by heightened expectations, they tend to focus more on what they're doing and lose the automaticity that guided their early play.

Shortly after taking over as England's national soccer coach Sven Goran Eriksson diagnosed his team's problem as fear of failing (see Heaton and Sigall 1989, for a formal exposition). He meant that the players were stricken by the high expectations of others and rarely performed to their best. Frequently among the favorites to win major international competitions, England typically failed to live up to expectations. In 1972, Matina Horner used a similar, though much-criticized, argument to explain why women didn't achieve at the highest levels. She described "fear of success" as a kind of horror some women athletes experience when they approach victory in a realm traditionally dominated by men. Winning carries with it an implied lack of femininity

None of this helps us understand why some athletes choke and others seal wins with cool efficiency and some others excel when actually facing defeat – the clutch players. R. W. Grant's (1988) argument that background factors, such as upbringing, athletic history, personal experiences, and interactions with coaches, have a bearing doesn't help much either. Maybe choking is more of a norm than we think. After all, tennis is a game that has to be won. In other sports, leads can be protected and choking players can disguise their conditions. A boxer with a points lead might choke over the final few rounds but still win, a football team might see its lead shrink yet still end the game with a winning margin. If there is more choking about than we notice, perhaps the athletes who manage to stave off pressure and close out games are the ones worthy of analysis. These are often thought to be immune to *stress*.

There is a spectrum of interpretations of what stress actually means, from a pressure or force that causes significant and unwanted changes to almost any form of discomfort (the latter is probably truer to the original meaning of its root *destresser*, an Anglo-French word meaning to make unhappy). Athletes are usually under stress when expectations of them are, as they see them, too high or, less commonly, too low. The effects include anxiety, tension, and a general apprehensiveness, particularly when approaching or during competition. It acts to the severe detriment of a sports performance – unless the athlete is able to accommodate it. Even top athletes, perhaps especially top athletes, experience the type of stress we read about so often. Yet, as they say, they don't let it get to them. They must be tough.

In contrast to physical toughness – which refers to durability and a high threshold of pain – mental toughness suggests qualities of mind or intellect. For example, Michael Schumacher presents an epitome of mental toughness, one incident in particular showcasing this. In 1996 at the Circuit de Catalunya near Barcelona, he won an astonishing race in treacherous hard rain that forced several of his rivals, including Damon Hill, to retire. Hill said: "I'm happy to be in one piece. You could not see the track. You are putting your life on the line more than normal." Hill's response seemed rational. Schumacher, trailing in sixth place, defied the poor visibility and slick track by driving with a total disregard for his own safety. At one point, he lapped at five seconds faster than the rest of the field.

In achieving a ferocious victory at the Nürburgring Grand Prix of Europe, in 2001, Schumacher all but squeezed his younger brother Ralf into the pit wall to defend his pole position. While technically permissible, it was a potentially perilous maneuver. Schumacher's almost inhuman resolve, his capacity to remain unflustered in even the most hazardous conditions, and his preparedness to take risks others wouldn't even contemplate separated him from his contemporaries.

How he came by these qualities, we can't be sure. But, there's at least a clue in his background. He was the German junior karting champion in 1984 and 1985 when aged 15/16. Competing at such a high level as a teenager must have required practically all the features we have covered so far in this chapter plus a capability for confronting physical danger without flinching or even allowing emotions to obstruct rational decision making.

There is no consensus on what constitutes mental toughness. But, were we to search for a living model, Schumacher would be a solid candidate; and, in some measure, all elite athletes need it. After all, very few sports careers are not punctuated with occasional setbacks: defeats, injuries, suspensions, and so on. Defeats can be especially damaging for some; for others, they are temporary reversals; for still others, they are stimuli, evoking a new response. How a setback is accommodated is crucial. An athlete buoyed by confidence will draw from it lessons that will help him or her avoid another.

Attributing the setback to, for example, lack of preparation or poor officiating enables the athlete to interpret the setback as temporary. Less able athletes are more likely to attribute failure to their own deficiencies, prompting the likelihood of further setbacks. So, being able to take the occasional setback is another aspect that complements the mental toughness that contributes to success. Perverse as it sounds, suffering setbacks can be one of the most beneficial experiences in an athlete's career. To be specific, the setback itself is not the source of value: the athlete's response *is*.

---

### Mental toughness

Mental toughness describes a bundle of qualities that include an unusually high level of resolution, a refusal to be intimidated, an ability to stay focused in high pressure situations, a capacity for retaining an optimum level of arousal throughout a competition, an unflagging eagerness to compete when injured, an unyielding attitude when being beaten, a propensity to take risks when rivals show caution, and an inflexible, perhaps obstinate, insistence on finishing a contest rather than concede defeat. Jean Côté writes: "Mentally tough athletes are able to keep their emotions in control and are calm and relaxed under pressure situations." This is a serviceable though narrower definition than the one drafted here.

Côté's review of research on "Coach and peer influence on children's development through sport" (2001) draws on 1996 work by Smith and Smoll, who describe mental toughness for children as "the ability to keep physical arousal within manageable limits."

---

We're now approaching a psychological profile of elite performers. Motivated strongly enough to commit themselves to a disciplined regimen and prepared to surrender themselves to a coach or advisor, they develop self-efficacy from early, modest success and assemble a self-confidence that will protect them from the occasional reversal of fortune. They'll attribute success and failure in a way that prompts them to strive rather than dwell. Instead of looking distantly into the future and dreaming of glory, they'll set themselves smaller, achievable goals, always remaining, or perhaps becoming, receptive to new ideas and strategies. All the time, they'll be readily accepting new challenges that will assist them in acquiring skills. Once those skills are mastered, they'll consign them to memory, so that they'll have no need to attend to them once in competition. The execution will be automatic.

In the midst of competition, they'll be aroused, yet rarely so anxious that their performance will deteriorate. Getting into a rhythm or flow becomes an important feature, so they might practice methods of gating out distractions, or self-talking themselves into an effective state. Performing at a peak becomes a self-sustaining habit. The kind of fears that can paralyze athletes are conquered or controlled. This is one of the key attributes of achieving athletes: maintaining control over emotions that might otherwise destabilize or ruin a game is a quality even the most seemingly headstrong athletes possess. Those who genuinely do "lose it" – as opposed to those who artfully appear to do so just to interrupt their rival's momentum – are rarely consistent winners. And those who fall prey to anxiety, fear, or some form of stress are always susceptible to choking.

Mentally tough athletes are not emotionless: they are just skilled in subordinating emotions to the greater requirements of winning competitions. Success in any sport typically requires making decisions and the best way to make them is by taking account of as much relevant information as possible and reacting to it in a rational way. Emotions are, in many ways, enemies of rational calculation. Sometimes an emotional choice pays off and, urged on by a loud crowd, an athlete attempts what might seem a suicidally ambitious move that wins a contest. It's hardly a prescription for long-term success, however.

Motivation ebbs away from many athletes once they have achieved their objective; though, for others, there is no loss. Success can function as a stimulant, firing the athlete to new levels of intensity. The longevity of some performers, though sometimes induced by avarice, is more probably the result of the pleasure competition and the attendant benefits bring.

Studying the psychology of athletes teaches us that there's no one-size-fits-all profile. Our distillation of the features that contribute either to success or failure over the short or long term provides us with an abstraction. The reason why the likes of Schumacher and Armstrong repeatedly won is as much to do with their adaptability as their psychology: they change to suit changing conditions of competition. In other words, we might say they're context sensitive. Environmental conditions, opposition, the vicissitudes of competition: these and countless other factors contribute to the context in which they must perform. And context never stands still. This is where intelligence matters.

Intelligence is the capacity to comprehend and understand in a way that enables successful adaptations to changing environments. There are abundant rival definitions, though this seems to capture the thrust of what intelligence is about – learning and abstracting from actual experiences and adapting accordingly when new demands arrive. Successful athletes have it. This doesn't mean to say that they score high on IQ tests, though some do; it means that they have what the psychologist Robert Sternberg describes as "the ability to make sense of and function adaptively in the environments in which one finds oneself" (1996).

"Adaptively" is the key here. A rookie learning a certain type of play in a football team, a boxer modifying his or her style to accommodate a cut that opens up during a fight, a basketball player traded from another club who tailors his or her game to fit in with new colleagues, a cricket captain who changes the field to discomfort batsmen, a baseball pitcher who alters every pitch to deceive different batters: these are examples of adaptive play that occur regularly in competition and are instances of what we might call sporting intelligence. The evidence suggests Van de Velde didn't have it.

A particular type and quality of intelligence operates in sports and, though it hasn't been measured by conventional tests, evidence of it is right there to be seen in competitions where tactics and good sense are required – which is almost all sports.

For every Armstrong or Schumacher who seem to present us with a blueprint of the perfect sporting mind, there is a Diego Maradona, extravagantly skilled but prone to dependencies which eventually consigned him to ill-health, or a Colin Montgomery, relaxed, confident, and technically superb but who couldn't win a major. In other words, there are elite athletes who achieve in spite of what a sport psychologist might identify as failings and other athletes who have no apparent failings, yet never win the big trophies. Identifying the features that are shared by achievers – and those shared by non-achievers – helps us understand the psychology of winners and losers, though never perfectly. One of the appealing qualities of sports is, as we've already noted, its incalculability. This applies as much to its competitors as anything else.

## OF RELATED INTEREST

Bruce Ogilvie and Thomas Tutko's *Problem Athletes and How to Handle Them* (Pelham) was first published in 1966 and it was followed in 1967 by *The Madness in Sports* by Arnold Beisser (Appleton-Century-Crofts). Both books showed how psychological theories could be used to enhance athletic performance and are popularly credited with precipitating interest in what became sport psychology.

"Motivation" by J. M. Silva and R. S. Weinberg in the authors' own edited collection *Psychological Foundations of Sport* (Human Kinetics, 1984) is a solid introduction to the concept of motivation. It should be read with the more advanced "Cognitive theories of motivation and the physical self" by S. J. H. Biddle in *The Physical Self: From motivation to well-being* edited by K. R. Fox (Human Kinetics, 1997) and Karen Hill's *Frameworks for Sport Psychologists: Enhancing sport performance* (Human Kinetics, 2001).

"Born-again sport: Ethics in biographical research" by Robert Rinehart in *Sport and Postmodern Times* (State University of New York Press, 1998) edited by Geneviève Rail is the study on how discipline is internalized by athletes quoted in this chapter.

*Psychological Dynamics of Sport and Exercise*, second edition, by Diane L. Gill

(Human Kinetics, 2000) is perhaps the best pound-for-pound textbook on sport psychology. Among the others are *Foundations of Sport and Exercise Psychology* by Robert S. Weinberg and Daniel Gould (Human Kinetics, 2004), *Psychological Foundations of Sport* edited by J. M. Silva and D. E. Stevens (Allyn & Bacon, 2002), and *Sport Psychology: Contemporary themes* by David Lavallee, John Kremer, Aiden Moran, and Mark Williams (Palgrave, 2003). *Sport Psychology: The key concepts* (Routledge, 2002) is my own A to Z and combines a dictionary-type approach with essay-style expositions, highlighting significant studies.

## ASSIGNMENT

You're a television critic for a newspaper; your main job is to write the television schedules. Due to the illness of a colleague, you're asked to write a psychological profile of an athlete of your choice. Your inclinations lead you to write the story in a style you're used to. So, choose your athlete and compile the profile, using the style of a tv schedule, like:

9.00pm **Nip/Tuck** Troy and Walsh offer surgery to twins with identity issues but Dr Grace Santiago has doubts about the wisdom of this. Cosmetic surgery drama, starring Julian McMahon and Dylan Walsh.

10.00pm CHOICE **Six Feet Under** Compelling drama set in undertakers. The multi-dysfunctional Fisher family has to take care of a druggy teenager who was convinced he could fly off a roof terrace (his relation to the events that follow is fitting, if tenuous, so watch out for the clues).

11.00pm **Young Doctors** Soap. A third-year medical student reaches crisis point as her exams loom, but, while Lizzy struggles to cope, others find success on their obstetrics attachments.

11.30pm FILM **Three to Tango** (Damon Santostefano 1999) A successful businessman mistakenly assumes a friend is gay and asks him to take care of his girlfriend – little suspecting the pair will fall for each other. Romantic comedy with Matthew Perry, Neve Campbell, and Oliver Platt.

1.30am **Major League Soccer** Highlights of today's games, including Kansas City Wiz at LA Galaxy.

2.30am **Law and Order: Special Victims Unit** The team are called in when an aspiring psychologist is found murdered in a convenience store and all the evidence points to one of her patients. Rerun of drama, with Christopher Meloni.

# sports emasculated

## why women had to break rules to get into sports

### WHAT HAPPENED TO THE LADIES?

To: e.e.cashmore@staffs.edu
From: h.g.wells@timemachine.org
Subject: women

Professor Cashmore: I recently stopped off in the late twentieth century and had the opportunity of reading the third edition your book *Making Sense of Sports* in which you make reference to the *Back to the Future* films and venture to imagine what sports might have been like in 1880. Before we continue, I should perhaps point out that in 1898, I wrote a book entitled *The Time Machine* which was popularly thought to be a work of fiction. You are probably already anticipating that this was not the case: it was based on factual experience. I was visited by a time traveler who had constructed an appliance capable of carrying her through the fourth dimension of time and who kindly allowed me to journey with her, at first to the year 802701, where I made the observations that were recorded in my book.

Since then I have undertaken voyages into the distant future, when the sun no longer shines, and to what is, to you, the recent past. All of which leads me to the point of this communication. When I first encountered the facility for time-shuttling I was an admirer of the practice of tennis, a practice that I understand you later called a sport. This was one of the few competitive activities women were believed to be capable of playing. Athletic competitions were the domains of men, who were more muscular and sufficiently robust to withstand the physical exertion required. In many ways, the position of women in competition reflected their position in the political arena. Women in Great Britain and the United States of America were campaigning for the right to vote.

Shortly after the publication of *The Time Machine* women became more militant in their attempts to secure political recognition. Emmeline Pankhurst's suffragettes, as they were called, suffered indignity and violence in their ultimately successful efforts, but their only excursion into sports was horrific: in 1913, Emily Davidson threw herself under a horse owned by King George V at the Derby race. It took until 1918 before the franchise was extended and the shackles of Victorian Britain were left behind. You can imagine my surprise when I paused in your time to review a game for which I have long held an affection. The gentle game of to-and-fro in which women, clothed in full length skirts and straw hats, transferred the ball from one side of the net to the other had been replaced by an altogether different type of activity.

The women, many taller and more muscular than men, play with strange-looking rackets and hit the ball with a barely believable force. Unlike their predecessors, they run about the court, not daintily, but like male sprinters. They also wear the most astonishing garb; and they grunt, sweat, and behave in a manner that would have been considered quite unsuitable in my day. I also had chance to see athletic women run distances that were once thought to be harmful; play ball games that leave their contestants bruised and pummeled; and even witnessed women engage in prizefighting with a fury one associates with men. Actually, I recall reading about female pugilists milling (as we used to call fighting) in the eighteenth century, though I didn't travel back to watch them. My question is this: how on earth did women become such fierce competitors, when they were once just decorative onlookers? Perhaps, when you write the next edition of your text, you might suggest an explanation. I will write to you again soon, next time with some observations from the future.

Cordially
Herbert George Wells

Imagine if Wells were to revisit the late nineteenth century and advise the then embryonic organizations that were governing sports that, contrary to the wisdom of the day, women were eminently capable of competing with men. The organizations might have allowed women admission, but not in separate events. They might have stipulated that if women could compete in tennis, soccer, track, and all the other major sports, then they would have to take their chances against men. In one stroke women would have been transformed from spectators to competitors. Of course, they would have been beaten time and again, especially in events in which muscular strength counted. That much is certain. After all, training, diet, rehabilitation facilities, and all the technologies that assist competitors today were just not available, nor even thought of, when Wells was writing at the end of the nineteenth century.

Still, it's interesting to conjecture what sports would be like now. One answer to this is: no difference. Women will always come second and, usually, a very poor second to men. An alternative is: they are able to hold their own in virtually every sporting matchup in which raw physical strength is not the sole determining factor. That's most sports, of course. I have a definite answer, but, to arrive at it, need to explain the logic guiding the argument.

First, we should consider why there are so few women in sports and why they have so little success compared to men. Today's women enter sport in considerable numbers and their achievements are many. But sportswomen are still a numerical minority and, in measurable terms at least, their performances do not match those of men. Nor do they earn as much.

Pressed to offer an immediate explanation we might take the simple, but misleading, natural ability argument, suggesting that women are just not equipped to handle sports and are always carrying a physical handicap. But the argument exaggerates physical factors and ignores social and psychological processes that either facilitate entry into or halt progress within sport.

We will see in the next chapter how a scientific discourse about the natural state of the female body gave rise to popular beliefs about the dangerous effects of vigorous exercise on women. For the moment, we should take note of three significant implications of this discourse. First, women were not regarded as capable either intellectually or physically as men; second, their natural predisposition was thought to be passive and not active; third, their relationship to men was one of dependence. All three statements are sexist and have been strongly challenged since the late 1960s, of course, but their impact on the entire character of sport is still evident today.

---

**Sexism**

Like racism, sexism is a set of beliefs or ideas about the purported inferiority of some members of the population, in this case, women. The inferiority is thought to be based on biological differences between the sexes: women are naturally equipped for specific types of activities and roles and these don't usually include ones which carry prestige and influence. Much of the scientific support for this type of belief derives from scientific and medical debates from the eighteenth and nineteenth centuries.

## BREAKING THROUGH

The first female sports champion was Cynisca, who won the *quadriga* (a chariot with four horses abreast) race in 396 BCE. In their book *Crossing Boundaries*, Susan Bandy and Anne Darden praise Cynisca for owning, training, and entering the horses, but note that "she was barred from attending and competing in any of the Panhellenic festivals of ancient Greece" (1999: 2). "Her victory, then was from a distance, from the outside." Cynisca was acknowledged as the winner of the event but, as Bandy and Darden put it, "Cynisca's experience as an outsider, not a participant, foreshadowed the role of spectator that women were to play for centuries in sport" (1999: 2).

Athletic contests were part of young women's education in ancient Sparta and Crete. In ancient Greek and Roman cultures, women would hunt, ride, swim, and run, but not (usually) engage in combat. Yet, they were not allowed to compete, nor, in Cynisca's case, even watch competitions. Women were assigned roles as spectators and outsiders.

In the medieval period, women were still seen not as active agents but as objects to be placed on a pedestal, protected and revered and, if necessary, fought for. But, there were exceptions in the Age of Chivalry: some women, certainly noblewomen in parts of Europe, jousted. In his book *The Erotic in Sports*, Allen Guttmann gives examples of women, not only jousting, but fighting men with staffs. He also cites "a titillating contest between two naked women armed with distaffs, one upon a goat, the other on a ram" (1996: 41). And, apparently, foot races between women were common attractions in parts of Europe in the thirteenth century, the condition of entry being that the competitor must be a prostitute (1996: 43).

Typically, these races took place after men's archery contests. It is also probable that women competed in a forerunner of the modern game of darts which involved throwing 18-inch hand weapons at a barrel. Certainly, many women were adept archers and, by the eighteenth century, shot on level terms with men. Peter Kühnst's book *Sports: A cultural history in the mirror of art* includes a plate of a 1787 fencing match between a female and male (1996: 199). Returning to Guttmann, accounts from eighteenth-century England suggest that female pugilism, often of a brutal kind, existed and sometimes resulted in women with faces "covered with blood, bosoms bare, and the clothes nearly torn from their bodies" (1996: 53).

Activities before the nineteenth century, while resembling sports in content, were not strictly sports in the contemporary sense of the word. By the time of the emergence of organized, rule-bound activities we now recognize as sports, women were effectively pushed out of the picture. Frail of body and mind, women could not be expected to engage in any manner of physically exerting activity, save perhaps for dancing, horse-riding, bowling, and the occasional game of lacrosse. Out of the discourse on sexual difference (examined in the next chapter) came an image of the female as very distinct from the male, with totally different propensities and natural dispositions – a sexual bifurcation.

The Victorian ideal of the woman was gentle, delicate, and submissive. Women might let perspiration appear on their alabaster complexions, "glow" during exercise, but should never succeed in sport which was customarily associated with ruggedness, resilience, assertiveness, and a willingness to expend "blood, sweat, and tears." The occasional woman who would attempt to emulate men was risking harm to her body, particularly her reproductive organs.

Women, it was thought, were closer to nature than men: their duties should be confined to those nature conferred on them, like childbearing and rearing. Their role was to nurture. Far from being the product of a male conspiracy, this view was widely held and respected by men and women alike. Accepting that anything resembling strenuous exercise was detrimental to their well-being, women actually contributed, in a self-fulfilling way, to sexist beliefs about them. "The acceptance by women of their own incapacitation gave both a humane and moral weighting to the established scientific 'facts,'" writes Jennifer Hargreaves in her *Sporting Females* (1994: 47).

True, many women were campaigning forcefully and sacrificially in their quest for political suffrage, but their quest did not extend into sports. Women, particularly upper-middle-class women, sat ornamentally as they watched their menfolk participate in sports. But a closer inspection of women involved not so much in competitive sports but in active leisure pursuits, such as rock climbing or fell walking, would have revealed that women were as robust as men and their equals in endurance. Concordia Löfving, of Sweden, and her successor Martina Bergman Österberg both dedicated themselves to training women in gymnastics during the late nineteenth century.

Pierre de Coubertin, to whom so much is owed for his vision of the modern Olympics, embodied Victorian sentiments when he urged the prohibition of women's participation in sport. The sight of the "body of a woman being smashed" was, he recorded, "indecent." "No matter how toughened a sports-woman may be, her organism is not cut out to sustain certain shocks" (quoted in Snyder and Spreitzer 1983: 155–6). The Olympics were to be dedicated to the "solemn and periodic exultation of male athleticism . . . with female applause as reward," said Coubertin. Despite his reservations, women were included in the 1900 Olympics, four years after the inauguration, though in a restricted number of events and not in competition with men. Even as recently as 1980, Kari Fasting notes how women were not allowed to run a 3,000-meter event (just under two miles), the reason being that "it was too strenuous for women" (1987: 362.)

A year after women's inclusion in the Olympics, there was a second, this time relatively unsung trailblazer for female sports. Wealthy Frenchwoman

Camille du Gast was the first to challenge male supremacy behind the wheel. In 1901, she competed in the great 687-mile race from Paris to Berlin. Because her 20 horsepower Panhard was the smallest car in the race, she had to start last of the 127 entrants, but went on to finish ahead of many of the larger cars driven by some of Europe's top drivers.

Capital-to-capital races were popular in Europe in the early years of the twentieth century, but they often resulted in deaths and serious injuries and were discontinued, leaving Madame du Gast to pursue a different sport – motor boat racing – though not before she had inspired other women to take up competitive driving. Over the next 30 years, women made their presence felt at all the major European circuits. Gwenda Hawkes, of Britain, in the 1920s, and Australian Joan Richmond and Canadian Kay Petre, in the 1930s, were among the several women to campaign regularly on the racing circuits. Their involvement was curtailed by the cultural pressures on women to return to the home after the Second World War effort. Women were largely absent from motor racing until their re-emergence in the 1990s, when social changes made it possible for women to assert themselves in areas, including sports, that had been dominated by men.

Golf was a sport considered appropriate for women, at least ladies (as opposed to working-class women): it made minimal physical demands and could be played in full dress. The languid elegance of swing made the sight of female players pleasing to men's eyes; women were not expected to strike the ball with any force. England's Cecilia Leitch changed all that: she brought to the sport a power and competitive spirit that had previously been associated with only men's golf. In 1910, she played a highly publicized game against Harold Hilton, a renowned amateur who had won two Open championships. Leitch, having practiced hitting balls into the wind, won and was acclaimed by suffragettes. Although she went on to win many titles, her legacy was the style and sense of purpose she introduced to women's golf.

Style was also a hallmark of Suzanne Lenglen, the French tennis player; though it was the style of her outfits rather than her play that made most impact. Tennis was actually one of the few areas where women were allowed to compete, though only those of means could afford to. As well as full skirts, they wore tight corsets, high-necked, long-sleeved blouses, and boaters. It was a convention of Victorian society that women should appear decorative at all times, of course. Like golf, tennis was a seemly sport for women.

In the early 1920s, Wimbledon was the preserve of the elite, to whom even training was considered vulgar, if not outright cheating. Women were expected to be clothed head-to-foot. Lenglen, who dominated Wimbledon between 1919–26, shocked traditionalists when she appeared in loose-fitting, pleated skirts that finished just below the knee. Defying custom, she swapped the blouse for a T-shirt-style top that left her arms exposed. She also spurned the corsets and the hats, preferring a bandana not unlike those favored today. In 1931, Lili de Alvarez of Spain caused a rumpus when she appeared in shorts.

Tennis's related sport, table tennis or ping-pong, was not thought befitting women: too much scurrying about and aggressive bursts of activity. The breakthrough player in this sport was Maria Mednyanszky, a Hungarian, who became the first women's world champion and went on to win 18 world titles. Her all-backhand style which saw her crowd the table was strikingly different in its day. In the 1920s, Mednyanszky elevated what was once a parlor game into a serious competitive sport for women.

Baseball has never been considered a suitable sport for ladies. "Unladylike" is one of those words with a certain ring to it: the many activities to which it refers are to be avoided by any female who favors keeping her dignity. In the nineteenth century, the application of the term to behavior that involved some degree of physical exertion was commonplace, unless the behavior was performed by females out of necessity. Washing, cleaning, fetching coal, and emptying chambers were activities performed by working-class women, but they could have few pretensions to being ladies. These were typically the kind of women whose daily duties were so draining that they wouldn't have the inclination to add to their physical workload. Gentlewomen and the wives of the emergent bourgeoisie would have time for croquet, tennis, and perhaps archery, but were self-consciously "ladies."

But, as the nineteenth century passed and women were made to play a vigorous role in the First World War, the flimsy illusion of women as delicate creatures in need of men's protection was eroded. A vocal and effective suffragette movement was prying open new areas in politics and education for women. "Furthermore the 1920s was an era when many feared that the Industrial Age had 'feminized' American culture by sending men to offices and factories and leaving responsibility for socializing young males in the hands of women. Athletics became a way for men to prove their manhood, especially because it allowed them to pursue 'manly' sporting activities in the company of other men," writes Heather Addison (2000: 31).

The Second World War effort also drew women to factories, trucks, and areas of work traditionally reserved for men. The war periods also left a gap in sports that women filled. One famous example of this was the All-American Girls Baseball League, which was started in 1943. The brainchild of Philip K. Wrigley, of the chewing gum company and owner of the Chicago Cubs, the league was made up of women's teams. Major League Baseball's ranks were depleted by the number of male players who were drafted into the armed services in the war effort and it was feared that a substandard competition would drive away fans.

Women had been playing baseball and softball at a competitive level at colleges from at least the turn of the century and possibly before. The war demanded that many women leave their traditionally defined domestic duties and work in factories or other parts of industry; it seemed perfectly consistent for women sports performers to occupy positions previously held by men too. The league's popularity waned when men returned home from war and resumed playing, though attendances were poor in the postwar period. But, there was a legacy, as Susan Cahn points out in her *Coming on Strong: Gender and sexuality in twentieth-century women's sport*: "Women ballplayers offered the public an exciting and expanded sense of female capabilities" (1994: 163). The women's league was the subject of the Penny Marshall film *A League of Their Own* (1992).

While women were allowed to enter the Olympic Games from 1900, their track and field competitions were regarded as a sideshow, lacking the intensity and vigor of men's. This perception persisted regardless of the quality of competition. The woman who more than any other was responsible for changing this was Fanny Blankers-Koen, of Holland, who amassed four gold medals at the 1948 Olympics when aged 30 and a mother of two.

As we'll see in Chapter 8, one of the typical strategies used to discredit female sports performers was to defeminize them either through innuendo or allegations of homosexuality. In the 1930s and 1940s, Babe Didrikson, the American track and field star and golfer, worked hard at presenting a feminine and heterosexual front in spite of suspicions – suspicions that were not actually confirmed until years later with the publication of her biography, which contained details of her friendship with Betty Dodd. By contrast, Blankers-Koen's public persona was enhanced by her motherhood and, in this sense, she was an important harbinger: a heterosexual woman who could also break world records (and at several events).

Swimming prefigured a later fusion of sports and showbusiness. Johnny Weissmuller, who won a total of five gold medals at the 1924 and 1928 Olympics went on to a successful film career after landing the part of Tarzan in 1932. He played the part 12 times. The man who broke Weissmuller's 400-meter freestyle record at the 1932 Olympics, Buster Crabbe, also played Tarzan, though he became better known for his portrayals of Flash Gordon and Buck Rogers. Hollywood repeated the success with swimmer Esther Williams who made her debut in the 1942 movie *Andy Hardy's Double Life* and went on to become a fully fledged star, though mostly in swim-related roles. Like Lenglen before her, Williams visibly embodied a popular, male-defined image of femininity. While they had their detractors, both helped changed perceptions of women: freer, possessed of great exuberance, and unafraid to display their bodies. Yet, there were other women who were uninterested in conforming to men's expectations and made forays into sports for which they were considered hopelessly unsuited.

In the 1930s, women from provincial badminton and tennis clubs in New Zealand got together and played rugby. It was planned to coincide with a men's matchup played on the same day and had no serious intentions: it was a sort of exhibition, almost a spoof of the men's game. Although women had played a version of rugby football in Wales in the nineteenth century, the NZ game was the first recorded competition played according to rugby union rules and, as such, was something of a breakthrough for women's sports.

Rugby had traditionally been a byword for macho sport, the type of game for which women were thought ill-suited. After the Kiwi women had broken the taboo, women all over the world set about doing likewise. Organized matches in the USA and France started in the 1960s, leagues sprung up in Canada and all over Europe in the 1970s, and a Japanese women's league was established in 1983. The Women's Rugby Union was founded in 1983 in response to growing enthusiasm for rugby from women in Britain. It staged its first World Cup competition in 1991, Wales hosting a 12-nation tournament which was won by the USA "Eagles" who beat England in the final game.

At various points over the past hundred years or more, there have been women or teams that have broken new ground in sport. Whether wittingly, or not, they became feminist emblems. We have surveyed just a few of the more conspicuously influential figures in women's sport. But, as the 1960s drew to a close and a vital new form of feminism known as "Women's Liberation" surfaced, sportswomen who were prepared to challenge male traditions were

---

### Fanny Blankers-Koen (1918–2004)

No woman track athlete has managed to match Blankers-Koen's four gold medals, won in the 100 and 200 meters, 80-meter hurdles, plus $4 \times 100$ meters relay, at a single Olympics. Yet, as the rules stood in 1948, she was barred from entering more than three individual events. She held world records in high jump and long jump at the time. Blankers-Koen was then 30 and a mother of two. Her feats, including 20 world records, advanced the cause of women's sport appreciably in the twentieth century. Competing in an era when running 800 meters was considered unsafe for women, Blankers-Koen defied conventional expectations about combining family life with an athletic career. Track and field was an amateur sport in her day. After a promising start in which she appeared at the 1936 Olympics in Berlin, her athletic career was interrupted by the Second World War, in which her native Holland was occupied by Nazis. It was not until the 1946 European championships that Blankers-Koen was allowed to compete internationally again; she won two golds. After her triumph of 1948, she continued to compete, winning three more European titles and setting her final world record, in the pentathlon, in 1951. In 1999, the IAAF honored her as the woman athlete of the twentieth century.

immediately recast as political icons. This was not because of who they were, nor even what they did, but because of the perfect synchronicity of their timing. Of the two most prominent feminist sports icons of the two decades from 1967, one was an averagely talented marathon runner who was never championship material; the other was one of the most consummate champions of her generation. We will examine them and their impact next.

## DE-GENDERING BEGINS

On April 19, 1967, a 20-year-old Syracuse University student entered the Boston Marathon as "K. V. Switzer" and was given the number 261. About four miles into the race, a race official noticed that K. V. Switzer was a woman; as women were not allowed in the race, Jock Semple tried to remove her from the field He was stymied and Switzer went on to complete a historic marathon. Her well-publicized run demonstrated to the world that women were capable of competing in an endurance event that had, up to that point, been officially men-only. Women, it was thought, were not physically able to withstand the rigors of over 26 miles of road-running.

The International Olympic Committee did not even include a 1,500-meter event for women until the Munich Olympics of 1972 – the same year as the passing of Title IX. It was 1984, 17 years after Kathrine Switzer's historic run, before there was a women's Olympic marathon. Switzer maintained that she was unaware that women were not legally admitted to the event in the 1960s. She filled out her application form and signed her usual signature, enclosing this with a medical certificate. "I wasn't trying to get away with anything wrong," Switzer later insisted. "I wasn't trying to do it for women's rights." But, her impact on women's sports was immense. Her disingenuous use of initials, she claimed, was due to the fact that: "I dreamed of becoming a great writer and it seemed all the great writers signed their names with initials: T. S. Eliot, J. D. Salinger, e. e. cummings, W. B. Yeats."

Switzer became world famous for her run, which grew in symbolic terms over the next several years. The picture of Semple attempting to abort her run took an almost iconic status: a male vainly trying to thwart a determined woman trying to break into male territory. Switzer ran eight Boston marathons in total and used her success as evidence in her campaign to have a women's marathon established as an Olympic event. She also approached the cosmetics company Avon, which sponsored a series of high-profile marathons for women 1978–85.

There is often special providence in an event. Seven months after Switzer's run, the United States National Organization for Women (NOW) under the presidency of Betty Friedan held a conference which drew publicity from all quarters in its attempt to create an agenda for women's issues. Although it was actually the second annual conference of NOW, the inaugural meeting had nowhere near the same impact. News of the conference reached Britain at a time when legislators were debating reforms and stimulated interest in the incipient women's movement.

Among the eight-point "Bill of Rights for Women" there were demands for the enforcement of laws banning sex discrimination in employment, more day-care centers, equal educational and training opportunities, and the right of women to control their reproductive lives. This final demand effectively called for greater contraceptive facilities and for the repeal of laws that limited abortion – demands that were already satisfied, at least partially, in Britain.

The conference functioned as a clarion call for the feminist movement which was to have resonance in every sphere of cultural life, including sports. Switzer may not have been self-consciously feminist, but, in practical terms, her contribution to the feminist cause was extremely valuable. As well as attracting media attention, she effectively undermined sexist myths about the fragility of women and their inability to complete marathons without incurring physical damage. Because of the circumstances in which she made her run, she was virtually forced into becoming a spokesperson for feminism, a position she filled with growing assurance.

The marathon is rather an instructive case-study. Between Briton Dale Greig's first official run in 1964 and 2004, the world record for women improved by over 1 hour 12 minutes. In the same period, the men's record has been reduced by 7 minutes 16 seconds. Women are nearly 92.25 percent as fast as men over the distance today, compared to 1925 when they were only 67.6 percent as fast as men.

The moral of this would seem to be that, when women are allowed legally to compete in an event, they can perform at least on comparable terms with men. One wonders how great or small the marathon time differential would be had a women's event been allowed in the Olympics at the time of Violet Percy's first recorded run. "The same as it is today," might be the skeptic's answer, marshaling the support of significant differences in all women's and men's track records. But marathons, though separate events in major international meets, regularly pitch men and women together and, in this sense, they provide a meaningful guide. From the 1970s and the boom in popular marathons and fun runs, women have mixed with men, competed against them, and on many occasions beaten them. The gap shown in the marathon figure would surely have been narrower had television not intervened and insisted that women started their races prior to the men, thus removing the opportunity for females to test their mettle against the world's fastest males.

It's misleading comparing performances in male and female events which have developed separately. Tennis has for long been open to at least those

**the progression of men's and women's marathon records**

women of resources sufficient to afford it. Only in the most playful mixed doubles have they been allowed to confront male adversaries. One-off exhibitions between the likes of an aged Bobby Riggs and Billie Jean King (and, before her, Margaret Court) owed more to theater than competitive sport, though "The Battle of the Sexes," as it was hailed by the media in 1973, was a victory of sorts for King. But, it was a minor struggle compared to the one she faced eight years later.

"My sexuality has been my most difficult struggle," King reflected on her conflict-strewn career. It had been known in tennis circles that many of the world's top female players engaged in lesbian relationships, though few had come out voluntarily. In 1981, King's former hairdresser and secretary Marilyn Barnett took legal action against her to ascertain property rights; in other words "palimony." King at first denied that she had had an intimate relationship with

Barnett, then acknowledged it. The case was thrown out after the judge heard that Barnett had threatened to publish letters that King had written her.

King won her first Wimbledon title in 1966, when aged 22. Her prize was a £45 ($30) gift voucher for Harrods. She went on to win 39 Grand Slam titles. Echoing the remonstrations of "women's liberation," King began demanding prize moneys for women players. Professionalism was already under consideration in tennis. Although ostensibly an amateur (she worked as a playground director), King was "professional" in her approach to the sport. Her preparations were careful and disciplined and her on-court behavior was often belligerent. It was she rather than John McEnroe who introduced the histrionic protests against umpires' decisions. Admired for her ruthlessness in some quarters, crowds turned against her.

King's major professional initiative was to organize an exclusively women's tennis tour which began in 1968. Operating outside the auspices of "official" organizations, King's tour was openly professional in much the same way as pro men's tours such as the Kramer Pro Tour. BJK was able to recruit fellow player Rosie Casals, but few of the other top players. Interestingly, Wimbledon allowed professionals within three months of the start of the King/Casals tour; and the rest of the world's tournaments went open soon after.

Having taken charge of her own career, King aligned herself with the pro-abortion campaign that had grown in momentum and the Title IX legislation of 1972. And, as if to cement her position as a feminist champion, she negotiated a deal with the Philip Morris tobacco company to set up the women-only

---

### Title IX

In 1972, the United States Congress passed Title IX of the Educational Amendments and so instituted a law that would seriously affect all educational institutions offering sports programs. The law specified that: "No person in the United States shall, on the basis of sex, be excluded from participation in, be denied the benefits of, or be subjected to discrimination under any educational program or activity receiving federal financial assistance." At first, this was unpopular among the male-dominated sports officials of schools, colleges, and universities. In 1979, three women athletes from the University of Alaska sued their state for failing to comply with Title IX in providing better funding equipment and publicity compared to the male basketball team. This set in train more actions, so that by the end of 1979, 62 colleges and universities were under investigation by the Office for Civil Rights. The resistance to offering equal opportunity to women has continued to the present day.

Virginia Slims tour. Virginia Slims cigarettes were marketed in such a way as to appeal to newly independent women. King had no compunction about accepting sponsorship money from a tobacco company, in fact very few people considered the combination of sports and tobacco sponsorship objectionable. The United States Tennis Association (USTA) set up a rival women's tournament, though it was clear that King's ascendancy during 1972–5, her most prodigious championship-winning period, and her sheer notoriety made the Virginia Slims the major attraction in women's tennis.

After BJK's sexual proclivities had become a matter of public record, her finances collapsed: heavy legal bills and the withdrawal of sponsorship money forced her into resuscitating her playing career. Actually, she made quite a fist of her comeback, progressing to a Wimbledon semi-final at the age of 40.

The zeal with which King levered away the control of tennis from men was almost matched by her initial reticence about her homosexuality. Her first ineffectual denials gave way to a reluctant admission of her affair, though she maintained she was not a lesbian. In the 1980s, outings were not yet in vogue. After King, they became commonplace, especially among female tennis players; though, less frequently among male sports performers. (See burning question: why don't more gay athletes come out? p. 173)

The question we asked of marathons stands with tennis: how would, say, Serena Williams fare in a head-to-head with Roger Federer had women been playing competitively against men for the past 60 or 50 years? Again, the skeptic might argue that the results would be basically the same, the support this time coming from the copious amount of evidence on the physical differences between the sexes – that is, differences which do not refer to social or cultural influences.

We can gain some measure of the rate of women's progress in sports over the past couple of decades by glancing back at what was once a standard text, *Social Aspects of Sport*. In the 1983 edition of their book, Snyder and Spreitzer wrote about the types of sport women have been encouraged or discouraged from pursuing. "The 'appropriateness' of the type of sport continues to reflect the tenets of the Victorian ideal of femininity," they wrote (1983: 156). They went on to identify three types, all drawn from a 1965 essay written by Eleanor Metheny, "Symbolic forms of movement."

1   *The categorically unacceptable* includes combat sports, some field events, and sports that involve attempts to subdue physically opponents by body contact, direct application of force to a heavy object, and face-to-face opposition where body contact may occur.

2   *Generally not acceptable* forms of competition include most field events, sprints, and long jump; these strength-related events are acceptable, the

authors believe, only for the "minority group" women, particularly, we presume, ethnic minorities.

3   *Generally acceptable* for all women are sports that involve the projection of the body through space in aesthetically pleasing patterns or the use of a light implement; no body contact is possible in sports such as swimming, gymnastics, figure skating, and tennis.

The division suggested a continuity between Metheny's original arrangement of the 1960s and the way things stood almost two decades on. Basically, sports that emphasized aesthetics and grace as opposed to strength and speed were acceptable. The rougher pursuits involving head-on collisions were not. Now, the whole formulation seems about as fresh as disco music and mullets. Types (1) and (2) no longer exist. Women compete in every sport, even those that were once strictly "men only." Even the once-exclusive male preserve of combat sports has been breached. Professional women boxers appear regularly on major boxing bills; some, like Laila Ali made over a million dollars from boxing. Taekwondo, an exhibition event at the 1988 Olympics, was featured as a competitive event in the 2000 games. Women are involved in virtually every form of combat sport, including the total fighting forms.

The inclusion of marathons and 10,000-meter races in the Olympics indicates that women are now seen as capable of handling endurance and strength events as capably as men. Nor are these events dominated by black women. Leadership has circulated among Europeans, Africans, and Asians. Of course, black women, especially, have achieved excellence, for reasons we will come to in Chapter 9.

Over the years, women have not achieved as much as men; yet the conclusion that women can't achieve the same levels doesn't follow logically from the original premise that they are biologically different. In fact, it could be argued that if women had been regarded as equally capable as men physically, then they would perform at similar standards, and that the only reason they don't is because they've been regarded as biologically incapable for so long. In previous editions of this book, I have included a section on the physical differences between men and women and how these affect sporting performance. I highlighted the areas of skeletal and cardiovascular systems and body composition, comparing the typical women's body with the typical male's.

It would be ridiculous to deny that there are differences, though I now believe they are of significantly less importance than our conceptions about them. The body is a process, not a thing: it is constantly changing physically and culturally. Sporting performance promotes changes in terms of muscular strength and oxygen uptake; changes in diet and climactic conditions induce bodily changes too, of course. In our particular culture and this stage in history we understand women and their association with men in one way; in another place and at another time, this relationship may be understood quite differently. It is a matter of convention that we organize sports into women's and men's events, just as it's a convention to award Oscars for the "best actor," a man, and "best actress," a term that's still used to describe the best female actor.

It seems contradictory then to itemize the differences in adipose tissue, respiratory volumes, activity of sweat glands, etc. To do so would fall into the same trap as those who went to so much trouble to "prove" that women were simply not capable of sporting endeavor.

There can be no argument about the fact that the experience of women in sports virtually replicates their more general experience. They have been seen and treated as not only different to men, but also inferior in many respects. Historically, women's position has been subordinate to that of men. They have been systematically excluded from high-ranking, prestigious jobs, made to organize their lives around domestic or private priorities, while men have busied themselves in the public spheres of industry and commerce. Being the bread-winner, the male has occupied a central position in the family and has tended to use women for supplementary incomes only, or, more importantly, as unpaid homeworkers, making their contribution appear peripheral. Traditionally, females have been encouraged to seek work, but only in the short term: women's strivings should be toward getting married, bearing children, and raising a family.

Since the late 1960s and the advent of legal abortion and convenient female contraception, women in the West have been able to exercise much more choice in their own fertility and this has been accompanied by feminist critiques of male dominance. Empirical studies showed wide discrepancies in earning power and this prompted legislation on both sides of the Atlantic designed to ensure equality in incomes for comparable jobs.

One of the loudest cries of feminists was about the abuses of the female body: women, it was argued, have not had control over their own bodies; they have been appropriated by men, not only for working, but for display. "Sex objects" were how many women described themselves, ogled at by men and utilized, often dispassionately. Against this, they recoiled. Even a respectable magazine like *Sports Illustrated*, ostensibly interested in what women do as opposed to what they look like, devotes an annual issue to photographs of women posing in swimwear.

Women are underrepresented in politics compared to their total number in the population. They consistently earn less than their equivalent males and are increasingly asked to work part-time. Despite recent changes in the number of places in higher education occupied by women, they tend to opt for subjects (like sociology and art) that won't necessarily guarantee them jobs in science and industry. When they do penetrate the boundaries of the professions they find that having to compete in what is, to all intents and purposes, a man's world, has its hidden disadvantages – what many call the glass ceiling.

Some argue that this state of affairs has been brought about by a capitalist economy geared to maximizing profits and only too willing to exploit the relatively cheap labor of women who are willing to work for less than men, mainly because they've been taught to believe that their work is unimportant and subsidiary to that of men, and that their "real" work is domestic not industrial. Others insist that women's subordination has a larger resonance that transcends any political or economic system and is derived from patriarchy, a state in which men have continually sought to maintain the grip they have had on society and have found the deception that "a woman's place is in the home" a great convenience which they wish to perpetuate. Whatever the motivation behind the successful effort to keep women subordinate, its effects have been felt in sport, where women have for long been pushed into second place.

Like it or not, women who succeed in sport do not always succeed in the popular imagination: where are the female Beckhams, Bryants, or Mannings? In recent decades, only Nancy Kerrigan, Mia Hamm, and Gabrielle Reece have generated enough interest to guarantee portfolios of endorsements and, in Kerrigan's case, a movie. For a while she was America's favorite covergirl. Had she been pear-shaped with carious teeth, scrubby hair, and pimples, only skating fans would have ever heard of her. Her athletic ability on the ice alone would have quickly been overlooked. Well, not entirely: her conflict with arch-rival Tonya Harding would have guaranteed headlines. But the soft-focus treatment reserved for Kerrigan, in spite of her failure to gain an Olympic gold medal, indicates that her physical appearance was uppermost in the minds of those who bombarded her with contracts. Harding, who never shirked from mixing punches, had an athletic renascence in the 2000s when she reinvented herself as a boxer.

Women, like black people, have never managed entirely to shrug off their stereotypes: each group is in the process of redefining itself in a way that suggests they are much more capable than popular images suggest. But old ideas die hard. Black competitors in sport have unwittingly contributed to the stereotype of a brawny and physically adept specimen but with little "upstairs." They've grasped the only opportunity they were offered for escaping deprivation and, in the process, have become so brilliant that their prowess appears natural.

Women's experience has been one of denial: they simply have not been allowed to enter sports, again on the basis of a mistaken belief in their natural predisposition. Because of this, the encouragement, facilities, and, importantly, competition available to males from an early age hasn't been extended to them. In the very few areas where the gates have been recently opened – the marathon being the obvious example – women's progress has been extraordinary. Given open competition, women could achieve parity with men in virtually all events, apart from those very few that require the rawest of muscle power.

The vast majority of events need fineness of judgement, quickness of reaction, balance, and anticipation; women have no disadvantages in these respects. Their only disadvantage is what men believe about them. To close this chapter, I want to consider another set of beliefs produced – not entirely, but mostly – by men that purports to explain why, in sports as in life, women will simply never catch up.

## MEN'S 10 PERCENT ADVANTAGE

Imagine a man attempting to park a car. He looks at the space, then quickly uses mental imagery to assess whether his car will fit, pulls forward, then backs into the spot. A woman's approach to parallel parking is different: she mentally converts the picture into words, estimating the car's length, the size of the space available, then takes time to evaluate whether one will go into the other. At least that is one interpretation of what happens. According to Anne and Bill Moir, men can form a spatial image easily, while women cannot; they need to reduce the situation to a verbal form. And this constitutes a "fundamental" difference between the sexes. As the Moirs put it, "women are generally more verbal, men are more spatial" (1998: 116).

This has clear implications for sports. Able to assess spaces, judge distances, and coordinate hand and eye, men are well equipped to tackle the demands of athletic competition; they are, as the Moirs say, "good with things." Women, by contrast, are not: they are "good with words" – which is not a great deal of help in sports. In their book *Why Men Don't Iron: The real science of gender studies*, the Moirs pull together a number of studies, all of which purport in some way to confirm the view that the difference between males and females is not a matter of cultural convention, nurturing, stereotyping or, indeed, anything to do with the environment.

"The truth is that the brains of the two sexes are organized in different ways, and it is this difference which gives rise to the differences in ability," argue the Moirs (1998: 119). The sources of this structural and chemical difference are biological. A typical six-week-old embryo is exposed to a cascade of genes – a sort of hormonal soup – that affect later sexual characteristics. Many of these characteristics are obvious. Others are not. Marshaling support from researchers into brain functionality and morphology, the Moirs insist that we have neglected more fundamental, though less visible, differences between men and women. Brain differences give rise to different abilities. "Real science" shows that permanent differences in brain capacity can never be removed. Men will always be better at some things than women and vice versa.

In itself, this sounds retro, though not especially threatening. After all, some science, as we discovered earlier, has found genes that predispose some individuals toward homosexuality and others that determine that the person will become an alcoholic. We'll also see in Chapter 9 how one theory explains the differences between the abilities of black and white athletes as due to biological differences. These have been controversial because they imply that no amount of social change can do much to alter constant differences and the inequalities that turn on them.

For instance, the Moirs believe that the equal sports facilities mandated by Title IX is the "most ludicrous application" of the doctrine of "absolute equality between the sexes" (1998: 144). On their account, it is not surprising that young men are better at physical events: they are more aggressive, impatient, and competitive than young women and they have brains suited to high-speed, high-pressure situations. These are traits likely to be of service in sports. And the reason why men typically have them is not because they are socialized into them, but because they have the right neurological equipment and ten times more testosterone than women. "For boys there should at least be more active and practical learning; more action and stress; a firmer structure and more competitive (virile) tests," they argue, as if confirming that men truly are from Mars (1998: 152).

On this account, the male is an adventure-seeker, attracted to "dangerous sports and physically risky activities involving speed or defying gravity (like parachuting or skiing)" (1998: 161). A woman's "instinct is to avoid risk" (1998: 163). Again differences in the engineering of the brain explain all, including why women underperform compared to men in, well, just about everything that matters, including sports. The Moirs directly answer the question I set at the outset. They cite two marathon times: that of Boston marathon winners Moses Tanui, 2:7.44, and Fatuma Roba, 2:23.21, who were 15.37 apart. "In track and field events, on the whole, males have a 10% advantage, and nature will keep it that way" (1998: 165). In addition to the physical advantages of greater lung capacity, faster metabolic rate, and proportionately more hemoglobin, men have a brain with "triggers" that prompt their bodies to pump out more testosterone and "testosterone in competition is what oxygen is to fire" (1998: 166).

This type of argument has been used before, though the Moirs are careful to support their claims with evidence from studies by, among others, Roger Gorski whose studies demonstrated that male rats, if starved of testosterone in fetal stage, become female in later sexual orientation (1991). Other researchers who are cited approvingly include Munroe and Govier: their work on sex differences and brain organization indicates that females use both hemispheres of their brains to process language, while men involved in verbal tasks utilize only the left brain (1993). Ernie Govier, in particular, argues that males who are verbally gifted (one assumes he means professors, like himself) have female brain patterns (in his 1998 essay "Brainsex and occupation"). But, the crucial insight about boys doing better than girls in spatial tests comes from Gina

Grimshaw who has worked with several co-researchers and discovered a correlation between exposure to testosterone in the womb and "male-typical brain patterns." Interviewed by the Moirs, Grimshaw confirms that male and female brains are neither the same, nor equal, and this has consequences for the way boys and girls learn (1998: 125).

Any number of social scientists agree that there are significant learning differences between young males and females, though most would maintain that the differences are due, not to brain organization, but to cultural determinants. The learning process begins from the get-go: the way children are named, dressed, rewarded, punished, taught, in the most general sense, dealt with – these are all influenced by the different expectations people have about males and females. This does not necessarily mean that the research used by the Moirs is misguided or invalid. It just means that it is less earth-shattering than the authors suppose.

Say there are biologically driven differences in brain structure: a sophisticated social scientist will accept the possibility, at the same time adding that the biggest influences on our lives come not from within but from without. Our parents, peers, and "significant others" bear heavily on us; the institutions that surround us and enter our consciousness induce us to think and behave in ways that strike us as perfectly natural, but which are, in all probability, social. Differences may appear so deep and distinct that they have sources in biology, but it is often the shaping effect of culture that makes us who we are. Culture has a habit of overpowering biology. And, as culture is constantly changing, so are we.

In other words, it doesn't take a sledgehammer to crack the Moir's nut: while their argument exaggerates the effects of biological factors, we do not have to reject out-of-hand the evidence they gather but to substantiate it in order to arrive at a different conclusion. Perhaps the reason why men and women are not equal is *not* because they are different biologically, but because they are treated differently. The parallel processes of exclusion that have operated in sports and in society generally should alert us to the possibility that, over time, cultural conventions have a tendency to be accepted as natural inevitabilities.

Women have underachieved in sports relative to men. We have seen how sports were originally intended exclusively for men and how, for most of their history, stayed exactly that. Women were warned off either forcibly or by medical scares and those who did have the temerity to venture toward the male domain were stigmatized as freaks. So, when they eventually broke onto men's turf, female athletes started from a position of weakness. Even then, they were, and are still, reminded by many that they occupy a secondary status. Paid less, with fewer representatives in senior administrative, coaching, media, and academic positions, women are left in little doubt that they remain trespassers rather than tenants.

That's history, though. Women are now well ensconced in sports. They may not enjoy the same amount of media coverage as men, nor equitable prize money, and they may even endure the sneers of those who continue to look at women's basketball, soccer, rugby, and so on as inferior versions of men's sports. But, women have made their impact felt everywhere. Sports have been emasculated.

## WOMEN'S NEW PARADOX

In 1995, the *New York Times* columnist Robert Lipsyte wrote a story on what he called "The emasculation of sports" (April 2, 1995). Lipsyte mourned the passing of "manly virtues of self-discipline, responsibility, altruism and dedication" (1995: 52). "Sports were promoted as the crucible of American manhood . . . after the closing of the Western frontier in 1890, there was no place left for American men to transform themselves into the stalwarts who would keep democracy alive and lead the country to global greatness." Sport effectively became the "new frontier"; an artificial one, perhaps, but one that could still function as a proving ground.

How did women fit into sports? "Not comfortably," answered Lipsyte. Those sportswomen who didn't look aesthetically pleasing were assumed to be mannish, or full-on lesbians. Gradually at first, then more quickly from 1980, the role of women – and by implication men – in sports changed. No longer were they mere spectators, subordinates, or underachieving versions of their male counterparts. In sports like tennis, golf, and track and field, they copied the examples of men, training hard and competing unsparingly. Whether on court, track, or anywhere sports were played, women started to "exhibit the same killer instincts that we thought were exclusive to men," as Lipsyte put it.

We might add to Lipsyte's account the impact of a number of gay male athletes who decided to declare their sexual preferences from 1980s. Tom Waddell, the Olympic decathlete, was one of the first and, while he didn't start an avalanche of disclosures, his example seemed to embolden a few other high-profile sportsmen. This further complicated the picture: as well as women who revealed features traditionally associated with manhood, there were male athletes who openly defied older conceptions of red-blooded masculinity.

Coinciding with the changes in gender roles, was a change in the institution of sport itself. It became entertainment. Lipsyte believes that sports once had a "moral resonance" in the sense that its central figures were supposed to embody rightness, rectitude, and decency. And while he conceded that there is a "rose-colored prism" through which sportswriters view the world, he lamented the disappearance of sports that conveyed key values, such as "honoring boundaries, playing by the rules, working together for a common goal, submitting to authority" (1995: 51). As sports mutated into pure entertainment, Lipsyte believes that the moral lessons that sports once taught were squeezed out by the mandates of money. People watched sport for amusement, not instruction. They participated for money, not for honor.

Even allowing for the idealized view of sports, Lipsyte's point about the role reversal, or role disarrangement (as we might more properly call it) is a strong one. At a time when sport itself was undergoing something of a trans-formation to an overtly commercial entertainment and shedding whatever moral imperatives it once held, women were forcing their way into the mainstream. They were doing so by demonstrating their ability to compete just as well as their male equivalents. We will cover the process through which sports became a division of the entertainment industry later. For now, we should note the fortune of the timing.

While women were making their presence felt, so sports was becoming showbusiness-like. Women were welcome performers on the new stage. Perhaps they didn't command as much interest as male athletes, maybe interest in some of them centered on features other than their athletic prowess and certainly their achievements in many cases were seen as inferior to those of men. But, sport, to use Lipsyte's phrase, was emasculated: its days as a purveyor of all things fine about manhood were over. No longer the exclusive preserve of men, sports, reluctantly at first, became a gender-neutral arena. And despite all the criticisms that women continued to occupy a marginal status, there could be no denying that every step made by women advanced them toward the center. But, there is a backstory to the progression.

Even as late as 2001, Patricia Clasen was asking the question: "Why is it that women who compete in highly competitive physical activities need to express their femininity so overtly?" Her answer: "Western dualisms have created a paradox for women in athletics . . . women need to emphasize their femininity to the point of commodification" (2001: 36). Even in the twenty-first century, Clasen believes, "the presence of women threatens definitions of masculinity." She argues that the traditional dualism in which women are obliged to conform to certain expectations of what it means to be a woman, has created a paradox for women who want to be successful in sports. A paradox occurs when a person or thing conflicts with preconceived notions of what is reasonable or possible (the word comes from the Greek *para*, for beyond, and *doxa*, meaning opinion).

With Lipsyte, Clasen agrees that the commercialization of sports has introduced new opportunities and demands, but, where Lipsyte sees change, Clasen sees permanence, especially in "patriarchal discourse." Sports continue to constitute a masculine domain, she argues. As such, successful female athletes feel under pressure to reassert their femininity, aided and abetted by a media ablaze with words and images that accentuate the way an athlete looks rather than the way she performs. In other words, women have submitted to a kind of "commodity feminism" in which they have broken with older notions of woman-hood, but surrendered to a new kind; one in which they allow their bodies to be objectified. (Question: don't all athletes allow their bodies to be objectified? After all, when we watch sports, we're admiring bodies in motion.)

Clasen's argument draws support from several other scholars, including Michael Messner who maintains that women are marginalized, sexualized, put down, or just plain left out of sports coverage. What images of women escape into public discourse "come out of the masculinist cultural center of sports," writes Messner (2002: 93). The effect is to preserve sports as a vehicle for reproducing conceptions of manhood.

Other studies have lent conditional support to this type of view. For example, a 2001 study by Christeen George *et al.* concluded that women are still squeezed out to the peripheries of sports: "The media is not necessarily the cause of this marginalization but plays a vital role in its maintenance."

Other research suggests matters are not quite as straightforward as this. Jennifer Knight and Traci Giuliano in 2003 disclosed a pattern in the media's coverage of female athletes: they are "heterosexualized." This means "empha-sizing their relationships with men" (2003: 272). "This pattern is not frequently found in coverage of male athletes," comment the authors, presumably not intending the innuendo. According to Knight and Giuliano, being a successful athlete contradicts a woman's prescribed societal gender role, women are required to "overcompensate for their masculine behavior on the field by acting in traditionally feminine ways off the field" (2003: 273).

Another study, this time by Darin Arsenault and Tamer Fawzy in 2001, examined Nike's advertising. Nike is, of course, a corporation intent on retaining market leadership and maximizing its profits. Women present a sizeable and growing portion of its potential market; so advertising has to reflect this. Arsenault and Fawzy argue that: "Nike attempted to offer women the opportunity to throw off the chains of patriarchy through its provision of a vision of a woman as athletic and competitive, yet nurturing, capable of change, and cognizant of her role as a link between past and future" (2001: 74). Remember, advertising is a key part of the media that many scholars insist is keeping women at the margins. In this study, representations of women break violently with the tradition that portrays women as "soft, effeminate, yielding, compliant and submissive to men" and shows them instead in sex role reversals. Women are authority figures. Yet the authors believe Nike was not bold enough: its use of symbols and images, such as flowers, plaid backgrounds, and smiley faces, "are indicative of women's rather than men's experiences," argue Arsenault and Fawzy.

The study is low in key but perhaps of high importance. Nike is very much part of the transformation of sports since the 1980s. It has played no small part in bringing about many of the changes that have turned sports into popular entertainment. Women's encroachment on the inner circle of sports has not only been affected by this transformation: it has assisted it. As an influential organization, Nike has cultivated a market among women and then exploited that market. Its advertising has reflected this. Envisioning women as strong, vigorous, formidable and, in almost every way, the equals of male athletes suggests a symmetry. The authors of the study criticize the advertising's construction of women, positive as it is in many respects, for failing to disconnect it from its patriarchal past. But, it also shows how advertising in particular and the media in general have *had* to respond to the progress of women in sports.

Women were once marginal in sports. The media were once culpable in maintaining that status. This is no longer the case. Of course, there are residues of the past. Female athletes are, as some writers call it, "sexualized": they are admired less for their skills, more for their aesthetic qualities. Many female athletes seem willing to further their personal interests by displaying themselves in a way that almost encourages this. This may be because they feel obliged to overcompensate, as the Knight and Giuliano study indicated. But a great many more women are valued for no other reason than their athletic prowess. Spend any day poring over the newspapers, or viewing ESPN or Sky Sports and the evidence of your senses will confirm this.

Those who insist that female athletes are still stuck on the margins of sports and that the media continue either to ignore them, "heterosexualize" them, or turn them into objects of desire have either not been looking or are relying on critiques from the 1980s. In the early twenty-first century, awareness of the likes of Justine Henin-Hardenne and Annika Sorenstam rank with that of Condoleezza Rice or J. K. Rowling. They are known for their accomplishments, not their appearance or sexual proclivities.

The media haven't quite managed to suppress their tendency to drool over model lookalikes, with or without athletic ability. And the day when women's sports command equal coverage with men's is still some way off. Yet, change is undeniable. Well, perhaps not undeniable. For instance, in the 2003 edition of his *Sports in Society*, Jay Coakley argues that "sports celebrate a form of masculinity that leads to the social marginalization of women and many [gay] men" (2003: 279). In 1978, when the first edition of Coakley's text was published, perhaps. But in the twenty-first century? Sports have witnessed profound changes since the 1980s, driven by the conversion of competition into entertainment, the pressure of the women's movement, and perhaps even the redundancy of sports as a way of authenticating manhood.

Where did that leave masculinity? After all, if sport was originally conceived as a place where a man could prove himself, what should be made of the growing number of women who were proving themselves? If the incursions of women into sport disarranged conventional notions of femininity, then notions of masculinity were thrown into corresponding disarray.

## Integrated sports

While the physical advantage men are said to have over women has been exaggerated, differences in strength and power preclude women from competing head-to-head in some sports, such as weightlifting. In most sports, however, physical differences are less important than skill. How do women fare in integrated sports?

*Equestrianism* Women and men compete on equal terms in a completely integrated sport. Whether in show jumping, three-day eventing, dressage, enduring and driving disciplines, women regularly beat men.

*Sailing* There is integration in solo ocean-racing, though, since 1988, women compete in a separate category in Olympic sailing events.

*Motor racing* Although there are no rules that prohibit mixed races, there are no female Formula 1 drivers. The Italian Lella Lombardi is the only woman to have scored points in an F1 race, the Spanish Grand Prix, of 1975.

*Snooker* In the early 2000s, the women's number one, Kelly Fisher, played on the men's Challenge Tour, which is one level below the main tour. Fisher was not ranked among the world's leading 100 men.

Several other sports allow integrated competition, though not at all levels. For example, Margaret Thompson Murdoch was the first woman to win an Olympic shooting medal in 1976, though most Olympic events are now segregated. There are also separate Olympic events for women and men in bowls, though, at club level, the sport is completely integrated. Similarly, in darts, women compete with men at club level, but have their own major events.

## CALLING MANHOOD INTO QUESTION

A practice predicated on manhood, patriarchy, and myths about women has a lot to answer for. Its only excuse is that it's given a lot of people an awful lot of pleasure. Sport never pretended to be an equal opportunities pursuit. It never needed to: for the largest part of its history, it was a realm populated by men, all eager to test their spirit against another's and, in the process, exhibit their manly fortitude. Up to the mid-1980s and perhaps beyond, it would have been unimaginable to allow women to compete at the same kind of level as men.

Don't forget: there was no women's marathon event in the Olympics until 1984. Once the demon of women's frailty had been exorcised, sports began its own form of spiritual cleansing, starting with the problem of masculinity.

Actually, there is no problem of masculinity as such: only when masculinity is asserted in distinction to femininity and assumes a superiority, often of an aggressive kind – as many considered it did in and through sports. The particular conception of masculinity propagated in sports was that of the macho male, red in tooth and claw, antagonistic toward gays, contemptuous of women, and robust in the defense of a rigid separation of gender roles. At least, that's one version of masculinity. There are many, many others. In his book *From Chivalry to Terrorism* (2003), the historian Leo Braudy spends 550 pages detailing the various conceptions of what it is to be a man; he even names some of them, "the adventurer," "Don Quixote," "the patriot," "the pirate" (one doubts if he had Johnny Depp's mascara'd Captain Jack Sparrow from *Pirates of the Caribbean: The curse of the black pearl* (2003) in mind). There's no single type of masculinity: there are innumerable versions.

"The sports hero" is one of Braudy's types and this is the version that's typically wheeled out by critics like Mariah Burton Nelson, whose book *The Stronger Women Get, the More Men Love Football* proposed that sports are like incubators for misogyny, and Robert Connell, who, in his *Masculinities*, argued that sports are a leading definer of masculinity in Western culture. Admittedly both books were published in 1994 and have self-obsolesced more quickly than their authors would have wished for. Yet, they epitomized a style of thinking that was popular in the 1990s, one that visualized sports as a monolith on which there hung a "Women not welcome" sign.

Also written in 1994 was an essay by David Whitson in which a rather different vision emerged. According to Whitson, a variety of forms of masculinity and femininity coexisted in sports, especially in newer events, such as mountain bike racing, snowboarding, and skateboarding. Older macho conceptions surfaced in more overtly physical sports, including collision sports, but even these were to change as the end of the millennium approached.

Forms of masculinity that "explicitly critiqued the more traditional form" became apparent in skateboarding, as Becky Beal explained in her "Alternative masculinity and its effects on gender relations in the subculture of skateboarding" (1996). This was complemented by the "ambivalent masculinity" discovered in windsurf culture by Belinda Wheaton in 2000. Both studies found incongruities, Beal especially noting the creation of different roles for men and women. This finding was echoed in a research review by Lee McGinnis *et al.*: "Gender significations are less limiting in some ways than they were in the past," concluded the research team; but, "gender still matters" (2003: 7).

True. And it should, argue some writers, including Susan Faludi, who, in 1999, wrote of an unseen war on men. Traditional codes of manhood are

---

### Crisis in masculinity

According to many writers, men have been in crisis since the late nineteenth century. As the factory system became more dominant, fewer men owned their own businesses or controlled their own labor. Women began to enter the job market in increasing numbers. Fears that culture was becoming "feminized" were stoked up when, following the end of the Second World War, women receded from the workplace, leaving them responsibility for socializing their young. Participation in sports has been seen as one response to the crisis: it allowed men to prove their value in the company of other men. The newer crisis appeared in the wake of the women's movement, when displays of manhood considered appropriate in the post-war period were rendered inappropriate. Overtly aggressive, dominant, and emotionally repressed behavior was derided, if not stigmatized, reducing men to what Stephen Whitehead and Frank Barrett, in their *The Masculinities Reader* (2001), describe as a "confused, dysfunctional and insecure state."

---

no longer honored, observed Faludi. Men have been, as the title of her book suggests, *Stiffed*. (One can almost hear Faludi's publishers pleading with her to choose a title that would convey her sentiments without causing too much offense. "*Screwed? Shafted?* Come on, Susan. Think of something we can sell.")

Faludi's argument, in a way, complements Lipsyte's statements about the emasculation of sports. Both writers agree that the arrival of an age when the media and entertainment industries predominated effectively ended the traditional gender division. There were other factors, of course; but the upshot was that "ornamental culture," as Faludi calls it, called for less doing and more showing. Men were once doers: those who were honored were astronauts, military heroes, even breadwinners. Now, "we are surrounded by a culture that encourages people to play almost no functional roles, only decorative or consumer ones." Culture has reshaped our conception of manhood to the point where men are valued less on their "internal qualities," more on their appearances.

This has led to what we called role disarrangement. Men are eagerly rushing into roles that were once designated as trivializing and humiliating – when women performed them. Think about sportsmen: they have no hesitation in appearing in photoshoots, on catwalks, in celebrity magazines, none of which has any interest in athletic ability. They flex their biceps, curl their lips, smile, or sneer for the cameras. They affect a gangsta attitude or a glamor boy pose and purr "because I'm worth it" in L'Oreal commercials. In other words, they exhibit the same traits that used to be attributed to women. Far from resenting the idea of being objectified, men seem to love it. Women rebelled against what used to be the "feminine mystique"; men show no such insurgency. Perhaps it's because the women's movement had a clearly defined enemy in the form of men. If men have been destabilized and reduced to a state of confusion, they do not seem to mind. This seems to be a case of "Crisis? What crisis?"

So, how do we distil manhood in this era of ornamentation? Is it personified in Dwayne Johnson a.k.a. The Rock? Michael Jackson? Frankie Muniz, the diminutive Agent Cody Banks? Sean Hayes, who plays Jack in *Will & Grace*? The question might once have been answerable; now it's hardly worth asking. Mainly because of the reasons we have covered earlier. Stephen Whitehead and Frank Barrett summarize them: "A combination of, firstly, rampant, soulless consumerism; secondly, women's (feminism's) successful assault on male bastions of privilege; and, thirdly, more widespread social and cultural disapproval of traditional displays of masculinity" (2001: 6).

Sports may well have been emasculated, as Lipsyte suggested. Not castrated, nor sterilized, nor even weakened. Emasculated in the sense that the all-male preserve where misogynist values and sexist assumptions were allowed to go unchecked has been replaced. Not that gender divisions have been wiped away. But, there has been change and the likelihood is that change will continue.

## OF RELATED INTEREST

*Sport and the Physical Emancipation of English Women, 1870–1914* by Kathleen McCrone (Routledge, 1988) looks at the entry of women into sport during the Victorian period. It was a crucial time in the development of sport and also one in which myths about women abounded. At public schools, the new sports with rules and timescales were meant to instill character and decisiveness fitting for future purveyors of the empire. Women were not seen as purveyors. There are several other histories of women in sports, including *Coming on Strong: Gender and sexuality in twentieth-century women's sport* by Susan K. Cahn (Free Press, 1994). More recent histories are: *Feminism and Sporting Bodies* by M. Ann Hall (Human Kinetics, 1996) and *Women in Sport* edited by Greta L. Cohen (Sage, 1993).

"Gender typing of sports: An investigation of Metheny's classification" by Brenda A. Riemer and Michelle E. Visio (in *Research Quarterly for Exercise and Sport*, vol. 74, no. 2, June, 2003) revisited Metheny's postulates nearly 40 years after the original publication. The twist in this research was that they asked schoolchildren to assess Metheny's formulation. "Although we may see girls participating in what Metheny viewed as masculine sports, the opposite does not seem to be true for boys and feminine sports," the authors concluded, adding that "this does not mean that girls and women are socially accepted when they participate in masculine sports . . . but they see the opportunity to participate."

*The Masculinities Reader* edited by Stephen Whitehead and Frank Barrett (Polity, 2001) is a collection of essays predicated on the view that masculinity and indeed gender are defined and sustained by culture, rather than biology. The book contains a short chapter on "how contemporary black males utilize sports as one means of masculine self-expression within an otherwise limited structure of opportunity"; it's complemented by Kenneth MacKinnon's *Representing Men: Maleness and masculinity in the media* (Hodder Arnold, 2003).

"The emasculation of sports" by Robert Lipsyte was published in the *New York Times* (April 2, 1995, section 6) and might profitably be read in conjunction with Susan Faludi's *Stiffed: The betrayal of the modern man* (Chatto & Windus, 1999). Together they advance an image of today's male, in and out of sports, under pressure. "Men aren't simply refusing to 'give up the reins of power,' as some feminists have argued," argues Faludi. "The reins have already slipped from most of their hands."

"Comparing perceived sex role orientations of the ideal male and female athlete to the ideal male and female person" by Beth Ann Martin and James H. Martin (in *Journal of Sport Behavior*, vol. 18, no. 4, 1995) is a slightly dated but revealing study that concludes: "The ideal male athlete and the ideal male person are not perceived as particularly different in rating of their masculinity/femininity." But: "It is clear that ideal female athletes are attributed many masculine characteristics which ideal female persons are not." Readers should consider how much this has changed since the mid-1990s.

## ASSIGNMENT

You are H. G. Wells and it's 1890. Your publishers have asked you to write about the future. In particular, they want you to turn your attention to the pursuits that are currently occupying the population: athletic competitions. You know from your time-traveling that these are set to become immensely popular in the coming century. Your publishers believe that the suffragettes will go from strength to strength and one of their demands will be for open competition, with men and women going head-to-head in all the major sports. Write the synopsis, plotting the progress of women and men to the present day. Remember: sports authorities do not recognize separate gender-based events. Extrapolate creatively from known evidence, which may be drawn from sports and social histories, using statistics where appropriate.

*burning* **QUESTION**

### why don't more gay athletes come out?

Because, in most sports, being gay still carries a *stigma* – a negative imputation attaching to a person's reputation (from the Greek *stigmatos*, for a mark made by a pointed instrument). As Esera Tuaolo declared in his first post-coming out press conference: "If I would've come out in my early career in the NFL, I don't think I would have had the opportunity to play for nine years. I think my career would have been cut short. And also, I think it would've been dangerous for me" (quoted in Steele, 2002).

The danger, as Tuaolo saw it, would have been from fans as well as fellow players. Like David Kopay before him, Tuaolo took the safer option of revealing his sexuality at the end of his playing career. So few athletes, male or female, come out during their competitive years, that it's almost impossible to determine whether or not Tuaolo is right and that it actually is dangerous. But, as a player with the Minnesota Vikings and the Atlanta Falcons, his conjecture has credence.

Money is another strong factor. Cultural prohibitions on revealing one's homosexuality may have receded in recent years, but many athletes who take part of their income from endorsements are hesitant about losing lucrative contracts if they come out. But, there are at least two other related reasons: a homophobia that permeates many male-dominated sports; and the spread of popular misconceptions about Aids – both of which we will deal with later. All the reasons have sources in the stigma associated with being homosexual.

Plenty of showbusiness stars, such as Elton John and George Michael, have stepped out the closet, suggesting that much of the stigma once associated with being gay has disappeared. But not all of it: commercial companies who sign high-profile celebrities to endorsement and sponsorship contracts are notoriously wary about having their products linked to anything to do with gay issues.

In 1997, the famous "coming-out" episode of the sitcom *Ellen* drew impressive viewing audience rating; yet the majority of advertisers pulled their commercials, leaving only Volkswagen, a lesbian tour operator, and advertisements for forthcoming films in the breaks. There is no conclusive evidence that advertising in the show would have had a negative impact on sales, but advertising agencies are not typically adventurous and err on the side of conservatism.

Companies rarely opt for genuinely subversive figures. Possessors of remunerative contracts break rules and defy traditions, but only on the surface. David Beckham and, before him, Dennis Rodman, cut sexually ambiguous figures, but neither was gay. Athletes who venture to overthrow traditions are usually penalized by either having contracts cancelled or never getting offered any in the first place.

The first athlete to suffer financially after coming out was Billie Jean King. There was irony in the icy reception she received from fellow women professionals after her outing. King was the singlemost important figure in the movement that secured prize money comparable with that of men's for women. At a time when the incipient women's movement was making demands for equal pay, reproductive rights, and an end to sexist discrimination, King was a vocal campaigner for women's rights in sports.

Reflecting on her conflict-strewn career, King observed: "My sexuality has been my most difficult struggle." In 1981, King's former hairdresser and secretary Marilyn Barnett took legal action against her to ascertain property rights; in other words "palimony." King at first denied that she had had an intimate relationship with Barnett, then acknowledged it. The case was thrown out after the judge heard that Barnett had threatened to publish letters that King had written her.

Despite this and the fact that King was married (she divorced in 1987), King's sexual proclivities had become a matter of public record and her sponsors dissociated themselves from her, leaving her with the task of making a comeback to meet her legal costs. King was the first major sports star to open up about their sexuality. In the 1930s and 1940s, Babe Didrikson, the track and field star and golfer, worked hard at presenting a feminine and heterosexual front in spite of suspicions – suspicions that were not actually confirmed until years later with the publication of her biography, which contained details of her friendship with Betty Dodd.

Martina Navratilova's relationship with writer and lesbian activist Rita Mae Brown was revealed in a 1981 *New York Post* article. Navratilova never concealed her lesbian relationship, though she probably missed out on the kind of commercial opportunities available to other, more conspicuously heterosexual players. By the time of Navratilova's era in the 1980s and 1990s, there had been a liberalizing of attitudes toward homosexuality and recognition that lesbianism was prevalent among tennis and golf players.

In 1999, Amélie Mauresmo, of France, became famous not only for her world-class tennis and muscular body, but for her candor about her lesbianism: at the age of 19, she talked freely to the media about her relationship with a woman. But, more typically, athletes come out either toward the end of their careers, or even in retirement, or after innuendo. It was something of an open secret for many years before golfer Muffin Spencer-Devlin's announcement that she was gay in 1996. She chose to do so through the pages of *Sports Illustrated*. In the aftermath of the magazine's revelation, other golfers and officials acknowledged that there were other lesbians on the women's tour.

Mariah Burton Nelson was – and is – one of the most effective advocates of gay pride in sport. A basketball player-turned-writer, Nelson became a self-styled role model for lesbians, who encouraged gay players in all sports to declare their sexual preferences. Despite the limited acceptance of gay female athletes by commercial sponsors, male homosexuality has been a different matter and two examples illustrate this.

In 1998, two Canadian Olympians came out within months of each other. Stung by the cancellation of a contract as a motivational speaker on the grounds that he was "too openly gay," Mark Tewksbury, the gold medal-winning swimmer from the 1992 Olympics, who set seven world records in his athletic career, came out voluntarily in a television interview.

Tewksbury, like other gay athletes before him, suffered financially and figure skater Brian Orser claimed his career would also be "irreparably harmed" if his homosexuality were made public. Involved in a palimony suit with his former partner, Orser requested to an Ontario Court Justice that records of the case be sealed. When the request was denied, Orser was effectively outed. One immediate consequence was that he lost his job as a television commentator, yet again underscoring the financially ruinous consequences of coming out.

Figure skating is unusual in the sense that it condones or exculpates male homosexuals in a way that many other sports will not. We have seen elsewhere in this book that most contemporary sports were created largely for the purpose of validating masculinity. Inviolable heterosexual norms might be expected to endure even in spite of liberalization outside sports. In many sports, there is a conspicuous zero tolerance of values, beliefs, or behavior that contradict heterosexual standards. For instance, when confronted by the prospect that he would be outed without his consent, Australian rugby league player Ian Roberts chose to foreshadow the news by declaring himself to be gay through the publication New Weekly. Roberts withstood the predictably hostile response and continued playing.

British soccer player Justin Fashanu also chose to come out via a news story (in The Sun, a sensationalist British newspaper) but with less fortunate consequences. His club terminated his playing contract and he moved to several others, including a club in the USA. He committed suicide in London in 1998 after fleeing the States where he allegedly assaulted a teenage male. Fashanu had earlier claimed he had slept with a Tory party politician, which may not have helped his case.

The reactionary attitude toward homosexuality has been reinforced by the spread of Aids in the last two decades of the twentieth century. While the pandemic was by no means confined to the gay population, fears of the "gay plague" lingered. One of the first gay male athletes to come out actually died with Aids in 1987: Tom Waddell, the Olympic decathlete from the 1968 Mexico Olympics, who was one of the founders of the Gay Games in 1982. He became involved in a legal case with the US Olympic Committee, which refused to let him use the word "Olympics" to describe the gay tournament. Waddell was aged 49 at the time of his death.

Glenn Burke also died with Aids; he was the first Major League Baseball player to declare his homosexuality. After playing in the Dodger's World Series-winning team in 1977, Burke refused to take part in a marriage of convenience to allay rumors of his homosexuality and was traded to Oakland Athletics. He later competed at the Gay Games, winning sprint medals, and, later, turned to basketball. Burke died in 1995.

Greg Louganis's public declaration of his homosexuality came through the publication of his autobiography *Breaking the Surface: A life*, in 1995, which contained details of his HIV+ diagnosis. Louganis revealed how, in the 1988 summer Olympics, he cut his head and spilled blood into the pool when attempting a reverse two-and-half pike. The doctor who treated Louganis's wound did not wear protective gloves. Louganis's disclosure came after an acrimonious split with his former partner Tom Barrett who threatened to reveal details of Louganis's medical condition. Louganis came to a court settlement with Barrett and pre-empted any disclosure with his book.

While these are isolated cases, associations between Aids and gays in sport persist and hinder the efforts of campaigners like Burton. It is unlikely that gay male athletes will volunteer information about their sexuality. Despite this, a body of scholarly evidence suggests that at least 10 percent of men have had some form of homosexual experience and there is no reason to suppose that athletes are exceptions.

*More questions . . .*

- Does the mass media inhibit or encourage honesty among athletes about sexual proclivities?
- Why don't more referees, umpires, and other officials come out?
- Are sponsors right in assuming gay endorsers would not help sales?

*Read on . . .*

- Mary Jo Festle, *Playing Nice: Politics and apologies in women's sport* (Columbia University Press, 1996).
- Pat Griffin, *Strong Women, Deep Closets: Lesbians and homophobia in sport* (Human Kinetics, 1998).
- Tyler Hoffman, "The umpire is out" in *The Advocate*, issue 877, pp. 9–18, 2002
- Billie Jean King and Frank Deford, *Billie Jean* (Viking, 1982).

# control of the body

## how science, sex, and cyborgs affect sports

### BEAUTIFUL IN MEN, UGLY IN WOMEN

There's no such thing as a natural human body. Never has been; the body has changed physiologically over the years: improvements in nutrition, better sanitation, healthier living conditions, and better understandings of its structure and functions have made an impact on the body. These physical changes have cultural counterparts: changes in the popular comprehension of the body. The story of Bernarr Macfadden reminds us that the way we make sense of our and other people's bodies is open to sometimes quite considerable changes.

Macfadden was, among other things, a publisher, an advocate of vigorous exercise, and a campaigner for the relaxation of censorship. In 1893, Macfadden watched a demonstration of strength by Eugen Sandow, in Chicago. Sandow pulled a few strongman stunts and posed in a way not unlike today's body-builders. Sandow (real name, Friedrich Müller) had built an international reputation, posing near-naked for rapt audiences, designing training programs for the British army, and editing several publications on health and exercise. Macfadden was so inspired, he went away and invented an exercise machine consisting of cables and pulleys. He also wrote a manual on how to use "The Macfadden Exerciser," as it was called.

Macfadden toured the United States and Britain, exhibiting himself as evidence of the machine's efficacy. He lectured on the benefits of physical exercise and struck up poses, much as Sandow had done. Soon he became a rival to Sandow, who had made money from a mail order training program. Macfadden's manual changed into a free-standing magazine with articles on training and diet. In 1899, he published a second magazine, *Physical Culture* (retail 5¢). Later, he launched the first women's physique magazine *Women's Physical Development*, which was changed in 1903 to *Beauty and Health*.

One of the premises of Macfadden's philosophy of physical culture was that a oneness with nature is absolutely vital to a healthy life. It followed that a natural act like sex should be practiced as often as possible. He advocated sex in his publications – much to the annoyance of censors who objected particularly to the illustrations that accompanied his articles on sexual activity. According to Macfadden, a healthy sex life was highly conducive to physical fitness. What's more, he publicized this through his magazine.

The magazine was so successful that, in 1919, Macfadden expanded his business interests with another publication, this time a more tabloid-like venture specializing in confessions. Again the magazine was decried, especially by censorious church groups, which insisted that sexuality and the body were private issues and should be kept that way.

Macfadden published copious articles about physical beauty, how to achieve it and how to show it off to your best advantage. A sedentary life was the worst enemy of beauty: good looks came through exercise and plenty of sex. Macfadden was years ahead of his time, of course: the prevailing wisdom was that women were naturally fragile and ill-equipped for the kinds of activities applauded by Macfadden. In fact, Macfadden's training prescriptions were seen as downright dangerous for women.

The popular view of the day was that women were naturally beautiful the way they were: the kinds of physical changes brought on by regular exercise were liable to make women unsightly. "To men and women in the first half of the nineteenth century, any sort of muscular development on women was seen as useless and unattractive," writes Jan Todd in her article "Bernarr Macfadden: Reformer of the feminine form" (1987a: 70). "Strength was beautiful in men and ugly in women."

Todd traces how the ideal female form was in the throes of change. "Ethereal frailty," as she calls it, was on its way out in the 1870s and, by the turn of the century, the hourglass figure had evolved into an "S" shape, with more prominence given to women's busts. The prettiness associated with women during the Victorian era "had given way to height, grandeur and sturdiness." The emerging ideal woman was described as a "Titaness."

Macfadden set out to find his perfect woman in 1904, when he promoted a contest eventually won by Emma Newkirk, of Santa Monica. Run like a beauty pageant, but with quite different criteria, the contest was augmented with other competitions, all featuring women. Foot races, wrestling, and, bizarrely, fasting competitions were held. As expected, in an age when the role of women at sports events was thought properly to be ornamental, Macfadden's project proved controversial.

One of Macfadden's particular dislikes was the Victorian corset, which was both a harmful and constricting article of underwear and a symbol of female captivity, confinement, and downright servitude. Even when playing tennis, women were obliged to wear corsets under their full-length skirts, long-sleeved blouses, and boater hats. And tennis was one of the few sports in which women were allowed to compete in the early years of the century.

Todd points out that while Macfadden was campaigning, unprecedentedly high numbers of American women were going to work: "The number of women who entered the work force increased at a rate faster than the birth rate" (1987: 74). So, conceptions of women were changing. The time had not yet arrived when women could enter a full team at the Olympic Games. But, it was all right for a woman to work a full day in a factory.

Popular understanding of the purposes and limits of a woman's body was in the process of change and, while Macfadden may not appear in anybody's "Who's Who?" of feminist reformers, Todd believes he made a "significant contribution" to the aesthetic shift that encouraged a more energetic, active role for women. By projecting images of strong, fit, and vigorous females, he paved the way for a reconsideration of women. Specifically, he initiated new perspectives on women's bodies. For Macfadden, firm, healthy, and toned bodies were not simply for decorative purposes; they were active, agile, mobile, and could perform as athletically as men's.

We'll never know Macfadden's intentions. Maybe he was a shrewd entrepreneur with an eye for an opportunity; having witnessed Sandow's success, he set about improving on it. Courting controversy as he did served to improve his business position. But, even if his motives were tainted, the effect he had on provoking discussions on the female body is undoubted. Subsequent popularizers of what we might call the cult of the body beautiful borrowed from Macfadden's portfolio. Angelo Siciliano a.k.a. "Charles Atlas" made his fortune through his "dynamic tension" system of bodybuilding. A champion bodybuilder himself, Atlas's claim that "You too can have a body like mine" was featured in mail order advertisements the world over.

In the 1940s, Joe and Ben Weider tried to extend bodybuilding from its exhibition format to a fully fledged competitive sport. This was quite an innovation, as it carried no connotation of strength. Unlike, for example, weightlifting, bodybuilding focused solely on the look of the human body, its symmetry of shape, the sharpness of muscle separation, the tone of the skin, and so on. The brothers' intention was to make bodybuilding the legitimate competitive sport it now is.

Introducing their collection of essays *The Making of the Modern Body: Sexuality and society in the nineteenth century*, Catherine Gallagher and Thomas Laqueur observe of the human body:

> Not only has it been perceived, interpreted, and represented differently in different epochs, but it has also been lived differently, brought into being within widely dissimilar cultures, subjected to various technologies and means of control, and incorporated into different rhythms of production and consumption, pleasure and pain.
>
> (1987: i)

Their point is that there is no single understanding of the human body that holds good for all cultures at all times. Of course, every body is made of flesh, blood, and bones and, nowadays, the odd piece of metal or plastic. But, the significance of the body and the purposes it serves change as our interest in it broadens, or narrows. The way we care for it, nourish it, adorn it, display it, represent important statements about our culture. The space it occupies, the curves it defines, the manner of its regulation, the methods of its restraint; its fertility and sexuality: these and other features make the body a potent instrument for understanding ourselves and our culture.

From today's standpoint, Macfadden's ventures appear to be ludicrously tame. After all, what was he saying? That beauty and fitness go together and that sex can be healthy. His infamous magazines featuring the partially clad female form that incurred the wrath of the censors were as innocuous as a DC comic and probably less exciting. Macfadden, though, was doing something more than peddling mags and exercise machines: he was pushing people to a new awareness of their own and others' bodies. He was urging women in particular to experience their bodies differently.

In many ways, Macfadden anticipated the changes that came about during the growth of what historian Christopher Lasch, in the title of one of his books, called *The Culture of Narcissism* (1979). As the promise of the 1960s radicalism waned and the anti-Vietnam movement gradually wound down, people looked for a therapeutic intervention in their own lives, rather than theirs *and* others. A new movement in the 1970s was driven by a quest for self-understanding or self-perfection; in other words, personal growth. Lasch argues that people became preoccupied with themselves: they admired themselves, pampered themselves, attended to themselves. Like Narcissus of the Greek myth who fell in love with his own reflection, people became emotionally and intellectually fixated with their own images.

The almost obsessive self-centeredness translated into a demand for physical perfection; an avoidance of substances that were obviously harmful; and a fascination for any new product that promised youth. If maintaining the body was once a privilege, it became a binding duty. The preoccupation intensified, giving rise to an industry dedicated to the requirements of keeping in shape and attending to body maintenance.

The term body maintenance itself reveals how we came to regard the body as analogous to a machine, particularly a car that requires regular servicing and repairs to perform efficiently. The analogy works both ways: diagnostic checks are now advised for cars between major services. But, if the term itself is relatively new, the concept behind it is not. "In traditional societies, religious communities such as monasteries demanded ascetic routines with an emphasis upon exercise and dietary control," writes Mike Featherstone in his "The body in consumer culture" (1991: 182). Denying the body more earthly gratifications meant that higher, spiritual purposes could be pursued. The whole Christian tradition emphasized the primacy of the soul over the body, which needs to be repressed. It was, after all, the body not the soul that succumbed to temptation. Perversely, one of the main intentions of body maintenance is to maximize the opportunities to succumb to such temptation. People restrain and care for their bodies in order to feel good about their appearance. In other words, they want to believe they look attractive to others. The often unstated purpose of cultural imperatives to become fit, healthy, and toned is sexual. An athletic body is a sexy one; a dissipated one is definitely not.

We have now entered a stage that we might call the culture *beyond* narcissism. Lasch was writing of a period slightly before the body became such a focal point of people's lives; when we were less absorbed about the status and appearance of our bodies. Now, we have idealized forms to which we are supposed to aspire. Television commercials, magazines, movies, videos, and many other media heave with images of supermodels and hunks, who, three decades ago, would have been regarded as freaks of nature and muscle-bound monstrosities, respectively. Now many people want to mimic them.

Macfadden was hounded for publishing pictures of women and men who would be overdressed by today's magazine standards. Pick up any copy of a respectable publication, like *GQ* or *FHM*, and you'll find about a dozen pictures of women in swimwear or underclothes, the kind of shots that would have embarrassed Macfadden himself.

Today's culture has fostered a self-awareness of our own bodies that has produced its own corollary: we're interested in other people's bodies, not for licentious reasons, but just out of curiosity. This is part of the same mentality that allows us to declare often highly personal details about ourselves in the interests of security, but fires our interest in the lives of others – as the success of confessional tv programs suggests. We do not mind disclosing more of ourselves just as long as we can inspect more of everybody else. Their bodies included.

The hundred years or so after Macfadden first saw Eugen Sandow's act saw changes of such enormity in the way people related to and experienced their own and others' bodies that it is laughable to imagine how his projects caused offense. The fact that they did and that Macfadden was forced to operate like an early Larry Flynt reminds us of an important point: that when people thought and looked about bodies in Macfadden's day, they were thinking and looking very differently than we do today. So differently in fact that we might as well say they were thinking and looking about two different things.

How about the bodies of female sports performers? After Florence Griffith Joyner in the 1980s and Gabrielle Reece in the 1990s, we have a generation of women athletes who are often indistinguishable from fashion models or rock stars. But, never mind their looks: they perform to standards and have capacities that are not far behind – and are, in some cases, ahead – of men's. Rarely, if ever, do we doubt their durability, resilience, or downright toughness. We're probably not sure why we ever wondered at these features. There are reasons.

## WHEN THERE WAS ONLY ONE SEX

Macfadden flew in the face of popular wisdom when he maintained that women not only could, but *should* do vigorous physical exercise. This was in stark contrast to what most felt was appropriate to women, who were simply not naturally suited to such endeavors. It was a matter of scientific fact established by an intellectual tradition in which women's bodies were defined by scientists as objects of sexuality and reproduction.

Nelly Oudshoorn's extraordinary book *Beyond the Natural Body: An archeology of sex hormones* (1994) analyzes how this conception of the female body dominated medical discourse through the eighteenth and nineteenth centuries. In this period, intellectual curiosity centered on the dissimilarities between men and women: in what respects were they different? This may strike us as perfectly obvious; the fact that it does illustrates again just how dramatically understanding of the human body can change. Oudshoorn's work underlines that new knowledge does not just make the body more transparent: it actually alters its nature – nature being the order we impose on our physical environment to help us make sense of it.

Oudshoorn acknowledges that her account was influenced by the work of two scholars, Thomas Laqueur and Londa Schiebinger. Laqueur's studies of medical texts indicate that the concept of a sharp division between male and female is a product of the past 300 years and, for 2,000 years before that, bodies were not visualized in terms of differences. Think about this: the division of the world into men and women based on sex is a relatively new convention. Previously, there were just people, some of whom could have children, others of whom could not. Hormones had not been discovered, sexual difference was not a concept, so it was impossible to conceive of a distinct bifurcation of types based on sexual characteristics. Even physical differences we now regard as obvious were not so obvious without a conceptual understanding of sexual differences. In some periods, a woman's clitoris was thought to be a minuscule protuberance, an underdeveloped version of the equivalent structure in men – the penis.

For most of human history, the stress was on similarities, the female body being just a "gradation," or nuance of one basic male type. "Medical theory taught that there was but one sex," writes Jeffrey Weeks in his book *Sexuality*, "with the female body simply an inverted version of the male" (2003: 43). Needless to say, this vision complemented and bolstered a male-centered world view in which, as Laqueur puts it in his *Making Sex: Body and gender from the Greeks to Freud*, "man is the measure of all things, and women does not exist as an ontologically distinct category" (1990: 62).

The tradition of bodily similarities came under attack, particularly from anatomists who argued that sex was not restricted only to reproductive organs, but affected every part of the body. Anatomists' interest in this was fired by the idea that even the skeleton had sexual characteristics. Schiebinger's medical history *The Mind Has No Sex: Women in the origins of modern science* (1989) shows that anatomists in the nineteenth century searched for the sources of women's difference and apparent inferiority. Depictions of the female skull were used to "prove" that women were naturally inferior to men in intellectual capacities. In the process, the concept of sexual differences was integrated into the discourse; so that, by the end of the nineteenth century, female and male bodies were understood in terms of opposites, each having different organs, functions, and even feelings.

Oudshoorn's work picks up the story by identifying how the female body became conceptualized in terms of its unique sexual essence in the 1920s and 1930s. In these decades, sex endocrinology created a completely new understanding of sexual differences based on hormones. Eventually, hormonal differences became accepted natural facts. Knowledge, on this account, was not discovered but produced: research on hormones created a different model of the sexes, which was adopted universally and served to reshape our most fundamental conceptions of human nature. Women were different to men in most profound, categorical, and immovable way.

So, women were not only discouraged from participating in sports and exercise, but were warned against it. "Medical advice concerning exercise and physical activity came to reflect and perpetuate understandings about women's 'abiding sense of physical weakness' and the unchangeable nature of her physical inferiority," writes Patricia Vertinsky in her essay "Exercise, physical capability, and the eternally wounded woman in late nineteenth century North America" (1987: 8). In this and her later book *The Eternally Wounded Woman: Women, doctors and exercise in the late nineteenth century* (1990) Vertinsky explores how physicians' interpretation of biological theories of menstruation led them to discourage taxing physical exertion.

Menstruation – the eternal wound – was seen as a form of invalidity and its beginning meant that young women would need to be careful in conserving energy. Growing up had quite different meanings for young males and females, as Vertinsky observes: "Puberty for boys marked the onset of strength and enhanced vigor; for girls it marked the onset of the prolonged and periodic weaknesses of womanhood" (1987: 17). Remember, this was the popular view at a time (1880s) when the full ramifications of sexuality were the subject of great debate.

Disabled by menstruation, women were less-than-perfect when compared to men. Their physical inferiority prohibited them from competing against each other, let alone men. As in so many other instances of exclusion, the justification was based on patronage: it was for women's own sake. If they tried to emulate their physically superior male counterparts, they would be risking damaging themselves.

Scientific studies of how menstruation defined and delimited a woman's capacity for physical activity shaped popular thought, their credibility enhanced by their apparent symmetry with folk beliefs and taboos concerning impurity and contamination. Vertinsky notes that scientific and medical theories were "strongly colored by these traditional beliefs" (1987: 11).

Women were thought to be so handicapped during monthly periods that they were prone to accidents and hysteria, making sport and exercise unsuitable areas of activity. Another scientific view was that women possessed a finite amount of energy and, unlike men, were "taxed" biologically with special energy demands necessitated by menstruation and reproduction. Women could never aspire to the kind of intellectual and social development pursued by men because they were simply not built for that purpose: they were naturally mothers.

There were some schools of thought that held that the enfeebling effects of menstruation could be offset by cold baths, deep breathing, and mild exercising, such as beanbag-throwing, hoops, or golf. Especially appropriate, according to Alice Tweedy, writing in *Popular Science Monthly* in 1892, were "homely gymnastics," i.e. housework. Other physicians prescribed rest and energy conservation. While these may sound like (if the reader will pardon the phrase) old wives' tales, they had the status of scientific fact in the period when organized sports were coming into being. Sports were intended for men only.

Vertinsky quotes a passage from influential physician Henry Maudsley who, in 1874, wrote that "women are marked out by Nature for very different offices in life from those of men . . . special functions renders it improbable she will succeed, and unwise for her to persevere in running over the same course at the same pace with him . . . women cannot rebel successfully against the tyranny of their organization" (1987: 25).

The same natural tyranny that dictated women's exclusion from sports and exercise restricted women's activities in all other areas of social life.

"Scientific definitions of human 'nature' were thus used to justify the channeling of men and women . . . into vastly different social roles," writes Schiebinger in her article "Skeletons in the closet: The first illustrations of the female skeleton in eighteenth-century anatomy" (1987: 72). "It was thought 'natural' that men, by virtue of their 'natural reason,' should dominate public spheres of government and commerce, science and scholarship, while women, as creatures of feeling, fulfilled their natural destiny as mother, conservators of custom in the confined sphere of the home."

One can imagine why Macfadden's startling ideas caused such a stir. In proposing a more active capability for women, he was unwittingly undermining a whole set of roles that had been reserved for women and which supported an entire configuration of social institutions. Even the most tremulous suggestions about activities for women were likely to incense those whose interests were best served by passive women.

For example, toward the end of the nineteenth century, cycling was a popular pastime in North America and Europe. Both men and women cycled, though to mixed reactions from the medical community. While the advantages to men's health were acknowledged, there was suspicion about the uses of cycling to women. Peter Kühnst quotes a physician, who, in 1897, pointed out that cycling offered women the "opportunity for frequent and clandestine masturbation" (2004: 37). Medical experts doubted whether women's bodies were up to the rigors of cycling. Many doctors believed that the pedaling motion when operating a sewing machine gave women sufficient exercise, according to Helen Lenskyj (1986: 30). One wonders what those doctors would have thought about the six-day, 274-mile Hewlett-Packard International Women's Challenge pro biking race, or the women's Tour de France (and particularly about Canada's Linda Jackson, who competed regularly in and won some of these events when approaching her fortieth birthday).

As we have seen, up till relatively recently, women's bodies were seen as ill-equipped to cope with the physical and mental demands of sports. An entire discourse devoted to the subject of the effect of exercise and competition on the body and minds of women threw up all manner of reasons why women should not enter sports. The same discourse served to justify women's subservient position in society generally.

This did not stop women who wanted to get involved in sports and in her *Out of Bounds: Women, sport and sexuality* (1986), Lenskyj provides examples of competitors in several sports and women's organizations that would cater for them. She also points out that sportswomen were generally seen as odd. Labeled as tomboys or hoydens, they were thought to lack "femininity" and even represent a moral degeneracy that was thought to be creeping into society. Macfadden, incidentally, had pointed out that almost all beautiful women had been tomboys in their youth. "Although some doctors advocated exercise therapy in the early 1900s, a time when rest, not exercise, was the accepted medical treatment for virtually all diseases and injuries, they rarely made the connection between exercise therapy and women's full sporting participation," writes Lenskyj (1986: 30).

Despite the fears, women were cautiously admitted to the more taxing track events of the Olympics, though the sight of exhausted females fighting for their breath as they crossed the line of the 800 meters in 1928 was so repugnant to Olympic organizers that they removed the event from women's schedules. Not until 1960 was the distance reinstated for women.

Yet, women continued to steal their way into competition, giving rise to a different scare. Contemporary biologists Lynda Birke and Gail Vines use a cautionary quotation from a 1939 book on women and sport: "Too much activity in sports of a masculine character causes the female body to become more like that of a man" (1987: 340). *Virilism* is the term that describes the development of secondary male sexual characteristics in women; and there is evidence that continued use of synthesized testosterone-based products is responsible for facial hair, deep voice, broad shoulders, muscle mass, and other typically male features. In the 1930s, this evidence was not available. The assumption was that exercise and competition in themselves would cause female genital organs to decay and so pervert woman's true nature.

Not only was a woman's body regarded as too weak and liable to serious hormonal dysfunction if she went into sports, "but the competitive mentality was antithetical to her true nature," reported the respected *Scientific American* journal as late as 1936, adding that women had an "innate tendency to shun competition." By this time, women were already showing competence in a variety of Olympic sports, including track and field, swimming, and many team sports. Yet, fears about the long-term effects persisted and physical prohibitions were reinforced by social ones.

---

### Virilism

This refered to the theory that exercise affected a woman's endocrinal system, possibly leading to virilism – the development of secondary male characteristics. The idea was based on the fact that testosterone, the hormone responsible for facial hair, deep voice, broad shoulders, muscle mass, and other typically male features and which is produced primarily in testes, is found in both sexes, though significantly less in females' adrenal glands. Prolonged exercise, it was speculated, induced an imbalance in women's hormones, causing an overproduction of testosterone and a resultant "de-feminization."

---

Lenskyj's study reveals how sneering comments about tomboys added to alarm over the masculinizing effects of sport and grew into fully fledged condemnations of sporting females' alleged sexual proclivities. Women aiming to succeed in sports were freighted with scientific and popular beliefs and images about the rightful place of women. Any achievement of note was a subversion of established wisdom. Lenskyj's thesis is that, in all other social contexts, women's femininity served to validate male identity and male power at both individual and social levels. A woman who defied scientific orthodoxy and excelled in areas defined by and for men, was threat.

Women who managed to negotiate a successful passage into sports, or any other traditionally male domain, for that matter, were snagged in a paradox. Lenskyj argues that male heterosexual standards were applied to sports and women who succeeded were immediately suspected of being lesbians. If they were not lesbians before they went into sports, they would be before long. Their achievements were undermined by the presumption that they were not natural women at all; or, as Lenskyj puts it, by "the equating of any sign of athletic or intellectual competence with masculinity, and by extension, with lesbianism" (1986: 74).

Those who failed escaped allegations, especially if they had conventionally good looks (as defined by heterosexual males, of course). "Thus, the unathletic or unintelligent woman suffered no handicap in men's estimation as long as she was attractive. Although beauty redeemed a lack of intellectual ability, the reverse was not true," writes Lenskyj. "Moreover, it seemed that athletic ability did not redeem any feminine inadequacies. Beating a man at golf was hardly conducive to a harmonious relationship" (1986: 74–5).

No culture that promotes masculinity could surrender one of its bastions of masculine pride to women. But, preaching conformity to male standards requires a transgressive influence as an example of otherness. It appeared that women athletes might fill that position; their transgressions being punished with the stigma of homosexuality, or the stain of virilism. All this would be grossly offensive today; but, as mid-century approached, it was nothing of the sort. In fact, it was common sense and rested on a scientific discourse that had been in progress for a couple of centuries.

The thought of female sports performers functioning within these kinds of restrictions was not a promising one. Yet, women showed that their talents were more supple than they may have appeared. Struggling through the fears and prejudices, women showed that their bodies were sturdier than they appeared and their minds as competitive as any man's. Besmirching sportswomen remained commonplace through the 1940s and 1950s. At the 1952 summer Olympics, the achievements of brawny Soviet field athletes and tenaciously competitive Japanese volleyball players were regarded with skepticism: were they women at all? Appeals for sex tests followed.

Actually, the calls for some standardized sex-testing had been growing since 1946 when three female medal winners at the European Athletic championships declared themselves to be men. They had "male-like genitals" and facial hair as well as chromosomal indicators of maleness. In 1952, two French female medalists were later exposed as males. The cries for testing reached full pitch in 1955 when it was revealed that the German winner of the women's high jump at the 1936 Berlin Olympics was in fact a man who had been pressured into competing for the glory of the Third Reich.

Other individual competitors, like Stella Walsh, the Polish-American track and field athlete, were the subject of widespread speculation in the 1930s and 1940s. It was not until her death in 1981 that it was discovered that she had male-like testicles. The innuendo about Walsh was mild compared to that about Irina and Tamara Press, of the former Soviet Union. Irina won the 100-meters gold and Tamara triumphed in the shot and discuss. They both disappeared suddenly from active competition soon after the introduction of mandatory sex testing in 1966.

---

### Barr bodies sex test

This was designed to establish unambiguously whether contestants were male or female. The test required that a sample of cells be scraped from the inside of a competitor's cheek, or hair follicle, and subjected to a laboratory examination to determine whether a minimum number contain what are called "Barr bodies" (collections of chromatins). Although the exact number of these chromatins varies from woman to woman and may change over time for any given woman, usually about 20 out of 100 cells contain these characteristics. If the count dropped below a minimum percentage, the athlete would be disqualified from competition. The test was dropped before the 2000 Sydney games, partly because not all women have standard female chromosomes.

---

Prior to this, certificates from the country of origin were sufficient proof. But visual examinations from gynecologists replaced this at the European Athletic championships in Budapest. Chromosomal testing was introduced in 1967, when Polish sprinter Eva Klobkowska was disqualified from competition after failing such a test. To her apparent surprise, she was found to have internal testicles (a condition that is not as uncommon as it sounds).

At the time, knowledge of the extensive performance-enhancing programs that were being pursued in Soviet bloc countries, especially the Soviet Union and

East Germany, was obscure. The connection between taking anabolic steroids and the acquisition of male features was not widely known. In retrospect, it is probable that many of the female athletes who were suspected of being men had been inducted into steroid use, probably at an early age.

Lenskyj's comment that "it has served male interests to stress biological differences, and to ignore the more numerous and obvious biological similarities between the sexes" (1986: 141) returns us to where we were before the emergent scientific discourse of the eighteenth century started kicking in. The implication of Lenskyj's statement is that women's experience in sport would have been radically different if they had not been the subjects of an intense yet tortuous debate on the precise nature of the woman's body.

Historically, sports, particularly those that involve strenuous competition, have certified masculinity: by providing the kind of unmediated athletic challenge rarely encountered in working days, sports made possible a strong and assertive proclamation of men's strength, valor, and, above all, physical superiority over women. Industrial society brought with it, among other things, a less physical life, one in which manual labor, while still essential in many spheres of work, was less dangerous and taxing than in pre-industrial times.

The proliferation of organized sports toward the end of the nineteenth century is due in large part to the desire for an expression of canalized aggression to counteract what was becoming an increasingly sedentary lifestyle. Sports had the added benefit of providing a sense of traditional masculinity, which was in the process of erosion as the seas of industrial and urban change swept against it. The developing scientific discourse over the female body elevated two themes that fitted perfectly the masculine purposes of sports. Lenskyj summarizes them as: "Women's unique anatomy and physiology and their special moral obligations" (1986: 18). Both derived from nature and were immutable; both effectively disqualified women from sport. As we have seen, the perils of competing in sports lay not in the effects of exercise on women's bodies, but in the reaction of society to their achievements. Jennifer Hargreaves summarizes the wider relevance of this when she writes: "The struggle over the physical body was important for women because control over its use was the issue central to their subordination: the repression of women's bodies symbolized powerfully their repression in society" (1994: 85).

## MORE SELF-CREATION THAN IMPOSITION

In Chapter 3, I examined the body as a collection of about 60 billion cells, organized into substances like muscle and tissue, flesh and bone. In this chapter, I am presenting an alternative way of approaching the same thing: not as a physical entity, but as a subject of a discourse, the center of scientific debate and public discussion. Women's bodies in particular have fascinated scientists and philosophers for the past 300 years: the search for the "true nature" of women led to the female body becoming something of a terrain on which competing versions contested their claims.

Overwhelmingly, favor swung toward a conception of the female body that was capable of certain types of function but either incapable or unsuited to others, usually those that were regarded as male undertakings. These included not only sports, but, to repeat Schiebinger, the "public spheres of government and commerce, science and scholarship." The symmetry was consummate.

Think for a moment about the ways in which men have sought to restrain women. The ancient Chinese practice of footbinding was ostensibly to prevent women developing large and therefore (in Chinese males' eyes) ugly feet: small feet were the epitome of beauty in Chinese culture. It also effectively confined them to the boudoir away from the gaze of men other than husbands. As feet were generally first bound when the woman was 7 years old, she would be hobbled. The custom was abolished by imperial decree in 1902; it had lasted for more than a thousand years.

As cultures define physically appropriate shapes for women, so women have been obliged to conform. Witness the neck brace used by Ndebe women, or the plates that are wedged between the lower lips and the mandible of Ubangis in equatorial Africa. Neither practice has the practical utility of footbinding, which restricted women's physical mobility so that it was virtually impossible to escape servitude. In these cases, women voluntarily mutilate their bodies for the pleasure of men.

Clitoridectomy is widely practiced in many parts of the Middle East and in North and sub-Sahara Africa. About 74 million women have currently undergone this procedure, which involves excising part or all of the clitoris. The catalog of infections, complications, and long-term effects of this mutilation is immense. It reminds us of how far men will go to reaffirm the subjugation of women through the control not only of their reproductive functions, but of their ability to experience sexual pleasure (in one form of clitoridectomy, the clitoris is excised, as is the labia minor, before the sides of the vulva are sewn together with catgut, to be ritually opened with a dagger on the eve of the woman's wedding). The process is defended as an integral part of some sections of Islamic faith, but, as Linda Lindsey writes in her *Gender Roles: A sociological perspective*, "Regardless of how it is justified, it is a grim reminder of the subjugation of women" (1990: 104).

What we must ask ourselves is: are these kinds of gory activities so different from the things women do to themselves even today? Victorian women and their daughters self-destructively squeezed themselves into whalebone-lined corsets that were so tight that they stopped blood circulation and distorted the spine. Now, women have swapped this contraption for liposuction (vacuuming

## Pregnancy and motherhood

While scientists once cautioned that exercise might damage women's reproductive functions, the potential benefits of the hormones produced in early pregnancy were realized in the 1950s. During the first three months of pregancy, the mother's body generates a natural surplus of red corpuscles rich in hemoglobin. These assist cardiac and lung performance and improve muscle capacity by up to 30 percent. A pregnant woman also secretes increased amounts of progesterone to make muscles suppler and joints more flexible. Oxygen consumption, a measure of fitness also known as aerobic capacity, can rise by as much 30 percent during pregnancy. It has also been argued that childbirth can permanently raise pain barriers.

Olga Karasseva (now Kovalenko), a gymnastics gold medal winner at the 1968 summer Olympics, later revealed that she had become pregnant and had an abortion shortly before the games to prepare her body. She also claimed that, during the 1970s, females as young as 14 were ordered to have sex with their men friends or coaches in an effort to become pregnant (reported in the British *Sunday Times*, S1: 23, November 27, 1994). Suspicions that female athletes from the former Soviet Union planned abortions to coincide with competitions first surfaced in 1956 at the Melbourne summer Olympics, then eight years later at Tokyo. One estimate at the time suggested that as many as 10 out of 26 medal winners might have manipulated their pregnancies, though no conclusive proof ever came to light.

Yet, the fact that not all mothers return as better athletes weakens the physiological argument and suggests there may be psychological changes that follow childbirth. Having children changes athletes' perspectives, in some cases precipitating a more relaxed attitude and less pre-competition anxiety. For some, this might improve performance, though for others it could be counter-productive, leading to a drop in motivation and a corresponding slackening-off in training. Sports history is full of females who have improved their performances after becoming mothers. Fanny Blankers-Koen, whom we covered in Chapter 7, is perhaps the most celebrated, but there are others, including: **Shirley Strickland De La Hunty** (Australia), won seven medals in three successive Olympics between 1948 and 1956, including three golds. At 31 and the mother of a 2-year-old, she won two golds at the 1956 Melbourne games.

**Wilma Rudolph** (USA), was a bronze medal winner in the 4 × 100-meter relay at the 1956 Olympics when she was 16. She had a daughter then triumphed at the 1960 Olympics, winning three golds.

**Irena Szewinska** (Poland) competed at five Olympics, 1964–80. Her best form came after she gave birth to a son in 1970. Four years later, she broke the world 400 meters record, then broke it again two years later at the Montreal Olympics where she won gold.

**Ingrid Kristiansen** (Norway) was a formidable distance runner before becoming a mother and virtually invincible after, setting world records for 5,000 and 10,000 meters and the marathon, all within two years of giving birth.

**Valerie Brisco-Hooks** (USA) won 200 and 400 meters gold medals at the LA Olympics of 1984, two years after giving birth to her son.

**Evelyn Ashford** (USA) won two golds at the 1984 Olympics, then had a daughter and returned to the track to finish second in the 100 meters at the 1988 Olympics. She also won golds in the 4 × 100 meter relay at the same and the subsequent Olympic Games.

**Liz McColgan** (Scotland) gave birth to a daughter in 1990, having won a silver at the Seoul Olympics two years before. Four months after giving birth she came third in the 1991 world cross-country championships and, later that year, won the 10,000 meters at the IAAF world championships in Tokyo.

**Svetlana Masterkova** (Russia) had a daughter in 1994, then won both the 800 and 1,500 meters at the 1996 Olympics in Atlanta.

**Derartu Tulu** (Ethiopia) won Olympic gold for 10,000 meters in 1992, came fourth over the distance at the 1996 Olympics, then took a three-year break, during which time she had a daughter. At the 2000 Olympics, she recorded a personal best time in winning gold in the 10,000 meters.

*With thanks to Quentin Webb, of Reuters.*

fatty tissue from the epidermis), rhinoplasty (slicing open the nose and filing down gristle), and all sorts of cosmetic surgery designed to bring women's bodies into alignment with men's expectations (breast implants being a supreme example; the American Federal Food and Drugs Administration severely restricted these after the damaging effects of them became known, though they are still available).

Then we still have to reckon with the less invasive, but no less disabling, attempts women make to meet with men's approval. By defining ideal shapes in ways that please them, men actually force women into near-starvation diets or, worse still, chronic eating disorders like anorexia nervosa and bulimia. The burgeoning popularity of aerobic classes and their progeny, step classes, boxercise, etc., are related to changes in how men define the perfect shape. The 1950s Monroe model looks podgy by comparison with the lean supermodels of today. Women remain willing to connive with men: they are still prepared to risk their health to chase what Naomi Wolf calls *The Beauty Myth*. But, the myth is "not about women at all," argues Wolf. "It is about men's institutions and institutional power" (1991: 10, 13).

---

## Anorexia nervosa and bulimia

Research has shown that anorexia nervosa and bulimia are more prevalent in certain sports than in the general population. Sports that emphasize the importance of physical appearance, such as gymnastics, ice dancing, and synchronized swimming, harbor more eating disorders and competitors have been encouraged by coaches and trainers to restrict food intake, use purgatives, or induce vomiting in an effort to maintain nymph-like bodies.

While it may contradict popular expectations of healthy young people with, one assumes, a keener sense of their own bodies than most, several studies in Europe and the USA have indicated that they are more rather than less prone to eating disorders. Since the early 1980s, researchers have reported an increase in clinically diagnosed eating disorders and eating disorder tendencies (like faddish dieting, diuretics abuse, and overdosing on diet pills). The rates have varied between 1 and 4 percent in the general population, with an increase in anorexia occurring primarily in white females between the ages of 15 and 24 years. In 1983, Puglise *et al.* coined the term *anorexia athletica* to indicate the particular eating disorder that affects competitive sports performers. Estimates of the prevalence of eating disorders in the female sporting population vary between 4 and 22 percent, with gymnasts, long-distance runners, and synchronized swimmers being most affected.

Monitoring weight is normal in most sports: in some, leanness is considered of paramount importance. Sports that are subject to judge's evaluation, like gymnastics, diving, and figure skating, encourage participants to take care of all aspects of their appearance. About 35 percent of competitors have eating disorders and half practice what researchers term "pathogenic weight control." In some sports, looking young and slender is considered such an advantage that competitors actively try to stave off the onset of menstruation and the development of secondary sexual characteristics; or to counterbalance the weight gain that typically accompanies puberty. Menstrual dysfunctions, such as amenorrhea and oligomenorrhea, frequently result from anorexia.

In endurance events, excess weight is generally believed to impair performance. Athletes reduce body fat to increase strength, speed, and endurance, though they risk bone mineral deficiencies, dehydration and a decrease in maximum oxygen uptake ($VO_2$max). The Norwegian biologist Jorunn Sundgot-Borgen suggests that the training load typically carried by endurance athletes may induce a calorific deprivation which, in turn, elicits "certain biological and social reinforcement leading to the development of eating disorders" (1994a). But, the prevalence of bulimia is more difficult to explain.

Sundgot-Borgen also argues that competitors most at risk tend to be characterized by "high self-expectation, perfectionism, persistence and independence." In other words, the qualities that enable them to achieve in sports make them vulnerable to eating disorders. The same researcher reports (1994b) that a change of coach can trigger an eating disorder, as can an injury that prevents the athlete training at usual levels. A further finding of Sundgot-Borgen and several other scholars is that coaches actually recommend the use of pathogenic control methods, including vomiting, laxatives, and diuretics.

Coaches and trainers in weight-sensitive sports need to keep an eye on their charges' eating habits in preparation for competitions. For example, lightweight rowers and jockeys must meet weight restrictions before competition. In their article "Weight concerns, weight control techniques, and eating disorders among adolescent competitive swimmers" (1992), Diane Taub and Rose Benson write that: "Excess body fat and body weight in both males and females are widely considered by coaches, parents and participants to hinder performance." See also: Chapman (1997), Petrie (1996), and Ryan (1998).

In her essay "Femininity as discourse," Dorothy E. Smith reminds us that: "We must not begin by conceiving of women as manipulated by mass media or subject passively to male power . . . when we speak of 'femininity'" (1988: 39). Femininity, she argues, is more a matter of self-creation, not just imposition. This allows for a conception of femininity, or, perhaps, more accurately femininities, that is not fixed but always in the process of redefinition. No one is suggesting that there is an equally weighted balance of power with men and women trading ideas on how the body should look. Men have had their own way in most areas of society and this is no exception. But, where the female body is concerned, they have had either to resort to coercion (footbinding, clitoridectomies) or secure the complicity of women themselves.

As we have seen, transgressive bodies have been liable to penalties, whether through the application of stigma, or disqualification. Rewards went to the soft and weak. The unwritten rules or codes of the discourse dictated that women whose bodies and exploits did not conform were not "real" women at all. The 1980s witnessed the emergence of a number of women athletes who defied the coded expectations and, in the process, began to rewrite a different code.

## CROSSING NATURAL BOUNDARIES

Almost as newsworthy as Ben Johnson's expulsion from the 1988 Olympics, was the spectacular performance of US sprinter Florence Griffith Joyner. "Flo-Jo," as the media dubbed her, had risen from relative obscurity of a so-so track athlete in a couple of years; her personal best times for the short sprints tumbled and her physical appearance altered visibly. Not only was she bigger and more conspicuously muscular, but her outfits were more suited to a catwalk than a running track.

Had she not won a bagful of medals, detractors would no doubt have dismissed her, perhaps in the way they did Mary Pierce, the 1990s tennis player: as a bellwether of fashion who looked aesthetically pleasing, but could not compete consistently at the highest level. Or Anna Kournikova, whose tennis never matched her achievements in music videos and fashion shoots. If that had been the case, there would have been no violation of the popular image of female athletes: the ones that look like women have limited athletic ability.

Griffith Joyner's egregious track presence challenged the media: would they concentrate on her record-breaking speed, or her flamboyant appearance? In the event, they escaped the double bind by integrating sexuality and athleticism. Anne Balsamo calls the media's treatment of Flo-Jo "the process of sexualization at work" (1996: 44). Hard-bitten newspaper hacks were forcibly turned into fashion correspondents as they prefaced reports of her track triumphs with detailed fashion itineraries, right down to the color of her nail varnish.

Of course, sports history is full of unconquerable females. Yet none had resisted type as much as Flo-Jo. Far from being a delicate-looking creature, she was chunky, strong, and radiated power; *and* she still managed to conform to heterosexual standards of female attractiveness. It was as if she was stamping out the message that women can be big, good-looking, well dressed, and still produce in the competitive arena.

In her *Coming on Strong: Gender and sexuality in twentieth-century women's sport*, Susan Cahn argues that: "A reservoir of racist beliefs about black women as deficient in femininity buttressed the masculine connotation of track and field" (1994: 138). African American achievers not only in track and field but other sports, were regarded as "mannish" and, as Cahn calls them, "liminal figures."

There was some ambivalence about Griffith Joyner even before the 1988 games. Linford Christie, the men's 100-meter winner at the 1992 Olympics, reacted to her win in the US trials in which she took a massive 0.27 seconds off the existing world record: "No woman can run 10.49 legit," he pronounced. "I know what it feels like to run 10.49 and its hard" (quoted in the British *Sunday Mirror Magazine*, September 4, 1988). She further astonished the world by breaking the 200 meters world record twice at the games. Slurs faded when she retired with a lucrative portfolio of modeling contracts. Despite the gossip, she never failed a drugs test. Her world records remained intact, Marion Jones's 10.71 in 1998 being the closest time.

She retired with her "real woman" status preserved, having changed some of the rules of the discourse irredeemably. Gone was the quality of otherness usually afforded big, strong women. Griffith Joyner herself may have elicited confusion by mixing the athletic with the erotic, but subsequent women in track and many other areas of sport normalized the image of the powerful female body. Almost immediately after her death in 1998, journalists turned rumors into claims: Griffith Joyner's body and her track performances were almost certainly enhanced by drugs, many writers charged, presumably in the safe knowledge that they could not libel a dead person.

Four years before Flo-Jo's triumph, the film *Pumping Iron II: The women* (1984) was released. Directed by George Butler, who had co-directed the Schwarzenegger vehicle *Pumping Iron* (1976), the docudrama focused on the lead-up to the 1983 Caesar's Cup bodybuilding competition in Las Vegas. The film introduced the world to the astounding Bev Francis, an Australian woman whose body pullulated with "manly" characteristics. Tall, flat-chested, and square-shouldered, Francis was so vasculated that snakes seemed to be crawling beneath her skin.

Female bodybuilding had been around for years before. As a sport, female bodybuilding began in 1979, a product largely of Doris Barrilleaux who was formerly a physique photography model. Barrilleaux started the Superior Physique Association, which set down competition rules for female body-building contests. In 1980 she was asked to head a national American Federation of Women Bodybuilders. Butler's movie not only took the sport to a global audience, but it dramatized one of the questions that had tormented the sport since about 1980. The Francis model was clearly transgressive: she had a woman's body that for intents and purposes looked like a man's, not just any man's, but one of a latter-day Hercules.

In technical terms, Francis was an obvious winner: her body fulfilled all the criteria of muscle development, separation, symmetry, etc. She had also made it her avowed intention to take women's bodybuilding to its next level. The problem was: she just did not look like a woman. Neither were her nearest rivals feminine in the traditional sense; but Carla Dunlap – an African American who was the ultimate winner – and Rachel McLish were recognizably women.

In terms of strict bodybuilding criteria as applied to men's competitions, neither Dunlap nor McLish came even close to the extraordinary, imposing Francis. But, the debate in women's bodybuilding was whether to reward someone who, while superior in terms of musculature and skin tone, would be seen widely as a steroid-pumped malformation or a raging dyke, or both.

In all probability, most female bodybuilders were seen in the same way. To date, they are the mightiest transgressors of the traditional feminine ideal. The fragility, vulnerability, and passivity of the eternally wounded woman are effaced. Instead, female bodybuilders present powerful signifiers of strength, resilience, and activity. Linda Hamilton famously prepared for her role in the movie *Terminator 2* (1992) with a specially designed training program that left her with a hard, yet lean physique, complete with the now *de rigueur* corrugated abdominals. Looking at the DVD now, Hamilton seems very ordinary; yet, in the early 1990s, her look was something of a breakthrough – an example of how a woman's body can be masculinized while still looking unmistakably female. Bodybuilders did not manage to do this.

When they first came to public attention, women bodybuilders were derided as freaks by men, who found them repulsive. Anne Bolin suggests why when she writes that bodybuilding "exaggerates Western notions of gender difference – muscles denoting masculinity and signifying 'biological' disparity between the genders" (1996: 126).

Women bodybuilders were encroaching on the domain historically defined as male. Men are supposed to be the ones with the muscles. Putting their male colleagues to shame did them no favors: the typical male response was to reject them as "unnatural." And, in a sense, they were: after all, natural, as coded by a discourse that had been in operation for the previous three centuries, meant weak.

It would be tempting to regard the women who paraded their striated bodies in the 1980s as *ur*-feminists. For instance, in their paper "Pumping irony," Alan Mansfield and Barbara McGinn write: "Because muscularity has been coded as a fundamentally masculine attribute, its adoption by women has offered a threat and a challenge to notions of both the feminine AND the masculine" (1993: 65).

As head of a research project based in Tampa, Florida, and Birmingham, England, I, with my co-researcher Amy Shepper, interviewed competitive female bodybuilders. The pattern that emerged from the case studies was that most had taken up the sport after a personal trauma, such as the breakup of a relationship, a bereavement, or a serious accident. Changes in the body wrought by intense training and strict dieting occasioned a change in self-assurance. Their confidence up after competing, they immersed themselves more deeply into what might allowably be called a bodybuilding subculture. Here the reactions of fellow bodybuilders were important and the often hostile responses of outsiders were disregarded. Standing on line at a supermarket checkout, one woman heard the sarcastic question of a male behind her: "Is that a *woman*?" he asked his friend rhetorically. She turned, looked at him, and asked no one in particular: "Is that an *asshole*?"

But, while their bodies may have been transgressively masculine, their behavior when not training was not. Away from the gym, most slid comfortably into traditional roles as carers and houseworkers. The majority were involved in heterosexual partnerships and cooked, laundered, cleaned, and performed the whole panoply of duties associated with the natural woman. Some of those who were not involved in heterosexual relationships functioned in traditional ways for their brothers. Gaining control over one's body, it seems, does not imply gaining control of one's life. This tells us something about the pervasiveness of male hegemony: a woman can release herself in one very important sphere, while at the same time retaining attachments, identifications, and dependencies in another.

Balsamo believes there are other ways in which female bodybuilders are domesticated. In her *Technologies of the Gendered Body: Reading cyborg women*, Balsamo reasons that, while their bodies transgress gender boundaries, they are not reconstructed according to an opposite gender identity. "They reveal, instead, how culture processes transgressive bodies in such a way as to keep each body in its place," she writes, suggesting that, for white women, their bodies are subjected to an idealized "strong" male body. "For black women, it is the white female body" (1996: 55).

Women who tread on the hallowed male turf of bodybuilding do not have their bodies "recoded according to an oppositional or empowered set of gendered connotations," Balsamo writes. In other words, they are seen less for what they are and more for what they are not. So, any threat they might appear to pose has been rehabilitated and the gender hierarchy remains intact.

Studies of female bodybuilding following Balsamo grappled with the contradiction of what B. Christine Shea called "resistance and compliance." For Shea, bodybuilding is both empowering and disempowering in three distinct ways. First, although women used bodybuilding as a "site of resistance to traditional gender norms . . . by allowing women to build muscle and blur the lines between masculinity and femininity . . . society has normalized the muscular woman in such a manner as to render her 'non-threatening' and even 'sexy'" (2001: 46). Second, women experience boosts to their self-esteem when they first begin bodybuilding, but they can get depressed when their bodies don't live up to their own, perhaps unreasonably high, expectations and further depressed when they suspect they are losing their sex appeal. Third, contests provide a showcase where women can display the results of their work in the gym, but the criteria used in judging often involves what some call "heteronormative" elements. In other words, even the most muscular women are expected to exhibit the softness and curvature conventionally associated with women. Shea concludes that, far from being a transgressive force, female bodybuilding has been hijacked and now reinforces "hegemonic femininity" "by normalizing, objectifying, and sexualizing the female bodybuilder" (2001: 47).

Marcia Ian, herself a bodybuilder-turned-scholar, agrees with some of this, but points out that in male bodybuilding "the central activity is exposing to view the passive and objectified male physique" (2001: 77). So, the male bodybuilder makes himself available for public inspection rather than actually doing anything. That is, he is engaging in something passive and feminine (Ian points out that the word passive derives from the same Latin root as passion, which means to suffer and be acted upon).

On this account, sport inscribes dominant narratives of gender identity on the material body by providing the means for exercising power relations on female flesh. Not only bodybuilding: in some measure, all sports operate to perpetuate gender divisions. They do so in two ways. (1) By intervening in the physiological functioning of female bodies, scientific theories and experiments on sexual differences had the effect of opening up women's bodies to surveillance, as we have seen. (2) By institutionalizing subordinate status for women's events and competitions, women's sport has been separated from men's in all but a very few contemporary events. Both confirm that while the female is more durable and capable of exertion than once thought, there is still a natural state, corporeal boundaries that cannot be crossed, at least not safely.

The reaction to French tennis player Amélie Mauresmo's rise to prominence at the 1999 Australian Open could have been designed to hold up this argument. "*Sie ist ein halber Mann*," said Martina Hingis of Mauresmo, her opponent in the final: "She is half a man." Mauresmo had already been stung by Lindsay Davenport who reflected on her, "I thought I was playing a guy." The then 19-year-old French player was tall and muscular but hardly ripped and she spoke freely about her relationship with another female. The old appellation "mannish" looked set for a return once the media got involved. "Oh man, she's good" declared the Melbourne tabloid *Herald Sun* in its headline; the paper's story featured two photographs of Mauresmo, including one shot from the rear that showed off her musculature.

The body is both natural and unnatural. Sports show us that we are constantly redefining the limits of the body. Not only can we remake our bodies in ways that we consciously control, but we can move it faster, higher, and longer, lift heavier weights and propel objects farther. The whole project of sport is based on the assumption that their are no natural confines of the human body; and if there are, we have not yet approached them. Watching sports reminds us that there is no such thing as the natural body: the body is what we make it.

## MAKING THE BODY

Many of us are already cyborgs. Some of us will wear contact lenses. Others will have steel plates in their heads, plastic joints and graphite replacements for cartilage. A friend of mine walks round with a plastic panel inside him after having an abdominal hernia fixed; he's also had his myopia fixed with laser surgery. Another friend's father has a pacemaker to regulate his heart. My own dad should wear a hearing aid, but could never get used to it. How many people do you know who have nose jobs, face lifts, botox injections, lip augmentations, or breast enlargements? This is even before we get to amputees who have some form of prosthetic, or those people who have undergone transplant surgery and now have someone else's vital organs. Then there are people who have microchips inside them. The list goes on. If we really wanted to stretch a point and insist that a cyborg is any fusion of body and technology, we could round up recipients of drugs, including vaccines. Very few of us have not had our bodies modified in some way. Cyborgs are not half-human/half-machine creatures from science fiction: they're us.

Cyborgs are already in sports, of course. I'm not referring to athletes who enhance their performances with dope, licit or illicit. I mean people like Sean Elliott, who played for San Antonio Spurs after an kidney transplant and reconstructive surgery on both knees (his brother donated one of his kidneys). And Aron Ralston, who competed in Adventure Duluth, a six-discipline (kayak, canoe, run, swim, mountain-bike, and skate) race in Minnesota, with a prosthetic arm and hand. Or Neil Patton, who played on San Jose State University's football team with a prosthetic leg, becoming the first non-kicker ever to suit up for NCAA football. Moving slightly outside the orbit of competitive sports, there was also the mountain climber with a prosthetic leg, who scaled Everest and whose venture was recorded by Chris Hables Gray in *Cyborg Citizen* (2001). Every week, athletes who might qualify as cyborgs record new feats.

Gray defines a cyborg as a "self regulating organism that combines the natural and artificial in one system" and "any organism that mixes the evolved and the made, the living and the inanimate" (2001: 2). We are, it seems, in the throes of "cyborgization": there's a sort of co-evolution going on, human bodies adapting to a changing environment with the aid of technology. There's nothing terribly new about this: bifocals and false teeth were early instances and artificial limbs were, as any reader of *Treasure Island* knows, popular among pirates like Long John Silver in the eighteenth century. The Napoleonic Wars in Europe, 1803–15, and the American Civil War, 1861–5, left many combatants disabled, leading to a demand for replacement limbs. These were rudimentary when compared to the possibilities offered in the twenty-first century. Again the supervening necessities of war played an important part.

The concept of fixing humans with spare parts was a far cry from the possibilities offered by science fiction, of course. While the idea of robots and hybrids had been entertained for years, the first film actually to use the term cyborg was Franklin Adreon's *Cyborg 2087*, released in 1966. The plot is familiar to fans of the later *Terminator* series that featured Arnold Schwarzenegger: a cyborg, played by Michael Rennie, is sent back from the future to save civilization. In the late twentieth century, the idea of a fusion between human and machine captured many imaginations, including that of the makers of the television series *The Six Million Dollar Man*, the 1973 pilot of which was entitled *Cyborg: The six million dollar man*. The premise of this was that an injured war hero is put back together using technology that enables him to perform extraordinary feats, like running as fast as a train. A glut of movies followed similar themes, the most celebrated being Paul Verhoeven's 1987 *Robocop*, which spawned two sequels. (The replicants of Ridley Scott's *Blade Runner*, 1982, were not cyborgs, but completely fabricated androids.)

Fascinating as the prospects are, humans were, for long, ambivalent about cyborgs. The Greek myth of Prometheus is a cautionary one. After stealing fire from Olympus and teaching mortals how to use it, Prometheus was punished by being chained to a rock and left to the vultures. "A little knowledge is a dangerous thing," is a slogan that has a similar meaning. The *Frankenstein* story too: the obsessed scientist creates life from an assembly of human parts, only to lose control of his creation. Today, we seem less cautious. Perhaps, it's because we sense we're approaching the limits of human possibility. To go further, whether in sports or any other sphere of endeavor, we need not only to assist our efforts but to augment them – make them greater.

---

### Cyborg

The term itself is from the Greek *kubernetes*, meaning one who steers vessels, which was anglicized to cyber, cybernetics being the science of systems of control in animals and machines; if a system is *cybernated*, it means it is controlled by machines. Added to this was "org," short for organic, as in parts of the body adapted for special functions, from the Greek for tool, *organon*. The word entered the popular vocabulary of the late twentieth century via science fiction. The growth of people who emerged from surgery with synthetic parts replacing their original organs suggested that the cyborg was not just a fictional creature. Bionic parts were mechanical productions that performed like living organs and appendages. Appropriated by scholars, such as Donna Haraway and Chris Hables Gray, cyborg came to define a political reality, a way of challenging traditionally accepted divisions supposedly based on natural arrangements.

---

Some writers welcome the fusion of human and machine as an emancipation. Donna Haraway, in her *Simians, Cyborgs and Women* (1991), argues that, in cyborgs, we have the nucleus of a society freed of stifling gender roles. In this and her earlier work, Haraway called for a recognition that we are all, in some respect, cyborgs and that we should take advantage of this. Why continue respecting the traditional divisions between animal/human/machine, asks Haraway? We should be transgressing them: using all available technologies to take control of our bodies in ways that give us satisfaction.

This wouldn't be music to the ears of drug-testers in sports, nor those who favor the continuation of separate events for men and women. As Brian Pronger points out in his essay "Post-sport: Transgressing boundaries in physical culture": "In sport this means encouraging people to experiment with the cybernetic boundaries of their bodies, thus resisting the boundary project of a sports system that requires athletes to technologize their bodies but punishes them if they are caught doing so" (1998: 286).

Doping aside, athletes are well engaged in cyborgization. The effects of injuries and disabilities are often overcome with technologies. It's a small step away from actively using similar technologies to go beyond maximal performance. Structural, biochemical alterations to the body may sound drastic, but, as we will see in the chapters ahead, genetic engineering is already on the agenda. We'll return to this in Chapter 10 and in the conclusion. For now, we recognize that the body is natural and artificial, physical and cultural.

*Out of Bounds: Women, sport and sexuality* by Helen Lenskyj (Women's Press, 1986) traces the massively hindered progress of women into mainstream sports from the 1880s, paying special attention to the various ways women's achievements were discredited, typically by accusations of impropriety or unnatural status. It can profitably be read in conjunction with Patricia Vertinsky's excellent *The Eternally Wounded Woman: Women, doctors and exercise in the late nineteenth century* (Manchester University Press, 1990).

*The Making of the Modern Body: Sexuality and society in the nineteenth century* edited by Catherine Gallagher and Thomas Laqueur (University of California Press, 1987) is a collection of essays all devoted to exploring different aspects of the body's changing meanings.

*Beyond the Natural Body: An archeology of sex hormones* by Nelly Oudshoorn (Routledge, 1994) is a detailed exploration of how the "discovery" of sex hormones established as a scientific fact the precise natural differences between men and women.

*Technologies of the Gendered Body: Reading cyborg women* by Anne Balsamo, (Duke University Press, 1996) focuses on the cultural meanings of body technologies: quite apart from performance-enhancing substances and other aids to competition, we have bionic technology that was once thought fanciful when featured in television shows like *The Six Million Dollar Man* and *The Bionic Woman*. Now, the artificial reconstruction of the human body is underway.

*Sexuality*, second edition, by Jeffrey Weeks (Routledge, 2003) has a chapter on "The meanings of sexual difference" in which the author discloses several perspectives including one that suggests that "heterosexuality and homosexuality are not emanations of the genes or hormones or anything else: they are regulative fictions and ideals through which conformities are generated, reinforced and 'normalized' . . . The norms are inscribed on the body in a variety of ways through the relations and rituals of power which prescribe and proscribe appearance, physicality, who and what is desirable and so on."

*Sport and Postmodern Times* edited by Geneviève Rail (State University of New York Press, 1998) has a section on "Sport and postmodern body invaders" in which there are chapters on cyborgs and body technologies. This might be read against the background of Robert Pepperell's third edition of *The Posthuman Condition: Consciousness beyond the brain* (Intellect, 2004) which examines how genetic modification, intelligent machines, and synthetic creativity challenge traditional assumptions about humanity.

## ASSIGNMENT

Renee Richards played on the women's tennis tour before it was discovered that she was formerly Richard Raskind. Hastily, the United States Tennis Association and the Women's Tennis Association introduced a Barr bodies sex test, which Richards refused to take. S/he was excluded from competition. In 1977, the New York Supreme Court ruled that requiring Richards to take the Barr test was "grossly unfair, discriminatory and inequitable, and violative of her rights" (see Renee Richards's biography *Second Serve* (with J. Ames), Stein & Day, 1983; and Susan Birrell and Cheryl Cole's "Double fault: Renee Richards and the construction and naturalization of difference," in *Sociology of Sport Journal*, vol. 7, 1990). In the 1990s, Canada's Michelle Dumaresq made news competing as a mountain bike racer. Formerly Michael, Dumaresq had sex reassignment surgery in 1996 and competed for Canada at the World Championships in Austria. In 2003, the IOC's medical director Patrick Schamasch announced that, in regard to transsexuals, "We will have no discrimination . . . the IOC will respect human rights . . . after certain conditions have been fulfilled, the athlete will be able to compete in his or her new sex." Discrimination against transsexuals appears to be receding. But, has it disappeared?

Perhaps surprisingly, Richards criticized the decision: "Sex-assignment is based on putting materials into your body." But, the IOC insists safeguards are in place to prevent an athlete reaping competitive benefits from a sex change. Hormone treatment should have ceased at least two years before competition.

Construct a narrative in which it is revealed that several members of the current tennis circuit, the WNBA, the US track and field team, and some beach volleyball players have undergone similar surgery to Richards. Take careful note of Balsamo's reminder that "gender is not simply an effect of the circulation of representations and discourse, but also the effect of specific social, economic, and institutional relations of power" (1996: 162).

# behind on points

## why black athletes are symbols of failure

## A MILLION DREAMS, ONE STAR

In March 1995, two of the most potent black sporting symbols were released, one from prison, the other from baseball's backwaters. Mike Tyson and Michael Jordan were the most successful African Americans in sports. They earned more money, more respect, and, in Tyson's case, more notoriety than any previous black athlete in history. Their absence from sport's big league was agonizing. Tyson's was enforced: he was found guilty of raping a beauty queen contestant in an Indianapolis hotel room and banished in ignominy. Jordan quit the Chicago Bulls with the plaudits ringing in his ears; he wanted to conquer his second sport, baseball, but fared poorly with Chicago White Sox. Even after a second departure from basketball, Jordan found the lure of competition irresistible and returned, this time with Washington Wizards. Tyson never recaptured the indestructible menace of his early career, but remained the biggest attraction in boxing even as he advanced on his fortieth birthday. His presence, like Jordan's, had promoters rubbing their hands and advertisers reaching for their check-books. In many ways, Tyson and Jordan were opposites. In one important way, they were similar: they inspired the dreams of millions.

But, are they realistic dreams, or just dangerous fantasies? In this chapter, I'll address not only this question, but, perhaps more importantly, why we should be asking it at all. After all, whose business is it if someone wants to channel all his or her energy into the pursuit of an ideal? Sports themselves thrive off the zeal and ambition of millions of "wannabes," the vast majority of whom never approach the level where they can make a living, let alone a fortune, out of sports.

Tens of thousands of young African Americans and African Caribbeans who grew up in American and British inner cities in the 1970s and 1980s are now reflecting on a sports career that never was. They, like literally millions before them, had watched television, listened to radios, read newspapers and magazines, and logged onto the Internet. There was the evidence before their eyes: Kobe Bryant, Lennox Lewis, Sol Campbell; black sports stars lauded all over the world, winning titles, medals, and making the kind of money that qualifies you for a place in *Fortune* magazine.

But appearances are often deceptive and these highly unrepresentative superstars unwittingly create an illusion. As American sports writer Jack Olsen observed in his classic 1968 book, *The Black Athlete*: "At most, sport has led a few thousand Negroes out of the ghetto. But for hundreds of thousands of other Negroes it has substituted a meaningless dream."

While the time and effort demanded in trying to become another Bryant or Campbell is so great that it may ruin a young person's prospects of doing anything else, the actual chances of emulating them are infinitesimally small. Failed sports performers have quite frequently destroyed any other career possibilities they might have had. No sports performer can avoid making sacrifices; the black athletes' sacrifices are just greater than most.

But, the gains are greater too, the reader might argue. Take Justin Gatlin (the sprinter), Louis Saha (soccer player), or Michael Olowokandi (basketball player): these are not names that spring to mind when you think of top black athletes. Yet, they're all successful and have enough money to last them a lifetime. Sport is such a lucrative area, nowadays, that even modest success earns a lot of money. And, no matter how you interpret the evidence, many black athletes achieve success relative to the number of black people in the total population. African Americans account for little more than 13 percent of the total US population; African Caribbeans are, by the largest estimate, only 3 percent of the British population. Yet, the NBA has 80–90 percent majority of black players, and one in five professional soccer players in Britain is black. At any one time, 50 percent of world boxing champions are black. We could marshal other figures to support what is an obvious fact: black people overachieve in sports; it's also a fact that far more leave sport in failure and disappointment. We need to uncover some of the processes at work beneath these facts.

The experience of women as we covered in Chapter 7 is comparable with that of the black community. Being minorities, both have marginal positions, meaning that they are largely excluded from many of the key areas of society. Neither features prominently in politics, the professions, or other areas of society where important decisions are made that affect people's lives. Their exclusion is usually the product of an "-ism": as black individuals are discriminated against and their accomplishments diminished through racism, so women are prohibited from competing on equal terms with men through sexism. Both remain on the underside of a lopsided structure of inequality and this has affected the involvement of both in sport in quite different ways. We've already dealt with the ways in which women have been pushed to the margins of society and how they've responded to this, particularly in sports. The focus in this chapter is on the experience of black people.

There is quite a story to the involvement of black athletes with organized sport in the West. It begins in the late eighteenth century during the American War of Independence, when General Percy of the British forces captured the Virginian town of Richmond. Impressed by the fighting prowess of a slave who worked on the plantations there, Percy took Bill Richmond – as he named him – under his tutelage and groomed him for prizefighting. While it could not have been an easy life, prizefighting had its perks (like extensive travel in Europe) and must have seemed far preferable to plantation work. Richmond was something of a prototype, his modest success encouraging slave owners and merchants to scour for potential fighters whom they might patronize.

The celebrated Tom Molineaux was one such fighter. Once a slave, he was taken to England and trained by Richmond, eventually winning his freedom. Molineaux built on his predecessor's success, rubbing shoulders with the nobility and generally mixing with the London beau monde. It was in his classic fight with all-England heavyweight champion Tom Cribb that he created his niche in sports history. Moulineaux was beaten and died four years later. He is the subject of George MacDonald Fraser's historical novel *Black Ajax*, which takes the form of eyewitness "reports" of the epic fight in 1811.

Peter Jackson was born on the West Indies island of St. Croix and traveled to Sydney and San Francisco before settling in England in the late nineteenth century. He, more than any pugilist of his day, embraced fame, though world champion John L. Sullivan's refusal to fight him denied him the ultimate title. Yet his decline was abrupt and he became a habitual drinker and was made to play in a stage version of Stowe's *Uncle Tom's Cabin*.

Some slaves continued to leave America to campaign as prizefighters in Europe, but the majority were pitted against each other locally. The years on either side of emancipation in 1865 saw black athletes filtering into other sports; they were most successful at horse-riding and baseball. In the latter, they were not permitted to play with or against white players. Ninety-eight years after the first Molyneaux–Cribb clash, a black man ascended to the apogee of sporting achievement. John Arthur Johnson in 1908 challenged and beat Tommy Burns, a white man, to become the heavyweight champion of the world. Fighting as "Jack Johnson," he broke the "color line" which segregated the black community from white in all areas, including sport. In fact, after Johnson eventually lost the title in 1916, the line was redrawn and no black man was allowed to fight for the world title until 1937 when Joe Louis started a succession of black champions interrupted in the twentieth century only by Rocky Marciano (1952–5), Ingemar Johannson (1959–60), and Gerrie Coetzee (1983–4).

Johnson and, in an entirely different way, Louis were black icons of their day. Especially Johnson who cultivated a reputation as a "bad nigger," a moral hard man who, as Lawrence Levine puts it in his *Black Culture and Black Consciousness*, "had the strength and courage and ability to flout the limitations imposed by white society" (1977: 420). Johnson's imagery was based as much on his penchant for the company of white women as his boxing. This was a time when the Ku Klux Klan was in its ascendancy and black men were lynched for far lesser deeds than consorting with white females. Far from being "bad," Louis was obsequious, apolitical, and exploitable – as his poverty, despite vast ring earnings, demonstrates. Yet, he too was a potent symbol for black Americans who were short of heroes or role models on whom to style their own lives. Both were anomalies: conspicuously successful black men in a society where success was virtually monopolized by white men.

The other outstanding black sportsman of this period was Jesse Owens who, like Louis, was "a credit to his race" – which meant he was self-effacing and compliant to the demands of white officials. Well, not totally compliant: after returning a performance of theatrical proportions at the 1936 "Nazi Olympics" in Berlin (covered in Chapter 17), where he won four gold medals and shamed Hitler into a walkout, he was expelled from the American Athletics Union for refusing to compete in a Swedish tour. Owens was eventually reduced to freak shows, racing against horses and motorcycles. Donald McRae's book, *In Black and White* (2003), assesses the experiences of Louis and Owens during the 1930s.

Other black sports performers were similarly brought to reduced circumstances. Johnson suffered the indignity of imprisonment, of fighting bulls in Barcelona, of performing stunts in circuses, of comically playing Othello, and of boxing all-comers in exhibitions at the age of 68. Louis ended his days ignominiously in a wheelchair, welcoming visitors at a Las Vegas hotel. The careers of all three followed a comet's elliptical path, radiating brilliance in their orbit, yet fading into invisibility. Plenty of other black stars have followed the same route. Sports history is full of dreams turning to nightmares. But black sportsmen seem particularly afflicted. Not even "The Greatest," Muhammad Ali, could maintain his dignity in later years.

While boxing was the first sport in which black athletes were able to cross the color line and compete with white colleagues, others followed the form. In 1946, when Joe Louis was nearing the end of his reign as heavyweight king (and the year in which Jack Johnson died), Jackie Robinson became the first black person to play major league baseball. He was sent death threats and his teams, Montreal and the Brooklyn Dodgers, were sometimes boycotted by opponents. The hostility of his reception may have initially daunted administrators from recruiting black players, but by the 1950s the numbers entering major league were multiplying.

Nowadays, basketball is dominated by black players. The trend began in 1951 when Chuck Hooper signed for Boston Celtics and precipitated a rush: within 16 years, over half the National Basketball Association (NBA) players were black. The specter of freak show that had hung over Owens and the others visited basketball in the shape of the Harlem Globetrotters whose goals were more in making audiences laugh than scoring hoops. The comic Globetrotters' popularity with white spectators was probably because of the players' conformity to the image of black athletes as physically adept, but too limited intellectually to harness skill to firm objectives. James Michener, in *Sports in America* (1976), wrote of the Globetrotters: "They deepened the stereotype of 'the loveable [*sic*], irresponsible Negro'" (1976: 145).

Civil rights legislation in 1964 and 1965 erased the color line, in a *de jure*, or legal, sense at least. As the segregationist barriers in education tumbled down, so black youngsters began to mix and play competitively with white students. College football came within reach of more black athletes and this, in turn, translated into more black professional players. By 1972, African American players comprised 40 percent of the NFL.

---

### Stereotype

An image or depiction of a group based on false or, at best, incomplete information, which can be used as the basis for gross generalizations about members of such groups. Typically, a stereotype extracts alleged features of a culture or a "race" and elevates these to prominence, making them into defining characteristics. The stereotype is usually insulting, frequently demeaning, and occasionally hostile.

---

In Britain, the historical developments were similar, though compressed into a shorter timespan and with considerably fewer numbers, of course. The old prizefighters Richmond and Molineaux were followed by a succession of prizefighters, one notable being Andrew Jeptha, who migrated from Cape Town, South Africa, in 1902, and became the first-ever black boxer to hold a British title in 1907 (this was before the formation of the British Boxing Board of Control). On the track, sprinters from the British Caribbean, like Arthur Wharton, Jack London, McDonald Bailey, and Arthur Wint, established reputations from the end of the nineteenth century to the 1950s.

Wharton transferred to professional soccer with Preston North End, thus becoming the first-ever black player; though the person popularly credited with that distinction is Lloyd Lindbergh Delaphena, who played for Middlesbrough and Portsmouth in the 1950s. This period was one of mass migration from the Caribbean and, as a consequence, many migrants, such as Trinidad's Yolande Pompey and Guyana's Cliff Anderson, were active in British rings. Hogan "Kid" Bassey, originally from Nigeria but based in Liverpool, won the world featherweight title in 1957.

But one boxer embodied all the elements of the black sportsman in this period. Born in the Midlands town of Leamington Spa in 1928, Randolph Turpin had a Guyanese migrant father and an English mother. Inspired by the example of his older brother Dick, who in 1948 won the British middleweight title, Randolph had a shimmering boxing career that came to a climax in 1951 when he upset Sugar Ray Robinson to become the world middleweight champion. Lacking any financial acumen, he ran into trouble with the Inland Revenue which filed a bankruptcy petition against him for unpaid tax on his considerable ring earnings. His career plunged to humiliating depths when he engaged in "boxer *vs* wrestler" bouts and even consented to a fully fledged comeback in an unlicensed boxing promotion at the age of 35. On May 16, 1966, he committed suicide by shooting himself, though rumors of a gangland murder were rife, according to his biographer Jack Birtley (1976: 140–53). His fall resembled that of other black champions.

Marilyn Fay Neufville broke the world's 400-meter record in 1970 when she was 18. Born in Jamaica, she ran for Cambridge Harriers, a London club, and became the first black female to make an impact on British sport. Sprint events were later virtually dominated by black women, but less conspicuously, judo and volleyball also benefited from the growing participation of black women.

Unlike the USA, Britain has never had formal segregation, so black schoolchildren have competed in sports with peers from a variety of ethnic backgrounds. Soccer, as the nation's most popular game, has been played in high schools throughout the country so it was not unexpected when, in the late 1970s and early 1980s, black players began appearing in Football League teams. First, the trickle: Albert Johanneson, a Leeds United player in the 1960s; Clyde Best, who played for West Ham United in the 1970s. Then the flood: dozens of professional players, including Viv Anderson, who in 1979 became the first black footballer to represent England, began to appear, prompting reactions from the racist fans, who frequently pelted them with bananas and targeted them for abusive chants. Through the 1980s, black footballers continued to make their mark on British soccer often to the ambiguous rejoicing of newspapers whose "Black Magic" and "Black Power" headlines were more than faintly reminiscent of a London paper's banner after a promotion in June 1946 when five black boxers posted wins: "Black Night for British Boxing" (quoted in Henderson 1949: 340).

At the close of the 1980s, a "second generation" of British-born black athletes was established in British sport. Over half the British boxing champions were black as were more than 40 percent of the Olympic squad of 1988, and virtually every Football League club had two or three black players on its books. It is no coincidence that the major sports in which black athletes have excelled – boxing, track and field, football, and basketball – are ones which demand little in the way of equipment. They can be practiced away from any formal organization and with minimal resources. A strong pair of legs, fast hands, sharp reflexes, and a desire to compete are basics. Much more than this is needed to progress in the club-oriented sports, like cricket, golf, and tennis, which tend to be accessible only to the middle class. It might be argued that cricket has some possibilities for players of working-class backgrounds – and black athletes in the main come from such backgrounds – but the very structure of the sport and the educational institutions in which it is encouraged make it more available to the more affluent class. The same argument applies to Rugby Union.

In the more accessible sports, black athletes have grown to a prominence that belies their numerical minority status in both the USA and Britain. Their sometimes overwhelming success in certain sports is quite disproportionate to their numbers within the total population. The ratio is most pronounced in boxing, track and field, and basketball. But in sports in which black performers have either been allowed to compete or have been attracted to, they seem to approach a mastery that is difficult to match; their apparent predilection for sport, and the high orders of success they have achieved, has been the subject of bar-room discussion and academic controversy. Why so many in sport and why so many champions? The answers are intertwined.

## SMALL BUT MEANINGFUL DIFFERENCES

One of the simplest and most influential explanations of black excellence has been supplied by Martin Kane in an article entitled "An assessment of black is best" in the magazine *Sports Illustrated* (January 18, 1971). At the center of Kane's argument is the "insight" that black individuals are endowed with a natural ability that gives them an advantage in certain sports. Around this lie a number of other related points, many culled from Kane's interviews with medical scientists, coaches, and sports performers. An important, though oddly dated, point is that there are race-linked physical characteristics.

Black people as a "race" have proportionately longer legs to white people, narrower hips, wider calf bones, greater arm circumference, greater ratio of tendon to muscle, denser skeletal structure, and a more elongated body. Typically, they have power and an efficient body-heat dissipation system. Kane inferred these features from a small sample of successful black sportsmen – that is, a minority with proven excellence rather than a random sample from the total population. And he concludes that black people are innately different and the differences, being genetic in origin, can be passed on from one generation to the next.

So, cold climates are said to affect all black people badly, even ones who are born and brought up in places like Toronto. Weak ankle bones would account for the relative absence of black ice hockey players. The disadvantages are transmitted genetically, as are natural advantages which equip black athletes to do well in particular sports where speed and power are essential. Kane argues that black competitors are not suited to endurance events. Since the publication of the article, hundreds of African distance runners have undermined this point, though Kane tries to cover himself by claiming Kenyans have black skin, but a number of white features.

Kane's arguments border on the absurd, especially when we consider anthropologists' dismissal of the concept of race itself as having any analytical value at all. Black people are descended from African populations, but, over the centuries, their genetic heritage has become diversified and complicated by various permutations of mating. There is no "pure" race. Kane ignores this when he examines the area of psychology, emerging with a set of personality traits that are supposed to be determined by race. Black athletes have the kind of yielding personality that puts them, as one coach told Kane, "far ahead of whites . . . relaxation under pressure" (1971: 76).

This has a common-sense authenticity about it, for coaches and spectators seem to associate black athletes with a cool approach to competition, never stressing-out, or growing tense. But competitors themselves actually work at portraying this: they consciously try to convey an image that reflects coolness. That is all it is – image. Beneath the surface, black performers are as tense and concerned as anyone else. Possibly more so: sport for many black youths is not a casual recreation (as it may be for white youths), but a career path and every failure represents a possible sinking to obscurity. Every event has to be approached as if it were the most demanding of one's life; defeat is not easily assimilated as a result. Kane mistook impression management for deep psychological profiles.

Slavery is the key to the third part of Kane's argument. "Of all the physical and psychological theories about the American black's excellence in sport, none has proved more controversial than one of the least discussed: that slavery weeded out the weak" (1971: 80). Here Kane introduces some homespun Darwinism, his view being that, as only the fittest survived the rigors of slavery, those best suited to what must have been terribly harsh environments passed on their genes to successive populations, who used them to great effect in sport. There are two drawbacks to this. First, it is preposterous to suggest that black individuals bred for generations in such a controlled way as to retain a gene pool in which specific genes – related to, for instance, speed, strength, and agility – became dominant. Second, these properties were probably of less significance in matters of survival than intelligence, ingenuity, and anticipation and Kane considers none of these as essentially black features.

While Kane's views might have been controversial in the early 1970s, they were inadmissible by 1988. That's when a CBS pundit named Jimmy "The Greek" Snyder expressed similar observations during an NFL pregame show. He was fired after suggesting that slave owners had bred black slaves for sporting endeavors.

In 2000, nearly 30 years after the publication of Kane's article, another writer asked: "Was Jimmy 'The Greek' right?" By then, theories that purported to link athletic excellence with racial factors, while not forbidden, were discouraged; Jon Entine broke what he called the *Taboo*. This was the title of his book, the subtitle of which provides an idea of his central question: *why black athletes dominate and why we're afraid to talk about it*. Entine asked and answered the question about Snyder negatively, pointing out that breeding patterns during slavery couldn't possibly have led to differences in athletic ability. "Scientists who are convinced that innate differences exist between races unavoidably walk a very slippery slope of exaggeration and conjecture," wrote Entine. "It is important to remind ourselves that genes set parameters, but it is life experiences that 'express' biological capabilities" (2000: 263).

This is a promising advance on Kane's argument, though Entine still maintains that "West African-descended blacks are naturally faster and better jumpers than whites" (2000: 279). He agrees with those that argue a case for social factors when he contends that the conspicuous success of some black athletes in sports encourages others and discourages white competitors. This is what leads to patterns, with, for example, many black middle-distance runners and few black swimmers. But, these are not causes but consequences of an uneven distribution of natural talent. As Entine concludes: "Cultural conditions exaggerate the small but meaningful differences that led to the athletic edge" (2000: 279).

While Entine writes in terms of what he calls "bio-cultural factors," his argument rests as unmistakably as Kane's on fundamental natural differences, which may be embellished and overstated by cultural influences, but remain the primary causes of differences in athletic achievements.

The simplicity and comprehensiveness of this approach to explaining differences have made it appealing to many. Harry Edwards is not one of them: he has even suggested that the explanation itself has effects for white competitors who, believing black athletes to be innately superior, start off at a psychological disadvantage. "The 'white race' thus becomes the chief victim of its own myth" (1973: 197).

But, for Edwards, it is exactly that: a myth. Its appeal disguises something more sinister because, if we accept as proof of the natural ability argument the outstanding results recorded by black sports performers then what are we to infer from the underachievement of black students in formal education? That they are naturally limited intellectually? If so, it could be argued that they should be encouraged to develop their gifts and possibly neglect areas in which they haven't much aptitude. Sadly, this is what has happened in the past and it gives us the first clue in answering the question of the sporting success of black performers all over again, this time with an entirely different approach.

## LOSERS AND STILL CHAMPIONS

History alone tells us that sport has been one of the two channels through which black individuals have been able to escape the imprisonment of slavery and the impoverishment that followed its dissolution; the other being entertainment. In both spheres, they performed largely for the amusement of white patricians. This holds true to this day: the season-ticket holders or cable television subscribers, no less than old-time slave masters, have decisive effects on the destinies of sports performers. For this reason, slaves were encouraged; the incentive might be freedom or at least a temporary respite from daily labors.

There is an adage that emerged during the 1930s depression in Yorkshire, England, a county famed for its cricket and its mining industry: "Shout down any coalpit and half a dozen fast bowlers will come out." The theme is similar: that material deprivation is an ideal starting point for sporting prowess. "Hungry fighters" are invariably the most effective. As we have seen, many fight their way out, only to return to indigence; but they're not to know that as they're striving for improvement. The supposed predilection of black individuals for sport is more a product of material circumstances than natural talent.

Whether or not sport is a viable avenue from despair is not the issue: it has been seen as such by people who lacked alternatives. And the perception has stuck, and probably will continue to stick as long as obstacles to progress in other avenues remain. The argument here is that the early slave prizefighters began a tradition by setting themselves up – quite unwittingly – as cultural icons, or images to be revered and copied; in today's parlance, role models. The stupendous success of black competitors in such sports as boxing and athletics has clearly been inspirational to countless black youths over the decades.

Racism and racial discrimination have worked to exclude black people from many areas of employment, restrict their opportunities, and, generally, push them toward the "marginal" or least important areas of the labor market. Experiencing this at first hand or anticipating it through the stories of others has set young people thinking about alternative sources of employment. "There aren't too many successful black tycoons, professionals, or politicians, so where should I look for an example?" black youths might ask themselves. Answers spring to mind readily: Kevin Garnett – six-year contract worth $125 million

(£76 million); Roy Jones – estimated career earnings: $100 million (£61 million); Serena Williams – designer tennis queen; the list goes on. Black individuals can make it, but only in certain areas. Evaporating into insignificance are the millions of other aspirants whose fortune never materialized and whose career ended shabbily. No matter how remote the chances of success may be, the tiny number of elite black sports stars supply tangible and irrefutable evidence that it can be achieved.

---

### Racism

A set of beliefs or ideas based on the assumption that the world's population can be divided into different human biological groups designated "races." Following on from this is the proposition that the "races" are ordered hierarchically, so that some stand in a position of superordinacy, or superiority, to others. This is a classic type of racism; nowadays, ideas of superiority are often veiled in arguments concerning culture, nationalism, and ethnic identity. Quite often, these contain connotations of racism that are not specific, but only inferred. When ideas, or beliefs, about racial superiority are translated into action, we speak in terms of racial discrimination, or simply racialism. Racism is the idea; racialism is the practice, though racism is often used to cover both.

---

By their early teens, black youths showing potential become draft horses, drawing along the displaced ambitions of parents, sibling and human cargo of others who, for some reason, have had their own ambitions blighted and remain fixed in the underclass, their only hope of redemption lying in the success of the would-be champion. Encouraged, even cajoled, by physical education teachers at high school who might subscribe to the popular if mistaken view that sports black students have "natural talent," young persons might, while running or fighting, discover new dimensions of themselves. Zealous scouts for colleges pump up the youths with inflated claims when they attempt to woo them into their programs. Many youths understandably find comfort in the view that they do possess natural advantages. The fact that such views are based on stereotypes not realities doesn't enter into it: beliefs often have a self-fulfilling quality, so that if you believe in your own ability strongly enough, you eventually acquire that ability. I can illustrate the point.

A few years ago, I received a call from a journalist from the British *Sunday Times*. He was writing a story on black overachievement in sports and wanted to know why no one actually expressed what he felt was an evident truth: that there is a natural edge that black athletes possess. Was it because of political

correctness? he asked. Partly, I answered, but also because it has racist implications and mainly because it is just wrong. Then, I qualified my response: the
fact that a journalist, who happened to be black himself, writing for a prestigious
newspaper was prepared to entertain the idea was testimony to its power. It is
not only white people who have bought the myth of black natural talent in sport:
black people have accepted and, in some cases, even clung to a defective theory
that has actually performed a disservice.

Actually, it's not the myth itself that has performed the disservice so much
as the culture in which it has stayed credible; one in which black people have
been regarded as unsuited to or just unwanted for work that demands intellect
and imagination – cerebral rather than physical skills.

Study after study in the USA and Britain – and, more recently, in parts of
continental Europe – has chronicled the extent and intensity of racism in today's
society. We need not dwell on specific examples; suffice it to say that in the
postwar years in Britain and for many more years before that in the USA, black
students and wokers have been systematically squeezed out of education and
employment opportunities for reasons that derive from, in its rawest form,
racist hostility.

The origins of this hostility lie in the European colonial expansion of the
seventeenth century, the settlement of the West Indies, or Caribbean, and
the expansion of trade in slaves, gold, and sugar between Africa, the Americas,
and Britain. Slavery meant that white masters maintained their domination over
black slaves and so kept a rigid inequality. The inequality has been modified
and lessened in the decades following emancipation, but black populations have
never quite shed the remnants of their shackles and white people have passed
on their colonial mentality. Seeing black athletes as great sports performers
might seem a compliment, but, as Harry Edwards memorably observed in his
*The Revolt of the Black Athlete*: "The only difference between the black man
shining shoes in the ghetto and the champion black sprinter is that the shoe shine
man is a nigger, while the sprinter is a fast nigger" (1970: 20).

Historically, sport, along with entertainment, was one of the areas in which
black individuals were allowed to maximize their prowess, and circumstances
haven't changed sufficiently to permit a significant departure. Black students
still approach sport with vigor and commitment at least partly because persistent
racism effectively closes off other channels. Even if those other channels have
become freer in recent years, black youths have become accustomed to anticipating obstacles to their progress. So that, by the time they prepare to make
the transition from school to work, many have made sports as a career their
first priority.

With sights set on a future filled with championships, black youths fight
their way into sports determined that, slim though their chances may be, they
will succeed. And they usually do, though mostly in an altogether more modest

way than they envisaged. Few attain the heights they wanted to conquer and even fewer surpass them. An unstoppable motivation and unbreakable commitment are valuable, perhaps essential, assets to success in sport and this is why so many possessors of these achieve some level of distinction. But titles are, by definition, reserved for only a very small elite and, while black athletes are always well represented among the elite of all sports in which they compete, there are never enough championships to go round. The majority inevitably fail.

The success of many black performers in sports may look impressive, but, compared to the numbers of youths entering sport, their interest primed, their success is not so great, even when their chances are affected by "stacking" and other racialist maneuvers. Sheer weight of numbers dictates that a great many African Americans and African Caribbeans will rise to the top of certain sports. When the phenomenon is approached this way, the reasons are less opaque. There is no need to resort to imprecise ideas such as natural ability: the sporting success of black athletes is actually constructed in history and contemporary culture. Let me summarize.

Cultures on both sides of the Atlantic have fostered strains of racism that, while less virulent now than 20 years ago, are still bitter enough to convince young black people that their future in mainstream society may be curtailed by popularly held stereotypes about their abilities. Weighing up the possibilities of a future career, many opt for a shot at sports, where it has been demonstrated time and again that black people can make it to the very top and command the respect of everyone, white players and spectators included. Respect is a sought-after commodity by people who have been denied it historically. Ideas of the "White Men Can't Jump" variety are conveyed to young black people by possibly well-meaning, but mistaken, coaches and high school teachers who enthuse over a career in sports. Then the story separates into two contrasting plots. Some tread the road to respectability, even stardom, making a living they can be proud of from professional sports. Others dissolve into oblivion, never to be heard of.

What this scenario doesn't seem to account for is the scarcity of black competitors, let alone winners, in certain sports. Their exclusion from more expensive pursuits like golf, shooting, skiing, and so on is obvious: you need money to get started. But swimming, tennis, or some field events pose more of a mystery. One might reasonably suppose that, over the years, a percentage of black youths would gravitate toward areas not traditionally black-dominated. Perhaps they will, but so far the pull of the icons has been irresistible. Black stars today have been recast into idols by corporations, watchful of an emergent black middle class with plenty of disposable income. Having their products endorsed by successful black players can help them gain a piece of the developing African American market.

---

### Icons

The term "icon" is from the Greek *eikon*, meaning image. Its application to culture refers to the image that is conferred, granted, or attributed to an individual by a collection of others. In a sense, the cultural icon exists almost independently of the individual, who may be a sports or rock star: popular perceptions, expectations, and beliefs define the icon much more powerfully than the person. Jack Johnson, for example, "was not merely a fighter but a symbol," as Levine puts it (1977: 430). In 1912, it was widely believed that Johnson had been refused passage on the doomed *Titanic*, and this enhanced his status even further. Contemporary cultural icons also have beliefs built around them that contribute to their status; there is a willingness to believe almost anything about either of them. Similarly, some contemporary black sports stars command iconic status.

---

In the 1980s, Eldon Snyder and Elmer Spreitzer reported that world-ranked tennis players Lori McNeill and Zina Garrison were missing out on sponsors to inferior white players (1983: 339). Since then there has been a steady march of black athletes into higher tax brackets. By 1995, it was possible for the Wall Street value of stocks in the five companies endorsed by Michael Jordan to swell by $2.3 billion (£1.4 billion) amid rumors that he would return to basketball. In the early 2000s, the French soccer player Thierry Henry led an ad campaign for Renault that was believed to have been worth €5 million to him. The endorsement of a recognizably successful sports performer can add enormously to the marketability of a product. Advertisers have been guided less by fine spirits, more by the argument that affluent black consumers can be persuaded to part with their money by other, more successful black celebrities.

The result is the transformation of the likes of David Robinson and Sheryl Swoopes into something much more than sports performers: they have become representatives of an aspirational culture in which people are prepared to emulate them in nearly every respect. If they chase the same dreams and seek the same praise, they might eat the same breakfast cereal or wear the same sneakers. If those dreams have long since gone, they might still buy the products they endorse. Whatever the logic behind the advertisers' ploy, the effect is to create a televisual pantheon for living sports stars. The majority of young black people will structure their ambitions around the icons of success they see before them, all but deified by tv culture.

# BETWEEN MIND AND MUSCLE

But there is a heavy cost and one which John Hoberman emphasizes in his book *Darwin's Athletes*, which bears the subtitle "How sport has damaged black America and preserved the myth of race" (1997). Hoberman's thesis is that the "fixation" on the athletic achievements of African Americans has led to a glorification of the physical aspects of black people, a glorification that degenerates, as Orlando Patterson once put it, "into a vulgar exoticism" and "inverted racist claims of superior sexual potency and greater zest and passion for life" (1971: 303).

Hoberman believes there exists what he calls the Law of Compensation which states that there is "an inverse relationship between mind and muscle, between athletic and intellectual development" (1997: 225). America has perpetuated falsehoods about black people's biological propensities; and "black athleticism has served . . . as the most dramatic vehicle in which such ideas can ride in public consciousness" (1997: 225).

Prominent black sports performers have been used as living evidence of a not-so noble savagery: virtually every sports star embodies concepts of racial evolution that are enthusiastically accepted by both white and black populations as support for the view that black individuals are naturally good athletes, but not much good at much else. Among Hoberman's examples are Joe Louis "who was granted messianic status by his fellow blacks [and] was also depicted as a savage brute to his white audience" (1997: 115–26) and Mike Tyson whose "well-publicized brutalities in and out of the ring have helped to preserve pseudo-evolutionary fantasies about black ferocity that are still of commercial value to fight promoters and their business partners in the media" (1997: 209).

Black boxers are bit part players in a "Darwinian drama par excellence, in that portraying the black male as an undisciplined savage confirmed both his primitive nature and his inevitable failure in the competition with civilized whites in a modern society" (1997: 209). They are joined by an all-star cast that includes all top black athletes and the millions more who want to follow in their footsteps.

Hoberman argues that black people in the States and, to a similar degree in Britain, have been depicted in an unending series of images that have contributed toward a social pathology. White people are society's stewards. The typical image of the black community in the media is that of a violent physical people, habitually involved in criminal activity, entertainment, or sports. In the late twentieth century, the slayings of black musicians and the vulgar misogynist material of rap artists contributed to a "merger of the athlete, the gangster rapper, and the criminal into a single black male persona" that the sports, entertainment, and advertising industries have made into the dominant image of black masculinity – a single menacing figure. The high-profile sports figures who have courted ambitions in music and movies supports Hoberman's point.

## Tyson's cases

On September 19, 1991, heavyweight boxer Mike Tyson was indicted by a Marion County grand jury of raping Desiree Washington, a contestant at a Miss Black America pageant, who claimed Tyson had forcibly had sex with her in an Indianapolis hotel room. Tyson had attended the pageant. On February 10, 1992, Tyson was convicted of rape and sentenced to six years in prison. Washington later alleged that Tyson had given her a venereal disease. During his imprisonment, the boxer converted to Islam. Tyson was released from prison in March 1995, and resumed his professional boxing career five months later under the guidance of Don King. Richard Hoffer believes: "He [Tyson] was the perfect man for King's purposes, though, smart enough to be actively complicit in the con, but emotionally disorganized enough to defer to King in its execution" (1998: 266). The "con" was a series of easy fights spread over two years which earned Tyson $135 million. By 1998, Tyson was back in prison again for assault, having served a suspension from boxing for the infamous ear-biting incident with Evander Holyfield. Another spell in prison after a road rage incident looked to be the end for Tyson, but, despite being banned in some states, he continued to fight and, even in an obvious state of decay, remained the biggest draw in heavyweight boxing.

The power of Hoberman's argument is not so much in its dismantling of the myth of athletic prowess, which has been done before, nor in discerning the racist implications of exalting black athletic accomplishments; but in analyzing the ways in which cost of black success, whether in sports or entertainment, far outweighs its benefits. Back in 1997, I was spending a sabbatical at the University of Massachusetts, Boston, when Tiger Woods became the first black player to win the US Masters. As a Fellow of the William Monroe Trotter Institute, I was in the company of several distinguished African American scholars, many of whom greeted Woods's success heartily. But, why? After all, how badly does black America need yet another sports champion? For Hoberman, this is not liberation, but entrapment.

Woods, no less than Joe Louis, Willie Mays, or Michael Jordan, was a symbol of black potential that has been continually adapted to changing circumstances. The media visibility of successful black sports stars discourages thinking about what black individuals have accomplished in areas such as education, politics, the professions; perhaps, more pertinently, what they have *not* accomplished in these areas.

There is a scene in the movie *Hoop Dreams*, in which a basketball coach addresses his protégés with some sobering statistics (directed by Steve James, Fred Marx, and Peter Gilbert, 1994). Each year, 500,000 boys play high school basketball, he tells them. Of the 14,000 who progress to intercollegiate basketball, fewer than 25 percent ever play one season in the NBA. Don't reach for your calculator: it works out at about 1:143. Some American writers, like Jack Olsen and Nathan Hare, have looked at the underside of this "shameful story" (as Olsen calls it) which begins with visions of wealth and glamor but frequently ends in poverty, crime, and, sometimes, insanity. Their conclusions concur with those of Hoberman in the sense that they believe that black youths are seduced into sport and, in the process, ignore their formal academic and vocational studies. They invest so much energy in sport that little is left for other pursuits. So, by the time dreams fade, they are left with few if any career alternatives and join the gallery of "also-rans."

Sports that attract black athletes are always expensive in terms of people: wasteful, profligate even. If it takes 143 ambitious kids to make one NBA player for one season, how many to produce a Jordan? Entering sports is less a career choice, more a lottery. As I noted earlier, the idea of recruiting bowlers from Yorkshire coalpits might have proved workable in the 1930s. Now, young white players are told to enjoy their cricket, but, first, get a degree and qualify as a lawyer or a doctor. The same piece of advice doesn't reach as far as inner London, or South Central LA.

There are always a small number of outstanding performers with naturally endowed faculties, but there's no reason to suppose that the black population has a monopoly or even a majority of them. Success in sport is due much more to non-physical qualities such as drive, determination, and an ability to focus sharply. Given that black workers see the job market as a maze of culs-de-sac, they may well accrue more than their fair share of these qualities. Failure has potentially direr consequences for them than for their white, working-class counterparts who, while still having limited opportunities, at least escape racialism.

Returning to *Hoop Dreams*, we hear the familiar cliché from one of the school players: "Basketball is my ticket out of the ghetto." One can almost hear a chorus of others saying the same thing. It is explosive motivational fuel. Add the "push" of outsiders, the magnetizing influence of black icons and you have a heady mixture – one which sends young black performers into sport year after year. If and when this slows, it's been suggested that this would reflect a quickening of the rate at which opportunities arise in the job market. In other words, if racialism disappeared completely there'd be only a few black sports stars. That is not the case at present and, while discrimination persists, sport is bound to prosper from the contributions of black athletes.

## THE REBECCA MYTH

When Minnesota Vikings failed narrowly to make it to Super Bowl in the 1999 NFC championship game against Atlanta Falcons, the club's head coach Dennis Green missed out in his attempt to become the first African American coach to take his team to American football's ultimate prize. Despite the high percentage of black players, Green was one of a tiny number of African Americans who successfully transferred to senior coaching positions. Since 1999, several black coaches, including head coaches, have made an impact, though still nothing like the impact made by black players.

This situation proved so embarrassing for the NFL that, in 1998, the governing organization hired a recruitment agency to stage and video interviews with other black coaches and aspiring coaches and distribute the tapes around the league. This was part of an effort to raise club owners' awareness of the abilities of black coaches and stimulate more enlightened hiring policies. Players like Doug Williams and, later, Warren Moon helped destroy the fiction that black football players did not have the intelligence to play quarterback, so needed to be "stacked" in other positions. The success of people like Green, Tony Dungy, Ray Rhodes, and others, may have helped dispel the similar fiction that existed about black coaches.

We know about the "before" part of the black experience in sports, how and why athletes make it to the pros, or fail in the process. The "during" phase can be read about in the sports pages of any newspaper. But, what happens "after"? Green *et al.* are exceptions. More usual are rags-to-riches and back-to-rags stories. Boxers especially have a knack of earning and blowing fortunes: Razor Ruddock was one of many millionaires-cum-bankrupts when he was declared financially insolvent in 1995. Others go on to become sportcasters, movie stars, and all-round media personalities; the most successful of these combined all three and became the most famous black sports star ever – but for the wrong reasons, of course. I mean O.J. Simpson.

Considering the heavy investment of black people in the playing side of sport, one might expect many to stay in sport and serve in officiating or administrative capacities. Here, there is an unevenness. Although there has been a steadily growing number of black game officials since 1965 (when Burt Tolar became the NFL's first black official), the number of black coaches and administrators has been few. Green was the first African American head football coach when he joined Northwestern University in 1981. Art Shell was the first black NFL coach when he joined Los Angeles Raiders in 1989. In Britain, Viv Anderson successfully transited from playing to managing, first at Barnsley, then as assistant manager at Middlesbrough. Black people are certainly appearing in the front offices, but not in the numbers one might expect from a glance at the number of active players.

One of the main reasons why owners and general managers have failed to appoint more black people is highlighted by Douglas Putnam, in his book *Controversies of the Sports World*: "Team owners and general managers, as businesspeople, prefer to hire candidates who are similar to coaches who have already achieved success or are similar to coaches they have known personally and admired" (1999: 27). If so, they might think in terms of a Parcells, a Jackson, or, in Britain, a Ferguson. "Consequently," writes Putnam, they "often pass over qualified blacks and hire whites with whom they are familiar . . . and to conform to their long-held ideal about what a successful coach should be" (1999: 27).

This is sport's equivalent of what the sociologist Alvin Gouldner once called the "Rebecca Myth," after Daphne du Maurier's famous novel. In the book *Rebecca* and Alfred Hitchcock's 1940 film of the same name, a young woman marries an English aristocrat, but, after moving into his mansion, meets an unfriendly housekeeper, Mrs. Danvers, who idolizes the late mistress of the mansion, Rebecca. Entranced by the thought of the dead Rebecca, Mrs. Danvers makes her new mistress's life a misery. In his *Wildcat Strike: A study in worker–management relations*, Goulder transposes this theme to an industrial setting and shows how the succession of personnel in senior positions can be impeded by the expectations of colleagues. "The successor may fail to show the old lieutenants proper deference, willfully or through ignorance of their expectations, but in either event making them dissatisfied," writes Goulder (1965: 158). They resist the new boss as a "legitimate heir" to the position once held by someone they knew and trusted and withhold legitimacy unless he conforms to their ideal (Goulder's study was an all-male affair).

The Rebecca Myth has obvious applications to players' responses to a newly appointed coach or manager, but it also helps clarify why owners and chairs fail to hire more black staff in senior positions: because they have what Putnam calls a "subliminal perception." Consciously or unconsciously, they desire to appoint someone who resembles a past manager/coach, who has brought success to their organization. And the historical chances are that this person will be white. This creates special difficulties for aspiring managers/coaches from ethnic minorities who need to convince prospective employers of their capabilities, but may also need their approval as someone who resembles a successful predecessor.

In his *Offside Racism: Playing the white man*, Colin King uses a similar approach to explain the paucity of black managers, coaches, or administrators in British soccer. Black ex-players wishing to make the transition are forced to perform to standards, that is "play the white man," in order to gain admission (2004).

Interestingly, there are (literally) one or two African Americans who have bypassed the salaried positions and headed straight for the seats of power. Beginning as a boxing promoter in the 1970s, Don King became one of the most powerful figures in sport: a man at the center of an extensive web of business interests stretching over a range of sports and sports-related areas. Peter Bynoe and Bertram Lee aspired to King-like powers in 1989 when they bought the Denver Nuggets of the NBA for $50 million (£31 million); they were the first African American owners of a major sports club. The deal went sour when Lee had cashflow problems and was made to sell his share. Bynoe also sold out in 1992, leaving the sports without a black owner. It took until 2002 before an African American became the owner of major league franchise. Robert Johnson, the publishing billionaire, opened up the NBA expansion franchise, Charlotte Bobcats.

---

### Don King

The world's leading sports promoter has summed up his own rise thus: "I was an ex-numbers runner, ex-convict who received a full, unconditional pardon. I am, what they would say in America, what everyone's supposed to be – when coming from the wrong side of the track to the right side of the track" (quoted in Regen 1990: 115). After serving a prison sentence for manslaughter, King's first promotional venture was in 1972 when he staged an exhibition by Muhammad Ali in an African Americans' hospital in Cleveland. His first major promotion in 1974 (when aged 43), also featured Ali, when he regained the heavyweight title from George Foreman in Zaire. After this, King kept an interest in the heavyweight championship, either by promoting bouts or managing the champions. Mike Tyson left his manager Bill Cayton and entered into a business relationship with King. Tyson refused to criticize King, even when many of his boxers, like ex-champion Tim Witherspoon, turned against him. King has also co-promoted rock stars, such as Michael Jackson, and began his own ppv tv system, KingVision. His biggest promotion never materialized: Tyson's conviction and imprisonment for rape meant that a fight with Evander Holyfield (originally scheduled for November 8, 1991) fell through. It was expected to gross more than $100 million (£62 million), with the ppv operation alone drawing $80 million, foreign sales $10 million, and the promotional fee from Caesar's Palace $11 million. Former heavyweight champion Larry Holmes once said of King: "He looks black, lives white and thinks green." See Jack Newfield's *Only in America: The life and crimes of Don King* (1995).

---

Vince Payne was the first African American president of a major league club when he took over at the Milwaukee Brewers. Bill Duffy is a bigtime sports agent in the USA. These are success stories and, while there are only a few of them, there will be more in the years to come. Hoberman would be ambivalent about this: good news – black people breaking ground by demonstrating intellectual abilities; bad news – they stay in sports. However many success stories emerge about black individuals in sport, whether on the field or in the front office, they should not disguise the practices and processes which effectively produce the black sports star, who is both a champion and loser. From the 1770s to the present, sport has been a route to fame and material fortune for thousands of black youths and will continue to be that in the future. For tens of thousands of others it will be only a route to nowhere.

Sport conceals deep inequalities and, for all the positive benefits it yields, it remains a source of hope and ambition for black people only as long as those inequalities remain. Sports coopt black people into the racist belief that they do have some natural aptitude for sports, while convincing white people that the success of a few counts as proof that they are right. But perhaps sports' vilest function is in persuading the white population that, as long as blacks continue to succeed athletically, the American dream is still alive, and race poses no barrier to achievement.

**OF RELATED INTEREST**

*A Hard Road to Glory: A history of the African-American Athlete 1619–1918 Vol 1; 1919–1945 Vol 2; Since 1946 Vol 3*, by Arthur R. Ashe (Amistad Warner, 1993) is a three-volume history of the participation of African Americans in sports. Ashe himself, during and after his tennis career, was a constant advocate of academic study over sports and spoke publicly on the need for black children to temper their sports ambitions.

*Darwin's Athletes: How sport has damaged black America and preserved the myth of race* by John Hoberman (Houghton Mifflin, 1997) includes the insight that both black and white communities have bought into the "myth" and how identifying with black sporting success has made black professional achievement "a seldom-noticed sideshow to more dramatic media coverage of celebrities and deviants." Also worth reading in this context: Marek Kohn's "Can white men jump?" which is chapter 4 of his book *The Race Gallery* (Vintage, 1996). And, for contrast, Jon Entine's *Taboo: Why black athletes dominate and why we're afraid to talk about it* (Public Affairs, 2000).

*Glory Bound: Black athletes in a white America* by David K. Wiggins (Syracuse University Press, 1997) critically examines the achievements of black Americans in sport against a historical background of racism and segregation.

*In Black and White: The untold story of Joe Louis and Jesse Owens* by Donald McRae (Scribner, 2003) is the book cited in the text and, as the title suggests, narrates the experiences of two prominent African American champions in the midst of segregated America.

## ASSIGNMENT

In 1947, psychologists Kenneth and Mamie Clark conducted a famous experiment: they asked 253 black children to choose between four dolls, two black and two white. The result: two-thirds of the children preferred white dolls. Conclusion: that black children had internalized the hatred society directed at all black people and so suffered from poor self-esteem. But this was before the rise of so many African American and African Caribbean sports icons. Imaginatively repeat the experiment using a smaller sample of children, but use dolls in the likeness of famous sports stars: two black and two white. Document the results and draw out the implications, taking note of major social changes over the past 50 years.

# champs and cheats

## why attempts to eliminate drugs might prove futile

### AS OLD AS SPORT ITSELF

Which name will be best remembered from 2004's sporting calendar? Dave Andreychuk? The 40-year-old captain of Stanley Cup winners Tampa Bay Lightning, which triumphed over Calgary Flames in the seventh and deciding game of the NHL playoffs, gained his first major trophy in 22 years as a pro. Angelos Charisteas whose goal gave 80 to 1 outsiders Greece a fairytale victory in the European soccer championships? Maria Sharapova, Wayne Rooney, or Michelle Wie, the teenagers who emerged as worldbeaters. Lance Armstrong, who won his sixth straight Tour de France and, in so doing, established the nearest thing to an unbreakable record in sports? Yang Tae-young, the South Korean gymnast who lost the all-round title to the USA's Paul Hamm at the Athens Olympics due to a scoring error?

Or Balco? It's not the name of an athlete, a racehorse, or a Latvian soccer club, but a company: it stands for Bay Area Laboratory Cooperative and it specialized in producing dietary supplements that, when taken as part of a nutrition program, helped athletes build muscle, endurance, and speed and helped recovery. Why is Balco so important? Because, according to its proprietors, it supplied its products to several of the world's leading athletes, including NFL and Major League Baseball players as well as track and field athletes – not just any old track and field athletes, but Olympic stars, including the much-garlanded Marion Jones and world 100-meter record-holder Tim Montgomery. Not forgetting Kelli White, who was banned from competition for two years after admitting she'd used undetectable performance-enhancing substances.

Balco, which had operated since 1984, claimed its formulations had been used extensively by clients from around the world. Some of the products were acceptable to governing organizations. Others were either on the banned list or were related closely to substances on the list. The implications were potentially immense: if many of the athletes we had admired and respected for their achievements were boosting their performances with supplements that had escaped detection, how many more were there out there? How many world records, Olympic golds, baseball championships, boxing titles, football trophies, or other major prizes were won with a little assistance?

Contemporary sports have taken on a Manichean character in which good coexists with evil: the evil is represented by the spread of doping among athletes willing to risk chemical side effects, or even direct effects, in the attempt to build muscle, steady the hand, flush out body fluids, speed up the metabolism, improve endurance, or spark more aggression. There are substances available that can assist in all these, but woe for any athlete caught taking them. Before addressing the issues of today, let's trace the history of drug use in sports. It's a common mistake to assume that doping in sport is a recent innovation: it's been around for as long as sport has.

## Balco

The company was started in 1994 by Victor Conte, a one-time musician turned entrepreneur, who developed a legal dietary supplement called ZMA (zinc, magnesium, aspartate) that purported to build muscle and accelerate recovery after exercise. The product was used by several athletes and approved of by coaches, including the Ukranian veteran Remi Korchemny. Conte formed the ZMA Track Club. Among the athletes who used Balco products were Barry Bonds, Bill Romanowski, Marion Jones, and Dwain Chambers. In 2003, an informant anonymously sent a syringe with residual amounts of a substance known as "the clear" to the United States Anti-Doping Agency (USADA) in Colorado, naming Balco as the source. The substance was the hitherto unknown THG. Traces were discovered in one of Chambers's urine samples and he was subsequently banned. In the same year, a federal grand jury initiated investigations into Balco for tax evasion, money laundering, and illegal distribution of controlled substances. In February 2004, the US Attorney General announced a 42-count indictment against Conte, Korchemny, Greg Anderson, a trainer, and James Valente, a Balco director. The USADA notified several US athletes, who had not failed drug tests, that they were either being investigated or charged with dope violations.

Taking supplements as a way of improving physical or mental performance in sports is arguably as old as sports themselves. Competitors in the ancient Greco-Roman games were known to eat animals' parts, such as horns or the secretions of testes, which they thought would confer the strength of bulls, for example. It's probable that Greeks habitually used plants and mushrooms with chemically active derivatives either to aid performance or accelerate the healing process.

In the modern era, as sports became professionalized, evidence of the systematic use of stimulants arrived initially through the six-day cycle races in Europe. Riders in the late nineteenth century favored ether and caffeine to delay the onset of fatigue sensations. Sprint cyclists preferred nitroglycerine, a violently explosive chemical later used in conjunction with heroin, cocaine, strychnine, and others. In his *Journal of Sport History* article, "Anabolic steroids: The gremlins of sport," Terry Todd records "the first known drug related death of an athlete" after a cyclist had taken a "speed ball" of heroin and cocaine (1987b: 91).

"The most famous early case of drug enhancement, however, occurred in the 1904 Olympic Games in St. Louis," writes Todd. (Actually, Arthur Linton, a cyclist, had collapsed and died earlier in 1886 after taking stimulants.) Marathon winner Thomas Hicks, of the USA, collapsed after the race. "Hicks' handlers, who had been allowed to accompany him throughout the course of the race in a motor car, admitted they had given him repeated doses of strychnine and brandy to keep him on his feet" (1987b: 91). Hicks was allowed to keep his medal. (While known principally as a poison, the vegetable alkaloid strychnine was also used as a stimulant.)

There's irony in the fact that sports medicine's role in contemporary sports was given impetus by the efforts of sports federations to eliminate the use of the very products that medicine gave to sports. This is the conclusion of Ivan Waddington, whose article "The development of sports medicine" (1996) shows clearly that medicine was originally invoked by sports to help improve performance. It did so, of course. Medicine's largess included pharmaceuticals, many to treat sports-related injuries, but many others to promote competitive performance. In the 1950s, colleges in Germany and the United States were established to exploit the applications of medicine to sports.

*The Male Hormone*, a book by Paul de Kruiff, which was published in 1945, covered research into the impact of testosterone on the endurance of men involved in muscular work; and this alerted some coaches to the potential of what was supposed to be a medically prescribed treatment. After returning from the 1952 Olympics convinced that the successful Soviet weightlifting team had used "hormone stuff," US coach Bob Hoffman sought something similar for his own squad. The product he obtained was Dianabol, an anabolic steroid first produced by the CIBA company in 1958 and intended for patients suffering from burns. The gains in weight and strength were impressive enough to convince him and observers of the value of medical science in sports. During the 1950s and 1960s, there were no rules forbidding the use of pharmaceuticals and, as news of Dianabol circulated in the sports world, strength-reliant performers, like field-eventers and football players, started using steroids. Other sports were not slow to realize the importance of testosterone and, through the 1960s, it was commonplace for cyclists, skiers, and an assortment of other athletes to use the substance.

---

### Testosterone

From *testis* + *o* + *sterol* + *one*, this is a steroid androgen formed in the testes. The basic function of testosterone is to control the natural production of sperm cells and this, in turn, affects the male's masculine appearance. A feedback control system is at work involving the hypothalamus; this secretes a hormone called LHR which stimulates the pituitary gland to secrete luteinizing hormone (LH) and this, in turn, stimulates the testes to produce the testosterone. A high concentration of testosterone inhibits the secretion of LHR by the hypothalamus, which causes a drop in the level of testosterone, triggering the hypothalamus to release more LHR, LH, and ultimately testosterone in a smoothly regulated system.

---

If there was a turning point in attitudes toward the use of drugs in sport, it was on July 13, 1967, when Tommy Simpson, then 29, collapsed and died on the 13th stage of the three-week long Tour de France. Simpson, a British rider, was lying seventh overall when the race set off from Marseilles. The temperature was well over 40°C (105°F). Simpson fell and remounted twice before falling for the final time. Three tubes were found in his pocket, one full of amphetamines, and two empties. The British team's luggage was searched and more supplies of the pills were found. At the time, the drugs element did not cause the sensation that might be expected today: the death itself was of most concern. In continental Europe, there was substantial and open advocacy of the use of such pills to alleviate the strain of long-distance cycling. There is little doubt that many of the leading contenders in the 1967 and other tours were taking amphetamines. Seven years before, in a less publicized tragedy, another cyclist, Knut Jensen, collapsed during his race and later died in hospital where amphetamine was found in his system. (His was the second Olympic death after Portuguese marathon runner Francisco Lazaro died from heatstroke in 1912.)

An attempt in the previous year to introduce drug testing was opposed by leading cyclists, including the five-times Tour winner Jacques Anquetil, who told the newspaper *France-Dimanche*: "Yes, I dope myself. You would be a fool to imagine that a professional cyclist who ride 235 days a year in all temperatures and conditions can hold up without a stimulant." Interestingly, Simpson was not denounced as a cheat at the time; his death opened up a rather different discourse about the perils of drug taking rather than the morality of it.

The International Olympic Committee (IOC) had actually set up a Medical Commission in 1950, mainly to investigate the medical effects of the use of stimulants, especially amphetamines, to increase endurance. Simpson's death prompted the introduction of testing, which came into being at the 1968 winter Olympics, though it was, as Barrie Houlihan calls it, a "modest effort" and largely for research purposes (1997: 180). Todd cites an American decathlete at the Mexico Olympic Games of 1968, who estimated a third of the US track and field team used steroids at training camp (1987b: 95). Writer Jack Scott (1971) reported that drugs were circulated quite freely at Mexico and conversations revolved not around the morality of taking them, but which ones were most effective.

The games themselves were memorable, with some athletes collapsing with exhaustion in the rarified atmosphere and others producing extraordinary performances. In particular, Bob Beamon improved the world's long jump record by 21.75 inches with a leap of 29ft 2.5in (8.90 m). In the previous 33 years, the record had progressed by only 8.5 inches; it took a further 23 years before Mike Powell broke Beamon's record.

Beginning in 1960, East Germany had operated a systematic program of inducting about 10,000 young people into sports academies where they were trained, conditioned, and supplied with pharmaceuticals intended to improve their athletic performance. State Program 1425, as it was known, was responsible for some of the world's outstanding track achievements, including Marita Koch's 47.60-second 400 meters record set in 1985 and rarely threatened ever since. After the end of the cold war, a special team of prosecutors began sifting through capture files of the Stasi secret police and uncovered details of often abusive treatment accorded young athletes. Offenders were later prosecuted.

Drug use in American sports was less systematic: stories of baseball and football players' use of amphetamines, narcotic analgesics, and other substances were escaping via books such as Scott's *The Athletic Revolution* and Paul Hoch's *Rip Off the Big Game* which concluded "that the biggest drug dealers in the sports world are none other than team trainers" (1972: 122). Ted Kotcheff's 1979 film *North Dallas Forty*, which was based on Pete Gent's account of pro football, showed football players trotting onto the field as near-zombies after taking copious amounts of painkillers and sundry other drugs.

Coaches were doling out amphetamines to pep players up and analgesics to help them play without the sensation of pain while carrying injuries before a game. After a game the players were, as Hoch puts it, "tranquilized to get their eyeballs back in their head – to even get a night's sleep" (1972: 123). Hoch cites two players who filed lawsuits against their clubs for administering drugs "deceptively and without consent" and which eventually proved detrimental to their health (1972: 123).

Estimates about the amount of drug use are so vague as to be useless, but it is at least suggestive that, in 1983, a *Sports Illustrated* (May 13) article stated that between 40 and 90 percent of NFL players used anabolic steroids. Several deaths were attributed to steroids in the years that followed. In 1987, the IOC recorded 521 positive tests for steroid use; this was 16 years after the introduction of anti-drug legislation by the International Association of Athletics Federations (IAAF). Anabolic steroids weren't added to the IAAF's banned list until 1976; the organization didn't have a reliable test until 1974, anyway.

Recreational drug use was also widespread among athletes. In his 1986 book *Fractured Focus*, Richard Lapchick referred to an "epidemic in American sport" and highlighted several athletes who were either in prison or fighting additions. The NBA, in particular, was infamous for the number of cocaine-using players and, as we'll see in Chapter 15, improved its marketability only after introducing drugs testing. A succession of boxers, football players, and other athletes were penalized for cocaine use. While cocaine use was probably recreational rather than performance enhancing, the term "drugs" was used indiscriminately. Using such an emotive word had the effect of heightening the feeling that sports were adrift in a moral sea with no terra firma in sight.

Unquestionably, the case that converted concern over drug use in sports from concern to hysteria was the ejection of Canadian sprinter Ben Johnson from the 1988 Seoul Olympics after he had won the 100 meters in a world record 9.79 seconds. Stanozolol, an anabolic steroid, was detected in Johnson's urine sample; he was stripped of his gold medal and his time expunged from the records. Overnight, Johnson went from the "world's fastest man" to the "world's fastest cheat." While he was the thirty-first competitor to be disqualified for drug use since the IOC instituted its systematic testing in 1972, Johnson's stature in world sport ensured that his case would make news everywhere and that he as an individual would carry the sins of all. As well as his medal and record, he instantly lost (at the most conservative estimate) $2 million in performance-related product endorsement fees.

Fifteen years later, it was revealed that Carl Lewis, who was awarded the gold, had tested positive for three stimulants, including ephedrine – two months before the 1988 Olympics, but was allowed to compete after the United States Olympic Committee (USOC) accepted his appeal that he was unaware of the contents of a herbal supplement he'd used. Of the other sprinters in the fateful race, third-placed Linford Christie was banned for two years in 2000 after a positive dope test, fifth-placed Dennis Mitchell was banned for two years after testing positive in 1999, and sixth-placed Desai Williams was implicated in the

Dubin inquiry into the use of banned substances by Canadian athletes. In retrospect, Johnson appears a convenient scapegoat.

Following the Johnson case, the use of drugs to improve athletic performance was universally condemned by sporting authorities. Lists of prohibited substances lengthened so that many prescription drugs and perfectly legal products that could be purchased at drug stores were banned. Alexander Watson, an Australian pentathlete was disqualified from the same Olympics as Johnson, for having an excessive level of caffeine in his system; to have reached such a level he would have needed to have drunk 40 regular-sized cups of coffee.

---

**Dubin inquiry**

This was the official inquiry headed by Charles Dubin set up following Ben Johnson's ejection from the 1988 Olympics. Among the inquiry's conclusions was the fact that there was a conspiracy of silence among athletes, coaches, and physicians. Dr. Jamie Astaphan, Johnson's physician, referred to "the brotherhood of the needle." Dr. Robert Kerr, author of *The Practical Use of Anabolic Steroids with Athletes* (1982), testified that he had prescribed anabolic steroids to about 20 medalists at the 1984 summer Olympics. At the hearings, IOC vice-president Richard Pound famously answered the question why, with rumors abounding, he did not ask Johnson if he took drugs: "As a lawyer, I felt I was better off not knowing" (Houlihan, 1997: 194–5).

---

The expulsion of Argentinian player Diego Maradona from the 1994 soccer World Cup was the biggest "bust" since Johnson. He'd tested positive before in 1991 (and, would again fail drug tests in 1997 and 2000). Maradona all but had his cleats exchanged for cloven hooves during a media demonization. Like Johnson, he was an exceptional athlete, a world-class performer who had, in the eyes of the world, resorted to cheating. But, there was a suspicion that, in another sense, he was not exceptional at all; he was simply one of countless others who systematically used substances to enhance their performance. They probably escaped detection through a variety of methods, such as coming off the drugs early, taking masking agents, or catheterizing (replacing the contents of one's own bladder with someone else's drug-free urine).

The Tour de France of 1998 disintegrated into chaos after the disqualification of one team, police raids on the hotels of several teams, and a go-slow protest by riders at the 17th stage. The expulsion of the entire Festina Watches team was unprecedented in the race's 95-year history. All nine Festina riders were taken into police custody, along with three more team directors. The specific charge against the masseur was for smuggling drugs, including anabolic steroids and erythropoietin (EPO). Four people connected with a second squad, TVM, were also questioned over a seizure of banned substances.

The Festina manager, Bruno Rousel, told a police inquiry of "the conditions under which a co-ordinated supply of doping products was made available to the riders, organized by the team management, the doctors, the masseurs and the riders. The aim was to maximize performance under strict medical control to avoid the riders obtaining drugs for themselves in circumstances which might have been seriously damaging to their health." Rousel reported that the drug war chest amounted to £40,000 ($65,000) per year, or 1 percent of the team's £4 million annual budget.

Rider Frederic Pontier confessed to the French sports daily newspaper *L'Equipe* that he had used EPO and knew that an "important number" of other cyclists were also using performance enhancers. Police sweeps resulted in a number of other riders and officials being held for questioning. The crisis deepened when competitors sensed they were being, as rider Jeroen Blijlevens put it, "treated like animals, like criminals." Their snail's pace demonstration forced organizers to annul the Albertville to Aix-les-Bains stage of the race.

By the time of the Tour de France scandal, drugs-testing procedures were in place in all major sports and each had policies, most derived from the IOC's. The list of proscribed substances had lengthened to the point where athletes

---

### Massacre à la Chaîne: Révélations sur 30 ans de tricheries

This was the title of a book written by Willy Voet, the Belgian trainer of the Festina team that was disqualified from the 1998 Tour de France. Voet was stopped by French customs on his way to Dublin, the starting point of the race. It was alleged that the French government had been determined to create a test case and had been watching Voet for months. In his book, which became a best-seller in France, Voet argued that 90 percent of professional cyclists regularly take banned substances, not simply to enhance their racing performance, but to assist their recovery from perhaps the world's most grueling competition. He named over 100 athletes. Riders are obliged to fulfill excessively demanding commitments agreed by their teams in conjunction with sponsors and television. The publication of the English translation of the book, *Breaking the Chain: How drugs destroyed a sport* by Yellow Jersey Press, was held up by the criminal trial in France involving rider Richard Virenque, who denied allegations about him made in the book.

needed to be careful about reading the labels on over-the-counter headache or cold remedies in case they contained a banned constituent.

But anyone who thought the scandalous tour of 1998 would sound out a warning around the world and effectively put a stop to doping in sport was being naive. The positive tests kept coming – and from all sources.

# BANNED SUBSTANCES

The IOC's banned list includes over 4,000 substances, which are grouped into five categories. They are anabolic steroids, stimulants, narcotic analgesics, beta-blockers, and diuretics. I'll deal with them in that order, before moving to an examination of blood doping, peptide hormones, and procedures for detecting substances in sports performers.

*Anabolic steroids* In 1889, Charles Brown-Sequard devised a rejuvenating therapy for body and mind: the 72-year-old French physiologist had claimed he had increased his physical strength, improved his intellectual energy, relieved his constipation, and even lengthened the arc of his urine by injecting himself with an extract derived from the testes of dogs and guinea pigs. His discovery triggered a series of experiments that led to synthesis of testosterone, the primary male hormone produced in the testes, in 1935. The German military was impressed enough to feed it to soldiers in an effort to increase their strength and intensify their aggression. Since then, synthetic testosterone has been attributed with almost magical qualities and become the most controversial drug in sports. For this reason, it is worth reviewing its history.

There's nothing new about the concept of ingesting animals' sexual organs and secretions: Egyptians accorded medicinal powers to the testes; Johannes Mesue prescribed a kind of testicular extract as an aphrodisiac; the *Pharmacopoea Wirtenbergica*, a compendium of remedies published in 1754 in Germany, refers to horse testicles and the penises of amphibious mammals, like walruses and manatee. These and several other examples are given by John Hoberman and Charles Yesalis, whose *Scientific American* article (1995) on the subject is essential reading for students of the history of performance-enhancing drugs.

In 1896, an Austrian physiologist and future Nobel Prize winner, Oskar Zoth, published a paper, which concluded that extracts from bulls' testes, when injected in athletes, led to improvements in muscular strength and the "neuro-muscular apparatus." Here was the first official recognition of the significance of hormonal substances for sports performers. Zoth anticipated the objection that a placebo effect might have accounted for the change in his sample of athletes and denied it. Around the same time, other scientists were excited by

---

## Placebo

From the Latin *placere*, to please, this is a pharmacologically inert substance given to patients usually to humor them rather than effect any cure. Yet the substance often works as effectively (if not more so) as an active substance because the patient believes it will. The substance is called a placebo and its result is known as the placebo effect. This has many applications outside the clinical setting. Weightlifters have been told they were receiving an anabolic steroid while, in fact, only some of them received it – the others were given a placebo. Both groups improved leg presses, the first group by 135 lb, the other (receiving the placebo) by 132 lb. The sheer expectation of benefit seems to have been the crucial factor. A similar process can work in reverse. For example, subjects might be given active drugs together with information that they will have no effect: consequently the drugs might not have any effect. In other words, the direct effect of drugs alone might not be any more powerful than the administrator's or experimenter's suggestions alone. More recently, research has shown that high doses of testosterone given to healthy young men can increase muscle size but not necessarily strength. Increases in strength might come about as a result of the extra hard training the subjects were encouraged to do by taking the substance.

---

the prospect of finding the active ingredient in the male sex organ and specifying its effects.

Clinical applications were many. In 1916, two Philadelphia doctors transplanted a human testicle into a patient who was suffering from sexual dysfunctions, starting a spate of similar transplants, the most audacious being a mass removal of the testes of recently executed inmates for transplanting into patients suffering from impotence. Pharmaceutical corporations spotted the commercial potential and initiated research programs to isolate the active hormone and synthesize it. By 1939, clinical trials in humans were underway, employing injections of testosterone propionate. Early synthetic testosterone was used with some success by women suffering from a variety of complaints, the intention being to alter a female's hormonal balance. One of the problems was that the testosterone virilized the patients: they took on male secondary features, like facial hair and enlarged larynx.

From the 1940s male sex hormones (androgens) were used to treat wasting conditions associated with chronic debilitating illnesses and trauma, burns, surgery, and radiation therapy. Anabolic steroids' efficacy in accelerating red blood cell production made it first choice therapy for a variety of anemias (having too little hemoglobin) before bone marrow transplants and other treatments arrived. Between the 1930s and the mid-1980s, psychiatrists prescribed anabolic steroids for the treatment of depression and psychoses. Most recently, steroids have been used to arrest the muscle wasting that occurs during the progression of HIV infection and Aids. Testosterone treatment is currently in use for strengthening older bodies, rejuvenating an ailing libido, and improving a declining memory.

Steroids weren't considered a problem at all for sports until the late 1970s. After the 1988 Johnson case, they became high priority. German sprinters Katrin Krabbe, Silke Möller, and Grit Breuer submitted identical urine samples in out-of-competition tests prior to the 1992 Barcelona games, but escaped a ban on a technicality. The case served notice that the drugs issue would remain on the agenda at all future games.

Today, few people doubt the efficacy of anabolic steroids: they do work. Precisely what makes them work, we still don't know for sure. There is, for instance, a school of thought that argues that the critical component in the equation is our belief that they will enhance our performance. If, for some reason, we stopped believing in them, then maybe anabolic steroids wouldn't yield the results they apparently do. At present, so much money is spent on testing for drugs that there is little left for ascertaining exactly what they do to sports performers. If self-belief is the single most important factor, it might be that a placebo is at work. (For a fuller discussion of the purported effects of anabolic steroids, see Yesalis 1993.)

Not all products specifically developed to enhance athletic performance are condemned – at least not universally condemned. For example, creatine was sold legally and endorsed by sports performers and became popular as a result of its supposed muscle-building properties. Androstenedione, another product available over the counter at any health food store, was used by Mark McGwire during his history-making 1998 season. "Andro," to use its more popular abbreviation, had effects that many swore were identical to those of hormones: it stimulated the increased production of testosterone, but didn't appear on Major League Baseball's banned list. On the other hand, Randy Barnes, the 1966 Olympic shot put champion, was suspended for two years after andro was found in his sample – his second drugs test in eight years. The rights and wrongs of andro were discussed, but technically it was recognized as a food rather than a drug and McGwire, while criticized by some, used it with impunity.

Tetrahydrogestrinone (THG), on the other hand, landed its users in serious trouble. Developed by the previously mentioned Balco, the "designer drug" was detected in the sample of British sprinter Dwain Chambers, who was suspended as a result. He was also banned from Olympic competition. The unusual aspect of Chambers's ban was that it wasn't preceded by a regular test, but by an anonymous whistle-blower, who sent a syringe containing THG to the

US Anti-Doping Agency in June 2003. The dope testers had never seen and probably not heard of THG, but they identified it as related to banned steroids and tested urine samples retrospectively. This started the events that reverberated through every sport and caused observers to ponder: if THG was only stumbled across by accident, how many other substances with performance enhancing properties have escaped detection over the years?

---

### Anabolic steroids

From the Greek *ana*, meaning "up" and *bole* "throw," anabolism is the constructive metabolism of complex substances for body tissues, i.e. bodybuilding. Steroids are compounds whose molecules contain rings of carbon and hydrogen atoms; they influence cells by causing special proteins to be synthesized. So, an anabolic steroid is a compound considered to be responsible for the particular synthesis that causes the construction of muscle mass. The idea of using an anabolic steroid is to mirror the chemical action of the testosterone in the body and facilitate muscle growth.

---

*Stimulants* Evidence of the systematic application of stimulants arrived initially through the six-day cycle races in Europe. Riders in the late nineteenth century favored ether and caffeine to delay the onset of fatigue sensations. Sprint cyclists preferred nitroglycerine, a chemical later used in conjunction with heroin, cocaine, strychnine, and other substances.

The basic effect of stimulants is to get messages to a complex pathway of neurons in the brainstem called the arousal system, or reticular activating system (RAS). This system is ultimately responsible for maintaining consciousness and determining our state of awareness. So, if the RAS bombards the cerebral cortex with stimuli, we feel very alert and able to think clearly. Amphetamines are thought to cause chemical neurotransmitters, such as dopamine, to increase, so enhancing the flow of nervous impulses in the RAS and stimulating the entire CNS. The sympathetic nervous system is stimulated, speeding up heart rate, raising blood pressure, and dilating pupils. In sports terms, the performer is fired up and resistant to the sensation of fatigue, particularly the muscular pain associated with lactic acid.

One problem facing users active in sport who need nutrition for the release of energy is that amphetamines depress appetites. They used to be prescribed to dieters, though less so nowadays because dieters became dependent on the drug. This came about because the body quickly develops a tolerance, probably through the readiness of the liver to break down the drug rapidly. An obvious temptation is to increase the dose to achieve the same effect. So with increased use of the drug, the user becomes dependent. Weight loss and dependence are the more obvious side effects; others include irritability (probably due to irregular sleep) and even a tendency toward paranoia.

There is another class of stimulants called sympathomimetic amine drugs, such as ephedrine, or ephedra, which acts not on the brain but directly on the nerves affecting the organs. (This produces effects in the sympathetic part of the autonomic nervous system: it speeds up the action of the heart, constricts arteries, and increases lung inflation.) Ephedra was once commonly found in decongestants as well as over-the-counter dietary supplements with names like Ripped Fuel or BiLean. The US Food and Drug Administration accepted evidence that the ingredient raised blood pressure and could promote heart ailments and banned it from general use.

---

### Ephedra

In the early 1990s, ephedra, a herb with a long history of medicinal use to treat colds and respiratory ailments, and its main chemical component ephedrine gained widespread popularity as a dietary supplement to boost energy and promote weight loss. Reports of deaths attributed to ephedra raised concerns and prompted the IOC, NFL, and NCAA to ban its use. The ephedra-linked death of Baltimore Orioles pitcher Steve Bechler in February 2003 and the heatstroke death of Minnesota Vikings tackle Korey Stringer who was believed to have used an ephedra supplement, prompted the FDA to conclude that the sale of products containing ephedra posed "an unreasonable health risk" and instituted a ban on most products containing it (cold remedies that were labeled and were for short-term use were exempted).

---

*Narcotic analgesics* Painkillers are used in all walks of life, but especially in sports where injuries are commonplace and a tolerance to pain is essential. Soccer and American football are examples of games involving the "walking wounded." Derivatives of the opium poppy were probably used by ancient Mesopotamians around 3000 BCE; they left instructions for use on wax tablets.

There are now methods of producing such derivatives synthetically. Opium, heroin, codeine, and morphine, along with designer drugs, are all classified as narcotics, which relieve pain and depress the CNS, producing a state of stupor. Reflexes slow down, the skeleton is relaxed, and tension is reduced. The negative effects are much the same as those of amphetamines, with the additional one of specific neurons becoming dependent on the drug and so providing a basis for addiction.

The immediate effects of stimulants or narcotic analgesics would be of little or no service to sports performers who rely on fineness of judgment, sensitivity of touch, acuity of sight, and steadiness of hand. Success in sports like darts, archery, snooker, shooting, or show jumping is based on calmness and an imperviousness to "pressure." The Canadian snooker player Bill Werbeniuk was famed for his customary ten pints of beer to help him relax before a game. His CNS would become duller and tensions presumably disappeared. How he managed to coordinate hand and eye movements, stay awake, or even just stay upright is a mystery. Alcohol has serious drawbacks, which include nausea and impaired judgment, not to mention liver damage and a variety of dependency-related problems.

*Beta-blockers* The Vancouver-based Werbeniuk switched to Inderal, a beta-blocker that helped counteract the effects of a hereditary nervous disorder. After criticism from the British Minister for Sport, the World Professional Billiards and Snooker Association (WPBSA) reviewed its drug policy and included Inderal on its list of banned substances. Unable to find an alternative, Werbeniuk admitted to the WPBSA that he intended to continue using the drug and was eventually banned from tournaments.

Originally used by patients with irregular heartbeats, beta-blockers relieve anxiety by controlling the release of adrenaline and by lowering the heart rate; they are used by edgy showbusiness performers – and horses. In November 1994, a racehorse, Mobile Messenger, tested positive for propranolol, a beta-blocker, after winning a race at Southwell, England. The effect of the drug on the horse would have been similar to that on a human: to slow down the heart rate and thereby alleviate stress.

*Diuretics* Weightlifters and other sports performers who compete in categories based on body weight have to calibrate their diet and preparation carefully. A couple of pounds, even ounces, over the limit can destroy months of conditioning if the performer is made to take off the excess at the weigh-in. Jumping rope, saunas, and other methods of instant weight reduction can be debilitating and might drain cerebral fluid that cushions the brain against the wall of the cranium. Competitors in weight-controlled sports always check-weigh during the days preceding an event and, should their weight seem excessive, might take diuretics. These substances – widely used therapeutically for reducing fluid levels – excite the kidneys to produce more urea and, basically, speed up a perfectly natural waste disposal process. A visit to the bathroom is usually necessary after drinking alcoholic drinks or coffee; this is because they both contain diuretics.

Diuretics inhibit the secretion of the antidiuretic hormone which serves as a chemical messenger, carrying information from the pituitary gland at the base of the brain to parts of the kidneys, making them more permeable and allowing water to be reabsorbed into the body (thus conserving fluid). Hormones, of course, are carried in the blood. If the messages don't get through, the kidneys move the water out of the body. Continued use of diuretics can damage the kidneys. In recent years, the suspicion has grown that competitors have not only been using diuretics to reduce weight but also to flush out other substances, in particular the above-mentioned drugs.

It follows that competitors found to have diuretics in their urine immediately have their motives questioned. Kerrith Brown of Great Britain lost his Olympic bronze medal for judo despite pleading that the diuretic furosemide found in his urine was introduced into his system by a medical officer who gave him an anti-inflammatory substance containing the chemical to reduce a knee swelling.

*Peptide hormones* The values of altitude training are undoubted. In Chapter 3, we recognized the importance of the protein molecule hemoglobin, which is found in red blood cells. It has a remarkable ability to form loose associations with oxygen. As most oxygen in the blood is combined with hemoglobin rather than simply dissolved in plasma, the more hemoglobin present in a red blood cell, the more oxygen it can transport to the muscles. Obviously then, performers can benefit from having a plentiful supply of oxygen to react with glucose and release energy stored in food. The advantage of training at altitude, where the oxygen in the atmosphere is scarce, is that the body naturally compensates by producing more hemoglobin.

When the athlete descends to sea level, he or she carries a plentiful supply of hemoglobin in the blood, which gradually readjusts. Each day spent at lower altitudes diminishes the benefit of altitude training: a proliferation of hemoglobin ceases in the presence of available atmospheric oxygen. One way to "capture" the benefits is to remove a quantity of highly oxygenated blood during intense altitude training, store it, and reintroduce it into the circulatory system immediately prior to competition via a transfusion. This is known as blood doping and the IOC banned it in 1986.

The "doping" in this process doesn't refer to the administration of drugs but to the more correct use of the term, pertaining to a thick liquid used as a food or lubricant. There is, however, a synthetic drug that can achieve much the same effect. Erythropoietin (EPO) facilitates the production of extra red blood cells, which absorb oxygen, and leaves the user with no telltale needle tracks. As well as being more convenient than a transfusion, EPO has the advantage of being extremely difficult to detect once it has been administered. The biggest EPO case was uncovered when French police traced a delivery of EPO and some masking agents to a Paris address. Fifteen people including cyclists Frank Vandenbroucke and soccer player Jean-Christophe Devaux were arrested along with Lionel Virenque, brother of French cyclist Richard Virenque who was already under investigation for his alleged part in the Tour de France scandal of the previous year. In 2004, Philippe Gaumont admitted using and providing EPO to other riders, suggesting that this remained the drug of choice for professional cyclists. Cycling's governing organization *Union Cycliste Internationale* (UCI), employs a hemocrit test that measures the red blood cell ratio and is suggestive of the use of EPO. Riders who register a dangerously high ratio are suspended from racing for their own safety. Even a low count can be a problem if anomalies are discovered. For example, Gorka Gonzalez was declared unfit to ride shortly before the 2004 Tour: his hemocrit level was below the 50 percent set by the UCI, but the presence of reticulocytes – young blood cells – indicated doping.

In attempts to boost red cells, some athletes sleep in hypobaric chambers or use hypoxic machines that are designed to replicate high altitude atmospheres. Such devices are not prohibited by sports organizations, though the benefits accrued are much the same as if athletes had opted for illicit methods.

---

### Hypoxic

Hypoxic air contains 12–15 percent oxygen as opposed to sea level air, which contains about 21 percent. Athletes tend to use hypoxic facilities in two ways: sleeping in a confined unit – a hypobaric chamber or tent – in an atmosphere that simulates that at about 9,000 feet above sea level; or using a portable device intermittently, say, an hour a day, while awake. The expectation is that the body will respond by generating the production of red blood cells. Hypobaric chambers are also used for, among other things, preparing aircrews: atmospheres can be adjusted to simulate altitudes in excess of 100,000 feet.

---

Blood doping and EPO, in a sense, copy the body's natural processes and, at the moment, their long-term effects seem to be broadly the same as those of living at high altitudes. Another method of mimicking nature is by extracting the naturally occurring human growth hormone, somatotropin (hGH), which is produced and released by the pituitary gland, as discussed in Chapter 3. hGH controls the human rate of growth by regulating the amount of nutrients taken into the body's cells and by stimulating protein synthesis. Overproduction of the hormone might cause a child to grow to giant proportions (a condition referred to as gigantism), whereas too little can lead to dwarfism. hGH also affects fat and carbohydrate metabolism in adults, promoting a mobilization of fat, which becomes available for use as fuel, and sparing the utilization of protein. The potential of this mechanism for promoting growth has not been lost on field athletes, weightlifters, bodybuilders, and others requiring muscle build.

Illicit markets in growth hormone extracted from fetuses have been uncovered, though a synthetically manufactured version, somatonorm, has nearly made this redundant. In 1997, customs officers at Sydney, Australia, found 13 vials of Norditropin, the brand name of somatotropin, in a bag belonging to Yuan Yuan, a member of China's team in the World Swimming Championships. Yuan Yuan, at 21, was the youngest member of the team and ranked 13 in the world for the breaststroke. It was speculated that, as a relatively lowly member of the team, she was a guinea pig intended to ascertain whether hGH could be detected through conventional equipment.

This has led some to believe that drug users can always stay one step ahead of those wishing to identify them: the line between what is "natural" and "unnatural" for the human body is not so clear-cut as testers would like and science finds ways of replicating nature. By the end of the 1990s, substances such as insulin growth hormone (IGH) and perfluorocarbon (PFC), a type of highly oxygenated plasma, were impossible to detect through conventional methods. Others believe that drug-testing methods are keeping pace and not even the elite can escape detection, given a vigilant team of toxicologists and a sophisticated laboratory. But doubts remain.

## DOUBTS ABOUT TESTING

Hewlett-Packard, the multinational computer specialists, charged the IOC $3 million (£1.9 million) to set up the scientific testing equipment at the Korean Advanced Institute of Science and Technology in 1988. The system of gas chromatography and mass spectroscopy could, according to its makers, "detect concentrations [of banned substances] as low as one part per billion; roughly the equivalent to detecting traces from a teaspoonful of sugar after it has been dissolved in an Olympic swimming pool." A further claim was that it could check a compound found in urine against 70,000 held in a computer's database in "less than a minute." As new substances have been added to the banned list, so the equipment has been modified to detect them.

The entire testing process comprises four phases. (1) Within an hour of the finish of an event, two samples of a performer's urine are taken, one is tested for acidity and specific gravity so that testers can get a broad indication of any illegal compounds. (2) The sample is then split into smaller batches to test for certain classes of drugs, such as anabolic steroids, stimulants, etc. Testers make the urine alkaline and mix it with solvents, like ether, causing any drugs to dissolve into the solvent layer, which is more easily analyzed than urine itself. (3) This solvent is then passed through a tube (up to 25 meters long) of gas (or liquid chromatogram) and the molecules of the solvent separate and pass through at different rates, depending on their size and other properties (such as whether they are more likely to adhere to the material of the tube itself). More than 200 drugs are searched for in this period, which lasts about 15 minutes. (4) Any drugs found are then analyzed with a mass spectrometer, which bombards them with high-energy ions, or electrons, creating unique chemical fingerprints, which can be rapidly checked against the database. Should any banned substances show up, the second sample is tested in the presence of the performer. (Another method is radioimmunoassay, in which antibodies to known substances are used like keys that will only fit one lock; the lock is the banned substance which is found by the key that fits it.)

Encouraged by the Seoul experience, the IOC stated its intention to implement all-year-round testing and national sports organizations followed its example, though not without problems. By 1999, a catalog of cases involving athletes appealing their dope tests had accumulated. Among the most discussed was that of Harry "Butch" Reynolds who tested positive for the steroid nandrolone in 1991, was suspended by USA Track and Field (USATF) with the support of the IAAF. Reynolds challenged the decision all the way to the Supreme Court and was eventually awarded damages totaling $26 million (£16 million) and allowed to compete in the US Olympic trials.

Further doubts about the reliability of testing procedures were cast by the case of British runner Diane Modahl who was banned from competition for four years after failing a drug test at a meeting in Lisbon, Portugal, in 1994. The test was administered under the auspices of the Portuguese Athletics Federation. From the sample taken at the meet, Modahl's urine showed a testosterone to epitestosterone ratio (T–E ratio) reading of 42:1. Any ratio above 6:1 provides evidence of the presence of an excessive amount of testosterone and thus grounds for suspension. A reading of six times the permitted ratio suggested that Modahl had taken gross amounts of a prohibited substance – much more, in fact, than Ben Johnson had when he was banned after the Seoul Olympics in 1988.

After being banned, Modahl appealed to an independent panel constituted by the British Athletics Federation and an investigation opened up questions about the testing procedures followed. Lacking conclusive evidence, the panel determined that there was reasonable doubt over whether or not Modahl had taken proscribed substances. The British Athletics Federation (BAF) agreed, the International Association of Athletics Federations decided not to refer the case to an arbitration panel, and Modahl resumed her running career. Her ban lifted on appeal, Modahl sought up to $500,000 (£305,000) in damages from the BAF, which became bankrupt in 1997.

Further questions about the reliability of testing procedures were raised when German marathon runner Uta Pippig challenged the finding of her test by pointing out that she had recently stopped using oral birth control and this had affected her hormonal system; she also pointed out that each of her drug tests following her wins in the Boston marathon from 1994–6 came up clean. Mary Slaney used a similar defense, claiming that the abnormal T–E ratio in her sample might have been attributable to hormonal changes in women in their late thirties and early forties who were taking the pill. Slaney, who completed the 1,500 and 3,000 meters double at the 1983 World Championships, was 37 at the time of her test in 1996. After a three-year process, the IAAF arbitration panel discounted the claim.

Petr Korda escaped a one-year statutory ban from the International Tennis Federation (ITF) after testing positive for nandrolone by convincing the ITF independent appeals panel that he did not know how the substance found its way into his body. The ITF itself was not happy with the outcome, but was prevented by a London High Court ruling from appealing to the Court of Arbitration in Switzerland. Perhaps the most original appeal was that of American sprinter Dennis Mitchell, who claimed the high levels of testosterone found in his test sample in April 1998 were the result of having multiple bouts of sex and five bottles of beer the night before. Mitchell was suspended by the IAAF, but later cleared by the USATF drugs panel.

Tennis players Bohdan Ulihrach and Greg Rusedski were both cleared of drugs charges in 2003 and 2004 respectively after it was found that the Association of Tennis Professionals (ATP) through its trainers might have inadvertently caused as many as 30 players to have produced a unique ion chromatography pattern that appeared to suggest a doping offense under the ATP's own anti-doping rules. The Rusedski decision, coming so soon after the previously mentioned suspension of Dwain Chambers, threw up several doubts about the principle of strict liability, which the World Anti-Doping Agency maintains is central to a universally recognized policy. The principle places the complete onus of responsibility on the individual for any illicit substances found in a sample; the circumstances in which those substances were ingested (e.g. by accident; through a spiked drink) are irrelevant. The ATP decision destabilized this principle.

Efforts to stamp out drugs are obviously related to the degree of drug use in sport and, as I indicated earlier, there seems to have been a fairly sharp increase over the past 20 to 30 years. The reasons for that increase are to be found in cultural changes, as we'll see next.

> ## WADA (World Anti-Doping Agency)
>
> The 1998 Tour de France debacle underlined the inadequacy of governing organizations in controlling the use of dope: uncoordinated testing methods and different lists of prohibited substances rendered their efforts ineffective. This highlighted the need for an independent international agency, which would set unified standards for anti-doping work and coordinate the efforts of sports organizations and public authorities. The IOC took the initiative and convened the World Conference on Doping in Sport held in Lausanne in February 1999. Following the proposal of the conference, the World Anti-Doping Agency (WADA) was established. It was composed equally of representatives from the Olympic movement and governments and was divided into an 11-person executive committee and a 37-member foundation board. WADA received $25 million from the IOC for its first two years of operation. After 2001 when it moved its headquarters to Montreal, it was joint funded by the Olympic movement and national governments from around the world.

## DISCIPLINE AND CONTROL

Harsh denunciations of athletes found to be taking drugs began to appear from the 1980s. The deaths of Jensen and Simpson in the 1960s drew sympathetic responses quite unlike the treatment afforded Ben Johnson in 1988 or Dwain Chambers 15 years later. After the Johnson discovery, every competitor found guilty of doping violations was accused of cheating and incurred penalties, ranging from fines to life suspensions. Media opinion became unanimous: users were roundly condemned.

From the late 1980s, there was little disagreement over the use of performance-enhancing substances and recreational drugs in sports: it was wrong and should be eliminated. The position took acquired the status of an axiom – a principle that's so fundamental that it's self-evidently true. Statements such as "doping in sports is wrong" didn't invite argument; they seemed to state fact. Yet this did little to stem athletes' desire to gain a competitive edge through fair means or foul. Barely a week goes by without news of a positive dope test in some sport. To understand the censure that unerringly meets drug-using sports performers, we need to examine how the modern world has cultivated a wish for us to control ourselves.

The civilizing process, as Norbert Elias describes it, is a historical trend beginning in the Middle Ages (1300–1400) that has drawn us away from barbarism by bringing social pressures on people to exercise self-control (we covered Elias's theories in Chapter 5). At one level, this meant increasing our conscience as a means of regulating our behavior toward others. At another, it meant becoming enmeshed in a network of often subtle, invisible constraints that compelled us to lead ordered lives. One important result of this was the decrease in the use of direct force: violence was brought under control and the state became the only legitimate user of physical violence – outside of combat sports, of course (and these were subject to progressively strict regulation).

The civilizing process implicated humans in some form of control over their bodies. Elias focused mainly on the restraint in using physical violence, but notes the simultaneous trend for people to subdue bodily functions and control their physical being. The physical body became subordinated to the rational mind. While Elias did not discuss this, we might point to the literary fascination with the potential of science to complete this process. Mary Shelley's *Frankenstein* tells of a scientist obsessed by the possibility of reconstructing a total human being. In *Dr Jekyll and Mr Hyde*, Robert Louis Stevenson imagined another man of science experimenting with his own mind and body. These and other works of fiction suggest a fascination with trying to reshape the body in accordance with the imperatives of the mind.

Pharmacological advances in the twentieth century hastened the probability that the body could be brought under complete control. Not only could maladies be kept at bay, or even vanquished, but moods could be altered and physical well-being could be promoted. As we have seen, the early efforts of Brown-Sequard at the end of the nineteenth century were to find a rejuvenating therapy for body and mind; his work presaged the development of anabolic steroids. Any initial suspicions about introducing chemicals into the body faded with two world wars in which colossal and often horrific injuries were treated or palliated with medicaments.

The desire for good health that followed the end of the Second World War was complemented by the availability of drugs for the treatment of practically every complaint. A visit to the doctor was incomplete without a prescription, if only for antibiotics. An expanding range of over-the-counter remedies often made the visit unnecessary. The impact of drugs on people's self-evaluations was that ill-health, pain, or even mild discomfort became less and less tolerable. The good life, which seemed to beckon in the postwar period, offered both freedom from suffering and access to well-being. The latter became accessible through a variety of non-medicinal options, including supplements, dieting, and exercise – all of which combined in an enthusiasm in the self that Christopher Lasch characterized as *The Culture of Narcissism* (1979).

It was almost inevitable that athletes, themselves embracing aspirations to self-fulfillment through control of the body, would turn to dope. Many kinds of substances have been used historically to promote performance, though rarely so effectively as pharmaceutically produced drugs. One did not need to be a pharmacist to spot how the effects of, say, amphetamines or anabolic steroids, might be of use to a competitor specializing in speed or power.

The unanticipated, often tragic consequences of pharmacological products were not confined to sports. Thalidomide was given to pregnant women in Australia, Britain, and Germany in the 1960s as treatment for morning sickness and caused thousands of deformities in their children. The Jensen and Simpson tragedies, also in the 1960s, alerted the world to the dangers of ingesting chemical substances to affect changes in the body's condition. Yet, ironically, the imposition of controls by the IOC in the 1970s probably enhanced the appeal of many substances. In his book *Becoming Deviant* (1969), the criminologist David Matza reasoned that banning something immediately makes it more attractive than it would otherwise be.

As the importance of victory became more pronounced and professionalization made the rewards more extravagant, the value placed on winning replaced that of just competing. A success ethic came to pervade sports, making cost–benefit calculations simpler: the benefits of winning seemed greater than the risk of being found out, for many. As Michael Messner writes in his study *Power at Play*: "Many [competitors], because of the 'win at all costs' values of the sportsworld and the instrumental relationships they have with their own bodies, tend to feel that the short-term efficiency or confidence that is gained through drug use will outweigh any possible problems that may ensue from the drug" (1992: 78).

As the stakes in sports have changed, so the orientations of competitors have changed too: winning supersedes all other considerations, including *how* one wins. Today's athletes approach their events with a single-mindedness that would be alien to their counterparts of 50 years ago. They are prepared to train harder, focus more sharply, and risk more in the attempt to realize their ambitions. If pharmaceuticals can help, we can be sure many athletes will give only a sideways glance at moral warnings. The crucial edge that many drugs are thought to provide can be the difference between fortune and ignominy.

Advances in science; the growth of drug culture; an intensification of competitiveness. These are the reasons why so many athletes are prepared to use banned substances; and we know from the number of positive tests in almost every sport that even the most draconian measures do not deter them. So, why do sports governing organizations insist on trying to stop drug use? The answer is not quite so obvious as it seems.

## Seven cases that shook sports

| Who? | At? | What? | The impact? | What followed? |
|---|---|---|---|---|
| Tommy Simpson | 1967 Tour de France | amphetamine | Concern for athletes' health after Simpson's death, which follows that of fellow cyclist Knut Jensen. | Limited drug-testing introduced in 1968 to safeguard health of athletes. US swimmer Rick DeMont loses gold medal for 400m freestyle at 1972 Olympics after a positive test. |
| Ben Johnson | 1988 Olympic Games, South Korea | anabolic steroid (stanozolol) | Johnson stigmatized and alarm over cheating rather than health and safety mounts. | Gold medal taken, time expunged and suspended. Three years later, East German coaches admit giving anabolic steroids to athletes in their charge. |
| Diego Maradona | 1994 World Cup, USA | "cocktail" including ephedrine | By far the biggest drugs case in the global game prompts a recognition that soccer has a drugs issue with which to deal. | Argentina's captain sent home in disgrace, later suspended for 15 months. Stronger antidoping policies introduced by all major sports. |
| Yuan Yuan | 1998 World Swimming championships, Australia | hGH (somatotropin) | Awareness that synthetic versions of naturally occurring substances in widespread systematic use. | FINA, swimming's governing organization, sends China's 23-member team home. New tests for "undetectable" peptides pursued. |
| Festina Team | 1998 Tour de France | EPO (erythropoietin) | Evidence of organized doping programs for entire teams as 400 vials discovered in possession of coach and Festina team is expelled from Tour. | In same year, Mark McGwire breaks single season home run record after admitting to using a then-legal steroid precursor. Two years later, Manfred Ewald, ex-president of East Germany's Olympic Committee, goes on trial in Berlin charged with 142 counts of being an accessory to causing bodily harm. World Conference on Doping in sport sets up WADA. |
| Edgar Davids/ Fernando Couto | 2001 Italy | Anabolic steroid (nandrolone) | Other soccer players Frank de Boer and Jaap Stam also test positive for nandrolone. | Doubts over nandrolone persist, with several athletes claiming that ingestion of legal supplements leads to misleading test results. Two years later, British soccer player Rio Ferdinand suspended for 8 months for failing to give test sample. |
| Dwain Chambers | 2003 California | THG (tetrahydro-gestrinone | Realization that dope specifically designed to evade detection in use. THG not on IAAF's proscribed list but declared "chemically or pharmacologically related" to banned substances. | Two-year ban and lifetime Olympic ban. Documentary evidence used rather than positive dope test. Federal investigations into Balco, which cites several world-class clients from the USA. Several big names missing from the US Olympic team the following year. |

## BY ACCIDENT OR CHOICE?

The reasons why the IOC and other governing bodies of sport are prepared to go to quite extraordinary lengths in their efforts to solve the supposed drug problem might be self-evident to many. But, the sports analyst should never let "official reasons" go without interrogation. So, this is our next task: to evaluate each reason on its own merits, beginning with the most obvious.

*Drugs are not fair* They confer artificially induced advantages on the user; and competing with such advantages is tantamount to cheating. Fairness is a rather troublesome concept to define, but we can assume, with Peter McIntosh, author of the book *Fair Play*, that: "Fairness is related to justice" and "breaking the rules with intent to avoid the penalties" as a definition of cheating is too simple (1980: 2, 182). He favors the definition of Gunther Lüschen who believes that the "principle of chance beyond differences in skill and strategy are violated" when the conditions agreed upon for winning a contest "are changed in favor of one side" (1976: 67).

Drugs change the conditions for winning. But, then again, so do many other things. Take the example of blood doping for which athletes might draw penalties, including bans. In a strict sense, this is cheating. But, how about athletes born in Kenya or Ethiopia, both several hundred feet above sea level? Such athletes might be fortunate enough to be brought up in an atmosphere that encourages hemoglobin production in the body and they might find the transition to sea level really quite comfortable as a result. Witness as evidence the dominance of Kenyan middle- and long-distance runners over the past 20 years. Equipped with natural advantages, Kenyans capitalized on the track and cross-country circuits, leaving weary European and American athletes in their wake.

Another accident of birth meant that Jennifer Capriati was given every available coaching and equipment facility to help her develop his tennis skills since she was old enough to grip a racket. Her parents, being affluent, could afford to indulge their child and, as things turned out, their money was a shrewd investment for Capriati became a teenage world's number one and so unlocked a multimillion-dollar treasure chest. Imagine tennis produced a ghetto child from Brooklyn, who had the added disadvantage of being black. Were this imaginary figure to play Capriati, would it be a fair match? When they came face-to-face in matchup, the conditions might appear fair, but one would hardly say they were "fair" in a deeper sense. One player has benefited from social advantages in a similar way to Kenyan runners, who have benefited naturally from being born at high altitudes. It would be a naive person indeed who believed all is fair in sport, and that background, whether social or natural, is irrelevant to eventual success or failure.

Even doping itself is "unfair" in more than one sense: rich countries have more chemists and better laboratories, so athletes from poorer countries suffer disproportionately. But, perhaps drugs and a working knowledge of how to take them are more transferable than the developed world's high-tech facilities, Olympic-size pools, and college bursaries that enable full-time training.

*Drugs are taken by choice* There is a difference between the advantages bestowed by social background or place of origin and those that are enjoyed by the taker of drugs. Sports performers can, as the slogan goes, "say 'no' to drugs" in much the same way as many say "yes." Swallowing tablets or allowing oneself to be injected are voluntary activities over which individuals have a high degree of control. We presume – and only presume – that they realize the potential costs as well as benefits and they exercise volition when doing or agreeing to the action. Obviously, the same performers have no say in where they were born or the state of their parents' bank account. By contrast, using drugs involves procuring an advantage quite voluntarily.

Yet there is more to this: first, because there are many other forms of advantage that are actively sought out and, second, because some are better placed than others either to seek out or eschew them. Were you a Briton following home Kenenisa Bekele in a 5,000-meter race, you might wish you were born, like him, in Ethiopia, where he also trains at over 2,600 feet above sea level. Impossible, of course, so you might think about going to high altitudes and engaging in a spot of blood doping. Quite possible, but illegal. Another possibility is just to train in some part of the world high enough to give you some advantage, or at least to neutralize the advantage Bekele gets from preparing in Addis Ababa. Perfectly possible and legal. The probable result is an advantage quite legitimately obtained through voluntary effort. But an advantage is gained all the same.

Not that everyone is able to exercise choice in such matters: a dedication to competition, a determination to win, and an unflinching resolve to withstand pain are needed and these qualities are easier to come by if the alternative is a one-way ticket back to the ghetto. If your alternatives look unpromisingly bleak, then choices can be rather illusory. Ben Johnson was born in Jamaica and migrated to Canada in 1980 at the age of 19, his ambition being the same as any migrant – namely, to improve his material life. Lacking education, but possessing naturally quick reflexes (which couldn't be changed) and fast ground speed (which could), he made the best of what he had, so that, within four years, he was in the Canadian Olympic team. Sport is full of stories like Johnson's: bad news – poor origins, little education, few occupational prospects; good news – physical potential and the opportunity to realize it. There is no realistic choice, here. Countless young people with some form of sporting prowess when faced with the once-and-for-all decision of whether or not to sink their entire efforts in the one area in which they just might achieve success don't want to contemplate the alternatives. Given the chance, they'll go for it. And this means maximizing every possible advantage in an intensely competitive world. It's doubtful whether any athlete with a similarly deprived childhood would have any compunction about gaining an edge by any means. The choices they have are often too stark to need much mulling over.

Asking whether choice was exercised in trying to determine whether cheating took place is not adequate. Even if we were to dismiss the claims of a performer (who tested positive for a given drug) that his or her drink was spiked (or similar), the question of whether that person freely exercised choice remains. Is it feasible to argue that the choices of the university-educated daughter of an affluent North American family are roughly the same as those of a Mexican migrant worker's daughter in California whose one chance for some material success is through sport? To complicate matters further, compare both cases with that of someone insinuated into State Program 1425 as an 11-year old.

All this is not intended to exonerate those from deprived backgrounds who have sought an advantage through "foul" means rather than "fair." It merely casts doubts on the hard-and-fast distinction between fair play and cheating. If we want to sustain the distinction, we have to ignore the manifold advantages or disadvantages that derive from a person's physical and social background and which are beyond his or her power to change. We can attempt to get round this by isolating the element of choice and defining cheating only when a person has consciously and deliberately taken some action to gain advantage. This works up to a point if we cast aside doubts about the circumstances in which the decision was made. Again, backgrounds are important in influencing the decision.

So the pedestal on which sport stands when it tries to display itself as a model of fair play is not quite as secure as it might at first seem. Not only are advantages dispensed virtually at birth, but they operate either to limit or liberate a person's ability to make choices.

*Drugs are harmful to health* Picture this: a new drug is introduced. It has great recreational value, giving pleasure to the consumer. It's alleged that it relieves stress while boosting concentration and this is because of a similarity between one of its constituents and acetylcholine, a neurotransmitter that triggers the release of dopamine – the chemical messenger that controls pleasure and pain, among other things. As well as its calming effect, it's also believed to curb appetites, so it can assist dieting. A wide range of athletes spy advantages: the drug steadies the nerves of those who wish to remain relaxed under pressure and helps others unwind after stressful competition. But there's a downside: it contains a chemical that's extremely addictive, another that's carcinogenic; it also causes heart disease, bronchial complaints, and a number of related physical problems. Tobacco accounts for 4.9 million deaths worldwide every year. About 1,400 people in Britain and the USA die from it every day; 65 percent of its habitual users live in the developing world.

The doses of the anabolic steroid taken by Ben Johnson in the 1988 Olympics were allegedly lower than what the World Health Organization subsequently found safe to administer as a male contraceptive. Many of the substances banned from sport and condemned as harmful to health are condoned, and even prescribed in other circumstances, prompting the thought that the banned drugs might not be so dangerous as some of the legal ones.

Sport's central philosophical point seems to be that, whatever people's backgrounds, if they are given the chance to gain advantages over others, they might fairly do so as long as they stop short of knowingly using chemical substances (at least some chemical substances). Some might counter the argument that supports this by saying that acupuncture, hypnotism, psyching techniques, and – in the case of the England national soccer team in 1998 – faith healing might yet prove to have long-term consequences. And there is a growing school of thought that supports the view that the quantity and intensity of training needed in today's highly competitive sports might depress natural immunity systems, exposing performers to infection. Sports clubs themselves acknowledge that players in need of surgery will often postpone operations in order to compete in key games. They do so with the full consent if not encouragement – and perhaps, in some cases, at the request – of coaches or managers, who are surely aware of the probability of exacerbating a condition by delaying corrective treatment.

This has led some observers to believe that the use of drugs is no better or worse than some other aids to performance. They are certainly no worse than many of the drugs commonly available outside the world of sport. Most sports frown on smoking and drinking too, though some, like motor racing and cricket, have been grateful for sponsorship from tobacco companies. Others, like English soccer, have openly embraced breweries, at the same time committing itself to clamping down on drugs, both performance enhancing and recreational. Alcohol kills about 100,000 people a year, significantly more if alcohol-related road deaths are included. The positive effects of alcohol in oxidizing blood, making it less sticky, are outweighed by the physical and social consequences of its excessive use.

The dangers of paracetamol and Prozac are well known. Even everyday drugs such as aspirin and antihistamine, which we presume to be innocuous, are not completely without potentially harmful consequences. Caffeine found in coffee, tea, and soft drinks is mildly harmful, but who, apart from governing bodies in sports, would dream of banning its general use?

The world is full of harm. We don't reject every thing or practice because it's potentially harmful. In fact, sometimes our choices about what and what not

253

to reject seem arbitrary. The same medical organizations that approve of legal prescription drugs, often advise against the use of others. They also disapprove of and mount campaigns against practices that are quite legal. For instance, the British and American Medical Associations have urged a ban on boxing. Prolonged involvement in boxing exposes the boxer to the risk of brain damage and many other less severe injuries, is the claim of the anti-boxing lobbyists. This we know. Medical associations maintain that boxers should be protected, if necessary from themselves, in much the same way as any other athletes contemplating actions that might result in harm to their health. The effect on health of many banned drugs is small compared to that of boxing.

But to make boxing illegal because of this presumes that all the young and physically healthy young men and women are oblivious to the hazards of the sport when they enter. It assumes they are not rational, deliberating agents with some grasp of the implications of boxing – a grasp sufficient for them to do a cost–benefit calculation and weigh up the probable rewards against the probable losses.

Were information about the long-term consequences of boxing or drug use concealed, then the medical associations would have a very strong case. But the results of scientific tests are available and to assume that competitors are so witless as to know nothing of this is insulting and patronizing. If young people with a chance to capitalize on their sporting potential are informed of the dangers involved in their decision to pursue a line of action, then it's difficult to support a case for prohibiting this, at least in societies not prone to totalitarianism. Boxers might well judge the brain damage they risk in their sport preferable to the different kind of "brain damage" they could sustain in a repetitive, unsatisfying job over a 40-year period, or in an unbearably long spell out of work. The judgment is theirs. The alternative is to present those judgments to guardian agents.

But, boxers and, for that matter, any other kind of athlete, don't reach judgments unaided. We've noted previously that all manner of influence bear on an individual's decision and, quite apart from those deriving from background, we have to isolate coaches and trainers. Bearing in mind the case of American football in the 1960s when coaches were assuming virtual medical status in dispensing drugs, we should remind ourselves of the important roles still played by these people in all sports. We must also realize that sports are populated by many "Dr. Feelgoods" who are only too happy to boost performance without necessarily informing the competitor of all the possible implications. It's quite probable that many competitors are doing things, taking things, even thinking things that might jeopardize their health. But do they know it? Perhaps sports authorities might attempt to satisfy themselves formally that all competitors in sports which do hold dangers are totally aware of them and comfortable about their involvement. This would remove the educational task from coaches and trainers and shift the onus onto governing organizations.

Some drugs certainly are harmful to health – as are many other things. Governing organizations quite properly communicate this, though the distinctions that are often made between harmful substances and activities and apparently innocuous ones are frequently arbitrary and difficult to support with compelling evidence. Further, the assumptions carried by governing organizations in their efforts to regulate the use of drugs can be seen in some lights as demeaning, suggesting that performers themselves are incapable of making assessments, judgments, and decisions unassisted.

*Athletes are role models for the young* It follows that, if athletes are known and seen to use drugs of any kind, then young people might be encouraged to follow. While the substances which competitors use to enhance performance are often different to the ones that cause long-term distress at street-level, the very act of using drugs might work as a powerful example. But the argument can't be confined to sports: many rock musicians as well as writers and artists use drugs for relief or stimulus. Rock stars arguably wield more influence over young acolytes than the sports elite. The shaming of an athlete found to have used drugs and the nullifying of his or her performance is a deterrent or a warning to the young: "Do this and you will suffer the same fate." But the Red Hot Chili Peppers are not disgraced and their albums would not be expunged from the charts if it were discovered that they recorded them while Flea was using heroin. No one considers asking Pavarotti for a urine sample after one of his concerts. The music of Chet Baker, a heroin addict, the acting of Cary Grant, who used LSD, the writing of Dylan Thomas, an alcoholic: all have not been obliterated.

Athletes are different in the sense that they operate in and therefore symbolize a sphere where all is meant to be wholesome and pure. But this puts competitors under sometimes intolerable pressure to keep their haloes straight and maintain the pretense of being saints. Clearly, they are not, nor, given the competitive nature of sport, will they ever be.

An argument advanced by parents of promising athletes is that dope-using champions set a bad example. The counter is that, if the young person progresses in sport, he or she will eventually be disabused of all innocence. Gone are the days portrayed in *Chariots of Fire* when winners were heroes to be glorified and losers were good sports for competing. Hard cash spoiled all that. A yearning for money has introduced a limitless capacity for compromise and previously amateur or shamateur sports organizations, including the IOC, have led the way by embracing commercialism rather than spurning it. Competitors too are creatures of a competitive world and probably more preoccupied with struggling to win than with keeping a clean image. They too were once innocents with dreams of emulating their heroes. Yet ambition and money have ways of reshaping values.

*Drugs are not natural* In an interesting essay, "Blood doping and athletic competition," Clifton Perry argues the case for and against blood doping, which, as we've seen, facilitates sporting performance through the introduction of a natural material that is indigenous to the body – blood. He offers the distinction between "performance enhancers" that do not cause lasting changes to the body of the user and "capacity enhancers" that do have long-term effects.

This means that anabolic steroids are ruled out – not on the grounds that they are capacity enhancers but because they have deleterious effects (there is evidence that they elevate enzyme levels in the liver). But does this mean that blood doping should be allowed as it enhances capacities without harmful consequences? Perry says no. His reason is based on the body's response to coming off the enhancer. "There is a difference between the loss of performance output through the loss of a mere performance enhancer and the loss of a capacity through inactivity" (1983: 43). After coming off an enhancer, the body returns to homeostasis: "There is nothing the athlete can do by way of performance to retain the former level of performance. This is not the case when a performer simply stops training" (1983: 42).

There are many things that are allowed in sports that are deemed acceptable, but which are artificial: if we ran only on natural surfaces performance would be diminished, as they would be if we stripped any sport down to its "natural" basics: archery without sights, sprint cycling without the banked track of a velodrome, etc. Sports utilize any number of devices that don't actually make us faster or better, but certainly enhance performance. Pole-vaulters are not better vaulters when they use a particular type of pole, but they achieve better performances.

These don't just facilitate the exploitation of the body: they supplement it for specific periods of time. We have accepted world record times without dismissing them as due in large part to the wearing of lightweight, air-inflated spikes on fast synthetic surfaces. When pressed, we would have to agree that the same times couldn't have been achieved in flats on cinders. Blood doping, one might argue, is actually only the reintroduction of our own blood into our systems, albeit by means of transfusion and, in this sense, is more natural than some of the other devices that are commonplace in sports.

We might anticipate that Perry's reply to this would be that blood doping and other banned methods of enhancing performance involve the ingestion of substances. This is true; but it doesn't make them any more or less natural. No one accuses a 300-lb defensive lineman or an Olympic heavyweight weightlifter of being unnatural. Yet, they've achieved the bodies they have through a combination of resistance training and high carbohydrate diets. The activities we perform – or don't perform – affect our bodies, as do the physical environments in which we live and the cultural definitions we try to live up to (or reject). Biochemical changes are affected by virtually everything we do. There is no natural body state: just living means changing our bodies.

*Drugs are bad for business*  None of the arguments presented is airtight enough to convince a skeptic. Yet sports governing organizations' pursuit of dopers has taken on the status of a crusade: all-year-round surveillance, invigilation, regulation, and punishment are now institutional features of sport and their maintenance is costly. Yet athletes continue to take dope and testers keep spending more time and money trying to catch them. Why? If none of the previous answers ring true, we might turn to the motives of the IOC, an infamously corrupt organization which was involved in bribery, cover-ups, and various other malfeasant activities under the presidency of Juan Antonio Samaranch.

After the financial debacle of the 1976 summer Olympics at Montreal, the IOC became much more of a commercial organization. All subsequent games were heavily supported by the likes of Coca-Cola, McDonald's, Panasonic, and a host of other mainly American and Japanese companies. While the IOC continued to present itself as embodying the spirit originally revived by Coubertin, its ideals became progressively diluted. Samaranch had made clear his intention to extricate the Olympic movement financially from governments and become economically independent. In doing so, he made pacts with companies and the mass media; these, in a sense, surrendered the Olympics' independence to other more overtly commercial organizations and, more generally, to market forces.

Increasingly, the IOC grew reliant on money from not only sponsors, but from television companies. NBC paid the IOC $3.7 billion (£2.64 billion) over 12 years from 2000. Commercial organizations do not donate their money out of the goodness of their hearts; they do it to attract further business for themselves. By encouraging their potential market to associate their products with a clean and wholesome activity that commands the respect and affection of billions, they hope to promote sales. Once that healthy activity is sullied by "drugs" – and remember: the term suggests no distinction between illicit recreational substances and pharmacological products – sponsors quickly move their money. Ben Johnson lost a fortune overnight; Michelle De Bruin failed to land endorsement contracts despite winning three swimming gold medals at the Atlanta games. Rio Ferdinand missed out on a lucrative European soccer championship tournament (though he compensated by appearing in tv commercials that parodied his drugs ban). Many other athletes have suffered financially after being positively tested. The IOC and other organizations that follow its lead in drug testing realize that the money they receive is always conditional.

Long before the scandal of the Salt Lake City winter Olympics broke in 1999, the writers Vyv Simson and Andrew Jennings had exposed the lengths to which the IOC had gone to conceal wrongdoings (1992; see also Jennings 1996). Simson and Jennings revealed how many positive dope tests at Olympic Games in the 1980s and 1990s had mysteriously failed to reach the light of day, leaving the image of a squeaky clean IOC that had eradicated drug use. It wasn't until April 2003 that Wade Exum, USOC's director for drug control between 1991 and 2000, released documents suggesting that, between 1998 and 2000, 100 athletes, including 19 Olympic medalists, competed despite failing dope tests.

The big name catch at Seoul was, of course, Johnson. It is interesting that the female 100-meters winner Florence Griffith Joyner was declared clean, despite hearsay that she had used performance enhancers to achieve her prodigious 10.47 seconds 100 meters record, set in 1988. After her death in 1998, writers around the world were emboldened to declare that she had probably used drugs habitually. Had both winners of the Olympic track program's blue riband events been disqualified for drugs, then it's likely the Olympic movement would have lost credibility with its sponsors and might never have recovered. In the event, Griffith Joyner retired suddenly and unexpectedly, aged 29, in the months following her triumph.

Subsequent Olympics were scandal-free, but as John Andrews, of *The Economist*, put it: "It would have been commercially disastrous – for athletes, organisers, sponsors and broadcasters – to have them declared anything else" (1998: 14). It's this kind of perception that gives weight to the argument that there is a commercial motive behind anti-drugs policies in sport.

The IOC, for long, paved the way for other sports organizations. Its initiative in clinching lucrative sponsorships acted almost as a template for other sports; but, it also had to lead the way in doping policies. Most of the world's sports governing organizations adopt the IOC's banned list and accept the reliability of its methods of detection. While they'll never admit that their purposes in trying to eliminate drugs from their sports are anything but pure, the argument has a plausibility that is, as we've seen, conspicuously absent from all other explanations.

These then are the main reasons why governing bodies have sought to eliminate drugs from sports and discredit those found using them. The reasons are not as straightforward as they appear and all are open to objections. Whatever the argument, we need to recognize: (1) that drugs are part of contemporary sports; and (2) whatever attempts are made to extirpate them, ways and means will be found to continue to use them. In a decade's time, it is possible that there will be no way of preventing competitors from taking drugs which doesn't involve prison-like supervision in training as well as competition: inspection, invigilation, regulation, and punishment would become features of sport. This would be costly and punitive.

| ARGUMENT | EVIDENCE | COUNTER |
|---|---|---|
| DRUGS ARE NOT FAIR | Decent corroboration: drugs can supplement, assist, or compensate in athletic performance. | a. Historically, other performance supplements (like spikes) have been regarded as unfair. b. Circumstances of birth may confer advantages. |
| DRUGS ARE TAKEN BY CHOICE | Yes: often on advice and with support of peers, coaches, and trainers. | Often, the only alternative is lack of success at the highest level. |
| DRUGS ARE HARMFUL TO HEALTH | Some have negative effects; others do not. | a. Some sports activities are also dangerous. b. Many legal drugs are more damaging than banned substances. |
| DRUGS ARE NOT NATURAL | Partial support: many drugs are synthetic versions of natural products. | There is no natural body state: training, diet, environment, etc. elicit biochemical change. |
| ATHLETES ARE ROLE MODELS | Strong support: young people try to emulate sports stars. | a. Rock stars and actors are also emulated. b. Once a certain level is reached, young athletes realize that drugs are used, possibly by their role models. |
| DRUGS ARE BAD FOR BUSINESS | Good support: sponsors avoid contracts with athletes who have used, or are suspected of using, drugs. | Sports' governing bodies maintain that commercial motives do not guide drugs policies. |

**the reasoning behind sport's anti-drugs policy**

Debates about drugs and how to eliminate their use and their impact on sports will continue, at least for a few more years. Discussions about the obligations of athletes, especially celebrity athletes, the impoverishment of sporting ideals, and the loss of simple pleasures will exercise the minds of all interested parties. Typically, the effects of business interests in sports on drug use are set aside, though, as I've suggested in this chapter, they are germane to the debate. What of the future? When will drugs become obsolete? As we've seen in previous chapters, research in genetic science is proceeding at pace and the desire to engineer a body to order has been around at least since 1816, the publication date of *Frankenstein*. This project has also picked up pace in recent years. Combine the two and you have some idea of what's to come. "Athletes will try to alter their genes so that they don't need designer drugs," says Arlene Weintraub in *BusinessWeek* online.

> What's especially frightening about the emergence of new doping methods is that athletes who use them may be putting their lives on the line. Underground manufacturers of designer steroids don't go through the normal US Food & Drug Administration testing rigmarole to prove the drugs are safe.
>
> (June 14, 2004, p. 1)

Frightening enough to persuade some writers to urge a rethink on sport's approach to drugs. In his *Genetically Modified Athletes*, Andy Miah points out that: "Perhaps the strongest argument against doping in sport . . . remains the concern for the health of athletes" (2004: 31). Yet, "harm often seems integral to the activity" in sports (2004: 10). Just training or competing involves the athlete in potentially harmful endeavors.

*Newsweek*'s Oliver Morton acknowledges that athletes take risks all the time and that taking dope is an extra risk. But: "Drugs taken voluntarily, openly and with professional advice will add to these risks far less than they do when taken in a culture of hearsay and secrecy" (July 12, 1999, p. 4).

Morton maintains that athletes will continue to use dope, possibly ill-suited to their purposes and designed in ways to conceal them from drug testers. Referring to the 1998 Tour de France episode (covered earlier in this chapter), Morton writes: "The Festina team's approach of systematic and supervised drug enhancement, though it broke the rules, at least tried to ensure a certain amount of safety for the cyclists" (1999: 4). "In an Open Olympics [in which doping was allowed] . . . there would be a strong incentive for effective but comparatively safe dosing regimes to be found and promulgated," reasons Morton (1999: 4).

Miah's argument is compatible with this. He urges a recognition of athletes "as autonomous agents, capable of making their own life decisions, where such decisions do not harm other individuals or devalue the practices within which those choices take place" (2004: 164).

Objectors might contend that dope taking does "devalue" sports, though Miah points out that: "Ethical discussions have focused solely on the drug issue, to the neglect of a vast number of other technologies that confer a similar kind of effect" (2004: 175). Hypobaric chambers, air-inflated spikes, and FastSkin swimsuits , as introduced by Speedo in the 2000 Olympic pool, would fall into this category.

Like Morton, Miah believes that in sports, as in all other areas of life, we are continually reshaping human bodies, moving them farther and farther from "the imperfect state in which evolution left them," as Morton puts it. Both writers see anti-doping policy as inimical to the interests of athletes, forcing them – however inadvertently – to take dope in clandestine circumstances and so endangering their well-being. It also denies them the ability to make informed decisions about their own lives: as research on the efficacy and effects of dope is never commissioned, athletes are left in the dark and grope their way along almost by trial and error.

As arguments such as these grow, sports governing organizations will have to respond, either through redefining what doping actually means, or adding evermore draconian measures to the already rigorous apparatus of control and punishment. If the latter option prevails, then companies like Balco will prosper. Even anti-doping agents accept that theirs is an unwinnable fight. Weintraub advises that "drug testers assume that there are dozens of designer steroids for sale, or in the labs" and interprets their comments to her as meaning that tests are always destined to be behind the curve: it's simply too easy to design undetectable drugs. She concludes by likening testers to dogs chasing their own tails.

---

**OF RELATED INTEREST**

*Drugs in Sport*, third edition, by David Mottram (Routledge, 2003) is a serviceable introduction to the field and can be augmented with a collection of essays edited by Wade Wilson and Edward Derse, *Doping in Elite Sport: The politics of drugs in the Olympic movement* (Human Kinetics, 2001).

*Mortal Engines: Human engineering and the transformation of sport* by John Hoberman (Free Press, 1992) is a masterly thesis on the relationship between medicine, technology, and the human body and can be read in conjunction with *The Steroids Game: An expert's look at anabolic steroid use in sports* by Charles Yesalis and Virginia Cowart (Human Kinetics, 1998) which traces the history of drugs testing, examines educational programs designed to curb drug use, and presents some of the legal issues relating especially to steroid use.

*Sport, Health and Drugs: A critical sociological perspective* by Ivan Waddington (E & FN Spon, 2000) argues that doping is banned from sports because it offends our sense of right and wrong. But there is irony in the role played by sports medicine: "The development of performance-enhancing drugs and techniques is not something that is alien to, but something which as been an integral part of, the recent history of sports medicine."

*Philosophic Inquiry in Sport* edited by William Morgan and Klaus Meier (Human Kinetics, 1995) has a section "Drugs and sport" that contains five searching (and previously published) articles, all of which probe the moral issues underlying drugs policies. Every argument has the kind of bite missing from most standard textbook discussions of drugs in sport. Morgan and Meier (together with Angela Schneider) have updated their argument, though without actually advancing it, in their *Ethics in Sport* (Human Kinetics, 2001).

Andy Miah's argument is presented in the overall discussion of *Genetically Modified Athletes: Biomedical ethics, gene doping, and sport* (Routledge, 2004) and may valuably be read with Oliver Morton's short but incisive *Newsweek* story "As the Tour de France begins, it's time to rethink the way we treat drugs in sports" (July 12, 1999).

## ASSIGNMENT

You are asked to review research that indicates that 98 out of 100 young athletes interviewed in confidence would be prepared to take a banned substance that guaranteed them success. Even when presented with the prospect that the substance would mean certain death within a couple of decades, over half still said they would take it (Bamberger and Yaeger 1997). After the review, you decide to do your own research along similar lines. Anticipate your results and interpret them.

# *burning* **QUESTION** ⸮

---

## *do cheats epitomize today's sports better than fair players?*

Yes. It might plausibly be argued that the athlete who is prepared to risk disqualification and the defeat, shame, and abject humiliation that often follow embodies the very qualities that define competitive sports in the twenty-first century.

To cheat is to act fraudulently, to deceive, swindle, or flout rules designed to maintain conditions of fairness. In the context of sports, fairness may be defined as in accordance with specified rules. As professionalism has crept into virtually every major sport, often irresistible incentives have been offered to competitors. The temptation to do "whatever it takes" to win has meant that the competitors – as opposed to those who are gratified by participating alone – have broken the rules whenever they believed they could escape being penalized for their infraction.

Cheating is endemic in professional sports, though the actual form it takes changes. There are three main classes of cheating: (1) an intentional infraction designed and executed to gain an unfair advantage; (2) an unintentional infraction that goes unnoticed by game officials and which the offending player fails to report – and so exploits his/her advantage; (3) an instance when rules are observed, but the spirit of competition is compromised, a tactic often described as "gamesmanship." All three feature strongly in today's sport.

1  Several former NFL and British Premiership players have made reputations from their dirty play. As *Sports Illustrated* puts it: "There's a nasty breed of NFL players who follow one cardinal rule: Anything goes, and that means biting, kicking, spearing, spitting and leg-whipping" (October 26, 1998). Kevin Gogan epitomized this type of player. Soccer's Vinnie Jones held a similar distinction. But there are less obvious methods of cheating.

   Perhaps the most notorious unpunished instance of disguised cheating was Diego Maradona's "Hand of God" goal, when he palmed the ball into the goal of the England soccer team in a 1986 World Cup game. Video evidence showed clearly that the Argentinian player deliberately used his hand illegally. The referee did not see it and awarded a goal amid much protest. Maradona didn't confess his sin to the referee. As his biographer Jimmy Burns wrote: "Neither in the immediate aftermath of the game nor in the years that followed did Maradona ever admit to his folly" (1996: 163). Nor did New York Jets players own up to referee Phil Luckett, whose crew allowed a touchdown call to stand on quarterback Vinny Testaverde's play which finished over a foot shy of the endzone in the Jets' crucial 1998 game against Seattle Seahawks.

Cheating is not confined to competitors. Owners, managers, and coaches want to win just as fiercely as those who play under their guidance do. Tall stories of cornermen slipping horseshoes into their boxers' gloves may be laughable, but the most notorious instance of tampering with gloves was the Resto–Collins case of 1983. The unbeaten Billy Collins, then 21, took a terrible pounding from the normally light-hitting Luis Resto, who was 20-7-2 at the time. Collins's injuries were so bad that he did not fight again and was killed in a car accident nine months later. It was found that padding had been removed from Resto's gloves. Resto was banned from boxing and, later, convicted of assault, conspiracy, and criminal possession of a deadly weapon (his fists). His cornerman, Panama Al Lewis, was convicted of assault, conspiracy, tampering with a sports contest, and criminal possession of a deadly weapon. They both served over two years in prison.

Less serious in its repercussions was the case in 1963 when Henry Cooper was poised at the brink of an upset victory over a dazed Cassius Clay (as he then was). Clay clung on until the end of the round at which point his cornerman Angelo Dundee claimed that a tear in his charge's glove occasioned a replacement. In the several minutes it took to change the glove, Clay's head cleared and he went on to defeat Cooper. Years later it was revealed that the tear was Dundee's own handiwork, posing the question, was this the action of a brilliant, quick-thinking strategist, or a crass cheat? Or both.

Willie John McBride's revelation about the British Lions touring rugby team is a telling illustration of how the pragmatism typically associated with coaches can become wholesale cheating. Players were told to strike members of the opposing teams whenever they heard a coded instruction from the sideline. The foul tactic was rationalized as a defense against referees who favored the home sides.

2   It is difficult to imagine an instance when a coach would not condone cheating if there was a guarantee that it would go undetected. In a 1997 game of soccer between two English teams, Liverpool player Robbie Fowler was awarded a penalty after the referee ruled that he had been fouled by Arsenal's goalkeeper David Seaman. Fowler risked censure by insisting to the referee that Seaman had not fouled him. The referee was adamant that the penalty stood and Fowler duly took it. While Fowler's spotkick was saved and driven home on the rebound, one wonders what might have happened had the player remained true to his original confession and deliberately sliced the ball wide of the goal. It strains credibility to believe that Liverpool's head coach would have commended him on his uprightness. More likely, he would have

disciplined him for failing to act in the best interests of his team. In the event, the player was congratulated by teammates and was hailed as triumphant.

This was a rare case when a player actually owned up to an official but was overruled in such a way that he prospered. Players are discouraged from making such disclosures, not only by teammates and coaches, but by game officials themselves, who may interpret the player's confession as an attempt to undermine his or her authority. Even if the original intention of the athlete was not to cheat, the structure of the game actually inhibits him or her from doing much else.

3  Intention is never clear in instances of "gamesmanship": when rules may be observed but the spirit of competition is broken. Exaggerating the effects of low blows to gain time to recover when under pressure is a stratagem sometimes employed by boxers. Soccer players are so notorious for this that Fifa introduced rules that forced all injured (or pseudo-injured) players to be stretchered off the field of play before they could resume playing. These maneuvers are right at the margins of fair game: strictly speaking legal, but designed to gain a benefit or relieve pressure. For example, during her losing match against Steffi Graf in the French Open final of 1999, Martina Hingis (a) demanded that the umpire inspect a mark on the clay surface after her forehand landed adjacent to the baseline, (b) went for a 5-minute restroom break at the start of the third set, and (c) served underarm when facing match point on two occasions. While the actions did not contravene the rules, they prompted Graf to ask the umpire: "We play *tennis*, OK?"

Instrumental qualities such as prudence and calculation have seeped into sports and one effect of this has been the loss of the abandon with which competitors once pursued their goals – which were gratuitous before the onset of professionalization. The underpinnings of sport have been destroyed, says William Morgan in his book *Leftist Theories of Sport* (1994). Market norms have come to prevail: sports "practitioners," as he calls them, have no compelling reason to value or engage in competitive challenges save for extrinsic rewards – money. They are provided "with no reason not to cheat and every reason to cheat in order to obtain the external goods they desire."

For Morgan, rules have become little more than technical directives that enable practitioners to acquire the external goods they seek. Any moral power the rules of sports once had has disappeared. So, sports performers break every rule they can get away with and comply with every rule they cannot. If a player gets caught, he or she is rightly accused of not being clever or adept enough, or even being plain stupid. This is either a technical infraction or a miscalculation. Morality does not enter into it. Morgan believes that the institutional imperatives of professional sports "underwrite and legitimate such rule breaking."

Those same imperatives seem to drive amateurs too. In 1976, for example, Boris Onischenko, in a desperate bid for gold in his last Olympics, wired a switch under his leather grip which triggered a hit when pressed during the fencing event of the modern pentathlon. He was disqualified after officials noticed that hits were registering even though his foil wasn't even touching his opponent. Rosie Ruiz watched the 1980 New York marathon from the 25-mile mark before mixing in with the mass of bodies and crossing the finish line as the first female – and with a new course record. She was the "champion" for a week before her chicanery became known and she was disqualified.

*More questions . . .*

- Should we admire rather than castigate the cheat who escapes penalties?
- Is fair play compatible with professional sports?
- Do coaches/managers influence players' approaches to cheating?

*Read on . . .*

- Oliver Leaman, "Cheating and fair play in sport" in *Philosophic Inquiry in Sport* edited by William J. Morgan and Klaus Meier (Human Kinetics, 1988).
- Gunther Lüschen, "Cheating" in *Social Problems in America* edited by D. Landers (University of Illinois Press, 1976).
- Peter McIntosh, *Fair Play* (Heinemann Educational, 1980).

# not for the fainthearted

where violence in sports comes from

## A BALL GAME WITH A PUNCH

None of the players could have expected it when they turned up for practice on December 1, 1997, but they were going to witness "one of the most outrageous acts on the court or field of play that American professional sports in the modern era has known" – at least that's how *Sports Illustrated*'s Phil Taylor saw it (1997: 62).

Latrell Sprewell, then with the Golden State Warriors, threatened to kill his coach, P. J. Carlesimo, dragged him to the floor, and choked him for between 10 and 15 seconds. Having been pulled off, Sprewell disappeared, returning after about 20 minutes. Taylor describes what happened next: "According to several Warriors players, he went after Carlesimo again and threw punches at the coach, connecting with one glancing blow before he could again be hauled away" (1997: 62). In 1999, Sprewell was fined $10,000 for making obscene remarks to fans during a Knicks' victory at Golden State. He was in trouble again in 2003, when, having moved to Minnesota Timberwolves, he got involved in a heated exchange with Knicks chair, James Dolan, and was fined $25,000.

You might argue that Sprewell is exceptional: a hothead who has trouble keeping his emotions under control. Then again, a great many other athletes have the same trouble. Think of Mike Tyson's notorious ear-biting in 1997. He was disqualified after taking a chunk out of Evander Holyfield in a world title fight. Boxing is, of course, an often brutal sport; but the universal condemnation of Tyson's behavior underlined how even the most aggressive of sports is sensitive to violence that occurs outside the framework of rules. Tyson, like

Sprewell, was fined and suspended by his relevant sporting organization and absolutely castigated by the world's media.

The reason sports' governing organizations and media alike are sensitive to illicit violence is because so much of sports competition is in itself very violent. There are plenty of people and groups who have no interest or empathy with sports who are only too willing to decry sports for their excessive emphasis on aggression. Detractors blame sports for bringing out those nasty, brutish impulses that we manage to keep under control in other walks of life. Sports seem to license us to let rip.

Boxing, in particular, has been singled out by the American and British Medical Associations for its alleged barbarism, which is why even boxing fans damned Tyson. "Boxing is not an expression of ghetto criminality or primitive aggression or some innate human propensity for violence," insisted Mike Marqusee in his *Redemption Song: Muhammad Ali and the spirit of the sixties*. "Though when a Mike Tyson comes along, it is all too easy to paint it in those colors" (1999: 15). But several other sports that call for offensiveness prompt criticisms, especially when they result in serious injury to competitors.

Parties with an interest in sports – like governing organizations and the media – are usually quick to point out that serious injuries occur in a minority of cases and that cases like Sprewell's and Tyson's are extremely rare. Actually, anyone with a reasonable memory can recall comparable cases: Eric Cantona's detour into the crowd to fight a fan during a Crystal Palace *vs* Manchester United game in London in 1995; Vernon Maxwell's similar pursuit of a fan during a Houston Rockets game, also in 1995; Scottie Pippen's dangerous hurling of a chair across the court; Deion Sanders's on-field fight with Andre Rison in the 1994 49ers *vs* Falcons game; the near riot after the first Riddick Bowe–Andrew

---

### Violence

Action involving the exercise of physical force to hurt, injure, or disrespect another human, or property. The term derives from the Latin *violare*, which has essentially the same meaning. In sports, as in many other areas, violence is equated with the unlawful use of force, though many sports either tacitly condone or explicitly encourage violence. Hockey is an example of the former and boxing the latter. In both sports, however, the transgression of boundaries is still punishable, as this constitutes a rule *violation* (from the same Latin root). The word has been prefixed with, for example, "emotional" and "mental" to convey a sense in which action, which is not physically damaging, can result in less visible injuries.

Golota fight. There are too many others to be able to dismiss the Sprewell and Tyson affairs as untypical.

Sports provide a context for the sanctioned expression of violence. That much is clear. But that same context frequently encourages the *unsanctioned* expression of violence, too. The line between them is a fine one. The context, in this instance, refers to both history and the surrounding environment in which fans view, cheer, boo, and experience vicariously the same adrenaline rush competitors get when the competition is in progress. Let's deal with them separately before moving to the competitive situation itself. After this, we'll move to a consideration of "quasi-criminal violence" and then to an explanation of collective violence among fans, particularly soccer fans.

## History

We saw in Chapter 4 how the early folk games of England were raucous and perilous affairs, frequently ending with several casualties. Blood sports such as cockfighting and bear-baiting were nothing if not violent, spectators jostling to get a view of animals which would either be killed or mutilated. The prize fights that crowds flocked to see bore little resemblance to the boxing we see today: pugilists would try to pound opponents into either submission or unconsciousness (padded gloves were introduced not to minimize the damage, but to protect the hands of the fighters, enabling them to land harder punches without hurting their fists).

From the late nineteenth century, when governing federations began to impose formal structure and control on what were loose assemblies of competitive activities, restrictions of the outright use of violence were introduced. The brutal content of many sports decreased systematically as governing organizations moved with the times: as society's threshold of acceptable violence changed, so did sport's. Late football hits, overly savage beatings in the ring, unlimited head-high balls in cricket: these once acceptable practices were reviewed and modified during the twentieth century. Even sports that weren't ostensibly violent were assessed: whip abuse in horse racing was banned, as was racket abuse in tennis.

Mindful of changing attitudes, sports federations adjusted their limits of tolerable violence, penalizing violators with fines and suspensions. This quasi-legal function of sports organizations became a more prominent feature of their operations. Sports defended their right to police themselves and to safeguard their own standards. Their administration of justice served to insulate them from the attentions of the wider judicial system. In other words, sports involved action that would almost certainly be punishable by law if it took place outside the sports arenas – and removed from the auspices of the official governing organization. Can you imagine what would happen if a tackle that's common-place on the football field took place in a crowded department store?

In effect, sports ruling organizations realized the violence inherent in many competitive activities and the potential violence in practically all of them. To keep in sync with the rest of society's standards, they had to regulate them and penalize infractions. Even then, it didn't keep away the legal eagles that were poised to swoop on behavior that appeared to violate not only sports' rules, but the rules that lay beyond. This type of behavior has been called quasi-criminal violence.

## Environment

No fan wants to attend a game of football, hockey, soccer, or any other sport, and sit quietly for the duration. The whole buzz about being there is to get wrapped up in the atmosphere of the occasion; to feel the elation, the depression, and all the emotions in between. The fan can get all the thrills and still get home without stitches.

Being a fan is a relatively safe experience. Only relatively: as the example of British soccer reminds us. In some situations, there is more violence off the field of play than there is on it, much more. The pitched battles in the streets of many Portuguese towns during the European Championship tournament of 2004 was no blip: soccer's fandom has a well-deserved reputation for violence. Soccer the world over seems to elicit peculiarly intense passions among its fans and violence has become a staple feature of the sport. While there's always the possibility of getting hurt in any large gathering, especially of rival groups of fans, injuries among fans of sports other than soccer are less common.

---

### Aggression and aggressiveness

Aggression is behavior, or a propensity to behave, in a way that is either intended as harmful or carries with it a recognizable possibility that a living being will be harmed, physically or psychologically. Its Latin root is *aggressio*, to attack. By contrast, aggressiveness means expressing assertive, forceful, offensive, dominant tendencies when pursuing goals but without necessarily engaging in intentional harmful behavior. In sports, aggressiveness is typically applauded and carries a positive connotation, unlike actual aggression, which is directed at hurting others and is approved of only in particular circumstances.

---

This doesn't negate the central point: sports are conducive to violent behavior and aggressive conduct. We want them to be. After all, whoever praised an athlete or a team for passivity? We don't expect tranquil attitudes or good-natured approaches: in fact, we demand aggressiveness, which is not the same thing as aggression or flat-out violence, but is never far away from them.

# FRUSTRATION

Let's expand the argument to discover what theorists of aggression tell us about its causes. Ethologists (who study humans in the same way as they would any other animal and whose approach to sports we covered in Chapter 5) contend that we are born with an aggressive instinct that has been quite serviceable in our survival as a species. So, we defend our "natural" territory when it is under threat. Konrad Lorenz (1966) wrote that human aggression is like other forms of animal aggression, only we have learned to route it into safe outlets, sports being an obvious one.

Sigmund Freud (1963) too viewed sport as a way of discharging aggression. In his theory, we all have a *death* instinct that builds up inside us to the point where it must be discharged, either inwardly (self-destructive acts), or outwardly. Because we don't always have socially acceptable opportunities for turning our aggression outward, we displace it into acceptable channels. Sports are perfect: we can get all our aggression out of our system either by participating or just watching; either way, we rid ourselves of the aggression.

Without denying that aggression has its source in a biological drive, other accounts focused on the context in which aggression materializes, noticing that some environments seem to have more potential for eliciting aggressive behavior than others. Sports, of course, are crucibles of frustration: individuals pursue aims, while others try to stop them. Several theorists have argued that frustration creates a readiness for aggressive behavior.

The frustration–aggression hypothesis, as it's called, states that, when goal-oriented behavior is blocked, an aggressive drive is induced. Further frustrations increase the drive. On this account, all aggressive behavior is produced by frustration. The hypothesis was introduced as an alternative to theories of aggression based on innate characteristics. Scholars such as John Dollard *et al* (1939) and his colleagues rejected the notion of human behavior as programmed by nature and argued instead that the way we act is the product of stimuli in the world about us – frustration being the stimuli that produces aggressive behavior. Unlike Lorenz, Freud, and others who portrayed sports competition as a cathartic experience, allowing all the aggressive energies to blow out, frustration–aggression theorists interpreted sports as heightening the possibility of aggression. Frustration of some order is inevitable in any competition. But, while this might help explain why aggression of some kind is likely to appear in sports, it leaves the issue of why some sports seem to have developed a tradition of violence, raising the possibility that there's a cultural element to violence too.

Albert Bandura's (1973) famous experiment with Bobo dolls involved asking groups of children to watch an aggressive model beating up a toy Bobo doll or treating it kindly. The tendency of the children was to copy the model they observed, especially when they witnessed the aggressive model being rewarded for the assault. Bandura concluded from this and other studies that we learn aggression and, in this sense, it's a cultural rather than natural phenomenon. Clearly, this finding is totally at odds with the view of many coaches and players who believe (presumably, with Lorenz) that sports are a good way of letting off steam, or getting our aggression out of our system. The aggression has never been in there, according to social learning theorists: we acquire it during our interactions with others. Crudely summarized, sport is an outlet for aggression in biologically based approaches, a mediating factor in the frustration–aggression hypothesis, and an environment in which aggression is acquired in social learning theory.

This doesn't exclude frustration from the social learning account: frustration is one of several experiences that lead to an emotional arousal. But there may be others, including physical discomfort, or even pleasant circumstances, such as dancing in a club. Aroused by the physical exertion of dancing and a feeling of well-being, a person may be aggressive toward someone who accidentally bumps into them and makes them spill a drink. It may well be that the aggressor has learned this response through observing others at the same club, whose behavior was rewarded. Even if the person had been thrown out, his or her peers may have been suitably impressed. Several studies indicate that emotional arousal, regardless of the source, can increase aggression when the requisite stimuli are present. The consequences of the reaction to the aggression can have decisive effects in shaping future behavior.

The lesson is that much aggression is preceded, if not caused, by frustration and frustration arises from not being able to get one's own way. Isn't that what sports are all about? One person or group trying to get their way, while another tries to stop them. Whether viewed from a historical or contemporary perspective, sports are either violent or carry the potential for violence. Basic logic tells us that this will always be the case. The primary goal of sporting competition is to do one's utmost to win in the face of opposition. The opposition's primary aim is exactly the same. Each party is continuously trying to achieve the goal, while preventing the opposition from achieving theirs. It means that the competitive environment is alive with cues for aggression. And that can often tip over into violence – but not just any old violence.

*Instrumental* violence is used with a specific purpose beyond the violence itself. Its counterpart is *hostile* violence, which is designed to cause harm to another, plain and simple (see Husman and Silva 1984). A football player might believe he or she has been hit by another player in an unfair way, which goes unnoticed by the referee. Incensed, the player chases the offender and lunges feet-first at his ankles with the sole intention of causing him harm. This is hostile.

The same player, later in the game, might jump to meet the ball in the air, at the same time, deliberately elbowing an opponent in the face. His aim in this instance is primarily to get to the ball first and his elbow action is a way of deterring another player who might otherwise obstruct him. In both cases, aggressive behavior inflicts harm, but, in the latter case, it's a means to an end and the end is defined by the purpose of the competition. The aggression serves as an instrument. The distinction in sports is not always so clear-cut. Even an enraged athlete who intentionally bites an opponent's ear does so in the context of competition in which he or she has the overarching aim of victory.

Now that we've examined how sports have thrummed with aggression and violence through the ages and how the context of sports encourages the kind of frustration that leads to aggression, we arrive at an interesting question. Not, why is there so much violence in and around sport? But, why isn't there more?

## BY FAIR MEANS OR FOUL

Given the amount of money at stake in professional sports, it's hardly surprising that many competitors are prepared to do what it takes by fair means or foul to get the desired results. A win can mean an awful lot to competitors. Winning or losing a title fight can be the difference between boxing for several million dollars or a dozen or so thousand in the next fight (though it didn't for Tyson: in his first fight after the Holyfield debacle, he earned $10 million – not exactly chump change). Most ball players have bonus agreements built into their contracts. So playing a role in a major championship victory can make a big impression on your bank statement, especially when you have a clause like the New York Yankees: each member of the baseball team was offered $322,578 (£226,896) if it won the World Series in 2000. It did. The Swiss soccer team was incentivized with a cow per player if it beat England in the 2004 European championships. It didn't. As incentives go, hard cash seems to work better than bovine stock.

The growth of commercialism brought about by television, especially from the 1960s, as we have seen, introduced to sports more money than could have been dreamt of 25 years earlier. In Chapter 10, I argued that the increase in the use of performance-enhancing drugs by performers is one result of this. Coaches over the years have driven competitors as hard as they could, pushing and prodding them to their peak performances. But the carrot is mightier than the stick. There's no better way to get the ultimate effort out of a performer than to offer irresistible incentives.

The results of this are obvious: perfectly conditioned, highly motivated, tunnel-visioned, win-oriented performers, who continually frustrate critics and sometimes governing authorities with the excellence of their play and the tenacity of their approach. The "give-it-your-best-shot" approach gave way to a "must-win" orientation as athletes were encouraged to achieve, rather than just strive.

In many sports where competitors are physically separated, the changes in orientation manifested only surreptitiously. In tennis and billiards, for example, competitors exhibit their prowess in relative isolation. They don't, for example, break tackles, knock opponents out, or dribble pucks around opposing players. In sports where contact or collision is inevitable, either by design or default, the effort to win by any means necessary takes on a different complexion. Physical encounters are less restrained than they might have been where only pride was once at stake. Serious injuries are accepted as part and parcel of today's sports. Illegal play is seen as permissible as long as it goes unnoticed by officials. When the price of failure is measured in terms of what might have been gained, success is pursued with a fury.

In other words, the efforts of sports to curb overly aggressive play hasn't been accompanied by a corresponding change in players' motivations or behavior. They're more motivated to win than ever and are prepared to bend if not break the rules to do so. This isn't to say that competitors from past eras didn't have ferocity, single-mindedness, or callous disregard for others. These were qualities that might have been permissible, or even lauded. Today, sports governors realize that they're qualities that have to be kept in check. They don't want to neuter the competition, but they know that the bar has been raised: consumers want aggressiveness without being repulsed by unjustifiable and obnoxious violence.

The National Hockey League in the 1970s reset its bar and with interesting results. Watch the hockey played at the Olympics, where there is a high degree of technical competence but none of the almost theatrical fighting that punctuates a typical NHL game. The experience is quite different and, I dare say, not as entertaining for an NHL fan. The George Roy Hill film *Slap Shot* (1977) is a satire on commercialism and violence in hockey. Manager Paul Newman tries to revive his club's fortunes by drafting-in three goons with limited skill, but a lot of butt-kicking ability. The team's principles are sacrificed; but the results improve and the crowd loves the roughhouse tactics.

The film was made in the mid-1970s, when the Philadelphia Flyers dominated the sport, winning two straight Stanley Cups, with a ferocious brand of physical hockey in which the "hit" was a central weapon (the NHL defines a "hit" as contact that "significantly impedes" a player's progress). The Flyers' expert use of the bodychecking changed the character of the game: the crushing hits they put on opponents were calculated to intimidate; though, as with all forms of intimidation, once opponents started to hit back with interest, Philadelphia's superiority was broken.

Hockey at the time was a perilous sport: sticks were wielded like axes, fists flew furiously, and players got slammed with bone-rattling hits. In their *Hockey Night in Canada*, Richard Gruneau and David Whitson wrote "hockey actually seems to celebrate fighting outside the rules as a normal part of the game" (1993: 189). Not so, said Ted Green, of Boston Bruins, who almost died as a result of a stick blow to the head that fractured his skull. The game in which it happened took place in 1969. In the following year, both Green and his attacker, Wayne Maki, of St. Louis, appeared in separate trials in Ottawa, charged with assault causing bodily harm. It was alleged that Green provoked Maki. Both were acquitted on grounds of self-defense.

Within months of the Green–Maki case, a Canada-wide poll conducted by *Maclean's* magazine indicated that almost 40 percent of the respondents, male and female, liked to see physical violence in hockey. They were not disappointed over the next several years as the amount and intensity of what Michael Smith calls "quasi-criminal violence" increased – as, incidentally, did the popularity of hockey. The NHL's attendances grew by about 40 percent over the 15 years from the mid-1970s; tv revenue increased about twelvefold.

Violence in sports is not a phenomenon to which Canadians are unaccustomed. "The belief that violence sells and that eliminating fighting would undercut the game's appeal as spectacle has been the official thinking among the NHL's most influential governors and officers," detect Gruneau and Whitson (1993: 185). Yet, in 1976, the Attorney-General of Ontario ordered a crackdown on violence in sports after a year that had seen 67 assault charges relating to hockey. In the same year, a particularly wild bust-up occurred during a World Hockey Association playoff game between Quebec Nordiques and Calgary Cowboys, whose player Rick Jodzio was eventually fined C$3,000 (US$2,200, or £1,360) after pleading guilty to a lesser charge than the original of causing bodily harm with intent to wound. There were also convictions arising from a Philadelphia–Toronto game in 1976: the interesting aspect of this one was that, in legal terms, a hockey stick was designated a dangerous weapon.

Despite the commercial success of the NHL after the mid-1970s and the rise of the Philadelphia Flyers, the league remained mindful that too much on-ice brawling could easily turn television away. Big-hit players threatened to overrun the game, making more skillful players less likely to survive. The NHL's crackdown on violence did not eliminate fights, but between the 1987/8 season to 1998/9 the average number of altercations dropped from 2.1 to 1.2.

Concern over the violence prompted the NHL to rethink its policies and clamp down. By the early twenty-first century, it had slipped from its position as North America's fourth major league sport and tv viewing figures collapsed, leaving it without the gargantuan contracts to which it had become accustomed. Maybe NHL without the big hits and the fist fights was just not the same.

Basketball is another sport that has benefited from more physical aspects. At the start of the 1980s, the sport lagged way behind hockey in terms of popularity in the USA. It now vies with baseball and football as the most-watched sport in the USA and has a large tv following around the world. Much of its success has been based on marketing strategies that have worked like a charm and a format that suits television perfectly. But, again, compare your experiences: watch a game of basketball from any Olympics before 1992, when an all-professional American "dream team" dominated. The action is fast, nimble, and precise; yet there is something lacking; and I don't mean the climactic slam-dunks. The physical contact is almost polite alongside the bumps, knocks, shoves, and jostling we are used to seeing. Players don't get sent splaying after running into a colossus like Shaq O'Neal. None of the players has the mien of a pro boxer, as do any number of NBA all-stars.

The NBA purveys a different game from the basketball played by the rest of the world 15 years ago. It's harsher, more physical, and brings with it an undertow of violence that has made it commercially attractive. Small wonder that tv networks have clamored to throw money at the NBA, which has in turn plowed it through the clubs which have been able to pay players salaries to rival those of the best-paid boxers and baseball players. This has pumped up the stakes even higher, reinforcing the intensity of competition that characterizes the NBA.

The phrase "only in America" springs to mind when we come to comparing this trend with sports elsewhere in the world. Or, perhaps, only North America, because efforts south of the Rio Grande and throughout Europe have been aimed at eliminating the violence that has been allegedly escalating in soccer. The sport has always been tough, of course; but soccer's world governing organization Fifa (*Fédération Internationale de Football Association*) in the 1980s, became concerned that the pre-eminent teams were those that employed particularly physical players, whose specialty was intimidation. This had commercial implications, though they were never spelled out: if the finesse players were succumbing to the "cloggers" as they were known ("clog" meaning to impede or hamper), then the shape of the sport would change fundamentally, skill being replaced by a more robust style of play in which only the strong would survive. Soccer was once described as a game of pianists and those who carry the pianos for them. At a time when Fifa was expanding into Africa and Asia to make the sport genuinely universal and needed television monies to fund its mission, it could ill-afford to lose its virtuosos.

Over a period of years, Fifa issued a series of directives to soccer referees to control not only violent play, but disagreements with referees' calls (classed as "dissent"), time-wasting (the clock runs continuously apart from half-time in soccer), and "professional fouls." The penalties for these and other violations were severe: without the hockey-style sin bins, soccer players were ejected from games for the duration and faced further suspensions as a result as well as heavy fines.

Despite attempts to contain aggressive behavior in many sports there remains a paradox. For many sports to be effective as competitive spectacles, some element of aggression has to be present. One only needs to see coaches before a game; they are never caught gazing reflectively out of a locker room window, whispering gently to their players, "Chill, we'll win if it's meant to be. Go with the karma." More likely, they'll be roaring with passion, using every device they know to bring their players to an aggressive peak.

Seen like this, sports create a milieu that sometimes endorses or encourages aggression, or at least creates conditions under which the possibility of violence is heightened. It then covers that milieu with a sheltering canopy as if to prevent outsiders interfering with internal affairs. Every sports governing organization condemns aggression and violence, though there is extreme variability in the punishments handed out to violators. In a way, the organizations are acknowledging the inherent potential for violence in a context in which frustration is inevitable. They're constantly trying to suppress it. Every so often, they simply can't contain the violence.

## ILLEGAL MEANS

The Green–Maki case wasn't the first famous instance of quasi-criminal violence. In a 1965 Giants–Dodgers game, the San Francisco hitter Juan Marichal whacked LA catcher John Roseborough with his bat. Marichal was fined by the league and suspended, but Roseborough sought the retribution through a civil suit that was eventually settled out of court. In basketball, a huge case in 1979 involved not only the fining and suspension of the Lakers' Kermit Washington, but an accusation leveled against his club for failing to train and supervise the player adequately. He was ordered to pay damages. The player whom he attacked, Rudy Tomjanovich, was effectively forced into premature retirement as a result of his injuries.

Boxer Billy Ray Collins was also made to retire as a result of injuries incurred during his fight with Luis Resto. Going into the 1983 fight a hot favorite with a 14–0 record, Collins was surprisingly beaten and finished with his eyes so swollen that he was temporarily blinded. He did not box again and was killed in an auto wreck the following year. In the aftermath of the fight, Resto's gloves were confiscated by the chief inspector of the New York State Athletic Commission (NYSAC), who had them inspected by the manufacturers, Everlast, and a state police laboratory. Each glove was meant to weigh 7.95

---

### Quasi-criminal violence

This is defined by Michael Smith as "that which violates not only the formal rules of a given sport (and the law of the land), but to a significant degree the informal norms of player conduct" (in his book *Violence and Sport*, 1983: 14). Typically, it will result in some form of injury that brings it to the attention of officials and, later, tends to generate public outrage when the mass media report it. Sometimes, civil legal proceedings follow, though, according to Smith, who it must be remembered was writing in 1983, "less often than thought." Nowadays, court cases are more prevalent. *Quasi* is Latin for almost.

---

ounces, but Resto's right glove was 6.92 ounces and the left 6.96 ounces. The Commission announced that unauthorized changes had been made to the gloves and permanently revoked the licences of Resto's trainer, Panama Al Lewis and Pedro Alvarado, who also worked his corner. Resto was suspended for a year. The fight was declared "No contest."

In October 1986, Resto and Lewis were brought to criminal court by the state of New York and convicted of assault, conspiracy, and criminal possession of a deadly weapon – Resto's fists. Additionally, Lewis was convicted of tampering with a sports contest. Resto was sentenced to a maximum of three years and Lewis a maximum of six; both served over two years. There was, as Jeff Pearlman of *Sports Illustrated* put it, "overwhelming evidence that the boxing career of Billy Ray Collins Jr. was ended by illegal means" (1998: 120).

Collins's estate filed a $65 million lawsuit against the NYSAC, arguing that the inspectors had an obligation not only to look at the gloves but also to feel them on Resto's hands, to look inside them – to do everything to ensure they had not been tampered with. The NYSAC counted that the term "inspection" was broad and added that the responsibility lay not with the Commission, but with the promoters, Bob Arum's Top Rank Boxing, which hired the inspectors. A further action by lawyers acting for Collins's estate was directed at Pasquale Giovanelli, an inspector provided by Top Rank. The case ended in a hung jury.

Another significant case of this kind occurred in an NFL game during the 1975 season. The plaintiff, Dale Hackbart of the Denver Broncos, suffered a career-ending fracture of the spine following a big hit from Charles Clark of the Cincinnati Bengals. Taking his case to the district court, Hackbart was told that, by the very fact of playing an NFL game, he was taking an implied risk and that anything happening to him between the sidelines was part of that risk. An appeals court disagreed and ruled that, while Clark may not have specifically intended to injure his opponent, he had engaged in "reckless misconduct." This paved the way for his employer, the Bengals, to be held accountable.

This case was to have echoes almost two decades later in England, when a Chelsea soccer player, Paul Elliott, pursued a case against Dean Saunders, then playing for Liverpool. Following a tackle from Saunders, Elliott sustained injuries that prevented him from playing again. The court found that the context of soccer mitigated the offense and that Saunders was not guilty of reckless or dangerous play. Elliott's case was weakened by the fact that the play was not penalized by the referee during the game and so the judge was effectively asked to use a video and other evidence to overturn the referee's decision.

John Fashanu was taken to court twice for play that seriously injured fellow soccer players: one was settled out of court and he was cleared of the other, underscoring the point that guilt in a law court and guilt on the playing field are two different things. It could be argued that a player who directs his or her aggression against another in a wild and reckless way is doing so out of a desire to win rather than malice. The relevant principle was originally stated in English law in the *Condon* v. *Basi* case of 1985, when it was decided that, even in a competitive sport whose rules indicate that physical contact will occur, a person owes a duty to an opponent to exercise a reasonable degree of care. In Condon, the court accepted the evidence of the referee in an amateur football game that the defendant had broken the plaintiff's leg by a reckless and dangerous tackle and damages were awarded.

Despite the experiences of Saunders and Fashanu, professional athletes in Britain were dealt an ominous warning in 1998 when Gordon Watson, a player for Bradford City soccer club, won an unprecedented negligence action in the High Court. He became the first player to win damages in spite of returning to soccer after recovering from a double fracture eighteen months before. Bradford's chair insisted that he attempted to settle the matter without going to court, but found no satisfaction with soccer's authorities. The club also brought an action for recklessness against the Kevin Gray, the player whose sliding tackle did the damage to Watson, but this was rejected.

In Elliott's case, the referee decided that Saunders attempted to play the ball and accidentally injured Elliott, which was how the game officials called it. In Watson's, the referee punished the violent tackle. This might suggest that officials' decisions are respected, though there are exceptions, the most remarkable coming in the aftermath of the European middleweight title fight between Alan Minter and Angelo Jacopucci in 1978.

A few hours after being knocked out, Jacopucci collapsed and ultimately died. In 1983, after a protracted and complicated series of legal actions, a court in Bologna, Italy, acquitted the referee and Jacopucci's manager of second degree manslaughter on the basis that they should have stopped the fight before the twelfth and last round. The ringside doctor, however, was convicted, ordered to pay Jacopucci's widow the equivalent of $15,000 (£10,000) damages and given a suspended eight-month prison sentence.

The courts have been wary of intervening in Britain, though the incidents involving Duncan Ferguson, Eric Cantona, and Paul Ince were exceptions that may prove to be the rule in future. Before examining this, let's retreat to 1975 and the case of Henry Boucha who played for the Minnesota North Stars of the NHL. During a home game against the Boston Bruins, Boucha got into a fight with Dave Forbes, for which they were both sent off for a period in the penalty box. On their way back to the game, Forbes lashed out with his stick, dropping Boucha to the ice. Concussed and bleeding, Boucha was helpless as Forbes leapt on him and, grabbing his hair, slammed his head onto the ice repeatedly.

Forbes escaped with a relatively light suspension of ten games from the NHL, but a Minnesota grand jury charged him with the crime of aggravated assault by use of a dangerous weapon. Forbes pleaded not guilty and the jury was unable to reach a unanimous verdict after 18 hours of deliberations. The court declared a mistrial and the case was dismissed. Boucha meanwhile needed surgery and never played again. Remember: *State* v. *Forbes* was a criminal case and its lack of a definite verdict left several pertinent questions unresolved. Smith believes the main ones revolve around whether Forbes was culpable or whether the club for which he played and the league in which he performed were in some way responsible for establishing a context for his action (1983: 20).

It's also relevant that the actual violent event took place as the players were re-entering the playing area rather than in the flow of the game itself, which is why it bears resemblance to the Cantona affair. At first Cantona committed a foul during his team's game with Crystal Palace; for this, his second serious offense, he was dismissed from play. While walking from the field he was provoked verbally by a fan who had made his way to the edge of the playing area. Cantona turned toward the fan, lurched at him feet first, and started to fire punches. Seeing the commotion, Cantona's teammate Paul Ince ran to the scene and engaged with another fan.

While only Cantona was singled out for punishment by his club and the FA, both players were charged with common assault, Cantona being sentenced to two weeks' imprisonment. More severe was the three-month prison sentence imposed on Ferguson for head-butting a fellow professional soccer player in a game between his club Rangers and Raith Rovers in Glasgow in 1994.

These were high-profile cases featuring top athletes. In contrast, Jesse Boulerice was a 19-year-old player for the Plymouth Whalers, an Ontario Hockey League (OHL) outfit from Michigan, when he found himself charged by the Wayne County (Michigan) Prosecutor's Office with a felony: assault with intent to do great bodily harm less than murder – a crime that carries a $5,000 fine and ten years' maximum imprisonment. In a 1998 game, Boulerice had swung his stick into the face of Andrew Long, also 19, a player with the Guelph

Storm, who sustained multiple facial fractures, a broken nose, concussion accompanied by seizure, a brain contusion, and a cut across his upper lip. The OHL decided that Boulerice had "used his stick in a most alarming and unacceptable fashion" and suspended him for one year. The incident itself was captured on videotape and observers estimated that Boulerice's stick was traveling between 50 and 75 mph when it made contact with Long. Boulerice denied that he meant to hurt Long.

The questions raised by the Boulerice–Long case are germane to all sports in which violence of some kind is integral. Was there any criminal intent in Boulerice's conduct, or was it simply part of the ebb and flow of a sport that trades on aggression? In strictly behavioral terms, was the action any different from the hundreds of other instances in the same game that either went unnoticed or did not result in such serious injuries? Should we consider other factors, such as a chanting crowd, an excitable coach, or even the cash incentives? Jeff MacGregor's point is similar to the one made earlier in this chapter: "What is most surprising about the Jesse Boulerice–Andrew Long matter is not that it happened, but that it doesn't happen more often" (1999: 114).

One of the usual protections afforded sports performers in similar circumstances is the context: players frequently behave in ways that would be alien to them outside of the sporting arena; they forge rivalries that have no meaning apart from in their sport; they consciously psyche themselves to an aggressive level in order to maximize their effectiveness. In other words, their disposition toward violent action is specific to the sport itself.

In the light of our earlier analysis of the history of sport and the frustration-steeped environment is creates, this seems reasonable. It's quite possible that the person might have violent tendencies that are only activated by competition. Or it could be that the player's "normal" character is at odds with the violent persona he or she feels bound to assume during a game. Or, it could just be that the player is aggressive in and out of sports. In a sense, none of this is relevant because the behavior itself is meshed into the context of the sport. Forbes, we presume, held nothing personal against Boucha and, if they met at, say, a party, they may well have got along together. Cantona would almost certainly have never met the man he assaulted had they not been player and fan respectively.

Sports are violent, but, as Michael Smith in his 1983 study *Violence and Sport* points out: "The fact is, sports violence has never been viewed as 'real' violence" and the public "give standing ovations to performers for acts that in other contexts would be instantly condemned as criminal" (1983: 9). Yet, in the years since the publication of Smith's book, many of those acts are being condemned as criminal and the impression is that governing organizations of sport have lost their ability to police themselves. Lawyers are already moving into areas that were once taboo. Sports can't be regarded as the sealed-in units they try to be. Legal eagles are circling.

## Soccer – a sport to die for

**Belgium, 1985** 95 fans were crushed to death and 200 others injured at the 1985 European Cup Final between Liverpool and Juventus, at the Heysel Stadium, Brussels. All English teams were suspended from European competitions as punishment.

**England, 1989** 96 Liverpool fans died as the result of a tragedy at the Hillsborough stadium, Sheffield, where Liverpool were due to meet Nottingham Forest in an FA Cup semi-final game. Police were blamed for allowing 658 too many spectators into a section of the stadium.

**Bosnia-Herzegovina,1993** 15 people were killed and 100 injured by Serb gunners who opened fire on a soccer match being played on a makeshift asphalt football pitch in a western suburb held by Muslim-led government forces.

**Colombia, 1994** Andres Escobar, a member of the Colombian team that had competed in the 1994 World Cup in the USA, returned home after his country had been eliminated from the tournament and was shot dead in the parking lot of a Medellin bar. Escobar had scored an own goal in the game against the USA.

**China, 1995** A 29-year-old fan of the Jinan Taishan club committed suicide by throwing himself out of the window of his fourth-floor apartment when his team's opponents, Beijing Guoan, scored an equalizing goal.

**Italy, 1995** Three Genoa fans died of heart attacks when their team was beaten in a relegation play-off game by Padova. Two fans died at the game, one while watching on television.

**Congo, 1996** 11 fans were killed by lightning while watching a game at Moutamba while perched on the branches of a mango tree.

**Turkey, 1996** Two fans of Trabzonspor killed themselves after their team had lost a crucial game 2–1 against Fenerbahce. In a separate incident, a Fenerbahce fan died when adjusting his television antenna to improve the reception of his team's game against Manchester United.

**Argentina, 1996** A Brazilian man was murdered in Buenos Aires after rooting for Nigeria when watching that country beat Argentina in the final of the 1996 Olympic soccer competition.

**France, 1998** Eric Fraschet, a French actor, was murdered while on a train traveling from Grenoble to Paris; the train stopped to pick up English fans who had watched their team lose to Argentina in the World Cup championships. Paul Birch, the man accused of killing Fraschet, apparently thought Fraschet was an Argentinian.

**Congo, 1998** All 11 members of a team were killed when lightning struck during a game at Basanga; curiously, the players on the other team emerged unharmed, though 30 other people at the game received treatment for burns. Because witchcraft is often blamed for adverse natural phenomena in western and central Africa, teams sometimes hire witchdoctors either to protect them or place hexes on their opponents.

**France, 2003** Playing for his country Cameroon in a Confederations Cup game against Columbia, 28-year-old midfield player Marc-Vivien Foé collapsed and died, the entire incident being captured on television. The player had no medical history and he had not been hit by another player prior to the collapse. Two autopsies revealed no evidence of drugs and concluded death through "natural causes," with probable cardiac origins.

## BEASTLIE FURIE

"fan" – fanatic adj. [<L *fanaticus*, of a temple, hence enthusiasm, inspired <*fanum*, a temple] unreasonably enthusiastic; overly zealous (*Webster's Dictionary*). Or: *a.* & *n.* (Person) filled with excessive and mistaken enthusiasm, esp. in religion; hence ~ AL *a.* (*Oxford English Dictionary*).

Excessively enthusiastic people sometimes get aggressive, particularly if their passion is fuelled by religious zeal. Sports fans often appear to be similarly motivated. The obsessive properties of fans are inspected in the Tony Scott film *The Fan* (1996) in which a fan, played by Robert De Niro, gets his spiritual nourishment only by following baseball: his job as a knife salesman holds no interest for him and he is prepared to sacrifice it in order to pursue his real love.

When he discovers that his team's recently signed superstar is interested primarily in money, he turns viciously against him.

The story has some basis in fact. For example, back in 1949, Philadelphia Phillies player Eddie Waitkus was shot by a fan. In the 1990s, Katarina Witt and Steffi Graf were harassed by stalkers. In 1993, Graf's rival Monica Seles was stabbed. The attacker kept a shrine to Graf in his aunt's attic. Less well known is the case of multiple world snooker champion Stephen Hendry: a female fan became fixated on the Scottish player and wrote him a series of letters which grew progressively abusive. In 1991, she threatened to shoot him, later claiming that her threat afforded her "power over people's lives . . . to know that you can cause such harm to people by doing something as simple as writing a letter" (quoted in the *Sunday Times*, September 29, 1996).

In her "A sociology of television fandom," Cheryl Harris argues that being a fan confers a sort of power; she writes of fandom "as a phenomenon in which members of subordinated groups try to align themselves with meanings embodied in stars or other texts that best express their own sense of social identity" (1998: 49–50). Following the exploits of others and perhaps displacing

---

### Fandom

From fan, or fanatic, and "dom," meaning a collectivity or the ways of (e.g. kingdom, officialdom), this refers to the condition in which whole congregations of people devote parts of their life to following, supporting, or just admiring an individual or sports team. Devotees of Madonna, for instance, were a fandom of "wannabes," trying to emulate or mimic the rock star. A fan of the Icelandic singer Björk arranged to send her a video of himself committing suicide. Sports fans exhibit traces of this, though their orientation typically lacks envy and is based more on devotion. In 1993, Günther Parche, a devotee of Steffi Graf, knifed Graf's rival Monica Seles in the back so that his idol could be no. 1 in the world. Often sports fandom revolves around loyalty to a club. Perhaps the largest fandom in the world belongs to Manchester United, a club which has won the European club championship twice. This is quite modest when compared to other clubs such as Real Madrid, AC Milan, Ajax, or Liverpool, all of which have won the accolade four or more times each. Yet the United fandom far outstrips these. Its fans travel from all over Europe to Manchester, and there are branches of its official supporters' clubs in virtually every Commonwealth and European country, as well as Japan, Malaysia, South Africa, and the USA. There is even a branch on the Indian Ocean island of Mauritius.

one's own perceived inadequacies in the process, fans can negate their feelings of powerlessness (see Henry Jenkins's *Textual Poachers*, 1992).

If we begin from this premise that fans try to align themselves with others as a way of expressing some part of their selves and that this can be experienced as empowering, especially for those who have little material power, then we can move toward an understanding of collective fan violence. The starting point for any discussion of aggression and violence among fans has to be soccer, a sport that attracts a singularly devout fandom almost everywhere in the world it's played (with apologies to Danes, who take pride in being the most peace-loving soccer fans in the world).

The mania aroused by soccer is not new. Back in 1314, King Edward II of England banned large ball games: "Forasmuch as there is great noise in the city caused by hustling over large balls, from which many evils may arise, which God forbid, we command and forbid, on behalf of the King, on pain of imprisonment, such a game to be used in the city in future." Frequent laws banning ball games followed the English types of football through the centuries, partly because of the violence that often erupted among its fans and partly because it was thought to distract young men from sports such as archery and boxing which, as we saw in Chapter 4, were useful for military duty. In 1514, the first published thesis on education in the English language described football, or at least its primitive equivalent, as "nothing but beastlie furie and extreme violence." Football, along with other forms of recreation, was banned under the Puritan regime of Oliver Cromwell in the seventeenth century, only to resurface again at the Restoration in 1660. As we've already seen, the folk games were insuppressible and were typically loud and rowdy affairs that left participants maimed or sometimes dead. Even when soccer, like other sports, became an organized competition in the late nineteenth century, it was still a rough, physical game that took few prisoners.

Of all the forms of football, only soccer has generated hooliganism in the sense we now understand it: a collective violent activity conducted principally in stadia, but often in surrounding areas, between rival fans. Soccer is the most popular sport in the world and, while the specific form of hooliganism originated in Britain in the 1960s, it quickly spread all over Europe and South America. The title of Janet Lever's book on the South American game captures the manic enthusiasm of fans, *Soccer Madness* (1983).

The term "hooligan" derives from an Irishman, Patrick Houlihan, who migrated to south-east London in the late nineteenth century and, by all accounts, enforced a reign of terror on the local pubs, many of which employed him as a bouncer. There's little evidence that Houlihan was even vaguely interested in ball sports, though ample to suggest he was a mean streetfighter. An undistinguished and disagreeable character, Houlihan had the questionable honor of giving his name to a social problem that was to endure for more than a century after his death.

---

### Football

Football is a generic term covering the world's most popular team game, known variously as soccer, *voetbal*, *fußball*, and other derivations; American football, sometimes called gridiron; rugby, which is divided into Rugby League and Rugby Union; and Gaelic football and Australian Rules football, which differ only slightly in terms of rules. Accounts of its origins usually include primitive kicking games using the inflated or stuffed bladder of an animal. In the Middle Ages, adjacent English villages would incorporate a version of this into their festivals celebrating holy days. These were, as David Canter and his colleagues call them, melees rather than games with no rules: the object being to move the bladder by any available means to the boundaries of one of the villages. The inhabitants of villages in Chester in the English north became so fierce in their efforts to move the bladder that the event had to be abandoned (Canter *et al.* 1989). Lack of transportation and mobility meant that the games remained localized until the mid-nineteenth century when common sets of rules emerged and standards were created. An unlikely but popular story that purports to explain the division into throwing and kicking games involves a certain William Webb Ellis, a pupil at Rugby school, who in 1823, became confused and picked up a ball in what was intended to be a kicking game. Legend has it that rugby was born that day and it was this game that had offspring in the form of American football, Australian Rules, and Gaelic football.

---

Early football violence normally took the form of trying to kill the referee. In 1921, a stadium in Bradford, Yorkshire, had to be closed for persistent violence. In the 1920s, fans of Arsenal and Tottenham Hotspur met in the streets of North London with knives and iron bars. Police baton charges on crowds were commonplace. One club took the view that a match should not be stopped unless the bottles being thrown were full rather than empty. In the 1930s, pitch invasions and attacks on players and the police were often the subject of public disapproval. The relative calm of 1945–60 was something of a rarity.

Many of the early eruptions of violence were at meetings between local teams, "derby games," such as Rangers *vs* Celtic in Glasgow, and Everton *vs* Liverpool. The rivalry between fans in these cities was intensified by a Catholic *vs* Protestant edge, Celtic and Everton having Catholic ancestry. At a time when sectarian conflict in Northern Ireland was raging, the soccer "wars" seemed a logical, if perverse, counterpart. Anti-Semitism was thought to be behind the age-old conflict between North London fans of Arsenal and Tottenham

Hotspur, the latter being traditionally a Jewish-owned club. But, then the violence, or "aggro" as it was called (short for aggravation), became, in the tabloid vernacular, mindless. Every weekend, local stores boarded up their windows, pubs were demolished, and hospitals filled up with casualties from the games. Every game of soccer carried with it the threat of open violence between fans, wherever it was played.

A new turn in the 1980s signaled a paramilitary tendency among many fans, who gave themselves names, organized their troops into divisions, and orchestrated their attacks on rival fans. Among the more notorious was West Ham's Inter City Firm, which is credited with the innovation of leaving behind specially printed business cards at sites of their fights. Other firms were Arsenal's Gooners, Burnley's Suicide Squad, and Chelsea's Headhunters. Soccer hooliganism reached its peak in the early 1980s.

The government, in response, adopted a number of measures which led to decline in violence at games throughout Britain: it was not reluctant to step into the sports arena and implement what might seem draconian legal measures to halt a problem that many felt had roots far beyond the sports stadium. Alcohol was banned from all stadia in 1985. The 1986 Public Order Act made provision for the exclusion from games of those convicted of offenses against the public order. The 1991 Football Offences Act and the introduction of surveillance cameras also reduced the incidence of criminal behavior at games.

None of these legal measures had too much impact on the behavior of fans traveling abroad, specifically to major European cities. Courts of law were empowered to prevent those convicted of hooliganism from traveling to games in countries outside England. But, this type of power was helpless to prevent the free travel of violence-seeking fans who had escaped prosecution.

In some ways, the English did the world a favor by creating, developing, and refining a sport, then taking it to the rest of the world, from Lima to Lahore. Years after it had exported the sport, it exported a grimmer cargo. During the 1980s, hooliganism was rife throughout Europe. British passions were hard to rival; but Italians came very close. So, when the top clubs of each country met on neutral territory to decide which was the top team in Europe, some form of fan conflict seemed inevitable. Few could have anticipated the scale of the disaster at the 1985 European Cup Final game between Liverpool and Juventus, of Turin, Italy, at the Heysel Stadium in Brussels, Belgium: 95 fans were crushed to death and 200 others injured in the worst tragedy in soccer's history. After blame was apportioned, English clubs were suspended from European-wide competition for five years and Liverpool for seven. Juventus and its fans were exonerated.

## WHAT'S BEHIND CROWD VIOLENCE?

... and we have some breaking news from Foxboro. We're getting accounts of crowd disturbances at the Patriots game. Our reporters there are telling us that rival groups of fans are fighting. We're going over live to see if we can pick up some of the action there. But, this is looking more and more like a scene from a British soccer game ...

The local tv station in Massachusetts gets a scoop.

Next morning the *Boston Globe* carries the story, along with the question: "Is this the first evidence that the kind of mindless violence that has afflicted soccer for decades is creeping into US sports?"

The tempting and thoroughly exploitable possibility has scholars rushing out of their offices, journalists calling frantically for soundbites, church leaders tut-tutting about the collapse of morality, politicians scrambling for the highest moral plateau, and, of course, the police chiefs promising that every football game will be subject to more stringent controls than ever.

The "serious crowd disturbances" might actually have been an old-fashioned fight between two sets of fans, whose inhibitions had been lowered by a few Budweisers and who were incensed by a couple of referee's calls that went against their team. But the images of their scuffle have been dramatically edited as if they had been picked off the cutting-room floor after the *Natural Born Killers* team had left for the day. (*NBK* was itself blamed for an outbreak of violence that coincided with its release in 1994 and delayed its opening in Britain.)

All this is very exciting for at least a segment of the football-following population who could use a little more action off-field and would welcome the chance to experience the same kind of thrill their European cousins have been enjoying for years. Next Sunday they go to their games ready for action, prepared for the kind of behavior the mass media have been focusing on for the past seven days. And, sure enough, the violence breaks out. The "prophecy," as sagely foretold by the media and an assembly of others, has duly been fulfilled.

An unlikely scenario perhaps; but one that illustrates the self-fulfilling potential held by the media. Events can be created as well as shaped or influenced by the way the media covers them. Those who swear the media is behind all the hooliganism in Europe and Central and South America have a tall order. The copycat effect has been invoked to account for a number of violent episodes over the years. Riots have been a stock favorite.

The uprisings in English cities in the early 1980s and the Rodney King incidents of 1992 were thought to have been perpetuated by the mass media which, in transmitting images of rioters, virtually invited people to duplicate them. Two murders in Britain in the early 1990s were blamed on the movie/video

*Child's Play 3*, which was watched by the culprits shortly before the crimes. Then President Bill Clinton appealed to America's entertainment industry to review its depiction of violence in response to the shootings at Columbine High School, Colorado, in 1999.

The theory holds that once the mass media get hold of a newsworthy topic their tendency is to amplify or exaggerate it, presenting the impression that the event, or events, are larger, more important, more serious, or more widespread than they actually are. But here the self-fulfilling prophecy kicks in: in creating distorted images, the media are actually establishing precisely the kind of conditions under which those images are likely to become a reality.

This doesn't explain why the first events occurred. Critics of this type of explanation complain that it reduces the actual incident to an almost motiveless reaction to an image or sound. It heaps blame on a movie or the media for initially showing the image and, in so doing, deters investigation into the more complex issues surrounding the incident. Perhaps it was an incident on the field of play that started it.

A 1987 study by Robert Arms *et al.*, "Effects on the hostility of spectators of viewing aggressive sports," concluded that "the observation of aggression on the field of play leads to an increase in hostility on the part of the spectators." Why? If we are exposed to models who are rewarded for aggressive behavior as opposed to models who are punished, we are likely to imitate them. Recall the Bandura research of the 1960s: it revealed the powerful part played by imitation in shaping our behavior. Simply observing aggressive behavior can affect our own behavior, if that aggression was positively sanctioned in some way, or, we should add, if the person interpreted the aggression as being positively sanctioned.

The kind of relationship Arms has in mind came to life in May 1999 when a game between the two Glasgow soccer teams, Rangers and Celtic, turned into a fearsome battle both on and off the field. A total of three players were ejected from the game and nine others were cautioned. The referee was hit by a missile during the game – and, later, had the windows of his house smashed. Violence on the field sparked violence among spectators. The crowd invaded the field and joined in a free-for-all. This works as support for their argument that violent play encourages, perhaps even causes, violent behavior among spectators. This is one account of the causes of fan violence, a phenomenon that's been relatively absent from North America, but follows soccer culture around the globe. The copycat effect is acknowledged to figure in the bewildering equation that results in collective violence, though other accounts have focused on the conditions under which the violence breaks out. Let's review some of the main accounts.

*The sociologist's account* Far from being a recent phenomenon, violence related to soccer has a history as long as the game itself. The origins of violent behavior lay in the neighborhoods, where status was often the reward for being the hardest, toughest, and meanest – the baddest – character around. Not having the money to acquire prestige through conventional resources, like cars, clothes, and other material possessions, inhabitants of the 'hood would fight their way to the top of the pecking order. Inspired by Gerald Suttles's American analysis of *The Social Order of the Slum* (1968), Eric Dunning (1988) and his colleagues discerned a status hierarchy and fighting was the way to climb it. Habituated to fighting, the slum dwellers, or the "rough" working class as they called them, were the same people likely to go to watch a soccer game.

Simon Jenkins, a writer for the London *Times*, complements this account with his own version of "risk displacement theory" (*Times*, February 18, 1995). "This states that most people need a certain amount of 'risk' and will find it where they can," writes Jenkins. "Every visit to a soccer game embraces an element of risk, including the danger of crowd trouble." English soccer's authorities thought they had virtually eliminated the possibility of violence in the early 1990s when they ordered all Premiership and Football League clubs to improve their stadia by installing seats instead of the old-style terraces on which fans used to stand.

This worked to an extent: but the violence transferred from the grounds to the streets and the pubs, creating what one writer called "landscapes of fear." The risk element is present in a number of sports and its complete elimination would probably detract from the enduring fascination we seem to have with danger and uncertainty. Jenkins's point is that spectators are clearly aware of the risks they take and, presumably, make a kind of cost–benefit analysis, concluding that the thrill is worth the risk. The "quest for excitement" that's so important to the figurational perspective remains.

*The psychologist's account* "Gratification" is the key word in psychologist John Kerr's (1994) theory: it's based on the individual's interpretation of the meaning or purpose of his or her own action. Basically, Kerr argues that young people who get involved in fan violence are satisfying their need for stimulation through forms of behavior that involve risk and novel or varied situations. One of the attempts behind this approach is to get away from theories that offer the impression that we are consistent. Kerr believes that human behavior is completely inconsistent. "This means that a soccer hooligan who on one occasion smashes a shop window may on another occasion do something completely different." This depends on our "metamotivational state": we can "reverse" between them as easily as a traffic light changes from red to green; it all depends on the situation, or contingent circumstances.

"The soccer environment provides a rich source of varied pleasure for those who wish to pursue and enjoy the feelings of pleasant high arousal," writes Kerr (1994: 47). Most regular fans reach a satisfactory level of arousal; others do not and develop their own extreme variation in their quest for excitement. Accordingly, there is destructive behavior, which can, given the right motivational state and a conducive situation, be as gratifying as watching a good movie or poring over a work of art. Kerr detects that one way of achieving a high arousal is through "empathy with the team."

*The ethologist's account* Focusing on the ritualistic elements of the violence, Peter Marsh (1978) and his associates viewed it as part of a huge dramatic performance in which youths acted out their parts without risking life and limb. Examining the sometimes quite elaborate hierarchies around which clubs' fans were organized (into troops, divisions, etc.), the researchers concluded that, while the belligerent behavior witnessed at football grounds appeared to be chaotic and unplanned, there were, on closer inspection "rules of disorder." Anybody who has been to a big game at a British stadium and witnessed first hand – or worse, been on the receiving end of – crowd violence, will be aware of the limitations of Marsh's approach. Nice idea when you're sitting in your ivory tower in the quiet university town of Oxford, where Marsh *et al.* did their research; ridiculous when you're in the thick of a brawl in London or Glasgow.

*The Marxist's account* The 1970s-style Marxists, like Ian Taylor, argued that the behavior was a working-class reflex: as British soccer became more commercialized and removed from the old communities where it had originated, it left behind a body of fans who felt the clubs were somehow theirs. The violence was seen as a symbolic attempt to confirm their control over the clubs. Not only hooliganism, but industrial sabotage, vandalism, gangs, and a variety of subcultural exotica were explained with reference to the breakup of the traditional working class in the postwar period. The argument may have appeared reasonable in the 1970s and 1980s, but has not worn well and is clearly inadequate to explain the continuing violence and its virtual universality.

*The historian's account* Like other major sports, soccer is played in an atmosphere charged with competitive intensity in which rationality is rendered vulnerable to emotion and self-control is put to the most stringent physical tests. But, attachments in soccer are unlike other sporting ties: they often have a lineage dating further back than the nineteenth century. Affiliations are inherited like family wealth, except in this case the families, being mostly working class, have no wealth to speak of.

Soccer fandom was once about rank, domain, a collective way of marking one's territory. And, while those features might have been modified over the decades, their essence remains: soccer fans call themselves supporters; they see themselves as representatives of their clubs, defenders of their names, bearers of their traditions. Feeling part of a unit capable of winning national and perhaps international honors, or at least challenging for them, has acted in a compensatory way for millions of soccer fans the world over. Once drawn from the industrial poor and deprived, the sport has never lost its base of support and continues to attract its most passionate following mostly from working-class people whose occupations are comparatively dull and unrewarding and offer little or no personal or professional gratification. By contrast, soccer does.

In this context, we might view approval given to soccer hardmen as a type of reward. In *Code of the Street*, a study of Germantown, in Philadelphia, Elijah Anderson writes: "In the inner-city environment respect on the street may be viewed as a form of social capital that is very valuable" (1999: 66). It becomes especially valuable "when other forms of capital have been denied or are unavailable." For many working-class soccer fans, fighting for their team may be one of the few resources they have for gaining respect of their peers. That in itself is "social capital." Inadvertently, Anderson suggests a way of understanding how aggression and violence were hard-wired into soccer culture from the beginning. Association football, to give it its correct name (the abbreviation "assoc" apparently led to the shorthand soccer), was never just a sport. It was a method through which entire communities could test their mettle. Way before the formation of the English Football Association in 1863, the forerunners of the sport had attracted players and spectators (there was no clear distinction) from local areas who challenged each other, for what we'd today call bragging rights; that is, civic pride, collective respect, and all-round esteem. Often the games would revolve around churches, adding another dimension to the competition. Later, factories started clubs, again with reputations on the line.

John Field argues that it isn't only violence that helps maintain social capital: "At least as important is the role of fear, sustained by folk tales of particularly memorable acts of violence," he writes in his 2003 book *Social Capital*. Although he's discussing Colombian drugs gangs rather than soccer fans, Field's comments about the benefits are spot on: "As well as self-efficacy and a sense of identity, the members were having fun . . . In a turbulent and risky environment, young men in particular found a survival mechanism . . . Violent gangs are the only network where they encounter people that they like and who in turn like them" (2003: 85). (We discussed *self-efficacy* in Chapter 6.)

Fans don't just watch a game of soccer: they vicariously participate in it; they are part of the overall culture of which the actual 90 minutes of play is but one part. And, as activities on the field of play have become more overtly violent, the responses of many sections of supporters in the crowd have become so, too. In other words, there is a relationship between the two, but it is mediated by a cultural change that has affected the context in which the link between players and fans exists.

The relationship is captured in Nick Hornby's *Fever Pitch* (1996), which charts the passage into adulthood of a fan of Arsenal, the North London soccer club. As a child, the first-person author is possessed of the kind of fanaticism that might be expected to dissolve in maturity. Not for Hornby: the ardor, fervor, and passion stay with him, often overwhelming more practical concerns: "Football is a context in which watching *becomes* doing . . . I am a part of the club, just as the club is a part of me" he writes. The players are merely "our representatives," as Hornby puts it. The "organic connection" he feels with Arsenal is both stronger and more durable than anything players can ever feel.

The organic connection is one that links today's fans with their predecessors. It helps explain the singular emotions aroused by soccer anywhere in the world. Like a contagion, the organic relationship is infectious. To watch soccer in a detached, analytical manner, misses the point of the experience. For the fans, watching, to repeat Hornby, becomes doing – it's living activity, not observation.

## OF RELATED INTEREST

*Sport Matters: Sociological studies of sport, violence and civilization* by Eric Dunning (Routledge, 1999) contrasts patterns of sports-related violence in North America with those in Europe, though they have a feature in common: "A hedonistic quest for enjoyable excitement is often expressed in social deviance."

"Sport and violence" by Kevin Young, in *Handbook of Sports Studies* edited by Jay Coakley and Eric Dunning (Sage, 2000), is a useful overview of all the main explanations of sports violence, spectator as well as competitor. John Kerr's *Rethinking Aggression and Violence in Sport* (Routledge, 2004) suggests an alternative approach to Young's.

*Sport, Physical Activity and the Law* by Neil Dougherty, David Auxter, Alan Goldberger, and Gregg Heinzmann (Human Kinetics, 1994) is a source book and, though dated, has utility for those practically involved in sports. Its value for students lies in its interesting use of case studies to illustrate its arguments.

*Code of the Street: Decency, violence, and the moral life of the inner city* by Elijah Anderson (Norton, 1999) is not about sports at all, but is full of insights that can be readily applied to the culture of sports fans, the rules by which many of them live, and the way their world confers reward and exacts punishment. This is complemented by John Field's more general discussion of *Social Capital* (Routledge, 2003).

*Fever Pitch* by Nick Hornby (Indigo, 1996) began a new sub-genre of "insider accounts" of soccer culture. Most of them reveal what it's like to be a member of a hooligan "firm." Among the better contributions are: *The Football Factory* by John King (Vintage, 2004), *Soul Crew* by Dave Jones and Tony Rivers (Milo, 2002), and *Blades Business Crew* by Steve Cowens (Milo, 2001).

## ASSIGNMENT

A bitter rivalry between two NHL teams has been given an extra edge by a facial injury suffered by Crawley, a player for the Saskatchewan Scorpions, after an aggressive encounter with Gaea of the Tacoma Terminators. The injured Crawley vows revenge and is reprimanded by his club for inflammatory remarks made to the media. The build-up to the next meeting of the teams is marked by the media's attention to the two players concerned and the "revenge" comments. In the game itself, Crawley is sent cartwheeling by a hard tackle from Gaea. His flailing skate catches Gaea across the throat. Gaea bleeds to death on his way to hospital. While it is a freak incident, there are strong reactions. Examine the fall-out from the point of view of (1) the two clubs; (2) the NHL; (3) the mass media; and (4) the criminal justice system. (The players and clubs in this example are fictitious, though the incident is based on the death of Sweden's Bengt Åkerblöm who died after an accidental collision with a fellow hockey player in a 1995 practice game.)

# representing the challenge

## how art has influenced our

## appreciation of sports

### MAKING SPORTS VISIBLE

Sports, as we know, never stop changing and, in the next two chapters, we will examine how visual media have reflected and inspired those changes. Chapter 13 will focus on electronic media, especially television, the function of which was intended to report rather than interpret sports. But, art has a different purpose and, in this chapter, I want to examine how artists have approached athletic competition. In the process, I will show how art provides us with a history of sport somewhat different from the history we have disclosed so far. This is a history as revealed through the eyes of painters, sculptors, and film-makers, many of whom were not interested in the significance of sport as a cultural institution; their interests were with images created in the movement excited by sports competition.

A related aim of this chapter is to recognize a continuity amid the change. Over the centuries, countless artists' impressions of athletic competition are testimony to the centrality of sports in human culture. The organization and content of the compositions have changed dramatically within and between periods. But, the effort to visualize facets of sports has remained strong.

A third design of this chapter is to suggest how representations of sport resonate with values and standards specific to times and places. We will see how cultural approaches to, for instance, violence, gender, and the cruelty, have been apparent in the work of artists focusing on sports. None of this suggests that art provides us with a straightforward document of sports or the cultures of which they were part. As painter Paul Klee once pronounced: "Art doesn't mirror the visible . . . It makes visible."

Klee, who worked in the 1920s using sports images as expressions of modernity, believed that art does not simply reflect reality. For him and, we can be sure, every other artist, art is an exposition, a way of witnessing the world, though not necessarily in a way we find comfortable or obvious. Art provokes and challenges as much as it pleases and reassures. This is not usually the purpose of illustrators, photographers, and camera operators. According to Guy Hubbard: "They are journalists and their purpose is to visually explain to people what happened as clearly as possible." In his article "Sports action," Hubbard distinguishes between this group and "Artists who express themselves through sports events [and who] are likely to be interested in portraying physical action and urge to compete and win." They feel no obligation to report what they see, argues Hubbard: "They are free to use their imaginations when interpreting sports action" (1998: 29–30).

Three aims, then: (1) to relate an "alternative history" of sport as told through the expressions, imaginations, interpretations of painters, sculptors, film-makers, and other artists who have focused on sports as their subject; (2) to understand how something resembling what Nikolaos Yaloris, in his *The Eternal Olympics: The art and history of sport* (1979), calls the "athletic spirit" has stirred artists' imaginations, albeit in quite different ways, for perhaps four thousand years and to highlight consistency across the ages; (3) to appreciate how art that focuses on sport can, indeed must, contain a record of the particular social milieux in which they were produced.

Faced with a cornucopia of materials, I have been extremely selective in my treatment. But, at the end of the chapter, there are recommended sources where the reader will find detailed accounts of the development of arts specializing in sports in specific periods. Peter Kühnst's *Sports: A cultural history in the mirror of art*, which covers the period from about 1450–1986, is a particularly solid collection of (mostly) paintings, graphics, and photography accompanied by an analytical text. While Kühnst does not include film in his analysis, there is strength in his thesis that: "By following the evolution of sports and sports-like physical activities, one can see the degree to which they have been the expression of changes in thinking and feeling. They can be understood as an index of individual and social historical transformation" (1996: 9).

## IMPRESSIONS OF COMPETITION

No genre has an official starting point, though it's tempting to identify 1766 as the year in which a warrantable artform called sporting art emerged, primarily through the work of the British painter George Stubbs whose landmark

---

### George Stubbs

Born in 1724 in Liverpool, Stubbs is generally regarded as the most influential artist of his period. Passionately interested in the study of anatomy in his youth, he was commissioned to illustrate medical textbooks with his engravings. In 1754, Stubbs visited Rome and, on his return, he was commissioned by several members of the English nobility to produce paintings of hunts and studies of horses. So exacting was Stubbs that he spent eighteen months dissecting horses in a Lincolnshire barn, producing his *Anatomy of a Horse* collection in 1766. Coombs (1978) describes Stubbs's *The Grosvenor Hunt*, 1762, as: "Arguably, the greatest of all sporting pictures." The scene depicts a dying stag surrounded by hounds and hunters on horseback. Stubbs died in 1806.

---

portfolio *Anatomy of a Horse* was published in that year and whose work is generally considered to have defined a new direction for artists. While Stubbs – to whom we shall return shortly – lent new shape and clarity to sporting art, he was by no means the first artist to have focused on sports. Indeed, artistic impressions of sporting events and competitors are as ancient as athletic competitions themselves.

Wall paintings and reliefs of men wrestling and lifting weights have been discovered in Egypt and dated to the second millennium BCE. There is evidence of other images showing figures seeming to play ball games and fighting with staffs. In later Cretan and Greek cultures there were engravings and frescos that suggested the presence of an athletic spirit: depictions of bull-leaping and combative activities on seals and walls indicate an interest in dangerous competitions. These tell us that the activities actually occurred, but little of their significance. In his essay "Athletics in Crete and Mycenae," J. Sakellarakis points out that, while there is evidence of combat and other athletic activity in ancient Egypt, "these and other similar sports practised in the East had essentially nothing in common with the Greek athletic contests except for the natural inclination to exercise a strong healthy body" (1979: 13–14). The purpose of the activities engraved on seal stones and rings or painted in frescos was to display athleticism and prowess and entertain spectators rather than convey ideals found in later Greek games.

The object of the earlier games was to exhibit a well-trained and skilled human body in contests against other humans and against animals. The games were performed at festivals in Minoan Crete in the second millennium BCE and had an almost ceremonial function which Nicolaos Yaloris likens to acrobatic display. Representations of bull-leaping – in which the leaper stands in front of an onrushing bull and grabs its horns so that the bull's momentum tosses him (women do not appear in the pictures) in the air – are found in ancient monuments. Scenes from the combat events, also popular in the Minoan period, are found on vases, especially *kraters* which were vases placed in the tombs of the dead, suggesting that the activities held some religious significance.

The lack of written evidence forced scholars to rely on bric-a-brac and artifacts as well as the stylized art forms that survived. Apart from combat sports, which seem to have endured through several different cultures and epochs, racing of some sort is found in the decoration of ceramics; this includes foot-racing, horse racing, and chariot racing, all of which in some way continue to the present.

Sculptures were characteristic of Greek art and, in this form, there is a pantheon of heroes, the most celebrated of which is Myron's *Discus Thrower* (*Discobolus*) in bronze from the fifth century BCE. The model for this work could well have been drawn from one of today's gyms. His body is lithe and cut, a flat midsection and prominent ribs giving him a very contemporary look. The position he takes in readiness of his discus throw is much the same as that of today's discus throwers, discus-holding arm outstretched behind him, other arm across his opposing knee, feet poised to rotate and thrust. It's a genuinely timeless piece.

For Greeks, sport, education, and culture were indistinct: they were all involved in the cultivation of the whole being; the mental and the physical were not dualities as the modern Western conceptions, but part of the same unity. So, sport, at least in the way we understand it, did not exist: it was not a separate sphere of activities sectioned off from many other parts of life. Once this is understood, it becomes clear why so many athletic images adorn Greek art and artifacts. Sport was revered in ancient Greece and found its fullest expression in the Olympic Games.

By contrast the Romans, who subjugated the Greeks in 146 BCE, were indifferent to sport and, indeed, to art; though their contributions to architecture and literature were immense. The only sporting endeavors encouraged by Romans were those that contributed to the preparation for war. Whereas Greeks had idealized athletic pursuits and endowed them with spiritual purpose, Romans saw them as a kind of military training and undeserving of the cultural attention Greeks had afforded them in their art.

The Romans' lust for gladiatorial conflict is famous: trained, armed men fought in mortal combat against each other, or against animals. At Naples' National Archeological Museum, there is a fresco from Pompeii showing a Roman amphitheater and a number of other activities, some of which appear to be gladiator fights. While the Romans did not leave largess of art, contemporary reconstructions of gladiatorial contests have been memorable. Jean Léon Gérôme's 1874 oil on canvas *Pollice Verso* is a frightening, dramatic depiction of the climax of a duel in which the triumphant gladiator, wearing a helmet and arm mail, stands over the fallen *netarius* (net-thrower), his foot on his throat. The viewer sees from the floor of the Colosseum and witnesses the imposing crowd baying for blood. As was the custom, the gladiator looks to the emperor seated in his box; to his left are six vestal virgins, all signaling their wishes as to the fate of the victim – thumbs down.

It's probable that director Stanley Kubrick consulted Gérôme's work when he recreated a gladiatorial contest for his 1960 film *Spartacus*. Gérôme was painstaking in his research, obtaining casts of antique armor and weapons in his quest for authentic detail. In *Spartacus*, the similarities are pronounced, though Kirk Douglas did not wear the formidable headgear of the Gérôme victor. Ridley Scott's 1999 film *Gladiator* also recreates the visceral excitement of the Roman combat sports.

The Roman fascination with gory death manifested again in chariot racing. The floor of the huge Circus Maximus was often strewn with bodies as races progressed. Without doubt the most memorable reconstruction of such a chariot race is in William Wyler's 1959 epic *Ben-Hur* in which Charlton Heston and Stephen Boyd lead a field of racers, most of whom come to a bloody end. The race stands the test of time as one of the most exhilarating pieces of dramatized sport ever.

The fall of the Roman Empire in the fifth century ushered in a period of a thousand years that became known as the Dark Ages and then the Middle Ages. Artistic evidence of *les tournements* were preserved in the forms of great medieval tapestries that held narratives of the chivalric conflicts in which honor, glory, and reputation were at stake. More durable were the woodcuts that proliferated, particularly in what is now Germany, in the sixteenth century. Albrecht Dürer was one of the foremost artists of his time.

Dürer was well versed in fighting sports, including wrestling and swords-manship. He illustrated the *Wallerstein Codex*, which was a manual of fighting, first published about 1470. Like some later artists of boxing, he believed that he needed to train with competitors in order to gain the insights necessary to produce his art. Germany led Europe in printing and woodcuts were used to illustrate manuscripts which could then be duplicated and disseminated. Jost Amman's 1565 *Emperor Maximilian's Tournament at Vienna* produced a celebrated vista that reveals much of the organization of tournaments. Eight jousts take place simultaneously in an enclosed courtyard outside of which are thronged spectators, some on horseback. Overlooking the courtyard are balconies from which the nobility watch in comfort. Guards patrol the area to keep order. In the competition, some of the knights have been unseated and have progressed to a ground battle with swords. The atmosphere of the scene is part sporting and part carnival, suggesting that tournaments were occasions for festivities as well as stark competition.

This type of mixture of activities gains full expression in Matthias Gerung's oil on wood *Melancholia* (1558) which features a vortex of activities, some of which resemble sports, others of which seem more like pure entertainment, still others of which appear to be celebrations. Knights in combat are also visible in Gerung's work, as are archers and bowlers, but there is no clear differentiation between the clearly ordered sport of Amman's work and other forms of recreation.

Contemporary visualizations of tournaments are commonplace thanks to the popularity of films, such as Jerry Zucker's *First Knight* (1994), in which Richard Gere plays the medieval knight Lancelot, and Kevin Reynold's *Robin Hood: Prince of Thieves* (1991) which was one of several films to feature the Nottingham outlaw of yore in the legendary archery contest.

## ORDER AND TRANSFORMATION

Europe was in the midst of the Renaissance in the sixteenth century. The profound changes that transfigured the cultural and, eventually, scientific landscape mobilized the desire for creative self-expression which in turn led to new ways of explaining, understanding, and appreciating the world. Some of the activities that we now distinguish as sports had links, however tenuous, with games that were played in Europe in this period. Kühnst detects an early visual representation of a ball game in a Venice ceiling fresco produced in the 1550s: the players wear gauntlets and exchange a leather ball in what appears to be an early type of handball.

At the same time, the rough game *calcio*, which has some similarities with latter day soccer, rugby, and its derivatives, like American football, was played by the working class. In northern Europe, woodcuts produced around 1520 feature ball games that appear to be have been played for amusement. These type of games gradually gained in popularity, superseding the chivalric combat characteristic of the tournaments. Some of the tournament events, such as horse riding, running, and spear (later, javelin) throwing, mutated and survived; others, like jousting and vaulting, did not, at least not in competitive forms.

But, the tournaments rapidly became anachronisms as the Renaissance spirit diffused throughout Europe, stimulating the progress, discovery, and a new sense of wonder with the natural world. This inevitably led to changes both in sports and in the way those sports were represented. In art, we find competitive sports signifying the desire for order, the rationalization of society, and the mastery of the self. The Baroque style epitomized this: competitors define geometrical patterns, suggesting an order and control of space. The work of Johann Christoph Neyffer and Willem Swanenburgh in the early 1600s are works of art constructed like architectural plans, so that fencers and riflemen appear as lifeless points rather than active human beings. Their conduct is not spontaneous, but ordered.

Order was even brought to the chaotic and often violent *calcio*. A 1689 copperplate by Alessandro Cecchini shows a game being played: the field of play is clearly demarcated by perimeter fencing and guards are stationed strategically; even the players occupy set positions, much like they do in contemporary ball games. Sports, like every other aspect of European society, was affected by the new model of knowledge known as science. Far from being mysterious if not unfathomable, nature was becoming comprehensible: theories about the world could be tested empirically, that is by appealing to human senses of observation, touch, taste, and sound.

Sports are often thought of as diversions from the rational planning and scientific rationality of other areas of life. This is only partly true: in the eighteenth century, as it became clear that the natural world was governed by laws, sports too underwent a revision. Luck, randomness, and a certain ineffability have always been vital ingredients in sports, of course. But some of these could be subordinated or controlled using scientific understanding.

From 1800, sports began to devour the fruits of science. The same technologies that served industry aided sports. Races took place over prescribed distances, times were measured, results were recorded; sports acquired the same rationality as industry. The importance of the stopwatch, which was first used in 1731, can scarcely be exaggerated. We find the scientific impulses to analyze, quantify, and record in the art of the period, art which became known as "sporting art."

All three impulses come together in the art of George Stubbs, who specialized in commissioned portraits of race horses. As we have noted, Stubbs's *Anatomy of a Horse* was published in 1766: it was not only work of great aesthetic beauty but of scientific precision. As its title suggests, Stubbs's art lay at the borders of medical knowledge: he brought to his subject a surgeon's skill and a thoroughness that few of his peers could match. Stubbs seemed to have investigated the minutest of detail in his quest for the perfection of objective accuracy and his masterwork has been likened to da Vinci's studies of human cadavers two hundred years earlier.

Stubbs's work chronicles some of the race horses of the day, reflecting a desire to record sporting achievements rather than just enjoy them and let them pass. There was also an element of exhibitionism, as Martin Vincent detects in his article "Painters and punters": "This kind of art had the triple advantage of showing off the patron's land, his horses and his sporting prowess" (1995: 32).

In his *Sport and the Countryside*, David Coombs refers to Stubbs and his fascination with horses: "His art sprang naturally from its environment, a prosperous, country-based economy in which the horse was the prime means of transport and a major source of motive power" (1978: 56). The horse was central to eighteenth- and early nineteenth-century life and commanded the attentions of many artists. Their work provides a documentary of Britain's changing society between 1700 and 1900, when agriculture was emerging as the primary industry and sporting customs responded to the changes.

The horse was arguably of even greater importance in America, though it was not until 1822 that it became as embodied in art as it had been in England. Charles Hall, an agriculturist and breeder, commissioned paintings of thoroughbreds by, among others, Alvan Fisher, whose *Eclipse, with Race Track* is displayed at the National Art Museum of Sport at Indianapolis.

"At the end of the eighteenth century the countryside was becoming softer and more orderly as wild areas were conquered and cultivated," writes Anthony Vandervell and Charles Coles in their *Game and the English Landscape* (1980: 61). British sporting art bore a close relationship to the changing context, depicting races and hunts against a landscape that was being prepared for the coming of industry.

Other changes were delineated in sporting art. For example, William Powell Thomas's oil *Derby Day* was created in 1858 and captures the atmosphere of the race track, members of different social classes segregated from each other: sports events were attended by all social classes, though they could not always mix. One area where they were free to mingle was the animal pit. William Hogarth's intimidating *Pit Ticket* (1759) shows male patrons, from aristocrats to thieves, huddled together around a cockpit, their devilish zeal for the fight apparent in their grotesquely drawn faces. *The Rat Pit*, by an unknown artist around 1860 (after the prohibition of cockfighting in 1849), shows members of different social classes stratified as if according to rank from the top of the canvas. The picture bears a striking resemblance to Peter Blake's artwork for the cover of *Sgt. Pepper's Lonely Hearts Club Band*, the motley characters looking like lifeless cut-outs congregating around a central attraction, in this case a pit filled with 50-odd rats and a tenacious terrier (reproduced by Coombs 1978: 186).

Théodore Géricaux's *The Derby at Epsom*, painted in 1821, on the other hand, focuses on the thrill of a horse race in progress, the horses speeding toward the finishing line; and this too gives some indication of the changes afoot in society. Kühnst argues that this and other works that communicate speed, tension, and the excitement of competition "show the transformation of physical exercises from static exhibitions of skill to lively achievement-oriented contests" (1996: 140).

This achievement orientation spread across the whole sporting spectrum from the beginning of the nineteenth century, and the stylized poses of earlier art gave way to scenes of action in which competitors strove, not just to compete, but to win. Gustave Coubert's oil *The Wrestler* painted in 1853, for example, shows two men clearly struggling for all they are worth. Frederic Remington's

*Touchdown, Yale vs. Princeton, Thanksgiving Day, November 27, 1890, Yale 32, Princeton 0* suggests a less-than-friendly rivalry between the two teams as the players strain for supremacy. In these and in countless other works of the time, competitors are no longer statuesque, but dynamic and goal-directed. In a sense, the change mirrored the transition in art from Romanticism to Impressionism which animated its subjects with a variety of techniques.

Impressionism originated in and refracted a world agitated by the twin forces of industrialization and urbanization. Advances in the natural sciences, especially chemistry, propelled a move toward the mechanization and other technological processes. The same processes that revolutionized economies all over Europe made their presence felt in sports – and art. In 1896, when Coubertin launched the modern Olympic Games, the factory system was in full swing and populations were herding together in cities. European societies were at pains to restore stability in the face of fundamental economic and cultural shifts. Industry demanded order.

Rational progress, uniformity, and standardization were the hallmarks of industrialism. It is no coincidence that they were also key features of Coubertin's vision: a comprehensive program of sports events carefully organized, each performance being quantified, ranked, and rewarded according to standards of excellence. The effects of modernity, industrialism, and the technology they fostered were felt in sports; they were also felt in the modes through which sports were represented.

In the early 1880s, two artists, one American, one British, both of whom shared an interest in technology, came together at the University of Pennsylvania, their purpose being to apply science to art and produce objectively accurate representations of sports. Thomas Eakins was a celebrated oils painter who created some of the most evocative images of boxing and wrestling of the nineteenth century. His nude and near-nude studies of prizefighters formed part of a tradition of homoerotic sports art that found later expression in the sculptures of Eakins's student Charles Grafly and, later, in the art of John De Andrea, David Rohn, and Bruce Weber, the director of the film *Broken Noses* (1987).

Eakins's collaboration with Eadweard Muybridge, a British photographer who emigrated to the United States in 1852, yielded work that changed artists', indeed everyone's, conceptions of sports. Exploiting the potential of the relatively new technology of photography, Eakins and Muybridge sought to create the most physiologically precise record of sports action using the most technically efficient methods. *Studies of Human Movements* included over 100,000 stroboscopic photographs, each capturing a moment of sporting action.

Photography was arguably the most influential of all media in sports history. Prior to the pioneering work of Louis Daguerre, it had been difficult to capture a moving image without blurring, mainly because of the lengthy exposure time required. Also, the amount of equipment involved made it impracticable for sports events, and images faded with age, anyway. But improvements in photographic paper reduced the exposure time and sharpened the images. Poses of people such as Bernarr Macfadden and Eugen Sandow, whom we covered in Chapter 8, were widely circulated, adding to the reputations of both. We'll return to photography in Chapter 16 when we consider the importance of image diffusion in the rise of celebrities. For now, we should recognize the crucial role played by photography, not only in spreading interest in sports, but in advancing our understanding of athletic movement.

Let's take an obvious example. To the naked eye, a great deal of sports action is indistinct and uncertain. Artists had no way of knowing whether their work faithfully represented what actually happened. Stubbs and his peers, who were fascinated by horses, always imagined and represented them galloping in what's called the "rocking horse" position, all four hooves planted on the ground. Photography exposed the absurdity of this. Muybridge's work showed how all four feet sometimes left the ground as the same time. Though it seems obvious to those of us who have grown up with the benefit of slow-motion tv, it was astounding to people who depended on their eyesight alone. Next time you watch a sports event, try imagining what it would be like if you were relying only on what you see as your guide.

The art of Eakins and Muybridge had aesthetic beauty, but it also had practical application, enabling an understanding of the mechanics of motion and so establishing a base point for later studies. Their techniques were adopted and refined by photographer Étienne-Jules Marey who used time exposure experiments to disclose the minutiae of athletic actions. Among his more notable studies were *Fencing* (1890) and *Mounting a Bicycle* (1891) which were both educative and picturesque. Similar techniques were used by Harold Edgerton who produced stop-motion studies of, among other sports, pole vaulting and tennis in the mid-twentieth century. These artists brought to sports a punctiliousness and fidelity that was to resurface in later film documentaries, such as *Visions of Eight* (1973) and *Hoop Dreams* (1994).

Photography became popular in the twentieth century and artists of sport were adventurous in their use of the medium to portray sports in entirely new ways. Painters made use of photography to achieve a new level of naturalism and photographers innovated with new techniques to steer clear of naturalism. The photo-collages of John Heartfield in the 1920s extended earlier work, but introduced satire. For example, his *A Specter is Haunting Europe* features a runner made up of industrial parts, the head a stopwatch, pistons for limbs, and what seems to be a clock card in place of a chest. The work satirizes both the preoccupation with industrial production and its effects on sports, which were becoming joyless affairs, interested in records and measurable achievements. The changes in organization and focus in sports is also a theme in the photo-collages of Laszlo Moholy-Nagy, Irene Hoffmann, and Willi Baumeister. In all their work, there is a concern with the apparent mechanization of the modern athlete and the dehumanizing possibilities it entailed. A similar pitiless angular drive toward geometric perfection informs the work of William Roberts, particularly his 1967 "Goal" in which football players appear compressed into unison, their limbs bent like levers. We find the same concerns at the core of Jean-Marie Brohm's 1978 critique, the title of which sums up the author's thrust, *Sport: A prison of measured time*.

Modernity and the trends it ushered in continued to have salience with other artists, many either intrigued with or disgusted by its impact on sports. The reduction of what was once a playful, expressive activity to flat-out competition was a popular subject for many members of the avant-garde. Paul Klee, whose insight opened this chapter, produced his *Runner–Hooker–Boxer* in 1920: this aquarelle is structured like geological layers, its figure seeming to run through the strata; the sprinting figure wears a boxing glove on one hand and has an arrow jutting from the other. Robert Delaunay's oil *The Runners*, 1926, visualizes its characters similarly: the faceless athletes run in unison. Even celebrated athletes can do little to distinguish themselves in a postwar culture that renders everyone anonymous, the artists seem to say.

## THE GAZE OF HIS LADY

Among the vestiges from fifth-century BCE Sparta is a vase decorated with a scene from a woman's foot race. The barefoot runners wear long skirts and short-sleeved tops. Yaloris records that: "Women's sport was a feature of the education of girls in Sparta and Crete" (1979: 59). The same author also reproduces a mosaic depicting women training with dumbbells, practicing discus-throwing, and sprinting. "Women's sport was quite widespread in the Roman period," observes Yaloris (1979: 279).

Even in the medieval period when it is generally assumed women's presence at sporting events was purely decorative, there are artworks that show women in active roles. There are several illuminated manuscripts depicting women competing in jousts. As Allen Guttmann writes, in his *The Erotic in Sports*: "Robert de Borron's *Histoire du Graal* and the anonymous *Lancelot de Lac* are ornamented with pictures of mounted women wielding distaffs and spindles and charging at obviously disconcerted knights and monks" (1996: 41).

Kühnst includes in his impressive text a reproduction of Nicolas Arnoult's 1698 *Le Jeu du Volant* with three figures, two female, playing "featherball," which was a precursor of badminton. He also has a plate of Jean-Baptiste's oil *Girl with a Shuttlecock and Battledore* from 1741. In both works, the women appear to be middle class. A copperplate by Victor Marie Picot features, as

305

its title suggests, *The Assault or Fencing Match which took place between Mademoiselle La Chevalière d'Eon de Beaumont and Monsieur de Saint Georges on the 9th of April 1787*. The female contestant is seen thrusting decisively at her male opponent.

In the late eighteenth century archery became popular with affluent English women who competed on level terms with men. The etching *A Meeting of the Society of Royal British Archers in Gwersyllt Park, Denbighshire* by Robert Smirke and John Emes, which is now in the British Museum, shows women archers in competition. In the sense that it allowed head-to-head contests between males and females, archery was unusual, and a more telling picture from the same century is James Seymour's *A Coursing Scene* in which a woman sits side-saddle on her horse while a male inspects a dead hare presented to him by his servant. "This is not a painting for feminists," remarks Coombs. "There is no doubt who is the master, as much from the nature of his expression as the gaze of his lady and stance of his huntsman" (1978: 20).

Hunting scenes in nineteenth-century works continued to depict women riding side-saddle to protect their modesty. Sir Francis Grant's opulent canvas *Lady Riding Side-Saddle with her Dog, circa* 1840, is an example. The idea of women opening their legs to ride in the same way as men was an outrage to Victorians. But, in 1861, Pierre Micheaux and his son Ernest invented a machine they called a *vélocipède*, a riding machine that offered a cheaper, simpler, and more efficient mode of transport than the horse. The mass production of the *vélocipèdes* in France in the 1860s was quickly followed by what became known as the "cycling craze." Curiously, given the time in history, cycling was seen as a safe pastime for women.

Sir John Lavery's *The Tennis Party* (1885) and Winslow Homer's *Croquet Scene* (1866) chronicle the more typical sporting endeavors of women in the period and, even then, tennis and croquet were sports of the affluent. Cycling was relatively inexpensive and available to all classes. By the turn of the century, women all over Europe and America were taking to the road on bicycles. Spurning the reserve associated with side-saddle riding, women made a hugely symbolic gesture by cycling – they opened their legs. Kühnst believes that of all the developments in sports, the bicycle "contributed the most to the emancipation of women by increasing their physical independence and personal freedom" (1996: 208).

Jean Béraud's 1900 canvas *The Cyclists' Café in the Bois de Bologne* shows women and men sharing drinks and inspecting each others' cycles during a break from their recreations. Bruno Paul's lithograph *Die Frau vor dem Rad: Hinter dem Rad: und aus dem Rad* ("The Woman in Front of the Wheel, Behind the Wheel, and on Wheels") cleverly essayed women's relationship with technology by displaying the same women cycling, working a sewing machine, and pulling an agricultural appliance.

## Cycling and Art

Cycling has held a special appeal for several significant artists, including Henri Toulouse-Lautrec. The coming together of human and machine in competitive racing seemed to offer unique possibilities at the end of the nineteenth century when races spread across Europe and the USA. Toulouse-Lautrec was drawn to the cycling milieu: he regularly attended velodromes and race tracks and stood at the roadside in an effort to absorb some of the atmosphere that he then translated into his art, much of it commissioned by bicycle manufacturers, like Simpsons. Other significant artists of cycling include Jean Metzinger, Natalia Gontscharova, and the Futurist, Umberto Boccioni, in the early twentieth century, Fernand Léger in the mid-twentieth century, and, more recently, Alex Colville. A great many other prominent artists have pictures of cycling in their portfolios.

Kühnst includes in his collection an anonymous photograph from 1910 that anticipates the later trend to mix sexual and sporting imagery: the female stands besides her bicycle, her skirt and petticoat caught on the handlebars and saddle so that her bare genitalia is revealed. While usually not as risqué as this study, many later works ventured toward the lewd, showing athletic women more as models than as active performers and often wearing skimpy clothes.

Picasso's gouache *The Race* (1922) features two running women, each of whom displays a breast, their tops having slipped from their shoulders. Anton Räderscheidt's several studies of naked female sports performers in the 1920s typically incorporated a fully dressed male voyeur in the background. In the same period, Willi Baumeister depicted naked women running on tracks and diving from rocks, not perhaps for prurient purposes, but with the effect of sexualizing the image of the female athlete. Even the celebrated Canadian artist Alex Colville's paintings of sports performers, include *Skater* (1964) which invites the viewer to inspect the rear of a gliding skater, her arms clasped at her back, right leg raised perpendicular to her left and lycra-clad buttocks conspicuously displayed. There is a minor tradition in art that depicts women athletes engaging in competition but positioned, dressed, or undressed in a way that tempts salacity.

Robert Towne's 1982 film *Personal Best*, in which Mariel Hemingway and Patrice Donnelly play two pentathletes involved in a lesbian relationship, does not entirely escape this convention. As Guttmann remarks: "Although the film does justice to sports as physical *contests*, Towne never hesitates to underscore the erotic element" (1996: 119). Guttmann has in mind slow-motion studies of bare thighs and midriffs of female high-jumpers in mid-air, a bench-press session in which the spotter stands invitingly astride her prostrate training partner, and a bout of arm-wrestling that turns into a bout of sex.

## LITE AND DARK

Hailed by some, denounced by others, the film *Olympia* (or *Olympisch Spiele*) was undeniably a monumental work of art. Ostensibly, a chronicle of the 1936 Olympic Games held at Berlin, Leni Riefenstahl's film was a propagandist disquisition that attempted to immortalize Nazi visions of Aryan supremacy. Commissioned to make a film of the games, Riefenstahl, perhaps naively, produced a stylistic masterwork with cinematographic innovations to rival those of *Citizen Kane*. Despite its seminal artistry, the film is still an ideological frame to showcase Aryanism: so glaring is the Nazi iconography that the viewer can almost sense Hitler himself at Riefenstahl's shoulder.

The IOC had encouraged art and, at Coubertin's urging, integrated a program of artistic competition into the games with medals awarded for different art forms. So, a filmic record of the Olympic Games was welcomed. Jacob Lawrence's gouache for the poster commemorating the 1972 games at Munich was one of a series that have been acknowledged as stand-alone works of art.

---

### Leni Riefenstahl

Famed German director of *Olympia*, which is hailed by many as the greatest-ever sports documentary and reviled by many others as a glorification of Nazism. Born in 1902, Riefenstahl was a dancer and actor who turned to directing in 1932 when she made *The Blue Light*. Influenced by Fanck's 1926 silent film *Mountain of Destiny*, she used specially imported lenses and film stock to further her experiments with lighting and composition. Having seen Riefenstahl's work, Hitler commissioned her to film the 1933 National Socialist Party Congress, a film that was released as *Victory of Faith*. Dissatisfied with the results, Riefenstahl filmed the following year's Congress at Nuremberg; this time, the end product was a visually stunning documentary, *Triumph of the Will*. Riefenstahl's *Olympia*, which was ostensibly the filmic record of the 1936 Berlin Olympics, was another work of brilliance, though its exaltation of Aryan manhood ultimately marred its critical reception. Wagnerian in atmosphere, the film's majesty is in its narrative construction, each scene building toward the thunderous climax. After the Second World War, Riefenstahl was boycotted. She died, aged 101, in 2003.

---

But it is another Olympic-themed work, Claus Mattyes's collage *Olympia* (1978) that Kühnst singles out as the most revelational piece of contemporary sporting art. In it, a Magritte-style figure, bowler-hatted and wearing an IOC lapel pin, stands in front of a faux Greek statue which someone has defaced with a drawn-on beard and mustache. In the background, there is a bunting, but the flags are not just those of nations – they bear the logos of Coca-Cola, IBM, and the Playboy Club. There is even a dollar bill dangling from the bunting. The significance of these needs no explanation. And, as if to connect his work with that of Baumeister, Hoffmann, and, indeed, the writer Brohm, Mattyes positions a clock centrally between the two figures.

Such cynicism informs much of the art on sport over the past 70 or so years. The age of innocence, when art glorified sport, had been drawing to a close for several years before Riefenstahl's film. Shortly after its release, the Second World War occasioned a re-evaluation of sport's merits. It was not long before virtually every Olympic Games became political as well as sporting events. Coupled with this came the realization that more and more sports were becoming professionalized and the Corinthian ideals that had once motivated competitors were extinct.

The darker side of sports was explored exquisitely by George Bellows in the first two decades of the twentieth century. His usually grim images, often of boxing matches, feature faces in the crowds that seem to have spilled straight from a Hogarth canvas. Fighters collide viciously, blood spattering their bodies as fans frantically make wagers. A fighter's left hook sends a hapless opponent crashing through the ropes. The dim and dingy atmosphere of boxing halls is a

---

### George Bellows

Born in 1882, in Columbus, Ohio, Bellows moved to New York in 1904 where he studied art under Robert Henri, a radical artist of his time. Bellows became associated with what was known as the Ash Can School because of his choice of subjects: in contrast to many studies that emphasized the dignity of competition, Bellows stuck to the sordid, often shameful, side of sports. His characters were frequently rough, common people battling savagely in what often looked like a war zone. He inherited the mantle of art's greatest interpreter of boxing with works such as *Both Members of this Club (A Nigger and a White Man)*, an oil painted in 1918 which pictured a black and a white fighter locked in combat, both literally and metaphorically. His *Dempsey and Firpo*, 1924, remains one of the most stirring works of sports art. Bellows died of a ruptured appendix aged 42, in 1925.

fitting backdrop to a sport that enthralled Bellows in much the same manner that pedestrians are enthralled by car wrecks. For Bellows, boxing simultaneously repels and attracts.

It was probably only logical that, as film became a more established art form, directors would try to adapt features of Bellows's work for the screen. In the late 1930s and 1940s, films such as *Kid Galahad*, directed by Michael Curtiz and released in 1937, probed the dirtier aspects of the fight game. Robert Wise's *The Set-Up* (1948) examined how a fixed fight goes wrong when no one tells the fighter he is supposed to take a dive. The short (72 minutes) film, shot in black and white, casts shadows across virtually every scene to evoke the gloomy atmosphere of bleakness and moral uncertainty; a radio commentary punctuates the soundtrack as if to remind the viewer that the media has made its malevolent presence felt on a once-noble sport. Mark Robson's 1949 *Champion* was another portrait of a sport callously corrupted by avaricious businessmen. The familiarly dire portrait of boxing continued with films such as *Somebody Up There Likes Me* and *The Harder They Fall*, both 1956, and *Requiem for a Heavyweight* (in Britain, *Blood Money*), 1962. In these and other films, romanticism was jettisoned and a savage realism was brought to the subject. Like the bronzes of Mahonri Mackintosh Young and Richmond Barthé, boxers are disfigured by the strains of competing in a sport that has long forgotten the principles of fairness and "sportsmanship."

This misanthropic approach was by no means confined to boxing. Paul Cadmus's oil and tempera work *Aspects of Suburban Life: Golf* (1936) was one of four panels created during the Depression. Here golf is a putrid metaphor for the social inequalities of America: a well-heeled, cigar-smoking golfer sits while his supine caddy holds his clubs. The caddy is poverty personified; his shoes have holes in their soles, his jeans, which are a few sizes too big for his undernourished body, are tied with string. He tends to the needs of the conspicuously rich, all overweight and either ignoring completely or peering down their noses at the caddy.

Other disagreeable aspects of sports are dealt with by A. Paul Weber's *The False Penalty Shoot*. Weber envisions a game of soccer as disintegrating into a horrifying riot with the bodies of hundreds of spectators strewn about the field and thousands more pouring forward. The lithograph was produced in 1964 and bears an eerie similarity with the scenes evidenced at the Hillsborough stadium in 1989 when 96 fans died resulting from the worst tragedy in British sports history.

Sports fans have not escaped the critical attentions of film directors. *The Fan* (1996) featured Robert De Niro as a knife salesman turning on a baseball star who seems to have sacrificed sporting values for money. Tony Scott's film was a study in how contemporary sports are able to destroy the very things they build: devotion, loyalty, and hero-worship. A playful pitching competition between fan and player is shot like a gunfight in a 1950s western, the duel escalating as the fan vents his wrath. Fanaticism is also the focus of Philip Davis's undervalued account of a British police officer who goes undercover to penetrate a gang of hooligans: *i.d.*, 1994, communicated the dubious attractions of gang affiliation and organized violence. Particularly powerful are scenes in a British pub used as headquarters by the gang: here the *esprit de corps* that fuels the fanaticism is dramatically realized and the viewer is made privy to the attractions of fandom. Nick Love revisited London's hooligan pubs in 2004: his *The Football Factory* makes us onlookers to the violent subculture of soccer fans.

The photographer Tom Stoddart used a close-up of the blistered, calloused, and cut palms of a female gymnast's hands to convey the punishing effects of training regimes. Regarded by most as a beautiful and edifying sport, gymnastics was exposed by Joan Ryan's book *Little Girls in Pretty Boxes: The making and breaking of élite gymnasts and figure skaters* (1998) as hideously cruel. Stoddart's *Hands of a Seven-Year-Old Gymnast* (1994) presents this ugly side of the sport and, like most quality sports photography, is capable of prodding viewers to regard sports in new ways.

Film, more than any other medium, has been able to expose the darker side of sports graphically and in often disturbing detail. In the fight films mentioned earlier, the decay of the sport was almost palpable; and, in later works, boxing served as an ungodly background against which to paint a larger human drama. John Huston's *Fat City* (1972) is a piercingly miserable exploration of two losers and the exploitation of one by the other. *Raging Bull* (1980) is Martin Scorsese's harrowing, monochrome biography of the middleweight champion, Jake LaMotta.

The very nature of the art form permits much more indulgence in the circumstances surrounding sports: the event itself is often filmed in a way that deliberately avoids *reportage*. Scorsese, for example, shot some fight scenes from the perspective of a boxer rather than a spectator, often dwelling on small effects like blood dripping from a ring rope. Scorsese hurls naturalism away, using LaMotta's fights as parts of a narrative that maps out his personal conflicts, especially with his belittled wife Vicky.

Perhaps the most earnest portrayal of the degradation of sports was John Sayles's film of the scandalous 1919 World Series, *Eight Men Out* (1988). In it, the poorly paid and virtually indentured Chicago White Sox players are depicted as fodder for greedy owners and corrupt gamblers. Baseball action is shown sparingly, most of the plot centering on the bars and boardrooms where the real "action" is played out. Venality is at the heart of several other films on sports, one of the most celebrated of which is Robert Rosen's 1961 *The Hustler*, which moves in and out of the grimy poolhalls of the 1960s; as its title suggests, gambling provides the mainspring of the plot. Most of the film is shot indoors and the black and white cinematography accentuates the grubbiness of both the sport and its milieu. Gambling and the opportunities for corruption it offers are themes in Norman Jewison's *The Cincinnati Kid*, 1965, in which Steve McQueen plays a hot-shot poker player in the 1930s, and in Stephen Frears' *The Grifters* (1979) which involves a horse race track scam. A similar scam forms the nucleus of Stanley Kubrick's *The Killing* (1956). In these films, the camera dwells on images of dollar bills, being bet, exchanged, or, in *The Killing*, being swirled around, the black and white photography making them appear like leaves in a gale.

One of the most underrated attempts to uncloak the malignancy of contemporary sport is *Blue Chips*, a 1994 film by William Friedkin, in which an NCAA basketball coach played by Nick Nolte is pulled into offering money to secure college players. The movie's plot was uncomfortably similar to several real-life incidents involving illegal payments and points shaving. The film is an almost natural partner of the epic, 2 hour 50 minute documentary *Hoop Dreams* (1994) in which directors Steve James, Fred Marx, and Peter Gilbert track the progress of two African American youths who aspire to be pro basketball players: they are but two of countless young black men who single-mindedly pursue what is for most only, as the title implies, a dream. The *in situ* scenes at the home of the aspirants make the viewer feel like an eavesdropper on a private conversation.

Often neglected is *The Club* (1980) an Australian film directed by Bruce Beresford which tells of the travails of an Australian Rules football club owner who trades in a star player only to find his man has undergone a conversion and despises the competitive machismo of contemporary sports. A comparable conversion is the plot device of *Jerry Maguire* (1997) director Chris Columbus's tale of an avaricious sports agent who discovers a conscience and tries to mend his ways.

These are but a sample of the ways cinema has ripped away the sentimentality and honor traditionally associated with sports to disclose the grimmer, unethical aspects that are integral to professional sports. They find a kindred spirit in Armand Arman's dissection of football helmets, produced in 1972: 24 helmets split in half are mounted on Plexiglas. Gone is the sheen, the insignia, and smooth curves that athletes are meant to wear with honor; instead, Arman presents a jumbled mess of dismembered metal, plastic, and rubber parts. By literally deconstructing the helmets, Arman is exposing the innards of American sports.

It is tempting to add the silkscreens of Andy Warhol to this myth-shattering tradition in sports art. In 1978, Warhol produced portraits of Muhammad Ali, Chris Evert, Pelé, O. J. Simpson, and several other distinguished sports performers. The work has an ambiguity in the sense that each of the portraits is daubed over and modified, some might say defaced. Much of Warhol's work was intended to distort as a way of revealing hitherto unknown truths that lurk behind the images or façades we habitually confront. The Warhol symbols consecrate and condemn simultaneously.

Several films have used sports as metaphors for other areas of social life. There is a vital British tradition that starts with Lindsay Anderson's 1963 *This Sporting Life* set in the North of England, where Richard Harris's mud-spattered struggle on the rugby field parallels the rest of his life and, in many senses, that of the northern working class in the 1960s. *The Loneliness of the Long Distance Runner*, directed by Tony Richardson, in 1962, cross-country running is a simile for a young working-class offender's gutsy clamber out of a correctional facility. There is a resemblance between this and Robert Aldrich's 1974 film *The Longest Yard*, also known as *The Mean Machine* which features Burt Reynolds as a pro football player who winds up in prison and leads a team of inmates against a team of guards. In all three, images of sport are coarse and unpleasant. Anderson's film, like Aldrich's, makes great use of shots that are unavailable to the spectator: inside scrums and scrimmages, where players spit and trade sly punches.

Oliver Stone's 1999 movie *Any Given Sunday* used an allegorical NFL franchise to illustrate the manner in which corporate interests overpower all others and, in the process, threaten the integrity, principles, and ideals that once lay at the heart of honest competition.

A big part of our enchantment with sports is their ability to evoke extremes and for every work of art that exposes dim and recondite areas, there is at least another that illuminates the glorious, heroic, and even spiritually uplifting qualities of honest competition. The choice is vast, though some films all but select themselves if only because they correspond so perfectly to what David Rowe describes as a "source of mythologies, allegories and narratives" (2004a: 200).

The five *Rocky* films (the first and fifth directed by John G. Avildsen, 1976, 1990; the others by Sylvester Stallone, 1979, 1982, 1985) were collectively a saga of a down-at-heel fighter who is plucked from obscurity to challenge for the world heavyweight title. The fable follows Rocky Balboa, "The Italian Stallion" through his ascent, descent, and beyond. The fight action scenes are outrageously choreographed so that they have a comic book quality: ablaze with color and gravity-defying action; the fights that made the series so successful bore little resemblance to boxing. They are counterpointed by Rocky's delicate relationship with his lover and, later, wife. Boxing's dark corners are never fully explored and the film suggests that human courage and perseverance are the qualities needed to triumph. There are just deserts for those with the will to win; merit never goes unrewarded.

*Rocky* won the Academy Award for the Best Picture in 1976 and it is no accident that the Oscar winner of 1981 embodied similar ideals about the ethic of competition and the glory of victory. Hugh Hudson's *Chariots of Fire* (1981) is set in the twilight of the British Empire and has no plot to speak of: it simply traces the build-up to the 1924 summer Olympics through the experiences of two real British track athletes. Harold Abrahams was a Jewish university student at Oxford. Eric Liddell was a Scottish working-class Christian who ran because he believed it was for the greater glory of god. In a sense, both were outsiders and the film rejoices in their achievements, employing slo-mo running sequences and a stirring Vangelis soundtrack to amplify all that is good about clean athletic competition. The famous scene of a joyous training group running along a beach, hair swept by the breeze, ocean waves lapping against their ankles, captures the wholesomeness of sport purveyed by *Chariots of Fire*.

If there is a painter whose work embodies the sentiments of these two films it is LeRoy Neiman. His work, particularly in the 1970s, was straightforward fast-moving narrative action. Neiman's characters seem to scorch the canvas: boxers' punches whiz toward their opponent, horses gallop almost into the viewer, tennis players throw themselves across the court. Compositions appear to occur so rapidly that there is no time for thought, less still criticism. Neiman's art is pure, glorious competitive energy.

Baseball films – and there have been dozens – typically gorge on narrative action. But not so Phil Alden's gently fantastic *Field of Dreams* (1989). Hearing the mandate "if you build it they will come," farmer Kevin Costner clears a section of his plot in Iowa and constructs a baseball diamond. Sure enough, "they," the ghosts of great baseball players, appear from beyond the grave. Every frame is bathed in autumnal tones of greens and browns appropriate to a film that pines for a bygone age. Costner established himself in part through his sports roles. He also featured in two Ron Shelton films: *Bull Durham* (1988) another baseball film, and *Tin Cup* (1996) which was about golf. Other notable Shelton efforts include *White Men Can't Jump* and *Cobb*, the latter of which used an interview between a writer and the old baseball player, Ty Cobb, as a framing device; the narrative proceeds in a series of flashbacks.

Sports have often supplied raw material for the subgenre of fantasy-comedy, the most influential of which was *Here Comes Mr Jordan* (1941) directed by Alexander Hall and featuring Robert Montgomery as a boxer prematurely called to heaven due to a clerical error; returned to earth as an angel, the boxer seeks out his incredulous manager and seeks to resume his career. The plot was updated in 1978 and the boxer was replaced by a football player for Buck Henry's *Heaven Can Wait*, with Warren Beatty playing the deceased athlete. The cinematic conceit was to show the audience the returned player even though he was supposed to be invisible to the cast of the film. Much the same story was reprised again in 1997 with *The Sixth Man*, this time the departed-and-returned being a basketball player.

Slightly less whimsical were two comedies directed by David S. Ward, *Major League* (1989) and *Major League II* (1994) which followed the adventures of a baseball team of misfits who somehow contrived to win the occasional game.

Another pair of baseball films were based on the real All American Girls'
Professional Baseball League which was formed in 1943 to fill the void left by
male baseball players who were involved in the war effort. Penny Marshall's
*A League of Their Own* (1992) led to a less successful sequel. The baseball
sequences were colorful and exaggerated, lending the films their phantas-
magorical quality.

---

### Ron Shelton

Born in Whittier, California, in 1945, Shelton is the world's premier
director of films with sports themes. His *Bull Durham* (1988) featured Kevin
Costner as an experienced baseball player coaching a promising young
player (Tim Robbins) who is being seduced by Susan Sarandon. It was
followed by *White Men Can't Jump* (1992) in which Wesley Snipes and
Woody Harrelson play a couple of basketball hustlers plying their trade
around parking lots. Returning to baseball, Shelton made *Cobb* (1994),
a biopic of the irascible stand-out player of the period either side of the
First World War, with Ty Cobb played by Tommy Lee Jones. *Tin Cup*
(1996) centers on a golf pro, played by Costner, who enters the US Open,
comes within a whisker of winning it, and blows it by refusing to play safe.
Shelton focused on boxing in his *Play it to the Bone* (2000), in which
Woody Harrelson and Antonio Banderas play the leads. Shelton also
wrote the underrated *Blue Chips* (1994) which tells of corruption in NCAA
basketball, and co-wrote the tv movie *The Great White Hype* (1996),
memorable for Samuel L. Jackson's portrayal of a Don King-type promoter.
In Shelton's work, sports are more than the competitive activities that
provide their material substance: they are opportunities for mere mortals
to test themselves against invincible forces that constantly challenge them.

---

Light comedy became outright farce in Harold Ramis's *Caddyshack* (1980)
Dennis Dugan's *Happy Gilmore* (1996) and Frank Coraci's *The Waterboy* (1999)
all of which treated sports as a burlesque show. A similar playful mischief
is evident in the work of pop artist Red Grooms. His *Fran Tarkenton* (1979) is
described by Louis A. Zona: "Grooms chooses to create a 'schtick' right out of
vaudeville, as the greatest quarterback of his time tiptoes through a flower patch
in search of a receiver . . . giving American pictorial art that sense of humor and
humanity which has been missing" (1990: 122).

While Riefenstahl's *Olympia* had its ideological shortcomings, there was
no doubt about its aesthetic triumph and it is still arguably the benchmark
against which sports documentary features are measured. The previously

mentioned *Hoop Dreams* was acclaimed as one of the finest documentaries in recent times: young black males become beasts of burden, laden with their failed parents' vanquished ambitions, as they strive to make it in pro basketball. In Leon Gast's *When We Were Kings* (1997) Muhammad Ali's upset win over George Foreman in 1974 is embellished in a way that enriches the viewer's appreciation of the wider issues surrounding the fight, which took place in Zaire. Edited in such a way that observers of the fight function like a Greek chorus, the film intercuts footage of the boxers in training with clips of them in unguarded moments and scenes from the James Brown concert that preceded the boxing promotion.

Less inventive but still insightful was George Butler's *Pumping Iron II: The women* (1984) which was a follow-up to the same director's 1976 *Pumping Iron* (which he made with Robert Fiore), but which is altogether more challenging, as it observed women competing in a ruthless yet sisterly way for the 1983 Caeser's Cup. The viewer seems to be secluded in hotel and locker rooms and made privy to personal conversations; the tight camera shots serve to convey competitor Bev Francis's torture and her trainer puts her through near-Procrustean schedules.

But, in terms of lineage, perhaps the rightful heir to *Olympia* is *Visions of Eight* (1973) which brought together eight noted directors from around the world, each concentrating on a particular event or athlete at the Munich Olympics of 1972. Only John Schlesinger's segment incorporated the Palestinian terrorist hostage deaths into a sports story, this one about British marathon runner, Ron Hill. Others directors included Arthur Penn (of *Bonnie and Clyde* fame) who examined the pole vault, Mai Zetterling, who dwelled on weightlifting, and Kon Ichikawa, who scrutinized the men's 100-meter sprint. This sports documentary, like some others, shares many aims with the photography of Muybridge and his followers: by scrupulously attending to particularities the artist invites viewers to build their own vista. As in all art, it is the person attending to the work that is actually doing the work: making connections, filling in blanks, comprehending the meanings of the image. And so it has been with all art based on sport.

Were it not for our preoccupation with sports, then the art we have covered in this chapter would have less meaning, less value, and less significance culturally. The fact that the art I have referred to here is only a fraction of a much more formidable corpus of work bears witness to the seemingly perpetual interest in both sport and the art it has in some way inspired. Our fascination is not only with the activities themselves, but with the minute moments of a contest and the larger dynamics of the context in which it takes place. Art has enlarged our appreciation of both.

*Motion Studies: Time, space and Eadweard Muybridge* by Rebecca Solnit (Bloomsbury, 2004) makes a good case for Muybridge as "a bullet shot through a book. His trajectory ripped through all the stories of his time . . . He is the man who split the second, as dramatic and far-reaching as the splitting of the atom."

*The Eternal Olympics: The art and history of sport* edited by Nicolaos Yaloris (Caratzas Brothers, 1979) alerts us to the vital importance of athletic competition to the culture and civic life of ancient civilizations by examining the evolution of sports and sports-related art from the second millennium BCE to the end of the ancient Olympic Games in CE 510.

*Sport and the Countryside* by David Coombs (Phaidon Press, 1978) concentrates on the period from the seventeenth century to the middle of the nineteenth, when hunting was virtually synonymous with "sports" and supplied the inspiration for a great many artists, especially painters. This may profitably be read in conjunction with *Game and the English Landscape: The influence of the chase on sporting art and scenery* by Anthony Vandervell and Charles Coles (Debrett's Peerage, 1980).

*Sports: A cultural history in the mirror of art* by Peter Kühnst (Verlag der Kunst, 1996) is a marvelous narrative exposition of the story of sports from the Renaissance onwards as told through art. "The artist's vision is a unique clue to historical change," argues Kühnst. The same author has compiled another revealing collection *Physique: Classic photographs of naked athletes* (Thames & Hudson, 2004).

*Sport in Art from American Museums* edited by Reilly Rhodes (Universe, 1990) reproduces exhibits from the National Art Museum of Sport, Indianapolis; most of the art is from the nineteenth and twentieth centuries and includes the work of Stubbs, Eakins, and Bellows.

*Sport on Film and Video: The North American Society for Sport History guide* edited by Judith Davidson and compiled by Daryl Adler (Scarecrow Press, 1993) is one of a number of reference books on the subject; others include *Sports in the Movies* by Ronald Bergan (Proteus Books, 1982) and *Sports Films: A complete reference* by Harvey M. Zucker and Lawrence J. Babich (HM & M Publishers, 1976); there is an entry on "Films" in my own *Sports Culture: An A–Z* (Routledge, 2000).

"Screening the action" is a chapter in the second edition of David Rowe's *Sport, Culture and the Media* (Open University, 2004a) and the author sees the various ways in which tv, radio, film, and other media have depicted sports as evidence of "sport's amoeba-like cultural capacity to divide and re-form."

## ASSIGNMENT

> As the curator of a museum, you are charged with the responsibility of organizing an exhibition *Sports: The heroes and the villains*. You may commission glass displays of artifacts, waxwork models, performance art, installations, and other forms of contemporary art (*à la* Damien Hirst, Tracey Emin, or Gillian Wearing), as well as more traditional art forms. Imagine the works you would include; these can include anything you consider suitable. Then write an account justifying the inclusion of your pieces.

# a match made in heaven

why television and sports are

inseparable

**SUPER BOWL L**

To: e.e.cashmore@staffs.edu
From: h.g.wells@timemachine.org
Subject: the wonders of the media

Professor Cashmore: It's 2016 and I'm in the USA. Today is a huge day over here: World Super Bowl Sunday. This year the rival teams are Tokyo Samurai, appearing in their first Super Bowl and the Las Vegas Fortune. Vegas is going for its second championship this century, having won three years ago under their old name Las Vegas Bengals. The old Cincinnati Bengals owner sold out in 2011 and the new owners, a consortium in which News Corp. has a 36 percent stake, moved the franchise to Nevada. Now, the city of Cincinnati has been promised an expansion team and has been granted permission to reclaim its original name. So, the Vegas outfit changed to the Fortune – quite an appropriate name in several ways, including the investment that went into building the franchise and an 85,000-seater stadium which has 70 percent of its capacity taken up by luxury boxes. Still the investment has paid off handsomely and the club has been estimated as worth $4 billion – almost as much as the super-rich Italian soccer club Juventus.

I've been noticing how the NFL has expanded: it seems to get bigger every year. In 2010, it decided to globalize the game by setting up franchises all over the world. The abortive World League and its unsuccessful

319

offspring NFL Europe were never more than job-creation packages for players who did not quite make the cut (as they say) with the NFL. But today's operation has the backing of several big media interest groups and the television audience around the world is guaranteed. It's still nowhere near soccer in terms of global popularity, of course: big soccer events can draw 40+ billion viewers to their screens for really big games. But, the World Super Bowl is beamed around the world and brings in near 3 billion.

I'll watch the game on the RayZ, a recent invention based on the old hologram principal in which a pattern is produced by interference between a lightbeam and light broken up into a series of colored spectra (diffracted is the technical term for this). The result is a moving full-color three-dimensional holographic image of the game. The RayZ sits in the middle of the room and viewers can sit anywhere around it, as the images are formed in the beams of light that shoot upwards from the appliance. It's a tremendous improvement on the old 4 × 3 foot plasma screens, which provided only two-dimensional images. When you think of it, what took them so long? The first domestic television sets were available in the late 1940s and we had to suffer flat 2-D images for nearly 70 years. Now, program makers use technology that allows 360° views. The viewer can freeze the action at any time and take a close look from whatever angle they choose.

The *Matrix* movies used a primitive form of this, but, back then, we used to watch on screens, so our ability to move around the image was illusory. Now, we just walk around the beams of light. Although the technology behind it is quite old, it's only in recent years that it's become available as a domestic appliance. At least, that's what they tell us. You suspect there are powerful economic forces too. Think about television: they reckon we could have had it in our homes 20 years before we did, but the big business interests that had invested heavily in radio feared that radio would be wiped out by tv. Radio clung on, though television is already beginning to look redundant. They used to say that watching sports on tv was better than being there: slow-mos and action replays, together with the so-called expert analysis made televised sports a superior all-round package. However, nobody was convinced and people still flocked to the "live" occasions. But, this new technology is something different. It really is like being there. With the atmospheric audio, it's easy to imagine yourself actually at the event.

The established media corporations still own the rights to broadcast action from professional sports, but the Super Bowl no longer rotates around the networks. Pay per view had never quite realized its potential through cable or satellite; but the opening up of digital television and

DIRECTV in the 1990s offered clues for the future. Deal after deal, many of them involving European broadcasting corporations – Deutsche Telecom, Canal+, Telecom Italia, and others – produced a web of business alliances, some permanent, others temporary. The name of the game is to control the broadcasting rights of events, or individual teams, and then sell straight to the consumer.

The USA's FCC and the broadcasting governing organizations of other countries around the world were predictably against this development: they were powerless to prevent the media conglomerates broadcasting wherever they wanted. Even now, governments are busy trying to formulate laws that will stop games like today's being sent around the world. Universal distribution used to be the central aim of media organizations, like AOL Time Warner and Disney; but the scramble in recent years has been for control of content. Once you have a product that people want to see and the network through which they can access it, you have a colossal market. My operator is UMC (United Micro-Cable), which has its origins in a deal between Microsoft and AT&T in 1999.

Today's game will cost $250. Of course, this is a special event; packages for regular season games are less expensive. If I had the money, I could watch every single game in the NFL season (there are now 22 games per team in the regular season and four rounds of play-offs). I can access practically any sporting event in the world. Of course, I have to pay for each event; the days when you could get sports free-to-air have long since disappeared.

The British terrestrial networks dropped most sports by the end of the twentieth century. By 2008, the only events that had not been scooped up by either satellite, cable, or digital pay tv were so minor that advertisers lost interest and the networks decided to concentrate on drama, news, and quiz shows. In the USA, Fox steadily upped its stake in the NFL and the other main leagues, at the same time buying into local stations and sports clubs themselves. Fans were weaned off the idea of getting sports for free. It's amusing to talk to old-timers when they reminisce about the old days when they were able to watch sports for free. They were probably amused by their parents who could remember the days when there was no tv at all. Now attendances have slipped right down: who wants to brave the elements when you can see more games, from all angles, with informed commentary and analysis in the comfort of your own home?

Today, I will have a choice of commentators. Some viewers still like those old-fashioned views from the perspective of players, so you can almost see through the athlete's eyes. Soccer fans love to view the referee's view. Fans can see the action from the perspective of whoever they choose. Baseball catchers and wicket keepers included. As you watch, you can order changes on your voice-activated remote control. For example, you say "quarter-back's view" or "slo-mo" and you can change the size of image. Or you might say "tighten" or "widen" and this lets you get either a close-up shot or a panoramic vista. And it takes about 1.5 seconds to change. Just think how long it used to take to download something as simple as a screensaver from the internet at the start of the century.

Cordially
H.G.

Is this how we will be watching televised sports in the near future? It would still be televised, even if the receiving apparatus was called something else (*tele* is Greek for far off). Technologically, the scenario is still some way off. But, even if everything was in place, the hard part would be in persuading consumers to part with even more of their hard-earned cash. NBC thought it could do it back in 1992 and got its fingers burnt. It offered 24-hour coverage of the summer Olympic Games from Barcelona to those prepared to pay $125 (£78) for a 15-day package, or $19.95 (£12.50) for a single day at a time. The meager number of viewers and the resulting losses did not inspire confidence. But, it was all part of a steady process of gently breaking a habit that television audiences had got used to over the previous four decades, that of getting televised sports for nothing. It's been tough, but the signs are that sports fans are finally getting used to the idea that they are going to have to pay for more and more of their televised sports in future.

If ever there was a marriage made in heaven it was between television and sports. The commercial success of each was almost directly attributable to the other. From the 1940s to the present sports have grown in proportion to tv. Not only have they grown in scale and popularity, but they have become modified into virtual theater. And television's efforts at dragging sports toward the popular entertainment end of the market have paid off in terms of record-breaking viewing ratings. High-profile sports events draw audiences comparable with televisual phenomena, like the moon landing, the funeral of Princess Diana, or the finale of *Friends*, which drew 52.5 million viewers in 2004 (advertisers were charged $2 million per 30 seconds).

In this chapter I am going to investigate the origins and development of what became an unexpectedly prosperous relationship. Both television and sports have grown rich and influential as a result of their partnership; in the process, they have transformed each other, television validating its place as the premier communications channel, sports mutating into an entertainment medium on par with showbusiness. The beginnings of this alliance lie in the 1950s, but its sources go back further; to the early nineteenth century, in fact.

## LET THERE BE TELEVISION . . .

Founded in 1822, the British news-sheet *Bell's Life in London* found its circulation rising as it included sports reports. Sports were hardly news, at least not in the hardest sense of the word, but reports of them had the desired effect and sales continued to rise. The paper held a monopoly until 1865 when *The Sporting Life* issued what was to be a potent challenge. The success of *The Sporting Life* with its quick and detailed reporting and varied advertising prompted other publications to dedicate sections to sports coverage. The North American equivalent of *The Sporting Life* was *The American Farmer* which first appeared in 1819 and was followed by many others, including *The Spirit of the Times*, founded in 1831.

Newspaper proprietors were interested in selling their publications and sports did the trick; but the coverage also primed further interest in sports and, as Tony Mason points out: "It was the press who first elevated a minority of sportsmen and women into national celebrities, whose names and faces were recognized by people uninterested in sport; performers whose mere presence on the pitch would tempt people to the event; the exceptional performer" (1988: 50). Here lay the sources of what we now call the sports celebrity, whose fame relies as much on the mass media as on athletic performance (as we'll see in Chapter 16).

There was a clear symmetry of interests between those with an interest in exploiting the mass spectatorship potential of sports and those who could sell newspapers with stories about sports. Reporting in the press had the useful consequence of raising public awareness, so enlarging the mass spectator market. Newspaper's value to sports was undoubted, but there was uncertainty about radio, which came to the fore in the 1920s, when a warrantable mass spectatorship for sports was emerging.

Radio could relay information on any event, but the main advantage it held in terms of boosting interest was its immediacy: instead of attending an actual event, fans may have opted for listening to "live" commentary on the radio. Radio's capacity to excite was enhanced by the social atmosphere it generated, listeners huddled together whooping and yelling as the commentator's voice crackled through the airwaves.

Despite possible drawbacks, radio had one big plus factor: it paid, sometimes quite well. For instance, in 1935, the radio rights to the Joe Louis–Max Baer world heavyweight fight were a record $27,500 (then about £9,000). Fears that radio commentary would hurt the gate were unfounded as 88,000 spectators attended the event. By this time, radio coverage of sports was commonplace and, as this involved issues of proprietorship and copyright, it gave rise to a economic relationship between the mass media and sports organizers. Newspapers did not pay to cover events because they were regarded as good publicity.

Radio's effect was more ambiguous: it may well pump up interest, but it could also keep people away; so it was asked to stump up money.

Radio still saw a profit in sports: it existed to make money and could attract large listening audiences for its sports programs. This meant that advertisers and sponsors were tempted to pay more to have their products associated with the event and so reach a large potential market. Sponsors of radio shows were among the first commercial companies to realize the financial benefits of linking their commodities with sports. We see evidence of this link all around us every day. But, of course, radio has been eclipsed by television.

Filmed news of sports events occupied a segment of newsreels shown in movie theaters even before radio transmissions, but the films were at least a week after the event and could not compare with the thrill of a "live" radio broadcast. In the USA, a 1912 ban on showing fight films was relaxed in 1939 when the Senate passed a bill to permit the transfer of boxing films from state-to-state. But, by this time, a new medium had crept into the homes of a select few. In 1937, a few hundred Londoners were the first to see the first outside broadcast coverage of British sport, when 25 minutes of a men's singles match was televised from Wimbledon. It was strictly an experimental service from the BBC which had improved on an earlier, unsatisfactory, attempt by CBS to broadcast a fight by "sight and sound."

The main technical shortcoming of televising events was that cameras were fixed and were fitted with lenses that made the performers appear as tiny figures. Boxing, whose action takes part in a small, finite territory seemed reasonably suitable for the new medium and, in 1939, BBC and NBC both broadcast fights, the BBC being fortunate enough to capture the British lightweight title fight between Eric Boon and Arthur Danahar, which is regarded as amongst the best-ever fights on British soil. In the same year, the BBC, still in its infancy, showed its first FA Cup Final and NBC telecast baseball, at first with one camera and, later, with two, which was a significant innovation as it permitted close-ups not even visible to audiences watching the game live.

Television was still only a futuristic luxury of the rich, with just 5,000 sets being sold in the USA in 1946. Within ten dramatic years, 75 percent of the country's households had a set. John Goldlust, in his book on sport and the media *Playing for Keeps: Sport, the media and society*, argues that "The significance of sports for this phenomenal rate of penetration should not be underestimated" and that the televising of major sports events was "a key element in launching the television industry" (1987: 8).

Goldlust cites the transmission of the Melbourne Olympics in 1956 as a key event that greatly assisted the sale of television receivers. After this, the television industry of continental Europe and Latin America developed within the framework of either the BBC, which considered the televising of sport one of its statutory obligations in order to provide as many aspects as possible of the "national culture," or the American companies, which geared their schedules so as to maximize demand from advertisers. If manufacturers had products to sell and wanted exposure for their products, then placing commercials in the "natural breaks" of a high-profile event was rational and effective.

Even with a minute fraction of its potential audience, televised sports were attractive: as early as 1947, Ford and Gillette paid $65,000 (then about £20,000) for the rights to sponsor baseball's World Series on television, despite the fact that less than 12 percent of US households could receive it. Sports governing organizations were wary of tv, thinking its impact could only be detrimental. As if to illustrate the point, between 1948 and 1956, the Cleveland Indians baseball team won a World Series and a pennant, yet suffered a 67 percent drop in attendance. The Boston Braves' crowds plunged by 81 percent following their National League victory in 1948, immediately after which they signed a tv deal for the next three years. The situation needed drastic remedial action, so the owner Lou Perini moved the franchise to Milwaukee and banned television cameras, apart from the World Series winning games of 1957 and 1958.

The gates stayed healthy, prompting Perini to announce smugly: "We have come to believe that tv can saturate the minds of the fans with baseball. We would very much like to guard against this." Perini relaxed his strictures after 1962 and eventually sold out to a group which wholeheartedly embraced television by relocating the club in Atlanta where a tv–radio guarantee of $1.25 million (then over £600,000) per year awaited.

Another sport whose gates were hit severely was college football. Between 1949 and 1953, attendance declined by almost 3 million. The National Collegiate Athletic Association (NCAA) formed a special television committee and instituted rigid rules for limiting the number of telecasts. Even then, it took ten years before gates rose to their 1949 levels.

North American television feasted on boxing, which it left as a carcass in 1964 after 18 years of the kind of saturation Perini had feared for baseball. In some areas of the United States, boxing was on every night of the week, with promoters eagerly accepting television monies to augment profits. Gradually, the tv fees became the profits: live audiences dwindled. As tv was interested only in "name" fighters, the bigger promoters who had the champions under contract were able to capitalize, while the smaller promoters went to the wall. In the period 1952–9 alone, 250 of the country's 300 small boxing clubs shut down. At the height of its power in 1955, boxing was watched by 8.5 million homes, about one-third of the available viewing audience in those days. By 1959, boxing commanded only 10.6 percent – which sounds much more impressive now than it did then when the market was uncluttered by cable channels. NBC was the first to cut boxing from its schedules in 1960.

The other networks followed suit. But the sport and the medium had merely obeyed the logic of the market. The signs were clear: many sports were being tempted by a cozy and highly profitable relationship; but, in doing so they were exposing themselves completely to television and risking becoming totally and possibly ruinously dependent on the networks.

Apart from boxing, North American television's sporting energy in the 1950s came from wrestling and roller derby. From a production viewpoint, these were perfect sports for the technically naive tv companies of the day, CBS and NBC. All that was needed was a fixed orthicon camera trained on a small finite area of action, insulated from natural weather conditions. The two networks enjoyed a relatively peaceful coexistence, carving up the major sporting events between them. ABC's entrance changed all that. Not having access to the big sports, ABC decided to feature minority sports and activities that were barely sports at all and treat them in such dramatic ways that even those with no interest in sports would be converted.

Rodeos, demolition derbies, and even the bizarre fireman's bucket-filling championships were all fair game for ABC's cameras, which wouldn't just document what happened but would take the viewer to where it happened. Cameras would venture to the tops of cliffs, peer over the edge, then draw back to view a diver hurtling into the seas below, where another camera joined him or her in the water. Sports were drama. Inspired by the iconoclastic philosophies of Roone Arledge, ABC vandalized the established traditions and made an overt appeal to younger audiences which were not bound by the fidelities of their parents. Women viewers were wooed, as they were demographically

---

### Roone Arledge

As ABC television's producer of network sports, Forest Hills-born Arledge mapped out a direction for television in the 1960s and, at the same time, established his tv network as a rival to the USA's then duopoly, comprising CBS and NBC. Instead of following sports events, Arledge believed television should take the initiative. Instead of accepting that sporting occasions had a "natural" appeal that should be reflected in television coverage, Arledge created interest across the widest possible range of the population. He recognized no barriers set by class, gender, or age. His premise was much the same as that of the advertisers on whose patronage ABC ultimately depended: if the demand is not there to begin with, build it. The way Arledge built is was by taking obscure sports and adding something to them, something that only television could provide. Among Arledge's ideas were the weekly Wide World of Sports and Monday Night Football, both of which were instrumental in drawing the hitherto neglected female sports fan to television screens. Arledge died in 2002.

attractive to advertisers: research showed that women make decisions about household purchases.

ABC's approach was unashamedly populist, projecting personalities, highlighting unusual characteristics about them, and reducing almost any competitive activity to its most basic elements. Frog-jumping contests were not out of place in ABC's sports panoply. Gillette, one of television's biggest sports sponsors, hooked up with ABC on a Friday night boxing series and, encouraged by the response, fed in more money, which enabled ABC to capture NCAA football in the 1960–1 season. This was the first of many coups, the biggest being the American Football League (AFL), a second-rate rival to the NFL, but one which, given the ABC treatment, rose in popularity. So much so that, in 1966, the two merged to produce the NFL as we know it today.

One significant innovation in the AFL–ABC deal was the pooling of broadcast rights. By dealing with the television as a league, the AFL eliminated the kind of interclub competition that arose when selling local broadcast rights of individual clubs. In his book *The Market Structure of Sports*, Gerald Scully suggests: "One could argue that the survival of the AFL as a league was made possible by access to national television, which helped financially in its own right and brought recognition and fan interest" (1995: 27). The other innovation was the introduction of the television time-out in 1958. This allowed stoppages specifically for tv companies to screen commercials.

In the same year as the NFL–AFL merger, BBC television in Britain screened soccer's World Cup staged in England. It was a prestigious tournament and the BBC beamed its pictures all over the world. The advantage of the camera over the naked eye had been appreciated since 1877, when Eadweard Muybridge published his serial photographs of human bodies in motion from different perspectives, using shutter speeds of less than 1/2000th of a second. The series disclosed new ways of understanding the movement of bodies (as we saw in Chapter 12). Television offered even further possibilities.

In the championship game, the English team's third goal arrived gift-wrapped for television. The ball thundered against the underside of the West German team's crossbar, appearing momentarily to bounce over the goal line before rebounding into the field of play. If the whole ball had crossed (not just broken as in American football) the plane of the goal line, then it was a goal. The German players said "no." But, the referee said "yes," and the goal stood. This was a cue for television to go to work: BBC slowed down the action, freeze-framed it, reversed the angle; and it could still not prove conclusively whether or not the ball had crossed the line. The arguments raged and the footage rolled and rolled. Even today, the debate continues. Were it not for television, the game would have been consigned to history.

## CONTROLLING THE CONSUMER

Unlike early British television which was once intended to become a "theater of the airwaves," American television has always been a business, like any other: whether they derive income from sponsorship or advertising, from cable subscriptions, from production, or from station ownership, for-profit corporations have always dominated the industry in the USA. During television's formative years, it followed the successful formula of radio stations, selling space in its programs to advertisers. Ford, General Electric, Singer, and other giants of the expanding industries of peacetime seized the chance of reaching a genuinely mass market of potential consumers.

---

### Subscription television

Unlike terrestrial television and basic cable, subscription television operates on the principle that viewers will pay extra monthly fees for the privilege of watching movies and events that are unavailable on other tv stations. Home Box Office (HBO) is the leading subscription service in the world. It was founded in November 1972 when it broadcast a hockey game from Madison Square Garden, New York, to 365 subscribers. It now has more than 27 million subscribers across America and screens 24 hours a day (this is still a relatively small number compared to terrestrial network tv ). Beside being a major screener of international sports events, HBO (which is owned by AOL Time Warner) has become actively involved in the promotion of events, particularly world title fights. In France, Canal+ fulfills a similar function. In Britain, BSkyB is the foremost subscription channel.

---

British television originally took a rather snooty attitude, attracting funding not through advertising, but through licenses, which viewers were obliged to buy in order to receive tv signals legally. BBC television even today resolutely refuses to screen commercials, even though its rivals operate on much the same lines as their American counterparts, which have always operated on a simple but effective idea. Television offers to deliver to advertisers an audience of several million consumers, many of whom will be influenced enough by the "commercial messages" (as they were once politely called) to spend their money on the advertised product, whether it be soap, cars, financial services, or whatever. Advertisers pay their money to the tv company, which in turn pays the cost of the production and distribution of its programs. The difference is, of course, what keeps the tv company in business.

While viewers are sometimes referred to as the customers of the television companies, the real customers are the advertising agencies who handle the affairs of product manufacturers and do business with the networks. Customers are actually part of the deal: the tv companies are selling several million sets of eyeballs trained on the screen. If they can include programs that command the attentions of several dozen million viewers, then they can raise the price of advertising slots. If the program draws only small viewing audiences, then advertisers are less inclined to part with serious money. If, as is sometimes the case nowadays, commercial time is sold on the supposition that x-million viewers will be watching and, in the event, less than that number view the program, the television network offers rebates. We'll return to this, as big sports events nowadays frequently fail to attract projected audiences and tv companies are being hit as a result.

A complicating factor in this concerns demographics: some television shows attract high audience ratings (the measurement of viewers), but not of the right type. In the 1950s when television was building its following, content didn't discriminate too much between audiences and advertisers were eager to have their messages seen by as many potential customers as possible. A show such as *I Love Lucy*, which drew as many as 44 million viewers, was priceless to advertisers. Well, not quite priceless: its stars, Lucille Ball and Desi Arnez signed a contract worth $8 million with CBS and the show's sponsors Philip Morris, the tobacco company. It was, by far, the largest contract written for a tv show, but then again, it was, as the Philip Morris president put it, "the all-time phenomenon of the entertainment business" (quoted in Landay 1999: 30).

As market research techniques developed, it became possible to identify which demographic segments of the market watched which programs. General Foods, for example, may wish to target young people with a new cereal; advertising in slots during a show that draws an audience typically aged between 55–70 wouldn't be too attractive to the advertising agency handling the account for the product. Instead, the ad agency would analyze what kind of programs are watched by their target consumers. Reality shows or pop idol-type contests would be more likely to draw younger viewers, as would all of MTV's output. So, healthy viewing figures are no guarantee of success: advertisers may opt for smaller audiences of the right type. All of which brings us to sports.

"Sports programming is extremely valued by the television networks," writes Scully. "The demographic profile of viewers is attractive to a certain class of advertisers, whose willingness to pay some of the highest advertising fees in the industry has propelled the growth of network television revenues to the leagues" (1995: 28). It is no accident that early sponsors of television and radio sports programs were manufacturers of shaving products and brewers. Followers of sport were predominantly male and working class. Sports audiences are now more variegated, but the essential point remains: they are likely consumers for a wide range of goods and services. Within the wide category of sports, there are variations. Golf and cricket, for example, tend to draw more affluent consumers to their screens, while soccer and baseball cross socio-economic boundaries.

Some events draw spectacularly huge viewing audiences. For instance, 175 million households regularly watch at least some part of the Super Bowl. This allows the television company to charge about $1.5 million per 30-second advertising slot, anticipating 56 units that yield a total of $84 million, a figure reduced to $74 million after advertising agency commissions. The commercials reach a immense number of people, but can they be worth $3 million per minute?

An answer of sorts comes from Macintosh, which, in 1989, launched its new computer with a series of spots during the Super Bowl. The very next day, $3.5 million-worth of said computer went over the counter and the sales figure grew to $155 million over the next 90 days. This is impressive, though Jib Fowles doesn't think it's typical. In his *Advertising and Popular Culture* (1996), Fowles is skeptical about the supposed power of tv advertising. He quotes another Super Bowl commercial, this time from 1991. A healthy 70 percent of the television audience recognized that Joe Montana had appeared in the commercial, but only 18 percent remembered what the ad was for. It was Diet Pepsi. (See also Rick Burton's "Sports advertising and the Super Bowl," (1999).)

All the same, we have to consider why so many corporations are willing to shell out over a million dollars for a commercial that's over in less time than it takes to make popcorn in the microwave. If their impact is so negligible, why don't all the big companies that squander their advertising budget on television commercials go out of business? The fact that they don't suggests that tv does influence our spending habits.

Even if the jury is still out, advertisers and tv execs alike seem convinced that commercials shown during sports events move goods off shelves. This means that, from television's point of view, the fan is a resource; an article used in a trade with advertisers. So, for example, an ABC executive in negotiation with an advertising agent is not going to discuss Peyton Manning's fabulous 40-yard touchdown pass in last Monday night's game: more likely the conversation will converge on how many people watched it, what were their class backgrounds, sex composition, ages, ethnic identities, incomes, and zip codes? It's as if television companies sell the fans to the advertisers.

No one has understood this better than Rupert Murdoch whose operations are more fully covered in Chapter 14. In 1992, he carved open what had previously been a relatively cozy rivalry between BBC television and Independent Television (ITV – the commercial terrestrial network of British stations). Eager to sell subscriptions to his BSkyB satellite network, Murdoch negotiated a £304-million ($575 million) deal for exclusive "live" coverage of English Premiership soccer. BBC had to settle for tape-delay highlights, while ITV got nothing.

In the States, legislation prevents collusive arrangements between the leagues and television (the European Union, in the early twenty-first century, grew uncomfortable with the control Murdoch has appropriated and instructed him to put some events out to tender, effectively subcontracting them to other television companies). Most leagues distribute their product among various television companies. For example, the NFL allocates its games to the major networks and one or two cable companies and draws revenues from Fox, CBS, and Disney totaling $17.6 billion (£10.75 billion) over seven years (ending 2005). Similarly, the NBA split its games between Disney and AOL Time Warner for a total of $4.6 billion over six years (ending 2008).

The National Hockey League is unusual in that it signed an exclusive $600 million deal with Disney that distributed its games through three channels, ABC, ESPN, and ESPN2. This is the type of arrangement the English Football Association favored. The soccer contract was one of several seemingly extravagant contracts between television and sports leagues in the 1990s. Major League Baseball negotiated several contracts worth a total of $1.587 billion (just under £1 billion) in 1996; the NBA's 1998 deal with NBC was worth $1.75 billion over four years. And, by the time the FA deal came up for renewal in 1996, the stakes were pushed up to £670 million ($1.1 billion) over the next four years. Scully observes of the value of broadcasting rights: "A fourteenfold increase in baseball, a sixteenfold increase in football, and a seventeenfold increase in basketball since the mid-1970s" (1995: 3). This tells us something about how much the tv companies holding the contracts expected to earn from advertising or subscriptions. But expectations do not always square with reality.

The original soccer deal worked well for BSkyB in Britain: subscriptions soared immediately, then leveled off at about 7 million, or about 8.5 percent of the population. Major advertisers like Ford and Carling beer sponsored segments of the soccer coverage. On the other hand, the Murdoch-owned Fox dropped $350 million on its first four-year contract with the NFL. NBC lost $40 million in the games leading to the Super Bowl in the 1992/3 season and emerged with a profit of between $6–10 million derived from spots during the 150 minutes of pre- and post-game analysis plus commercial fees from NBC-owned stations. Few sports events can have the potential to gross $46 million (£65 million) and counting in three hours; but, the Super Bowl has become, as *New York Times* writer Richard Sandomir puts it, "like a luscious *crème brulée* after a long dyspeptic dinner" (January 26, 1993). Take away the dessert and all you have left is the kind of bellyache that may make certain sports less attractive.

CBS whined about the kind of money demanded by the leagues when reflecting on its estimated loss of $450 million (over £280 million) over the period of its early 1990s contract with Major League Baseball. There are skeptics, one of them being Andrew Zimbalist, author of *Baseball and Billions*, who writes: "The [CBS] network's sudden diffidence might arouse some suspicion about whether it is engaging in a public relations game in a bid for smaller contracts the next time round" (1992: 160).

---

### ESPN

The all-sports cable tv channel was the creation of Bill Rasmussen, who, in the 1970s, dreamt up an original idea for a regional network of radio stations to broadcast the University of Massachusetts' football games. Cable broadcasting was then in its infancy and Rasmussen was able to buy time on a communications satellite (transponder) inexpensively. He filled the time with small-scale sports commentary, interviews, and analysis. The Entertainment Sports Programming Network operated out of Plainville, Connecticut, and gained permission from the FCC (Federal Communications Commission) to begin broadcasting in September 1979.

Getty Oil sensed the potential of the enterprise and invested heavily; in fact, it assumed effective control and sold out to Texaco, which, in turn sold out to ABC television. ABC's interest transformed ESPN from a local operation to a national network, reaching 34 million homes by 1984. This was the year David Stern became the NBA commissioner and Michael Jordan made his debut for Chicago Bulls. ESPN had held a contract with the NBA for the previous two years and had shown NCAA games from the start in 1979 – which had the effect of familiarizing tv fans with the players before they transferred to the pro game.

Perhaps inadvertently, ESPN had hitched its wagon to the NBA star, which went into orbit over the next several years. By 1998, ESPN was taken by about 70 percent of all US television-owning households; of the total televised sports, ESPN carried 23 percent. In addition, the network's reach extended to 160 different countries around the world; it provided services in 19 languages. In 1996, it set up a second ESPN channel specializing in news items; and, to complement its extensive tv coverage, started ESPN Radio. It is now owned by Disney.

---

In 1993, with baseball's popularity waning and CBS licking its wounds, rival networks ABC and NBC actually joined forces to reach an agreement with Major League Baseball. For the first time, the league did not receive an up-front tv rights payment, but entered into a package venture with the television companies for administering, marketing, and selling the sport. The following years, disaster struck when the baseball players went on strike and the World Series was aborted.

Zimbalist, like Scully, predicted that a prudent sports executive should not expect as much television revenue in the future. Yet, in 2001, Murdoch's Fox splashed out $2.5 billion for Major League Baseball, which it shared with ESPN, which paid $851 million. The Fox deal was for five years, ESPN's for four.

Fox's deals seemed to defy commercial wisdom. It also lashed out $4.4 billion on the National Football League's NFC Eastern division which includes the Dallas, Washington, and New York Giants franchises, despite its losses on the previous deal; this represented a hike of around 30 percent over the contract Fox signed with the NFL in 1993. There were other huge deals in the late 1990s. In 1998, CBS doubled what NBC had previously paid (on annual average) for the AFC's television rights. The prices the NFL charged ABC and ESPN (both Disney-owned) for Monday Night Football and the Sunday game respectively was three times more than their annual payments under the previous 1993 agreements. Cablevision paid New York Knicks $486 million over 12 years.

---

### Monday Night Football

This has become something of an institution since its inception in the 1970s. ABC's innovation was an attempt to broaden the appeal of football by incorporating elements of drama and popular entertainment into its coverage. Unusual camera angles, personality close-ups, half-time interviews: these were all used to distinguish ABC's football from that of the other networks. It quickly commanded a one-third share of the viewing audience. ABC paid the NFL $8.5 million per year for 13 games and claimed this back by charging advertisers $65,000 per minute during the game. By the end of 1979, it was regularly the eighth most watched program in the USA, enabling ABC to charge $110,000 for a 30-second commercial slot. In 2005, the show was moved to ESPN (like ABC, part of Disney) in a deal reported to cost the cable channel $1.1bn (£525m) per season over eight years.

---

Advertising revenues remain attractive: there are few safer bets than sports when it comes to pulling in viewers. Even shows like *Sex and the City* and *Friends* lost popularity over time. But, sports are fairly consistent. Fox and BSkyB's motives in paying over the odds were transparent. As marginal players alongside the established giants of the tv industry, they wanted to position themselves more centrally and major sports coverage was an instrument designed to do exactly that. Fox lost money, but it gained an awful lot of prestige. BSkyB won subscribers and a reputation as the leading sports channel in Europe.

CBS's willingness to absorb losses of $450 million on its baseball contract was thought to be based on the assumption that it could use the World Series to include October promotions for its prime-time shows in the crucial fall, or autumn, schedule from which ratings are extrapolated. CBS effectively wanted to use sports as a means of generating interest in future programs – from both advertisers and audiences. Not that the leagues themselves care about the motives. Television deals mean that each team can start the season with an assured amount (e.g. $77 million for each NFL club) before a season ticket has been sold. But, the fact remains that television hemorrhages money on sports. The US networks' combined loss between 2001 and 2006 is probably near $6 billion ($400 million or so of those losses due to the ABC/ESPN/ESPN2 deal with the NHL). In Britain, an entire channel (ITV Digital) collapsed under the strain of Football League contracts, leaving 72 clubs without tv income and many of them facing bankruptcy as a result. The sports marketing agency ISL went belly-up after paying €2.3 billion for the tv rights to two soccer World Cups, 2002 and 2006, and discovering that its clients, the European networks, wouldn't pay its asking price.

Perhaps the most spectacular flat-out miscalculation was that of Dick Ebersol, who was head of sports at the tv-rights holding NBC, when he paid a jaw-dropping $3.7 billion (£2.64 billion) for the 27th, 28th, and 29th summer Olympics. In 2000, viewing figures were nearly a quarter down on the previous Olympics, which were held in Atlanta. His network drew more than $900 million worth of advertising, which translated into a $200 million profit on the $700 million outlay for the Sydney segment of the 12-year deal with the IOC. Disappointing viewing figures obliged NBC to calculate rebates for the aggrieved advertisers. Ebersol, it seems, believed he could redefine the demographics of televised sports in the way that Kerry Packer had, as we'll see in the next section: by packaging the Olympics like just another prime-time tv show. At Atlanta, US tv focused so much on American competitors that actual winners of events, if they came from outside the USA, were sometimes effaced. Cameras opted for close-up examination of homegrown athletes. But, this was only part of the problem: the huge American tv market was interested in baseball, but not Olympic baseball; basketball, but not Olympic basketball. Why watch so-called "dream teams" when organized leagues offered what fans considered more authentic competition? Sports that are integral to the Olympic movement, such as archery or weightlifting, were of no significance at all to North American viewers. The historic defeat of the US $4 \times 100$ meters men's swimming relay by the Australian team was the final nail in NBC's coffin.

Presumably, this kind of chastening experience was on NBC's mind when it brokered an inventive deal with the NHL in 2004. It offered no front-end money, only the promise of a share of advertising revenues when the figures went into the black. In other words, the television company had grown so wary of the harsh costs of overspending on sports, it decided to divide the risk with the sports league involved. The league had guaranteed income from ESPN, however: the cable channel paid $60 million for a year's coverage, to be followed by $70 million for each subsequent year, this being the equivalent of half of the value of the previous NHL contract with ABC/ESPN.

While the NHL is regarded as the fourth major league in the USA, it was in no position to argue with the tv companies. Sliding in television popularity, it had been passed by golf, NASCAR, and college football, among others. So the drop in its tv revenues was hardly surprising. All the same, the deal would have prompted nervousness among sports leagues. The apparent disappearance of television's munificence after so many years might have been a sign of change.

Sports were once cheap production numbers that drew viewers to their screens in millions. Those days have long since gone. While negotiating various deals with television, major sports governing organizations must have been taking notes. They quickly learnt that the same principles that applied to marketing beer or shaving foam, also applied to sports. Marketing, as Mark Gottdiener states, "has gone from a rather straightforward affair involving the *distribution* of goods to potential customers that existed as a generic mass, otherwise known as 'sales,' to a knowledge-based, purposeful effort at controlling consumer buying" (1997: 70).

From the 1980s, sports began marketing themselves, turning themselves into commodities; not commodities with use-values, but ones with symbolic values. Consumers were sold images they could blend with their personal histories or their identities: sports became a means of self-expression, a statement of lifestyle. While Gottdiener does not refer to sports, his observations about how consumers pursue particular kinds of lifestyles through their consumption patterns has obvious application. The NBA, more than any other sport, used television not only to rebrand itself, but to offer its followers a lifestyle option. Other sports on both sides of the Atlantic followed suit.

Licensed baseball caps became ubiquitous, replica shirts became staples of leisure wear, endorsed products became mandatory for clued-up youth. It seemed almost serendipity when Nike came on the scene at exactly the right time in history; but, as we'll see in Chapter 15, the sports goods firm was actually a factor in the whole process through which sports became commodities. None of this was possible without the exposure provided by television. Sports used the same techniques as car makers, soft drink manufacturers, and computer companies, attempting to manipulate consumer "needs," using art and design to create agreeable images and packaging their products to make them appealing. Today, it is virtually impossible to find a major sport that does not have a logo.

The evidence of many sports' marketing successes is abundant in the form of players' status and salaries, colossally expensive stadiums, stock exchange listings (for many British clubs), not forgetting the high-priced tv deals of the late

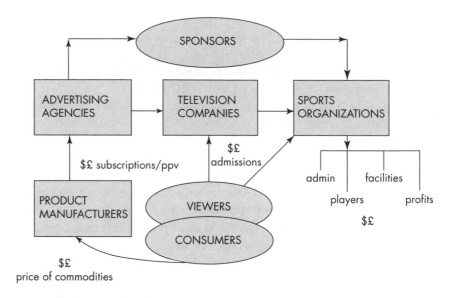

**how we pay for televised sports**

1990s and early twenty-first century. Even if the 2004 NHL deal prefigures less lavishness from tv corporations, there's still likely to be keen competition for the premier sports, even if it involves taking losses. As David Rowe writes in his *Sport, Culture and the Media*:

> The struggle for television sport can be seen to be more than a fight for profit: it reveals the cultural power of sport, particularly in the higher ranks of large corporate enterprises, where aggressive, competitive masculinity is as evident in the boardroom as in the locker rooms.
>
> (2004a: 78)

Credibility is always on the line when tv companies bid for sports. Such is the cultural power of sports that few major networks would dare risk cutting them from their schedules. And sports have prospered extravagantly as the tv money has flowed in.

## MADE FOR TELEVISION

In 1976, Kerry Packer, the head of an Australian television company, offered the Australian Cricket Board (ACB) a deal for the exclusive rights to screen Australian cricket for five years. The offer was refused. Determined to press ahead and feature cricket on his tv channel, known as Network Nine, Packer signed up 35 international class players and organized his own "rebel" tournament. Few sports respect their own history as much as cricket: it is one of the oldest and most traditional games and, for most of its existence, worked carefully to retain links with its past.

Packer was a television man; he knew what drew audiences. Horrified traditionalists watched as Packer dressed his players in brightly colored uniforms, scheduled evening games under floodlights, and introduced yellow cricket balls. He used eight cameras, some trained on players' faces, and several microphones strategically positioned to pick up the players' often blasphemous comments. The games were played in a single day, using limited overs, its format being, as John Goldlust puts it, "unabashedly spectator oriented, geared towards providing entertainment, tight finishes, big hitting and aggressive play . . . ideally suited for television" (1987: 163).

The cricket Packer promoted was barely recognizable as the age-old pursuit of English gentlemen, but television fans watched it. After a nervous first season, viewing figures and attendance both rose, enabling Network Nine to attract more advertisers. Established governing organizations, like England's MCC, opposed the wanton commercialism, but eventually capitulated in the face of the tournament's rising popularity. In 1979, Packer's marketing subsidiary secured a ten-year contract to organize the sponsorship of official cricket. Packer's attempt to capture exclusive broadcasting rights succeeded and, by the mid-1980s, he had virtually taken control of Australian cricket.

Crowds continued to flock to the stadiums and, more importantly for Packer, tv audience ratings stayed healthy. The players earned more money, the governing organizations took substantial fees for broadcasting rights, and Network Nine increased its advertising revenue by selling more commercial time during the ordinarily quiet summer months. Those who still thought cricket should be played with a straight bat and a stiff upper lip were offended by the changes Packer had instigated, but there was no going back.

Packer acted as a catalyst, instigating changes that were to transform cricket from a sport that might be described as television-hostile (played over five days, often at a ponderous pace) to a shorter and frequently explosive game that provided nail-biting finishes. One-day cricket did not replace the more conventional format: it coexisted with it. By the end of the century, World Cup cricket was a well-established part of cricket's calendar. It was played over a day, with a white ball, with players dressed in various colors, and was watched by television viewers all over the world. It was, as David Rowe puts it, "moulded well to the demands of television in terms of its structure and guaranteed result" (2004a: 183).

The Packer case gave early evidence of how television could change a sport radically. Cricket was a game that had remained largely unchanged since the formation of the MCC in 1787. Yet it could not resist the challenge of a tv magnate bent on fashioning the sport to his own requirements. Rugby League struck a television deal in 1996, the terms of which obliged the sport to dismantle a 100-year structure and switch to a summer schedule to comply with Rupert Murdoch's plans for a Rugby Super League. The new league was to include European and Australasian teams and culminate in play-offs that could be broadcast around the globe by Murdoch's many media networks. Rugby League agreed, underlining how commercial considerations can supersede those intrinsic to the sport itself.

Murdoch, whose impact on sports will be covered in the next chapter, was decried for instigating this historical change, though he was not the first media magnate to have pushed through changes in sports schedules simply to accommodate television's demands. The length of the NFL season was extended from 1990 after the signing of a $3.6 billion (£2.25 billion) contract. The reasoning behind it is spelled out by Jerry Gorman and Kirk Calhoun in their *The Name of the Game: The business of sports*: "The plan for extension was to sell more advertising over a longer period, that space filled not by more games but by more televised games" (1994: 242).

The additional games, which were broadcast by the ESPN and TNT channels, earned the NFL about $900 million. In the same year, the play-off format was changed to accommodate ABC television. The net effect was to double the tv network's payments to $225 million, according to Gorman and Calhoun, but "it all amounted to a serious strain on the trust and devotion of the fans" (1994: 242). Then again, fans take low priority when it comes to major issues such as these. As we have seen, the networks are sports' real customers – and advertisers theirs.

Television's influence has not always been so obvious. Boxing's scaling down of championship fights from 15 to 12 rounds was motivated ostensibly by safety considerations, though there was little conclusive evidence that the serious injuries associated with boxing occurred in the final three rounds. A more probable explanation was that boxing changed to suit tv requirements. In its traditional form, a boxing match involved 15 three-minute rounds, 14 one-minute intervals, plus preamble and post-fight interviews, yielding an awkward 70–75 minutes. Twelve rounds gave 47 minutes and, say, 13 minutes for padding, which fitted neatly into a one-hour slot.

The Association of Tennis Professionals (ATP) implemented changes in 1994 that were even more clearly motivated by television's needs. It reduced the time allowed in preparing to serve by five seconds to 20 seconds, so speeding up the game. This followed the introduction of the tie-break, which reduced the chances of protracted games that were difficult for tv to schedule. A repetition of the epic five hour, 12 minute, 112-game match between Pancho Gonzales and Charlie Pasarell in 1969 was rendered almost impossible. Though not quite: while it consisted of only 71 games, Fabrice Santoro's win over Arnaud Clément at the 2004 French Open took six hours, 33 minutes (beating the previous record held by John McEnroe and Mats Wilander, who were on court for six hours, 22 minutes during a 1982 Davis Cup match).

The ATP also loosened up on its strictures concerning spectators: they could react freely and spontaneously and wander about during play, instead of sitting still and gasping "oohs" and "aahs" as at Wimbledon. Perhaps the biggest concession was that in allowing broadcasters to place microphones on the umpire's side of the court so that conversations between players and officials could be heard by a television audience.

The commercial imperatives of television have led to a proliferation of time-outs, which George Ritzer believes, "alter the nature of some sports, and [may] affect the outcome of a game." For Ritzer, this is just one instance of "the attempts to McDonaldize sports" (1998: 71). Like fast-food chains, television emphasizes speed and quantity over quality. "In basketball this has taken the form of the 24-second clock for professionals and the 45-second clock for college athletes," writes Ritzer about initiatives designed to maximize points-scoring. Ritzer notes other changes in sports, such as baseball's introduction of livelier balls, artificial turf that makes ground balls travel faster, outfield fences that are closer to the home plate, and the AL's designated hitter; all moves that make bigger scores probable.

Television's influence can extend beyond the competition itself and into the ambience. Darts started life as a late nineteenth-century pub pastime. It took place in a confined space, allowed tight shots of the players' faces, and generated plenty of alcohol-fueled passion. Potential sponsors and advertisers became uncomfortable about the habitual smoking and drinking in the crowd and made their concerns known to the British television company which in turn approached the British Darts Organization (BDO). Spectators and players alike were instructed by the BDO to refrain from their normal activities in front of the cameras. Considering that the sport's origins were in pubs, the change must have been tantamount to sacrilege to die-hard fans.

With very few exceptions, televised sports have changed as a result of their relations with tv companies. There are critics for whom "television is a corrupting parasite that latches onto the host body, sport, and draws life support from it while giving nothing back in return," as Michael R. Real characterizes their view (1998: 16). The "corruption" of sports involves the various changes of rules, schedules, and formats instigated by television. It must be saddening for those who mourn the days when sports were real "sports." There again, as Sut Jhally points out: "This seems to imply that before the influence of the media there was something that was pure sports" (1989: 80).

Roone Arledge, who inspired ABC's sports coverage, often defended his network's use of synthetic sports by reminding critics that sports were not delivered by god with rules inscribed on tablets of stone. All sports, even those in ancient Greece, are in some way artificial. Teams of firefighters competing

| BIG FIGHT—BIG EARNERS | | | | |
|---|---|---|---|---|
| | IN | $m | OUT | $m |
| TELEVISION COMPANY | 700,000 ppv units @ $50 | 35 | Promoter's fee | 15 |
| | | | Other staff costs | 5 |
| | Foreign sales | 5 | Administration | 4 |
| | | | Production costs including communications network, plant and equipment | 4 |
| | | | Advertising and marketing | 3 |
| | | | Commissions | 2.5 |
| | | | Overseas partner services | 2 |
| **Earnings before tax $4.5 million** | TOTAL | 40 | TOTAL | 35.5 |
| PROMOTER | Fee from television | 15 | Boxers' purses | 28 |
| | Ticket sales | 13 | Publicity | 2 |
| | Site fee | 6 | Legal fees | 2.5 |
| | Sponsorship | 2.5 | Sanctioning fee to WBA or other governing organization | 1.5 |
| | Merchandise | 2.5 | Insurance | 0.5 |
| **Earnings before tax $4.5 million** | TOTAL | 39 | TOTAL | 34.5 |
| BOXER | Champion's purse ($9m for challenger) | 16 | Manager's commission @33% of gross income | 5.9 |
| | 4% of ppv gross | 1.4 | Trainer's commission @10% of purse | 1.79 |
| | 33% of merchandise sales | 0.5 | Training expenses | 2.5 |
| | | | Other operating expenses, including insurance cover | 0.5 |
| **Earnings before tax $7.21 million** | TOTAL | 17.9 | TOTAL | 10.69 |

- The site fee is paid to the promoter for staging the fight at, for example, the Mirage in Las Vegas, the casino owners estimating that the interest generated by a big promotion will draw gamblers, who will collectively lose more than the site fee.
- A manager may take up to 33 per cent commission from a boxer's gross purse (25 per cent in Britain) and a trainer usually 10 per cent; payments to other aides are included in the training expenses in the above example. A big promoter, such as Don King, may also manage one of the main boxers, so that his take is even greater than represented here.
- Financially, the risk is taken by the tv company: if the promotion fails to sell through the ppv agency, the promoter and boxers are still guaranteed fixed fees (though some boxers occasionally prefer to negotiate a commission-only deal).
- The figures represent a typical world title promotion rather than a megabuck heavy-weight extravaganza in which the main boxers might split anything up to $80 million.

**big fight earners**

over how many buckets of water they can carry from point A to point Z is no more or less of a pure sport than 11 men trying to move an inflated ball in the opposite direction to another 11 men, or eight women running hell-for-leather along a strip of track. The comparison reminds us that television has not so much corrupted or even transformed sports as extended and reshaped them.

The change is not always so dramatic as many writers seem to think: over the past fiftysomething years there has been a drip-by-drip transition, some sports gradually changing from one state to another. Grand, sprawling, majestic sports, like cricket and golf, no less than the cramped, frenetic basketball, have been changed through their commerce with television, but also just to stay popular with new generations of fans who demand instant gratification. As previous chapters have shown us, all sports are evolving entities, anyway – with or without tv. Rules, durations, start times, methods of evaluation, and so on have been changing for decades, centuries even. Sports never stand still. Television has imposed change rather than waited for it to happen. And audiences have responded.

## IS WATCHING TELEVISION A CREATIVE ACT?

Sport, for the television executive, is a way of ensuring audience ratings stay healthy and of keeping the advertisers' money rolling in. From the point of view of the consumer, televised sports mean something different: it's a form of entertainment that allows the fan to satisfy personal desires, pursue a type of fulfillment, and even reach a form of self-actualization, if writers like Mark Gottdiener are to be believed. In his book *The Theming of America: Dreams, visions and commercial spaces*, Gottdiener argues that, far from being passive consumers conditioned by advertising into behaving as producers wish, television viewers are engaged in "the creative act of consumption" (1997: 158).

So far, I have looked at the industrial processes of production and distribution. Now, I want to turn to the consumers. For years, tv fans were led to believe that they received televised sports for free. In fact, they have always had to pay one way or another, usually by a few more pennies on, for example, the retail price of a bar of soap, the manufacturers of which advertise their products in the breaks of sports programs. Or, a few more dollars or pounds on the sticker price of a car. The cost of buying the broadcasting rights are built into the price the customer pays. But, they surely get something back in return. Consistently high viewing figures tell us how sports vie with soaps as the most-watched genre on television.

Sport in the raw is insufficient for the tv viewer: he or she wants it packaged and presented, just like any other commodity. After all, when viewers are asked to pay for the product, as increasingly seems to be the case, they want more than roving-eye-style presentation. In sports, the action doesn't speak for itself: it needs the direction and narration that produce drama. If you disagree, try hitting the mute button on your remote control next time you watch sports and see how long you can take it.

There is now a mature second generation of people reared on televised sports, the kind of people who prefer waiting for DVD instead of going to the movies and playing computer games at home instead of playing ball in the park. Attendance at sports events must seem pretty one-dimensional to them. Some will insist the tension in the atmosphere of a packed stadium or arena can never be even remotely approximated by watching at home. Yet you can almost hear the groans: "Where are the captions and statistics?" "I missed that piece of action; how about a replay?" "I'd like to see that from a different angle, or slowed-down, or explained to me by an informed commentator."

Expectations and perceptions of sports have changed, as have patterns of viewing. Television has gently encouraged us to *read* sports differently: we may be watching the same piece of action as our grandparents, but we won't necessarily interpret it in the same way. We're also likely to watch more of it, if only because of the volume on the air, or through the cables. Television's facilities for replays allows us to relax our concentration. Missing a touchdown, a goal, a knockdown, a homer, or a hole-in-one is not a disaster when we can see it reviewed again and again from different vantage points. This, plus the comments, summaries, and statistics that accompany the action, encourages a certain detachment and predilection for analysis.

Today's sports-watcher sits like an argus, assimilating all manner of information, audio as well as video. One hesitates before suggesting it, but the pre- and post-event features have all but supplanted the actual competition. Analyzing has become an integral part of televised sports and the better-informed viewer can cast a clinical eye on proceedings. The irony is: they can do so with less play-by-play concentration on the activity itself.

Perhaps I generalize too much: a 1998 study by Lawrence Wenner and Walter Ganz found that: "Many sports viewers are active, discerning, engaged and passionate." Yet: "Because sports spectators come to the viewing situation with different levels of sporting interest, knowledge and experience, they look for and receive different benefits from the experience" (1998: 250). Beyond the "engaged" viewer, there are those who value the social dimensions of watching sports, those who use it as an emotionally cathartic blow-out, and those who just "use sports viewing to kill time." While Wenner and Ganz report on "The television sports viewing experience," they actually discern a series of different experiences and for different sports.

For all the different orientations, there are basic competencies that viewers bring to sports shows and rewards they take from them. Whether or not this fulfillment measures up to Gottdiener's self-actualization is not clear, but what *is* clear is that we shouldn't underestimate the amount of critical intellectual work that gets done when watching televised sports, nor the appreciable gratification derived from the experience. All this suggests that, when we're asked to pay more for sport to be delivered to our home, we'll grimace, complain, then pay up. And, it's certain that we'll have to pay more directly for our sports.

In the golden years between the 1960s and 1980s, sports were as valuable a commodity as television executives could have imagined: relatively inexpensive (no salaries or heavy production costs) and very watchable, as the ratings bore out. Some sports were elevated to international stature as a result of television. It was a match made in heaven. Now, the relationship is much more conflict-torn and the possibility of a divorce looms.

Established television networks have sought a bigger interest in the cable/satellite systems, giving rise to a compex multi-tiered mesh of alliances, often between rival media corporations. In the USA, all the networks have not only cable interests, but pay per view (ppv) links. As major sports find tv money harder to come by, they may buy into cable/satellite themselves or extend the kind of shared risk relationships. Whatever the future, we can anticipate much more interlocking between governing bodies and media groups in sports, rather than straightforward buying and selling of rights. The big leagues and big clubs will want more say in their own destinies. And this means we, the consumers, the fans, the television-watching public, are going to have to pay more for our sports.

---

### Pay per view (ppv)

The first ppv event was in 1980 when the Sugar Ray Leonard–Roberto Duran fight drew 170,000 customers who paid $15 (£10) each. Rock concerts and operas followed sporadically, until the advent of TVKO, an agency owned by Time Warner, which also owned HBO. TVKO struggled to establish itself as an alternative, more selective way of viewing until 1991 when it sold the Evander Holyfield–George Foreman fight to 1.45 million homes at $34.93 (£22). The Mike Tyson–Peter McNeeley fight in 1995 was an even greater success, going into 1.52 million households and grossing $63 million (£42 million) in the USA alone ($96 million worldwide). By comparison, less than a tenth of this number chose to buy a Guns 'n' Roses concert for $24.95 (£15.60) in 1992 and just 34,000 homes took a Pavarotti concert in 1991. NBC's 1992 "Olympic Triplecast," a 15-day event was the biggest disaster to date: out of a potential 20 million homes equipped with the receiving equipment only 165,000 took the whole deal, with 35,000 taking single days.

Since the 1940s, tv viewers have expected sports for no more than the nominal charge of a few pennies on the price of an advertised product, or the cost of a license in the British case. Sports have been as much a part of television's stock-in-trade as soaps, news, and cop shows. But we have already seen some of the grander sports events either being lured away from the terrestrial networks by competing cable/satellite companies or passed over to the ppv services of the media giants themselves. The ppv route has already been explored by boxing and English soccer, with promoters and clubs sharing some of the risks. It's likely that other major sports will pursue similar packages with media giants rather than just selling rights in bundles.

Digital, or DIRECTV, signal ways ahead, with viewers exercising more individual choice in the market: they can select not only camera angles, replays, and so on, but actual events. And, of course, the investments several television groups have made in the internet suggest that the day may not be far off when we can download programs as swiftly and efficiently as we open our email. If this is so, it will be convenient for the consumer, but also profitable for the program providers: viewers will pay for their chosen sports directly. There again, in sports, nothing is for nothing. It never has been.

## OF RELATED INTEREST

*Sport, Culture and the Media: The unruly trinity*, second edition by David Rowe (Open University Press, 2004a) is the most comprehensive treatment of "the sport–media nexus," examining the production and content of mainstream media sport; the same writer has edited a companion volume *Critical Readings: Sport, culture and the media* (Open University Press, 2004b).

*Representing Sport* by Rod Brookes (Arnold, 2002) is a short examination of "the cultural and social significance of the increasingly important role of sport within a global media industry" and can profitably be read in conjunction with "Sport and the media" by Garry Whannel in *Handbook of Sports Studies* edited by Jay Coakley and Eric Dunning (Sage, 2000).The slightly dated *MediaSport* edited by Lawrence Wenner (Routledge, 1998) contains the studies by Whitson and Wenner/Ganz referenced earlier in this chapter.

"Sports advertising and the Super Bowl" by Rick Burton in *The Advertising Business* edited by John Philip Jones (Sage, 1999) is one of several interesting essays in this handbook and may profitably be read in conjunction with *Advertising and Popular Culture* by Jib Fowles (Sage, 1996) which is an intriguing analysis of the power and limitations of advertising and its centrality in contemporary culture, and Arthur Asa Berger's *Ads, Fads and Consumer Culture*, second edition (Rowman & Littlefield, 2003).

*The Theming of America: Dreams, visions and commercial spaces* by Mark Gottdiener (Westview Press, 1997), while not specifically about sports, makes several interesting points about "the powerful compulsions of the consumer society that pressure people to make certain choices in the marketplace"; twenty-first century sports would qualify as one such compulsion.

For historical interest, other books dealing with the media and sports include: *Games and Sets: The changing face of sport on television* by Steven Barnett (British Film Institute, 1990); *Sports for Sale: Television, money and the fans* by David Klatell and Norman Marcus (Oxford University Press, 1988); *Television and National Sport: The United States and Britain* by Joan Chandler (University of Illinois Press, 1988); *In its Own Image: How television has transformed sport* by Benjamin Rader (Collier-Macmillan, 1984); and John Goldlust's *Playing for Keeps: Sport, the media and society* (Longman, 1987).

---

## ASSIGNMENT

Imagine the kind of futuristic scenario depicted at the start of this chapter – but with a difference. Major sports have come under the total control of the mass media. So much so that there is no need for "live" audiences and events are viewed only via the media. When people refer to the spectators, they mean the people watching at home. What were once mass open-air sports, like football and baseball, are now played behind locked doors. Indoor sports are performed in studios. How realistic is this? Support your argument with evidence from current trends.

# *burning* QUESTION ?

## *why do we like to bet on sports?*

Three reasons. (1) The obvious one: it adds to the thrill; watching, or listening to, sports events is arousing in itself and it becomes even more arousing if we have money riding on their outcome. (2) Competition lends itself to gambling; it lacks the randomness of games of chance such as roulette and cards, and invites the bettor to measure his or her own judgment against those of another person or firm. (3) Historically, sports and gambling have been intertwined; the entire development of sports features a coupling with betting. Many sports would not exist at all were it not for gambling and it could be argued that many others would not be so popular if we could not bet on them, whether legally or illegally. In fact, anthropologist Kendall Blanchard argues that to gamble is one of three prime objectives of sports, the others being to compete and to win prizes (1995: 122).

In all but five American states, betting is illegal. Yet Douglas Putnam estimates that as much as $120 billion is unlawfully wagered on sports every year. He reckons that: "the Super Bowl alone generates about $4 billion in illegal bets each January" (1999: 134). In other parts of the world, where sports betting is legal, particularly East Asia, the figures are much higher. The internet has opened up gambling on a global scale: a credit card, online facilities, and an awareness of sports events are all that are needed. Clearly, the betting is a powerful component of the commercial world of sport. A first step to understanding its appeal is to trace its origins.

Betting's underlying motive probably dates back to antiquity. Two great minds of the seventeenth century, Isaac Newton and Gottfried Wilhelm Leibniz, inadvertently contributed to our understanding of this motive. Like Einstein who followed them, Newton and Leibniz were committed to a view of the world as ordered mechanically and moving according to definable principles with potentially predictable outcomes. As with all Enlightenment thinkers, reason and rationalty lay behind all affairs, natural and social. As Galileo had shown in his *Starry Messenger*, first published in 1610, forces that work to render the sky predictable were also at work on earth.

Chance had no place in this ordered universe. Ignorance was merely imperfect knowledge. Everything is potentially knowable; Newton and Leibnitz were both prominent in the advancement of both theoretical and practical science. Given greater knowledge, we could apply the "infinitesimal calculus," a method of calculating or reasoning about the changing world. The seeming mysteries of nature could be comprehended and subordinated to the rational, calculating mind.

Gambling is guided by such reasoning: admittedly, the conscious thought that lies behind rolling a dice or drawing lots is hardly likely to resemble any kind of calculation; these are games of chance, played with the intention of winning money (though many claim to have discovered systems or formulae for winning). But, the motive behind betting on sports is very much influenced by a more rational style of thinking – that it is possible to predict the outcome of an event by the employment of a calculus of probability. No one wagers money on a sporting event without at least some inkling that they are privy to a special knowledge about how a competition will end. A suspicion, a taste, a fancy, a "feel"; all these add to the calculus at work in the mind of even the most casual of gamblers when he or she stakes money on a competition.

Orientations of gamblers differ widely: some always feel a tingle or adrenaline rush, whether it is in watching a horse romp home or a dice roll; others observe from a position of detachment, their interest resting on only the result. The sports gambler bets with head as well as heart; the reward is both in the winning and in the satisfaction that he or she has divined a correct result from the unmanageable flux of a competitive event.

The seventeenth-century philosophers' concerns were not with gambling, though, in fact, they may well have observed the surge in popularity in games of chance in the pre-Enlightenment period. The philosopher Nicholas Rescher locates this popularity in wagering on contests of skill and chance during the English Civil War, 1641–5, and the Thirty Years War, 1618–48 in continental Europe. Starved of entertainment, soldiers and sailors killed time by wagering on virtually any activity. Rescher cites a seventeenth-century soldier's remembrance of betting on a race between lice. Returning to civilian society, the militia brought with them their habits and the enthusiasm for gambling diffused, aligning itself quite naturally with the games of skill that were growing in popularity in England.

In the seventeenth century, laws were passed both in England and in the New World to outlaw gambling, principally to restrict the debts that were being incurred as a result of the growing stakes. Some activities had attracted gambling for decades, perhaps centuries. Swordplay, for example, was a pursuit that was viscerally thrilling to watch and stimulated the human passion for prediction. As the military use of swords declined, so the contests continued simply for recreation and entertainment. Engaging in competitive contests simply for the satisfaction they afforded the competitor and observer was exactly the kind of wasteful and sinful behavior despised by Puritans, who passed an anti-gambling law shortly after their arrival in the New World.

Gambling was actually the basis of many early sports, especially blood sports, in which the amusements of watching animals fight or be ravaged was enhanced by a wager. This was by no means confined to the West. Clifford Geertz's (1972) classic study of cockfighting in Bali emphasizes the significance of betting to the meaning of the event. All forms of animal sports were fair game for gaming. Western-style dog racing which has its origins in eighteenth-century coursing (and involved highly bred and trained dogs which chased and – usually – killed a fleeing hare) became an organized sport, complete with its own organization in 1858, when a National Coursing Club was established in the USA. The betting norm became pari-mutuel, from the French, meaning mutual stake. In the 1930s, this also took off in on-track British horse racing, though it was known as the totalizator, or just "tote" – betting, in which winners divide the losers' stakes, less an administrative charge.

Appealing as it may be to link the rise of gambling with modern capitalism and the ethos it both embodies and encourages, sports betting is not confined to cultures characterized by materialism and acquisitiveness. Blanchard's work documents the centrality of betting, in some cases as an obligation, to sports in several cultures, many in the underdeveloped world. Yet Western influences brought different aspects. Blanchard gives the example of a Mississippi Choctaw sport to which betting was integral. In the 1890s, "local whites frequented the 'Indian ballgames' and with the whites came a new type of betting, whiskey, and a threat to the safety of Choctaw women" (1995: 175). After appeals from missionaries, the state of Mississippi outlawed gambling at all the ball games. The sport faded away. While there were other factors, it is believed the elimination of betting from the sport was responsible for its demise. This suggests that the very existence of some sports is predicated on betting. Horse and dog racing are contemporary instances.

In Britain, a form of gambling on soccer came to life in the early 1930s and captured the British public's imagination almost immediately. Newspapers had been publishing their own versions of "pools," as the bets were known, for many years, but the practice was declared illegal in 1928. Dennis Brailsford (1997) notes how the £20 million staked in the 1934/5 season doubled within two years. The outlay was usually no more than a few pence and the bets were typically collected from one's home. The aim of pools was to select a requisite number of drawn games (ties), so it was not classified as a game of chance, but one of skill, thus escaping the regulation of gaming legislation. By the outbreak of war in 1939, there were 10 million players of the pools. The popularity the pools enjoyed with working-class bettors stayed intact until the introduction of the national lottery (modeled on the US state lotteries) in the early 1990s.

Nowadays, betting on the spread is one of the most popular gambling forms. The bettor can wager not only on the result of a contest but on any facet of it: for example, how often Mark McGwire spat or the total positive drug tests at an Olympic Games or even something like how many times British soccer commentator Mark Lawrenson said "very, very" during a game. Betting on sports, legally and illegally, was facilitated by the spread of the internet in the late 1990s. Because of the difficulty in regulating it, online betting became attractive where local laws prohibited or restricted most forms of betting, such as in the States, or where gaming taxes were once high, as in Britain.

*More questions . . .*

- Should the USA acknowledge that betting is an integral part of sports' attraction and legalize it?
- Does televising sports make it more possible that people want to bet on them?
- Why are some sports, like jai alai or horse racing, less interesting, if not meaningless, without betting?

*Read on . . .*

- Kendall Blanchard, *The Anthropology of Sports: An introduction* (Bergin & Garvey, 1995).
- Dennis Brailsford, *British Sport: A social history* (Lutterworth Press, 1997).
- Mike Huggins, *Horseracing and the British, 1919–39* (Manchester University Press, 2003).
- Nicholas Rescher, *Luck: The brilliant randomness of everyday life* (Farrar Straus Giroux, 1995).
- Howard J. Shaffer (ed.) *Journal of Gambling Studies* (Human Sciences Press, since 1984).

# at the business end

## how Rupert Murdoch became the

## most powerful man in sports

# 1

Rupert Murdoch started the twenty-first century as the most powerful person in sports. There were other contenders, such as Michael Eisner, the head of Disney, and John Malone, the chief of Tele-Communications. But no one came close to Murdoch; his worldwide influence in almost every facet of sports was undoubted. And yet, he had no particular passion for sports. A glance at his career reveals that he only took an active interest in them in the 1990s, when he realized that he could use sports, as he put it, as a "battering ram" to smash down people's doors and install his television services. For Murdoch, sport was strictly a means to an end; a very effective means, we should note.

In 2003, he acquired the final piece in his global jigsaw of satellite platforms when he closed a deal with General Motors worth $6.6 billion (£4.3 billion) for a controlling 34 percent interest in GM's Hughes Electronics, owner of DIRECTV. The deal gave Murdoch leverage far beyond the US tv industry: even before the deal, he had assembled the most formidable combination of sports clubs, production operations, and media outlets the world had ever known. Through his media empire, he had the kind of leverage "undreamed of by bush-leaguers like William Randolph Hearst," as Thomas Frank puts it in his "The new gilded age" (1997a: 25). The meshing of media and sports into a combined network was either the masterstroke of a genius or the evil work of a mega-lomaniac.

It is, of course, no accident that Murdoch conquered both domains of sports and television. At the cusp of the twenty-first century, the two had become so symbiotically attached that virtually any media entrepreneur had interests in sports, almost by default. Sports and the media became convergent fields: Murdoch's ability to unite them into a single business established him as the single most important player in the entire sports business – and I use the term to embrace the whole province of sports.

But, how was it possible for a person such as Murdoch to rise to a position of virtually unrivaled power in sports? What were the conditions under which he rose? And what would sports be like if RM had become, say, a priest or a politician? To answer these questions, we need to backtrack to a time when sports were exactly that – sports, not businesses. The introduction of money into pursuits or pastimes that were once played for enjoyment only set in motion a series of processes that changed sports irreversibly and, some would say, abominably. Money corrupts; that much we know. Some misty-eyed romantics will always complain that the filthy stuff has corrupted the ideals that were once integral to sports. Others will point out that the commercialization of sports is only part of an inexorable movement that has affected every aspect of contemporary culture. If people enjoy watching and appreciating something and, in some circumstances, are willing to pay to do so, then there will always be others eager to profit from their willingness.

Murdoch is but one of countless entrepreneurs, competitors, managers, and other personnel associated with sports who have profited handsomely. Where there has been a demand and a raw supply, there has been no shortage of enterprising people with ideas on how to connect the two and appropriate the surplus. This is a business approach to sports and one that conflicts with the cardinal rules of sport as they were originally laid out.

## THE RISE OF THE PROFESSIONALS

All sports that are watchable have potential for commercial exploitation. An after-dinner game of snooker played in private without even a side-bet would not have this potential. Nor would a one-on-one basketball matchup in the privacy of a high school gym. Make the snooker players Stephen Hendry and Ronnie O'Sullivan and transport them to Sheffield's Crucible, or the ball players Kobe Bryant and Grant Hill and pitch them together in Madison Square Garden, and they become spectator sports. If contests can draw crowds, they qualify as spectator sports. And, if they are spectator sports, then people are usually willing to pay for the privilege of spectating.

It's perfectly possible to have mass spectator sports without the taint of money that many argue pollutes the central values of competition. The NCAA is strictly amateur and celebrates this fact. The organization's approach to sports is pure in the sense that harks back to an age when sports were for, as the name implies, love (from the Latin *amatorious*, "pertaining to love"). Fondness for the activity itself or the satisfaction drawn from winning fairly were the motivating principles, though participation was, or should have been, regarded as more important than achievement.

Nowadays, "amateur" is almost a pejorative term, implying a lack of refinement or clumsiness – the opposite of professional. In the eighteenth and nineteenth centuries, the reverse was the case and the amateur symbolized all that was good in sport; while the professional was despised as a vulgarian who competed just for money. "Sports had as their ideal aim the production of pleasure," write Eric Dunning and Kenneth Sheard, "an immediate emotional state rather than some ulterior end, whether of a material or other kind" (1979: 153–4).

It was regarded as "unsportsmanlike" and "ungentlemanly" to show elation in victory and disappointment in defeat. Compare that with today's response to a touchdown or a goal. British public schools and universities were the wellsprings of the amateur ethos and there was concern at the prospect of the dignified ball games practiced at Rugby, Harrow, and other upper class schools, being copied by the lower classes, whose desire to win rather than just compete amounted to a defilement.

"Subsidized" players who were reimbursed for work time lost while playing, or who accepted straight cash for their services were a threatening presence in some sports, especially rugby. Amateurs could not devote so much of their time to their game as professionals and would be hard-pressed to maintain their superiority. There was also the suspicion that dangling a carrot in front of players would encourage them not only to play harder and forget the joy of it all, but to raise their ability levels through training. In the eyes of the nineteenth-century amateur, this was unfair: it produced a competitive advantage for those who committed themselves to self-improvement. Sports were meant to be about enjoyment, whereas "to train for sport and take it too seriously was," as Dunning and Sheard observe, "tantamount to transforming it into work and, hence, to destroying its essence" (1979: 148).

Of course, sports did eventually become like work: by the second half of the nineteenth century, cricket and other ball games, prizefighting, and pedestrianism (the equivalent of competitive walking) paid contestants. Sports that were played by affluent classes, like golf, were rich enough to employ coaches; while other sports could pay expenses simply because they were popular enough to attract paying spectators. This caused the amateur gentlemen to confound the trend toward professionalism with greater fervor. Mass gatherings of working-class spectators, some of them partisan, posed what was seen as a threat to public order. So much so that such assemblies were outlawed in some circumstances.

Spectators didn't benefit from sports in the same way as participants. Quite the contrary: they suffered by degenerating into an excitable, amoral mass. At least, that is what the affluent classes thought. The gentlemen amateurs' reaction to spectator sports presents a type of metaphor for the changes that were occurring in society generally. The industrial working class was getting organized and showing signs of cohesion and solidarity in the face of employers who were worried by the prospect of having their authority challenged from below. Class antagonism, or sheer prejudice, manifested itself in several notable incidents, all designed to cocoon the exclusive elite of gentlemen from others. As well as the landowning English aristocracy, gentlemen would have included *nouveaux riches*, merchants, physicians, lawyers, politicians, and others with new-found prestige rather than inherited wealth.

Let's segue to an actual incident that illustrates the class tension of the period. In 1846 at Lancaster, in the northwest of England, there was a dispute following a Manchester crew's victory in the Borough Cup rowing competition. It was alleged that two of the crew, a cabinetmaker and a bricklayer, were not acceptable entrants because "they were not known as men of property." The debate continued until, in 1853, when the category of "gentlemen amateur" was distinguished from just plain amateur, for the Lancaster Rowing Club's purposes. Other clubs followed suit, stipulating that those who worked as mechanics, artisans, or laborers would not be eligible for competition as their employment, being physical in nature, equipped them with advantages.

This may have seemed a subterfuge to members of the working class, but it was perpetuated by the Amateur Athletic Association which, in 1866, officially defined an amateur as a person who had either never competed (1) in open competition, (2) for prize money, (3) for admission money, (4) with professionals, (5) never taught or assisted in the pursuit of athletic exercises, or (6) was not a mechanic, artisan, or laborer. Condition (6) was removed in 1880, but the intent of this typical pronouncement was clear: to exclude working-class competitors and so stave off the evils of professionalism. This applied only to track and field; in several other sports professionalism looked unstoppable.

By the 1880s, rugby and soccer became so popular, especially in the English north and the Midlands, that spectators were prepared to pay hard cash to watch organized games between the best players. The money made it possible to pay those players. The Rugby Union was intractable in its opposition to this and, by 1895, had effectively forced the formation of a professional organization, which became the Rugby League in 1922. Soccer prevaricated, but, by 1885, had agreed to a controlled professionalism, with a maximum wage limit (what we'd call a cap today) and, stipulation about the movement of players between clubs.

This was a similar restriction to baseball's "reserve clause" which prevented out-of-contract players moving on and depressed salaries overall. Baseball itself had much the same matrix as cricket and rugby, but, as Peter Levine points out, in his *A. G. Spalding and the Rise of Baseball*: "Almost from the outset, however, this amateur gentlemen's game was transformed" and baseball became one of the first professional spectator sports (1985). In 1858, fans were charged 50¢ admission to watch a three-game championship series between teams from New York and Brooklyn. In 1862, enclosures were specially built to accommodate paying fans and exclude those who wanted to watch games for free. As gate fees went up, so players began to reap some benefits, though their salaries were to prove a source of dispute for many years.

The subject of Levine's book, A. G. Spalding, was instrumental in the early development of baseball. Spalding, an American, had no respect for the English gentlemen's customs and approached baseball as if it were an industry – and he a captain of that industry. Spalding was puzzled by the amateur ethos: "I was not able to understand how it could be right to pay an actor, or a singer, or an instrumentalist for entertaining the public, and wrong to pay a ball player for doing the same thing in his way" (quoted in Levine).

---

### A. G. Spalding

Spalding was the man who started the first sports goods manufacturing and retail industry. In 1876, Spalding opened what was then a unique store specializing in sports goods. Spalding's Baseball and Sporting-goods Emporium was based in Chicago and stocked baseball uniforms and equipment. The firm also manufactured baseball bats, croquet equipment, ice skates, and fishing tackle. Capitalizing on the cycling craze, Spalding published an *Official Cycling Guide* featuring pictures of bicycles, sweaters, and shoes, which he also sold. He anticipated later trends to sign players to endorsement deals and signed three pro cyclists to a contract that required them to use his cycles. Spalding, who had played professional baseball, had several other business interests, though his name is forever linked with recognizing and exploiting the demand for sporting goods and apparel.

---

By 1910 – five years before Spalding's death – attendance had soared to 7.25 million, though players' salaries were still kept artificially low, averaging under $2,500. In Britain, spectators were flocking to sports and stadiums were built to accommodate them. Professionalism was well established and organizers and promoters openly exploited the business opportunities offered by sports. Boxing, for long a pursuit of professionals at some level, whether in fairground shows or streetfighting, evolving into two coexisting organizations, amateur and professional, with boxers transferring from the former to the latter. Other sports refused to condone professionalism.

Prosperous gentlemen of New York, concerned over professionalism, helped organize the National Association of Amateur Athletes of America in

1868. This became the Amateur Athletic Association in 1888. Intercollegiate sports, which gained in currency during the 1880s, were very much amateur affairs and kept a safe distance from the dishonorable baseball leagues. As soccer had emerged as primarily an upper-class sport which was appropriated by the English working-class, so American football began life as a derivative of rugby played in the main by sons of the wealthy during their university years. The Intercollegiate Athletic Association (IAA) was formed in 1906 in response to an early-century crisis in college football: players were "moonlighting," playing for money under assumed names. The IAA was a precursor of the NCAA (National Collegiate Athletic Association) which was formed to protect amateurism and regulate college sports.

American football's career was not unlike soccer's, early professional outfits growing out of factory teams and cultivating a working-class following. The Indian Packing Company, of Green Bay, Wisconsin, had its own team in the first decade of the twentieth century; as did the Staley Starch Company, of Decatur, Illinois. Players were paid about $50 per week and given time off to train. In 1920, both companies affiliated their teams to a new organization that also harbored teams from New York and Washington. The teams evolved into the Packers, Bears, Giants, and Redskins respectively. Quite soon it was possible for the teams to divorce themselves from their industrial backgrounds and become independent employers: players who had learnt their skills at colleges could earn a decent living once their years of study were over. This seamless transition from university to pro club has been a feature of American football ever since, the draft being brought into play in 1936.

Some sports were slower than others to accept the inevitability of professionalism. Tennis adamantly refused to allow professionals into its prestigious competitions until 1968 when it went "open." From that point, players like Rod Laver, who had previously turned pro and been barred, reintegrated with amateurs whom they dominated so overwhelmingly that amateurism vanished from top levels over the next few years. Track and field for long assumed the ostrich position, burying its head in the sand despite widespread knowledge of "shamateurism" with athletes accepting generous gifts and exaggerated expenses for their services. In 1983, the International Association of Athletics Federations (IAAF) accepted reality but insisted that payments should go via a subvention into a trust fund and be dispensed later to the athlete. By the end of the century, there were millions to be earned in both sports.

## SPORTS ENTREPRENEURS: FROM FIGG TO TURNER

In some dark and distant age, an enterprising witness to a contest noticed a crowd react excitedly to the sight of competition and thought: "Lo! The gathered masses act as if 'twas them joined in battle!" Inspired by this, the first sports entrepreneur would have brought the same contestants together again, but this time charging a fee for watching – the assumption being that the pleasure taken in just observing was worth a small amount. So, the sports business was started.

No one is officially credited with being the first person to spot the potential for earning money from sports. James Figg was one of the first to establish an organization to exploit the potential when he opened his Amphitheatre in London, in 1743. Figg attracted large crowds to watch his combat events which were arranged on a regular basis and supplied him with a successful business, as we noted in Chapter 4. His concept was adopted from that of the ancient Romans, except that his motive was merely to take a profit. His patrons' motives were mixed: to identify with and cheer on their favorite, to extract vicarious pleasure from watching, to wager, or just to meet other members of the "fancy," as patrons of prizefighting were collectively known (possibly an early form of the word "fan"). This reflects much the same mixture of impulses of fans today.

The correlation between high-caliber athletes and large crowds would not have been lost on early promoters. Figg's natural successors were the prize-fight organizers of America in the 1800s. Some states, such as Massachusetts, outlawed prizefighting and this prompted organizers to stage illicit contests behind locked doors with a small, invited crowd.

In his history of boxing *Beyond the Ring*, Jeffrey Sammons discovers that the first unofficial world heavyweight championship between Paddy Ryan and Joe Goss, in 1880, was "fought in virtual secrecy at Colliers, West Virginia." Sammons explains: "Organizers chose the tiny Brooks County town for its proximity to the Ohio and Pennsylvania state lines: if raided by hostile law officers, participants and followers could scatter across the border to escape arrest" (1988: 6).

In the same period, Richard Kyle Fox, an Irish migrant who was scratching a living by writing about events such as oyster-opening and one-legged dancing competitions, ventured into promoting events that he could then write about for local newspapers. In 1881, he had a chance encounter with John L. Sullivan, a prizefighter, who, so folklore had it, spurned Fox's offer to promote him. Sullivan went on to become the most famous athlete of his day and Fox's determination to secure his services or ruin him drove him to the position of American sports' first major promoter, offering either purses (fixed payments) or percentages of gate receipts to fighters. By the mid-1890s, top pugilists fought for what were then enormous purses of thousands of dollars. Sullivan is known to have charged in the region of $25,000 per championship fight (then more than £50,000) – remember, pro baseball players averaged only a tenth of this amount per year by 1910.

The legalization of prizefighting in New York in 1920 opened up new commercial possibilities for sports entrepreneurs. Sammons notes that, in 1922 alone, gate receipts in New York state totaled $5 million (in those days, about £1.5 million), a sum that made some conclude presciently that boxing was "an industry, financed by banks, and licensed and supervised by state laws and officials just as banking and insurance" (quoted in Sammons 1988: 66).

If this was so, then boxing was a prototype for other sports. Opportunistic entrepreneurs were key agents in the process of establishing sports along business lines. Unquestionably, the most visionary was George "Tex" Rickard, who promoted all but one heavyweight title fight that resulted in a new champion from the reign of Jack Johnson to that of Gene Tunney and whose elaborate publicity stunts and gargantuan promotions (regularly attracting 100,000+ spectators, with receipts of nearly $1.9 million for one show in 1926) established him as *the* sports promoter of his era.

Allegations that many of Rickard's contests were not only run as but actually *were* showbusiness events complete with scripts and stage directions were commonplace. But, the controversy only added to Rickard's notoriety and he was able to exploit the growing enthusiasm for sports which featured not only contestants but a sense of occasion – an atmosphere that drew together the blue-collar and the plutocracy, the anonymous and the famous.

Rickard's promotions were huge but occasional extravaganzas. The market for everyday pro sports was also buoyant. Baseball's National League (NL) was having to stave off the challenges of several rival leagues which were prepared to undercut it with lower admission prices. The most formidable of these was the Western League, which later became the American League (AL). In 1902, the AL attracted 2.2 million fans to its games, compared to the 1.7 million who attended NL games. A truce was signed in January 1903, and this agreement established the framework of what became Major League Baseball (MLB). By the 1930s, baseball had become America's most popular sport, regularly attracting five-figure crowds. In the midst of economic depression, star players, like Babe Ruth, were able to command staggering salaries of $80,000.

The big-earning athletes were able to command such money not simply because they had more talent than their colleagues, but because (1) they had market appeal; and (2) they were surrounded with entrepreneurs who knew how to capitalize on that appeal. Promoters and owners of ball clubs were about as philanthropic in the 1930s as they are today. In the mid-1970s, Jonathan Brower's research into the subject concluded that they are "neither accustomed to nor comfortable with losing money in business ventures" (1976: 15).

They were and are in sports to make money; to them it was and is a business. Not surprisingly, promoters and owners have run sports organizations as if they were any other business, the only problem being that many ventures fail to make money. Ball clubs in particular are not typically great investments, though, of course, there is great prestige and a certain celebrity status that attaches to owners. Ask Wayne Huizinga or George Steinbrenner; or Victor

Kiam, owner of Remington, who apparently liked the New York Patriots so much that, in 1988, he bought the club. "He saw the acquisition as a good way to draw attention to himself and to Remington," suggest Jerry Gorman and Kirk Calhoun, who quote Kiam: "I felt that with any exposure I got, there would be some falloff benefit for Remington" (1994: 30).

Whatever the motives of promoters, owners, or any other entrepreneur in sports, their impact has been to transform sports into a unique collective enterprise. Why unique? Because sports may have veered toward but has never become pure entertainment. Its packaging and merchandising may be indistinguishable, but sports' abiding appeal lies in an essential unpredictability. The outcome of a competition is never known, at least nearly never. During the 1950s, organized crime had such a stranglehold on North American boxing that the results of a great many title fights were prescribed. Promoters of sports events and owners or chairs of clubs are integral parts of a landscape filled with sponsors, agents, and hard-boiled marketing executives, all seeking to manipulate competitive sports to their own requirements. Yet, they are not simple conveyers of public demand: they originate the demand, shape it, manage it, and, occasionally, destroy it.

---

### Mark McCormack

Chicago-born McCormack is credited with being the first sports agent. When, in 1960, he created his company International Management Group (IMG), he sparked a series of changes that would transfigure sports. McCormack's principle was simple and can be summed up in an episode that followed Tony Jacklin's victory at the 1969 Open Golf Championship. Bollinger asked to photograph Jacklin holding a bottle of its champagne. McCormack intervened, twisting the bottle so that the label wasn't visible. "If Bollinger wanted to photograph Jacklin with their champagne . . . that has value to them and they ought to pay for it." He applied the same principle when negotiating for any of his many luminary clients, including Tiger Woods, Serena Williams, and Andre Agassi. He also handled television and marketing rights for Wimbledon and other tournaments. As well as representing athletes (and entertainers, like Placido Domingo, and scholars, such as Stephen Hawking), McCormack promoted his own golf tournaments, like the World Match Play Championship. Once described by *Sports Illustrated* as the "most important man in sports," McCormack saw his influence abate in the 1990s as sports agents began, at first, to proliferate, and, then, consolidate into major corporations, such as SFX (itself part of Clear Channel Communications).

---

Market forces being what they are, it is unlikely that sports would have grown into the massive business it now is without the assistance of the mass media. As things transpired, sports entrepreneurs did enjoy such assistance. Newspapers, radio, and, later, television were not slow in realizing that they too could turn a penny by extensively covering sports. This both responded to demand and stimulated further interest. As we saw in Chapter 13, television seized the commercial opportunities offered by sports and quickly extended its interest and influence in ways that would have been considered pure fantasy to any one of the 120,757 people who watched the Jack Dempsey–Gene Tunney fight in 1926.

The complementary nature of interests between sports entrepreneurs and media companies was too obvious to miss. If sports were popular, people wanted to watch them, if not in the flesh, then on the screen. Media magnates were never willing to part with the kind of money demanded by promoters and league commissioners (who represented the interests of clubs), but they usually did. Ever-grudgingly, they paid more and more for every new contract. Then Ted Turner, the head of a media corporation, hit on the novel idea: buy the clubs.

In 1972, the owner of Turner Communications agreed to pay the Atlanta Braves baseball club $2.5 million for the rights to games for five years. A year before the end of the arrangement, Turner offered the club's owners $9.65 million for the whole shebang. The new owner was called the Atlanta National League Baseball Club, which was a subsidiary of Turner Communications. The same company acquired a 75 percent interest in the Atlanta Hawks NBA franchise, in 1977; and, the following year, it bought a partnership in the Atlanta Chiefs soccer club.

An obvious advantage of owning the Braves was that their games had high ratings and gave Turner's tv station a strong presence in the local market. Perhaps more significantly, Turner was able to avoid the hard-fought negotiations that typically accompany a tv–ball club deal. The reciprocity was enhanced by the boost television exposure gave to home game attendance. Eventually, this gave the Braves more money to attract better players and so contributed to the playing performance. Improving performances brought more viewers to their tv screens and enabled Turner to crank up his advertising rates. As the team's W–L record improved, so tv and radio broadcast rights rose, becoming the single biggest source of revenue; in the 1990s, this regularly exceeded $22 million per annum.

The Hawks were a poor team when Turner took over. Its owners were prepared to move the franchise out of Atlanta. As in baseball, clubs received a pro rata distribution of television revenues from telecasts by the national networks but, unlike baseball clubs, they received none of the gate receipts from away games. It took only till 1979/80 before the Hawks began averaging 10,000+ for home games and, although this subsequently slipped, attendance picked up again after 1988/9. This was the period when the NBA generally gained widespread popularity. Encouraged by this, NBC paid the NBA $600 million for four years' broadcast rights, 1990–4. The Hawks's share of this was $22 million. TNT (Turner Network Television) retained broadcast rights for the 50-game regular season and, if appropriate, 30 play-off games; for this it paid the NBA $275 million, of which the Hawks saw about $10 million.

Turner's strategy could not be faulted: it was a no-lose situation. And one which other media owners were observing carefully. So that, by the time Turner stepped up to plate with his bid for the Los Angeles Dodgers, in 1996, several other media corporations had taken active financial interests in sports clubs and Turner found himself in competition with News Corporation owner Rupert Murdoch. Turner bitterly opposed Murdoch's ultimately successful attempt to buy the Dodgers, though he was outvoted when the 16 National League franchises took the decision in 1998. Turner's enmity was apparent when he

---

### Ted Turner

At the age of 24, Turner inherited his father's billboard business and, with it, $6 million worth of debt. After turning the business around, Turner bought two radio stations in Chattanooga and retitled the business the Turner Communications Corporation. He floated the company on the local stock exchange in 1970 to finance the acquisition of Channel 17, an Atlanta television station. At first, he filled its schedules with old movies and tv show reruns, but, in 1972, he bought the rights to the Atlanta Braves games. In 1976, he bought the ailing club and turned round its fortunes. The Major League Baseball authorities despised Turner's flamboyant conduct. In 1976, he was suspended from all baseball activities for a year. But Turner was undaunted and continued to spend more money in the ultimately successful attempt to bring the World Series to Atlanta.

Turner's flagship television network CNN started life in 1979: it was a highly innovative 24-hour all-news cable station. He augmented this with a movie tv cable, TNT, and, in 1992, split the Turner Broadcasting System (TBS) into five divisions, one of which concentrated on sports activities. In 1996, CNN/SI was launched: this was an all-sports news cable in competition with ESPN's second channel. Turner's mega-deal with media giant Time Warner was one of a number of a series of mergers and transactions in the late 1990s. Turner continued to handle Time Warner's cable networks, including HBO, and ran the Braves, Hawks, and Thrashers. In 2003, he sold 60 million AOL Time Warner shares for $784m.

promised: "I'll squish Murdoch like a bug." But, Turner must have soon felt like a character in Roland Emmerich's 2002 movie *Eight Legged Freaks* in which spiders are pumped up into giant people-eaters by a toxic waste spill.

## VERTICAL INTEGRATION, OR HOW SPORTS BECAME "MURDOCHIZED"

Murdoch's purchase of the 20th Century Fox film and television studio signaled his arrival as a key player in the North American media. But, for many years before, he had been steadily building his interests. He had already assembled a bundle of British newspapers to add to his collection of Australian titles. Although, a successful television company escaped him. Having been thwarted in an attempt to buy London Weekend Television, he turned to the States where he had been impressed by the ascent of cable channels, especially ESPN and MTV. In 1983, he bought a struggling satellite operator, Inter-American, which he turned into Skyband. The purchase proved a disaster and Murdoch lost $20 million within six months. In the same year, he tried unsuccessfully to buy Warner, the Hollywood studio (later to merge with Time).

Fox was then struggling and, in 1985, Murdoch took advantage to buy at first a 50 percent stake and, later, full control from its owner Marvin Davis. Fox was insignificant in the tv market, but Murdoch grew it into the fourth major network. One of the reasons he was able to do this was by outbidding the established trio of ABC, CBS, and NBC for the rights to screen the plum NFL games. The 1993 deal cost Murdoch what many thought an absurdly high $1.6 billion; Fox lost an estimated $100 million in broadcasts in the 1994/5 season alone. Undeterred, Murdoch also signed contracts with Major League Baseball and the National Hockey League.

Murdoch's logic? By wresting the popular Sunday afternoon games from CBS, he had established Fox as a major network. Many local television stations changed their affiliations as a direct result of the coup and, of course, advertising revenue soared. Solid audience ratings helped Fox advertise its other shows in the commercial spots, thus increasing viewer awareness of the station's menu.

Then, Murdoch changed the formula: he beat off Turner's challenge to buy the Los Angeles Dodgers, admittedly one of sport's astral franchises, but not worth $350 million (£217 million) in the estimation of most market analysts.

On the heels of this deal, Murdoch, through his 50/50 joint venture with Liberty Media, bought a 40 percent interest in LA's Staples Center, the only arena in the States to house three major franchises, including the Los Angeles Kings, of the NHL. The deal included an option on 40 percent of the Kings. As the Kings announced their intention to exercise their own option on just under

10 percent of the Los Angeles Lakers, who also played at the Staples Center, Murdoch became a minority owner in an NBA franchise too.

Over on the other coast, Murdoch's Fox Entertainment Group's 40 percent ownership of Rainbow Media Holdings Inc., a subsidiary of Cablevision – which held a majority interest in Madison Square Garden, the New York Knicks, of the NBA, and the New York Rangers hockey club – meant that Murdoch had his fingers deeply in the pies of the NBA and the NHL on both coasts. Like Turner's strategy, Murdoch's was to control the media distribution networks *and* the content of the programs to run through them.

His attempt to repeat the strategy in Britain was stymied when a £600 million ($1 billion) bid for Manchester United, though accepted by the owners, was blocked by the Monopolies and Mergers Commission, an official body set up to guard against anti-trust arrangements. Murdoch's BSkyB subscription network had earlier bought the exclusive rights to screen English soccer's Premiership games "live" and was, at the time, experimenting with pay per view transmissions. As Turner had earlier discovered, owning a ball club simplified broadcasting negotiations.

As we have seen, Murdoch was not the only media owner to have sensed the advantages in owning clubs: in the late 1990s, media companies owned at least 20 top clubs in baseball, football, basketball, and hockey. The process was known as *vertical integration*. Time Warner (later AOL Time Warner) acquired baseball's Atlanta Braves and the Atlanta Hawks basketball club after its takeover of Turner's holdings, which included his several cable channels; it also became owners of the Atlanta Thrashers hockey team. Disney owned the NHL's Mighty Ducks and the Anaheim Angels baseball club; it also owned ABC and ESPN. Wayne Huizinga, former owner of Blockbuster Video, owned baseball's Florida Marlins and the Florida Panthers hockey club. *The Chicago Tribune* owned the Chicago Cubs; Cablevision owned the New York Knicks and the New York Rangers (and tried to buy the Yankees); Ascent Entertainments owned the Denver Nuggets; and Comcast owned the Philadelphia 76ers. Italian media magnate Silvio Berlusconi owned the AC Milan soccer club of *Serie A*. The French cable television company Canal+ owned the Paris St. Germain club. These are but a few illustrations of the media–sports cross-ownership patterns in North America and Europe. But, on a global scale, Murdoch's operations had no counterpart.

In addition to Fox in the States and BSkyB in Europe, Murdoch had Star TV that stretched from Saudi Arabia to Australia and included the gigantic Chinese market, as well as Japan (24 countries in total). Think of all the sports Murdoch had access to through his American and British set-ups, then contemplate the size of the sports diet he could offer to markets in the rest of the world. It is estimated by Kevin Maney that, at any one time, Murdoch could "reach more than two-thirds of the world's television households and touch

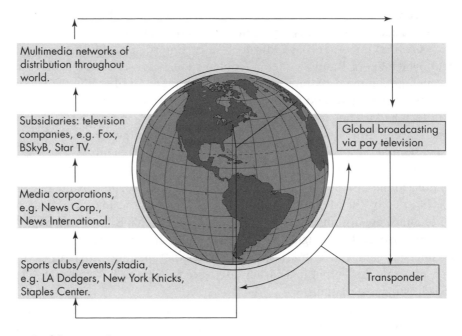

Multimedia networks of distribution throughout world.

Subsidiaries: television companies, e.g. Fox, BSkyB, Star TV.

Media corporations, e.g. News Corp., News International.

Sports clubs/events/stadia, e.g. LA Dodgers, New York Knicks, Staples Center.

Global broadcasting via pay television

Transponder

**vertical integration**

yet more people through movies and newspapers" (1995: 173). In his book *Megamedia Shakeout: The inside story of the leaders and the losers in the exploding communications industry*, Maney characterizes Murdoch's "awesome basket of assets" as: "The intertwining of the two trends of megamedia and globalization" (1995: 173).

Apart from the scale of Murdoch's empire, which frightened many, his methods of construction were also alarming. With his cross-ownership of several media, Murdoch would typically sacrifice profits from one medium and underwrite costs from another. An example was the London *Times*, one of four quality national newspapers in a somewhat congested British market. Murdoch also owned the *New York Post*-ish *Sun*, which he had bought cheaply in 1969 and, within nine years, turned into the nation's best-selling daily. He did so by featuring bare-bosomed models, a bingo game, and sensationalist stories, many about the Royal family. Profits from the *Sun* allowed Murdoch to use *The Times* as a sort of loss leader by dropping its cover price to about two-thirds of its rivals'.

Could the same tactic be applied to sports? Consider: Florida Marlins' owner Wayne Huizinga split up his 1997 World Series-winning team because the salary demands were too great. Faced with a similar situation, might a Murdoch-owned team underwrite salary costs with money from other ventures just to ensure the team stays ahead of the field and draws more television viewers?

(As the Marlins fragmented, the LA Dodgers' payroll totaled a league high of $90 million.)

Any club owned by Murdoch was eligible for *The Times* treatment. In other words, it could become the beneficiary of cash from other outposts of the empire. Even with salary caps, the consequence of this would be to weaken rival clubs and media groups by driving up wages. Such possibilities gave rise to the suspicion that Murdoch's goal was not ownership of clubs or media companies, but of sport and the communications industry. His track record suggested that, if he wanted something, he was prepared to pay over-the-odds for it. This is why *Big League, Big Time* author Len Sherman, writing before Murdoch clinched the Dodgers, trembled at the prospect: "Murdoch could, if he gained control of the Dodgers, deploy his newspapers and TV networks to forcefully thrust baseball into the international arena, forever upsetting the power structure of Major League Baseball, remaking the industry and the sport from top to bottom" (1998: 35).

In 2003, Murdoch vastly consolidated his command over the distribution of tv programming in the USA with the acquisition of a controlling interest in Hughes Electronics, whose DIRECTV had 11.3 million subscribers in the USA, making it the biggest distributor of programming.

Murdoch revolutionized sports' marketplace by investing for long-term value rather than short-term profits and building globally rather than nationally. If he had begun his campaign ten years, or perhaps even five years before he did, his grand project may have quickly disintegrated and you would not be reading this much about him in *Making Sense of Sports*. He may still overreach himself, of course. But, for him to have risen even as far as he did tells us something about the social changes of the past 20 years. In the final part of the answer to the "what if . . .?" question posed earlier, we will look at those changes.

## BETTER THAN SEX

Addressing the 1996 AGM of News Corp., Murdoch announced that sports "absolutely overpowers film and all other forms of entertainment in drawing viewers to television." Comforting stockholders with the news that the company held long-term rights to major sports events in most countries, he revealed future strategy: "We will be doing in Asia what we intend to do elsewhere in the world – that is, use sports as a battering ram and a lead offering in all our pay television operations." It was a widely quoted remark and, as it turned out, an honest one. Murdoch's acquisitive quest for leadership, if not ownership, of the sports market, reflects both sports' crucial role in generating television ratings and television's equally crucial role in the healthy cashflow of sports.

As we noted before, during the 1980s, Murdoch became impressed by the ways in which dedicated cable channels, such as ESPN and MTV particularly, were able to isolate specific portions of the population. This was an agreeable development for advertisers; and the enduring commercial success of both of these confirms this. While he had no intrinsic interest in sports, Murdoch realized how effective these were in attracting a particular group of consumers, which he could, in turn, deliver to potential advertisers. At Fox and at BSkyB, Murdoch was prepared to bear brutal initial losses in anticipation that sports would ultimately woo demographically desirable viewers – the kind that drink alcohol, drive cars, and have private pension plans, for example.

The concept of using sports to sell products, possibly products only tangentially connected to sports (like beer, cars, and pension plans) seems blindingly obvious today; but, in the 1960s, it was a daring innovation. Even in the 1970s, the possibilities were never totally explored. Only in the late 1980s and through the 1990s was sport's marketing potential fully realized. In retrospect, the linking of consumerism with sports may be the single most influential development since the advent of professional sport itself in the late nineteenth century.

The link was strengthened by the emergence of a new cultural equation in which sports' stock soared. In the early 1990s, "Sports had arguably surpassed popular music as the captivating medium most essential to being perceived as 'young and alive,'" according to Donald Katz, author of *Just Do It: The Nike spirit in the corporate world*. "Sports, as never before, had so completely permeated the logic of the marketplace in consumer goods that by 1992 the psychological content of selling was often more sports-oriented than it was sexual" (1994: 25–6).

Companies such as Nike, Coca-Cola, and McDonald's in some measure hitched their wagons to sports' star; and profited enormously as a result. While Nike was not the only company to have exploited the new status of sports performers, it did more than any other to enhance the status (we will open this out in the next chapter). The new cultural equation encouraged the interest of all manner of companies in sports, especially televised sports. Car firms, clothes makers, food manufacturers, and other organizations with no particular interest in sports apart from the ability to sell their products began to express interest. This took the form of both signing athletes to endorse products and advertising in the commercial spots that punctuated sports competitions.

The zest with which Murdoch bought television rights, often for sums that other major networks believed to be suicidal, attests to his confidence in the cultural power of sports to deliver its followers to his programs and, by implication, his customers – the advertisers. His ability to deliver grew out of his belief in thinking globally. Murdoch's master plan was never confined to one country, nor indeed one continent. Early in his career, he realized that Australia was simply not big enough for his ambitions. Moving to Britain, then the States, he recognized that markets had no natural boundaries: unlike nations, corporations, especially media corporations, were not confined by government and the limitations of any single polity.

The postcolonial world was one in which old empires had disappeared and new forms of interdependency had grown: nations relied on each other's support, not only militarily, but politically and, of course, commercially. Advances in telecommunications, particularly in satellite and fiber optic technologies, enhanced the capacity and flexibility of media networks to carry services (data, video, or voice) around the world. No other phenomenon possessed this unique capability.

While no entity could actually *own* a nation's political system or economy, it was perfectly possible to own a telecommunications network that encircled the earth. The power this conferred on the potential owner was unequaled. Owners of the means of communications could exert influences in any number of countries. By the end of the twentieth century, the technologies that could make this theoretically possible were well advanced. They included: digital methods of encoding, transmitting, and decoding; multimedia cable and satellite networks to carry and disseminate information; and a single international collection of computer networks from which users could access information from computers anywhere in the world – the internet. Murdoch's various organizations had invested in all these and more.

One of the many consequences of the global expansion of the mass and multimedia has been the sharpening of awareness in other cultures. "Awareness" probably understates the case, because there has been a convergence of tastes, consumption patterns, and enthusiasm for lifestyles, many of which have origins in the United States. Witness the eagerness of young people all over the world to follow the NBA, wear replica clothes, and devour any artifact connected with basketball. Yet it is soccer, a sport largely ignored in the States, that has become the first truly global game, capturing the interest of every continent, especially at the time of its World Cup championship. Neither of these sports would have occupied their current status without television.

The global convergence manifests itself in several other areas, of course. Like: the proliferation of fast-food restaurants, the ubiquity of Hollywood movies, and the prevalence of American-English as a language that serves as a medium between different nations – indeed, many of the phrases in the new *lingua franca* derive from a sports idiom. Telstar, the first communications satellite, went into orbit in 1962; since then a miscellany of different transponders have been launched, offering a daily bill of fare of news, sports, and entertainment to a planetary audience. This has been interpreted as part of a generic pattern in which Western powers have sought to conquer and control developing countries and maintain their dominance in a non-economic, non-military way: through the imposition of cultures.

Sport, no less than religion, television, and movies, has played a vital part in this process, occasionally called "Coca-colonization." The meaning of this is that, after the old Western colonial powers ceded their control, multinational corporations took over and introduced a different form of control, this one based on the culture their products carry with them. Coca-Cola is the supreme

---

### Sponsorship

"Sponsorship is the support of sport, sports events, sports organizations or competitors by an outside body or person for the mutual benefit of both parties." This was how former British Minister for Sports, Denis Howell, once serviceably described sponsorship (quoted in Neil Wilson's *The Sport Business*, 1988). It is not a new phenomenon: there are examples of commercial companies financing events, especially cycling tours, in the late nineteenth century. But, the significant possibilities of mass exposure through the television opened up new relations between sports and corporations. Breweries were among the first and most enduring sponsors of sports to recognize the potential of televised sports. Pabst Riband, in the USA, and Whitbread's, in Britain, sponsored competitions in the 1950s.

Gillette has maintained an interest in sports on both sides of the Atlantic since the early twentieth century when it sponsored radio coverage of baseball. In the early twenty-first century, it signed the prolific endorser, David Beckham, to a deal worth up to $70 million. Beckham also had contracts with, among others, adidas, Pepsi, and Police. The majority of leagues and major world competitions have sponsors, sometimes several. Grand Prix, for example, is sponsored by dozens of companies, each with its logo plastered over cars. The Olympics are officially sponsored by a group of blue chip companies, which receive in return the right to use the Olympic rings on their merchandise.

Individual athletes often have portfolios of sponsorship contracts, most with companies that have no obvious connection with sports, but wish their products to be associated with a popular and ostensibly wholesome pursuit or person. Athletes endorse products regardless of whether they actually use them. Sponsors seek sports performers with images that signify something about their product. Anna Kournikova's contract with Berlei to endorse the Shock Absorber sports bra is an example: although Kournikova had won only one title (Australian women's doubles), her youth, looks, and style of dress suggested a perfect match with the bra-makers.

example: an American product that became arguably the best-known brand in the world. It sourced materials, set up plants, employed labor, and exported its products all over the world. It was also the most prodigious sponsor of sports and one of the biggest beneficiaries of sports' worldwide appeal.

These then are the conditions under which Rupert Murdoch was able to rise to his unique position. His influence developed out of an extraordinary combination of changing global conditions and a corporate set-up flexible enough to be able both to respond to the changes and push them in the direction Murdoch desired. All of which leads us back to the question asked at the beginning of this chapter: were Murdoch not around, would sports be as they are?

The answer is a tentative one: probably. There have been transformations underlying Murdoch's rise, including a technological revolution in the communications field, corporate realignments in the media industry, an expansion of world commerce, a confluence of culture, and a new-found marketability of sports. All of these have established circumstances conducive to the growth of media–sports empires. Vertical integration, as we have seen, was by no means the sole preserve of Murdoch. Turner had turned around his television stations by incorporating sports clubs into his complex. Several other media giants also employed the strategy of gathering clubs and other sources of program content in their efforts to control the entire supply–demand chain. Murdoch's strategy was on a grander scale and perhaps with a higher purpose; there were those who suspected his efforts to produce, transmit, and sell events were part of a plan to control all sports. Yet, the strategy was not unique.

Coming from a relatively isolated country with a small market probably gave Murdoch a more global perspective than contemporaries, like Disney's Michael Eisner or James Dolan, of Cablevision, both Americans who had little experience or interest beyond the States. Murdoch was also well versed in other media beside television. His father was a newspaper proprietor and his first few enterprises were in the Australian and British print media. The advantages of cross-ownership were not lost on Murdoch: profits from a lucrative medium could be used to underwrite short-term losses in another. Additionally, newspapers were useful as a way of publicizing other media. So, Murdoch held a competitive advantage when the predacious pursuit began. Were he not around, the other corporate predators would surely have extended their interests though perhaps not at the hellfire pace they did in the late 1990s. The power in sports would still be distributed between about four or five media execs though no individual would reign as supremely as Murdoch.

What we once called spectators or audiences are now markets; what were once measured in thousands are now measured in dozens of millions. The global technological and commercial developments at the end of the twentieth century ensured that the shape and character of sports would be changed more radically than at any stage in organized sports' history. It is possible that entrepreneurs were slow in realizing the genuine commercial potential of sports. If so, they made up for it. They did so by opening out the potential market of those who wanted to sell products with sports and by turning sports themselves into products that could be transported around the world like articles of trade. Nike offers us an object lesson in this. We will look at its development in the globalization process in the next chapter.

## OF RELATED INTEREST

*Virtual Murdoch: Reality wars on the information highway* by Neil Chenoweth (Secker & Warburg, 2001) and *SkyHigh: The inside story of BSkyB* by Mathew Horsman (Orion Business, 1997) chart Murdoch's business exploits. For more straightforward biographies, there are: *Rupert Murdoch* by William Shawcross (Chatto & Windus, 1992) and *Rupert Murdoch: A paper prince* by Georg Muster (Penguin, 1985).

*Big League, Big Time: The birth of the Arizona Diamondbacks, the billion-dollar business of sports, and the power of the media in America* by Len Sherman (Pocket Books, 1998) is a fascinating case study of the MLB expansion franchise; as its subtitle suggests, the influence of corporate business and media conglomerates is apparent throughout. Also dealing with the business of franchising, though not as strong as Sherman's account, are: *Home Team: Professional sports and the American metropolis* by Michael Danielson (Princeton University Press, 1997) and *Major League Losers: The real cost of sports and who's paying for it* by Mark Rosentraub (HarperCollins, 1997).

*The Economics of Sport and Recreation: An economic analysis* by Chris Gratton and Peter Taylor (Routledge, 2004) is an introduction to the sports industry and *The Name of the Game: The business of sports* by Jerry Gorman and Kirk Calhoun (Wiley, 1994) is quality analyses of the changing relationship between sports and big business.

*Newszak and News Media* by Bob Franklin (Arnold, 1997), *Global Television: An introduction* by Chris Barker (Blackwell, 1997), and *Megamedia Shakeout: The inside story of the leaders and the losers in the exploding communications industry* by Kevin Maney (Wiley, 1995) provide examinations of how the globalized media industry took shape in the late 1990s.

You are appointed head of marketing services at a worldwide credit card company, not unlike American Express. For years, your brand has marketed itself on class and privilege. Despite competition from other credit cards, the cachet your company has enjoyed has kept it among the market leaders. Recently, however, your exclusivity has become dated. Even your advertising slogans, such as "never be without it," and "that will do adequately" have become the target of comedians' jokes. Market share has declined sharply. After studying the spending and lifestyle habits of each of your 1 million cardholders your research department has concluded that there is a growing interest in sports among them. Design a series of initiatives that will exploit the sports connection and report the result.

# the 🗸 that conquered the world

## why Nike was a key player

## in the globalization of sports

*There was once a sea anemone called Adamsia palliata. Being a plant with tentacles, he could trap food but couldn't travel far to get it. One day, he met a hermit crab named Pagouros. "How about if I live on your back and let you carry me around?" he asked Pagouros. "That way, I can get to all the scraps of food I need." "And?" answered the crab. "Well, this seabed is a dangerous place for crabs," said the seaplant, "but, with me on your back, you'd be well camouflaged." The crab thought for a second, then agreed: "Deal." The two species lived together in a mutually beneficial partnership until the day when they got scooped up in a trawler's net. Resourcefully, Pagouros extricated himself, but only after the trawler had dragged the two way, way off their turf. "Actually, that wasn't so bad, was it?" said Adamsia after pulling himself together. "And look around you," Pagouros responded. "We're in new territory. This is all pretty exciting. Let's check this place out and, when we get bored, I'll snap onto a net with one of my claws and we'll let it carry us somewhere else." And so the symbiotic pair became world travelers, clinging onto trawler's nets but without ever getting snared up. The moral of this story is: if there's reciprocal advantage in working together, do it, but never pass up the opportunity of a free ride around the world.*

## THE SEDUCTION OF SNOW WHITE

Cast your eyes around; it won't be long till you see ✔ . You might even be wearing something that bears it. Nike has built such a formidable presence in the sports and leisure industry that it's ubiquitous: everywhere at the same time. It's impossible to find a major sports event anywhere in the world that does not bear the Nike imprimatur, either as a competition sponsor, or the supplier of footwear and apparel, or as an advertiser at the competition venue. It's equally as impossible to visit a major city anywhere in the world where there aren't dozens of stores that sell Nike products. Most of them will have mini-department stores called Nike Towns that carry nothing but Nike. The millions that wear or carry Nike products presumably think this is a good thing. Others don't.

As we'll see later in this chapter, a chorus of Nike critics has grown louder and louder since the early 1990s. Nike wasn't alone, of course. The Gap and Blockbuster were a couple of the several other corporations that came under attack for their role in the globalization that has shaped the world economy over the past few decades. Shell and BP too came under fire. Yet Nike had more cultural power than most. It managed to withstand the most severe criticisms, the boycotts, the traffic-stopping rallies, the anti-Nike movement, the hundreds of thousands of letters of protest, the dozens of hypercritical websites, and still stay at the forefront. How?

Unlike many of its contemporaries, Nike's brand was built on figures who were known, respected, and trusted. If you had a reputation as a stand-up guy, clean-living, wholesome, and honorable and you not only approved of, but lent your name to and unreservedly endorsed Nike, then consumers would take attention. And, of course, they didn't come any more clean-living, wholesome, and honorable than Michael Jordan.

From the mid-1980s, Nike and Jordan lived in symbiosis in the manner of two different organisms attached to each other to their mutual advantage. Just like the hermit crab and the sea anemone (the first part of the fable is based on aquatic fact; the part about the trawler net is made up). Jordan was an exceptional athlete; with Nike he became an icon. Nike made decent sportswear; with Jordan it too became an icon. In this chapter, I'll trace the history of Nike, particularly the period of its growth with Jordan and its relationship with other developments in the sports world. In the process, I'll be addressing the question of whether Nike is responsible for the momentous changes, good and bad, that have changed not only sports but the world economy. Or whether it was and is just a sportswear manufacturer that tapped into the mood of the times.

Phil Knight was neither a sprinter, nor a marathon runner. Authors of *Swoosh: The unauthorized story of Nike and the men who played there* (1993), J. B. Strasser and Laurie Becklund, believe this is significant: when he started his business, Knight was not seeking instant gratification, but nor did he want to

---

### Brand

Brand comes from a pre-twelfth-century English word *brant*, meaning burn; it came to mean a burned-in mark on, for example, slaves or cattle. Later, it referred to goods of a particular make, though today it has a wider resonance. It's still a mark or distinguishing characteristic and it has its origins in goods, or commodities, made by or for a particular company. But, the brand is now an identity and one portable enough to migrate across products. The value of a brand is in its ability to elicit recognition across several sectors and add value to virtually any product that bears it. For example, Giorgio Armani is known essentially for high-quality clothes. Affix the Armani label to wristwatches and value is added. Attaching adidas to men's skincare products makes them recognizable: adidas is a name associated with sportswear, but its brand value is strong enough to migrate to sectors away from sports. ESPN is another powerful brand that has its sources in television, but has transferred to magazines and restaurants, all themed around sports. Evidence all around us suggests that consumers respond positively to brands: they dress in clothes bearing the names of fizzy drinks, football teams, universities, construction equipment, or anything with which they feel an affiliation.

---

wait an eternity for success. He wanted to distribute his energies evenly, pace himself and exercise strategy – all elements of middle-distance running. Knight himself was no more than an able middle-distance runner on the track; but his application of the elements to sportswear manufacturing and marketing revolutionized the industry.

After working with Bill Bowerman, who became head coach of the US Olympic team at the 1972 summer games (and who, incidentally, was played by Donald Sutherland in Robert Towne's 1999 film *Without Limits*), Knight moved on from the University of Oregon and enrolled at Stanford University, where he studied to be an accountant. Here, Knight designed a class project in which he headed a hypothetical company that specialized in sports footwear imported from Japan. His premise was that labor costs in East Asia were far less than those in Europe and the USA.

During the early 1960s, the sports footwear and apparel market was dominated by a sibling rivalry between Adi Dassler, at adidas, and his brother Rudi, of Puma. The Dassler brothers grew ever more competitive in their attempts to establish leadership of the field. American and British manufacturers lagged way behind, specializing in flat-soled sneaker-type shoes, as opposed to the sturdy leather purpose-built jobs with arch and ankle supports that were being produced by the German brothers.

Knight was an admirer not only of adidas' product, but the style in which it promoted its goods. But, he thought he could produce something as good, yet cheaper. His first forays into the industry were tentative: he asked Tiger, a Japanese sports goods manufacturer to copy the adidas design and send him shipments of its version; he would then sell for them in the USA. He consulted his ex-coach Bowerman who suggested improvements, particularly in terms of material. Bowerman was a great believer in lightened shoes, his theory being that, if you count the number of paces a runner uses, say 880 strides over 1,500 meters and multiply by the number of ounces you can save by making his or her shoes lighter, then the runner carries less weight and can travel faster. Take an ounce off the weight of the shoes and the runner is unburdened by 54 pounds.

Japan, in the postwar period, had made significant progress in developing nylon and leather substitute materials, this being made necessary by the lack of land suitable for cattle breeding – and hence no leather. This proved rather beneficial for Knight, who, in 1964, entered into a partnership with Bowerman. Blue Ribbon Sports (BRS) with a starting capital of $1,000. Knight and Bowerman intended to import Japanese-made Tiger footwear made to their own specifications, though modeled on adidas, and sell in 13 western states.

Selling out of a car trunk and taking orders from his father's basement, Knight built his reputation for selling shoes designed by athletes for athletes. The industry giants were warring with each other over big international meetings. It was suspected that adidas was actually giving away its footwear simply to enhance its brand recognition: the distinctive three stripes on either side of the shoe was world renowned. As Olympic and world championships were becoming global media events, thanks to the interest of television, so the athletic footwear market was expanding. Puma responded by taking the unheard of step of paying athletes to wear its products. While this is commonplace today, it was a breakthrough idea in the 1960s, when track and field was ostensibly amateur.

But the matrix for Nike's extraordinarily successful endorsement program was set in 1972 when Blue Ribbon Sports paid tennis star Ilie Nastase $3,000 to use its shoes. Nastase was an interesting choice: an exciting and excitable player, he seemed to personify an attitude that Nike shared: always prepared to challenge decisions, often belligerent and frequently preferring to lose with style rather than win without it. Nastase, while fondly remembered as a baroque character, was never a tennis great; but everything he did, he did with flamboyance. He was also an inveterate risk-taker. And this made him perfect for Nike. As with many seemingly inspired decisions, its motive was much baser than one might expect. Both Nastase and the then promising teenager but relatively unknown Jimmy Connors had the same agent. Knight was offered both in a sort of package deal. Knight, wanting to save a few dollars, signed only Nastase.

Nike's other key athlete at the time was Steve Prefontaine, a white American middle-distance runner, who competed at the 1972 Munich Olympics, and commanded a following usually reserved for rock stars. Fans wore T-shirts emblazoned with "Go Pre" and followed him to track meets. Were he alive today, he would have probably made CDs and appeared in movies. Tragically, he died in a road crash in 1975. Nike had subsidized his training, his coach being Bowerman.

After the Amateur Sports Act, of 1978, Nike was able to subsidize athletes: with most major sports abandoning their amateur status, track and field went open, though it had been known for years that under-the-counter payments had sustained the sport and that, in Soviet bloc countries, athletes were practically full-time professionals, anyway. Nike set up its own track club called Athletics West in Eugene, Oregon, and gave athletes enough support to pursue their sports without having to take part-time jobs. Knight resisted the temptation to include Nike in the name of the club, preferring to allow the worst-kept secret about Nike's financial involvement to circulate. Still, it was a crucial move in Nike's development because it was able both to subsidize and sponsor – which is tantamount to owning – a sport without violating any codes.

The beginning of Athletics West was also the beginning of Nike's transition from a private company worth $28 million to an international public corporation that capitalized, in 1980, at $240 million. Blue Ribbon Sports had been producing goods called Nike for some time, the name being taken from the Greek goddess of victory. In 1972, having disentangled itself from its original Japanese supplier and set up alternative manufacturing sources, it changed its name to Nike.

The whole sports shoe market was buoyant as the health craze of the 1970s swept through North America and Europe. As some measurement of the jogging boom's growth, Strasser and Becklund note that, in 1970, there were just 156 entrants in the annual New York Marathon. By 1977, this had increased more than 32-fold to 5,000. And, to indicate Nike's presence in this boom, Strasser and Becklund point out that 11 of the first 20 finishers in 1977 were wearing Nike shoes. Even then, it would have been impossible to predict the scale of Nike's project over the next several years. Its products had earned a reputation for being runner-friendly: light mesh uppers and the characteristic waffle sole had found favor among joggers and pro athletes alike. But the sportswear market had limits.

Knight's biggest signing in 1978 was John McEnroe whom he reportedly paid $25,000. McEnroe was an even better fit for Nike than Nastase: his temperament ensured that even meaningless early round matches of tennis tournaments were likely to become explosive. McEnroe's histrionics gained him the kind of reputation that Knight wanted for his products: insubordinate, brassy, and defiant. With adidas still leading the market, it was Knight's ambition to position Nike as its most audacious contender. In one memorably tasteless sales meeting address in 1978, Knight likened adidas to Snow White. "This year, we became the biggest dwarf," he told his sales team. "And next year, we're going to get into her pants" (quoted in Strasser and Becklund 1993: 271).

A central thrust of Knight's assault was the Tailwind, at $50 the most expensive running shoe to date and a technological innovation, incorporating a sealed module of air in its sole. Launched in 1978, it was a disaster initially, tiny particles of metal in its silver dye rubbing against the shoe's fibers and cutting the uppers. But Knight was undeterred and opened a sports research laboratory with the brief to its staff to come up with concepts like the air module every six months. It won't have escaped any reader's attention that the original idea behind the Tailwind later became the basis for the gargantuan Air Jordan line.

The link with Michael Jordan was forged amid concern about the future of Nike. In 1985, after eight years of market growth and increasing profits, Nike reported two consecutive losing quarters. The market had expanded and new players had entered the fray. While the supremacy of adidas and Puma had been ended, Reebok, a company started in England in the late nineteenth century, had come to the fore. In 1979, Paul Fireman bought the rights to the Reebok name and began a US operation. Within two years, sales were up to $1.5 million and, by 1984, $65 million. Its sudden rise had caught Nike and indeed the whole sector unaware.

Nike's brand credibility was based on the testimonies of sports performers. If people like Bo Jackson and Andre Agassi wore Nike and spoke on its behalf, then their endorsements carried weight. At least they carried weight with those who played football or tennis – or ran or engaged in any other sports, for that matter. Strasser and Becklund reckon that: "Even in 1980, most consumers were still not aware that many pro athletes were paid to wear shoes" (1993: 258). They probably learnt very quickly over the next few years; but, by then, it did not make much difference, anyway.

Reebok's strategy was different: rather than aim at sports followers, it targeted the apostles of aerobics. Aerobics was a new subsector of the sports market and one that Nike and the others had failed to exploit. For Reebok, the great outdoors did not beckon: its stomping ground was the sprung timber floors of health clubs.

After a shaky start to his enterprise, Fireman did a trading deal with Stephen Rubin, of Liverpool, and took advantage of Nike's apparent apathy. By 1983, Nike was leading the athletic footwear market, but was not producing any lines designed specifically at women's aerobics. The policy of signing high-profile sports personalities had stood Nike in good stead, but there were suspicions that it had outlived its usefulness. Reebok's campaign included giving away its products to aerobics instructors, whose pupils would take notice.

With profits taking a pounding, Nike needed to cut back its endorsement budget: it opted to go after a few key athletes and offer them money, while just giving away free gear to others. In 1984, the NBA was making gains in the television viewer ratings. It only boasted a small number of stars – Larry Bird, Magic Johnson, Isiah Thomas – and they were under contract to the sports goods maker, Converse. Nike wanted to isolate a name player and tie its colors to him. At one point, it actually released many members of its roster, allowing them to find new sponsors.

By the time he signed his endorsement deal in 1985, Michael Jordan was already an Olympic gold medalist (in the days when the USA sent amateur basketball players, not "dream teams") and had left the University of North Carolina in his junior (third) year to sign for Chicago Bulls in a deal worth $3 million. Both adidas and Converse were interested in doing business, though Jordan eventually signed with Nike in what was then a ground-breaking arrangement.

---

### Logo

An abbreviation of logotype (from the Greek *logo* for word), this was largely advertising jargon 20 years ago, but has come into popular use in recent years. It describes an unbroken strip of type, lettering, badge, or insignia used by organizations to promote their corporate identities in advertising and publicity material. Today, it is difficult to find a sports performer or team that does not bear at least one, and, more usually, many logos. For example, a pro cyclist, tennis player, or racing driver will typically wear several logos on their uniforms signifiying their sponsors. Logos have been especially important in licensing sports-related products. Sports governing federations strictly control the use of logos by manufacturers and will seek redress from any company using, for instance, the "W" of Wimbledon or the silhouette of the basketball players of the NBA without permission. The growth of the sports logo is, in many ways, a symbol of the corporateness of contemporary sports.

---

## THE AIRBRUSHED ICON

Like the majority of other players in the league, Michael Jordan was an African American. So, he didn't have the same credentials of other American sports icons: Babe Ruth, Jack Dempsey, Joe Namath, *et al*. The reverence in which many now hold Muhammad Ali disguises the fact that, in the 1960s, he was regarded with contempt and described by one sports writer as: "a vicious propagandist for a spiteful mob that works the religious underworld" (Jimmy Cannon, quoted by Thomas Hauser in his *Muhammad Ali: His life and times*, 1997). For all the adulation he received in the 1930s, Joe Louis was accepted as a sports hero in an era when black people could not vote, attend the same schools, or live in the same areas as white people; the fact that Louis did not vocally oppose such arrangements earned him the epithet "a credit to his race."

After Jordan left his university without graduating, David Falk, of the ProServ agency, secured him a five-year deal with the Bulls and opened negotiations with all the main sportswear manufacturers. The emergence of athletes as product endorsers, a process hastened by Nike, of course, meant that pro sports performers regarded their salary as only one and not necessarily the biggest component of their income. Falk demanded that Nike paid Jordan in excess of his salary.

Nike's reply was to offer Jordan a guaranteed minimum plus a royalty. In other words, Jordan would receive a percentage of every piece of apparel or footwear sold. Not just items bearing his name, but all those in the Air range. That clinched it for Falk: adidas and Converse failed to match the terms and Jordan began the most remunerative commercial relationship with a sports goods manufacturer in history.

With sales rising, Knight embarked on one of the most aggressive advertising campaigns ever. In the year following his signing of Jordan, Nike's advertising budget leapt from $231 million to $281 million (almost 22 percent). It seemed like manic extravagance. But, the first year's sales of Nike's Air Jordan range, complete with a Jordan-silhouette logo, hit $130 million. And, as if to underline the importance of Jordan's tv presence, sales dropped off in the second year when Jordan missed 62 games through injury. Knight knew how to take risks: even Nike's first toe in British waters was more of a triple pike: in 1992, Knight signed a reported £4 million deal to supply Arsenal with training and competition wear.

Jordan himself said nothing in the first Nike advertising campaign featuring him. "Who said man wasn't meant to fly?" was the question strapped across the screen after a slo-mo clip of him in mid-air. Another famous campaign featured Jordan with the fictional character Mars Blackmon, who was drawn from Spike Lee's 1986 film *She's Gotta Have It*. Lee also directed the commercial, which was steeped in signifiers of urban street culture, including rap music. The triumph of this campaign was not only in sales, but in its projection of an African American as wholesome and unthreatening and yet still irreverent enough to hold his own on the streets.

At the time, Nike had just slipped behind Reebok in the global trade war. Four years later, Nike had regained the lead and forced Reebok into one of its most embarrassing moves. Recognizing the value of Jordan to Nike, Reebok tried to repeat the trick for itself, signing Shaq O'Neal for $15 million over five years. It was an expensive lesson. Not only did it pass on a renewal of O'Neal's contract after it expired in 1998, but Reebok cut Emmitt Smith for a $1 million buyout fee. In the three years leading to 1998, sales of sports shoes dropped and Reebok trimmed its roster from 130 endorsers to just 20. Incorporating players into the brand was no guarantee of cachet, nor of sales. The choice of player, the style of promotion, and the social conditions under which the promotion takes place were all important factors that Nike managed to judge to perfection.

"No company enriched Michael Jordan more than Nike or benefited more from his career. Jordan had made around $130 million from Nike over his career by 1998," writes David Halberstam in his *Playing for Keeps: Michael Jordan and the world he made*. "Not all of Nike's growth was attributable to Jordan's presence, of course, but in 1984 the company had revenues of $919 million and a net income of about $40 million, and by the end of 1997, Nike's revenues were over $9 billion, with a net of around $800 million" (1999: 412–13).

What these bare figures conceal is the work Jordan's agent, David Falk, and Nike put into projecting Jordan and the role played by David Stern in turning the NBA from an unfashionable collection of forlorn clubs into one of the USA's major leagues. As the trawl net dragged the crab and seaplant around the world, so television made the NBA and, by implication, Nike/Jordan globally famous.

---

### David Falk

Falk is the agent for a fleet of leading sports performers, including many of the best-known NBA players. Because of his influence over so many stars, he has often been portrayed as a puppeteer, pulling the strings of professional basketball. Falk joined the ProServ agency in 1975 and began specializing in negotiating contracts for pro athletes. His major coup was in signing Michael Jordan. Falk was something of an architect, designing a complex structure of corporate links for Jordan: endorsements for the likes of McDonald's, Gatorade, Wheaties, etc., positioned Jordan at the fore of every television viewer's mind. Falk masterminded what might be called the commodification of Jordan, the crucial phase of the process being Jordan's association with Phil Knight's Nike. Falk's own agency, Falk Associates Management Enterprises (FAME) is based in Washington, DC.

## STERN: THE MAN WHO SOLD THE NBA

1984 was a key year in the globalization of sports, though it wouldn't have seemed so at the time. David Stern took over as the Commissioner of the floundering NBA, Jordan entered the professional league and the then fledgling cable television network ESPN decided to sell out to the ABC network for $237 million. Two years previously, ESPN had broadcast its first NBA game as part of a two-year contract; it had been featuring NCAA games since 1979 and, because it reached (by 1984) 34 million homes, could fairly claim to have primed interest in college and pro basketball. The draft arrangement made it possible for viewers to map the progress of young, aspiring amateurs before they transferred to the pros and grow familiar with the style and personalities of the players.

Since the 1970s, America's (not just North America's) televisual landscape had become a lattice of cables, some underground, some on poles, all connected to stations which received signals from satellites. Cable viewers all over the continent were able to pick up television shows that originated in the USA. ESPN had exploited America's penchant for sports, serving up competitive action all day, every day.

Stern realized the infrastructure was in place to transmit NBA far and wide, but was also aware that his league lacked the legitimacy of the NFL or Major League Baseball, mainly because it lacked the backing of mainstream corporations. And the reason it lacked them was that, as one advertising agency put it to Stern, "the pro game is too black" (quoted in Halberstam 1999: 118).

The NBA, it was thought, was a sport played by black men and watched by black men. As the United States' black population was over-represented in poorer socio-economic groups and had less disposable income than most, it was not a demographic sector much sought after by advertisers. Stern's first attempts to persuade ad agencies that the NBA's audiences were not predominantly black, but were as mixed as audiences for the college game, cut no ice. Halberstam argues that the enthusiasm for NCAA basketball was because: "The college game was perceived, perhaps unconsciously, as still operating within a white hierarchy, under powerful white supervision, a world where no matter who the foot soldiers were, the generals were still white" (1999: 118).

As professionals, black athletes were contractually as powerful as their coaches and able to dictate their own destinies. And this was troubling to white America, especially when coupled with the stories of drug abuse among professional sports performers, many of whom were African American. Overpaid young black males and cocaine seemed to go together in the consciousness of many Americans. Major corporations steered clear and the NBA's few backers were those interested in selling their products primarily to black consumers. Stern addressed this problem by introducing a league drugs policy: he struck an agreement with the Players' Association that allowed players with drug habits to own up without penalty. If they persisted in using illicit drugs, they could get expelled from the NBA. It helped clean up the image of the league.

A second major innovation of Stern's was the salary cap, which was introduced in 1984. The NBA cap was set at 51.8 percent of the league's "defined gross revenues." While salaries were comparatively meager in early years, by 1998, this translated as $26.9 million (£16.5 million) per 12-man team; or an average of over $2 million per player per year. Rather than let franchises operate independently (as, for example, Major League Baseball and, to a lesser extent, the NFL did), the NBA subordinated its members to the central organization and demanded compliance.

His new structure in place, Stern secured the sponsorship of the Miller Brewing Company and aggressively went after other corporations eager to tap into the youth market. The NBA was sold as a fast, exciting game with points racked up at a pace never approached by most other sports. It was also blessedly easy for the uninitiated to understand. Quite unlike the statistically laden baseball and the intricately ruled football, basketball was a straightforward game with a playing area that could have been designed as a stage for the more extravagant characters.

Two of the most famous players of the period were Earvin "Magic" Johnson and Larry Bird, whose frequent clashes became a staple feature of the NBA. Both high-class players, Johnson, of the LA Lakers and Bird, from the Boston Celtics on the opposite coast, had a rivalry that helped the credibility of pro basketball in much the same way as Ali–Frazier and Navratilova–Evert had helped their respective sports. Johnson and Bird first met in the 1984 Finals; three years later when they again met in the Finals, the television viewing share more than doubled to 16 (i.e. 16 percent of the total viewing population). Johnson was an African American and Bird a white player; they were both intensely competitive and vied for the mantle of the league's best player.

Stern oversaw the early globalization of basketball: a total of 75 different countries received NBA telecasts in 1988. But, by 1989, when Stern was ready to renegotiate a new domestic television deal, the Johnson–Bird rivalry had lost its old potency. CBS had held the broadcasting rights since 1972 and was coming to the end of its four-year $188 million contract. NBC poured out a staggering $600 million to secure rights to the NBA for four years starting 1991. It seemed profligate; but NBC's head Dick Ebersol believed the demographics augured well. The NBA was followed avidly by young people of all ethnic backgrounds. NBC could offer its advertisers a direct route to the youth market at a time in history when young people were becoming the most sought-after consumers (sought after, that is, by ad agencies and their clients). One of the most revealing acknowledgments of this is an ad for MTV that ran in the business sections of newspapers and was quoted by Thomas Frank: "Buy this 24-year-old and get all his friends for absolutely free" its headline read (1997b: 150).

## Sheryl Swoopes

Swoopes was the athlete Nike tried to turn into a "female Jordan," in the sense that it designed a range of shoes and apparel especially for her and called it "Air Swoopes." Nike had earlier used Gabrielle Reece in an advertising campaign, but her image was used in poses rather than action shots. Unlike Reece, Swoopes was better known for her play than her looks. A formidably productive college player (for Texas Tech), she broke all manner of scoring records and won a gold medal with the USA team at the Atlanta Olympics. She turned pro with the Houston Comets in 1997, the first season of the Women's National Basketball Association (WNBA).

Ebersol may also have sensed the potential selling power of Jordan, a player who seemed well equipped to replace any interest lost by the disappearance of Johnson–Bird and whose mannerisms and style was being emulated by young people. Today, the NBA is televised to 206 countries in 42 languages. It has also started up the Woman's National Basketball Association (WNBA), its first big star being signed up, almost inevitably, by Nike.

Nike, Jordan, the NBA. Take any one of these figures out of the equation and Jordan would probably be regarded as a good player; but certainly not as a globally recognizable icon. Take away Jordan and there would be no NBA, at least not a universally popular league that boasts more celebrity players than any other sport. And Nike?

At the time of signing Jordan, Nike had around 20 percent of the world market in sports shoes and apparel that was led by Reebok. It's possible that Reebok, having ridden the crest of the health wave, would have suffered as the wave broke; it's also possible that another brand might have stolen its way into the hearts, minds, and pockets of young people. Nike picked the perfect intersection of history and personality. At a time when America was still mortified by its never-ending racial problems, it was comforting to know that black individuals, however humble their origins, could soar to the top.

Jordan's play could mesmerize audiences, his persuasive advertising could enchant markets. He didn't talk politics and his comments about the condition of black people were platitudinous. His followers stayed spellbound as long as he didn't grow up: while he continued to play the game everyone played in their childhood or youth and acted as a role model of sorts for children, appearing in commercials with young people who sang that they wanted to "be like Mike," his supporters were happy. Were he to have chosen "adult" subjects to talk about in public, or criticized Nike's employment practices, or got involved in the kinds of activities typically attributed to black males, then he might not have been so media-friendly. Jordan's success was conditional on his remaining well-behaved man-child in the promised land: a black American who resisted every conceivable negative quality and remained virtuous in the eyes of white people. And the collective forces of Nike, the NBA, and his agent were involved in this process; so too was NBC, which, as *Sports Illustrated* writer Rick Reilly put it, "airbrushed every Jordan zit into a dimple for 10 years" (vol. 90, no. 2, 1999).

So different was Jordan from the image of the black male that stalks the popular consciousness, that it was almost possible to forget he was black at all. The dread engendered by a virile young black man did not apply to Jordan: he was a symbolic eunuch when it came to women: happily married and strictly unavailable. The goody-two-shoes image took a few knocks when details of Jordan's gambling habit were disclosed, but, if anything, the revelations helped in reassuring the world that this all-too-perfect being had all-too-human failings.

Jordan came to prominence as a black man with no ax to grind, someone who had risen to the top on merit. In a way, he was proof that the civil rights of the 1960s and days of what was once called an American dilemma were gone for ever. Not all black people, he seemed to suggest, were preoccupied with racism and the obstacles it strewed in their paths. White America was in a kind of racial torment in the mid-1980s. The vigilante-style shooting by Bernhard Goetz of black assailants in 1984; the Howard Beach incident of 1986 when white youths assaulted three black men, chasing one to his death on a busy parkway. These had stretched racial tensions. A year later black teenager Tawana Brawley reported that she had been kidnapped and raped by a gang of white men; her story turned out to be a hoax but it added to the mounting psychodrama. The image of Jordan brought comfort amid an atmosphere of challenge and confrontation.

Jordan didn't so much exit as recede into the background. He remained contracted to Nike through his ill-judged retirement and his comeback with the Washington Wizards. Nike's quest for a replacement was never going to be easy, though, in 2003, Knight closed arguably his most ambitious and audacious deal ever, signing a high school basketball player to a reported $90 million endorsement contract. LeBron James had never thrown a professional basketball; in fact, he'd never thrown a hoop in college either. Nike fended off Reebok, which, industry rumors suggested, had offered James an even larger sum. It was the kind of jaw-dropping deal that made Nike *Nike*. Within months, it launched the Air Zoom range of footwear and apparel, which it saw as the natural successor to the all-conquering Air Jordan range. Nike had bigger contracts – it reportedly paid Tiger Woods $100 million (£70 million) – but the James deal had symbolic importance: it demonstrated that, unlike other global corporations, it still had the same risk-taking tendency that lay behind its early success.

## ANTICORPORATE BACKLASH

You don't get to be a brand like Nike without a backlash. For critics of globalization, Nike has become shorthand for exploiting populations in the developing world, creating internecine violence in city streets, and turning sports into a gigantic showcase for its high-priced wares. Along with other multinational companies, international banks, and other agents in the global market economy, Nike has been vilified by critics of capitalism, labor unions, farming lobbies, Friends of the Earth, and a variety of other organizations, as well as writers such as Naomi Klein whose 2001 book *No Logo* captured the heartbeat of the "anticorporate attitude," and film-maker Michael Moore, whose *The Big One* subjected Nike to the same kind of scrutiny afforded George W. Bush in *Fahrenheit 9/11* and the National Riflemen's Association in *Bowling for Columbine*. Few corporations have aroused passions like Nike. Those that love the brand make their ardor visible by wearing its products and carrying its accessories. Those that hate it either just don't buy anything emblazoned with the signature ✔ or organize themselves in protest.

Klein describes one of Knight's first encounter with his detractors. Invited by Stanford University Business School to deliver a guest speech in May 1997, Knight was greeted by pickets who screamed at him to "pay your workers a living wage" (2001: 366). Public notice was served that an international anti-Nike movement was gathering momentum. Later in the year, a day of action resulted in protesters zeroing in on Nike Towns and Foot Locker outlets in 13 countries.

In Australia, anti-Nike demonstrators once wore plain cloth sacks with "Rather wear a bag than Nike" daubed across them. Students at the University of Colorado held a fundraising run, the admission price of which was the equivalent of a day's wages for a Nike worker in Vietnam, $1.60; the winner received a prize of $2.10, the cost of three square meals in Vietnam.

Nike's response included sponsoring community schemes, gifting equipment to schools and colleges, and inviting human rights groups to inspect its factories anywhere in the world. It argued, though not to everyone's satisfaction, that, while its wages were low compared to those in Western economies, they were actually higher than local rates. It also cleaned up its factories to create better working conditions for its labor. Its boss Phil Knight insisted that his company had been unfairly made the "poster boy for the global economy."

Apart from the antiglobalization and the anticorporate movements, Nike was considered by some to be complicit in the so-called "Sneaker wars" in which young people attacked others and robbed them of their desirable footwear. In fairness to Nike, it was hardly culpable for initiating violence; it was simply that its products were regarded as the most desirable. They became the shoes of choice for African American youths, a fact that spurred Jesse

Jackson to action. On behalf of his Operation Push (a strategy for securing equal opportunities for ethnic minorities), he protested to Nike that, while it profited from sales to black people and used black people in its advertising, its management structure remained white. In 1990, he warned of a boycott of Nike products if Knight did not promise more contracts with minority businesses and jobs for black people. Jackson claimed, though without evidence, that Nike sold up to 45 percent of its products to inner-city youths, many of whom were African Americans, though Nike itself estimated only 13 percent of sales were made to ethnic minorities. Knight was able to call Jackson's bluff, though he promised to re-evaluate Nike's equal opportunity program.

Over the next several years, Nike was criticized for other forms of exploitation. Investigators exposed the menial wages Nike paid to workers in developing countries and compared these to the retail prices of its products in the West. The *New York Times* was swingeing in its attacks of Nike's labor practices. Nike was one of several sports goods manufacturers which made use of poorly paid Asian labor; in fact, it was revealed that some of its products were actually made under the same roof as its competitors', often by the same personnel. Nike's response was to get together with other sports goods manufacturers and draw up a code of practice.

As if to underline its social conscience, Nike formed NEAT (Nike Environmental Action Team) in 1993. This project encouraged the recycling of worn shoes and created inner-city playgrounds and sports areas at the same time serving as a concession to environmentalists. It prevented millions of pairs of used shoes occupying landfills and provided sports surfaces for hundreds of facilities all over the world.

PLAY (Participate in the Lives of American Youth) was launched in 1994 with Jordan and Jackie Joyner-Kersee as figureheads: this was aimed at reclaiming public spaces for youth. A skeptic might interpret these initiatives as part of Nike's strategy to offset the harm done to its reputation by reports of its labor exploitation in underdeveloped countries, though it should be pointed out that Nike held contracts with factories that paid wages relative to the countries in which they were based. While the wage levels would amount to exploitation if paid to workers in the US or UK, they were in line with other industries in the countries concerned.

## SHAPING AND SHAPED BY THE TIMES

In Chapter 14 we took note of Donald Katz's insight about sports surpassing pop music as a vehicle for selling and how it even eclipsed sex as an orienting consumer theme in the early 1990s (1994: 25–6). In more recent years, the demarcation line between sports and sex has become less distinct, especially in the marketplace where sports and sex permeate, well, everything. The market is not confined to palpable goods and services: it peddles ideas and beliefs, including what Katz and indeed the people at Beavertown called "the Nike spirit."

In the 1990s, sports became "sexy" in more than one sense. Quite apart from the more overt pandering to male libidos by using female athlete models in erotic poses, sport sold itself as inescapably chic: wearing the right label on clothes was a virtual requirement. Sports clothing became leisurewear. No one was seriously going to spend $200+ on a pair of shoes decorated with all the right appliqués and then wear them for football practice. In the 1970s, people would have balked at the idea of becoming a mobile advertisement for a sportswear company; in the 1990s, they had to pay extra to have the name and logo plastered across their tops. And not just any name and logo: Timberland might have been cool last year, but 12 months on, it could be passé.

adidas was quicker to notice the potential of melding sports and entertainment, but slower to capitalize fully on it. In 1985, the then aspirant rap music entrepreneur Russell Simmons invited adidas representatives to a hip-hop concert featuring his band Run DMC. Unimpressed, the adidas people wondered what Simmons's point was until the impresario turned their attention to the crowd. One of the band members urged the audience to throw their adidases in the air. The result was a volcanic eruption of sports shoes, all bearing the trademark three stripes. adidas realized how their shoes, far from being just sportswear, were now fashion accessories; it signed a deal to sponsor the next Run DMC tour. The band itself responded by releasing its track "My adidas."

Whether Knight himself had prescience and knew sports were going to acquire a new status, or whether he contrived to make this happen, we may never know. Maybe he just happened to have the right product at the right moment in history. One thing we can be sure of: he understood the ephemera of taste. Never content to let a line succeed, he constantly replaced them with new lines of the same brand, forcing the brand to migrate and mutate. The changes came with head-spinning speed. No doubt he learnt this tactic from fashion houses which organized their output in terms of seasons. The label may have been a signifier of quality, but the collection from which it came was also material.

This meant that Nikes became collectible: they could be dated, even cataloged. Connoisseurs – and they still exist – were able to date and value Nike items by just looking at them. A pair of first issue 1987 Air Max's, for example, was eminently collectible; these were the first model to make the air pocket in the sole of the shoe visible. On reflection, they were the shoes that kickstarted Nike's resurgence. With Reebok owning a 30 percent market share and Nike 21 percent, Knight gambled with the Air Max, paying Bo Jackson, who played both football and baseball, a reported $100,000 to endorse them. The ad agency

Wieden & Kennedy created the celebrated "Bo knows . . ." campaign to push the product, which was instrumental in Nike's return to market leadership. Hence, the historical significance of the Air Max.

Nike was able to pull through the 1986 crisis and another in 1993. But, in 1998, a third major slump in sales forced the company to issue a profits warning. The problem this time looked less to do with Nike, its products, or its advertising; more to do with a structural shift in the market. Jordan's retirement may not have helped, but changes in fashion hurt all sports goods manufacturers. Consumers turned away from athletic gear and toward other brands. Despite Knight's insistence that Nike was a sports goods firm, the evidence suggested differently: some 80 percent of Nike sales are for nonsports purposes. When sales slumped and Nike profits plummeted to unprecedented depths, Knight's assertion looked especially weak. The fashion that had served him so well for over a decade turned on him. The Nike swoosh that had once signified voguish rebellion changed into a symbol of conformity, the kind of logo that young people would expect to see their fathers wearing.

Knight had made provision for this: knowing soccer, as the most popular sport in the world, offered a mature and prosperous market, Knight wished to establish Nike's presence. Nike contracted the Brazilian Football Federation to a reported £250 million ($400 million) arrangement which included the right to organize matches, promote tournaments and sell television rights. The deal formed the core of Nike Sports Entertainment (NSE), the company's event management arm. NSE promoted and produced five Brazil exhibition games per year around the world as well as several other events featuring the company's roster of sports stars. It also promoted the first World Championship of Beach Volleyball. NSE seemed to herald the development of the world's first sports and media conglomerate: the inclusion of the word "entertainment" revealed something of Knight's ambitions.

Time and again, Knight had pointed out his products' functionality over style. In 2004, a self-employed weaver on a tiny island in the Sea of the Hebrides off the coast of Scotland, was approached by Harris Tweed. The maker of the famous coarse-checkered fabric had been approached by Nike to produce some samples for a range of sportswear. Tweed may be a great cloth for winter jackets, caps, and overcoats. But, sports shoes? Then introducing about 200 new lines every season, Nike had presumably looked on with interest as Burberry had licensed out its distinctive check design to such great effect. Nike had been in the fashion business for years before, of course; it just wouldn't admit to it.

In some senses, the ascent of Nike is attributable to the gnomic wisdom of Phil Knight, a man who seemed to know more about the mysteries of changes in youth culture and how to exploit them than any other entrepreneur. In another sense, Knight was just part of a new cultural equation that transformed the relationship between supply and demand.

---

### Globalization

This has been used to refer to the emergence of a global economy, cosmopolitan cultures, the expansion of world media, and, more generally, to the interdependence of societies around the world. Malcolm Waters provides the most useful definition in the 2001 edition of his book *Globalization*: "A social process in which the constraints of geography on economic, political, social and cultural arrangements recede, in which people become increasingly aware that they are receding and in which people act accordingly."

For critics, it typically refers to the capitalist exploitation of the developing world whose labor and material is used for the production of commodities that are sold with enormous mark-ups everywhere. Two of the least desirable effects of globalization, from this perspective, are the manner in which local cultures are homogenized into a single, featureless, anodyne blend; and that local consumers are persuaded into buying products that have little relevance to their own cultures. Corporations like Nike are sometimes held accountable for this.

---

Cultural tastes and fashions may not be totally controllable; but they can be heavily influenced. To take an uncomplicated example from Malcolm Waters's book *Globalization*: "The British taste for tea . . . could not have been cultivated in that damp little island had it not been possible to export its cheap textiles to Southern Asia, albeit to sell them in captive colonial markets, along with common law, cricket and railways" (2001: 66–7).

Nike did not make sports fashionable, though its role in that process is undeniably significant: it extended, expanded, and even exaggerated them in accordance with his own priorities. Sports drew alongside the entertainment industry as one of the most longed-for means through which young, predominantly working-class people imagine becoming successful. Television, movies, and even educational institutions were all parts of a changing cultural configuration in which sports became more glamorous than at any stage in its history. All sorts of products could be sold merely by associating them with sports; which is why endorsement contracts became so lucrative.

Nike emerged after a rude awakening. America had learned that its hitherto unquestioned military and economic supremacy could be questioned after all. Defeat in Vietnam was a hurtful reminder that pride goeth before a fall. America reflected on itself and saw a nation that had gone flabby, a citizenry that ate too much, exercised too little, and accepted comfort as if by divine right.

Nike's invocation to "just do it" might have been intended for every American who had ever comforted him or herself in the thought that they were a citizen of the richest, most unassailably powerful nation in history – and had been exposed.

In a sense, the rise of that other colossus of brands, Coca-Cola, might also be seen in the context of the USA's upheaval. In his *For God, Country and Coca-Cola*, Mark Prendergrast writes: "Coca-Cola grew up in a country, shaping and shaped by the times. The drink not only helped to alter consumption patterns, but attitudes toward leisure, work, advertising, sex, family life, and patriotism" (1993: 11). Similar claims could be made for Nike in the last three decades of the twentieth century.

In fact, the parallels between Coca-Cola and Nike are inescapable. Both emerged from turbulent periods of change in American society and both became globally recognizable brands (Coca-Cola enlarged its market during the 1930s Depression). Coke, like Nike, seized high-profile stars, in its case from Hollywood, to endorse its products: Joan Crawford, Clark Gable, and Greta Garbo were among Coke's panoply. Coca-Cola's links with sport are well known: it provided soft drinks for athletes in the 1936 Olympics and continued to align itself with health, vigor, robustness, and fitness, even when it became widely known that the drink itself did not promote any of these.

Jesse Jackson had famous conflicts with both Nike and Coca-Cola, in 1981 threatening a boycott of Coke if the demands of African American bottling plant owners were not met. Jackson reminded Coca-Cola that it had no black directors on its board. It was the second major boycott threatened: in the early 1960s, Jackson's mentor Martin Luther King accused Coca-Cola of using black models in only subservient roles in its advertising and of having no black sales personnel. African Americans formed about 11 percent of the total US population at the time, yet they consumed 17 percent of Coca-Cola.

In a similar way, Nike found itself at the center of an equal opportunities embarrassment when Jackson's Push organization revealed what some felt to be an irony – others, an outrage: Nike employed precious few black senior managers at a time when virtually every black urban male under 30 appeared to be wearing Nikes. Both Coca-Cola and Nike were able to schmooze their ways out of embarrassing situations and maintain their popular appeal with markets that were predominantly white.

Racial issues have beset the USA and sport has mirrored many of them. Nike's adeptness in defusing potentially explosive situations was a factor in its ascent. The NBA too faced a problem. As we have noticed, Nike's destiny was tied to that of the NBA and its star player, Michael Jordan. Each, in its own way, was able to exploit predicaments with racial implications to their own advantage.

## THE MYTH

Nike became brand leader thanks to Jordan. But Jordan took from Nike much more than money. "It was Nike's commercials that made Jordan a global superstar," writes Klein (2001: 52). There had been other gifted athletes before Jordan, but none reached what Klein calls "Jordan's other-worldly level of fame." Pre-Nike, sports stars, no matter how great, were athletes who happened to do commercials. They weren't synonymous with a brand, as Jordan was. Nike changed all that, creating lavish tv commercials that became the measure by which others were to be judged. Nike embarked on what Klein calls "myth-making," establishing an aura around Jordan. "Who said man wasn't meant to fly?" one of the ads asked, showing the gravity-defying Jordan in mid-air. It was almost possible to believe Jordan was actually capable of the unbelievable feats he performed in the commercials. No one's suggesting that Jordan wasn't great, perhaps the best basketball player ever. But, he wouldn't have been a global icon without Nike.

Then again, Nike wouldn't be the market leader without Jordan. In the June 1998 issue of *Fortune* magazine, Roy Johnson analyzed what he called "The Jordan effect" which described Jordan's impact on the overall economy of the USA. Nike developed the Air Jordan line of footwear and apparel and, over the 1990s, it was worth, in terms of sales, $5.2 billion. Read that again: $5.2 billion; that's over £3 billion. For that you could buy Manchester United, the New York Yankees, and the Orlando Magic – and still have change.

Money like this wouldn't have passed over the counter if Jordan had been playing to half-empty stadiums with his games shown on a modest cable network. Without the National Basketball Association and its television exposure, Jordan would have had less visibility and a less visible Jordan would have been of only limited value to Nike. Put the three together and they formed a perfect triangle; take any side away and all you have is an angle. Each owes its global success to the global success of the other two.

Nike's success, like that of the other global brands, including McDonald's and Disney, was based on an apparent understanding of cultural changes, the main one being the shift to consumerism. While others envisaged a market waiting to be exploited, Knight saw new markets waiting to be created; products that were to be displayed rather than just worn; commodities whose value lay less in what they were, more in who was wearing them.

Knight's market was simple: the planet. He wanted – and got – Nike in every corner of the world. He sourced his materials and manufactured his goods in East Asia and sold literally everywhere. Nike was a genuinely global operation. And an extremely profitable one. While its production costs were low, Nike's prices were high: the first $100 sports shoes, in 1986, may have been a flop, but they cleared the way for more extravagant ventures. Knight himself always denied that his company produced anything other than sportswear, but Nike was a fashion item. Nike was worn at the gym, on the track, and in any sports arena; but it was also worn in the clubs and bars, on the streets, and, for a while, in the early 1990s, in some boardrooms.

Its slogan "Just do it" had an odd resonance that seemed to appeal cross-culturally. Presumably prefixed by an unspoken "Don't think about it . . ." the phrase was a pragmatic appeal for action. Like other aspects of Nike's corporate persona, it was ideally suited to an age when theory was out of vogue, earning money was virtuous, and lunch was for wimps, as the stockbroker Gordon Gecko famously put it in the Oliver Stone movie *Wall Street*.

Right-wing governments under Ronald Reagan in the United States and Margaret Thatcher in Britain in the 1980s promoted a culture in which individualism and the ethic of personal achievement were paramount. Competition was not only healthy, but essential to the well-being of the individual; and this had ramifications at all levels. Cutbacks in welfare payments, affirmative action programs, and other areas of public spending were designed to decrease what many saw as a dependency culture.

Nike embodied much of this spirit. Its messages were in sharp contrast to early sporting morals that emphasized the importance of competing over winning. Nike mocked second-placers. Even winning was only one stop on a quest to fulfillment. "There is no finish line," one of Nike's ads reminded its potential customers.

Nike couldn't have succeeded globally without Jordan, or the NBA and the tv deals it brokered. The whole phenomenon was made possible by video. I use the term here in its generic sense, referring to the transmission of images via communications technology. Obviously, television has been the most effective and most encompassing form of video technology. By the end of the twentieth century, few, if any, parts of the globe did not have access to television. Since the 1960s, sport and television have existed in a synergetic relationship, each depending on the other to create bigger revenues. The interest of sponsors, advertisers, and manufacturers seeking endorsements from sports performers is strongly linked to gaining the widest possible exposure to consumers.

As we have seen in Chapter 13, sports were appealing to television companies, principally because they were a lot cheaper than drama; when the viewing figures started climbing, the sports organizations began to hike their prices. Television responded by paying the asking prices, but needed to guarantee viewer ratings to make sports a viable proposition. One way was to make televised sports as, if not more, attractive than actually being there.

To state that Jordan would not exist were it not for television sounds frivolous; Jordan the player would; but not Jordan the icon – the image that has been relayed around the world countless times, plastered across billboards and buildings, stamped onto millions of food packets, and even digitally mixed into cartoons. This is a Jordan that exists independently of Jordan the flesh-and-blood man; it is a phenomenon about which followers are prepared to believe almost anything, including the ability to fly.

Halberstam writes of Jordan's "other incarnation" borne of Nike ads: "The commercials were brief, but there were so many of them and they were done with such talent and charm that they formed an ongoing story. Their cumulative effect was to create a figure who had the power and force and charisma of a major movie star" (1999: 183–4). Of course, in contrast to movie stars, Jordan's deeds were not artificial.

So many pieces of information about the world reach our senses via electronic media that we might say we live in a videated culture in which entertainment and life have become not inseparable but the same. Images devour life so that our experiences are shaped by tv characters and tv coverage of news events.

The image of Michael Jordan was bigger, immeasurably bigger, than the man. Jordan would simply not have been possible without the cultural and technological transmutations that turned society into one vast network of coaxial cables, every home in the world connected to all others via some kind of link. And if this incarnation of Jordan was not possible without tv, then the same must be said of the NBA, whose big contract with NBC guaranteed it the kind of exposure it needed to compete with other major league sports, and Nike which exploited the cultural and commercial possibilities of television in a way no other company had contemplated.

"Circuits of promotion" is David Whitson's term to describe the endless loop-like way in which various forms of "recursive and mutually reinforcing" streams of communications "generate more visibility and more business for all concerned" and in which "cultural commodities, including celebrities, can become vehicles for the promotion of more than one producer's product at once" (1998: 67). The case of Nike, the NBA, Jordan, and, indeed, his club illustrate Whitson's point perfectly. He writes: "Nike . . . attached its corporate persona to images of Michael Jordan, but when Jordan appeared in Nike advertisements in the early 1990s, he was adding to the global visibility of the Chicago Bulls, the NBA, and the game of basketball, as well as promoting Nike shoes" (1998: 67).

There is no distinct effect to speak of; only another cycle, or circuit, of popular culture feeding back into an international "economy of signs" in which the symbolic values of products and images replace their use-values, so that a pair of Nikes can fetch ten times more than another pair made of the same materials and under the same factory roof. This was and is the global economy that Nike both helped create and dominate.

Two solid, if dated accounts of Nike and the changing social conditions that facilitated its growth are: *Swoosh: The unauthorized story of Nike and the men who played there* by J. B. Strasser (the widow of Rob Strasser, who left Nike to join adidas) and Laurie Becklund (HarperBusiness, 1993) and *Just Do It: The Nike spirit in the corporate world* (Random House, 1994) by Donald Katz, who has also written "Triumph of the swoosh" in *Sports Illustrated* (August 16, 1993).

"Nike's communication with black audiences" by Ketra L. Armstrong (*Journal of Sport & Social Issues* vol. 23, no. 3, August, 1999; reprinted in David Rowe's *Critical Readings: Sport, culture and the media*, Open University Press, 2004b) examines the way in which Nike targeted black consumers. Also worth reading in this context: *Nike Culture: The sign of the swoosh* by Robert Goldman and Stephen Papson (Sage, 1999) which also looks at Nike's advertising and marketing.

*No Logo* by Naomi Klein (Flamingo, 2001) is a trenchant critique not only of Nike but also of the corporate brands that encompass the globe. "Jordan and Nike are emblematic of a new paradigm that eliminates all barriers between branding and culture," argues Klein, meaning that it's become unthinkable for a music, art, film, sports, or any other kind of cultural affair not be associated with one or more brands. For a riposte to Klein, see *Wally Olins on Brand* by Wally Olins (Thames & Hudson, 2003), which argues that consumers have ultimate power to determine which brands succeed and which ones don't, so "we will get what we deserve."

*Playing for Keeps: Michael Jordan and the world he made* by David Halberstam (Random House, 1999) argues that Jordan possessed special qualities that carried him "more deeply into the psyche of the American public than any sports star had ever gone before." Less hagiographic are *Michael Jordan and the new global capitalism* by Walter LaFeber (Norton, 1999) and "Michael Jordan: Corporate sport and postmodern celebrityhood" by Mary G. McDonald and David L. Andrews, in *Sports Stars: The cultural politics of sporting celebrity* edited by David L. Andrews and Steven J. Jackson (Routledge, 2001).

*Globalization and Sport: Playing the world* by Toby Miller, David Rowe, Geoffrey Lawrence, and Jim McKay (Sage, 2001) argues: "Modern sport and the media developed simultaneously and symbiotically, supplying each other with the necessary resources for development: capital, audiences, promotion, and content."

"Nike" and "Michael Jordan" by Erwin Bengry are entries in my own *Sports Culture: An A–Z Guide* (Routledge, 2000) which also has relevant entries on the "NBA" and "ProServ."

## ASSIGNMENT

You are a sports reporter for a local television station in Tulsa which has had an NBA franchise for ten years, yet has won nothing and reached the play-offs only twice. One of the league's most colorful players has recently become a free agent and has expressed strong interest in joining the Tulsa Tempest, as the club is called. The player is a controversial character who has been the NBA's leading rebounder for the past five years, but who has had several brushes with the law, is in the middle of a stormy marriage with a supermodel, and stars in action movies. Many doubt he will fit in with the conservative suburban style of Tulsa. The team holds a press conference at which the owner announces that the player has signed. The player shows up wearing a glittering ankle-length evening gown which, he boasts, is a Donna Karan creation. You have five questions. What are they and how does the player answer them?

# buying into celebrity culture

## how athletes jumped onto the A-list

### KNOWN FOR BEING . . . WELL, *KNOWN*

**celebrify** *v.t.* Exalt; praise widely; make famous; invest common or inferior person or thing with great importance. So ~ FICATION [f. L. *celeber-bris* renowned + *ify* make or produce]

You won't find the above definition in *Webster*'s or the *Oxford English Dictionary*. Well, not yet. The verb *to celebrify* hasn't quite managed to penetrate popular language, though there are a number of academic writers already using it without actually spelling out its meaning. While we wait for an official version, mine will have to suffice. The word itself might sound clumsy; but its importance is indisputable. The age of celebrity is well and truly upon us. We live in times when the famous are like new gods. We – and I mean all of us, fans, analysts, and journalists – don't just admire the famous; we adore, adulate, and, in some cases, worship a class of people that have become known as celebs.

Celebrities haven't just emerged: we've created them. We, the idolatrous audience, have, as the definition suggests, invested them with great importance. In some cases, we attribute almost supernatural qualities to them. Of course, they're flesh-and-blood mortals like the rest of us. Yet, at times, they seem to exist in a different world.

We seem to like the division between Them and Us. They, the celebs, seem to live in a world so richly large, so showily opulent, so untouchably distant that we can never hope to get near, less still join it. Up till quite recently, celebrities were locked away in the Them camp: the celebrities themselves were remote, glamorous figures and being a fan was based on mystery and ignorance. In recent years, the mass media have not so much reported on the stars as demystified them: secrets are shared with magazines, close-up interviews are featured on television, biographies spare no detail of personal lives, exposés embarrass the high and mighty. Videos have made it possible for fans to capture moments of an individual's or a team's life for their own delectation. There is now an entire industry geared to selling proximity to celebrities. This is a relatively recent development, traceable to no earlier than the 1980s.

Where there were once sports stars, or even superstars, there are now celebrity athletes. In fact, they're just celebrities: their fame might have had its sources in sport, but, when they appear in the celeb magazines or on tv talk shows, they're indistinguishable from other celebrities, whether rock stars or fashion models. Their status is on par. How did all this come about? After all, it wasn't so long ago that athletes were judged as athletes: we evaluated them on their feats in the arena, not on whom they were sleeping with or what kind of designer underwear they favored.

There might have been extra-sporting intrigue created by marriages featuring prominent athletes and showbusiness stars, such as Joe DiMaggio and Marilyn Monroe, or England's Billy Wright and Joy Beverley. But these were exceptional unions. Ordinarily, athletes were confined to the sports pages.

Nowadays, athletes vie with showbiz types for the front pages and the gossip columns, let alone the celebrity magazines that have sprung up over the past decade or so. Top baseball and soccer players are every bit as newsworthy as actors or musicians. To be a celebrity means that you are *known*; for what doesn't matter. In fact, when you ascend to the A-list, being known supplies its own momentum and you become known for what Daniel Boorstin, back in 1961, tautologically called "well-knownness" (1961: 57). Well, it seemed a tautology – saying the same thing twice – when it was published; now it seems a reasonable assertion. Well-knownness has become an independent variable. It doesn't rely on anything else for its validity.

Athletes aren't just known for their well-knownness, of course. At least, not initially. The source of their renown is their prowess. Once that's noticed, they can garner recognition by their appearance, their partners, their presence at events, and practically anything that interests their audience, including exhibitions in porn videos. Even when their athletic performance declines, they can still draw attention. Falls from grace are eminently newsworthy, especially if they are spectacular falls. Witness Mike Tyson, Hansie Cronje, Marion Jones, Tonya Harding, or Paul Gascoigne. Even as they were brought to their knees, they retained the power to fascinate. The fact remains: we wouldn't have been interested in them in the first place if they weren't overachieving athletes. In this sense, sports celebrities differ from many others. Their public recognition is contingent on their performance, which means that they have to accomplish something that's widely accepted as having merit. That isn't necessarily the case with other celebs.

Celebrity culture has emerged, it seems, from some sort of magical vacuum. Out of nowhere came a plethora of tv channels, movies, DVDs, magazines, and websites, all dedicated to the exaltation of celebrities, many of whom had little to distinguish themselves – apart from their well-knownness, of course. Celebrities suddenly seemed to be everywhere. The word celebrity became prefixed to "ordinary" occupations, so that we were bequeathed with celebrity . . . chefs, lawyers, and hairdressers. Then there were the ubiquitous "tv presenters," people with no conspicuous talent besides being amiable and, of course, well known.

Censured by critics for being crass, superficial, meretricious, fraudulent, vulgar, and simple-minded, among other things, celebrity culture became none-theless pervasive. No area of society escaped the effects of celebrification: not politics (e.g. Arnold Schwarzenegger), not education (e.g. Stephen Hawking), and certainly not the church (e.g. Luis Palau). While our specific interest is with sports, we can't separate this sphere from all the others that have been absorbed into celebrity culture. It might have appeared to pop out of a vacuum, but, on analysis, there were specific conditions under which the age of the celebrity came into being. A clue to the first one is in the idea of the hero.

In the past, heroes came from the ranks of great political figures, military leaders, explorers, scientists, and even philosophers. Sporting heroes were the ones who could not just play, but who embodied values we held dear. They were fearless individuals who would prevail in the most unpromising circumstances, never flinching from pain, nor accepting defeat, always prepared to give up personal glory in the interests of a higher entity, whether the team, the nation, or even humanity.

Sports history abounds with characters like this. They commanded respect as well as attention: Babe Ruth, Jack Dempsey, Joe Namath in the USA; Stanley Matthews, Freddie Trueman, George Best in Britain; Muhammad Ali every-where. There are many, many more – their reputations were based on what they did in the diamond, the ring, or on the pitch. Their private lives might have attracted the attentions of gossip columnists every so often. But, in the main, fans followed them because of their great deeds in the field of play; fans weren't especially interested in their love lives, shopping habits, or egregious recre-ational activities (if they had any).

Ask yourself this question: would any sports star today be able to keep his or her private life "private"? In fact, there's a second question: is it meaningful to talk of a private life for celebrities? It's almost part of the definition of a celeb that you have to surrender all remnants of a private life to the media, which then make it available for public consumption. A sports celeb differs very little from any other kind of celebrity, whether from the domains of music, movies, or fashion. They are all there to entertain us.

---

### Hero

A person admired for achievements and noble qualities (*heroine* for women is now regarded as gendered and a bit passé). The Greek origins of the word expose its meaning: an illustrious warrior, who had earned the grace and favor of the gods. Competitors at the ancient Olympiad were striving for divine benediction and one of the rewards of victory was heroic status. In its more contemporary form, heroes are considered to be figures who have distinguished themselves for their courage and accomplishments, especially in war. In sports, heroes are largely historical characters recognized in retrospect. We can name heroes from virtually every decade of the twentieth century, but few from today, or perhaps not even the 1990s. Heroic status is conferred on athletes typically some years after they've ceased competing.

---

Professional sports today are constituents of the entertainment industry. The changes wrought in that industry by the twentieth-century revolution of media communications are all about us: the coming of television, the proliferation of film, the advent of digital technologies, the creation of cyberspace: these are some of the key developments that have changed the way we get our entertainment, the way we consume it, and the lifestyle patterns we make out of it.

We now consume sports in much the same way as we consume drama, music, and other forms of amusement: by exchanging money for commodities. Purists once abhorred the way film and, later, television corrupted live theater; connoisseurs deplored the phonographic cylinders that were used to reproduce music. Traditionalists were more ambivalent over the conversion of sports into packaged goods, though many probably lamented the passing of times when being a sports fan involved more than buying a baseball cap and sitting at home with a six-pack and a big screen tv; it meant actually going to see competitive action. However you analyze the statistics, younger people have tended to go to events less and watch more tv.

No matter what romantics tell us, sports are bigger than they ever were. Bigger, that is, in terms of worldwide popularity, awareness, and, importantly, turnover. Never in history have we spent more time watching sports, mostly on television. We have never been exposed to so many sports images in advertising and marketing. And we now spend much more money not only watching sports, but also buying the merchandise related to sports. Major League Baseball alone sells over $3 billion (£1.83 billion) worth of merchandise annually. That is over three times the value of the richest sports clubs in the world.

Our desire to compete and our even greater desire to watch others compete burns as brightly as ever. The difference is that, in the twenty-first century, sports with international appeal are competing among themselves for the attention and loyalty of fans. With the deluge of sports on our televisions, we might expect an imminent saturation. Yet, there is no sign: sports are poised to maintain their universal popularity for two reasons: on the demand side, we want as much sports as we can get; on the supply side, the sports industry is responding with ever more sophisticated ways of delivering the goods.

In other words, sports celebrities are delivered to us through exactly the same channels as other kinds of celebs: through the media. What's more, we consume them in the same way as we consume the other celebs: by watching them perform on tv, buying the merchandise, logging on to websites devoted to them. We even still go to the actual events in which they appear.

All of which leaves us with an obvious though essential question: how did celebrity culture start? The answer is: with the time–space compression. Go with this for a moment; I'll return to it in the next section.

## WATCHED, ADMIRED, PRIVILEGED, AND IMITATED

They're described by Len Sherman as "the most watched, admired, privileged, and imitated people" (1998: 189). Once celebrities were just famous, but, in the twenty-first century, they have acquired a kind of exemplary authority, an influence that they usually don't use to facilitate social change or promote good causes, but to sell commodities. A cynical public, having given up and been given up by old institutions, "gladly seizes upon this substitute, a substitute that might not provide a lot of benefits, but doesn't require a lot in return either" (1998: 189). Apart from money, we should add.

In times of national crisis, we're forced to place our faith in traditional leaders; what other choice do we have? Engaged in war or under siege, people look to their politicians, generals, and church leaders. These were active people, who based their reputations on what they said and did, the brave decisions they made, the steadfastness of their resolve, and the steeliness of their will. Like old sporting heroes, they were known for what they did.

In the absence of crises, our commitment became less secure and we had no need to trust them anymore. So, on Sherman's account, we looked to alternatives. Celebrities may not be obvious replacements, but they were functional equivalents of leaders: people who represented, influenced, perhaps inspired and commanded our attention, if not respect. This then was the first

## Fame

From the Latin *fama*, meaning reputation or renown, this is the condition of being recognized publicly, spoken of, and having one's actions reported. While it is often contrasted with infamy (notoriety or known for abominations), fame encompasses public recognition for all deeds, good and bad. Fame can be localized, in which case the subject is known by repute only within particular vicinities, or global, in which case knowledge of the subject is pervasive. Global fame was rare before the twentieth century. The growth of the mass media and, later, multimedia commissioned the development of genuine international renown. Television especially, from the 1950s, helped create a common culture in which figures from literally anywhere in the world could become recognizable everywhere. In his *Illusions of Immortality* (2000), David Giles emphasizes that today fame is frequently brought about purely by the media, i.e. rather than anything the famous person actually does: "The ultimate modern celebrity is the member of the public who becomes famous solely through media involvement."

condition under which celebrity culture came into existence: a loss of faith, trust, and confidence in established leaders. Now, we come to the time–space compression.

As we saw in the previous chapter, one of the many consequences of globalization has been a common culture, tastes, labels, languages being blended into a uniform whole. Not that we've all become submissive conformists: if anything, we have a greater range of choice than at any time in history. It's just that those choices come in neat packages and that they are mostly offered by global corporations, Nike being one of the principal ones, of course.

Globalization would not have been possible without a media capable of transmitting large volumes of information around the world, not just quickly, but instantly. By information, I mean news, entertainment, and advertising. "Advertising, in particular, seeks to sell products by depicting idealized Western lifestyles, often under the universalizing themes of sex, status and the sibling-hood of humanity," writes Malcolm Waters in his *Globalization* (2001: 203).

Satellites, or transponders, were the instruments of the media's global expansion. By wrapping the world in an invisible network of communications, satellite broadcasters were able to bounce information off satellites and send them literally anywhere. Satellite television companies recognized no national boundaries. This effectively meant that virtually everyone on earth was part of one huge market.

In Chapter 14, we saw how Rupert Murdoch, perhaps more than any other media figure, exploited the opportunities offered by the satellite technology pioneered in the 1960s, and the deregulation and privatization of the television industry in the 1980s and early 1990s. In February 1989, Murdoch's European satellite started beaming programs via satellite through his Sky network. By the end of the 1990s, his various channels reached 66 percent of the world's population (Stotlar, 2000).

The problem with having so many channels is content: what do you fill them with? MTV supplied a clue. To keep so much of the world glued to the screen, you need a formula. Sports, as we saw previously, was part of the formula designed to maintain people's interest. Televised programming detached itself from fixed content and began firing off in the direction of entertainment, by which I mean amusement – something that occupies us agreeably, diverting our minds from matters that might prompt introspection, analysis, or reflection. I'm not arguing that drama that provokes contemplation and critical examination can't be entertaining too, nor even that the narratives of soaps or cartoons aren't open to critical interrogation. And I'm certainly not underestimating the viewers' speedy acquisition of skills for screening and skimming information. But, for the most part, entertainment doesn't prompt us to modify ourselves in any way.

Light entertainment, to use a more indicative term, became a staple of a formula that demanded only a modest level of attention from viewers: music+movies+sport. Asked to respond to this in the 1990s, an informed person might have said: people will soon get sick of it; they'll feel bombarded, under siege, overwhelmed by too much entertainment. Yet here we are in the twenty-first century and, far from being overwhelmed, we can't seem to get enough.

Of course, the communications revolution didn't end with television and the proliferation of multimedia brought a further layer of information conduits. In a way, the internet worked as a kind of antidote to the potentially pacifying effects of too much televised entertainment. Lying on a couch for six hours a day watching undemanding programs is quite a different experience to sitting at a desk researching in an electronic database or following an online political debate. There are times when they complement each other too. Fans can watch a game on tv, then log on to analyze the game in a fans' chatroom, or even talk to players in "real time."

Let's remind ourselves of Sherman's plausible account of why we are now so devoted to sports. We've lost faith and confidence in established leaders, the central social institutions of state and government, and rescinded our memberships of other organizations that were once regarded as valuable, such as unions, political parties, and volunteer groups. This occurred at around the same time as the proliferation of global networks of communication and the increase

---

### Celebrity culture

This is characterized by a pervasive preoccupation with famous persons and extravagant values attached to the lives of public figures whose actual accomplishments may be limited, but whose visibility is extensive. It became a feature of social life, especially in the developed world, during the late 1980s/early 1990s, and extended into the twenty-first century, assisted by a global media that promoted, lauded, sometimes abominated, and occasionally annihilated figures, principally from entertainment and sports. Celebrity culture defined thought and conduct, style and manner. It affected and was affected by not just fans but by entire populations whose lives had been shaped by the shift from manufacturing to service societies and the corresponding shift from consumer to aspirational consumer.

---

in entertainment-themed programs to fill those networks. As the media grew in importance, so traditional leaders lost their former status.

A coincidence? Perhaps. Or maybe one hastened the other. In times of national emergency, what alternative is there to having confidence in political leaders, placing trust in military leaders, and having faith in religious leaders? In times of stability, skepticism turns either to cynicism and maybe to downright indifference.

Those baby boomers born in the immediate postwar period matured without the sense of crisis and foreboding that world war instills. But they had their expectations tempered by parents whose experience of war served to remind them of the deprivations as well as abundance. The offspring of that generation had no such brake on their expectations. In other words, a generation cooled on their leaders and turned their attention to a new class of people who seemed to embody everything they craved.

All of this looks a little too opportune. At that precise time when people were cooling, the new media turned up right on cue and started delivering light, or more appropriately, lite entertainment to everyone's living rooms. We quickly succumbed, dropping existing allegiances and devoting our energies to following and aping the new privileged class that was populating our screens. Too neat. Something else must have happened. Or perhaps *someone.*

# MADONNA: LIKE AN ANSWER TO A PRAYER

After the success of her fourth album *Like a Prayer*, in 1989, Madonna appears to have seen the future: it was a world in which a new type of celebrity would dominate as consummately as dinosaurs dominated the Jurassic world. The days when people got to be famous and stayed that way through just making movies, hit records, or writing best-sellers were approaching an end. The most important feature of the coming age was visibility: doing was less important than, well, just being right there in the public gaze. With so many channels of communication being filled up with all manner of entertainment, there was bound to be an overflow of entertainers, most of whom would make little impression on the public consciousness. The ones who did were those who would not just make themselves visible, but transparent – there was no contradiction.

Madonna not only epitomized this, but helped it materialize. She seems to have struck a bargain with the media. It was something like this: I will tell you more, show you more about me than any other rock or movie star in history; I will disclose my personal secrets, share my fears, joys, sorrows, what makes me happy or sad, angry or gratified; I will be more candid and unrestricted in my interviews than any other entertainer. In other words, I'll be completely see-through. In return, I want coverage like no other: I want to be omnipresent, ubiquitous, and pervasive – I want to be everywhere, all the time. It was a delicious *quid pro quo*. The media went for it; and the age of celebrity was upon us.

As the 1980s turned to the 1990s, Madonna was, as she wanted to be, everywhere. This was surely the meaning of Blonde Ambition, the title of her 1991 tour. The following year, she bared herself in her book *Sex*, accompanied by the album *Erotica*. Being famous was no longer sufficient: to be a celebrity, you had to strip yourself, make consumers privy to as many aspects of your life as you dare. And, no one did it better than La Ciccone.

The beauty of the age of celebrity, though, was that the consumers weren't hapless chumps: they were educated in the arts of celeb-production by the very channels that presented them. Put another way, they didn't just look at the pictures: they were able readers. They did most of the work. All the celebs did was make themselves available. Madonna was the first celebrity to render her manufacture completely transparent. Unabashed about revealing to her fandom evidence of the elaborate and monstrously expensive publicity and marketing that went into her videos, CDs, stage acts, and, indeed, herself, Madonna laid open her promotional props, at the same time exposing her utterly contrived persona changes.

From Material Girl to Monroe *manquée* to vamp to cowgirl, she made no attempt to conceal the artfulness of her constructions. Her 1991 movie called *Truth or Dare* in the USA and *In Bed with Madonna* in Britain, while ostensibly a fly-on-the-wall documentary of the Blonde Ambition tour, was a study of a maternally warm, generous, though impulsive woman, prone to the occasional but understandable bouts of bitchiness, yet with wit and charm enough to win over her doubters. In other words, a study in celebrity management. The risk wasn't that fans might not be taken in with the film; they obviously wouldn't be. It was that they might feel cheated: learning only what they already knew.

Today, fans may be in awe of celebrities, but they understand that there's an entire industry at work and that they have been coopted by that industry. The deal is that the fans will stay awed and curious, while the industry will disclose more and more about the celebrities.

Transparency is also apparent in movies, especially ones that employ special fx. Often, television documentaries on "The making of . . ." exposing the technologies that helped create fantastical illusions in the films, are shown either prior or just after the theater release of the main item. A blatant promotional device, maybe; but part of the new bargain: let the consumers in on the trick. As recently as the late 1970s, fans would be astonished by movies such as *Close Encounters of the Third Kind* or *Alien*, leaving theaters asking, "How did they *do* that?" Such wonderment wouldn't be tolerated today. Savvy fans are up to speed on the powers of digitalization and pixels. They want to know exactly how particular fx were achieved and with what consequences.

Madonna wasn't single-handedly responsible for moving the tectonic plates of popular culture. But there is a sense in which she was an archetype: others who aspired to become celebs were going to have to follow her example. Conspicuousness was everything. Someone like the fiercely reclusive Greta Garbo, who carved a career from her inaccessibility, wouldn't have survived as a celebrity in the 1990s. The media would just move onto someone more approachable. Fans would quickly tire of someone who wanted to maintain a private life. In the age of celebrity, the private life was merely another realm for inspection.

Accustomed to adventure, humor, sex, and violence in drama, fans developed an appetite for these in real life too. If they didn't find them in their own, they could at least experience them vicariously through the lives of the people they followed. Magazines like *Heat*, *People*, and *Hello* obliged, featuring tales of the celebs at play, which they spun into intriguing narratives for their readers.

Let's recap before we go on. I've identified three changes, two of which occurred round about the same time, the other of which had been in motion for several years before – this being the steady erosion of trust, confidence, and faith in traditional leaders. Of the other two, the proliferation of media, their encircling of the world, and their resolution to the problem of "what can we fill all these new channels with?" was utterly crucial. Without the global apparatus, there would have been no effective means to communicate instantly and ubiquitously. And without the overabundance of entertainment programs, there would have been fewer opportunities for anyone, talented or talentless, to become famous.

Madonna did have talent and not only singing talent: she also had the cunning to hatch a plan that would change the very nature of the media's relationship with performers. All right, that sounds more like a conspiracy than it actually was. But more than any other artist, Madonna uncovered herself to the media, making it less possible for others to engage the media without baring their all, so to speak. Not only this: Madonna also took the adventurous step of actually making her dealings with the media clear, as if she was involving fans in her manufacture. Actually, not "as if ": she was involving the fans in her manufacture.

Years later, we witnessed the effects of this when legions of young people of massively varying degrees of ability performed in front of tv cameras in often embarrassing attempts to win contests like *Pop Idol*, or *American Idol*. And when people volunteered to open their lives up to public inspection in reality tv shows like *Big Brother*. And when "ordinary people" would happily appear on shows like *Jerry Springer*, to disclose the most excruciatingly humiliating details of their personal lives and with no apparent embarrassment (presumably fortified by the knowledge that most of the audience would do the same if their positions were exchanged). And when once famous figures whose power to entrance had either faded or disappeared could leap back into the public imaginations simply by inviting television cameras to trail them around while doing nothing in particular. Anna Nicole Smith and Ozzy Osbourne are among those who can testify.

## RETAIL THERAPY

Walk around any shopping precinct in Britain and it won't be long before you run into someone wearing a replica shirt bearing the name of a soccer player. Replica shirts are less prevalent in the USA, though there are usually plenty of NBA tops to be seen. Of course, baseball caps are everywhere. It might seem perfectly obvious, but ask yourself why advertisers spend such fantastic amounts of money to persuade not only athletes but any celebrity, however minor, to endorse their products. The answer seems to be: because they help sell them. The tougher question is: how? What is it about seeing a celeb wear or use a commodity that makes us want to do the same?

The old purpose of shopping was to buy goods and services that we needed. It wasn't meant as an enjoyable experience: just something that had to be done to get through the week. We were consumers, but not in the sense that we are today. Maybe aspirational consumers would be more apposite: we consume because we yearn to be something, or even someone. This sounds faintly pathetic, but that's just the way contemporary consumer society works: not by supplying goods that we need, but by promoting desires, wishes, and passions that can never be satisfied, only temporarily satiated until the craving returns. That's why shopping is a joy. Retail therapy is the way to happiness, success, and even identity.

The cosmetics industry was something of a pioneer in this respect. As early as the 1930s, it marketed its products not according to their functional values, but according the benefit they were supposed to purvey. So, when you bought, say, Revlon products, you weren't buying foundation cream or lipstick, but glamor and attractiveness. Even as late as the 1960s, many advertisers hadn't caught on and were still marketing shampoo as stuff that cleans hair or cars as vehicles that go from A to B. By the 1990s, shampoo provided shine, silkiness, protection from UV rays, and, above all, radiance. And cars were to be experienced rather than driven. Today, every advertisement tries to sell something other than the actual product: a lifestyle, an image, or a solution to a problem with which it has no obvious association.

We know what the advertisers want: to move products off the shelves or out of the showrooms. What do consumers want – products? Obviously, but not just for their use-value. In his book *Celebrity*, Chris Rojek argues that fans "seek validation in imaginary relationships with the celebrity to whom they are attached in order to compensate for feelings of invalidation and incompleteness elsewhere in their lives" (2001: 52).

We don't have to agree with all of this: it's possible that fans (and we'll assume Rojek means all consumers who have an interest in celebrities) are not all searching for compensation for the emptiness of their own lives, but maintain "attachments," perhaps as a way of associating with people they admire, respect, or are just fond of. That probably applies to all the readers and the writer of this book. Whether we admit it or not, we all buy things that celebrities promote.

Even if they don't have lucrative endorsement contracts, celebrities are promoting. They're like walking, talking advertisement for the good life. I mean by this that their sheer presence advertises a version of the kind of life we should all aspire to. We can approach, though never reach, that good life through buying the kinds of products they conspicuously consume, all of which, when bought, can take us that little bit nearer to people who rarely acknowledge our existence.

Consumer culture was originally built on the materialism, envy, and possessiveness that flourished in the postwar years. Desire drove us towards appropriation: we wanted to have the things we saw dangled in front of us by advertising. The advertising industry had sensed that people didn't buy products just because they needed them: the needs had to be encouraged; desire worked much better. If you desire something, the second you have it, the desire is gone.

So, the trick was to keep pumping up new desires: as soon as you upgrade the fridge, you start thinking about a new car. As soon as you get the car, you start thinking about a new house. "The accelerator of consumer demand," as Zygmunt Bauman calls it in his article "Consuming life", is pressed hard down as new offers keep appearing on the road ahead.

Bauman argues that one of the triumphs of the consumer culture is in liberating the pleasure principle from the perimeter fence beyond which pleasure seekers once could venture only at their peril. "Consumer society has achieved a previously unimaginable feat: it reconciled the reality and pleasure principles by putting, so to speak, the thief in charge of the treasure box," Bauman concludes (2001: 16). What we used to think of as irrational now strikes us as perfectly normal. Max'ing out our credit cards, taking on gigantic mortgages, shopping for fun, vacationing in exotic places we can't afford: these might once have seemed instances of utter madness; now they seem quite normal. After all, seeking pleasure is a rational activity, isn't it?

Shopping is now considered glamorous, not utilitarian. The consumer is encouraged to declare his and her worth by spending money on items that will help them look like, play like, or in some other way, be like someone else. That someone else is the celeb, or more likely, celebs with whom they feel or want to feel an attachment. The second, let's say, Nicole Kidman appears in a certain marque of car or wearing a specific label gown or carries a distinct accessory, it's like a starting gun for people to jump out of their blocks. People quickly realize that the Maserati is too rich for their blood and the Prada number cost more than their entire wardrobe ten times over. But the Gucci snaffle bag she's carrying is within reach. It might be entry level, but, hey, it's the same as Nicole's *and* it's Gucci. Looked at in this way, shopping offers a way to strengthen our bonds with the people we admire and the good life they appear to luxuriate in. Shopping in the age of celebrity has undergone something of a transformation (compare Dittmar's account in 1992 with Goldberg *et al.*'s 2003 study).

Potentially, anything can induce us to shop. Watching a cookery program featuring a celebrity chef on tv, or a home improvement show, or even one of those "how to keep your house clean" series: they're not just there to be enjoyed. They also make us spend. There's a marvelously convenient "fit" between the requirements of the global media, the demands of a culture that turns celebrities into commodities, and the imperatives of consumer society. We watch, listen to, and, in many other ways, follow celebrities in the multiple media we have at our disposal, then go out and shop away our disposable income.

So, how do celebrity *athletes* specifically prompt us to shop? The kind of global changes we have covered over the past two chapters, 14 and 15, have had many effects, one of which is to turn sports into entertainment. Yet there is more drama in sports today. You might suppose that it no longer shares any DNA with its 4,000-year-old ancestor. But it does. The crucial *indeterminacy* that makes sports exciting and which we emphasized in Chapter 1, will always ensure it's never completely absorbed into pure entertainment. Yet celebrity culture has left its fingerprints all over sports and the people who play them.

Celebrity athletes have much in common with other celebs, including their ability to make us shop. Replica shirts and baseball caps are just the start. Sports celebs come into view in just the same way as other celebrities: through the media. How and what they consume is now staple fare for the magazines and tv shows. They are every bit as potent as Hollywood stars when it comes to advertising the good life. Seeing Serena Williams step out of a $200,000 Lamborghini wearing a $3,000 Balenciaga dress may not send people rushing to balenciaga.com, but that $150 necklace she's wearing is the same one you can get at the mall. And it's a Bvlgari. Well, not quite: her's actually cost $18,500, but the one at the mall looks just the same and, to authenticate our attachment, we'll get some Bvlgari perfume and Bvlgari sunglasses, which will set us back another couple of hundred or so.

Strange as it seems, we used to respect the gulf between the stars and us. We'd happily wait for those airbrushed pictures of the Hollywood crowd and their like wearing the best clothes and in the best hair and make-up money could buy. They had an otherworldly quality about them that we loved. It was Them and Us. There's still a gulf, of course. It's just that celebrity culture has narrowed it. The stars-at-their-best pictures are still printed in glossies like *Marie Claire*. But, *Star*, *Heat*, and the newer publications specialize in photos of celebrities in unguarded moments, looking rough, picking their noses, or just being seen in a way they would sooner not be made public. The celebrity-magazine has succeeded stunningly in showing celebrities appearing and behaving as ordinary people, aided by reality tv shows like *I'm a Celebrity . . . Get Me Out of Here!* They have closed the space between Them and Us though sometimes it's apparently possible to imagine Them as fundamentally different. Even Marie O'Riordan, editor of the aforementioned glossy, misjudged the ontological status of celebs when she advised, "the gap between celebrities and real people is diminishing" (in *The Independent Review*, August 2, 2004, p. 7).

The importance of the equivocal alliance between celebrity and magazine can't be overemphasized, the latter feeding off celebrities and the former needing the so-called oxygen of publicity to survive. Another example of the symbiosis we covered in Chapter 15. Theoretically, it might seem that athletes could survive without it. They could insist that only their sports performance is open for public exhibition and that their private life is strictly their own business. Whether or not this would be a successful strategy we don't know: nobody's tried it. Most athletes are too concerned about sinking like stones as they swim toward the shores of the good life. They grab every endorsement contract available, exploit every photo opportunity, and turn up to every opening (of a club, restaurant, movie, etc.) imaginable. Fame, money, and adulation may not be the initial motivation for a career in sports. But who would pass on them? Forgoing a private life seems a modest sacrifice.

For the others who actually do want to keep a portion of their lives private, this is not good news. The media is so habituated to probing the crust of outward appearances that they can't or won't discriminate. A withdrawn athlete is just as much fair game as an exhibitionist *Big Brother* contestant. Consider the most exhibited athletes. In the 1990s, Mike Tyson's life was opened up to visual inspection. His conduct away from the ring might not have militated against his having any semblance of a private life. But there was also a sense in which he lived in a Panopticon, a prison where cells are arranged around a central watchtower in which concealed authority figures can inspect without being seen – rather like *Big Brother*. Everyone was watching Tyson.

In the late twentieth century, the vigilant mediawatch on David Beckham worked as straightforwardly as cause → effect in turning him into the world's most famous athlete since Michael Jordan. That status earned him more comprehensive surveillance in the twenty-first century and stories of his playing away from home, so to speak, were reported not just to his wife but to the entire population of the world. What might, in many other circumstances, have been a private matter, became very public, with resounding repercussions for Beckham's professional life, too.

Like other celebrities, athletes gladly receive the attention while they're on the rise and remain appreciative at their peak. So, when they moan about the persistent intrusions into their private life and their inability to move without a retinue of photographers, we suspect they are either pretending they don't enjoy it, or unwilling to accept that, when you become public property, you lose the right to a private life. Unless, of course, the courts rule otherwise, as they sometimes do. Despite the successful legal claims to privacy of Naomi Campbell in England, Michael Douglas and Catherine Zeta-Jones in the USA, and Princess Caroline of Hanover in the European Court of Human Rights, there is little evidence that the media's love affair with celebrities has gone cold.

Still, we need to remind ourselves: athletes, unlike the more ephemeral celebrities, who flit in and out of our attention monitors, do something other than just appear. They perform. Admittedly, celebrity status can often overpower athletic performance. Tyson was still a pay-per-view performer in his late thirties when his time-eroded skills were all but gone. Other celebrities whose status originated in sports used that status to transfer into film: The Rock, Vinnie Jones, Dennis Rodman, included. The expansion of televised sports has also made it possible for celebrity athletes to prolong their sports careers long after retirement by becoming pundits (which actually comes from a Hindu term *pandit*, meaning a learned expert, or teacher).

The point is that, while athletes are different in some respects from other celebs, they're very similar in others, including their equivocal relationships with the media. In his *Illusions of Immortality*, David Giles writes: "The proliferation of media for publicizing the individual has been reflected in a proliferation of celebrated individuals. As the mass media has expanded, so individuals have had to do less in order to be celebrated" (2000: 32).

Giles is right in his first point: there *are* more celebrity athletes today. But does his second point apply to athletes? Some might argue that athletes of only modest abilities could become celebrities as long as the media take notice of them. They will probably point to Anna Kournikova as a prime example. Others? Well, there are probably other celebrity athletes whose status disguises their playing limitations. But athletes who become *somebodies* usually distinguish themselves competitively.

It's difficult to garner media attention without substance. Wearing outrageous clothes, looking like a supermodel, behaving aggressively, or raising hell in nightclubs are some of the ways athletes grab the headlines. But, if they're not good athletes as well, who cares? We should remember that, Kournikova apart, we are hard-pressed to name an athlete who has become a celebrity despite an absence of sporting prowess: most have earned initial recognition with something other than just well-knownness.

## CLOSER TO THE GODS

What's in it for the fan? Shopping might be gratifying. Using our purchases might be enjoyable, perhaps even rapturous. Every step we take toward the world of Them might fill us with pleasure. But, in a way, all this could be just a big con, designed to separate us from our money and maintain our dependence on commodities. Surely, there's something else. Following celebrities must satisfy us in a – dare we say it? – deeper way.

This is not quite as airy as it sounds. At least two contemporary writers, Chris Rojek and John Maltby, have discerned the resemblance between religious devoutness and celebrity culture. Rojek's sociological approach yields parallels between following celebrities and ritual, shamanism, and experiences of ecstasy (the exalted state, not the class A drug). Secularization has not led to the replacement of religion by science, but it has meant a displacement of religious activities and beliefs into other areas, such as animal rights campaigns and ecology movements. On Rojek's account, there has also been a "substantial convergence between religion and consumer culture" (2001: 57).

A godless world leaves a "terrifying meaninglessness" and celebrities help fill the void. Of course, you could argue that following celebrities is meaningless in its own right: it seems trivial, pointless, unimportant, and insignificant to an outsider. To someone who is involved in it, on the other hand, it can be tantamount to a religious experience.

Maltby's psychological research complements this. Celebrity worship syndrome is the expression Maltby uses to describe the condition of fans who adore celebrities. "Syndrome" isn't entirely appropriate, as it suggests a pathological condition that needs treatment. Maltby is not so judgmental: he is conveying an important point about the manner in which young people try to associate themselves with or affix themselves to their chosen celebs. There is a depth of devotion that mere observers just can't understand.

---

### Secularization

From the Latin *saeculum*, meaning an age, or generation, this refers to the growth in skepticism of religious knowledge and the corresponding decline in social significance of religion. Several influential theorists of the nineteenth century, including Sigmund Freud, Max Weber, and Karl Marx, predicted that the emergence of industrial society and the rise of science would make religion marginal and lead to a secular society, i.e. one in which sacred and ecclesiastical, or church affairs are subordinated to worldly, or profane matters. (A *secularist* is someone opposed to religious education.)

---

Giles traces the origins of the term "parasocial interaction" to a 1956 article in the journal *Psychiatry* (Horton and Wohl 1956). The 1950s was the decade of growth for television: at the start, few households had a tv; by the end over 90 percent of households in the USA and UK had at least one set. Viewers were forming unusual attachments. They were developing "friendships" with television characters, some fictional and others real (like announcers, or weather forecasters). Familiarity led to a sense of intimacy. Viewers actually thought they knew the figures they saw on their screens. They interacted with them parasocially.

It's called parasocial because *para* means beyond, as in paranormal. The attachment might only have been as strong as a beam of light from a cathode ray tube. Yet it was experienced as strong and meaningful. Consumers actually felt they knew people they had never met, probably never seen in the flesh, and who knew nothing of their existence. So there is no actual interaction (*inter* means between): it's oneway. This doesn't stop the consumer's feeling like there's a genuine interaction.

We often hear about fans who become stalkers after hearing a hallowed celebrity's voice commanding them. Fans regularly accost actors who play loathsome characters in the soaps. A devotee of the singer Björk believed he was acting out her will when he videotaped himself committing suicide. Of course, the celebs contribute to the feelings through their public performances but have no way of gauging the depth of fans' feelings toward them apart from fan mail or website conversations.

The point about parasocial interaction is that it's more relevant today than it was in the 1950s. At a time when there are more celebrities than ever, there are more fans experiencing feelings of emotional closeness and perhaps organizing parts of their lives around such feelings. There's an example of this in Gurinder Chadha's 2002 movie *Bend it Like Beckham* in which the central character Jess confides in no one, not even her closest friends. Yet David Beckham is her oracle: his face graces a poster on her bedroom ceiling and, at night, she lies in bed pouring out her heart to him, as ancient Greeks would once consult their deities for advice or prophecy.

Although, in the original meaning, parasocial interaction was unilateral, we need to revise it to allow for the possibility of bilateral interaction. Fans can really interact. It's almost become part of the celeb's job definition: interacting with fans, however fleetingly (like signing an autograph), however cursorily (in a radio or tv phone-in), or however remotely (through cyberspace, maybe), there is always a chance it will happen.

---

### Parasocial interaction

Interaction with imaginary, fictitious, legendary, or illusory beings, such as cartoon characters or dramatic figures, is unilateral (one-sided), affecting only one party. Film, television, and radio fans enter into relationships with figures with whom a bilateral (two-sided) relationship is improbable, though not impossible, as the Martin Scorsese 1982 movie *The King of Comedy* illustrated. In it, Rupert Pupkin obsesses over getting his own tv show, creating his own mock studio, complete with cut-out guests, at his apartment. Not only does he follow the stars: he uses them as his own, imagining he's with them, that he has what they have, that he can do what they do. It's a triumph of fantasy. At least, until he decides to buttonhole a real tv presenter, then fraudulently gain entrance to his home.

---

There are certainly parallels between religious devotion and the exaltation of gods, on the one hand, and the reverence and worship of today's celebrity culture. This is most evident in obsessional fans, including stalkers and those who are either deluded or fixated as fans to the point of becoming pathological. It's also apparent in organized groups of fans, such as Elvis devotees and those longstanding Trekkies (see Jindra 1994). So there is support for the idea that celebrities help relieve the "terrifying meaningless" of secular society, though we should guard against regarding celebrity culture as a kind of functional equivalent of religion.

For a start, it's possible that secularization has been exaggerated. The USA and Western Europe, which have often been cited as secular, have far from abandoned religion. And the post-communist resurgence of organized religion in eastern European countries suggests a spiritual comeback. Combine these with the Islamic revival that has swept across the world in the early twenty-first century, the emergence of New Age beliefs, the evangelical revival that swept through Latin America, and the widespread ethno-religious conflicts in international affairs, and you are left with an image of what we might call a de-secularization.

Far from disappearing, religion has acquired a new role in what Ronald Inglehart and Pippa Norris call "existential security." In their 2004 book *Sacred and Secular: Religion and politics worldwide*, they argue that, during the second half of the twentieth century, all advanced industrial societies moved toward a secular state, but the world as a whole now has more people with traditional religious views than ever before. That's because secularization has a substantial effect on human fertility rates. So, while Inglehart and Norris don't dismiss secularization, they marshal convincing evidence that it's not a straightforward process and that religiosity (being religious) persists, particularly in poorer nations and in failed states facing personal survival-threatening risks. Exposure to risks drives religiosity. The decline of religious practices, values, and beliefs is restricted to the more affluent sections of the most prosperous nations.

Also, we have to consider that, when we describe celebs as godlike or divine we are using similes, not explicit descriptions. Our enthusiasm for celebs might look like the devotion many have to a deity or deities. But that's as far as it goes; as we've seen, celebrities have become more available to us in recent years. In our eyes, they've become more flesh and blood and less godlike as the gap between Them and Us has closed.

But is this as true of sports as it is of other areas of entertainment? After all, athletes were latecomers to the celebrity parade. Even at the end of the 1980s, they were sportsmen and sportswomen, not celebrities: high-earners, to be sure; watched, followed, imitated, and a source of inspiration for many, certainly; but still "real people," to repeat Marie O'Riordan.

Fashion models, rock stars, and Hollywood actors might have occupied a position on the celestial equator, but athletes were down here on earth, organic parts of real, not imagined, communities, their roots in the same earth as ours. We weren't interested in their entire lives: just their conduct on the field of play. The term "superstar" was applied to a few overachieving athletes, but they were, almost by definition, a tiny minority. Only in the 1990s, did the transference begin in earnest and sports became showbusiness. In the process, the leading lights of sports became bone fide celebrities.

Yet, there is a paradox: long before the age of celebrity, sports had a spiritual dimension. It inspired writers like W. P. Kinsella to write *Shoeless Joe Jackson Comes to Iowa*, the source novel of *Field of Dreams* in which farmer "Ray Kinsella" hears a Voice whispering, "If you build it, he will come." Kinsella is able to resurrect the suspended players from the notorious 1919 Black Sox series. It inspired former Liverpool manager Bill Shankley to suggest that soccer was more important than life itself. It still inspires dozens of thousands to write into their wills requests that their ashes be scattered on the field of their favored ball club. The curiously positive and uplifting effect that sport has on its followers has an ethereal quality that bears resemblance to that of faith.

So, even if we allow that *worship* might exaggerate the adoration, honor, and respect afforded celebrities today, it still seems an appropriate way to describe the way in which fans regard athletes. The word worship comes from *worth+ship* (as in scholarship or friendship) and has no necessary link with religion. Yet, in the case of sports, there does seem to be a religious fire that ignites passions. The sacrifice of money, time, and energy might be the equivalent of burnt offerings. The manner in which fans defer to celebrity athletes, buying their memoirs, seeking their autographs, wearing shirts with their names across the back, is reminiscent of suppliants humbling themselves at the feet of holy men. And, if we really want to stretch it, we should remember the point made in Chapter 11: that the root of the word fan is *fanaticus*, meaning of a temple.

As faith brings its own sense of empowerment, so being a fan confers feelings of personal power on the otherwise dispossessed subordinates who feel deprived in many other areas of life (empowerment, in this sense, is close to the self-efficacy we discussed in Chapter 6: a belief in their ability to produce sought-after outcomes, making individuals or groups believe they have the capacity to bring about the results they want out of life). At least that's the view of several researchers, including Cheryl Harris (1998) and Henry Jenkins (1992) whose work we covered also in Chapter 11: fans feel stronger and more confident. Though some take this to bizarre extremes. The kind of weirdness that sometimes manifests in stalking and other forms of obsessive behavior evokes comparisons with the religious zealotry displayed by those seeking precisely the kind of empowerment sought by fans.

When Rojek concludes, "Celebrity culture is a culture of faux authenticity, since the passions it generates derive from staged authenticity rather than genuine forms of recognition and belonging," he surely confuses the theatricality of sports with fakeness (2001: 90). Of course, sports are staged events and, as such, provide showcases for the entertainers. This doesn't diminish the actuality or the verity of the experience and the passion aroused. In any case, aren't the rituals that are so integral to religious worship staged?

Who can say whether the parasocial attachment fans have to sports celebrities are more or less substantial or significant than those felt by acolytes, apostles, devotees, disciples, or zealots? Why is sport any more a "cult of distraction," as Rojek calls the assembly of celebrities, than religion, whether denominational, sectarian, or cultic? Celebrity culture can't produce "transcendent value" on this account. If by transcendent value we mean a quality that serves as both a guiding principle and an explanation of earthly matters, then celebrity culture fails. But do contemporary religious figures, including rabbis, evangelists, imams, ministers, preachers, priests, or any other type of cleric, provide any more succor, euphoria, and contentment than sports figures? Affirmation, unity, sense of belonging? Or grief, sadness, and disconsolation?

Sports celebrities may not knowingly engender these kinds of emotions in their devotees. They may not even care. They frequently absolve themselves from responsibility if such emotions lead to unfortunate consequences (like drinking, fighting, or even killing). Yet this doesn't make them any less potent. Remember: the parasocial relationship needs only one active party; the other can be oblivious – yet still evoke experiences, behavior, and, importantly, satisfactions in the follower.

Parallels between celebrity culture and religion may be strained, but, in the specific portion of that culture reserved for sports, the correspondence is compelling. Sports celebs are closer to the gods than they seem to recognize.

## NO GUARANTEES

Has it all changed since the end of the 1980s into the 1990s? Or, has there always been a celebrity culture, without its actually being called a celebrity culture? In the introduction to their edited collection *Sports Stars: The cultural politics of sporting celebrity*, David Andrews and Steven Jackson write: "Although at one point in time the emergence of celebrity figures was a haphazard and arbitrary voyage of discovery, today the process is considerably more proactive in its focus on the cultivation of potential celebrities" (2001: 4).

Over Chapters 13–15, we've seen how an entire sports industry has developed, principally around the demands of television. Without the commercial benefit of having sports relayed globally, there would be little point in calibrating the demands of competitive sports with those of other divisions of the sports industry. And, of course, it is, as we've seen, a proper industry: it provides habitual employment for millions, involves trade and manufacture, requires a high degree of organization, control, and regulation and runs on rational principles. In fact, the only thing about sports that isn't rational is the actual competition, as we noted in the opening chapter. For the duration of the competition, unpredictability, spontaneity, and sheer luck prevail; everything else is calculated, planned, and designed to minimize randomness.

Andrews and Jackson's point is that, in recent years, the industrial process that has steadily turned sports from an inchoate assembly of games into a fully fledged business sector has affected not only the structure of sports, but the athletes. "As with any cultural product, there is also no guarantee that celebrities will be consumed in the manner intended," caution Andrews and Jackson (2001: 5). Music and movie stars and fashion models can be manufactured like products to meet the specific requirements of a market. Athletes can't be produced to such fine tolerance. Their representations in the media, including advertising, tv talk shows, and other public appearances can be shaped according to an image. But, unlike actors, singers, models, and other members of the entertainment industry, athletes have to perform in an unscripted drama. If they don't compete well, their public presentations will eventually be seen as fraudulent. Consider the previously mentioned Anna Kournikova in the early twenty-first century. While she enjoyed unprecedented media attention and a bounty of endorsement contracts, consumers spied the deception when she failed to win any major tournaments.

Far from being "consumed in the manner intended," as Andrews and Jackson put it, she was sneered at or lusted after – but never respected, admired, or honored as an athlete. Some might maintain that this was never the objective, of course. But, looker that she was, there were any number of trained models who could outmatch her in the looks department. Her uniqueness was that she was a promising athlete. When her promise didn't translate into trophies, she was seen more as an artifice than a real player.

Consumers simply won't stand for frauds. Not consumers of sports, anyway. They're a far cry from the "one born every minute" suckers famously mocked by the great nineteenth-century showman P. T. Barnum. Today's fans are mostly astute, canny, knowing, and enthusiastic partners in the celebrity production process. Partners? Yes, that's the conclusion of an illuminating study in the 1990s by Joshua Gamson. In his *Claims to Fame: Celebrity in contemporary America*, Gamson explodes the idea that fans are helpless dupes who get taken in by the slick celebrity production. The closing gap between Us and Them means that fans are now able to examine the mechanisms of celebrity production: "Seeing evidence of the publicity machinery and marketing behaviors . . . increases [fans'] confidence in the fairness of their tacit 'agreement' with the celebrity industry," writes Gamson (1994: 124).

In other words, consumers know all about the maneuvers involved in producing a celebrity and are quite willing to accept rather than rebel against them. The reason is: they rather like being parts of the industry. Knowing that celebrities are made or broken, in the last instance, by them, is a source of satisfaction to audiences. Fans are simultaneously "voyeurs of and performers in commercial culture" (1994: 137).

In other words, consumers are "in on the game": the celebrity industry is no mystery to them. They've read the magazines, watched the tv shows, studied the internet sites, and demystified the whole production process. To outsiders, they're dupes, but, in actuality, they're accomplices.

Gamson's is a vision of the fan as inquisitive, investigative, and perceptive. Quite the opposite of the typical picture as a jerk who just soaks up all the hype without pausing for even a moment's reflection. Gamson discovered that fans are highly reflective, recognizing the façade of celebrity, but aware that they are integral to the façade's manufacture.

While Gamson's study concentrates on consumers of television and film celebrities, most of his points seem to hold good for sports fans. If anything, they are more self-reflective than Gamson's subjects. After all, they must realize that the celebrities they follow are susceptible not only to their fickle tastes, but to changes of form, injuries, capricious coaches, and several other contingencies that might sweep a well-planned showbusiness career off course. Celebrity athletes survive, prosper, or perish in a fast-changing and unstable environment, where the reference points are constantly shifting.

They sometimes shift in totally unexpected ways. Think "Eric the Eel" or "Eddie the Eagle," both inept athletes who leapt to eminence thanks to cutely ironic nicknames and the penchant of the media to laud abject failure at the Olympic Games. They proved that celebritydom beckons not only for winners; but also for willing failures. Neither athlete made much of a lasting impression, though they probably made a nice packet of money in the immediate aftermath of their "triumphs."

Celebrity culture has in some way affected every feature of sports. Skim back over the past chapters and imagine the impact it has had on, for example, the mental approach of athletes (Chapter 6). Are prospective sportsmen and women motivated by success in sports, or is success in sports the means to another end? Young people dream about becoming the next Woods or Beckham. Would they settle for being a champion golfer, or the England soccer captain? Or are they really aspiring to the adulation and zealotry inspired by these athletes? The emasculation of sports, as we called it in Chapter 7, is very much in harmony with celebrity culture. Celebrity culture emphasizes aestheti-cism, that is, an appreciation of the beauty, or art, of a performance, rather than its functionality or end result. Sports in which women have traditionally excelled were often regarded as borderline sports, not because they didn't involve skill, but because they were evaluated on aesthetic performance rather than goals, touchdowns, or tries: synchronized swimming, ice dancing, gymnastics. Men participate in all of these and many other sports in which women compete, of course. Yet, they have strong associations with women and this had the effect of maintaining their marginal status, a status that has undergone a revamp in recent years.

Celebrity culture has ushered in celebrity athletes whose ethnic identities might, at a different time, have limited their prospects of attracting the big endorsement deals that are so vital to celebrity status. It barely needs stating that the first genuinely global celebrity athlete was, of course, Michael Jordan, whose well-planned route to the top was mapped in Chapter 15. Celebrity culture would simply not have been possible without the advent of the global media and the intricate circuitry it established with sports (Chapters 13 and 14).

Has celebrity culture had an impact on doping, as discussed in Chapter 10? There's no obvious connection. But think: the prizes now available to elite athletes go far beyond medals and trophies, even far beyond the cash, much of it as there is. The risks are there, but the benefits are colossal. The difference between first and fourth place was once a variance, a margin by which the most excellent surpassed the very, very good. By the twenty-first century, it meant the difference between world renown and obscurity. Do you remember the men's Olympic 100 meters winner? Of course. How about the fourth placed runner? Or the third, or even second? Winners are fêted and revered in a way once reserved for showbiz stars. Is it any wonder, with such incentives on the line, athletes succumb to temptation?

Celebrity culture is all-pervasive and, though, I've dedicated a chapter to its inspection, it actually permeates the book. There's no facet of sports today that remains untouched by celebrity culture. Perhaps this helps explain why so many premier athletes are coopted into a world in which political issues are nullified or suppressed. It's difficult to imagine a figure like Muhammad Ali, who so stridently opposed the war in Vietnam in the 1960s, or a renegade like Tommie Smith, or even a friend of Fidel Castro, like Diego Maradona, surfacing today.

There is one more facet of celebrity culture that we should flag: that is, the body. The changing human body has, of course, been a central theme in this book and we will return to it yet again in the concluding chapter. One of the byproducts, or perhaps main products, of celebrity culture has been what we might call an organized dissatisfaction with the body. In its infancy, the cosmetics industry, as we have seen, fastened on to the insight that the way to sell products was by infusing them with values rather than actual things. It didn't take long for them to personify these values, largely through Hollywood stars, who were signed up to all manner of products that were supposed to make consumers look like them. This has been an enduring convention in the cosmetics industry, of course.

Prior to the 1980s, advertisers were involved in promoting an organized dissatisfaction with the human body, encouraging discontent with appearances and instilling concerns about personal hygiene. The plethora of products from toothpaste to deodorants to make-up was aimed at meeting this satisfaction. In the age of celebrity, there was less need for direct advertising. As we noticed before, the celebrities themselves were moving advertisements for the good life. Living that life involved having symmetrical features, full lips, clear skin, lustrous hair, narrow waists, and, of course, no cellulite. For women, ample breasts were favored; for men slab-like pecs and a six-pack. There are products to fix most of these; and, failing that, surgical procedure. If the arrangement had been designed, it would have been inspired: celebrities unwittingly promoting an entire industry – just by being there, being watched, and being admired.

We consume products that deliver desirability, sexual attraction being the main one, but also friendship, masculinity, health, and so on. Every celebrity that sashays across our tv screen doesn't necessarily personify all of these, but, in a sense, they are all purveyors of one or more of these appealing properties; if only because they are seen as successful – we're watching them, not vice versa.

## OF RELATED INTEREST

*Understanding Celebrity* by Graeme Turner (Sage, 2004) is one of a number of books devoted to exploring the reasons for the rise of celebrity culture and its consequences. Among the others are Chris Rojek's *Celebrity* (Reaktion, 2001) and David Giles's *Illusions of Immortality: A psychology of fame and celebrity* (Macmillan, 2000). Earlier works include P. D. Marshall's *Celebrity and Power: Fame in contemporary culture* (University of Minneapolis Press, 1997) and *Celebrity: The media as image makers* edited by James Monaco (Delta, 1978).

*Claims to Fame: Celebrity in contemporary America* by Joshua Gamson (University of California Press, 1994) proposes the fascinating argument that fans "participate more actively in the commodification and management of celebrities" than we typically acknowledge. They are, in fact, co-producers.

*Sports Stars: The cultural politics of sporting celebrity* edited by David A. Andrews and Steven J. Jackson (Routledge, 2001) is a collection of essays, each isolating a celebrity athlete. *Beckham*, 2nd edition (Polity, 2004) and *Tyson: Nurture of the beast* (Polity, 2004) are my own contributions to this area of study.

*Consuming Sport: The consumption spectacle and surveillance of contemporary sports fans* by Garry Crawford (Routledge, 2004) examines how fans engage with and experience sports. It traces how people become involved in sports and how it affects them over a life course. Tradition and locality might once have been important, but they have been overwhelmed by media and merchandising in their influence on fans.

## ASSIGNMENT

You are a sports agent. One of your clients is a leading football player who is eager to expand his portfolio of endorsement contracts. A new men's magazine, specializing in sports, sex, and cars requires the services of your client and he agrees to do a photoshoot. Weeks later, you receive the relevant issue and discover that your client is featured with a case of beer swinging from his penis. You call your client and he informs you that he happily consented to the shot. The circulation of the magazine soars. You are subsequently inundated with solicitations for him to do advertising spots for internet porn sites, condoms, and sex toys. He is agreeable, but you equivocate: while you'll gladly take your commission from all his earnings, you wonder if his long-term interests are best served by involvement in these kinds of promotions. Email him a message, explaining how the rewards of celebrity culture can often turn to punishment and why you are dubious about the abundance of offers.

*burning* **QUESTION**

---

### is being left-handed an advantage in sports?

According to at least two theories, yes. Considering that, in any given population and at any time, between 8 and 10 percent of people are left-handed, the number of top-class sports performers seems disproportionately high. Any survey of sports "greats" is bound to include Babe Ruth, Rod Laver, Martina Navratilova, Marvin Hagler, and Wasim Akram – all lefties. There are numerous others. To explain this, we need to understand why people are left-handed at all.

The word *sinistral*, meaning a left-handed person, has an interesting etymology, deriving from the Latin for "left," *sinister*, which also means an evil omen (sinister-looking person), or something malignant (sinister motive). Historically, there was little difference: left-handed people were associated with malevolence. As that myth receded, it was replaced by more enlightened empirical research, much of which still suggested some sort of undesirable characteristics or even pathology.

Left-handedness is a distinctly human trait: other animals show no bias or preference in claws, paws, hoofs, fins, etc. Most theories are based on the lateralization of the brain, that is the degree to which the right and left cerebral hemispheres of the brain differ in specific functions. The human brain is divided into two hemispheres, the left side often being described as the dominant half because that is where the centers of language and speech and of spatial perception are located in most people. Nerves on the two sides of the body cross each other as they enter the brain, so that the left hemisphere is associated with the right-hand side of the body. In most right-handed people the left hemisphere directs speech, reading, and writing, while the right half is responsible for emotions.

For years, it was thought that left-handedness was the result of a kind of reversal of the more usual pattern, with the main functions of the brain being on the right. But, in the 1970s, research by J. Levy and M. Reid (in *Science* vol. 194, 1976) showed that, in fact, most left-handers are still left-brain dominant and have their centers of language, speech, and spatial perception in the same place as right-handers.

Two lines of research led to the conclusion that there was a close connection between left-handedness and physical fitness. The most influential theory was that of Geschwind and Galaburda, who, in 1987, proposed that there was an association between left-handedness and immune or immune-related disorders. This stemmed from birth-related problems. Left-handedness was also related to

423

disabilities, such as stammering and dyslexia. Later studies cast doubt on these conclusions.

A second line of research came to light in 1991 in a widely reported article in *Psychological Bulletin* (no.109). In it, the authors Coren and Halpern claimed that left-handers die sooner than right-handers. The mean age of death for lefties was 66 compared with 75 for righties. Coren and Halpern gave two explanations for this. First, environment: we live in a world that has been designed and built with right-handed people in mind. Door handles, telephones, cars: the construction of these and countless other technological features reflects right-handedness. So, when left-handed people perform even the simplest of functions, they find them slightly more awkward and so have a higher risk of accidents (and accident-related injuries). Several subsequent studies confirmed that lefties were more prone to accidents.

Second, birth problems: referring back to the Geschwind and Galaburda studies, Coren and Halpern hypothesized that exposure to high fetal testosterone at birth may lead to developmental problems for left-handed people. This particular aspect and, indeed, the whole early-death theory did not go unchallenged and other studies both refuted the findings and uncovered others. For instance, Warren Eaton and a research team from the University of Manitoba took one strand of Coren and Halpern's research and argued that: "Indirect evidence for an association between sinistrality [left-handedness] and maturational lag can be found from the fact that males, who are more likely to be left-handed, are less advanced in language and skeletal development than are females" (*Journal of Child Psychology and Psychiatry and Allied Disciplines*, 37/5, 1996). On closer examination, however, direct evidence was not forthcoming.

The research supporting or refuting the relationship between left-handedness and early death, accident-proneness, physical immaturity, and other pathologies continues, though little light has been thrown on the exceptional sphere of sports. If, as most of the evidence suggests, lefties are disadvantaged in some way, how come so many of them rise to the top in sports? One interesting theory came from a French biologist, Michel Raymond, of the University of Montpellier, who published his views in the *Proceedings of the Royal Society* (December 1996). Marshaling data about athletes, including both amateurs and world-class professionals, Raymond concluded that, compared to their total size in the population, lefties are over-represented in sports.

The reason for this is: left-handers have an advantage in confrontation sports – those sports in which an opponent is directly confronted, including boxing, fencing, and tennis, as well as team sports such as baseball, cricket, and basketball. There is no over-representation of southpaws in non-confrontation sports, such as track or swimming, in which opponents compete alongside each other. Not only are lefties over-represented in confrontational sports, they are especially good at them. And, the closer the interaction between opponents, the greater the prevalence of left-handers. So, we would expect more southpaw boxers than lefty baseball hitters or pitchers and even fewer left-handed rugby players.

Yet even in sports like baseball and cricket where competitors face each other at several yards distance, there are more than the expected number of lefties. The researchers found that, over a six-year period, about 16 percent of top tennis players were left-handed and between 15 and 27 percent of bowlers in international cricket and pitchers in Major League Baseball. For close-quarter sports, the difference is more pronounced: 33 percent of competitors in the men's world foils championships, increasing to 50 percent by the quarter-final stage of the competition. Remember: this is a group that represents 10 percent of the total male population at most. The pattern was less marked for women, though there was still over-representation at the fencing championships.

One tempting thought is that, if left-handed people are disadvantaged in several areas of development and functionality, they may be overcompensated when it comes to sports skills, like hand-to-eye coordination, quick reflexes, astute judgment, tactical awareness, or just raw strength. Or, it could simply mean that the sheer fact of favoring one's left arm in a context geared to right-hand biases lends the southpaw a strategic advantage. Because of the frequency of right-handers in any given population, sports performers are habituated in training and in competition to facing other righties. So, left-handers, because of their relative scarcity, have an edge of sorts: they hit, run, and move in unexpected ways.

Certainly, sports are full of stories of orthodox (left leg forward) boxers who detest fighting southpaws because of the special problems they pose. These include having to jab along the same path as the opponent's jab and constantly having one's front foot trodden on. Baseball hitters swing at the ball in such a way that their momentum carries their bodies in the direction they want to move to get to first base; saving fractions of a second can be vital in a game where fielding is crisp and accurate. Pitchers, like cricket bowlers, can deliver at unfamiliar angles. Returning serve against left-handers is known to be difficult for a right-hander, especially defending the advantage court; lefties are known for their ability to cut the ball diagonally across the body of the receiver. In basketball, a portsider typically tries to pass opponents on the side they least expect; there is barely time to determine whether the opponent is left-handed or not.

The strategic advantage of playing against opponents who are used to a different pattern of play seems to be the answer to the preponderance of them in some sports. In others, where being left-handed counts for little, their prevalence is about the same as in the general population. According to Raymond et al. (1996), 9.6 percent of goalkeepers in soccer are lefties; and left-handed field-eventers account for 10.7 percent of all competitors. At the top levels of darts, snooker, bowling, and gymnastics, lefties are actually under-represented.

Somehow, they gravitate toward the sports in which they possess a natural advantage. There are, of course, notable exceptions: world champion pole vaulter Stacy Dragila is a lefty.

An anonymous journalist with *The Economist* magazine (in "Left-handedness: Sinister origins," February 15, 1997) adds an evolutionary level to this argument: over the years, the strategic advantage enjoyed by lefties outweighed the other possible disadvantage uncovered by the aforementioned psychological research. Natural selection, of course, favors the best physically equipped (strongest) species, which survived and were able to pass on their genes to their children. This would account, albeit in a crude way, for the persistence of left-handed people in an environment built largely by and for right-handers and in which social pressures (such as associating sinistrality with wrong-doing) might reasonably have expected to pressure lefties to change their biases.

*More questions . . .*

- Is left-handedness still an advantage in sports that involve less use of the arms, like soccer or diving?
- How might you set about changing a naturally left-handed child into a right-hander?
- Do left-handers pose particular problems for coaches/managers?

*Read on . . .*

- Stanley Coren, *Left Hander: Everything you need to know about left-handedness* (John Murray, 1992).
- Lauren J. Harris, "Do left-handers die sooner than right-handers? Commentary on Coren and Halpern's (1991) 'Left-handedness: A marker for decreased survival fitness'" *Psychological Bulletin* (vol. 114, no. 2, September, 1993).
- P. Muris, W. J. Kop, and H. Merckelbach, "Handedness, symptom resorting and accident susceptibility" *Journal of Clinical Psychology*, vol. 50, no. 3 (May, 1994).
- K. Pass, H. Freeman , J. Bautista, and C. Johnson, "Handedness and accidents with injury" *Perceptual and Motor Skills* vol. 77 no. 3 (December, 1993).

# same rules, different game

## why politics has always been a factor in international sports

### FREE OR FULL?

"Sport is completely free of politics." So said Avery Brundage in his capacity as president of the International Olympic Committee, in 1956. He was responding to an event that actually undermined his point: the withdrawal of six Olympic member countries from the Melbourne games in protest at the military conflicts in Hungary and Suez. Whether Brundage was being disingenuous, hypocritical, or just naive, we will never know. But, history has made his statement seem plainly absurd; far from being "free of politics," sport is full of politics.

The Melbourne protests were part of a general pattern established long before 1956 and which continue to the present day. In fact, since 1956, every summer Olympics has been implicated in some sort of political controversy. The most common form of political gesture has been the boycott. Countries absenting themselves from the Olympic Games, either as a sign of protest, or because of exclusion, have been a feature of Olympic history. Boycotts usually make headlines and attract the rhetoric of interested parties who talk regretfully about how unfortunate it is that sports and politics have become mixed up. But, then again, they mix so well. Why?

The Olympic Games have the kind of generic relevance that makes them a perfect theater in which to play out political dramas. Ostensibly sporting occasions, the games have continually managed grandly to capture tensions, protests, and sometimes atrocities that encircle the world. By celebrating the alleged unity, at least in spirit, of the world's population, the Olympic Games have sought temporarily to suspend terrorism, racism, imperialism, and other "worldly" matters that are the bane of our age. Instead, they have been hijacked by them. The setting and imagery of the games have been used to dramatize events seemingly unconnected with sports. So many of the themes inherent in sports have political and ideological potential: nationalism, competition, the pursuit of supremacy, the heroism of victory; all have a wider application. Differences between the contrived competition of the track and field events and the real conflict in the streets have often melted in the spectacle of the Olympics.

When political factions, or even whole nations, consciously manipulate events to make their points decisively and dramatically, they often opt for sports, in the safe knowledge that the rest of the world will be so outraged that it will take immediate notice. For example, a press conference in New York to announce that civil rights in the USA have amounted to nothing and that the majority of African Americans and Latinos are still struggling in poverty will gain a response from the media of "so what?" Announce the same message, this time silently and symbolically, with just two African Americans disdaining the US national anthem and wait for the media to go to work. You have a political event on a near-epic scale.

The difference? In the latter example, the two people in focus are Olympic track medalists and the moment they choose to make their gesture is after being awarded their medals on the victory rostrum at the 1968 Olympic Games in Mexico City. Sport worked as an instantly effective vehicle for what was obviously a political statement. The unspoken protest was louder and clearer than any other in the post-civil rights era. The event itself has a place alongside Martin Luther King's "I have a dream" speech as one of the most potent messages about racial inequality. The image of the two Olympians, their heads bowed to avoid looking at the stars and stripes, their fists pointed upward in an unequivocal act of defiance, is one of the most famous sporting representations of the twentieth century.

For Tommie Smith and John Carlos, the US athletes on the rostrum, and the organization behind them which orchestrated the protest, the Olympic Games were perfect: an effective vehicle for publicizing an openly political statement. The massive publicity it received and the fact that people still remember it today underscores the point: sport *is* political, if only because of its proven utility. It draws attention to particular issues, disseminates messages internationally, and occasionally eases or exacerbates diplomatic relations.

In this chapter, we'll see the diverse – and, to some, perverse – ways in which the development of sports has been and will continue to be influenced by political considerations. We will also see how sports are just too useful not to be used politically. Denials of this slip freely from the lips of those who have interests in presenting sport as an independent, transcendent force, one of few jewels decorating a tarnished crown. But, as we will also see later, those who have argued this are often the biggest culprits and their messages have been subterfuge, covering up their own misdemeanors.

# THE END OF OLYMPIAN INNOCENCE

In his book *Sport and Political Ideology*, John Hoberman makes the point: "Sport is a latently political issue in any society, since the cultural themes which inhere in a sport culture are potentially ideological in a political sense" (1984: 20). Nationalism, competition, and segregation are just three of the more obvious themes that spring to mind. They all came together in 1936. If sports ever had an age of innocence, it ended in that year: the Berlin summer Olympics were an occasion for Nazis to flex their Aryan muscles and demonstrate the physical supremacy of the "master race." Adolf Hitler had expressed his doctrine of racial superiority and sought an international stage on which to reveal tangible evidence of this.

In his original conception, Coubertin saw the Olympics as having bridge-building potential. He wanted to bring nations of various political ideologies together in a spirit of healthy competition. Participation was considered to be more important than winning and the only politics that mattered were the politics of unity. Hitler's visions were as ambitious, though less noble. The political ideology he wished to propagate concerned the dominance of one nation, or more specifically, one race, over all others; his philosophy was of the disunity rather than oneness of humanity. While the blatant use of sports as a propagandist tool was roundly denounced, subsequent hosts of the Olympics weren't slow to realize the potential of the games and often turned them into jingoistic extravaganzas. Still, it seems fair to suggest that the particular utility Hitler found in sports warrants special attention, if only as the benchmark against which to gage later expressions of nationalism.

Friedrich Ludwig Jahn's gymnastics *Turnen* movement of the nineteenth century was partly designed to prepare German youth to wage war against Napoleon. Jahn was a significant figure in fostering the "volkish" thought, which eventually gained political expression in Nazism, with its leitmotif of an overarching German essence. This was to be made visible through displays of physical control and strength, "a spectacle of masculine power." His sexism was complemented by racism. "Every real man must choose a mother from among his own people for his children," he asserted. "Any other marriage is an animal coupling" (quoted in Kühnst, 2004: 77).

Hitler had no interest in sports other than this: to express national superiority and internal unity. The Weimar Republic had assisted the growth of sports in Germany as part of the general restoration of morale after the First World War. But, under Hitler's National Socialism, it came to mean much more.

"Fitness was declared a patriotic obligation," writes historian Richard Mandell in his *The Nazi Olympics* (1971).

Nazism represented an extreme right-wing form of government organized to advance an aggressive brand of nationalism. Its particular virulence was provided by Aryanism, a philosophy of racial purity that informed much, if not all, of Hitler's endeavors. Among its manifestations was a commitment to rid Germany of its Jewish presence and an attempt to propagandize the supremacy of the Caucasian "race."

Sports surfaced as a perfect showcase for Nazism. During the 1920s, its potential for drawing not just audiences, but masses, had convinced organizers and promoters that the concept behind the Olympics could be adapted. Association football, in particular, had been exported from England and become *fútbol* in Spain, *voetbal* in Holland, *futebol* in Brazil, and *Fußball* in Germany. After the success of the inaugural World Cup in 1930, Italy, then under the fascist rule of Benito Mussolini, staged the 1934 tournament. It was a colossal triumph: not only did Italy win the trophy, beating favorites Austria in the process, but the slickness of the organization and the prestige associated with the competition reflected well on Mussolini's regime. Encouraged by this, Hitler sought an even more dramatic exploitation of a sporting event for political ends. Hosting a global event like the Olympics would, he anticipated, confer a certain legitimacy on Nazi Germany, symbolizing his own importance in international terms.

The anti-Semitism that characterized Nazism affected sport. In 1933, Hitler pulled Germany out of the League of Nations, an organization formed in 1920 in response to the destruction of life during the First World War. Its purpose was to stop war and disputes liable to lead to war (in 1946, its functions were taken over by the United Nations). When a boycott of Jewish businesses came into effect in Germany, the organizing bodies of sport excluded Jewish performers and officials. Two years later there was complete segregation in German sport, something that clearly contradicted Olympic ideals. In the USA, an abortive boycott campaign targeting the proposed 1936 Olympics failed to command support. Brundage, the then president of the American Olympic Committee, warned that: "Certain Jews must now understand that they cannot use these Games as a weapon in their boycott against the Nazis" (quoted in Hain 1982: 233). Germany reassured the world that the extent of anti-Semitism and segregation had been exaggerated and, to underline this, included the fencer, Helene Mayer, who was "half-Jewish", in the national team.

Newsreel depicts Hitler's leaving the Berlin stadium in apparent disgust as African American athlete Jesse Owens shook the ramparts of the Nazi's ideological platform by winning four gold medals. Doctrines of racial supremacy seemed ridiculous. Yet Hitler's departure was an uncomfortable moment in what was in other respects a satisfactory and rewarding Nazi spectacle. Not only did Germans lead the medal table, they "demonstrated to the whole world that the new Germans were administratively capable, generous, respectable, and peace loving," as Mandell puts it (1984: 244). "Hitler, particularly, was greatly emboldened by the generally acknowledged, domestically and internationally, triumph of this festival grounded on the pagan (though very new) rituals of modern sport" (1984: 245). In terms of propaganda, the entire Olympic project was of value to the Nazis: as the world exulted, Germany stepped up its rearmament program and stamped down on Jews.

Repercussions went beyond the Olympic movement. Before the games, in December 1935, an international game of soccer between England and Germany in London was opposed by Jewish organizations, supported by the Trades Union Congress and the Communist Party. In the event, the match went ahead. In a subsequent international game in 1938, this time in Germany, the England team was instructed to give the Nazi salute as the German national anthem was played before the match. Thanks to newsreel, the moment will live on as one of English sport's most mortifying moments, coming as it did so close to the outbreak of the Second World War

Only in retrospect was the full resonance of the "Nazi Olympics" realized. No single games since has approached it in terms of ideological pitch. Its sheer scale deserved the posterity afforded it by the openly propagandist film directed by Leni Riefenstahl, *Olympia*, which idealized German sportsmen as *übermenschen*, or supermen, as we saw in Chapter 12.

After 1936, no summer Olympics meeting escaped political incident. The defeated nations of Germany, Italy, and Japan were excluded from the first games after the war in London in 1948. Holland, Egypt, Iraq, and Spain boycotted the 1956 games in protest at the British and French invasion of Suez. In 1964, South Africa was suspended and subsequently expelled from the Olympic movement (in 1970). Zimbabwe, then Rhodesia, a country which adopted a similar system of stratification to apartheid, was barred in 1972, having made a Unilateral Declaration of Independence from the Commonwealth. New Zealand maintained sporting links with South Africa in the face of world opinion and the fact that it too wasn't expelled from the Olympics spurred 25 African nations to boycott the 1976 games in Montreal. Boycotts have since proliferated. Taiwan also withdrew after it was refused permission to compete as "China."

The USA team pulled out of the Moscow games in 1980 after the Soviet invasion of Afghanistan. British Prime Minister Margaret Thatcher exhorted British athletes not to go, but the British Olympic Association went ahead. Soviet bloc countries (except Romania) and their allies replied by steering clear of Los Angeles in 1984, though China sent a limited delegation of 200 athletes. The LA games were the most shamelessly nationalistic Olympics since 1936, though, as Rick Gruneau argues, "in no way a significant departure from practices established in earlier Olympics" (1984: 2).

In 1988, Cuba stayed away from Seoul after the South Korean government refused to share events with North Korea (which itself pulled out). In 1992, the political tensions were primarily internal, Barcelona, the host, being a municipality with a strong conservative tendency and nationalist Catalonian feelings. Its problem was in maintaining its autonomy while seeking the assistance of Spain's central government in Madrid. As Christopher Hill commented in the first edition of his *Olympic Politics*: "The political affinity one might expect it [Madrid] to have with Barcelona seems often to be strained by the rivalry between the two cities, as well as by the different traditions from which the national and local socialist parties spring" (1996: 219–20). Every Olympics has been associated with some form of political issue, which has often prompted boycotts.

Apart from boycotts, incidents internal to the games sometimes led commentators to suggest that the Olympics themselves were hemorrhaging so badly that they would have to be either stopped, or scaled down drastically. If any single event can be said to have provoked this, it was that at Munich in 1972 when eight Palestinians occupied the Israeli team's quarters and demanded the release of 200 Palestinian prisoners in Israel. Negotiations proved fruitless and gunfire opened up. Eleven athletes were killed. There followed a day's mourning before the competition resumed. Brundage, by this stage notorious for his blundering efforts to separate sport and politics, drew parallels between the politically charged incident with the equally political but quite different attempt to force the IOC into squeezing out racist Southern Rhodesia.

The games immediately preceding this, in Mexico in 1968, had underscored the point made so strongly by Berlin's "Nazi Olympics": that sport, given its world prominence, can be an effective stage on which to make a political point. The point in question was made by two black US track athletes, Tommie Smith and John Carlos, their fists clenched as if punching a hole in the American dream – as we covered previously.

Officials of the IOC have often arraigned politicians for urging their countries to use sporting occasions for political ends. Ascending to the moral high ground, they have stuck to the Brundage line and censured deviations from this. Yet, their bluster has obscured an inner politics of untrammeled corruption, greed, and manipulation at the very core of the IOC. While stories of venality in the ranks of the IOC had circulated since the publication of Vyv Simson and Andrew Jennings's *The Lords of the Rings: Power, money and drugs in the modern Olympics* in 1992, it was not until 1999 that a true measure of the degradation was revealed. We will return to this later in the chapter.

## Political Olympics

**1936, Berlin** Usually seen as the first games used for propagandist purposes. Hitler showcased his political regime with the most spectacular and well-run games to date.

**1948, London** The defeated nations of Germany, Italy, and Japan were excluded from the first games after the war.

**1952, Helsinki** The first games attended by a team from the communist Soviet Union. The difference in political ideology was reflected in the domestic arrangements: the Soviet team was housed in a separate village from teams representing Western nations.

**1956, Melbourne** Boycotts from Spain, Switzerland, and Holland over the Soviet invasion of Hungary and from Egypt, Lebanon, and Iraq over the takeover of the Suez Canal.

**1960, Rome** The last games for 32 years for a team from South Africa. The IOC impose its ban because of South Africa's maintenance of apartheid.

**1964 Tokyo** South Africa suspended from the Olympic movement and subsequently expelled (in 1970).

**1968, Mexico** The "black power" Olympics, where Smith and Carlos signaled their protest with heads bowed and defiant fists during the medals ceremony for the 200 meters.

**1972, Munich** Eleven members of the Israeli team taken hostage and killed by the Palestinian Black September group. Southern Rhodesia made Unilateral Declaration of Independence from the Commonwealth and was excluded.

**1976, Montreal** The most significant boycott to date: 25 African nations withdrew over New Zealand's inclusion in the games. The Kiwis had earlier toured South Africa. A year later, the Gleneagles Agreement blacklisted South Africa.

**1980, Moscow** The Soviet invasion of Afghanistan prompted US president, Jimmy Carter, to pull the USA team from the games, and several other nations followed suit.

**1984, Los Angeles** Retaliating for 1980, the Soviet Union withdrew its team, leading 13 other nations in a mass boycott.

**1988, Seoul** The democratized South Korea was boycotted by its neighbor, North Korea as well as Cuba, Ethiopia, and Nicaragua.

**1992, Barcelona** The first post-apartheid games, with the ban on South Africa removed. No boycotts for the first time since 1972.

**1996, Atlanta** One death and 110 injuries after the explosion of a pipebomb in the year following the Oklahoma bombing.

**2000, Sydney** North and South Korea marched under the same flag.

**2004, Athens** US team stayed on an ocean liner rather than in Olympic village because of the perceived threat of attack from Al Qaeda.

## POSTCOLONIAL CONFLICT

During the colonial era, cricket, one of the world's oldest organized sports, was both a symbol of Britain's imperial dominance and a conduit for civilization. The belief was that, if you can teach subordinate groups of the empire the rules, etiquette, and proprieties of the gentlemen's game, then you were helping civilize them out of their barbaric ways. For long, the administrative power of the sport, like that of the empire was in the grasp of England, though, in the postcolonial era, with the independence of what were formerly colonies and the replacement of the empire by the Commonwealth, changes introduced new tensions.

South Africa was declared a white dominion, that is, a self-governing state, in 1910. The majority black population was excluded from all areas of political influence. A rigid system of segregation known as apartheid was institutionalized in 1948 and vigorously enforced after 1958 under the leadership of Nazi sympathizer Hendrik Verwoerd (1906–66). In 1956, South Africa made a formal declaration of its sports policy program, which, it insisted, should stay within the boundaries of its general policy of apartheid. Justifications, unnecessary as they were in a country utterly controlled and dominated by the numerically small white population, included the arguments that black people had no "aptitude" for sport and the alleged potential for conflict in "mixed" teams and crowds of spectators.

On the second point: black people, who constituted over 70 percent of South Africa's total population, were barred from a new rugby stadium in Bloemfontein in 1955. In the following year, Bishop Trevor Huddleston, who was to become a prominent member of the anti-apartheid movement, observed that sports may be South Africa's Achilles heel, in the sense that its national teams were so obviously good in certain sports, particularly Rugby Union. To deny South Africa the opportunity to demonstrate its excellence would, as Huddleston put it in his *Naught for Your Comfort*, "shake its self-assurance very severely" (1956: 202).

Verwoerd's commitment to retain apartheid influenced his decision to withdraw South Africa's application for continued membership of the Commonwealth. In 1961, South Africa became a republic. Separate lands were apportioned to the black population and legislation in 1963 and 1964 ensured that black people were reduced to the status of chattel. The physical segregation

---

### Apartheid

An Afrikaans word, meaning "apartness" or total separation. In the context of South Africa, where it defined official policy, it referred to the segregation of white people and those defined as "non-whites." Apartheid has its roots in the white master/black slave relationships of seventeenth-century colonialism. The Dutch developed a small slave colony in Cape Town (on the Atlantic coast) in the 1650s and began to supply fresh produce to ships sailing from Europe to Asia. In the eighteenth and nineteenth centuries, Dutch settlers known as Boers (farmers) moved into the inner regions of Southern Africa. The Boers' incursions brought them into severe conflict with native peoples, such as the Khoikhoi (Hottentots, as they were called by the Boers) from the Cape and Bantu tribes from the southeast. The black native peoples were suppressed by the 1870s and the Boers constructed a series of all-white republics in the Orange Free State and the Transvaal. The division between the black and the white population was fully institutionalized in 1948 when the Afrikaner Nationalist Party came to power. In a technical sense, apartheid's dissolution began in 1990 when South Africa's Premier, F. W. de Klerk, authorized the release of Nelson Mandela and announced the attempted transition to a liberal, multi-ethnic, democratic nation.

was backed up by police brutality and a repressive state that dealt unsympathetically with any attempt to challenge its authority – as the slayings at Sharpeville in 1960 indicated. Individual athletes and teams visiting South Africa were expected to "respect South Africa's customs as she respected theirs," according to South Africa's policies (quoted in Horrell 1968: 9).

Another world power in rugby, New Zealand, had traditionally selected Maoris in its national team, but capitulated to South Africa by picking only white players to tour. This opened up a national controversy in 1960, especially when a New Zealand tour went ahead despite the atrocities at Sharpeville. This event crystallized many fears about South Africa, and a cricket tour in Britain in its aftermath prompted demonstrations. Sporadic protests continued, both at street level and at official levels.

The integration-oriented South African Non-Racial Olympic Committee (SANROC) was launched in 1962 with the intention that it should apply for recognition from the International Olympic Committee and officially replace the whites-only Olympic and National Games Association. The government pre-empted matters by banning SANROC. As the 1964 Olympic Games drew near, the IOC, whose charter forbids racial discrimination, demanded large concessions from South Africa before its entry could be approved. Some compromises were made in the trials, but the South African government maintained its insistence that sport comply with "custom"; so South Africa was denied entry to the Tokyo games.

New Zealand continued to send touring rugby sides to South Africa amid negotiations aimed at allowing the entry of Maoris. But, in a key speech in 1965, Verwoerd reaffirmed that no Maori players would be allowed to enter South Africa. Coming from the country's leader, the message was filled with political significance. In 1966, New Zealand finally declined an invitation to tour, but accepted another extended in 1968 under a new South African premier, John Vorster. In the interim, newly independent African states had begun to recognize South Africa's vulnerability to sporting boycotts and were strenuously trying to convince the rest of the world's sports organizations to expel South Africa. The Supreme Council for Sport in Africa, as the alliance was called, reminded the world that, while sport may conventionally have been regarded as trivial or unrelated to politics, "South Africans do not consider it minor" (quoted in Guelke 1986: 128). Outbursts from Verwoerd and Vorster confirmed this. They left no doubt that what was at first glance a sports issue was also one on which nations' premiers were obliged to dispense judgments.

Against this background, in 1968, an English cricket team arranged to tour the republic. Basil D'Oliveira, a black cricketer who was actually from South Africa's Cape and who had settled in England in 1960, reached the peak of his form. Selected for the English national representative team, he scored a triumphal century against Australia at London's Oval and was, almost without

> ### Sharpeville, 1960
>
> A black township (plot of land reserved for black people) in South Africa that, in March 1960, was the scene of a conflict that ended in 69 deaths (all black) and 180 wounded. It signaled the first organized black resistance to white political rule in South Africa. The Pan-African Congress (PAC) had asked blacks to leave their pass books at home and go to police stations to be arrested. They did so voluntarily, but refused to be dispersed by the police who, eventually, opened fire. Sharpeville triggered nationwide demonstrations. The reaction of the government was to arrest leaders of PAC and the other main black organization, the African National Congress (ANC), and ban both movements.

question, the most effective batsman in the country at the time. Yet when the national team for the winter tour of South Africa was announced, D'Oliveira's name was missing.

David Sheppard, a former England captain, later to become Bishop of Liverpool, led a protest, accusing selectors of submitting to the requirements of apartheid. D'Oliveira, having relatively pale brown skin, was officially classed by South Africans as "colored" and so had no legal right to share facilities with white players. South Africa's team comprised only white players. Several England team members threatened to resign as the protest gathered momentum, prompting the selectors to slip D'Oliveira into the squad as a replacement for an injured bowler, Tom Cartwright. It was an act of unheard-of nerve as far as South Africa's premier John Vorster was concerned: he smartly denounced the squad as "not the team of the MCC [Marylebone Cricket Club – the English governing organization] but the team of the Anti-Apartheid Movement, the team of SANROC [the South African Non-Racial Olympic Committee]."

In Peter Osborne's 2004 account, the MCC was inclined to accommodate South Africa to begin with, though, perhaps wounded by the accusation and certainly refusing to be dictated to, the English team's governing organization called off the tour. Vorster's intransigence and the MCC's pull-out were crucial: the former in hardening South Africa's policy in the face of suspicions that Vorster himself was beginning to soften; the latter in showing the rest of the world's sports governing bodies how they might in future react to South African policies.

The effects were not immediate and in the following January the MCC actually countenanced a projected tour by the South African cricket team in 1970. This was met with a "Stop the Seventy Tour" campaign and a series of disruptions of the Springbok's rugby tour of the UK, which served as a reminder of what would happen to any attempted cricket tour by the South Africans. The cricket tour did not take place. Progressively, more sports minimized or cut contacts with South Africa, effectively ostracizing that country's sport.

The episode itself wasn't the first to surface: it simply captured the elements more dramatically with statements from South Africa, and the refusal of the MCC to be commanded by a regime that had been widely condemned. By grabbing the attention of the world's media, the D'Oliveira case made the sports–South Africa link a significant political as well as sporting topic and one which would press governments into action. The political significance of South Africa in sports had been realized for at least ten years before D'Oliveira forced it into the open.

At a different time in history Vorster's conclusion that the MCC's selection of D'Oliveira was designed, as he expressed it, "to gain certain political objectives," may have passed virtually unnoticed by all those cricket devotees and anti-apartheid campaigners. In 1968, an *annus mirabilis* in which conflicting forces of protest gathered and collided all over the world, its effects were more far-reaching. The year had seen student demonstrations and protests from young people from all over Europe and the United States. Vietnam provided a focal point for the protests, though there was a more generic unrest underlying this. It was a time in history when people began to sense that collective efforts by "the people" could change world events. It was thought that not even apartheid was immune from "people power."

The IOC had already withdrawn its invitation to South Africa to attend the Mexico Olympics. A threat of boycott from about 50 member countries and protests from the black members of the American team were factors in the decision. British Rugby Union, a sport reluctant to dissolve its relationship with South Africa, entertained a Springbok touring team in the 1969–70 season and every match was seriously disrupted by mass demonstrations. The message from the tour was that any future visit by South Africans was likely to be met with a show of force. In May 1970, a planned cricket tour of South Africans to Britain was aborted quickly after the threat of uproar on the D'Oliveira scale in the lead-up to a general election. The same year saw the severance of more links with South Africa: expulsion from the IOC; elimination from the Davis Cup tennis competition; suspension from athletics; and a bar from gymnastics.

Isolation stirred Vorster into action and, in 1971, he announced what he called a "multinational" sports program in which "whites," "Africans," "coloreds," and "Asians" could compete against each other as "nations," but only in international competitions. This rather devious move effectively allowed black sports performers to compete, provided they were affiliated to one of the government's "national" federations. As such it served to divide blacks: some wishing to compete felt compelled to affiliate; others rejected the racist premise of the divisions and refused to affiliate. With international links receding, the government permitted domestic contests between "nations," and later club-level competitions between "nations."

Rugby Union resisted the international trend and, in particular, New Zealand set itself against world opinion by willfully maintaining contacts. During a tour of South Africa in 1976, the near-cataclysmic Soweto uprising (official figures: 575 dead, 2,389 wounded) prompted ever more searching questions. As New Zealand seemed intent on prosecuting links regardless of the upheavals, should it too be isolated? The answer from the black African Olympic member countries was affirmative and New Zealand's admission to the Montreal Olympics in 1976 caused a mass boycott. Thus the crisis deepened.

---

### Soweto, 1976

On June 16, 1976, South African police opened fire on protesting students in Soweto, a large African township near Johannesburg, killing two and injuring many. The students retaliated by attacking government property and officials. Police countered and soon violence spread to every part of the republic except Natal. For months, schools were closed. Students forced workers to stay away from their factories and offices in a series of one-day strikes. Some migrant workers refused and a battle between workers and students resulted in 70 deaths. The total number killed as a result of the conflict which began in Soweto was officially reported as 575 with 2,389 wounded – almost certainly an underestimate.

---

Commonwealth heads of governments met at Gleneagles in Scotland in 1977 to formulate a now-famous agreement "vigorously to combat the evil of apartheid by withholding any form of support for, and by taking every practical step to discourage contact or competition by their nationals with sporting organizations, teams or sportsmen from South Africa." The agreement was between governments not sports organizing bodies and, as subsequent events were to show, the ability of governments to overrule individual organizations was often tested. Rugby's robust stance against governments gave rise to several anomalies.

In 1979, Britain entertained a "mixed" Barbarians side (eight whites, eight "coloreds," and eight blacks). Critics dismissed the team, which was said to reflect the tripartite structure of South African society, as window-dressing. The British Lions' subsequent tours in which they competed with similarly composed teams, met with much the same skepticism. It was, so the argument went, a case of South Africa using sport to project a distortedly liberal image of itself while preserving its essential tyranny and oppression. The majority of black players belonged to the South African Rugby Union (SARU), which remained outside the aegis of the organization from which sides selected for international competition were drawn. Hence the sides were hardly representative.

It was a period of public relations initiated by Pretorian officials bent on convincing the world that every measure was being taken to desegregate sport – though not education, employment, and housing. For all its promises, South Africa fell short on delivery. Invitations went out to individual players of international repute who were drawn by the love of money to South Africa to engage in what were known as rebel tours. Cricketers, buoyant after the triumph of the individual over governing bodies, courtesy of Kerry Packer, went to South Africa in their scores, both to play and to coach, usually in contexts that were notionally "multiracial." British soccer players took short-term contracts to coach, some, like Stanley Matthews, working exclusively with black players. American boxing champions, like Bob Foster and Mike Weaver, both black, defended their titles in South Africa against white boxers. South Africa made no secret of the fact that it had an embarrassment of riches with which to lure top sports performers.

There were prices to pay, however. In 1981, the United Nations special committee against apartheid published its first "blacklist" (an embarrassing misnomer) of sports performers who had worked in South Africa. This served as an effective prohibition and ostracized South Africa further. Starved of decent-quality opposition, promising South Africans, like Sidney Maree, a black athlete, and Zola Budd, who was white, left to campaign abroad. Maree took US citizenship, while Budd was rapidly granted British citizenship. Controversies followed both those leaving South Africa and those who continued to flout the prohibition by going there. British cricketer Robin Jackman, who had played in South Africa, was deported from Guyana in 1981 just as a test match against the West Indies was about to begin. The match was abandoned. Others, like Geoff Boycott and Graham Gooch, were banned for a number of years from test cricket.

It wasn't until 1989 that the International Cricket Conference (ICC) passed a resolution, in defiance of a crucial summons obtained by the right-wing Freedom Association, to formalize sanctions against players, coaches, or administrators who worked in South Africa. Automatic suspensions from test cricket were the penalty. It was the most unambiguous pronouncement on sport and apartheid since the Gleneagles Agreement. The decision was reached after the cancellation of England's scheduled winter tour of India, when Indians refused to play a team that included players with South African connections. "A victory for sport over racism," was how the resolution was greeted by Sam Ramsamy of SANROC. Norris McWhirter, the leader of the Freedom Association, described it as "a crushing blow against cricketers' freedom to trade" and exhorted individual players to take out civil injunctions to prevent ICC carrying

> ## Gleneagles Agreement, 1977
>
> The issue of sporting links with South Africa prompted government involvement at high levels and, in 1977, at Gleneagles, Scotland, Commonwealth heads of government unanimously accepted to override the autonomy of sporting bodies by "taking every practical step to discourage contact or competition by their nationals with sporting organizations, teams or sportsmen from South Africa or from any other country where sports are organized on the basis of race, color and ethnic origin." Sanctions were to be applied to those ignoring the agreement. The full agreement was published by the Commonwealth Secretariat, London.

out its ban. It could be argued against this that the freedom of over 21 million black South Africans to trade – and not just in cricket – was of far greater significance than that of a relatively small number of cricketers.

The election of Nelson Mandela to South Africa's premiership in 1993, and the collapse of apartheid which preceded it, effectively ended the isolation of South Africa in all senses and sporting relations were resumed. South Africa was readmitted in the Olympic movement, its rugby teams were allowed to tour, and its cricket teams were permitted to play test series against the world's other major cricket powers. The West Indies cricket team was the first to tour South Africa after the announcement of apartheid's dissolution in 1991. Black representation in the country's national teams was still scant because of the imprint of several generations of "racialized" sports.

By 2004, when South Africa's apartheid had been consigned to history and the race issue seemed to have abated, another former colony contrived to torment cricket. Zimbabwe, like its neighbor South Africa, had once operated a political system in which segregation was legally enshrined. Also, like South Africa, Southern Rhodesia, as it was, incurred the wrath of the IOC after drawing up a constitution that allowed for white minority rule, then making a Unilateral Declaration of Independence from the Commonwealth in 1965.

Robert Mugabe, a guerrilla fighter who served ten years in prison under the white minority regime, took power in 1979 with the promise of reversing the injustices of colonial rule. He installed his Zanu PF in power and remained in command for over two decades. Yet, his policies were contested: quite apart from manipulating elections to ensure his own party's hold on power, he embarked on a land reclamation that displaced 3,000 white farmers. Critics were dismissed as "puppets of the western world" by John Nkomo, the Zanu PF chair (quoted in zwnews.com/issuefull.cfm, 2004).

From 1999, five straight years of recession left 80 percent of its 12 million citizens in poverty. Unemployment raced to 70 percent and inflation ran at a staggering 650 percent. Global reaction to Mugabe convinced him to take more control of the international media in 2003 and even Zimbabwe's own independent newspaper the *Daily Star* was closed down after mildly critical editorials. Mugabe's influence extended to all levels of society: when, in April, 2004, the Zimbabwe Cricket Union (ZCU) decided that its policy should be to develop black players, fifteen senior white players refused to play in a home test series against Sri Lanka. A depleted Zimbabwean team was hammered continually in the series, prompting the England and Wales Cricket Board (ECB) to consider the rightness of pressing ahead with a planned tour six months on. Cricket's global governing organization, the International Cricket Council threatened international suspension and a $2 million fine if the ECB pulled out, specifying security concerns or an instruction from a national government as the only legitimate reasons for refusing to tour. The British government offered only a recommendation that the tour should not go ahead, but drew short of actually mandating this.

Parallels between this and the South Africa situation were far from exact. Sports was, as Trevor Huddleston noted, the Achilles heel of South Africa, and, after the fall of apartheid, many reflected that the ostracizing of sports made possible by the Gleneagles Agreement had played its part. No one suggested that withdrawing from a tour of Zimbabwe would have remotely comparable effects. Nor was Zimbabwe in the grip of a centuries-old colonial regime under white rulers: it may have been a dictatorship, but a black African presided over it. This, in the eyes of many, made it more difficult to take action without precipitating reaction from some other African states.

The Zimbabwe affair thrust the general issue of sporting links back into focus. Was it legitimate to compete with, tour, and enjoy cordial sporting relations with countries that may have poor human rights records, or tyrannical political regimes, or unsavory cultural prescriptions (for example, about women)? If so, the world of sport would shrink considerably. Western nations would immediately find objectionable features with a great many other nations, which would, conversely, find fault with the likes of Europe and the USA.

## THE CORRUPTING POWER OF MONEY

If there was ever any purity in sports, it was when amateur ideas reigned supremc. As soon as money became involved, corruption followed with the same inevitability as night follows day. As one of the first sports to professionalize, in the 1850s, baseball was always a prime candidate for a major corruption scandal. The 1919 World Series destroyed the image of athletic integrity, perhaps not just for baseball either. If Chicago Black Sox players could be bribed to lose such a momentous and symbolic prize, who could be trusted? Only three years before, a world heavyweight title fight between Jack Johnson and Jess Willard ended inconclusively when the African American champion Johnson went down in the 26th round and made no attempt to regain his feet, virtually gifting the title to a white fighter.

### Corruption

Some form of deception or fraud has probably been present in all organized professional sports. Even amateur sports in which competitors officially receive no money are vulnerable: gambling has been integral to the sports experience and, while there are observers willing to wager on the outcome of a contest, the probability that they will try to control, manipulate, or determine the desired outcome will persist. In horse racing, this has been achieved through administering drugs to the horses, a tactic known as "nobbling." The most usual way of managing a result in a human sport is by bribing competitors, a practice that has been exposed historically in a number of sports, including baseball (Black Sox Scandal of 1919), boxing (the Jack Johnson–Jess Willard fight of 1916), and soccer (the Tony Kay case of 1963).

Soccer, another sport that was professional from its early years (1864), also has a history of venality. Match-fixing scandals have surfaced periodically, the most dramatic in recent history being in 1980 when AC Milan and Lazio were found guilty and relegated as a punishment. Among the players involved was Paul Rossi, the striker, who returned to inspire Italy to victory in the 1982 World Cup. In 2004, the Italian Football Federation launched an inquiry into suspected Mafia-linked illegal betting and match fixing, after two Seina players were suspended. In the same year, the Belgian federation investigated claims that Sporting Charleroi paid another team to help it avoid relegation. In France, Olympique Marseilles was suspended from European competition after its owner attempted to bribe members of the Valenciennes team. In Britain, three senior players were imprisoned and banned for life for fixing games.

But, money circles around rather than resides in some sports and even amateur pursuits attract gamblers. Both college basketball and football have been natural, if unwitting, allies to gambling. As such, they've lent themselves to points shaving, adjusting the score to accommodate spread bettors. Several cases have highlighted how *any* sport is amenable to corruption. But, surely, not the Olympic Games?

In December 1998, Marc Hodler, an IOC member, attended a routine meeting at the Lausanne headquarters of the organization. During press briefings, Hodler, then 81, made allegations about bribery in the IOC. Whispers of bribery and corruption had been heard for some time before Hodler's announcement. But Hodler astonished his colleagues by breaking ranks. There were, he said, four agents who, for a commission of between $500,000 and $1 million, offered to deliver blocks of votes to cities bidding for the right to host the Olympic Games. The agents, one of whom was an IOC member, charged the city that won the vote between $3m and $5 million. Subsequent inquiries, some by the world's media, others by the IOC itself (which produced a report on the subject within a month of Hodler's accusations) revealed a story that centered on the award of the 2002 Winter Olympics to Salt Lake City, Utah.

After Salt Lake City had been turned down in its attempt to stage the 1998 winter Olympic Games, it began to examine why its bid had failed. All cities vying for the right to host the games give IOC members (whose numbers vary, but usually between 95–115) gifts, such as laptop computers, designer luggage, or *objets d'art*. In the run-up to the voting, Nagano, Japan, had employed Goran Takacs as a lobbyist for a fee of $363,000 plus bonuses if the bid succeeded. Goran's father Artur Takacs was a Yugoslavian entrepreneur, and a close adviser to IOC President Juan Antonio Samaranch; he sat near Samaranch at IOC meetings and was influential among IOC members. The meeting to determine the site of the games was held in Birmingham, England, in April 1991. Prior to the voting, Takacs made it known that the president favored the Japanese bid; he later apologized for this impropriety. Nagano won.

Salt Lake City's bid committee set about correcting its mistakes. Over the next four years, it gave away nearly $800,000 in inappropriate "material benefits" to 14 IOC members. The benefits included cash, free housing, medical treatment, scholarships, and jobs. Two rifles valued at $2,000 were given to Samaranch who defended himself by explaining that, as president, he did not take part in the voting. Salt Lake City won the right to host the 2002 games.

The IOC's hastily assembled report in response to Hodler's statements confirmed that there was evidence that IOC members and their relatives had received "benefits" from Salt Lake City officials, in some cases more than $100,000. The report recommended disciplinary action, including expulsion for members involved. Among them was Jean-Claude Ganga, of the Congo, who was said to have made $60,000 profit on a land deal in Utah arranged by a member of the Salt Lake City bid committee. The committee also gave him $50,000 to help feed children in the war-riven Congo and paid for medical care for him and his mother. Another IOC member, Bashir Mohammed Attarabulsi, from Libya, had his son's education at Brigham Young University paid for by the committee, which also arranged living expenses.

The scandal surrounding Salt Lake City shook a few more skeletons out the closet. John Coates, the chair of the Australian Olympic Committee and leader of Sydney's bid for the 2000 Olympics, offered inducements estimated between $35,000 and $70,000 to the Kenyan and Ugandan IOC members at a dinner in Monte Carlo in 1993 – on the eve of the voting which saw Sydney beat Beijing by two votes for the right to host the games. Coates maintained that the money was a contribution toward helping the development of sports in Kenya and Uganda, though he admitted: "We didn't get the Games because of our great facilities or beautiful location" (quoted by Swift 1999: 34).

Melbourne failed in its attempt to host the 1996 games even though its bid committee arranged for the daughter of a South Korean IOC delegate to play with the Melbourne Symphony Orchestra. Atlanta eventually won the vote after high-profile power broker Andrew Young cultivated links with African IOC members to whom he had the bid committee provide athletic gear and other sports-related aid. The lobbying for this event became intense after Athens had reportedly prepared a dossier with details of IOC members' sexual preferences. Berlin allegedly repeated the operation when bidding for the 2000 Olympics.

Evidence, actual or inferential, was found to tarnish the bidding process for every summer and winter Olympics since 1988. There's no reason to suppose that backroom political deals and dubious gifts marked the elections before that date, though the stakes went up appreciably after the stupendous commercial success of the LA games in 1984. The huge costs of running the event are offset by a dozen key sponsors, including Coca-Cola and Kodak, which pay sums in the region of $14 million to use the Olympic five-ring symbol on their merchandise.

Added to this is the extra revenue generated by businesses in the city hosting the games and, importantly, the slice of the television revenues. NBC paid the IOC $3.55 billion for the US tv rights to all Olympics through 2008. The four-year Olympic cycle is estimated to generate some $10 billion. One can imagine, with this kind of money available to host cities, the temptation to leave no stone unturned is great. Perhaps we might also remember that the tv deal itself was not completely untainted by controversy: rival networks were not given the opportunity to submit proposals for the games beyond 2000; rumors of multimillion-dollar payments over and above the $3.55 billion circulated, though without substantiation.

It would be too simple to interpret the whole saga of corruption as the product of human avarice and overweening power. Greed has certainly been a factor, but the conditions under which that greed has been fed must be noted. The Olympic movement's embrace of commercialism, the proliferation of logo'd merchandise, the exorbitant television contracts, the bonanzas enjoyed by host cities: these are some of the other factors that made possible the fulfillment of individual greed. Being awarded an Olympic Games was like being given a cow that produced money instead of milk for its owner.

The International Olympic Committee was founded as a self-appointed association of ambassadors from national sports governing organizations. Athletics was amateur and it was thought the best way to protect amateur sports from corrupting influences was to insulate its members from outside influences; members were not even supposed to accept instructions from their home countries. The ideal was articulated by the Belgian ex-president Henri Baillet-Latour in a conversation with Hitler during the 1936 games. Baillet-Latour saw notices outside restrooms at all the venues warning that Jews and dogs were not allowed in. Hitler refused Baillet-Latour's request to have them removed on the grounds that no one who was invited to a friend's home would tell him or her how to run it. Baillet-Latour's riposte was: "When the five-circled flag is raised over the stadium, it is no longer Germany. It is Olympia and we are the masters here" (quoted in G. Morton 1999: 23).

The Olympic movement strove to remain independent for much of its history. The debacle of Montreal in 1976, in which financial losses were punitive and kickbacks from construction contractors were rife, was a turning point. For a while it looked as if the games had reached an end. The cost of staging what had become a quadrennial extravaganza, each successive host trying to outdo its predecessor, had become too great for even the world's biggest cities to bear. Determined not to let the games disappear, the IOC embraced commercialism, doing deals with sponsors, television companies, and, for many, sacrificing its original ideals. Had such a scandal broke when Brundage was making his pronouncements about sports and politics, it may well have ended the Olympic movement: the hypocricy would have been too much for the movement to bear. But, at the time, it seemed less earth-shattering, though still contemptible.

In a sense, fatigue has set in: we are no longer alarmed when sports are used like political instruments; we are not surprised when individuals get caught up in issues that are far beyond their control; we are not really shocked when we hear that the guardians of sports are themselves debased and dishonest. Perhaps our expectations of sport have changed. No longer do we regard sports as rising above the vileness that dwells in much of political life: sport is part of that political life and cannot help but be affected. Strenuous as efforts may once have been to protect the image of sport as independent and virtuous, the facts tell a different story.

## OF RELATED INTEREST

*Sport, Policy and Politics: A comparative analysis* by Barrie Houlihan (Routledge, 1997) selects five countries, Australia, Britain, Canada, Ireland, and the USA, and studies the different relationships between sports and governments; Houlihan takes particular note of how commerce and international sports federations influence policy making. The book forms a companion to the author's earlier work *Sport and International Politics* (Harvester Wheatsheaf, 1994) and, indeed, his later edited collection *Sport and Society: A student introduction* (Sage, 2003).

*Power, Politics and the Olympic Games* by Alfred E. Senn (Human Kinetics, 1999) is an account of the Olympic movement that deals with the controversies affecting many of the games; the author examines the way in which South Africa's apartheid impacted on several Olympic Games. Also useful, the second edition of Christopher Hill's *Olympic Politics* (Manchester University Press, 1996).

*Basil D'Oliveira* by Peter Osborne (Little, Brown, 2004) sets the cricketer's tribulation against the background of South Africa's politics, and should be read in conjunction with *Trevor Huddleston: A life* by Robin Denniston (Macmillan, 1999), which provides a perspective on the controversies through the life of the man responsible, perhaps more than anyone, for putting apartheid on the international agenda.

*The Lords of the Rings: Power, money and drugs in the modern Olympics* by Vyv Simson and Andrew Jennings (Simon & Schuster, 1992) and *The New Lords of the Rings: Olympics, corruption and how to buy gold medals* (Pocket Books, 1996) were criticized by the IOC when they were first published, but, on reflection, seemed a clear and fair account of the corruption and bribery that pervaded the Olympic movement.

*Football and Fascism: The national game in the international arena under Mussolini* by Simon Martin (Berg, 2004) is a historical account of the way in which football, or *calcio*, as it is called in Italy, was politicized as a way of enhancing Mussolini's international prestige, inculcating nationalist values, and reinforcing conformity in the 1930s.

*Baseball Babylon: From Black Sox to Pete Rose* by D. Gutman (Penguin, 1992) recounts baseball's catalog of crookedness; the book is complemented by Alan Wyke's dated but still impressive *Gambling* (Spring Books, 1964) which looks at the manner in which sports gambling has led logically to attempts to preordain results.

## ASSIGNMENT

You are a national volleyball manager-coach in the final stages of your squad's preparation for a major international tournament to be attended by the world's volleyball powers. In a newspaper feature profiling one of the squad's outstanding attacking players, he/she reveals that he/she is a member of the Order, a group opposed to what it calls ZOG (Zionist Occupation Government) and which, as the newspaper journalist uncovers, has links or sympathies with the Ku Klux Klan, the Posse Comitatus, the Nazi parties of Britain and the USA, and other anti-Semitic and racist groups. What is the likely fall-out and how will you, as manager-coach, deal with it?

# tomorrow's game

## what an ultra-human future

## might bring

### TECHNOLOGY AND THE BODY

To: e.e.cashmore@staffs.edu
From: h.g.wells@timemachine.org
Subject: human machines and science fiction

Hello prof: You can hardly credit it: the biggest debate in sports at the moment is over whether disabled sports should be discontinued. It is 70 years since the inaugural National Wheelchair Games in 1958. As you know, this led to athletic tournaments specifically for disabled competitors, which eventually evolved into the Paralympics. By the turn of the century, international events for the blind and partially sighted, paraplegics, tetraplegics, and amputees were commonplace. Some years ago, some competitors with handicaps demanded admission into the Olympics. Their times and distances were of the requisite qualifying standard and the IOC consented. It didn't take long before amputees (not a term that's used nowadays, by the way), were beating fully-abled rivals in events where you might not expect them to be competitive, such as cycling and the pole vault.

The reason for this is metal/bone integration. Prosthetists used to attach artificial limbs to the remaining portion of an athlete's arm or leg via a socket. We have known that bone melds with metal since the middle of the twentieth century, of course. But, the risk of infection was high. Once this was minimized, it was possible to affix titanium prosthetics in a way

449

that allowed them to bond with human bone. Recently, neuroscientists have perfected a way of tapping into the brain's cerebral cortex with electrodes and using electrical currents to direct the movements of the limb. Effectively, the bionic athlete uses the limb just like any other athlete. Because there is no muscle involved, there is no depletion nor build-up of waste products, making the athlete more efficient in biomechanical terms. This is the reason for the debate. Is it fair? people are asking.

Blind and partially sighted athletes are also being discussed. There have been breakthroughs in surgical procedure that involves implanting a wafer-thin electrode in the visual cortex and which enables what is, in effect, artificial vision. To make this possible, the individual had to carry around equipment that weighed about 25lb. A recent innovation has reduced this to just under a pound. Obviously, in some events this is still a disadvantage. In many others, it is no disadvantage at all and the individuals have argued that they should be allowed to participate in integrated competitions.

Even when I was writing what was to become "science fiction," I never anticipated anything quite like this. Fellow writers had conjectured that man and machine (I'm sorry, I still can't rid myself of the habit of referring to "man" when I mean human. I am after all, from the nineteenth century) would one day fuse, or artificial beings called robots would rule the world. But I'm sure they had nothing like this in mind.

Regards
H. G.

"High performance sport is increasingly contingent upon computer-revealed genetic potentialities . . . absorption of chemical substances, individualized diet and training, and publicity and marketing. The body becomes a means of production," according to Geneviève Rail (1998: 148–9). Rail was writing in the 1990s. The twenty-first century promises or threatens – depending on your perspective – to deliver new sporting bodies. With the help of prostheses, chemicals, electrodes, and, perhaps soon, some genetic tinkering, we could, in theory, engineer athletes to order. Prostheses are, of course, already prevalent in sports, as is doping, despite all efforts to extirpate it. But genetic modification poses all manner of possibilities and problems for the future.

Actually, the idea behind it isn't so new. In the late seventeenth century, English racehorse owners imported Arab stallions but not Arab mares and were forced to breed the prodigiously fast studs with comparatively sluggish English mares. They mated the female offspring of these unions back to other Arab stallions. After a few generations, the breeders had almost eliminated the English stock, leaving them with prime Arab bloodstock.

Today, that practice seems altogether too long-winded. It's also crude when compared to what breeders can do. And, in any case, producing a thoroughbred racehorse is one thing; but a human athlete? (Actually, selective breeding along the lines of the racehorse example has been tried on humans in, among other places, Australia, where, from the 1880s, people of mixed Aboriginal and European descent were forced into orphanages or introduced to white foster homes in an effort to produce a "white Australia".)

As we saw in Chapter 2, genetic research has laid bare the human genome and many of the hitherto unfathomable riddles of life. More than once, the possibility of applying genetic science to athletic performance has been raised. We're not referring to the old standby: could we clone Tiger Woods in the same way as we cloned Dolly the Sheep? Dolly was the product of reproductive engineering rather than genetic modification, anyway. But, there are other scientific breakthroughs that might have human applications.

Consider the case of the rhesus monkey into which was implanted the gene of a jellyfish, making it glow in the dark. Or the mouse which had a full-size human ear growing out of its back. Many pigs carry a gene for bovine growth hormone and show gains in weight and loss of fat. These make the racehorse example, or even the famous red canary of years ago, look antiquated. Now consider further: a mouse is injected with a synthetic gene that instructs its muscles to produce more insulin growth factor 1, commonly known as IGF-1. This is protein that promotes muscle growth and facilitates the repair of muscles after they've been damaged – as they are after hard training, or competition. The mouse is provided with a treadmill and other equipment. The mouse's muscle mass increases by 60 percent, its strength by 27 percent, and it stays like that, even when it grows old and its muscles would ordinarily deplete.

If genetic material could be delivered to the body just like cutting-and-pasting, then it would be possible to recreate organisms almost to order. Remember: the gene consists of DNA, the twin spiral ladder-like structure that contains the codes for development. As we saw in Chapter 3, there are many other mediating variables that affect how the body builds, but the DNA provides the potential. So, if, for example, the gene that signals the body to yield erythropoietin (EPO), which stimulates the body to produce red blood cells, could be identified and this could be transferred to, say, a virus, which could then be injected into a human being, the advantages to an endurance athlete would be many.

Having conducted the bodybuilding experiments with mice, Lee Sweeney told the American Association for the Advancement of Science, in 2004: "The prospects are especially high that muscle-directed gene transfer will be used by the athletic community for performance enhancement, just as many drugs are used and abused today" (quoted by John von Radowitz, *PA News*, February 4, 2004).

It was a view predicated on a fundamental shift in the ethos of sports and it's shared by, among others, Andrew Blake, who in his *Body Language: The meaning of modern sport*, argued:

> Body-builders and weightlifters, in order to succeed, routinely take drugs which drastically alter the physical structure and chemical composition of their bodies. There is no reason why other athletes should not equally resort to structural alteration, biochemical or microprocessor-based implants or the like.
>
> (1996: 161)

Actually, there is. Just because technologies are available doesn't mean they will be condoned by either sports governing organizations or fans. During the twentieth century, the effects of technology on sports was undeniable. Imagine ball games without the process known as vulcanizing, which increased the elasticity and strength of rubber. Now ball players themselves benefit from technologies that allow them to play with carbon fiber appendages. New technologies made an impact on the kind of materials and designs used in sports equipment in the late twentieth century. It's difficult to think of a single sport that hasn't been affected by new technologies, whether in terms of the materials it uses for its instruments (poles, javelins, rackets, etc.) or its apparel (shirts, footwear, headguards, etc.) or the means of conveyance (cycles, racing cars, wheelchairs, etc.) As sports themselves have changed, so have we the competitors and the equipment we use. But, there may be problems ahead.

As the end of the twentieth century approached, it seemed to many scholars that sports in the new millennium would be dominated by technology. The basis for this prediction was that the sports and, by implication, athletes, were increasingly geared to performance. Not a performance in terms of theater, spectacle, or display; but in terms of records, limits, results. Sports demanded that the boundaries of human performance were pushed back, then pushed back repeatedly. As we've noted in previous chapters, this demand is quite different from earlier conceptions of sports. But, of course, things change.

Once competition was about the search for excellence, either with or against others. As we now know, this nineteenth-century conception was vanquished by the cut-throat brand of professionalism that characterized sports, particularly from the 1930s. The meaning of competition today is the one that will probably persist for the remainder of the twenty-first century: to win. To this end, competitors will take advantage of whatever advantage they can, whether inside or outside the rules.

On both sides, we can expect technology to play a bigger and bigger part in the years ahead. The possibilities thrown up by cyborg technologies and the post-human future they promise have been covered earlier. Athletes augmented

## Competition

The word itself provides a clue as to its original meaning: it comes from the Latin *com*, meaning for, and *petere*, seek; it shares a common source with the word *competence*. In the nineteenth-century conception of the word, the aim was not to destroy or eliminate rivals: it was to try to excel by beating them. If they paid you the respect of trying their level best and you did likewise, it would bring all parties to their mettle and that was the aim – to perform at one's mettle. Winning, to reverse Vince Lombardi's famous declaration, was not the only thing. In fact, it was incidental to the main requirement, which was to strive as hard as possible and demonstrate proficiency. There was no disgrace, embarrassment, or regret in losing; the only cause for shame was if you didn't try to your utmost.

with all manner of technological appliances are already commonplace, anyway. Genetic engineering introduces the specter of Frankenstein athletes, but that may stay within the realms of fiction.

In their story "Advanced materials in sports: An advantage or ethical challenge," Sharon Kay Stoll *et al.* raise the possibility that the whole shape and experience of sports could be perverted by technology. "Electronically guided darts, heat-seeking missiles for grouse-shooting, solar energy-enhanced bicycles, and golf balls with terrain-following mechanisms that automatically find the lowest elevation on a putting surface – the bottom of the hole" are some of the possible developments they foresee (2002: 72).

Absurd as they sound, such technological innovations are only extensions of, for example, carbon fiber golf clubs or titanium wheels. Sports governing organizations have, on occasion, stepped in, often in the interests of health and safety. The most obvious example of this was the IAAF's ban on the Nemeth javelin, which was introduced in 1984 and led to a 20-meter improvement on the world record. The problem was that, even in the hands of a modest athlete, the new instrument was a danger to other athletes and even spectators at the other end of the field. Tennis, golf, and baseball are among the other sports that have ruled out the use of materials that add to performance but detract from other features.

But, surely drugs is the exemplar. As we saw in Chapter 10, the systematic application of drugs in sports was a product of the search for athletic excellence. It was introduced by medical practitioners, whose task was to discover ways of improving performance. If the sports enterprise was solely about performance – purely what an athlete *does* – doping would be a commonplace activity, acknowledged and approved by all parties. The fact that it still isn't tells us either that we still cling on to a residual, if misplaced, notion that sports competition is about purely human endeavor or that we just don't understand the extent to which sports are already dependent on technologies.

The IOC has long since issued its disapproval of gene doping. Jacques Rogge, of the organization's medical commission, in 2001, stipulated: "Genetic manipulation is there to treat people who have ailments, not there to treat a healthy person" (quoted in Swift and Yaeger 2001: 87). Of course, one athlete's "ailment" might be another's pretext. And, if there's any doubt over whether athletes would be unnerved by the unknown long-term consequences of gene doping, consider these cases. A female basketball player asked a doctor to break her arms and reset them in a way that would make them longer. A pediatrician was asked by parents to provide a child with human growth hormone to make him taller and more athletic (both reported in Longman 2001). And there is the study quoted by Bamberger and Yaeger: asked whether they would take a drug that would guarantee sporting success but bring certain death within twenty years, over half a sample of young athletes said yes. Athletes are risk-takers.

Maybe there is a risk-taker in all of us. If, say, 15 years ago, myopic spectacle-wearers were offered the chance to undergo a surgical procedure that involved shaving off a layer of their eyeballs with a laser beam, how might they respond? "OK, so the risks are minimal. But what about in 20 years time? Nobody had the surgery two decades ago, so you can't tell me with any accuracy about the longterm effects, right?"

We all probably know someone who has opted for the surgery. We might also know someone who has had cosmetic surgery, however minor (rhinoplasty sounds modest compared to today's extensive procedures). While we might not know someone, we probably know someone who knows someone who knows someone else who has undergone gender reassignment. It sometimes appears that there's no limit to what we can do to the human body. It would be strange if sports was out of sync with what's happening in the rest of society.

Sports have made accommodations for transsexuals and no one has accused recipients of laser eye surgery as cheats, not even if they compete in archery or shooting. In future, there will be major debates, not so much about the natural state of the body – only the naive seriously accept that there is such a thing – but about what constitutes humanity. The human body is being redefined as you read this book. What does it mean to be human? Surgery of one kind or another is changing us. Some of us walk around with chunks of technology. I don't mean carrying technology, but *with* technology. We might be alive because of that technology, or we might be able to function more effectively with it. Some argue that there will be a post-human future, though ultra-human might be more appropriate (*post* meaning after, *ultra* meaning beyond). There are countless ways in which we have changed our bodies and there is every reason to suppose that we'll go on changing them, perhaps in ever more radical ways. It flies in the face of reason to suppose that sports won't reflect this.

## PROGRESS AND PERFORMANCE

One of the consequences of modifying the human body is that sporting performance will change. Obviously, standards have been changing constantly and, while romantics might insist that, for example, the Pittsburgh Steelers of the 1960s was superior to today's best NFL teams, or that the indomitable Liverpool teams of the 1970s and 1980s would overcome the best contemporary soccer teams, the truth is that they wouldn't. In sports in which performance levels are measurable, the trend has been toward improvement by increments. It makes no sense to believe other sports have not progressed in a similar way.

In the first three editions of *Making Sense of Sports*, I paraphrased former Olympian Sebastian Coe's father and coach, Peter, who once ventured to suggest that there was no limit to how fast the mile could be run. "It's like taking a straight line, dividing it in two, splitting again, then again and again and so on *ad infinitum*," he argued. "The lines get smaller and smaller, but you're always left with something." In other words, there will always be the potential for improvement in competitive performances, but the improvements will be quantitatively smaller each time. I agreed with this prognosis, pointing out that it can be applied to any sport, not just track and field.

Huge improvements or long-standing records, such as Coe's 2:12.18 for 1,000 meters, set in 1981, Jarmila Kratochvilova's 1:53.28 for 800 meters, set in 1983, Marita Koch's 47.60 for 400 meters, set in 1985, or Randy Barnes's 23.12 meters shot, set in 1990, remain historically aberrant performances, explicable only in terms of freak atmospheric conditions, exceptionally fierce competition, or some undisclosed form of assistance. But, records have typically progressed smoothly and by decreasing increments in most events for most of the past century. But, in the mid-1990s, something unusual happened.

In August 1994, Algeria's Noureddine Morceli broke the world's 3,000 meters record when he ran 7:25.11, which equates to 8:01 for two miles. In other words, very, very fast; nearly four seconds faster, in fact, than the previous world record held by Kenya's Moses Kiptanui. In the 20 years immediately before Morceli's run, the record had been lowered by a yearly average of 0.307 seconds (6.14 seconds in total). Yet Morceli's was a portentous run.

The following year, Haile Gebrselassie, of Ethiopia, began to rewrite the record books. He lopped 1.55 seconds off the two miles record, which was more than it had been lowered between the entire 1972–94 period. He also destroyed Kiptanui's 5,000 meters record with 12:44.39, an improvement of 10.91 seconds, compared with an average improvement of just under 3.64 seconds every year

## Progress

Progress in sports is a uniquely human phenomenon, based more on intellectual abilities than physical ones. For example, over 1,500 meters, Hicham El Guerrouj in the early twenty-first century consistently ran about 40 seconds faster than his counterpart of 120 years ago. Yet, if we compare the Kentucky Derby or Grand National winner over a similar period, today's horses run only about 10 seconds faster. The reason for the difference is that a trained racehorse will maintain between 85 and 95 percent of its maximum speed, metabolizing anaerobic energy, which is, as we have seen, counterproductive in the long term as it produces lactic acid and retards muscle contraction.

Humans have improved their performances through advances in technique, training, rivalries, and supplements. They will run at between 70 and 75 percent of maximum speed for most of a middle-distance race, kicking over the final phase, e.g. 5,000m: 11 laps @ 61.5 seconds + 1 lap @ 56 seconds = 12:43.25. This requires timing, anticipation, and a tactical awareness, as well as the capacity to assimilate stress and discomfort – features that are built into training.

There is also incentive: a horse has only a whipped flank to motivate it in the final stretch, whereas a human has rewards for which he or she is prepared to suffer pain. Apart from the intellectual stimulus, we should note that humans are physically inefficient at running and have modest locomotion capabilities compared to horses, whose capacity for running is an evolutionary adaptation, probably resulting from their relative lack of defense. The human desire to run fast over distances and, indeed, achieve in any competition, is a product of self-induced challenge.

between 1972 and 1995. The Ethiopian later reduced this to 12:41.86, in 1997, and to 12:39.36, in 1998. But Gebrselassie's most extraordinary run was over 10,000 meters, in 1995, when he recorded 26:43.53. In the previous year, William Sigei, of Kenya, had shaken the athletics world when he ran a remarkable 26:52.23, which itself took a gigantic 6.15 seconds off a world record that had been brought down by about 15 seconds in the previous 15 years. So, Gebrselassie's 8.7 seconds improvement seemed to defy rational analysis.

The sequence of events did not stop. Gebrselassie's records were beaten by Daniel Komen and Paul Tergat, both of Kenya, and Salah Hissou, of Morocco, only for him to respond by breaking them again and again. Gebrselassie took the 5,000 meters mark from 12:58.39 to 12:39.36 and the 10,000 meters from 26:52.23 to 26:22.75 (in 1998). Then, after a period of relative calmness, during which Gebrselassie's dominance seemed consolidated and analysts began to adjudge him the greatest track runner in history, Kenenisa Bekele appeared. In a ten-month period in 2003/4, Bekele shattered Gebrselassie's 5,000 meters outdoor and indoor records, as well as his 6-year-old 10,000 meters record (he clocked 26:20.31, covering the second half of the race faster than the world record for 5,000 meters at the time he was born, June 13, 1982).

Collectively, the middle-distance records produced a pattern. The athletics equivalent of the law of diminishing returns held good up to around 1995; then the returns started to expand. Even if the pattern hasn't been replicated in other areas, the sharp and unexpected upturn in performance forces us to reconsider the orthodoxy about athletic progression and ponder on possible reasons for the disproportionate improvement.

Highly paid athletes often say money is the last thing they are thinking of in the midst of competition. This may be so, but it's tempting to advance cash incentives as at least one factor in the improvement. At the start of the twenty-first century, Bekele would not take his tracksuit off for less than $50,000 a race, top marathon runners could take home four or five times that and top male sprinters could command upwards of $100,000 a race. Bekele's middle-distance predecessors, like Lasse Viren and Henry Rono – both world record breakers – ran for expenses only in the 1970s. Money is a motivating force, however much people deny it, and it becomes an even greater force when you come from pestilential African countries. It is, of course, no coincidence that a growing number of soccer players from nations such as Ghana, Nigeria, and Sierra Leone are now playing at the highest levels of European competition and earning millions for their labors. Or that hockey players from war-ravaged or hard-up eastern European countries excel in the NHL.

A second factor is the knowledge we have about how to prepare athletes. We know more about diet and training cycles and, importantly, how to use technology to improve performance. Philosophies of training have changed. The brutal regimes instigated by Franz Stampfl in the 1950s now seem quite modest. Gebrselassie employed a version of Stampfl's philosophy which was to slice up a distance and repeatedly attack just one portion of it during training. He prepared for longer distances by running 400 meters at about 90 percent of his maximum (e.g. 46 seconds) about 20 times, with a one-minute recovery between reps. Bekele would typically do an even pace 8,000 meters training run in about 21:23. At about 2,600 meters above sea level, this would elevate his hemocrit level (percentage of red blood cells) to 49 (Gebrselassie's was usually about 42).

This reflects in actual performance. For example, distances up to a mile are now typically run quite evenly at about 96–97 percent capacity. Runners try to distribute their efforts in a way that replicates hard training. The first three laps of a fast 1,500 meters may each be run at even splits of 56 seconds, with the final three-quarter lap taking 41 seconds (equivalent of a 54.66 lap). This means that all distances up to 3,000 meters are likely to be less tactical affairs and more of sustained sprints.

Performance such as this requires training that accentuates quality as well as quantity. Combine better training with better nutrition and the supplementary aid of massage, acupuncture, and assorted methods of modifying cognition and you have potent factors that explain the improvements. But, there is perhaps one other point we need to contemplate.

In no other area of track and field has there been such a dramatic improvement as in men's middle distance. In some areas, there has actually been a deterioration in measurable performance. Few women's records are challenged nowadays, either in track and field, or swimming. The accepted reason for this is that many, probably most, records set by athletes from the former Soviet bloc countries were involved in state-run programs which involved taking performance-enhancing substances for which there were no rigorous tests. Anabolic steroids would have had an impact on virtually all strength-related performances, including throwing field events and track races up to 800 meters. Women have only recently begun to contest middle- and long-distance races. In men's events, the deterioration in power-based events is not so marked, though it is worth remembering that the best 21 throws in shot put history were all made before 1991, after which systems of gas chromatography and mass spectroscopy made it possible to check a compound found in urine against 70,000 held in a computer's database.

But, in the late 1990s, when the men's middle-distance records went tumbling, there was no effective test for EPO. The genetically engineered substance is a more convenient and more efficient alternative to blood doping, which was known to be favored by some middle- and long-distance men in the 1970s. The sharp upturn in distance records coincided with the greater availability of EPO. In his *Sports Illustrated* article "Distant thunder," Tim Layden quotes former marathon runner Alberto Salazar, of the USA: "I can believe that there can always be that one great person, that Superman who can run 45 seconds faster than Henry Rono . . . But all these people running so fast? That's incomprehensible to me" (1998: 37). (Gebrselassie's 1998 record for 10,000 meters was actually just under a minute faster than Rono's best of 20 years before.)

Perhaps it will become more comprehensible in years to come. Some will hold that the exponential improvement was the product of the genuinely gifted Superman referred to by Salazar, who inspired his rivals to greater and greater achievements. After all, rivalries tend to bring the best out of competitors. Others will dismiss it as a historical deviation. Cynics – and one suspects Salazar is among them – will wish to wait and see what happens when further tests for as-yet unknown substances come into force. If there is a tapering off in times, then we can draw obvious conclusions.

Brendan Foster, the British runner who held the 3,000 meters record, 1974–8, is also quoted by Layden: "You'd have to think these guys are approaching the limits of human endurance" (1998: 34). John Smith, who coached Maurice Greene, Ato Boldon, and others, disagrees. "I don't think a limit exists," he said to Mike Rowbottom, of *The Independent* (July 5, 1999). Ben Johnson's now-expunged time for the 100 meters at the 1988 Olympics was 9.79 seconds. It took only 11 years before the same time was clocked by Greene without the enhancement used by Johnson.

It seems my original forecast is in need of revision. The bit-by-even-smaller-bit progression I envisaged may be interspersed with periods of rapid and perhaps explosive improvements. Perhaps we have witnessed them in some sports, but have not been able to measure them. For example, the ascendant Chicago Bulls team of the 1990s may have taken the sport to new heights because of its special combination of coaching and playing staff, and appreciable cash incentives. Without these, it may have taken basketball another 10 or 15 years to produce a team capable of elevating the game to the same level.

Historically, we can identify intervals of superabundance in particular sports. The Duran/Hagler/Hearns/Leonard epoch of boxing in the 1970s stands out; there has been no evidence of such a sustained level of competition in the years since. Salazar's Superman theory seems to apply perfectly to Jean-Claude Killy, the best all-round ski racer in history, who glided to previously untouched planes of achievement and whose technical command has probably not been matched since (though fans of Alberto Tomba may wish to argue that point). But Michael Schumacher? For some, his achievements distinguish him as the greatest Formula 1 driver ever; for others, Schumacher's cars made him great. Technological changes often disguise progress: motor cars have been slowed-up; tennis balls have been deflated; javelins have been made less aerodynamic. The changes have usually been made in the interests of safety or spectacle, but, in both cases, their effect has been to mask quantifiable progress.

In other words, several sports may have passed through the kind of stage that middle-distance running went through in the late 1990s. But, because they are either not objectively measurable in the same way as track or they have changed the conditions of competition, the periods have not been acknowledged as exponential jumps forward.

Perhaps, these are the equivalents of Norbert Elias's "civilizing spurts" we encountered in Chapter 5: relatively short, but transformative bursts of activity in which human conduct is significantly affected. As we saw, Elias budgets for a reverse gear. Traditionalists maintain that sports also have that facility. It probably only seems that way. While there may be less intense rivalry and/or less talented individuals in some eras, it is unlikely that overall standards reverse; more likely that our retrospective interpretations deceive us. Jordan, Leonard, Killy, and many, many other athletes stand out as parts of "golden ages" in sports and, as I have argued, they were parts of periods of accelerated progress. But, the sports in which they participated would not have remained unchanged by their presence. They defined new standards of excellence in much the same way as Gebrselassie did in middle-distance running.

So, the revision to my prediction is simple. We need to allow for the fact that sports typically progress smoothly without denying the possibility of rapid spurts that violate all accepted criteria. The trick is to identify the conditions under which those spurts take place. A sharp upturn in the financial incentives on offer seems to help. There has always been money to be made in boxing; but in the 1970s, million-dollar purses became commonplace. We have seen in Chapter 15 how the NBA went from a struggling operation to a mega-billion-dollar sports from the mid-1980s.

The NBA was hardly in its infancy at the time, but, neither was it a mature major league sport. Being in the middle of a take-off period also seems conducive to rapid progress. Michael Jordan's NBA epitomizes this, but we should also consider the NFL in the early 1970s, still not the force it is today, but progressing very speedily toward it. The 1973 Dolphins who went 17–0 under Don Shulah represent this phase of the league's development. Sports that are either relatively new or have been reorganized are susceptible to spurts. Women's soccer is due for one. Beach volleyball is probably just coming out of one.

## A MATTER OF OBLIGATION

"It is little wonder that the relationship between sport and the media (especially television) is commonly described as the happiest of marriages," writes David Rowe, "with both institutions becoming mutually dependent in an increasingly extensive and expensive exchange of exposure and rights fees for sport in return for compelling content and audience capture for the media" (2004a: 32).

We simply can't hope to understand sports independently of the media. For that matter, we can't understand the media without examining its partnership with sports. As we saw in Chapter 13, television has enjoyed a productive relationship with sports virtually since it became a source of domestic pleasure in the 1950s. From the late 1980s, sports became increasingly important as content to fill the channels that multiplied at an almost bewildering rate. Already expensive, sports began to charge the television companies even more.

But there is still a mutual dependence. Sports needs tv: without it, the sponsorships dry up, salaries drop, and interest tapers off. Without sports, television struggles to find content that draws viewers to their screens so consistently. For commercial television, losing sports means losing advertising revenue. The problem is: what happens when the symbiosis becomes less beneficial to one of the parties? Sports was once hesitant about deepening its involvement with tv, fearing that extensive coverage would hurt its appeal as live action and depress attendance. It was a justifiable fear. Eventually, the money on offer was serious enough to dispel it. Even if attendance figures dropped, there was enough tv money to compensate amply. Now, television is beginning to wonder if it's paying too much.

Faced with growing demands from major sports, television has responded with alternatives to free-to-air transmission. Subscription, pay-per-view and other methods of enticing viewers to pay directly for live televised sports have exposed an elasticity in the demand for sports. Viewers seem prepared to pay to watch sports.

The day may not be far away when free-to-air sports will be a thing of the past. Even with pay television, the tv networks might not want to bear all the risks. Genuine partnerships, with both parties agreeing to profit-sharing, or loss-sharing, arrangements are already looming. Television companies will probably seek ways of involving major sports financially. Instead of just paying for the rights to televise football or boxing, for example, it might say to the league or the promoter: "You arrange the competition and we'll handle the production and screening. We'll add up how much revenue we take from advertising and ppv sales, subtract your costs and ours, and divide what's left over – or, in the event of a loss, split the deficit."

However sports and television modify their arrangements, one thing is sure: sports will remain on television. This alone will ensure its centrality as popular culture. Just being seen on television guarantees importance, culturally-speaking. In Chapter 16, we saw how celebrity culture was made possible by the media's remorseless pursuit of content for the ever-multiplying channels. Reality tv shows, in particular, were a kind of televisual equivalent of watching paint dry. But billions watched and new celebs came into being. The point is: television exposure makes bland people interesting, trivial information important, banal, tedious, and boring events engaging, exciting, and perhaps even fascinating. In the highly improbable event of sports moving off television, it would cease to be the compelling feature it currently is.

Television won't drop sports, of course. It can't. It needs a continual supply of new celebs to take our attention. Sports is a conveyor belt of such beings: every year, it delivers a new batch ready for our consumption. They appear in *Heat* and *People* as well as the sports publications. Their dirty little secrets are aired by tabloids. And, although we eventually tire of them, for a while, they enthrall us, perhaps infuriate us, and certainly inspire us to buy into the world of accessible luxury they portray.

The consequence of this is that, as Rowe puts it, "every sentient human being . . . willingly or unwillingly, must in some way come to terms with the sports behemoth" (2002: 1). A behemoth is an enormous beast, so Rowe's point is presumably that we have to live peaceably with it rather than fight it.

Those readers of this book who are using it for a university course won't be able to remember, probably not even imagine, a time when sports was equated with leisure. Sports were activities we engaged in during our leisure hours, whether watching or doing. It's now laughable to think that there was a virtual synonymy between sports and leisure. They're no more equivalent than clocks and grapefruit – some clocks are about the same diameter as grapefruit, but that's about the only thing they have in common. Some people watch sports during their leisure time.

Sports is a sphere of such colossal cultural importance that it needs analysis on its own terms. It's never been such a central component of popular culture. Its influence has never been so pervasive. Its intrusions into people's lives never so invasive. Its impact on high finance and national economies never so great. It perplexes, infuriates, enraptures; it elicits conflict, harmony, delight, and despair. It does this not because it's intrinsically important: but because we attribute it with importance. Those who argue that it really is, when all's said and done, just playful diversion might have a point. But they're wrong about the "just" part. Playful diversion it might be, but it's many, many other things besides.

To close, we should consider the subject that obviously occupies much of our attention: you wouldn't have got through 18 chapters unless you had a commitment to the study of sports. Over the final two decades of the twentieth century, sports studies and sports science were, sometimes grudgingly, accepted as legitimate academic pursuits. This reflected a more general recognition of sport as a central institution in contemporary society. Its historical association with frivolity, recreation, and leisure is virtually over. A lot of this recognition has grown not so much out of an appreciation of sports, but of a concern with the problems sports seemed to generate. Fan violence, racism, sexism, drugs: these were some of the issues that forced analysts to take sports seriously.

In 1996, I wrote in the second edition of *MSS* that a book such as this would not have been written ten years ago. The fact that it's now in its fourth edition is testimony to the success of sports as a field of academic inquiry and scholarly endeavor. The growth of sports-related degrees and programs of study strengthens the view that the study of sports is as relevant to today's curriculum as studies of crime, education, industry, religion, technology, and any number of other traditional subjects.

There are still areas of bewilderment: the apparent irrationality of some aspects of sports, the near-maniacal following they command, the almost suicidal tendencies of some of its participants, and the inexplicable political controversies they are prone to provoke. But, after 18 chapters, we're hopefully in a better position to comprehend these. For all their supposed lack of reason, sports are too important not to be understood. Making sense of sports is now a matter of obligation rather than choice.

---

## OF RELATED INTEREST

*Genetically Modified Athletes: Biomedical ethics, gene doping, and sport* by Andy Miah (Routledge, 2004) outlines both a future in which genetic engineering reshapes sports and presents a defense for such a future: "Genetic modification can enrich sporting performances by providing greater levels of excellence in performance, reducing the risk of unsafe drug enhancement, allowing athletes to express their authenticity through their relationship with technology, and to promote the acquisition of internal goods of sport."

*Post-Olympism? Questioning sport in the twenty-first century* edited by John Bale and Mette Krogh Christensen (Berg, 2004) concentrates specifically on the Olympics, charting the changes in the meaning of the Olympic ideals in the twentieth century and speculating on the future of the games against a background of globalization, drug use, and what the editors call "Disneyfication."

*Sport Business in the Global Marketplace* by Hans Westerbeek and Aaron Smith (Palgrave Macmillan, 2002) is written by two management consultants who examine the factors that will affect the future development of sport in an age of global uncertainty; these include "the rise of global super athletes and teams," as well as television, franchising, and further commercialization.

---

## ASSIGNMENT

France, 1568: You are calling for your friend Michel de Nostredame on your way to a big *torneiement* in nearby Provence, where a visiting court from Burgundy is due to appear. As he goes to grab his coat, you peer at de Nostredame's desk and read his scribbled notes. "Are you making more prophecies, Nostradamus?" you ask. "Yes, those are about the tournaments of the twenty-first century," he replies. You are dismayed:

"Not again. Didn't you get into enough trouble when you predicted King Henry's death in a joust?" "I was right, wasn't I?" he says. "Well, you might have got that one right, but all this business about a revolution in France in a couple of hundred years' time and a Great Fire in London and this whatsisname, Hister or Hitler or something in the twentieth century . . . it's ridiculous. People are laughing at you. Take that one you wrote recently:

*In the seventh month of 1999*
*From the sky will come a great King of Terror*
*He will resurrect the great King of Angolmois*
*Before and afterward war reigns happily*

"What was that supposed to mean? The end of the world?" Nostradamus responds: "Not at all: it refers to a type of tournament, except the riders will have mechanical beasts with wheels instead of legs and they will charge not at each other but in unison all over France and with a fury that resembles a war. And when they descend from the mountains, it will seem as if they come from the sky and the swiftest shall be a King." "Yeah, right," you scoff. "So, the tournaments will still be around in 2018." Nostradamus answers: "Not quite. But, the spirit that moves them will be." As you leave, you smile: "You don't seriously think people are going to be reading this stuff in 450 years' time, do you?" He just shrugs. What was Nostradamus writing?

# bibliography

Abernathy, B., Kippers, V., Mackinnon, L., Neal, R., and Hanrahan, S. (1997) *The Biophysical Foundations of Human Movement* Champaign, IL: Human Kinetics.

Adams, John (1995) *Risk* London: UCL Press.

Addison, Heather (2002) "Capitalizing their charms: Cinema stars and physical culture in the 1920s" *Velvet Light Trap*, issue 50 (Fall).

Anderson, Elijah (1999) *Code of the Street: Decency, violence, and the moral life of the inner city* New York: Norton.

Andrews, David L. and Jackson, Steven J. (eds) (2001) *Sports Stars: The cultural politics of sporting celebrity* London: Routledge.

Andrews, John (1998) "The world of sport: Not just a game" *The Economist* (June 6).

Anonymous (1994) *Cyclist's Training Diary*, seventh edition, Chambersberg, PA: Alan C. Hood & Co.

Arms, R., Russell, G., and Sandilands, M. (1987) "Effects on the hostility of spectators of viewing aggressive sports" in *Sport Sociology*, third edition, edited by A. Yiannakis, T. McIntyre, M. Melnick, and D. Hart, Dubuque, IA: Kendall/Hunt.

Armstrong, Ketra L. (1999) "Nike's communication with black audiences" *Journal of Sport & Social Issues* vol. 23, no. 3 (August).

Armstrong, Lance and Jenkins, Sally (2000) *It's Not About the Bike: My journey back to life* New York: Putnam.

Arsenault, Darin J. and Fawzy, Tamer (2001) "Just buy it – Nike advertising aimed at *Glamour* readers: A critical feminist analysis" *Tamara: Journal of Critical Postmodern Organization Science* vol. 1, no. 2.

Ashe, Arthur R. (1993) *A Hard Road to Glory: A history of the African-American Athlete*, 3 volumes, New York: Amistad Warner.

Bakhtin, Mikhail (1981) *The Dialogic Imagination* Austin: University of Texas Press.

Bale, John and Christensen, Mette Krogh (eds) (2004) *Post-Olympism? Questioning sport in the twenty-first century* Oxford: Berg.

Balsamo, Anne (1996) *Technologies of the Gendered Body: Reading cyborg women* Durham, NC: Duke University Press.

Bamberger, M. and Yaeger, D. (1997) "Over the edge: Aware that drug testing is a sham, athletes seem to rely more than ever on banned performance enhancers" *Sports Illustrated*, April 14.

Bandura, A. (1973) *Aggression: A social learning analysis* Englewood Cliffs, NJ: Prentice-Hall.

Bandy, Susan and Darden, Anne (1999) *Crossing Boundaries: An international anthology of women's experiences in sport* Champaign, IL: Human Kinetics.

Bane, Michael (1997) *Over the Edge: A regular guy's odyssey in extreme sports* New York: Gollancz.

Barker, Chris (1997) *Global Television: An introduction* Oxford: Blackwell.

Barnett, S. (1990) *Games and Sets: The changing face of sport on television* London: British Film Institute.

Bartlett, Roger (2005) *Introduction to Sports Biomechanics*, second edition, London: Routledge.

Bauman, Zygmunt (1979) "The phenomenon of Norbert Elias" *Sociology* vol. 13.

Bauman, Zygmunt (2001) "Consuming life" *Journal of Consumer Culture* vol. 1, no. 1.

Beal, Becky (1996) "Alternative masculinity and its effects on gender relations in the subculture of skateboarding" *Journal of Sport Behavior* vol. 19, no. 3 (August).

Beck, Ulrich (1992) *Risk Society* London: Sage.

Becker, Boris (2004) *Boris Becker – The Player: The autobiography* London: Bantam.

Beisser, Arnold (1967) *The Madness in Sports* New York: Appleton-Century-Crofts.

Bengry, Erwin (2000) "Nike" in *Sports Culture: An A–Z Guide* by Ellis Cashmore, London: Routledge.

Berger, Arthur Asa (2003) *Ads, Fads and Consumer Culture*, second edition, Lanham, MD: Rowman & Littlefield.

Biddle, S. J. H. (1997) "Cognitive theories of motivation and the physical self" in *The Physical Self: From motivation to well-being* edited by K. R. Fox, Champaign, IL: Human Kinetics.

Birke, Lynda and Vines, Gail (1987) "A sporting chance: The anatomy of destiny" *Women's Studies International Forum* vol. 10, no. 4.

Birrell, Susan and Cole, Cheryl (1990) "Double fault: Renee Richards and the construction and naturalization of difference" *Sociology of Sport Journal* vol. 7.

Birrell, Susan and Cole, Cheryl (eds) (1995) *Women, Sport and Culture* Champaign, IL: Human Kinetics.

Birtley, Jack (1976) *The Tragedy of Randolph Turpin*, London: NEL.

Blake, Andrew (1996) *Body Language: The meaning of modern sport* London: Lawrence & Wishart.

Blanchard, Kendall (1995) *The Anthropology of Sports: An introduction* Westport, CT: Bergin & Garvey.

Blue, Adrienne (1987) *Grace Under Pressure* London: Sidgwick & Jackson.

Blue, Adrienne (1995) *Martina: The life and times of Martina Navratilova* New York: Birch Lane Press.

Bolin, Anne (1996 ) "Body building" in *Encyclopedia of World Sport: From ancient times to the present* vol. 1 edited by D. Levinson and K. Christensen, Santa Barbara, CA: ABC-Clio.

Boorstin, Daniel (1961) *The Image: A guide to pseudo-events in America* New York: Harper & Row.

Brailsford, Dennis (1997) *British Sport: A social history* Cambridge: Lutterworth Press.

Braudy, Leo (2003) *From Chivalry to Terrorism* New York: Alfred Knopf.

Brill, A. A. (1929) "The why of a fan" *North American Review* pt. 22.

Brohm, Jean-Marie (1978) *Sport: A prison of measured time* London: Ink Links.

Brookes, Rod (2002) *Representing Sport* London: Arnold.

Brower, Jonathan (1976) "Professional sports team ownership" *Journal of Sport Sociology* vol. 1 no. 1.

Burns, Jimmy (1996) *Hand of God: The life of Diego Maradona* London: Bloomsbury.

Burton, Rick (1999) "Sports advertising and the Super Bowl" in *The Advertising Business* edited by John Philip Jones, London: Sage.

Cahn, Susan K. (1994) *Coming on Strong: Gender and sexuality in twentieth-century women's sport* New York: Free Press.

Canter, D., Comber, M., and Uzzell, D. (1989) *Football in its Place: An environmental psychology of football grounds* London: Routledge.

Cashmore, Ellis (2002) *Sport Psychology: The key concepts* London: Routledge.

Cashmore, Ellis (2003) *Sports Culture: An A–Z guide* London: Routledge.

Cashmore, Ellis (2004) *Beckham*, second edition, Cambridge: Polity.

Cashmore, Ellis (2005) *Tyson: Nurture of the beast* Cambridge: Polity.

Chandler, Joan (1988) *Television and National Sport: The United States and Britain* Urbana, IL: University of Illinois Press.

Chapman, Gwen E. (1997) "Making weight: Lightweight rowing, technologies of power, and technologies of the self", *Sociology of Sport Journal* vol. 14, no. 3.

Chenoweth, Neil (2001) *Virtual Murdoch: Reality wars on the information highway* London: Secker & Warburg.

Clasen, Patricia R. W. (2001) "The female athlete: Dualisms and paradox in practice" *Women and Language* vol. 24, no. 2 (Fall).

Coakley, Jay J. (2003) *Sport in Society: Issues and controversies* eighth edition, Columbus, OH: McGraw-Hill.

Cohen, Greta L. (1993) *Women in Sport* Newbury Park, CA: Sage.

Collins, Tony (1999) *Rugby's Great Split: Class, culture and the origins of rugby league football* London: Frank Cass.

Commoner, Barry (2002) "Unraveling the DNA myth" *Harper's* vol. 304, no. 1821.

Connell, Robert (1994) *Masculinities* Cambridge: Polity.

Coombs, David (1978) *Sport and the Countryside* Oxford: Phaidon Press.

Cooper, A. (1998) *Playing in the Zone: Exploring the spiritual dimensions of sport* Boston, MA: Shambhala.

Coren, Stanley (1992) *Left Hander: Everything you need to know about left-handedness*, London: John Murray.

Costa, Margaret and Guthrie, Sharon (eds) (1994) *Women and Sport: Interdisciplinary perspectives* Champaign, IL: Human Kinetics.

Côté, Jean (2001) "Coach and peer influence on children's development through sport" in *Psychological Foundations of Sport* edited by J. M. Silva and D. E. Stevens, Boston, MA: Allyn & Bacon.

Cowens, Steve (2001) *Blades Business Crew* Lytham, England: Milo.

Crawford, Garry (2004) *Consuming Sport: The consumption spectacle and surveillance of contemporary sports fans* London: Routledge.

Csikszentmihalyi, M. (1990) *Flow: The psychology of optimal experience* New York: Harper & Row.

Cunningham, Hugh (1980) *Leisure in the Industrial Revolution* London: Croom Helm.

Curtis, J. and Loy, J. (1978) "Race/ethnicity and relative centrality of playing positions in team sport" *Exercise and Sport Sciences Review* vol. 6.

Danielson, Michael N. (1997) *Home Team: Professional sports and the American metropolis* Princeton, NJ: Princeton University Press.

Dauncey, Hugh and Hare, Geoff (eds) (1999) *France and the 1998 World Cup* London: Cass.

Deneen, Sally (2001) "Designer people" *E: The Environmental Magazine*, vol. 12, no. 1.

Denniston, Robin (1999) *Trevor Huddleston: A life* Basingstoke, England: Macmillan,

Depasquale, Peter (1990) *The Boxer's Workout* New York: Fighting Fit.

Dittmar, Helga (1992) *The Social Psychology of Material Possessions: To have is to be* Hemel Hempstead, England: Harvester Wheatsheaf.

Dittmar, Helga, Beattie, Jane, and Friese, Susanne (1995) "Gender identity and material symbols: Objects and decision considerations in impulse purchases" *Journal of Economic Psychology*, vol. 15.

Dollard, J., Doob, L. W., Miller, N. E., Mowrer, O. H., and Sears, R. R. (1939) *Frustration and Aggression* New Haven, CT: Yale University Press.

Downes, S. and Mackay, D. (1996) *Running Scared: How athletics lost its innocence* Edinburgh: Mainstream.

Dunning, Eric (1999) *Sport Matters: Sociological studies of sport, violence and civilization* London: Routledge.

Dunning, Eric and Rojek, Chris (eds) (1992) *Sport and Leisure in the Civilizing Process* Basingstoke, England: Macmillan.

Dunning, Eric and Sheard, Kenneth (1979) *Barbarians, Gentlemen and Players* Oxford: Martin Robertson.

Dunning, Eric, Murphy, Patrick, and Williams, John (1988) *The Roots of Football Hooliganism* London: Routledge & Kegan Paul.

Dweck, C. S. (1980) "Learned helplessness in sport" in *Psychology of Motor Behavior and Sport – 1979* edited by C. H. Nadeau, W. R. Halliwell, K. M. Newell, and G. C. Roberts, Champaign, IL: Human Kinetics.

Edwards, Harry (1970) *The Revolt of the Black Athlete* New York: Free Press.

Edwards, Harry (1973) *Sociology of Sport* Homewood, IL: Dorsey Press.

Eitzen, D. Stanley and Sanford, D. (1975) "The segregation of blacks by playing position in football" *Social Science Quarterly* vol. 5, no. 4.

Eitzen, D. Stanley (ed.) (1993) *Sport in Contemporary Society*, fourth edition, New York: St. Martin's Press.

Eitzen, D. Stanley and Yetman, N. (1977) "Immune from racism?" *Civil Rights Digest* vol. 9, no. 2.

Elias, Norbert (1982) *The Civilizing Process*, 2 volumes, New York: Pantheon.

Elias, Norbert (1986a) "An essay on sport and violence" in *Quest for Excitement* edited by Norbert Elias and Eric Dunning, Oxford: Blackwell.

Elias, Norbert (1986b) "Introduction" in *Quest for Excitement* edited by Norbert Elias and Eric Dunning, Oxford: Blackwell.

Elias, Norbert and Dunning, Eric (eds) (1986) *Quest for Excitement* Oxford: Blackwell.

Entine, Jon (2000) *Taboo: Why black athletes dominate and why we're afraid to talk about it* New York: Public Affairs.

Evans, Marc (1997) *Endurance Athlete's Edge* Champaign, IL: Human Kinetics.

Faludi, Susan (1999) *Stiffed: The betrayal of the modern man* London: Chatto & Windus.

Fasting, Kari (1987) "Sports and women's culture" *Women's International Forum* vol. 19, no. 4.

Fazey, J. and Hardy, L. (1988) *The inverted-U hypothesis: A catastrophe for sport psychology?* British Association of Sports Sciences, Monograph No. 1, Leeds: National Coaching Foundation.

Featherstone, Mike (1991) "The body in consumer culture" in *The Body: Social process and cultural theory* edited by Mike Featherstone, Mike Hepworth, and Bryan S. Turner, London: Sage.

Featherstone, Mike, Hepworth, Mike, and Turner, Bryan S. (eds) (1991) *The Body: Social process and cultural theory*, London: Sage.

Festle, Mary Jo (1996) *Playing Nice: Politics and apologies in women's sport* New York: Columbia University Press.

Field, John (2003) *Social Capital* London: Routledge.

Finch, Laura (2001) "Understanding individual motivation in sport" in *Psychological Foundations of Sport*, edited by J. M. Silva and D. E. Stevens, Boston, MA: Allyn & Bacon.

Fowles, Jib (1996) *Advertising and Popular Culture* Newbury Hills, CA: Sage.

Frank, Thomas (1997a) "The new gilded age" in *Commodify Your Dissent: Salvos from* The Baffler edited by Thomas Frank and Matt Weiland, New York: Norton.

Frank, Thomas (1997b) "Alternative to what?" in *Commodify Your Dissent: Salvos from* The Baffler edited by Thomas Frank and Matt Weiland, New York: Norton.

Franklin, Bob (1997) *Newszak and News Media* London: Arnold.

Fraser, George MacDonald (1997) *Black Ajax* London: HarperCollins.

Freud, S. (1963) "Why war?" in *Freud: Character and culture* edited by P. Reiff, New York: Collier.

Furedi, Frank (1997) *Culture of Fear* London: Cassell.

Gallagher, Catherine and Laqueur, Thomas (eds) (1987) *The Making of the Modern Body: Sexuality and society in the nineteenth century* Berkeley: University of California Press.

Gamson, Joshua (1994) *Claims to Fame: Celebrity in contemporary America* Berkeley: University of California Press.

Gardenfors, Peter (2003) *How Homo Became Sapiens: On the evolution of thinking*, Oxford: Oxford University Press.

Geertz, Clifford (1972) "Deep Play: Notes on the Balinese cockfight" in *The Interpretation of Cultures* edited by Clifford Geertz, New York: Basic Books.

George, Christeen, Hartley, Andrew, and Paris, Jenny (2001) "Focus on communication in sport: The representation of female athletes in textual and visual media" *Corporate Communications*, vol. 6, no. 2.

Gibson, K. and Ingold, T. (eds) (1993) *Tools, Language and Cognition in Human Evolution* Cambridge: Cambridge University Press.

Giles, David (2000) *Illusions of Immortality: A psychology of fame and celebrity* London: Macmillan.

Gill, Diane L. (2000) *Psychological Dynamics of Sport and Exercise*, second edition, Champaign, IL: Human Kinetics.

Giulianotti, R., Bonney, R., and Hepworth, M. (eds) (1994) *Football, Violence and Social Identity* London: Routledge.

Goldberg, Marvin E., Gorn, Gerald J., Peracchio, Laura A., and Bamossy, Gary (2003) "Understanding materialism among youth" *Journal of Consumer Behavior*, vol. 13.

Goldlust, John (1987) *Playing for Keeps: Sport, the media and society* Melbourne: Longman Cheshire.

Goldman, Robert and Papson, Stephen (1999) *Nike Culture: The sign of the swoosh* London: Sage.

Gorman, J. and Calhoun, K. (1994) *The Name of the Game: The business of sports* New York: Wiley.

Gorn, Elliott J. (1986) *The Manly Art: Bare-knuckle prize fighting in America* Ithaca, NY: Cornell University Press.

Gorski, Roger A. (1991) "Gonadal hormones and the organization of brain structure and function" in *The Lifespan Development of Individuals: Behavioral, neurological and psychosocial perspectives* edited by D. Magnuson, Cambridge: Cambridge University Press.

Gottdiener, Mark (1997) *The Theming of America: Dreams, visions and commercial spaces* Boulder, CO: Westview Press.

Gould, Stephen Jay (2002) *The Structure of Evolutionary Theory* Cambridge, MA: Harvard University Press.

Gouldner, Alvin W. (1965) *Wildcat Strike: A study in worker–management relations* New York: Harper Torchbooks.

Govier, Ernie (1998) "Brainsex and occupation" in *Gender and Choice in Occupation and Education* edited by John Radford, London: Routledge.

Grant, R. W. (1988) *The Psychology of Sport: Facing one's true opponent* Raleigh, NC: McFarland Jefferson.

Gratton, Chris and Taylor, Pete (2004) *The Economics of Sport and Recreation: An economic analysis* London: Routledge.

Gray, Chris Hables (2001) *Cyborg Citizen: Politics in the posthuman age* London: Routledge.

Greenwood, Jim (1998) *Total Rugby: Fifteen-man rugby for coach and player* London: A&C Black.

Griffin, Pat (1998) *Strong Women, Deep Closets: Lesbians and homophobia in sport* Champaign, IL: Human Kinetics.

Groves, D. (1987) "Why do some athletes choose high-risk sports?" *Physician and Sportsmedicine* vol. 15, no. 2.

Gruneau, Richard (1983) *Class, Sports and Social Development*, Amherst: University of Massachusetts Press.

Gruneau, R. (1984) "Commercialism and the modern Olympics" in *Five Ring Circus* edited by Alan Tomlinson and Garry Whannel, London: Pluto Press.

Gruneau, R. and Whitson, D. (1993) *Hockey Night in Canada* Toronto: Garamond.

Guelke, A. (1986) "The politicisation of South African sport" in *The Politics of Sport* edited by Lincoln Allison, Manchester: Manchester University Press.

Gutman, D. (1992) *Baseball Babylon: From Black Sox to Pete Rose* London: Penguin.

Guttmann, Allen (1986) *Sports Spectators* New York: Columbia University Press.

Guttmann, Allen (1978) *From Ritual to Record: The nature of modern sports* New York: Columbia University Press.

Guttmann, Allen (1996) *The Erotic in Sports* New York: Columbia University Press.

Hain, Peter (1982) "The politics of sport and apartheid" in *Sport, Culture and Ideology* edited by John Hargreaves, London: Routledge & Kegan Paul.

Halberstam, David (1999) *Playing for Keeps: Michael Jordan and the world he made* New York: Random House.

Hall, M. Ann (1996) *Feminism and Sporting Bodies: Essays on theory and practice* Champaign, IL: Human Kinetics.

Hannigan, John (1998) *Fantasy City: Pleasure and profit in the postmodern metropolis* London: Routledge.

Haraway, Donna J. (1991) *Simians, Cyborgs and Women: The reinventon of nature* New York: Routledge.

Hare, Nathan (1973) "The occupational culture of the black fighter" in *Sport and Society* edited by J. Talamini and C. Page, Boston, MA: Little, Brown.

Hargreaves, Jennifer (1994) *Sporting Females: Critical issues in the history and sociology of women's sports* London: Routledge.

Hargreaves, John (ed.) (1982) *Sport, Culture and Ideology* London: Routledge & Kegan Paul.

Hargreaves, John (ed.) (1986) *Sport, Power and Culture* Oxford: Polity Press.

Harris, Cheryl (1998) "A sociology of television fandom" in *Theorizing Fandom: Fans, subculture and identity* edited by Cheryl Harris and Alison Alexander, Cresskill, NJ: Hampton Press.

Harris, Lauren J. (1993) "Do left-handers die sooner than right-handers? Commentary on Coren and Halpern's (1991) 'Left-handedness: A marker for decreased survival fitness'" *Psychological Bulletin* vol. 114, no. 2 (September).

Harris, Marvin (1997) *Culture, People, Nature: An introduction to general anthropology*, seventh edition, New York: Addison-Wesley.

Harris, Marvin (1998) *Theories of Culture in Postmodern Times* Walnut Creek, CA: AltaMira.

Hauser, Thomas (1997) *Muhammad Ali: His life and times* New York: Pan Books.

Heaton, A. W. and Sigall, H. (1989) "The 'championship choke' revisited: The role of fear of acquiring a negative identity" *Journal of Applied Social Psychology* vol. 19.

Henderson, Edwin (1949) *The Negro in Sports* Washington, DC: Associated Publishers.

Hill, Christopher (1996) *Olympic Politics,* second edition (first published 1992), Manchester: Manchester University Press.

Hill, Karen L. (2001) *Frameworks for Sport Psychologists* Champaign, IL: Human Kinetics.

Hoberman, John (1984) *Sport and Political Ideology* Austin: University of Texas Press.

Hoberman, John (1992) *Mortal Engines: Human engineering and the transformation of sport* New York: Free Press.

Hoberman, John (1997) *Darwin's Athletes: How sport has damaged black America and preserved the myth of race* New York: Houghton Mifflin.

Hoberman, John and Yesalis, Charles E. (1995) "The history of synthetic testosterone" *Scientific American* vol. 272, no. 2.

Hoch, Paul (1972) *Rip Off the Big Game: The exploitation of sports by the power elite*, New York: Anchor Doubleday.

Hoffer, Richard (1998) *A Savage Business: The comeback and comedown of Mike Tyson* New York: Simon & Schuster.

Hoffman, Shirl (ed.) (1992) *Sport and Religion* Champaign, IL: Human Kinetics.

Hoffman, Tyler (2002) "The umpire is out" *The Advocate*, issue 877 (November).

Hoggett, Paul (1986) "The taming of violence" *New Society* vol. 36 (October 17).

Holt, Richard (1989) *Sport and the British* Oxford: Oxford University Press.

Holt, Richard (1990) *Sport and the Working Class in Modern Britain* Manchester: Manchester University Press.

Hornby, Nick (1996) *Fever Pitch* London: Indigo.

Horner, M. S. (1972) "Toward an understanding of achievement-related conflicts in women" *Journal of Social Issues* vol. 28.

Horrell, M. (1968) *South Africa and the Olympic Games* Johannesburg: Institute of Race Relations.

Horsman, Mathew (1997) *SkyHigh: The inside story of BSkyB* London: Orion Business.

Horton, D. and Wohl, R. R. (1956) "Mass communication and parasocial interaction" *Psychiatry* vol. 19.

Houlihan, Barrie (1994) *Sport and International Politics* Brighton: Harvester Wheatsheaf.

Houlihan, Barrie (1997) *Sport, Policy and Politics: A comparative analysis* London: Routledge.

Houlihan, Barrie (ed.) (2003) *Sport and Society: A student introduction* London: Sage.

Hubbard, Guy (1998) "Sports action" *Arts and Activities* vol. 123 (March).

Huddleston, Trevor (1956) *Naught for Your Comfort* London: Collins.

Huggins, Mike (2003) *Horseracing and the British, 1919–39* Manchester: Manchester University Press.

Husman, B. F. and Silva, J. M. (1984) "Aggression in sport: Definitional and theoretical considerations" in *Psychological Foundations of Sport* edited by J. M. Silva and R. S. Weinberg, Champaign, IL: Human Kinetics.

Ian, Marcia (2001) "The primitive subject of female bodybuilding: Transgression and other postmodern myths" *Differences*, vol. 12, no. 3 (Fall).

Inglehart, Ronald and Norris, Pippa (2004) *Sacred and Secular: Religion and politics worldwide* Cambridge: Cambridge University Press.

Jackson, S. A. and Csikszentmihalyi, M. (1999) *Flow in Sports: The keys to optimal experiences and performances* Champaign, IL: Human Kinetics.

James, C. L. R. (1963) *Beyond a Boundary* London: Hutchinson.

Jarvie, Grant and Maguire, Joseph (1995) *Sport and Leisure in Social Thought* London: Routledge.

Jenkins, Henry (1992) *Textual Poachers* London: Routledge.

Jennings, Andrew (1996) *The New Lords of the Rings: Olympics, corruption and how to buy gold medals* New York: Pocket Books.

Jhally, Sut (1989) "Cultural studies and the sports/media complex" in *Media, Sports and Society* edited by Lawrence A. Wenner, Newbury Park, CA: Sage.

Jindra, M. (1994) "*Star-Trek* fandom as a religious phenomenon" *Sociology of Religion*, vol. 55.

Jiobu, R. (1988) "Racial inequality in a public arena" *Social Forces* vol. 67, no. 2.

Johnson, Roy S. and Harrington, Ann (1998) "The Jordan effect" *Fortune* vol. 137, no. 12 (June 22).

Jones, Dave and Rivers, Tony (2002) *Soul Crew* Lytham, England: Milo.

Katz, Donald (1994) *Just Do It: The Nike spirit in the corporate world* Holbrook, MA: Adams Media.

Kerr, John (1994) *Understanding Soccer Hooliganism* Philadelphia, PA: Open University Press.

Kerr, John (2004) *Rethinking Aggression and Violence in Sport* London: Routledge.

Kerr, Robert (1982) *The Practical Use of Anabolic Steroids with Athletes* San Gabriel, CA: Kerr Publishing.

King, Billie Jean and Deford, Frank (1982) *Billie Jean* New York: Viking.

King, Colin (2004) *Offside Racism: Playing the white man* Oxford: Berg.

King, John (2004) *The Football Factory* London: Vintage.

Klatell, David and Marcus, Norman (1988) *Sports for Sale: Television, money and the fans* Oxford: Oxford University Press.

Klein, Naomi (2001) *No Logo* London: Flamingo.

Knight, Jennifer and Giuliano, Traci (2003) "Blood, sweat, and jeers: The impact of the media's heterosexist portrayals on perceptions of male and female athletes" *Journal of Sport Behavior* vol. 26, no. 3 (September).

Kohn, Marek (1996) *The Race Gallery* London: Vintage.

Kühnst, Peter (1996) *Sports: A cultural history in the mirror of art* Dresden: Verlag der Kunst.

Kühnst, Peter (2004) *Physique: Classic photographs of naked athletes* London: Thames & Hudson.

LaFeber, Walter (1999) *Michael Jordan and the new global capitalism* New York: Norton.

Landay, Lori (1999) "Millions 'Love Lucy': Commodification and the Lucy phenomenon" *NWSA Journal* vol. 11, no. 2.

Lapchick, Richard (1986) *Fractured Focus* Lexington, MA: Heath.

Laqueur, Thomas (1990) *Making Sex: Body and gender from the Greeks to Freud* Cambridge, MA: Harvard University Press.

Lasch, Christopher (1979) *The Culture of Narcissism* New York: Norton.

Lavallee, David, Kremer, John, Moran, Aiden, and Williams, Mark (2003) *Sport Psychology: Contemporary themes* London: Palgrave.

Layden, Tim (1998) "Distant thunder" *Sports Illustrated* vol. 89, no. 3 (July 20).

Leaman, Oliver (1988) "Cheating and fair play in sport" in *Philosophic Inquiry in Sport* edited by William J. Morgan and Klaus Meier, Champaign, IL: Human Kinetics.

Lenskyj, Helen (1986) *Out of Bounds: Women, sport and sexuality* Toronto: The Women's Press.

Leonard, Wilbert (1988) *A Sociological Perspective of Sport*, third edn, New York: Macmillan.

Lever, Janet (1983) *Soccer Madness* Chicago: University of Chicago Press.

Levine, Lawrence (1977) *Black Culture and Black Consciousness* New York: Oxford University Press.

Levine, Peter (1985) *A. G. Spalding and the Rise of Baseball: The promise of American sport* New York: Oxford University Press.

Levinson, Daniel. and Christensen, K. (1996) *Encyclopedia of World Sport: From ancient times to the present* Santa Barbara, CA: ABC-Clio,

Lin, Carol (2003) "Interview with Lance Armstrong" *CNN Saturday Night Show*, October 18, LexisNexis Academic: Transcript # 101804CN.V88.

Lindsey, Linda (1990) *Gender Roles: A sociological perspective* Englewood Cliffs, NJ: Prentice-Hall.

Longman, Jere (2001) "Rise of the superathlete" *New York Times Upfront* vol. 134, no. 1 (September 3).

Lorenz, K. (1966) *On Aggression* New York: Harcourt Brace Jovanovich.

Louganis, Greg (1995) *Breaking the Surface: A life* New York: Random House.

Lukas, Gerhard (1969) *Die Körperkultur in frühen Epochen der Menschenentwicklung* East Berlin: Sportverlap.

Lüschen, G. (1976) "Cheating" in *Social Problems in America* edited by D. Landers, Champaign: University of Illinois Press

McDonald, Mary G. and Andrews, David L. (2001) "Michael Jordan: Corporate sport and postmodern celebrityhood" in *Sports Stars: The cultural politics of sporting celebrity* edited by David L. Andrews and Steven J. Jackson, London: Routledge.

McGinnis, Lee, Chun, Seungwoo, and McQuillan, Julia (2003) "A review of gendered consumption in sport and leisure" *Academy of Marketing Science Review* <www.amsreview.org/articles/mcginnis05-2003html>

McGinnis, Peter M. (1999) *Biomechanics of Sport and Exercise* Champaign, IL: Human Kinetics.

MacGregor, Jeff (1999) "SI view: Air and space" *Sports Illustrated* vol. 90, no. 13 (March 29).

MacGregor, Jeff (1999) "Less than murder" *Sports Illustrated* vol. 90, no. 12 (March 22).

McIntosh, Peter (1980) *Fair Play* London: Heinemann Educational.

MacKinnon, Kenneth (2003) *Representing Men: Maleness and masculinity in the media* London: Hodder Arnold.

McRae, Donald (2003) *In Black and White: The untold story of Joe Louis and Jesse Owens* New York: Scribner.

Malson, Lucien (1972) *Wolf Children and the Problem of Human Nature*, New York: Monthly Review Press.

Maltby, J., Houran, J., Lange, R., Ashe, D., and McCutcheon, L. E. (2002) "Thou shalt worship no other gods – unless they are celebrities" *Personality and Individual Differences*, vol. 32.

Mandell, Richard (1971) *The Nazi Olympics* New York: Macmillan.

Mandell, Richard D. (1984) *Sport: A cultural history* New York: Columbia University Press.

Maney, Kevin (1995) *Megamedia Shakeout: The inside story of the leaders and the losers in the exploding communications industry* London: Wiley.

Mansfield, Alan and McGinn, Barbara (1993) "Pumping irony" in *Body Matters* edited by Sue Scott and D. Morgan, London: Falmer.

Manzo, L. (2002) "Enhancing sport performance: The role of confidence and concentration" in *Psychological Foundations of Sport* edited by J. M. Silva and D. E. Stevens, Boston, MA: Allyn & Bacon.

Marqusee, Mike (1999) *Redemption Song: Muhammad Ali and the spirit of the sixties* London: Verso.

Marsh, Peter (1979) *Aggro: The illusion of violence* London: Dent.

Marsh, Peter, Prosser, Elizabeth, and Harré, Rom (1978) *The Rules of Disorder* London: Routledge & Kegan Paul.

Marshall, P. D. (1997) *Celebrity and Power: Fame in contemporary culture* Minneapolis: University of Minnesota Press.

Martin, Beth Ann and Martin, James H. (1995) "Comparing perceived sex role orientations of the ideal male and female athlete to the ideal male and female person" *Journal of Sport Behavior*, vol. 18, no. 4,

Mason, Tony (1988) *Sport in Britain* London: Faber & Faber.

Matza, David (1969) *Becoming Deviant* Englewood Cliffs, NJ: Prentice-Hall.

Mayr, Ernst and Diamond, Jared (1998) *What Evolution Is* New York: Free Press.

Mays, Willie and Sahadi, Lou (1989) *Say Hey: The autobiography of Willie Mays* New York: Pocket Books.

Messier, Mark, Gretzky, Walter, and Hull, Brett (1998) *Wayne Gretzky: The making of the great one* Dallas, TX: Beckett Publications.

Messner, Michael A. (1992) *Power at Play: Sports and the problem of masculinity* Boston, MA: Beacon Press.

Messner, Michael A. (2002) *Taking the Field: Women, men and sports* Minneapolis: University of Minnesota Press.

Miah, Andy (2004) *Genetically Modified Athletes: Biomedical ethics, gene doping, and sport* London: Routledge.

Michener, James (1976) *Sports in America* New York: Random House.

Miller, Stephen G. (2004) *Ancient Greek Olympics* New Haven, CT: Yale University Press.

Miller, Toby, Rowe, David, Lawrence, Geoffrey, and McKay, Jim (2001) *Globalization and Sport: Playing the world* London: Sage.

Moir, Anne and Bill (1998) *Why Men Don't Iron: The real science of gender studies* London: HarperCollins.

Monaco, James (ed.) (1978) *Celebrity: The media as image makers* New York: Delta.

Money, Tony (1997) *Manly and Muscular Diversions: Public schools and the nineteenth-century sporting revival* London: Duckworth.

Morgan, William J. (1994) *Leftist Theories of Sport: A critique and reconstruction* Urbana: University of Illinois Press.

Morgan, William J. and Meier, Klaus V. (eds) (1995) *Philsophic Inquiry in Sport*, second edition (first published 1988), Champaign, IL: Human Kinetics.

Morgan, William J., Meier, Klaus V., and Schneider, Angela J. (eds) (2001) *Ethics in Sport* Champaign, IL: Human Kinetics.

Morris, Desmond (1981) *The Soccer Tribe* London: Jonathan Cape.

Morton, Cole (1999) "The flame that died" *Independent on Sunday*, Focus section (January 24).

Morton, Oliver (1999) "As the Tour de France begins, it's time to rethink the way we treat drugs in sports" *Newsweek* (international edition) July 12.

Mottram, David (2003) *Drugs in Sport*, third edition, London: Routledge.

Munro, P. and Govier, E. (1993) "Dynamic gender-related differences in dichotic listening performance" *Neuropsychologia* vol. 31, no. 40.

Muris, P., Kop, W. J., and Merckelbach, H. (1994) "Handedness, symptom resorting and accident susceptibility" *Journal of Clinical Psychology*, vol. 50, no. 3 (May).

Murphy, P., Sheard, K., and Waddington, I. (2000) "Figurational sociology and its application to sport" in *Handbook of Sports Studies* edited by Jay Coakley and Eric Dunning, London: Sage.

Muster, Georg (1985) *Murdoch: A paper prince* Harmondsworth: Penguin.

Naison, Mark (1972) "Sports and the American empire" *Radical America*, vol. 6, no. 4 (July/August).

Nelson, Mariah Burton, (1994) *The Stronger Women Get, the More Men Love Football: Sex and sport in America* New York: Harcourt, Brace.

Newfield, Jack (1995) *Only in America: The life and crimes of Don King* New York: William Morrow.

Niednagel, J. (1994) *Your Keys to Sports Success* Nashville, TN: Nelson.

Novak, Michael (1976) *The Joy of Sport* New York: Basic Books.

Ogilvie, B. and Tutko, T. A. (1966) *Problem Athletes and How to Handle Them* London: Pelham.

Olins, Wally (2003) *Wally Olins on Brand* London: Thames & Hudson.

Olsen, Jack (1968) *The Black Athlete* New York: Time Life.

Osborne, Peter (2004) *Basil D'Oliveira* London: Little, Brown.

Oudshoorn, Nelly (1994) *Beyond the Natural Body: An archeology of sex hormones* London: Routledge.

Overman, Steven J. (1997) *The Influence of the Protestant Ethic on Sport and Recreation* Aldershot, England: Avebury.

Overman, Steven J. (2000) "The Protestant Ethic" in *Sports Culture: An A–Z Guide* by Ellis Cashmore, London: Routledge.

Page, Michael (1988) *Bradman: The biography* Sydney: Pan Macmillian.

Pass, K., Freeman, H., Bautista, J., and Johnson, C. (1993) "Handedness and accidents with injury" *Perceptual and Motor Skills* vol. 77 no. 3 (December).

Patterson, Orlando (1971) "Rethinking black history" *Harvard Educational Review* vol. 41 (August).

Paulsen, Gary (1994) *Winterdance: The fine madness of Alaskan dog-racing* London: Gollancz.

Pearlman, Jeff (1998) "Bare knuckles" *Sports Illustrated* vol. 89, no. 17 (October 26).

Pepperell, Robert (2004) *The Posthuman Condition: Consciousness beyond the brain*, third edition, Bristol, England: Intellect.

Perry, Clifton (1983) "Blood doping and athletic competition" *International Journal of Applied Philosophy* vol. 1, no. 3.

Petrie, Trent, A. (1996) "Differences between male and female college lean sport athletes, nonlean sports athletes, and nonathletes on behavioral and psychological indices of eating disorders" *Journal of Applied Sport Psychology* vol. 8, no. 2.

Poliakoff, Michael B. (1987) *Combat Sports in the Ancient World: Competition, violence, and culture* New Haven, CT: Yale University Press.

Prendergrast, Mark (1993) *For God, Country and Coca-Cola: The unauthorized history of the great American soft drink and the company that makes it* New York: Collier.

Pronger, Brian (1998) "Post-sport: Transgressing boundaries in physical culture" in *Sport and Postmodern Times* edited by Geneviève Rail, Albany: State University of New York Press.

Puglise, M., Lifshitz, F., and Grad, G. (1983) "Fear of obesity" *New England Journal of Medicine*, vol. 309.

Putnam, Douglas T. (1999) *Controversies of the Sports World* Westport, CT: Greenwood Press.

Rader, Benjamin (1984) *In its Own Image: How television has transformed sport* New York: Collier-Macmillan.

Rail, Geneviève (1998) "Seismography of the postmodern condition: Three theses on the implosion of sport" in *Sport and Postmodern Times* edited by Geneviève Rail, Albany: State University of New York Press.

Ravizza, Kenneth (1984) "Qualities of the peak experience in sport" *Psychological Foundations of Sport* edited by J. M. Silva and R. S. Weinberg, Champaign, IL: Human Kinetics.

Raymond, M., Pontier, D., Dufour, A., and Moller, A. P. (1996) "Frequency-dependent maintenance of left-handedness in humans" *Proceedings of the Royal Society of London* series 3, vol. 263 (December).

Real, Michael R. (1998) "MediaSport: Technology and the commodification of post-modern sport" in *MediaSport* edited by Lawrence A. Wenner, London: Routledge.

Regen, Richard (1990) "Neither does King" *Interview* vol. 20 (October 10).

Rescher, Nicholas (1995) *Luck: The brilliant randomness of everyday life* New York: Farrar Straus Giroux.

Rhodes, Reilly (ed.) (1990) *Sport in Art from American Museums* New York: Universe.

Richards, Renee and Ames, J. (1983) *Second Serve* New York: Stein & Day.

Ridley, Matt (2003a) *Nature via Nurture: Genes, experience and what makes us human* New York: HarperCollins.

Ridley, Matt (2003b) "Listen to the genome" *The American Spectator* vol. 36, no. 3 (June/July).

Rigauer, Bero (1981) *Sport and Work*, New York: Columbia University Press.

Rigauer, Bero (2000) "Marxist theories" in *Handbook of Sports Studies* edited by Jay Coakley and Eric Dunning, London: Sage.

Rinehart, R. (1998) "Born-again sport: Ethics in biographical research" in *Sport and Postmodern Times* edited by Geneviève Rail, Albany: State University of New York Press.

Ritzer, George (1998) *The McDonaldization of Society*, second edition, Newbury Park, CA: Pine Forge.

Robins, David (1982) "Sport and youth culture" in *Sport, Culture and Ideology* edited by John Hargreaves, London: Routledge & Kegan Paul.

Robinson, Sugar Ray and Anderson, Dave (1992) *Sugar Ray: The Sugar Ray Robinson story* London: Robson Books.

Rojek, Chris (2001) *Celebrity* London: Reaktion.

Rosentraub, Mark (1997) *Major League Losers: The real cost of sports and who's paying for it* New York: HarperCollins.

Rowe, David (2002) "Taking the sports brief: A review essay" *Theory and Event*, vol. 6, no. 1.

Rowe, David (2004a) *Sport, Culture and the Media*, second edition, Maidenhead, England: Open University Press.

Rowe, David (ed.) (2004b) *Critical Readings: Sport, culture and the media*, Maidenhead, England: Open University Press

Ryan, Joan (1998) *Little Girls in Pretty Boxes: The making and breaking of élite gymnasts and figure skaters* London: Women's Press.

Sakellarakis, J. (1979) "Athletics in Crete and Mycenae" in *The Eternal Olympics: The art and history of sport* edited by Nicolaos Yaloris, New York: Caratzas Brothers.

Sammons, Jeffrey (1988) *Beyond the Ring* Camden, NJ: University of Illinois Press.

Sandrock, Michael (1996) *Running with the Legends* Champaign, IL: Human Kinetics.

Schiebinger, Londa (1987) "Skeletons in the closet: The first illustrations of the female skeleton in eighteenth-century anatomy" in *The Making of the Modern Body: Sexuality and society in the nineteenth century* edited by Catherine Gallagher and Thomas Laqueur, Berkeley: University of California Press.

Schiebinger, Londa (1989) *The Mind Has No Sex: Women in the origins of modern science* Cambridge, MA: Harvard University Press.

Scott, Jack (1971) *The Athletic Revolution* New York: Free Press.

Scully, Gerald W. (1995) *The Market Structure of Sports* Chicago: University of Chicago Press.

Seligman, M. E. P. (1975) *Helplessness: On depression, development and death* San Francisco, CA: W. H. Freeman.

Senn, Alfred E. (1999) *Power, Politics and the Olympic Games* Champaign, IL: Human Kinetics.

Shawcross, William (1992) *Rupert Murdoch* London: Chatto & Windus.

Shea, B. Christine (2001) "The paradox of pumping iron: Female bodybuilding as resistance and compliance" *Women and Language* vol. 24, no. 2 (Fall).

Sherman, Len (1998) *Big League, Big Time: The birth of the Arizona Diamondbacks, the billion-dollar business of sports, and the power of the media in America* New York: Pocket Books.

Silva, J. M. and Stevens, D. E. (eds) (2002) *Psychological Foundations of Sport* Boston, MA: Allyn & Bacon.

Silva, J. M and Weinberg, R. S. (eds) (1984) *Psychological Foundations of Sport* Champaign, IL: Human Kinetics.

Silva, J. M. and Weinberg, R. S. (1984) "Motivation" in *Psychological Foundations of Sport* edited by J. M. Silva and R. S. Weinberg, Champaign, IL: Human Kinetics.

Simson, Vyv and Jennings, Andrew (1992) *The Lords of the Rings: Power, money and drugs in the modern Olympics* New York: Simon & Schuster.

Smith, Dorothy E. (1988) "Femininity as discourse" in *Becoming Feminine: The politics of popular culture* edited by Leslie G. Roman, Linda Christian-Smith, and Elizabeth Ellsworth, Philadelphia, PA: Falmer.

Smith, Ed (2004) *On and Off the Field*, London: Viking.

Smith, Michael D. (1983) *Violence and Sport* Toronto: Butterworth.

Smith, R. E. and Smoll, F. L. (1996) *Way to Go, Coach* Portola Valley, CA: Warde.

Snyder, E. and Spreitzer, E. (1983) *Social Aspects of Sport*, second edition, Englewood Cliffs, NJ: Prentice-Hall.

Solnit, Rebecca (2004) *Motion Studies: Time, space and Eadweard Muybridge* London: Bloomsbury.

Sowell, Thomas (1994) *Race and Culture: A world view* New York: Basic Books.

Spears, Betty and Swanson, Richard A. (1995) *History of Sport and Physical Activity in the United States*, fourth edition, Dubuque, IA: Brown & Benchmark.

Spivey, Nigel (2004) *The Ancient Olympics* London: Oxford University Press.

Staudohar, Paul and Mangan, James (eds) (1991) *The Business of Professional Sports* Urbana: University of Illinois Press.

Steele, Bruce C. (2002) "Tackling football's closet" *The Advocate*, issue 877 (November 26).

Sternberg, Robert J. (1996) "Intelligence and cognitive styles" in *Companion Encyclopedia of Psychology*, volume 2, edited by A. M. Colman London: Routledge.

Stoddart, Brian (1988) "Sport, cultural imperialism and colonial response in the British empire" *Comparative Studies in Society and History* part 30 (October).

Stoll, Sharon Kay, Prisbrey, Keith A., and Froes, F. H. (2002) "Advanced materials in sports: An advantage or ethical challenge" *USA Today Magazine* vol. 130, no. 2684 (May).

Stotlar, D. K. (2000) "Vertical integration in sport" *Journal of Sport Management*, vol. 14, no. 1.

Strasser, J. B. and Becklund, Laurie (1993) *Swoosh: The unauthorized story of Nike and the men who played there* New York: HarperBusiness.

Sundgot-Borgen, Jorunn (1994a) "Eating disorders in female athletes" *Sports Medicine* vol. 17, no. 3.

Sundgot-Borgen, Jorunn (1994b) "Risk and trigger factors in the development of eating disorders in female elite athletes" *Medicine and Science in Sports and Exercise* vol. 26, no. 4.

Suttles, Gerald (1968) *The Social Order of the Slum: Ethnicity and territory in the inner city* Chicago: University of Chicago Press.

Swift, E. M. (1999) "Breaking point" *Sports Illustrated* vol. 90, no. 4 (February 1).

Swift, E. M. and Yaeger, Don (2001) "Unnatural selection" *Sports Illustrated* vol. 94, no. 20 (May 14).

Taub, Diane and Benson, Rose (1992) "Weight concerns, weight control techniques, and eating disorders among adolescent competitive swimmers: The effect of gender" *Sociology of Sport Journal* vol. 9, no. 2.

Taylor, Ian (1971) "Soccer consciousness and soccer hooliganism" in *Images of Deviance* edited by Stanley Cohen, Harmondsworth: Penguin.

Taylor, J. and Demick, A. (1994) "A multidimensional model of momentum in sports" *Journal of Applied Sport Psychology* vol. 6.

Taylor, Phil (1997) "Center of the storm" *Sports Illustrated* vol. 87, no. 24 (December 15).

Todd, Jan (1987a) "Bernarr Macfadden: Reformer of the feminine form" *Journal of Sport History* vol. 14, no. 1 (Spring).

Todd, Terry (1987b) "Anabolic steroids: The gremlins of sport" *Journal of Sport History* vol. 14, no. 1 (Spring).

Turner, Bryan S. (1992) *Max Weber: From history to modernity* London: Routledge.

Turner, Graeme (2004) *Understanding Celebrity* London: Sage.

Van Schoyck, S. and Grasha, A. (1981) "Attentional style variations and athletic ability: The advantages of a sports-specific test" *Medicine and Science in Sport and Exercise* vol. 26.

Vandervell, Anthony and Coles, Charles (1980) *Game and the English Landscape: The Influence of the chase on sporting art and scenery* London: Debrett's Peerage.

Vanwalleghem, Rik (1968) *Eddy Merckx: The greatest cyclist of the twentieth century* Allentown, PA: Velo Press.

Vasili, Phil (1998) *The First Black Footballer, Arthur Wharton, 1865–1930: An absence of memory* Portland, OR: Frank Cass.

Vealey, R. S. (1986) "Conceptualization of sport-confidence and competitive orientation: Preliminary investigation and instrument development" *Journal of Sport Psychology* vol. 8.

Verma, Gajendra and Darby, Douglas (1994) *Winners and Losers: Ethnic minorities in sport and recreation* London: Falmer.

Vertinsky, Patricia (1987) "Exercise, physical capability, and the eternally wounded woman in late nineteenth century North America" *Journal of Sport History* vol. 14, no. 1 (Spring).

Vertinsky, Patricia (1990) *The Eternally Wounded Woman: Women, doctors and exercise in the late nineteenth century* Manchester: Manchester University Press.

Vincent, Martin (1995) "Painters and punters" *New Statesman & Society* vol. 8 (May).

Voy, Robert and Deeter, Kirk (1991) *Drugs, Sport and Politics* Champaign, IL: Human Kinetics.

Waddington, Ivan (1996) "The development of sports medicine" *Sociology of Sport Journal* vol. 9.

Waddington, Ivan (2000) *Sport, Health and Drugs: A critical sociological perspective* London: E&FN Spon.

Wankel, L. (1982) "Audience effects in sport" in *Psychological Foundations of Sport* edited by J. Silva and R. Weinberg, Champaign, IL: Human Kinetics.

Waters, Malcolm (2001) *Globalization*, second edition, London: Routledge.

Weber, Max (1958) *The Protestant Ethic and the Spirit of Capitalism*, trans. Talcott Parsons, New York: Scribner & Sons.

Weeks, Jeffrey (2003) *Sexuality*, second edition, London: Routledge.

Weinberg, Robert S. and Gould, Daniel (2004) *Foundations of Sport and Exercise Psychology* Champaign, IL: Human Kinetics.

Weintraub, Arlene (2004) "Commentary: Can drug-busters beat new steroids?" *BusinessWeek* online, June 14: <businessweek.com:/print/magazine/content/04_24/b3887096_mz018.htm?tc>

Weir, J. and Abrahams, P. (1992) *An Imaging Atlas of Human Anatomy*, St. Louis MO: Mosby-Wolfe.

Wenner, Lawrence (ed.) (1998 ) *MediaSport* London: Routledge.

Wenner, Lawrence and Ganz, Walter (1998) "Watching sports on television: Audience experience, gender, fanship, and marriage" in *MediaSport* edited by Lawrence Wenner, London: Routledge.

Westerbeek, Hans and Smith, Aaron (2002) *Sport Business in the Global Marketplace* London: Palgrave Macmillan.

Whannel, Gary (1992) *Fields in Vision: Television sport and cultural transformation* London: Routledge.

Whannel, Garry (2000) "Sport and the media" in *Handbook of Sports Studies*, edited by Jay Coakley and Eric Dunning, London: Sage.

Wheaton, Belinda (2000) "New lads' masculinities and the 'New Sport' participant" *Men and Masculinities* vol. 2 (April).

Whitehead, Stephen M. and Barrett, Frank J. (2001) "The sociology of masculinity" in *The Masculinities Reader* edited by Stephen M. Whitehead and Frank J. Barrett, Cambridge: Polity.

Whitson, David (1994) "The embodiment of gender: Discipline, domination and empowerment" in *Women, Sport and Culture* edited by Susan Birrell and Cheryl Cole, Champaign, IL: Human Kinetics.

Whitson, David (1998) "Circuits of promotion: Media, marketing and the globalization of sport" in *MediaSport* edited by Lawrence Wenner, London: Routledge.

Wiggins, David (1995) *Sports in America: From wicked amusement to national obsession* Champaign, IL: Human Kinetics.

Wiggins, David K. (1997) *Glory Bound: Black athletes in a white America* Syracuse, NY: Syracuse University Press.

Wilmore, Jack and Costill, David (2004) *Physiology of Sport and Exercise*, Champaign, IL: Human Kinetics.

Wilson, Neil (1988) *The Sport Business* London: Piatkus.

Wilson, Wade and Derse, Edward (eds) (2001) *Doping in Elite Sport: The politics of drugs in the Olympic movement* Champaign, IL: Human Kinetics.

Wolf, Naomi (1991) *The Beauty Myth: How images of beauty are used against women* New York: Morrow.

Yaloris, Nicolaos (ed.) (1979) *The Eternal Olympics: The art and history of sport* New York: Caratzas Brothers.

Yesalis, Charles E. (ed.) (1993) *Anabolic Steroids in Sport and Exercise* Champaign, IL: Human Kinetics.

Yesalis, Charles and Cowart, Virginia (1998) *The Steroids Game: An expert's look at anabolic steroid use in sports* Champaign, IL: Human Kinetics.

Zajonc, R. (1965) "Social facilitation" *Science* vol. 149.

Zimbalist, Andrew (1992) *Baseball and Billions* New York: Basic Books.

Zolberg, Vera (1987) "Elias and Dunning's theory of sport and excitement" *Theory, Culture and Society* vol. 4.

Zona, Louis A. (1990) "Red Grooms" in *Sport in Art from American Museums* edited by Reilly Rhodes, New York: Universe.

# name index

# subject index

# titles index